CANADIAN FIFTH EDITION

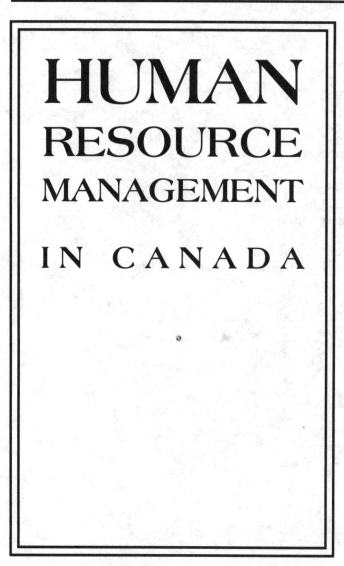

HUMAN
RESOURCE
MANAGEMENT
IN CANADA

Gary Dessler
Florida International University

Alvin Turner
Brock University

PRENTICE-HALL CANADA INC., Scarborough, Ontario

Canadian Cataloguing in Publication Data

Dessler, Gary
   Human resource management in Canada

Canadian 5th ed.
Previous eds. published under title: Personnel
management.
ISBN 0-13-435603-9

1. Personnel management.   2. Personnel management -
Canada.   I. Turner, Alvin, 1947 -   .   II. Title.
III. Title: Personnel management

© 1992 by Prentice-Hall Canada Inc., Scarborough, Ontario

Original U.S. edition published as *Personnel/Human Resource
Management* by Gary Dessler. © 1991 by Prentice-Hall, Inc.
A Division of Simon & Schuster, Englewood Cliffs, New Jersey 07632

Previous Canadian edition by Gary Dessler and John F. Duffy
published as *Personnel Management* © 1984 by Prentice-Hall Canada Inc., Scarborough, Ontario

Prentice-Hall, Inc., Englewood Cliffs, New Jersey
Prentice-Hall International, Inc., London
Prentice-Hall of Australia, Pty., Ltd., Sydney
Prentice-Hall of India Pvt., Ltd., New Delhi
Prentice-Hall of Japan, Inc., Tokyo
Prentice-Hall of Southeast Asia (Pte.) Ltd., Singapore
Editora Prentice-Hall do Brasil Ltda., Rio de Janeiro
Prentice-Hall Hispanoamericana, S.A., Mexico

ISBN 0-13-435603-9

Acquisitions Editor: Yolanda de Rooy
Developmental Editor: Linda Gorman
Production Editor: Jean Ferrier
Production Coordinator: Florence Rousseau
Cover and Interior Design: Aurora Di Ciaula
Cover Image: Supplied by Image Bank
Page Layout: Anita Macklin
Technical Illustration: Phillip Allen

1 2 3 4 5 AP 96 95 94 93 92

Printed and bound in Canada by Alger Press

Every reasonable effort has been made to find copyright holders. The publisher would be
pleased to have any errors or omissions brought to its attention.

TABLE OF CONTENTS

PREFACE

The aim of this book is to meet the needs of students, academics, and practitioners. However, the focus of the book is student oriented. We imagine that our readers are college and university students who intend to pursue a career in human resource management (HRM), or who may already be working in the field. This book provides our readers with comprehensive knowledge and understanding of all the essential concepts, techniques, theories, practices, principles, and functional activities of human resource management. Further, it provides our readers with a framework that offers both theory and hands-on applications to facilitate the acquisition of knowledge and expertise to apply to any particular circumstances.

We have based the structure and contents of *Human Resource Management in Canada* on our own research and teaching experience in HRM, on the research findings and published works of many individuals, and on the most current literature and major developments in the field.

We have endeavoured to be clear and interesting to ensure that we capture and hold the interest of our readers. We have written the book in easily readable, clear, and concise language using clearly defined, practical and concrete examples. We hope that our readers find the material that we present to be challenging, fresh, informative, stimulating, thought provoking, and as interesting as the field itself.

The turbulent economic conditions in Canada today, brought about by changing employment legislation, work force composition, changing markets and increased global competitiveness, rapidly changing technologies, and changing employee attitudes are challenging organizations to be more competitive. Doing so means becoming more innovative, proactive, and changing operating policies and processes to find and retain productive workers. Our readers will become familiar with how organizations use HRM functions and activities to meet these challenges by planning, designing, and implementing policies, procedures, and practices to attract the necessary human resources in sufficient quantity and quality. It also means being using effective techniques to recruit, select, train, develop, evaluate, compensate, manage, and stimulate employee performance. We also discuss how to achieve operational and strategic objectives and to control labour costs.

ORGANIZATION

The book is organized into five sections and grouped around different themes. These sections/themes are, of course, interconnected but, at the same time, they reflect different focuses of attention. The five sections are: Recruitment and Placement; Socialization, Training, and Development; Appraisal and Career Management; Compensation, Protection, and Motivation; and Employee Rights, Safety, and Representation. The individual chapters within each section provide readers with an excellent understanding of the dynamic concepts and techniques of human resource management, as well as with penetrating insights into some of the leading research findings, studies, and current practices.

KEY FEATURES

Throughout the book we provide a variety of special features and illustrations to aid readers in their understanding of the theory and applications of the principles learned. These include:

- **Chapter Objectives and Overviews** — to emphasize learning goals and principles to facilitate comprehension and retention of chapter contents.
- **Appendix** —in the Appendix (at the back of the book) titled "Interrelationships Between Human Resource Management Functions," we grouped all the major diagrams that describe the relationship of each essential HRM activity to other HRM functions. These diagrams provide an important coordinating link and will facilitate readers' understanding of how HRM functions tie in together. Readers also will find the diagrams beneficial because they illustrate and reinforce the significance of each chapter in relation to the others.
- **HRM: On the Front Line** — to provide a continuing examination of the problems, challenges, and HRM practices of a small organization
- **HRM In Action** — to spotlight real-life applications of current issues, recent developments and practices, or special topics in the HRM field
- **Computer Application** — to illustrate how computers are used in human resource management
- **Figures and Tables** — to visually identify and facilitate interpretation of key functions and activities of HRM
- **Discussion Questions** — to facilitate application of learned concepts as well as to test readers' abilities to recall information
- **Case Studies** — to facilitate the application of the theoretical material introduced in the text, and to help readers understand some of the problems and challenges faced

by HRM practitioners and organizations. They also are designed to test students' analytical skills and to serve as a springboard for group and class discussions

- **Experiential Exercises** — to give students the opportunity to meet in small groups and apply the concepts and techniques found in each chapter
- **Suggested Readings** — to provide critical elaborations of specific topics and core concepts discussed in the text and to enrich the readers' professional horizons beyond the coverage of this book
- **Glossary** — to provide a review and definition of the key terms used in the text.

Although there are many good HRM books available in Canada, we are confident that our text stands out among them because of a variety of distinguishing characteristics. For example:

Employment Equity: In Chapter 2, we provide the most extensive discussion of employment equity available in Canada. We provide a step-by-step approach that will enable readers to design, develop, implement, and manage an employment equity program.

Pay Equity: In Chapter 2 we also discuss the differences between federal and provincial (Ontario) pay equity programs. In Chapter 12 we discuss the implications of pay equity on compensation, and in Chapter 19 we discuss its implications on collective bargaining.

Sexual Harassment In Chapter 2 we define sexual harassment and discuss its human rights applications. In Chapter 16 we provide an expanded discussion of the subject including a variety of court and human rights cases. We also provide specific guidelines that employers should follow in developing, implenting, and managing a sexual harassment policy.

Organizational Choice: In Chapter 5 we discuss the series of decisions that an individual makes about joining an organization. We define the stages of the choice process and factors that an individual considers before making his or her decision.

Behaviour Description Interviewing: In Chapter 6 we discuss various aspects of behaviour description interviewing and how this type of interview should be conducted.

Employee Rights and Management Rights: In Chapter 16, we provide a comprehensive discussion of employee rights and management rights in Canada. We discuss issues such as just cause for dismissal, constructive dismissal, damages, sexual harassment, and discipline. We support our discussion with over 220 court cases.

Strategic Issues in Human Resource Management: In Chapter 20 we present a comprehensive discussion of the emerging issues of human resource management between now and the year 2000. In so doing, we spotlight the views of senior HRM executives from a variety of Canadian companies including: The Toronto Dominion Bank, William M. Mercer Limited, General Electric Canada Inc., British Columbia Telephone Company, Northern Telecom Canada, Canadian Pacific Limited, Westinghouse Canada Inc., Trimac Transportation System, and Canron Inc. We discuss general international issues in HRM, particularly the HRM practices in European countries. The topics examined include aspects of international HRM selection, training, and compensation.

SUPPLEMENTARY RESOURCES

Various supportive supplementary materials are offered to adopters of this text to make their teaching more effective. These include:

- Instructor's Manual — supplemental lecture material, sample syllabi, suggested term projects, a listing of chapter objectives, and overhead transparency masters
- Test Bank — multiple choice and true or false questions and answers
- Workweek Videos—30 minute programs discussing current Canadian workplace issues.

ACKNOWLEDGEMENTS

We are deeply indebted to a variety of individuals and organizations who provided assistance in the development of this book. Though we cannot name them all, a few deserve special mention. We wish to thank the Ontario Women's Directorate for the resources provided and used in our discussion of employment equity. We further thank both Canada Law Book, for allowing us generous access to Howard Levitt's research, and Butterworths, for Ellen Mole's research which we used in the chapter on employee and management rights. Additionally, we wish to thank the Conference Board of Canada for graciously allowing us to use Prem Benimadhu's research on strategic issues in human resource management. Eli Levanoni was a source of special inspiration and provided resources, help, guidance, constructive feedback, and insightful comments and other types of assistance too numerous to mention. Jila Boal's help was indispensable. She graciously typed the various drafts of the manuscript, and prepared the glossary as well as the index. To her we say a special thank-you. We are also grateful to Stephen Gibson, Publisher, The Employment Law Review, Maureen Duncan, Manager, Personal Banking, The Royal Bank of Canada, and Don Chamberlain, Senior Manager, The Bank of Montreal, for the special support and material provided. Finally, we also wish to extend a special thanks to Yolanda de Rooy, Managing Editor. We could not have done it without you. We also thank her editorial staff at Prentice-Hall Canada, and Joe March of Prentice-Hall's Business Information Services.

CHAPTER ONE
THE FIELD OF HUMAN RESOURCE MANAGEMENT

After studying this chapter you should be able to

1. Describe the field of human resource management.
2. Discuss the role of human resource management in modern organizations.
3. Explain the essential processes in human resource management.
4. Understand why the "human" dimension in an organization is important.
5. Understand the contemporary challenges facing human resource management.

OVERVIEW

This chapter defines the field of human resource management, explains its purposes and importance, and traces its historical development. We describe human resource management from a systems perspective and examine the impact of internal environmental forces such as organizational climate and culture on human resource management. We also examine the impact of external forces, such as labour market conditions, government, technology, and labour unions, on contemporary human resource management.

INTRODUCTION: WHAT IS HUMAN RESOURCE MANAGEMENT?

human resource
management (HRM)

Human resource management (HRM) refers to the management of *people* in organizations. The field involves those activities in which an organization engages to meet the individual's goals, society's objectives, and the organization's optimal productivity and effectiveness.[1] As such it comprises all the activities involved in attracting, recruiting, selecting, training, developing, utilizing, controlling, appraising, rewarding, motivating, retaining, directing, coordinating, negotiating with, and maintaining human resources. The term *human resource management* also covers the policies, processes, strategies, procedures, philosophies, activities, and practices used to manage all the human elements in the organization. Effective human resource management is the coordinative link of a comprehensive network of interrelated processes and systems that involve and affect all the employees in the organization. The major human resource management functions are recruitment and placement; training and development; compensation, protection, and motivation; appraisal and career management; employee health and safety, and labour-management relations.

Human resource management has been growing in importance for several reasons, including the dramatic development of innovative technologies; changing family structure; changing composition of the labour force; and increasing government involvement in the employer-employee work relationship. Top management has also grown to realize that human resources are important means of improving organizational effectiveness; that in order to survive, remain competitive and grow and diversify an organization must ensure that the interests of its human resources are managed carefully. Rather than addressing organizational needs and goals as distinct and separate from those of employees, they may be seen as compatible and mutual. Therefore the needs and goals of one party need not be satisfied or met at the expense of the other party. Human resources are now recognized as the organization's most important asset.

According to the Conference Board of Canada, in the 1990s the Canadian organization's competitive strength will be increasingly contingent on human resources. The effectiveness of traditional competitive tools, such as technology, product innovation, financial resources, and access to raw materials is slowly being eroded. As a result, the future competitiveness of Canadian organizations will be based less on these traditional elements, and more on human resources.[2]

The Conference Board of Canada also believes that the increasing recognition by organizations that their human resources are a fundamental source of competitive advantage is accompanied by major changes in the role and function of HRM. The Board conducted a recent survey of Canadian firms in which 86% indicated that changes have occurred in the role and importance of HRM during the last five years. Seventy-eight percent of respondents stated that the HR function wields greater influence within the organization than it did five years ago. The movement of the function from the "basement to the boardroom" is accompanied by senior management's recognition that HRM is a significant force in achieving organizational effectiveness.[3]

HUMAN RESOURCE MANAGEMENT IN ACTION

Human Resources Critical to Company's Success

TORONTO—Organizations today are operating in an environment in which the only resource that can make a significant difference is people, says Heather Reisman, Managing Director of Paradigm Consulting Inc. and a keynote speaker at the Ontario Society for Training and Development's tenth annual conference. Reisman says the current recession is part of a greater economic restructuring occurring world-wide, and the blind slashing of staff is a "ludicrous" response to change. "This is a period of fundamental restructuring," Reisman says, and the most important investment any organization can make is in its people: "Never before has it been so critical to recognize the importance of human resources, and of investing in human resources."

As we move from the industrial age into the information age, we are undergoing a "paradigm shift"— the working model of the successful organization in the 1990s is changing, Reisman says. The characteristics of industrial-age companies that have been unfortunately carried over into the new age, such as technological sources policies, are hindering organizations from transferring themselves into the "intelligent" companies they must become in order to meet the challenge of global competition and economic interdependence. The changing realities of the international marketplace mean organizations must become customer- rather than product-driven, and "people friendly" toward both employees and customers.

Intelligent organizations are learning-oriented, flexible, cross-functional, participative, and adaptive. The emphasis is on "value-added," Reisman says, but "value can't be added in hierarchical structures."

Reisman says that most organizations today are mired in the old paradigm and run the risk of becoming hopelessly out of date. Some of the symptoms of "old age" are dissatisfied customers, low productivity, poor employee morale, high turnover, and the inability to attract quality people. The challenge for HR practitioners is to try to reinvent the organization and help it stay "in sync" with the environment. Human resource policies must reflect the realities of the "new breed" of employers—workers who are more sophisticated and demanding than their predecessors—and HR professionals must help develop policies and practices to attract, attain, and motivate high-quality employees.

Reisman emphasizes that managers as well as workers must adopt a multi-disciplinary "head-set"— an understanding that even specialists must employ their skills in the greater context of the outside world. She adds that two of the most important tools for developing new corporate cultures are training and communication.

SOURCE: *Human Resources Management in Canada*, Report Bulletin no. 94 (Scarborough, Ont.: Prentice-Hall Canada Inc., December 1990), p. 4. Used with permission.

Purposes and Importance of Human Resource Management

The purposes and importance of human resource management are to

- Help the organization to design, develop, implement, and administer the type of policies, procedures, and activities which will enable the effective and efficient management of its human resources
- Help the organization to establish and manage a harmonious working relationship between itself and its employees
- Ensure that the organization complies with provincial and federal laws (e.g., human rights legislation, employment equity laws, labour laws)

- Help the organization to create the necessary climate that encourages employees to develop and utilize their skills to the fullest extent
- Help the organization to retain productive employees, and develop employees to current and future organization performance requirements to help increase productivity
- Develop policies and programs that meet the economic and emotional needs of the organization's human resources
- Help the organization to create a work environment that minimizes or eliminates risks to employee health and safety
- Assist the organization to maintain and/or increase its ability to attract the quality and quantity of job candidates needed in light of the organization's strategic and operational goals, staffing needs, and the desired organizational culture and climate

THE HISTORY OF HUMAN RESOURCE MANAGEMENT

The history of human resource management has generally reflected prevailing beliefs and attitudes held in society about workers. Industry in general has not led the way by introducing new directions in human resource management.[4] Generally, business has tended to react to trends rather than initiate them.[5]

In the early 1900s, human resource management, or personnel administration, as it was then called, played either a very subservient or a nonexistent role in organizations. It was generally held in low esteem where it did exist and was usually located at the bottom of the organization's chart. During this period there were very few laws that regulated or affected working conditions and the employer-employee relationship. Organizations generally operated in what was considered their own best interest (which was to maximize productivity and increase profits.) The human factor was generally considered unimportant or irrelevant. Two important developments that have had a dramatic impact on human resource management are scientific management and the human relations movement.

Scientific Management

scientific management

The **scientific management** of late 1800s and early 1900s has had significant impact on management and the management-employee relationship. The process of "scientifically" analyzing manufacturing processes, reducing production costs, and compensating employees was called scientific management. It has helped shape the managerial attitude that views workers as another factor in production—one that is motivated primarily by economic gain. Frederick Taylor was the driving force behind the scientific management. He emphasized systematic job design; task simplification; compensation tied to production; proper selection of workers with the skills, abilities, and capacities required to become superior performers; and the placement of the right individual in the right job. He emphasized the need for scientific job design, selection, training, and wage determination.

- *Scientific job design* entails observing, recording, and classifying job activities as they are performed.
- *Scientific selection* refers to the selection of workers who possess the required skills and abilities needed to perform the task (e.g., through aptitude tests).

- *Scientific training* refers to training workers for specialized tasks.
- *Scientific wage determination* refers to the creation of a wage differential, piece-rate incentive system whereby workers receive pay based on performance, and extra pay per piece produced in excess of the daily standard.

Taylor also felt that wage incentives would lead to higher wages for workers, increased profits for the organization, and harmony in the workplace. He also emphasized the need for cooperation which he felt could best be achieved through the use of scientific methods, rules, and procedures that were binding on both workers and management.

Taylor's application of scientific management focused primarily on using careful job analysis to identify the one best way to perform each of the organization's tasks. He believed that management had the responsibility to plan, organize, and determine the best methods for performing a job. Taylor felt that workers had the responsibility to do what they did best—labour.

The Human Relations Movement

During the 1920s and 1930s the concept of human relations emerged, and was fully embraced in the 1940s. The primary aim of the **human relations movement** was an examination of jobs from the perspective of workers. As such the movement focused on social solidarity, work group behaviour, and non-authoritarian supervisors. The Hawthorne studies, which were pioneered by Elton Mayo and other researchers, were the driving force behind the movement.

human relations movement

The human relations advocates believed that the attitudes and feelings of workers were important and therefore deserved more attention. These advocates criticized managers for treating workers as machines.

Between 1924 and 1933 a series of experiments known as the Hawthorne studies was conducted at the Western Electric Company on the type of factors that influence workers' morale and productivity. These studies were the most comprehensive experiments ever undertaken to evaluate the attitudes, behaviour, and reactions of workers in a field experiment. The conclusions had a significant and a far-reaching impact on the practice of management.

The researchers found that workers' feelings, sentiments, emotions, and morale were greatly influenced by factors such as working conditions, supervisory leadership style, and management's philosophy regarding workers. In addition, treating workers with dignity and respect was found to contribute significantly to the workers' job satisfaction and the attainment of higher levels of productivity. It also was asserted that economic incentives that had been considered the key motivator in scientific management theories were really of secondary importance to workers.

The researchers found that workers spontaneously formed groups, established group norms, and controlled productivity through these norms. These **group norms** were enforced by a variety of social pressures. Workers who produced in excess of group standards were called "ratebusters," those whose output was too little were called "chiselers," and those who complained to a superior were called "squealers." These norms provided solid evidence that peer group pressures influence workers' behaviour.

group norms

The human relations approach had wide appeal. It was embraced by many organizations and was considered instrumental in enhancing the working conditions of many workers.

The human relations movement came under severe criticism for over-compensating for the impersonal and dehumanizing effect of scientific management. It was charged that the human relations movement theories failed to recognize the importance of structure, standards, procedures, and work rules to control employees' behaviour and guide their conduct to achieve organizational goals. The movement was also criticized for oversimplifying the concept of human motivation and behaviour in an organizational environment and for failing to recognize the uniqueness of each individual (i.e., each individual has different beliefs, values, needs, expectations, interests, and abilities).

Modern Era

Human resource management has evolved in four main stages.[6] As noted previously, in the early 1900s (the first stage) personnel administrators first took over hiring and firing from foremen, ran the payroll department, and administered benefit plans. It was a job consisting largely of ensuring that procedures were followed. As technology in such areas as testing and interviewing began to emerge, the personnel department began to play an expanded role in employee selection, training, and promotion.

The emergence of a strong union movement as well as the depression in the 1930s drove the second expansion of personnel management's role. The rise of unions substantially increased the status and power of the personnel management function. Companies now needed the personnel department to counter the union's efforts to organize the company or (failing that) to deal effectively with the union. The depression of the 1930s led workers to seek government intervention to provide some form of financial protection, assistance, and protection of their rights to join unions. The government intervened and established various legislations. A minimum wage act was established, and an unemployment insurance program was established to help the unemployed meet their financial obligations until they could secure other forms of employment. Legislations also were passed to protect workers' rights to belong to unions.

As a result of these legislations organizations now had to take into account the need to ensure compliance with government legislations and the society's expectations and objectives. This led to an increase in the importance of the personnel department in organizations particularly in the 1940s and 1950s. During this era they had to help organizations contend with the impact of behavioural theories, and motivation theories in particular.

The third major change in personnel management came about as a result of government legislation of the 1960s, 1970s and 1980s. Various laws were passed that affected employees' human rights, wages, working conditions, health and safety, and benefits. This led to a dramatic increase in the role and function of personnel departments in organizations. Effective employment policies and practices became more important because of societal, governmental, and organizational challenges and objectives, and because of the penalties that could be imposed on organizations that failed to meet these challenges and objectives. It was during the latter part of this era that the term *human resource management* emerged. The change to human resource management from personnel administration was not just a change in name. The change represented a shift in emphasis: whereas personnel administration emphasized maintenance and administration, HRM emphasizes corporate contribution, proactive management, and the initiation of change.[7]

In this phase (as in phase two), human resource management continued to make a positive contribution by providing expertise in areas like recruitment, screening, and training. Thus the human resource management department could perform these staffing activities for the company, freeing line managers to concentrate on such primary responsibilities as production and sales. Whether dealing with unions (phase two) or equal employment (phase three), human resource management gained status in these two stages as much for what it could do to protect the organization from problems as for the positive contribution it made to the firm's effectiveness.

Today, "human resource management" is speeding through phase 4, and its role is shifting and must continue to shift from protector and screener to planner and agent of change. The evolution of human resource management reflects this, and in fact today's and tomorrow's human resource departments will be very different from those in the past.

CURRENT HUMAN RESOURCE MANAGEMENT FUNCTIONS

All managers are, in a sense, human resource managers, since they all get involved in activities like recruiting, interviewing, selecting, and training. Yet most firms also have a human resource management department with its own human resource manager. How do the duties of this human resource manager and his or her staff relate to the human resource management duties of the other "line" managers in the organization? In management, it is convenient to distinguish between two types of authority: line authority and staff authority.

Line Authority

Line authority, possessed by managers of operating departments, authorizes these managers to make decisions about production and about their subordinates. For example, production managers and sales managers are typically line managers. They are usually responsible for production output, job assignments, promotions, supervision, and performance appraisal. Human resource department managers also are line managers but only in certain circumstances (i.e., they are line managers of their own HR department subordinates, and of workers in service areas (like the plant cafeteria).

line authority

Staff Authority

Staff authority, possessed by service managers, allows these managers to assist and advise, but not direct, line managers. The human resource department managers are usually staff managers. They are usually authorized to assist and advise line managers in areas such as recruiting, selection, compensation, and training.

staff authority

Line Managers' HRM Responsibilities

According to one expert, "The direct handling of people is, and always has been, and integral part of every line manager's responsibility, from the president down to the lowest level supervisor."[8]

For example, one major company outlines its line supervisor's responsibilities for effective human resource management under the following general headings:

1. Placing the right person on the right job
2. Starting new employees in the organization (orientation)
3. Training employees for jobs that are new to them
4. Improving job performance of each person
5. Gaining creative cooperation and developing smooth working relationships
6. Interpreting the company's policies and procedures
7. Controlling labour costs
8. Developing potential abilities of each person
9. Creating and maintaining a high level of departmental morale
10. Protecting health and physical condition of employees

In small organizations, line managers may carry out all of these human resource management duties unassisted. But as the organization grows, these managers need the assistance, specialized knowledge, and advice of a separate human resource management staff.[9] The size and complexity of the organization are usually major factors in the decision of management to establish a HRM department. Another factor is determining when the benefits of doing so exceed the cost. As the growing organization must comply with increased government legislations, the burden of effectively managing its human resources also increases. Operating line managers often find that HRM activities are interfering with their other responsibilities, and thus they must delegate some of their work load to the HRM department.

The Role of the Human Resource Department

Human resource departments do not control many of the financial and material resources that influence employees' contributions to organizational goals. They also do not determine the organization's strategies nor the supervisors' treatment of their subordinates. Nonetheless they influence both because of their unique roles in the organizations.[10]

Human resource departments provide specialized service assistance[11] to other departments. In doing so, they carry out three distinct functions as summarized below:

1. *A Line Function.* First, the human resource management specialist exerts line authority within the human resource management department.

2. *A Coordinative Function.* The human resource management specialist also functions as a coordinator of human resource activities, a duty often referred to as **functional control**. Here the human resource management specialists and departments act as "the right arm of the top executive to assure him or her that human resource management objectives, policies, and procedures (concerning, for example, occupational safety and health), which have been approved and adopted are being consistently carried out by line managers."[12]

3. *Staff (Service) Functions.* Staff functions or service to line management is the "bread and butter" of the human resource director's job. For example the human resource department assists in hiring, training, evaluating, rewarding, counselling, promoting, and terminating employees at all levels. It also ad-

functional control

TABLE 1.1 Human Resource Activities: Line-Staff Assignments

Activity	Company Has Activity	(No. of Cos.)	RESPONSIBILITY FOR THE ACTIVITY IS ASSIGNED TO:[1]		
			HR Dept. Only	HR and Other Dept(s).	Other Dept(s). Only
Interviewing	99%	(681)	37%	61%	2%
Personnel recordkeeping/ information systems	99	(680)	77	22	1
Vacation/leave processing	99	(680)	51	35	14
Insurance benefits administration	99	(677)	87	8	5
Orientation/induction	99	(675)	61	37	2
Wage/salary adjustment processing	99	(674)	77	22	1
Workers' compensation administration	98	(672)	73	15	12
Promotion/transfer/ separation processing	98	(672)	71	28	1
Disciplinary procedures	98	(671)	43	55	2
Payroll administration	98	(669)	25	25	50
Recruiting	98	(668)	73	25	2
Job descriptions	97	(666)	62	35	2
Unemployment compensation	97	(666)	82	11	7
Wage/salary policy development	97	(665)	80	18	2
Performance appraisal, management	97	(665)	47	44	8
Performance appraisal, nonmanagement	97	(663)	47	45	8
Affirmative action	97	(662)	87	11	2
Administrative services	97	(662)	15	16	69
Purchasing	95	(654)	3	7	90
Maintenance/janitorial services	95	(653)	10	5	85
Safety programs/compliance	95	(650)	46	33	20
Job evaluation	94	(647)	70	28	2
Security measures	94	(646)	22	22	57
Training, nonmanagement	94	(641)	21	51	28
Supervisory training	94	(641)	48	44	8
Exit interviews	93	(639)	86	13	1
Complaint procedures	92	(633)	54	44	2
Job analysis	91	(626)	75	23	3
Employee communications/ publications	91	(624)	43	37	21
Award/recognition programs	91	(624)	66	29	5
Pension/retirement plan administration	90	(618)	73	18	8
Public/media relations	89	(612)	17	17	66

TABLE 1.1 (continued)

Activity	Company Has Activity	(No. of Cos.)	RESPONSIBILITY FOR THE ACTIVITY IS ASSIGNED TO:[1]		
			HR Dept. Only	HR and Other Dept(s).	Other Dept(s). Only
Travel/transportation services	89%	(608)	9%	14%	77%
Management development	88	(604)	49	44	6
Community service	88	(601)	30	31	39
Business insurance/risk management	88	(600)	12	17	72
Recreation/social programs	86	(590)	61	30	9
Tuition aid/scholarships	86	(590)	83	12	4
Human resource forecasting/planning	85	(580)	58	37	5
Preemployment testing	80	(551)	85	12	3
Executive compensation	80	(548)	55	26	19
Relocation	75	(512)	75	20	5
Office/clerical services	73	(502)	16	22	62
Organization development	73	(498)	46	44	10
Career planning/ development	72	(489)	51	45	5
Food service/cafeteria	70	(478)	36	6	58
Employee assistance plan/ counselling	69	(472)	83	14	4
Incentive pay plans	69	(472)	50	38	12
College recruiting	67	(462)	79	17	4
Productivity/motivation programs	67	(461)	26	61	13
Medical services	61	(414)	73	12	15
Suggestion systems	60	(408)	46	35	19
Health/wellness program	58	(400)	78	14	8
Outplacement	58	(396)	91	8	1
Attitude surveys	55	(374)	81	16	3
Thrift/savings plan administration	53	(364)	71	21	8
Preretirement counselling	52	(356)	90	4	5
Union/labour relations	50	(344)	71	27	2
Library	44	(301)	21	9	70
Profit sharing plan administration	39	(273)	59	23	18
Flexible benefits plan administration	36	(245)	87	11	3
Stock plan administration	33	(227)	57	20	23
Flexible spending account administration	29	(197)	83	11	6
Child-care centre	10	(67)	36	9	55

[1] Percentages are based on companies providing data on where responsibility for the activity is assigned. Percentages may not add up to 100 due to rounding.

SOURCE: "Personnel Activities: Line-Staff Assignments," Bureau of National Affairs, *Bulletin to Management* (September 1, 1988), p. 2.

ministers the various benefit programs (health and accident insurance, retirement, vacation, etc.). It further assists line managers in their attempts to comply with employment equity and occupational safety laws, and it has an important role with respect to grievances and labour relations.[13] As part of these service activities, the human resource director and department also carry out an "innovative role." They do this by providing career planning for employees. Human resource directors stay on top of trends and help their organizations implement the necessary programs.

Table 1.1 shows many of the organization's activities that are accomplished jointly by line and staff managers. As shown, in some areas, such as wage and salary policy development and job evaluation, the HR department plays the major role. In others, such as interviewing and disciplinary activities, the duties are split more evenly. It should be obvious that in practice good HRM is a joint, cooperative effort, with HRM specialists and operating managers working together.

Figure 1.1 illustrates a common placement of the human resource department in small organizations employing 200-400 workers. As indicated the manager of human resources usually reports to the head of the organization. Support staff usually have a wide variety of activities. The overall activities of the department would be to assist the operating departments with HRM processes such as recruiting, complying with government legislations, and maintaining human resources records.

Figure 1.2 illustrates the activities of the human resource department at a typical, medium-sized financial institution. These activities are structured by areas of specialization. As shown the positions usually found in medium organizations include a director of human resources, an employment manager, a human resources development manager, an employment equity coordinator, and a compensation manager. This indicates that in medium-sized organizations there is a need for expertise or specialization in each of the human resources positions. Human resource management specialists are expected to help formulate, recommend, and implement appropriate policies and procedures to ensure that the organization complies with government legislations and to make use of the human resources required to accomplish the organization's goals.

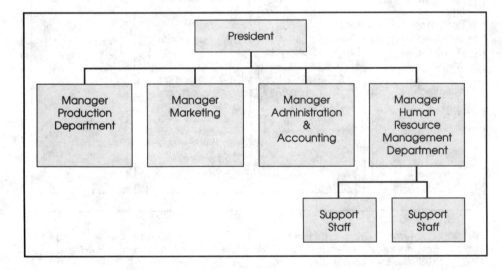

FIGURE 1.1
The Human Resource Department in a Small Organization

THE ORGANIZATION: A SYSTEMS VIEW

An organization is an open, social entity, which is goal directed, structured, and which has identifiable boundaries. It consists of resources that are transformed into outputs for users. All organizations fit this description whether they are public or private, profit or nonprofit, business or government, small or large, efficient or inefficient, or weak or powerful.[14]

As *open systems*, all organizations must interact with the environment to survive and prosper. The organization continuously has to find the resources it needs, and it must monitor, interpret, and act on environmental challenges, disturbances, and uncertainties.[15]

FIGURE 1.2
The Human Resource Department in a Medium-sized Canadian Financial Organization

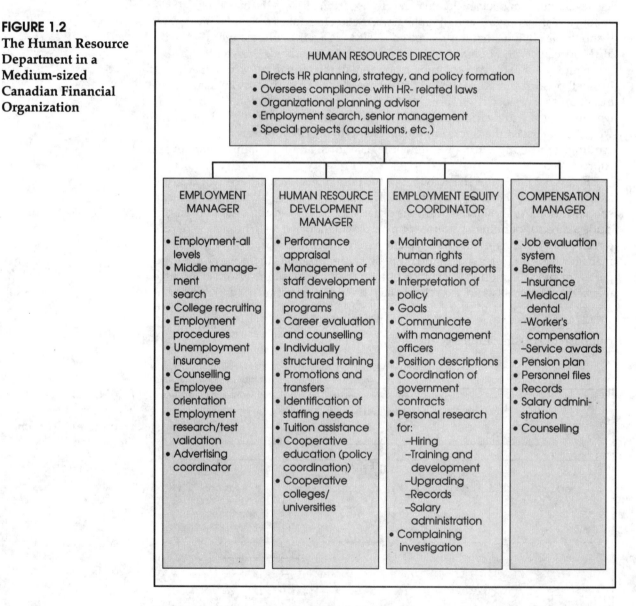

Source: V.V. Murray, "Organization and Administration of the Human Resources Management Function" in *Human Resources Management in Canada* (Scarborough, Ont.: Prentice-Hall Canada, Inc., 1990), p. 15,067. Used with permission.

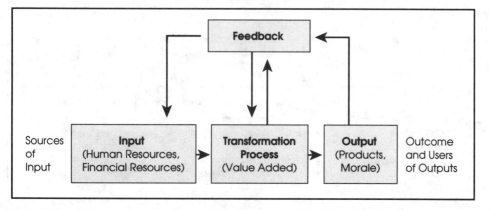

FIGURE 1.3
Organization as an
Open System: The
Input–Output Model

Figure 1.3 illustrates the open system model of the organization. The model represents the input—transformation—output (and feedback) processes. The framework presents a set of interrelated and interdependent parts that are arranged in such a way as to convey the relationships and information flow among the various parts in the organization.

The input consists of the human resources, financial resources, and material and other physical resources that go into the system in order for it to operate. Human resources are the most important input. It is through the utilization of its people's skills, knowledge, abilities, and other qualities that organizations are able to utilize, generate, and dispose of their resources, products, and services.

The transformation process involves changing or transforming inputs into something of value. It is through this activity that organizations plan, organize, and control human resources and the work processes; develop policies, procedures, and rules; and make decisions about such things as the allocation of resources.

The outputs result from the transformation process. This category represents such things as specific products and services for customers and clients, as well as employee morale. In other words output represents the end-goals or objectives of the organization.

The feedback loop is directly linked to the transformation process and outcome components. This loop provides information so that adjustments and corrective measures or changes may be undertaken in order to achieve desired results.

Strengths and Weaknesses

The systems approach has many strengths. It allows one to view an organization as a whole framework. It offers a rational and straightforward method of analysis of organizational strengths and weaknesses. It shows all the interrelations and interdependencies among the components in the organization and it shows the role and relevance of feedback. The weaknesses of the systems approach stem from the fact that it oversimplifies organizational relationships, both inside and outside the organization. Processes within the system are affected by influences outside the organization and in reality it is sometimes difficult to trace specific effects to specific causes.

FIGURE 1.4
Human Resource
Management: A
Systems View

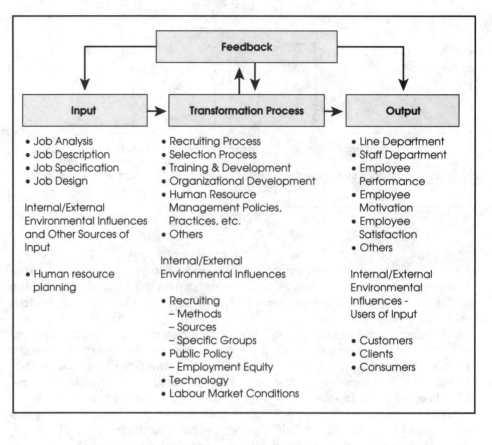

Human Resource Management: A Systems View

One of the primary functions of human resource management specialists is to facilitate the most effective use of human resources in the organization. The systems approach, despite its weaknesses, is very useful in showing how the different parts interact. This is illustrated in Figure 1.4.

The input component includes job analysis. Briefly, through job analysis the human resource management (HRM) specialist determines the nature of job, and gathers, analyzes, and records the activities and other essential characteristics of the job to be performed by the job holder. From job analysis the HRM specialist prepares the job description. The job description describes the duties, responsibilities, and other basic tasks associated with the job. The job descriptions are then used to prepare job specifications. Briefly, job specifications define the skills, knowledge, and abilities required to perform the job. Specific items usually defined are education, experience, training, and physical and mental demands. Another input factor is job design. It is the design of the function, content, and responsibility assigned to each member and the physical circumstances in which the individuals perform their jobs. Human resource planning also influences the input component.

The transformation process is achieved through the recruiting process, the selection process, and the other activities shown in Figure 1.4. The transformation process is influenced by the methods and sources of recruiting, government policies, and labour market conditions, among other influences.

The result is the output component. The line or staff department receives the new job holder who is assigned to perform required tasks to produce the organization's products or services. The output component also shows the level of the individual's job satisfaction or dissatisfaction, and the level of motivation or lack of motivation.

Next the feedback loop provides the HRM specialist with valuable information of success or failure. It may indicate what adjustment is required and where it should take place—whether at the input or transformation level—in order to achieve desired outputs. If job analyses, job descriptions, job specifications, and job designs are not done properly, they will have an adverse impact on the transformation process and the output level. For example, if the skills and education requirements are incorrectly defined, the result could be hiring the wrong person. It could either increase the organization's training and development costs, or result in increased recruitment costs to hire a replacement.

CONTEMPORARY CHALLENGES IN HUMAN RESOURCE MANAGEMENT

Internal and external environmental influences are having a dramatic impact on the field of human resource management. Internal factors such as the organizational climate, culture, and policies help determine the quality of job candidates the organization may attract, as well as the organization's ability to retain desired workers. External forces such as technology, government, and changing social and labour force demographics are also having an important impact on the quality and variety of employees that organizations can attract and retain. These influences intensify the importance of sound human resource management policies and practices.

INFLUENCES OF THE EXTERNAL ENVIRONMENT

Various external environmental factors have direct or indirect influences on human resource management. The most common external environmental influences are labour market conditions, labour unions, government, and technology. Effective human resource management requires HRM specialists to monitor the environment on an ongoing basis; assess the impact of any challenges, changes, and disturbances; and be proactive, rather than reactive, in the implementation of HRM policies and programs.

Labour Market Conditions

The **labour market** is the geographical and demographical area where an organization recruits employees and where individuals seek employment. It is the environment where the forces of supply and demand interact. One indicator of an organization's effectiveness is its demonstrated ability to compete successfully for high calibre human resources. Job candidates are motivated by a variety of factors to join organizations. These include the attractiveness of the organization, the organization's climate, compensation, location, job security, opportunities for advancement, working conditions, type of industry, and reputation.

The labour market is not controlled or influenced by any one factor. It is therefore unstructured and often unpredictable. Nevertheless, organizations must constantly monitor and track trends to determine the supply and demand of human resources. This is important for many reasons. The organization needs to find out the prevailing rate for needed talents, how difficult it is to attract and recruit staff,

labour market

and other relevant factors that must be taken into account in order for it to compete. The organization must also monitor the labour market conditions to determine and respond to present and emerging trends.

Recent trends include changes in the composition of the labour market as well as changing values. Beginning in the 1970s there has been a tremendous diversity and increase in the rate of participation of women, visible minorities, single-parents, and better educated individuals in the labour market. Organizations must therefore design programs and policies that recognize and take advantage of these trends.

Labour Unions

labour unions

Labour unions are an important external environmental factor and exert strong pressure upon the policies and practices of organizations. Labour unions are the organizations of individuals who are joined together for the purpose of presenting a united front or collective voice in dealing with management in order to secure and further the social and economic interests and well-being of their membership.

Labour unions exert significant influence and pressure on organizations' policies and practices in several ways. Within unionized organizations, labour unions reduce managerial discretion and flexibility in implementing and administering human resource policies, procedures, and practices. Wages, benefits and services increases, job security, and working conditions negotiated by the unions for their members create pressures on management to provide a similar or even slightly better package to their nonunionized staff in order to avoid dissatisfaction among those staff that could result in further unionizing of its labour force. Labour unions also influence the human resource policies and practices in nonunionized organizations. This is achieved through the perceived threat of unionizing those companies. As a result these organizations may be forced to establish some degree of parity in terms of pay, employee benefits and services, working conditions, and the way they treat their workers.

The existence of unions has important implications for the human resource manager. The manager must assist the organization to develop sound human resource management policies and practices that promote good union-management relations, and create and maintain a harmonious work environment. The human resource manager must be knowledgeable about negotiations, contract administration, and all pertinent labour legislations.

Government

Various legislations enacted by governments have had a dramatic impact on the employment relationship. The federal government, the ten provinces, and the two territories have all enacted various legislations and laws all intended to achieve certain societal and public policy objectives. Some of these laws include human rights laws, and health and safety laws.

Human Rights Laws

All 13 jurisdictions have enacted human rights acts. All of these acts differ in detail, nature of application, and methods of application but are similar in terms of their purpose, which is the prohibition of discrimination in employment practices. All of the acts prohibit discrimination in employment based on sex, race, colour, religion, national origin or marital status. The acts also prohibit discrimination in the terms and conditions of employment, transfer, promotion, termination, and sexual harassment. All jurisdictions make exceptions when a bona fide occupational requirement exists. (See Chapter 2 for a discussion of the human rights acts).

Health and Safety

All jurisdictions have enacted various laws designed to protect the health and safety of workers at work. All have established workers' compensation boards that require the employer to insure workers against personal injury, and other work-related accidents. These jurisdictions have also enacted legislations to protect workers from workplace health hazards. Each legislation varies in content and administration but includes common characteristics. (See Chapter 18 for a discussion of health and safety.)

All of these government laws and regulations have important implications for human resource management specialists. It is their responsibility to interpret the laws and to help shape the organization's policies to ensure compliance with them.

Technology

Technology is the use of available knowledge and techniques to produce goods and services. The complexity of technology influences the skill level and organization size required to use that technology.[16]

The present rate of growth of computers in the business field is having a significant impact on business operations. According to two writers,[17] the major challenge of the 1990s is innovation on two fronts: people and technology. Computers are revolutionizing organizations and the various processes within organizations. Through the use of computer technologies companies are able to become more competitive, strengthen manufacturing practices, enhance product quality, improve service to clients and customers, and produce large quantities of data.

Other recent technological changes include the increasing trend toward robotics. This innovation is the operation of programmable robots to perform a variety of routine and non-routine manufacturing assembly operations. The use of robots helps management streamline operations, increase speed, increase operational efficiency, ensure flexibility and predictability, increase productivity, reduce costs, use its human resources more effectively, and increase profit. The use of robots and other innovative technologies such as optical technologies, robotics engineering, and computerized X-ray scanners, Magnetic Renaissance Imagery (MRI), helps to reduce the need for certain jobs and also eliminates some jobs.

The computer's speed, on-line capability, storage and retrieval capacity, flexibility, array of software packages, and variety of desktop and lap top models enable the human resource manager to design and implement special and general purpose programs. Some of these purposes include:

- Human resource information system
- Salary, wages, and benefits systems
- Employee personal data
- Employee absenteeism, attendance, health, and safety records
- Employment equity programs
- Government statistics

The rapid growth of computerized technologies has created increased anxiety, tension, resentment, and worker alienation. Unions have consistently expressed concerns about job displacement as well as about health hazards. According to Statistics Canada figures,[18] between 1971 and 1981 more than half a million jobs were lost due to technological innovations. But this was offset by the more than 2.5 million jobs created as a result of the substantial growth in demand and use of new technologies. These developments have serious implications for human resource managers in terms of retraining programs and counselling employees.

Computerized Information System and HRM

human resource
information system
(HRIS)

The computer-based information system popularly known as **human resource information system (HRIS)**, is revolutionizing HRM departments. This system is being used to store detailed information on employees, HRM policies and procedures, government laws and regulations, and health and safety records. Computer information systems also help the organization to maintain qualifications inventories on large numbers of employees that could not adequately be done manually. Information that can be saved on this system includes: work experience, product knowledge, industry experience, formal education, training courses, foreign language skills, relocation limitations, career interests, transfers, promotions, and performance appraisals.

The computerization of essential information facilitates the retrieval and availability of information on a timely basis. It contributes to the organization's efficiency and effectiveness. However, the more computerized the organization becomes, the more intense the human resource manager's need to create better ways to actually control the security of the human resources data that are stored in the data banks. It is important to guard against unauthorized access to confidential employee information, particularly in an era when the expansion of end-users' computing capabilities offers more opportunities for more individuals to access information in computer data banks. This requires the HRM manager to implement appropriate safeguards to protect employees' privacy. HRIS will be discussed further in Chapter 3.

The Nature of the Canadian Labour Force

The Canadian labour force is said to be one of the most affluent among the major industrialized countries in the world. The growth in affluence is due to such factors as a substantial increase in the educational level of the labour force; significant increases in direct and indirect compensation; a decrease in the number of hours worked per week; increased jobs in the service sectors; and the increased availability of part-time jobs. The term **demographics** refers to the composition of individuals in the work force. This means the age, sex, marital status, education level, and any other important characteristic of the population.[19]

demographics

Age

The dominant characteristics of the Canadian labour force are shaped by the bulge created by the post World War II baby boom.[20] This has led until the 1980s to a domination of the work force by the **baby boomers**. These baby boomers began crowding into the labour market in the late 1960s. The number helped to expand the economy and made it easier for HR managers to focus on issues like cost contain-

baby boomers

FIGURE 1.5
Population Projections
for Canada

(Under Assumption of Fertility Rate of 1.5) % Distribution of Population by Age Group			
	0–14	15–64	65+	Mean Age
1991	20.5	68.1	11.4	35.5
1996	19.0	68.9	12.1	36.8
2001	17.2	70.2	16.6	38.2
2011	15.2	70.5	14.3	40.8
2021	14.3	66.7	19.0	43.2
2051	13.0	61.2	25.8	46.2

SOURCE: Statistics Canada, *Current Demographic Analysis: Fertility in Canada—From Baby Boom to Baby Bust,* Catalogue #91-524E (Ottawa, November 1984.) Reproduced with the permission of the Minister of Supply and Services Canada, 1991.

ment, since recruitment and screening (while important) were not the most critical problems. As can be seen in Figure 1.5, the baby boomers are rapidly advancing towards middle age. If fertility in Canada remains at the same rate, then the average age of the population will increase substantially. The implications for the HR specialists are that the buyers' market has now ended, and it is the (relatively few) sellers who now have the upper hand in selecting the firms that they will work for. The human resource policies that attract and motivate a predominantly young work force may not be appropriate for an aging population.

Education

The level of education of the Canadian labour force is increasing at a significant rate. This indicates that more Canadians are pursuing higher education through a variety of institutions. These include trade schools, community colleges, and universities. Adult Canadians are returning to evening part-time school in record numbers.[21] Many institutions are experiencing dramatic increases in part-time enrolment. For example, at Atkinson College of York University, part-time enrolment increased from 7507 in 1981 to 8879 in 1990, an 18% increase.[22] A better educated and better qualified labour market requires that the organization ensure that the talents and capabilities of its work force are being fully utilized and that appropriate channels of opportunities are available for career growth.

Minorities and Ethnic Groups

The proportion of visible and other minorities entering the Canadian labour market is growing. These visible minorities and ethnic groups work in a variety of tasks ranging from menial jobs, to skilled trades, to technical jobs, to professional jobs. A majority of these groups are immigrants. This has implications for human resource managers in that they must ensure that the organizations develop policies in addition to complying with human rights acts to accommodate the diverse cultural characteristics of these groups.

Women

The number of women in the Canadian work force has increased dramatically in the past 15 years and indications are that the number is growing. As a consequence of such factors as employment equity, pay equity, and society's changing values, more women are entering a variety of occupations formerly occupied by men. Some of the factors that have contributed to the dramatic increase in the participation of women in the work force include smaller family size, increased divorce rate, the need and desire for dual family incomes, increased educational level, and the availability of more flexible working hours and part-time jobs. The advent of an increase in women in the work force has created a pool of qualified job candidates that was not previously available. The increase of women in the work force is also creating a demand for a variety of other services such as day-care facilities.

Two separate projections confirm dramatic growth in female participation in the labour force. One projection indicates that by 1995, approximately 57% of Canadian women will enter the labour market.[23] The other study projects that by the year 2005, 85% of Canadian women between the ages of 25 and 54 will enter the labour force.[24]

Currently, over 44% of Canadian labour force is made up of women. By the year 2000, women's participation in the work force is expected to match men's. The average woman works a total of 30 to 45 years. Consequently, this group represents an enormous resource for organizations. At the same time there is strong evidence that women are under-utilized in the Canadian work force.[25]

It is important to note that women constitute 80% of the approximately 1.8 million part-time workforce in Canada today. These jobs are primarily located in the sales and service industry.[26]

Francophones

Canada is a bilingual country, and one of its provinces, Quebec, is predominantly French speaking. Other provinces such as Ontario and New Brunswick have a large French speaking population. There are 543 825 francophones in Ontario[27] and 225 590 in New Brunswick.[28] Organizations operating in these provinces, particularly in Quebec, must ensure that their policies, procedures, and practices conform to the requirements of the laws of those provinces.

Social Values

The combination of attributes that individuals bring to the job is greatly shaped by the beliefs, values, and attitudes employees acquired from their families and environments, before entering the organization. Many of these attitudes greatly influence an individual's motivation and level of productivity. V. V. Murray provides us with four important values that influence an individual's motivational stability and productivity.[29]

The Importance of Work in One's Life

For older workers, having a secure, well-paid job is of critical importance in their definition of a "good life," and leisure activities come well behind work in importance. For many younger employees (and managers) today, these priorities are reversed. The importance of having a job and keeping it is also less important for certain other cultural sub-groups in society. For example, people raised in chronic poverty have been known to become dependent on welfare and never develop the initiative to get and stay with a job, especially jobs that pay the minimum wage.

Work Characteristic Priorities

In addition to the general question of the overall importance of work in one's life, there are also very relevant differences among people with regard to what aspects or characteristics of a job are most important to them. At least part of these priorities is a reflection of more general sub-cultural values. There are ethnic, regional, generational, and social-class variations in the relative importance of such characteristics as job security, a high income, opportunities for promotion, autonomy in work methods, and congeniality of coworkers and supervisors. For example, traditional white, Anglo-Saxon, protestant, middle-class values give high priority to job security, high income, and "getting ahead" in terms of moving up the corporate hierarchy. Less importance is ascribed to the specific kind of work one has to do, or how one is treated by superiors or coworkers. Among certain groups of younger employees today, on the other hand, this ordering of priorities is quite different. The quality of working life in the form of interesting, varied, and challenging work and a congenial workplace comes first, while job promotion may be ranked quite low.

While the youth of the 1970s and early 1980s appeared to be less interested in income than their parents (preferring an interesting job to one that paid well but was not interesting), many sociologists believe that the youth of the late 1980s are increasingly materialistic and acquisitive. While still possessing a low tolerance for uninteresting, low-discretion work, they also gravitate more to jobs with high pay. Forced to choose, they are more likely to opt for the better paying but less interesting position. If neither is available, many simply opt out and return to live with their affluent, middle-class parents.

Organizational Discipline

Most members of society are conditioned, by a number of early experiences, to accept as "natural" the requirements of modern work settings that involve attendance at specified hours, at least five days of week throughout the year, and performing jobs according to largely predetermined methods at a certain minimum rate of speed. For others, the values according to which they were raised do not reinforce this kind of discipline, which can create major problems.

Attitudes toward Authority

One final important value is that governing the legitimacy of power: that is, "who can give orders about what and how" in a work setting. Groups vary as to who they will accept in positions of authority, in what matters they will accept direction, and the style or manner in which a supervisor may address them. Among those raised in the older European tradition, for example, anyone with a title can give orders concerning almost anything in the workplace, in as authoritarian a manner as possible, and expect to be obeyed. Younger people and those from certain occupational or other cultural backgrounds tend not to accept this type of management.

The important thing for the practising HR manager is to know the overall "value framework" held by the major groupings of employees in the organization and to realize how HR policies must adapt to the dominant values represented.

INFLUENCES OF THE INTERNAL ENVIRONMENT

Various internal environmental factors influence human resource management. The most common internal influences are HRM policies, organizational culture, organizational climate, and approaches followed to improve productivity. How successful the organization will be in meeting its objectives depends on how it deals with these challenges.

Human Resource Management Policies

Human resource management policies are specific guides to management action, and help achieve the organization's goals and objectives. Further, human resource management policies are specific statements of intention committing the organization to a specific course of action. Policies are extremely important; they communicate to all employees acceptable and unacceptable behaviour; define the organization's positions on given issues; assure consistency in the treatment of all employees; communicate management's expectations of employees; assure continuity and predictability of course of action; and serve as standards against which performance can be measured. To be effective, human resource management policies must be written. A well-written policy lets everyone know the type of treatment they can expect to receive from management, and helps to improve the supervisor-subordinate relationship.

Appendix 1.1 lists the specific areas that may require formal policies and procedures. Appendix 1.2 lists guidelines for developing a set of HRM policies.

Organizational Culture

organizational culture

Another important internal environmental influence is organizational culture. **Organizational culture** consists of the core values, beliefs, behaviour patterns, understandings, assumptions, norms, perceptions, emotions, and feelings that are widely shared by the members in the organizations. Further, organizational culture helps to foster commitment of employees to the organization's goals, by bonding their core values and core beliefs together for the attainment of the organization's goals and for the benefits of all members.

Organizational culture serves a variety of purposes. It provides employees with a sense of direction; a sense of what is expected of them in terms of acceptable and unacceptable behaviour. It creates a sense of identity, orderliness, and consistency for employees in the organization. It serves to enhance the organization's social system, and shapes employees' attitudes about themselves, the organization, and their roles in the organization. An effective organizational culture fosters employee loyalty, commitment, and good feelings and serves as the glue that holds them together. It communicates to employees "what the organization believes in," and "what the organization stands for."

Some of the most successful organizations in Canada have demonstrated that organizational culture can be a major asset. For example IBM Canada and Dofasco have created organizational cultures characterized by the shared belief in the value of team work; the belief that human resources are the most important asset and that employees must be treated with respect, dignity, and sensitivity; and the belief that their customers are also important.

The human resource management department has an important role in assisting management in creating and maintaining the type of organizational culture that facilitates a cohesive and integrated work environment for employees, as well as one that invites customer loyalty. HRM specialists can help develop policies that encourage a spirit of teamwork and cooperation within and among business units in working toward common objectives, with an emphasis on identifying, acknowledging, and rewarding personal and unit excellence. Such policies can also emphasize the commonality between workers and management.

Organizational Climate

Organizations have personalities just like people. They can be friendly or unfriendly, warm or cold, supportive or unsupportive, open or secretive, rigid or flexible, innovative or stagnant. **Organizational climate** refers to the prevailing atmosphere that exists in organizations and the impact it has on employees. The type of climate that exists in the organization will reflect in the level of employee motivation, job satisfaction, performance, productivity, and the organization's profits. There are three major factors that influence's organization's climate: management leadership style, human resources policies and practices, and effective communication.

organizational climate

A positive climate exists when organizations do the following through leadership, policies and practices, and communication:

- demonstrate a high degree of trust and confidence in employees
- encourage creativity
- provide effective feedback
- encourage risk-taking and entrepreneurship
- promote participative and creative approaches to problem solving
- practise open, two-way communication
- provide employees with greater job responsibility
- establish and preserve effective management-employee relationships
- support management

Of course a negative organizational climate exists when the reverse of the above is practised. The human resource management manager must assist top management to establish and maintain a positive organizational climate.

Improving Performance and Productivity at Work

In the 1990s *all* managers will have to find concepts and techniques to improve productivity and performance at work. The approach to improved productivity and performance focused on is this book is to improve human behaviour at work through the application of modern human resource management concepts and techniques. Explaining how to use the ones currently shown to be effective for improving the productivity and performance of employees is one of the purposes of this book. We explain, for example, how to use interviewing and other selection techniques to hire high-performers, how to train and motivate employees, and how to use incentives, benefits, and positive reinforcement to improve performance at work. In order to do so, there must be better training programs for employees; improved work environments; employee participation in decision making; improved planning; better management-labour relations; better channels of communications; improved performance incentives; appropriate rewards for desired levels of performance; increased investment in more modern equipment; and increased recognition of employee contributions.

GROWING PROFESSIONALISM IN HUMAN RESOURCE MANAGEMENT

The increasing importance of human resource management has led to a movement designed to establish and maintain professional standards among the individuals employed in the human resource management field. In 1989 more than 2500 members of the Human Resources Professionals Association of Ontario (HRPAO), formerly Personnel Association of Ontario (PAO), received the first professional designation for practitioners in North America, the Human Resources Professional (HRP).[30] Since then a number of associations including those in British Columbia, Alberta, Manitoba, and Nova Scotia have expressed an interest in certification.[31] The need to professionalize the HRM field came about as a result of many forces. These include the increasing demand for HRM expertise now that management recognizes the importance of human resources, the growing concerns regarding productivity; the increasing need for experts to design training programs since rapid technological innovations can suddenly leave many employees with obsolete skills; and the growth in government legislations establishing employment equity programs, pay equity programs, and various occupational health and safety standards. Several provinces have their own body which establishes professional standards for their members. The broad or common objectives of each body are similar. For example the objectives of HRPAO and the Association of Human Resource Professionals of the Province of Quebec are as follows:

Ontario

- To establish uniform standards of knowledge, experience, and ethics for all persons engaged in the field of personnel management.
- To promote and further the education of its members in personnel management.
- To provide a medium for communication and exchange of information and knowledge relating to the field of personnel management.
- To make representation to government with respect to legislation and programs affecting the personnel function.

Quebec

- To provide opportunities for those engaged in the practice of human resource management (HRM) to exchange information, thus providing a basis for co-operation in meeting and solving common problems.
- To assist in providing training for members in the field of human resources.
- To assist to obtain information concerning HRM, and to provide information concerning source material dealing with policies, practices, labour laws, etc.
- To submit recommendation and provide information, when appropriate, to government organizations.

A recent survey of 325 Canadian HR professionals found that 76% favoured the concept of professional designation in the field. Almost half of the respondents

FIGURE 1.6
Subject Areas in
Certification/
Accreditation Human
Resources
Professionals
Association of Ontario

HRPAO Tier I: HRM Foundations	Tier II (any 3)
1. Human Resource Administration	1. Compensation
2. Organization Behaviour	2. Training and Development
3. Finance and Accounting	3. Industrial Relations
4. Labour Economics	4. Occupational Health and Safety
	5. Human Resources Planning
	6. Human Resources Research and Information Systems (HRRIS)

SOURCE: D.A. Ondrack, "P/R Professional Certification in Ontario: The PAO Model," paper presented at a symposium on professional education in P/R, Canadian Industrial Relations Association (CIRA), Dalhousie University, Halifax, N.S., May 26, 1981. The HRPAO courses are listed from HRPAO 1989 "Program Information"—Certificate in Personnel Management.

(45%) favour a designation that would be applicable at both the provincial and federal level.[32] Canada does not as yet have a national body that establishes standards and sets national criteria for certification. However, many colleges and universities have created undergraduate programs with majors in human resource management, as well as many graduate programs specializing in HRM. Human resource management specialists may take their required courses for certification through their provincial associations or through colleges and universities. Figure 1.6 shows a list of courses required by the Human Resources Professionals Association of Ontario. Although HRM Associations in each province establish and offers their own programs, there is considerable similarity among the programs that are offered.[33]

THE FRAMEWORK FOR THIS BOOK

This book is organized into five major sections and grouped around different themes. These sections/themes are, of course, interconnected but, at the same time, they reflect different focuses of attention. The five sections are Recruitment and Placement; Training and Development; Appraisal and Career Management; Compensation, Protection, and Motivation; Employee Rights, Safety, and Representation.

Part One: Recruitment and Placement

This section covers the recruitment and placement component of human resource management. We discuss the activities or functions that influence the legal environment, human resource planning, and job analysis.

The Legal Environment

The legal environment is very important to the human resource management process. It includes an extensive network of federal and provincial laws and regulations that significantly shape an organization's HRM policies and programs. Many of these laws are enshrined in legislations such as human rights acts, the Charter of

Rights and Freedoms, the Employment Equity Act, the Canada Labour Code, and employment standards acts. The field of HRM is also influenced significantly by decisions of the courts and human rights commissions. Many of the laws and regulations are changed regularly by governments through the enactment of new laws, and by decisions of the courts and commissions through the interpretation of the laws and regulations. Effective HRM practices require HRM specialists to actively monitor the environment for these changes. The legal environment is the subject of Chapter 2.

Human Resource Planning

Human resource planning is the process of determining an organization's staffing needs, and providing important input into how, when, and where these staffing requirements are needed. The planning process includes forecasting the supply and demand of workers, determining net shortages and surpluses of workers by job category, department, and time-frame; knowing the organization's operational and strategic goals and objectives; and knowing internal work force demographics, skills, knowledge, abilities, and mobility.

Effective human resource planning facilitates replacement and succession planning, recruitment and selection strategies, as well as contributing to the attainment of other human resource management activities. Human resource planning is the subject of Chapter 3.

Job Analysis

Job analysis is the process of determining the skills, knowledge, abilities, and other essential characteristics required for effective job performance. The analysis of jobs entails identifying, collecting, documenting, and classifying job activity information. Job analysis provides the essential components for job descriptions and job specifications. Job descriptions detail the tasks, duties, and other criteria of the job. Job specifications describe the qualifications required for the job.

Job analysis performs a crucial role in all human resource management functions, particularly in human resource planning, recruiting, selection, compensation, and performance appraisal. Job analysis is the subject of Chapter 4.

Recruitment of Human Resources

Recruitment is the process of locating, attracting, and obtaining qualified individuals in adequate numbers, at the right place and time, to enable the organization and the individual to select each other. The recruitment process is characterized by a series of activities and strategies aimed at placing qualified job candidates in different positions at various levels in the organization.

Effective recruitment develops and maintains a wide variety of sources from which to recruit. Effective recruitment utilizes a variety of methods and sources to attract and secure job candidates. The larger the number of methods and sources utilized the greater the likelihood of locating the right individual with the required qualifications for the job. Recruitment is influenced by job analysis and human resource planning and influences selection. Among the many constraints on recruitment are legal considerations, the labour market, and organizational policies. The recruitment of human resources is the subject of Chapter 5.

The Selection Process

Selection is the process of choosing from among a pool of qualified applicants the best individuals to fill an organization's job opening. The selection process involves a variety of techniques, steps, and evaluative instruments. These include preliminary screening, reviews of completed application forms, employment interviews, and employment testing. All of these processes are aimed to enable the formulation of an objective assessment and an informed opinion of the individuals most capable of meeting desirable standards of performance.

Part Two: Training and Development

The major focus of this section is on the activities intended to improve the performance of the work force as well as to promote job competency and career development programs.

Orientation, Socialization, and Training

Orientation is a mixture of activities designed to acquaint new employees to the organization. It aims to reduce anxiety; develop positive attitudes; communicate the organization's policies, rules, and procedures, compensation and benefits, and physical facilities; increase employee satisfaction; provide an overview of the company; reduce employee turnover; and familiarize the new employee with job duties and responsibilities. Socialization is the process through which newcomers to the organization learn what is expected of them in terms of appropriate behaviours and acceptable performance.

Training is the process through which employees acquire new skills, technical knowledge, problem-solving abilities, and changed attitudes and behaviour for the purpose of advancing both organizational objectives and the individual's goals. Some of the benefits of training are improved performance; preparation for promotion; retraining to replace obsolescent skills; and filling human resources needs. The determination of training needs involves performing an analysis of current and required training skills, determining training targets and purposes, and deciding on training programs, content, and media.

Orientation, socialization, and training are the subjects of Chapter 7.

Management Development

Management development is the process of providing management education programs to managers to increase the company's current and future ability to meet its goals. Management development also involves providing formal programs specifically designed for high-potential management candidates so that they may acquire the skills, knowledge, and abilities to effectively manage and lead in today's highly competitive and dynamic business environment. Management development is the subject of Chapter 8.

Part Three: Appraisal and Career Management

This section covers the appraisal and career management component of human resource management. We discuss the activities required for effectively evaluating the individual's past and future development potential. We also discuss appropriate channels of career management.

Performance Appraisal

Performance appraisal is a systematic assessment of an individual's past performance and future potential for development. Performance appraisal serves a variety of purposes including communicating management's expectations to the employee, providing feedback on where he or she stands; documenting unsatisfactory and satisfactory performance; assessing problem areas; clarifying job expectations; and planning for future performance and development efforts. Performance appraisal is the subject of Chapter 9.

Career Management

Career management is the process of designing, implementing, and administering goals, objectives, plans, and strategies to facilitate the attainment of employees' career aspirations while enabling the company to meet its human resource needs. Career management is an inclusive process that involves human resource specialists, managers, supervisors, and the individual employee. It is a process that involves activities such as career planning; career development, and career management. Career management is the subject of Chapter 10.

Part Four: Compensation, Protection, and Motivation

The major focus of this section is on providing a rational method for designing, implementing, and administering an equitable system for attracting the desired quality of job candidates, maintaining a degree of work force stability, rewarding desired performance, and maintaining a motivated work force.

Fundamentals of Motivation

Motivation is the willingness of an individual to expend effort to achieve a desired goal, reward, or outcome. It is therefore an internal driving force that stimulates an individual to fulfil certain wants, needs, and drives. This internal driving force influences the direction, persistence, and maintenance of behaviour. As a result, an individual's motivation results from an interplay of many forces.

It is up to organizations to provide the type of organizational climate and culture, human resource policies and practices, as well as working environment and leadership style that motivate individuals to achieve desired levels of performances. Motivation is the subject of Chapter 11.

Compensation and Protection

Compensation constitutes one of the most important functions of human resource management. Its importance is demonstrated by the critical role it plays in recruitment, selection, motivation, satisfaction, productivity, retention, turnover, and the employees' perception of equity and fairness.

Broadly speaking, compensation refers to all financial rewards provided to individuals through their employment relationship with, or membership in, an organization. Compensation is provided to individuals as remuneration for services performed, to induce or reward desired behaviour. The design, implementation, and administration of compensation systems are influenced by various internal and external environmental factors, as well as essential instruments. Internal environmental factors include the organization's policies and its ability to pay. The external factors include the government, labour market, union, and the economy.

Essential instruments and mechanisms include job analysis, job evaluation, and surveys.

Performance-based rewards cover distinctly different segments of the compensation program and have a similar effect; that is, they promote increased productivity, enhance efficiency, job satisfaction, and motivation, and provide a direct link between performance and rewards. Performance-based rewards include a variety of plans, offering different types of rewards on a variety of bases. Some of the different types of plans include piece work plans, standard hour plans, profit sharing plans, premium pay, and commission pay.

Employee benefits are those compensation components made available to employees that provide financial protection against risks such as 1) health-related problem (e.g., illness, accident) and 2) income at future date or occasion (e.g., upon retirement, or termination of employment). Through the provisions of these benefits, organizations seek to increase morale, increase job satisfaction, attract good employees, and retain desirable employees.

Quality of Work Life Programs are designed to facilitate personal and organizational lifestyle enhancement for employees.

Compensation management, financial incentives, employee benefits and services, and quality of work life and nonfinancial motivation techniques are the subject of Chapters 12, 13, 14, and 15, respectively.

Part Five: Employee Rights, Safety, and Representation

This section takes a close look at two rapidly evolving areas of human resource management—employee rights and organizational due process. This section also focuses on government regulations and organization practices designed to protect the safety and health of employees. The final segment of this section deals with labour-management relations.

Employee Rights and Management Rights

Employee rights include formal contractual rights, implied rights provided under Canadian common laws, and rights protected by federal and provincial laws and regulations. Management rights include the rights to develop and administer those policies and procedures required to attract, recruit, and maintain an effective work force to help achieve organizational goals. Employee rights and management rights are the subject of Chapter 16.

Employee Health and Safety

There are a variety of government laws and regulations and health and safety programs implemented by management intended to ensure the physical well-being of employees in the workplace. Employee health and safety is the subject of Chapter 17.

Labour–Management Relations

Labour–management relations refers to a formal agreement that governs the relationship between management and its employees. In unionized companies, the policies, practices, and working conditions affecting employment relations that were previously decided solely by management are now subject to joint determination by management and the union. Other conditions of employment including salaries, wages, and hours are the subject of collective bargaining between the two

On the Front Line

The main theme of this book is that human resource management—activities like recruiting, selecting, training, and rewarding employees—is not just the job of some central human resource management group but rather a job in which every manager must engage. Perhaps nowhere is this more apparent than in the typical small service business. Here the owner/manager usually has no human resource management staff to rely on although the success of his or her enterprise (not to mention his or her family's peace of mind) often depends largely on the effectiveness through which workers are recruited, hired, trained, evaluated, and rewarded. Therefore, to help illustrate and emphasize the front-line manager's human resource management role, we will use throughout this book a continuing case based on a small business in central Canada. Each chapter's segment of the case will illustrate how the case's main player—owner/manager Jennifer Carter—confronts and solves human resource management problems each day at work by applying the concepts and techniques of that particular chapter. Here is some background information that will be necessary in order for the reader to answer questions that arise in subsequent chapters.

Carter Cleaning Centres

Jennifer Carter graduated from York University in June 1984, and after considering several job offers decided to do what she really always planned to do—go into business with her father, Jack Carter.

Jack Carter opened his first laundromat in 1980 and his second in 1982. The main attraction to him of these coin laundry businesses was that they were capital rather than labour intensive, so that once the investment in machinery was made, the stores could be run with just one unskilled attendant and none of the labour problems one normally expects from being in the retail service business.

The attractiveness of operating with virtually no skilled labour notwithstanding, Jack had decided by 1984 to expand the services in each of his stores to include the dry cleaning and pressing of clothes. He embarked, in other words, on a strategy of related diversification in that he added new services that were related to and consistent with his existing coin laundry activities. He added these new services in part because he wanted to utilize better the unused space in the rather large stores he currently had under lease and partly because he was, as he put it, "tired of sending out the dry cleaning and pressing work that came in from our coin laundry clients to a dry cleaner five miles away who then took most of what should have been our profit." To reflect their new expanded line of services he renamed each of his two stores "Carter Cleaning Centres" and was sufficiently satisfied with their performance to open four more of the same type of stores over the next five years. Each store had its own on-site manager and, on average, about seven employees, and annual revenues of about $300 000. It was this six-store chain of cleaning centres that Jennifer joined upon graduating from York University.

Her understanding with her father was that she would serve as a trouble-shooter/consultant to the elder Carter with the aim of both learning the business and bringing to it modern management concepts and techniques for solving the business's problems and facilitating its growth. On her first day on the job, Jennifer asked herself the following questions.

a) How important is effective human resource management to small businesses such as Carter Cleaning?

b) What internal and external environmental challenges are important to small businesses?

parties. Collective bargaining is a form of participative management in which management and labour negotiate the most affordable economic rewards and work environment for the employees. The process involves negotiation, administration, interpretation, and dispute settlement procedures. It is characterized by deliberation, persuasion, arguments, and attempts to influence the outcome more advantageous to either party.

Labour relations and collective bargaining are the subjects of Chapters 18 and 19, respectively.

Strategic Issues in Human Resource Management

The increasing recognition that people are a fundamental source of competitive advantage is accompanied by major changes in the role and function of human resource management. HR considerations are being incorporated into organizations' strategic plans. The major trends influencing the evolving role of human resource management include demographics, and technological, political, legal, competitive, and managerial trends. Strategic issues in human resource management are the subject of Chapter 20.

SUMMARY

1. In this chapter we have provided an overview of the growing importance of the field of human resources management. We discussed its evolution, focusing on significant events that have influenced the development of the field. Events such as the scientific and human relations movements, the growth of technology, the changing work force, and the influence of governmental legislation were discussed.

2. The chapter also examined the current human resource management functions and the dynamic role of the HRM departments in organizations. We also examined the various modern challenges facing human resource management from the perspectives of the internal and external environments.

KEY TERMS

human resource management (HRM)	staff authority	demographics
	functional control	baby boomers
scientific management	labour market	organizational culture
human relations movement	labour unions	organizational climate
group norms	human resource information	
line authority	system (HRIS)	

DISCUSSION QUESTIONS

1. Define human resource management.
2. Explain the importance and purposes of human resource management.
3. Compare and contrast the line and staff functions of human resource management.
4. Why is human resource management important to productivity?
5. Discuss four important external influences on human resource management.
6. List four major activities performed by a human resource manager.

CASE INCIDENT: The New Human Resource Department at Continental

It was late one afternoon when Carmen Tyndall was called into the office of the president of Continental Financial Resources (CFR). The president, John Adams, told Carmen that he has been pondering for some time the organizational structure of the firm. The firm, he said, has grown substantially over the past 15 years and is very successful financially. Yet, since the company was formed he has been acting as president, chief executive officer, and manager of human resources. He is concerned that because of the rapid growth of the company and demands on his time that the human resources area may not be getting the attention it deserves. He informed Carmen that he would like her to assume the position of manager of human resources. He authorized her to take whatever steps necessary to ensure the proper functioning of the new department.

Carmen is a very intelligent, ambitious, and hard-working individual who joined the company over three years ago as a special assistant to the president. She is a university graduate and is pursuing a CPM designation. She has worked in various administrative positions in the telecommunications, manufacturing, banking, and public sector fields.

CFR, a computer software and lending organization, has three divisions: financial, accounting, and payroll. It employs 175 individuals. The financial division offers mortgages and other loans to individuals. The accounting division offers computerized accounting services to companies. The payroll division offers computerized payroll services to companies. Each division has a manager, who reports directly to the president. Each division manager currently has full responsibility over all aspects of his or her human resource management functions.

The president did not talk to them about the creation of the new position. Neither did he talk to them about the creation of a new department nor about the impact that this change will have on their divisions.

Questions

1. Discuss the contributions that this new department will make to the organization.

2. How will the responsibilities of the managers change?

3. In what ways should Carmen go about setting up this department?

NOTES

1. Joyce D. Ross, "A Definition of Human Resources Management," *Personnel Journal* (October 1982), pp. 781-783.

2. *Human Resource Management: Charting a New Course* (Ottawa: Conference Board of Canada May 1989), p. vii.

3. *Human Resource Management: Charting a New Course* (Ottawa: Conference Board of Canada, May 1989).

4. V. V. Murray, "Organization and Administration of the Human Resource Management Function" in *Human Resource Management in Canada* (Scarborough, Ont.: Prentice-Hall Canada Inc., 1990), p. 15,047.

5. Murray, p. 15,047.

6. This is based on Edward E. Lawler III, "Human Resources Management," *Personnel* (January 1988), pp. 24-25.

7. R. Julian Cattaneo and Andrew J. Templer, "Determining the Effectiveness of Human Resources Management," *ASAC: Personnel and Human Resources Division Proceedings* (ed. T. H. Stone) (Halifax: St. Mary's University June 1988), p. 73.

8. The remainder of this section is based largely on Robert Saltonstall, "Who's Who in Personnel Administration," *Harvard Business Review*, Vol. 33 (July-August 1955), pp. 75-83; reprinted in Paul Pigors, Charles Meyers, and F. P. Malm, *Management of Human Resources* (New York: McGraw-Hill, 1969) pp. 61-73.

9. Saltonstall, p. 63.

10. Dennis R. Briscoe, "Human Resources Management Has Come of Age," *Personnel Administrator* (November 1982), pp. 75-77, 80-83.

11. For a detailed discussion of the responsibilities and duties of the personnel department, see Mary Zippo, "Personal Activities: Where the Dollars Went in 1979," *Personnel*, Vol. 57 (March-April 1980), pp. 61-67; and "ASPA-BNA Survey No. 49, Personnel Activities, Budgets, and Staffs: 1985-1986," *BNA Bulletin to Management* (June 5, 1986).

12. Saltonstall, p. 65.

13. Fred K. Foulkes and Henry Morgan, "Organizing and Staffing the Personnel Function," *Harvard Business Review*, Vol. 56 (May-June 1977), p. 146.

14. B. J. Hodge and William P. Anthony, *Organization Theory*, 3rd ed. (Boston: Allyn and Bacon, Inc., 1988), p. 58.

15. Richard L. Daft, *Organization Theory and Design*, 3rd ed. (St. Paul, MN: West Publishing Company, 1989), p. 11.

16. Daft, p. 48.

17. Newton and G. Betcherman, "Innovating on Two Fronts: People and Technology in the 1990s," *Canadian Business Review*, Vol. 14, no. 3 (Autumn 1987), pp. 18-21.

18. Newton and Betcherman, pp. 18-21.

19. Sylvia Ostry and Mahmood A. Zaidi, *Labour Economics in Canada*, 2nd ed. (Toronto: Macmillan of Canada, 1972).

20. Murray, p. 15,034.

21. *Maclean's* (August 9, 1982), p. 30.

22. *York University 1990 Enrolment Data* (Toronto: York University, 1990) p. 25; York University 1989-90 Fact Book (Toronto: York University, 1990), p. 7.

23. Woods Garden and Clarkson Garden, *Tomorrow's Customers*. 20th ed. (Toronto: 1986, pp. 1-8; see also Statistics Canada, *Labour Force Bulletin*, No. 71-001, 1987.

24. "In the Long Run: Good Reasons for Hope," *Financial Times* (March 26, 1984), pp. 21-25.

25. "Managing Employment Equity," Introduction to a Series (Toronto: Ontario Womens' Directorate, 1989), p. 3.

26. Labour Canada, *Part-Time Work in Canada. Report of the Commission of Inquiry into Part-Time Work* (Ottawa: Ministry of Supply and Services Canada, 1983).

27. Ontario Francophone.

28. Statistics New Brunswick 1990.

29. Murray, p. 15,038.

30. "PAO Gets Designation for HR Practitioners," *Human Resources Management in Canada*, Report Bulletin No. 82 (December 1989), p. 3.

31. "Desire for HR Professional Designation Growing," *Human Resources Management in Canada*, Report Bulletin No. 87 (May 1990), p 1.

32. "76% of HR Managers Favour Professional Designation," *Human Resources Management in Canada*, Report Bulletin No. 94 (December 1990), p 1.

33. Pradeep Kumar, "Professionalism in Canadian Personnel and Industrial Relations," *The Canadian Personnel and Industrial Relations Journal* (October 1980), pp. 34-41.

SUGGESTED READINGS

Beer, Michael, Russell A. Eisenstat, and Bert Spector. *The Critical Path to Corporate Renewal*. Cambridge, MA: Harvard Business School Press, 1990.

Benimadhu, Prem. *Human Resource Management: Charting a New Course*, Report 41-89. Ottawa: The Conference Board of Canada, 1989.

Cattaneo, R.J. and A.J. Templer. "Determining the Effectiveness of Human Resource Management." Administrative Sciences Association of Canada, Personnel and Human Resources Division Proceedings of the Annual Conference Meeting, June 1988, p. 72-82.

Dimick, David E. "Human Resources Development" in *Human Resources Management in Canada*. Toronto, Ont.: Prentice-Hall Canada Inc., 1989, pp. 35,011-35,065.

————. "The Control of Human Resources" in *Human Resources Management in Canada*. Toronto, Ont.: Prentice-Hall Canada Inc., 1987, pp. 70,011-70,082.

Dolan Shimon L. and Randall S. Schuler, eds. *Canadian Readings in Personnel and Human Resource Management*, St. Paul, MN: West Publishing Company, 1987.

Drunckel, Jacqueline. "Oral Communication and the HR Manager" in *Human Resources Management in Canada*. Toronto: Prentice-Hall Canada Inc. 1989, pp. 15,501-15,505.

Halcrow, A. "Operation Phoenix: The Business of Human Resources," *Personnel Journal*, Vol. 66, no. 9, September 1987, pp. 92-101.

Murray, V.V. "Organization and Administration of Human Resources Management Function" in *Human Resources Management in Canada* (Toronto, Ont.: Prentice-Hall Canada Inc., 1990, pp. 15,011-15,086.

Schein, Edgar H., ed. *The Art of Managing Human Resources*. New York: Oxford University Press, 1987.

Schneider, Benjamin, ed. *Organizational Climate and Culture*. San Francisco: Jossey-Bass Publishers, 1990.

Areas in Human Resource Management Which May Require Formal Policies and Procedures

Absenteeism
Accidents
Alcoholism
Anniversary Date
Appraisal
Attendance Awards

Benefits
Births and Adoptions
Birthdays
Blood Donation
Bonus

Cafeteria
Car Allowances
Charity Drives
Cheque Cashing
Christmas Shopping
Collections and Solicitations
Committees
Communication
Community Relations
Company Objectives
Company Property
Compensation
Confidential Information
Conflict of Interest
Contributions
Cost of Living
Court Service
Credit Union

Death of Employee
Dental Insurance

Discipline
Discounts to Employees
Dismissal
Downsizing
Dress and Grooming
Drug Abuse

Educational Assistance
Election Service
Employee Associations
Employee Attitudes
Employee Referrals
Employment Agencies
Employment Equity
Employment Policy
Employment Procedure
Exit Interview

Firearms and Weapons
Fire Procedure
First Aid
Flowers
Funeral Leave

Gambling
Garnishments
Gifts and Entertainment
Grievances

Handicapped Workers
Health
Holidays
Hours of Work
Housekeeping

Inspections

Job Classification and Evaluation
Job Security
Job Training
Jury Duty

Layoff and Recall
Leave of Absence
Legal and Financial Counsel
Library and Reading Racks
Life Insurance
Loans to Employees
Lockers
Lost and Found
Lunch Period

Mail, Personal
Major Medical Insurance
Make-up Time
Management Rights
Marriage
Maternity Benefits
Maternity Leave of Absence
Meal Allowances
Medical and Dental Appointments
Medical Department
Medical Examinations
Medical Insurance
Memberships and Dues
Merit Awards
Military Service

Military Training
Moving Allowance
Moving Time Off
Music at Work

Open House
Orientation
Outings
Outside Employment
Overtime
Overtime Pay

Parking
Part-time Employees
Patents and Inventions
Pay Advances
Pay Equity
Pay Increase
Pay Plan
Payroll Deductions
Personal Counselling
Personal Hygiene
Personal Property
Personal Time Off
Personnel Records
Plant Security
Plant Shutdown
Political Activities
Probation
Profit Sharing
Promotion
Publications

Radio and Television
Recreational Activities
Recruiting
References
Relatives, Employment of
Reporting and Call-in
Resignation
Rest Periods
Rest Rooms
Retirement
Retirement Counselling
   and Planning
Retirement Income
Retraining

Safety
Salary Continuation
Sanitation
Savings Bonds
Savings Plans
Scholarships
Seniority
Separation Pay
Service Recognition
Shift Premium
Sick Leave
Sickness and Disability
Smoking
Stock Purchase
Suggestions
Supervisor-Employee
   Relationship

Supervisory
   Development

Tardiness
Technological Change
Telephones
Temporary Employees
Termination
Testing
Time Clocks and Cards
Tools
Training and
   Development
Transfers
Transportation to Work
Travel Insurance

Unemployment
   Compensation
Uniforms and Laundry
Unions

Vacations
Vending Machines
Visitors
Volunteer Work by
   Employees
Voting Time

Weather
Work Assignments
Working Conditions
Workers' Compensation

SOURCE: V.V. Murray, "Organization/Administration of HRM Function," *Human Resource Management in Canada* (Scarborough, Ontario: Prentice-Hall Canada Inc., 1990), pp. 15,015-15,017. This list is an updated and amended version of the contents of *How to Write a Personnel Policy Manual* (Miami, Fla.: Management Information Center, Inc., 1973) (no longer in print).

Developing Human Resource Management Policies

Human resource management policies regarding such matters as how much to pay employees, how to screen candidates, how to deal with disciplinary matters, how to earn incentives, and how aggressively to pursue employment equity do not (or should not) emerge spontaneously. Instead they should be followed from and be consistent with the organization's basic mission and plan. They should enable the organization and its managers to better implement that plan.

Policies (and particularly written policies) are important for three reasons. They standardize decisions (for instance, regarding sick leave) which therefore need not be remade time and again. They ensure consistent and therefore fair treatment of employees, all of whom should be governed by the same set of disciplinary policies and rules. Finally, as extensions of the company's strategic plan, they should breathe life into general aims, like "let's maximize units sold and minimize costs," by providing specific guidelines for each department, such as "select only the most productive workers."

Policies for all their value can have their drawbacks, particularly when they get too restrictive. A policy manual should be in a sense a living document, evolving and changing as management's plans and philosophy evolve. Furthermore, it should not be forgotten that any policy is exactly that—a guide. Policies are not immutable laws, and in our society even laws tend to be applied by judges who remember the mitigating circumstances of the situation. It is important, therefore, not to poison the enormous usefulness of policies and policy manuals with the overly restrictive application of an unmanageable network of policy guidelines.

Legal Aspects

A policy manual should not be a formal contract with employees.[1] In both the policy manual and the employee handbook an employer should prominently display a disclaimer pointing out that the manual or handbook is not a contract and that employees may be terminated by the employer at any time, for any reason. It should also be noted that the manual or handbook may be revised, supplemented, or deleted at any time by the employer. In general any terminology that might be construed as limiting rights of an employer should be avoided, such as "permanent employee" or "termination for cause." Legal pitfalls like these, too, will obviously detract from the long-term usefulness of policy books.

THE POLICY DEVELOPMENT PROCESS

Most policies arise out of management's past practices.[2] The managers of any firm naturally have to make decisions and take actions as situations arise. As time goes by these tend to be codified either formally or informally in a network of policies for the firm. Even if the owner of a five-person store does not believe in written policies, his or her company will have policies nevertheless. They will emerge in response to the questions employees ask, such as, "How long do we have to work to take a vacation?" "How long that vacation can be?" "Are benefits paid?" and "How often?" Management's past practices are thus the place to start when formulating a set of written policies for the firm.

Good policies always flow from the basic strategic plan and philosophy of the owners and top management of the firm. Thus the firm that decides to stress cost reduction, efficiency, and specialized jobs should produce a very different set of human resource management policies than the firm in which creativity and entrepreneurial spirit are the guiding goals.

Developing a set of human resource management policies involves nine steps that are outlined below.

STEP 1: Define the Audience

First it must be decided what the purpose of the manual is and who the audience is. In general, human resource management policy manuals are aimed at those supervisory employees who are charged with implementing the policies, including the human resources manager, department heads, and supervisors. The policy manual contains the basic policies (regarding attendance, compensation, and so forth) that managers and supervisors need to administer the company's human resource management policies.

Beyond that, there are several other audience-related questions to consider. For example, many companies include an educational objective in their manual, thus recognising that the same managers that must carry out policies often also need a handy reference on such matters as "how to interview" and "how to appraise performance." In such a case the human resource management policies manual really becomes not just a policy manual but also a handy guide for how to carry out the manager's human resource management jobs. In any event, the purpose and target audience of the manual should be identified first.

STEP 2: Form a Policy Committee

The actual work of formulating, codifying, producing, and communicating the policies and the policy manual is usually assigned to a policy committee. The membership of such committees varies, but it is customary to appoint a high-ranking human resource management officer to chair the committee and to have representation from all the organization's key functional areas.

Exactly how the work is divided will vary too, but several guidelines should be kept in mind. One person is usually assigned the task of actually writing all the policies based on the information accumulated by the other committee members. It is then customary to have a second person—either on or off the committee—assigned the job of reviewing the actual policies to make any changes that are required. Someone should also keep track of the budget for the project and the schedule that must be adhered to.

STEP 3: Select Sources of Information

There are several sources of information available to use in developing the company's policies and policy manual.[3] Existing policy statements and policy manuals are a useful starting point. Other manuals and handbooks (such as employee handbooks from various departments or divisions, training manuals and any other written rules or procedures that various departments or divisions use) are valuable too. Other employers' policy manuals are another good sources that can sometimes be tapped by offering to trade or compare policy manuals between firms.

Several other sources can be tapped. In-house experts, including people like company attorneys, benefits administrators, and accountants, can provide useful information in their areas of expertise. "Packaged" human resource management policies, complete with numerous sample policies are also available.[4] Also, the organization's "unwritten" policies, the basic guidelines the owners and managers now use to guide their decisions but which have heretofore gone uncodified, must not be overlooked. People should be asked questions like what do they understand the company policy to be in this area, and what do they think it should be?

STEP 4: Determine Length and Writing Style

Next, some basic decisions must be made regarding the length of each policy and the writing style to be used. A human resource management policy on a matter like performance appraisals may range from a single paragraph to two pages or more, depending upon the amount of detailed information to be included. Here a decision needs to be made regarding how much detail there should be. The decision on detail, in turn, will hinge on the question of just how specific (and, therefore, restrictive) the policy has to be and on the extent to which the manual will be an education/training document that supervisors can use to bone up on how to perform some activity like appraising performance.

With respect to writing style, consistency from policy to policy is the aim. It is generally advisable to make the manual as "user friendly" as possible. Therefore, the sentences should be kept short and jargon should be avoided.

STEP 5: Organization and Format

The organization and format of the manual and of each policy statement should be decided on as well.

There are several specific issues to be addressed. In general, a table of contents and an index make the job of looking up the policies easier for all involved. Another important question involves deciding which specific policies are to be covered.

A number of things should not be included in the manual. Policies that do not apply to most of employees (such as special benefit plans for top executives), policies that are in the planning stages, and, of course, confidential information should be left out. Information that changes often, such as names and titles of individuals and telephone extension numbers, is also best left out.

A decision must also be made on the format of each policy itself. It is common to specify the subject on the top of the page and to present a rationale (often called "authorization") for the policy, followed by the policy itself. However, depending upon the use to which the policy is put, many organizations also include a detailed procedure for the supervisor to follow in implementing the policy.

STEP 6: Design Factors

Several practical considerations enter into the design of any manual. They should be easy to use, so heavy-grade paper, well-marked and reinforced tabs, and sufficiently wide three-ring binders are important to make sure the manuals do not start falling apart. Also, the eye appeal of the manual and the professionalism with which it is printed and produced may influence the extent to which it is used. It is necessary to accurately forecast the first printing (taking into consideration supervisory turnover), and to have the artwork and printing done as professionally as possible.

STEP 7: Approval Procedure

In smaller companies in particular the company president and even his or her board may want to make the final approval of all policies in the manual. After all, this may be the first time that these policies have been codified, and policies regarding matters like vacations, compensation, and discipline can have a big impact on the health and welfare of the firm. In larger organizations the president might want to review the manual, as would the head of human resource management. It is also wise to have copies of the preliminary manual distributed to department heads for their input and advice before anything is finalized.

STEP 8: Distribution and Copy Control

While it should not contain anything confidential, neither should copies of the human resource management manual be floating uncontrolled throughout or beyond the firm. It is therefore advisable to number each manual and maintain a master list in the HRM department showing each manual's location and to whom it is signed out. There will be a tendency for these manuals to drift away as managers leave. Therefore, a procedure should be in place for ensuring the return of the manual along with office keys and other property of the firm when supervisors leave.

STEP 9: Introducing the Manual to Supervisors

It is best to avoid the impression that there is some subterranean process going on aimed at changing all the human resource management policies in the firm. The new policy committee should issue a written announcement that the policy manual project is underway. In addition to heading off unneeded speculation, such an announcement can also elicit recommendations from the management and supervisory staff about the policies that currently exist and any policies that they feel should be added.

From a practical point of view, a brand new, set-in-store manual should not be foisted on managers and supervisors unannounced. Not only can this trigger unnecessary resistance from those who feel they were not consulted, but it also may happen that an important point has been overlooked that would have been uncovered by a more participatory approach. Therefore as the manual moves forward toward completion, small-group meetings within each department should be held among members of the policy committee and supervisors.

The manual itself will lose some of its effectiveness unless instructions and training are provided to explain its use. An orientation/training program explaining the manual to all managers and supervisors (either together or in groups) can thus ensure that the manual is used, and used properly.

NOTES

1. For discussion, see Thomas Hestwood, "Make Policy Manuals Useful and Relevant," *Personnel Journal* (April 1988), pp. 43-46.
2. Unless otherwise noted, this section is based on Thompson, *Encyclopedia of Personnel Policies*, pp. 1.07-1.40.
3. These are based on Thompson, pp. 1.12-1.40.
4. Thompson, pp. 1.12-1.40.

PART ONE
RECRUITMENT AND PLACEMENT

CHAPTER
TWO THE LEGAL ENVIRONMENT

After studying this chapter you should be able to

1. Define the provisions of the Canadian Human Rights Act.

2. Explain how the Canadian Human Rights Commission operates.

3. Cite at least five prohibited grounds of discrimination.

4. Understand what is meant by sexual harassment.

5. Describe pay equity.

6. Compare and contrast systemic discrimination with overt discrimination.

7. Explain the Federal Contract Compliance Criteria.

8. Explain the procedures an employer should follow to implement an Employment Equity Program.

9. Discuss the Charter of Rights and Freedoms.

OVERVIEW

This chapter discusses the comprehensive network of government laws and regulations that affect the employer-employee work relationship. We discuss in broad terms the main features of the Canadian Human Rights Act and the specific prohibitions as they relate to recruitment, selection, promotions, training, and development. We also cover sexual harassment, pay equity, systemic discrimination, employment equity, and the Charter of Rights and Freedoms.

INTRODUCTION: GOVERNMENT LAWS AND REGULATIONS

Government laws and regulations shape significantly human resource management policies, procedures, and practices. These laws and regulations are aimed at providing equal employment opportunities for all Canadians without regard to race, colour, age, sex, religion, marital status, or ethnic origin. They are also aimed at identifying and eliminating barriers and discriminatory disadvantages that deny opportunities and unfairly impede growth of many Canadians for reasons that have nothing to do with their abilities. The various government laws and regulations are often enacted in response to changing demands and expectations of society.

Legislative Jurisdiction

Under the provisions of the Constitution Act 1867 (formerly known as the British North America Act) both the Parliament of Canada and the provincial legislatures have the power to enact laws over various legislative areas. The provinces have been given exclusive control over property and civil rights. This is generally held to include the laws of contract and employment and most matters affecting human resources.[1] In practice, provincial employment and labour laws cover 90% of the Canadian labour force and the remaining 10% is covered by federal laws. The federal employment and labour laws cover employees in the federal government, crown corporations, banks, railways, and many organizations that operate in more than one province and those that operate internationally.

All 13 jurisdictions have established various boards and commissions for the purposes of enforcing compliance with government laws and regulations, to interpret the provisions of the legislations, to hear, investigate, assess, and rule on complaints and issues that fall under their jurisdictions.

THE CANADIAN HUMAN RIGHTS ACT

The **Canadian Human Rights Act** became effective in 1978. The Act states that

Canadian Human Rights Act

> every individual should have an equal opportunity with other individuals to make himself or herself the life that he or she is able and wishes to have, consistent with his or her duties and obligations as a member of society without being hindered in or prevented from doing so by discriminating practices based on race, national or ethnic origin, colour, religion, age, sex, marital status, or conviction for an offence for which a pardon has been granted or by discriminatory employment practices based on physical handicap.[2]

The act also prohibits discrimination with respect to recruitment, selection, promotion, transfer, training, and termination.

The Canadian Human Rights Act applies to all federal departments, agencies, crown corporations, banks, railways, airlines and businesses that operate under federal jurisdictions such as insurance companies and businesses within the communication industry.

Each of the ten provinces and the two territories have enacted their own human rights acts.[3] From a comprehensive point of view all these human rights acts are similar to the federal law. The provincial and territory government laws apply to jurisdictions that do not fall under the scope of federal law. Figure 2.1 illustrates the prohibited grounds of discrimination in employment.

FIGURE 2.1
Prohibited Grounds of Discrimination in Employment

	Federal	British Columbia	Alberta	Saskatchewan	Manitoba	Ontario	Quebec	New Brunswick	Prince Edward Island	Nova Scotia	Newfoundland	Northwest Territories	Yukon
Race	●	●	●	●	●	●	●	●	●	●	●	●	●
National or ethnic origin[1]	●					●	●	●	●	●	●		●
Ancestry		●	●	●		●	●					●	●
Nationality or citizenship				●	●	●						●	
Place of origin		●	●	●				●				●	
Colour	●	●	●	●	●	●	●	●	●	●	●		●
Religion	●	●		●	●		●	●	●	●	●		●
Creed[2]			●	●		●				●	●	●	●
Age	●	●	●	●	●	●	●	●	●	●	●	●	
		45-65	18+	18-65		18-65		18+		40-65	19-65		
Sex	●	●	●	●	●	●	●	●	●	●	●	●	●
Pregnancy or childbirth	●		●	●		●							
Marital status[3]	●	●	●	●	●	●	●	●	●	●	●	●	●
Family status[3]	●			●	●	●	●					●	
Pardoned offence	●						●					●	
Record of criminal conviction		●				●	●						
Physical handicap or disability	●	●	●	●	●	●	●	●	●	●	●	●	
Mental handicap or disability	●	●			●	●	●	●	●	●	●	●	
Dependence on alcohol or drug	●												
Place of residence												●	
Political belief		●			●		●		●		●		
Assignment, attachment or seizure of pay[4]												●	
Source of income													
Social condition[4]							●						
Language							●						
Social origin[4]											●		
Sexual orientation[5]						●	●						
Harassment[5]	●					●	●				●		

1. New Brunswick includes only "national origin."
2. Creed usually means religious beliefs
3. Quebec uses the term "civil status"
4. In Quebec's charter, "social condition" includes assignment, attachment or seizure of pay and social origin.
5. The federal, Ontario and Quebec statutes jban harassment on all proscribed grounds. Ontario, Nova Scotial and Newfoundland also ban sexual solicitation.

SOURCE: Labour Canada, *Worklife Report*, March 1987, p. 17. Reproduced with permission of the Minister of Supply and Services Canada, 1991.

Race and Colour

The Canadian Human Rights Act prohibits discrimination in an employer's employment policies and practices against an individual on the basis of that person's ethnic background (race) and/or on the basis of that person's skin colour (colour). The following decision illustrates the consequences of discrimination on the basis of race and colour.

> Five former employees of Majestic Electronics Inc. will share $300 000 in compensation for harassment they endured after refusing to carry out the racist and sexist orders of the company president. The settlement was announced after an Ontario Human Rights Commission investigation found that company president Curtis Ramsauer made "bigoted and racist remarks" and ordered that minorities and women be fired from the company. Four of the complainants, white males who held senior positions at Majestic, were threatened with dismissal when they refused to carry out Ramsauer's orders. The fifth complainant, an East Indian woman, resigned after only four days on the job when she was told she would be fired because of her race. All resigned between late 1986 and early 1987 before filling complaints with the OHRC.
>
> The settlement is the largest ever in a racial harassment case. Former vice-president of finance, Robert Lee, who earned $90 000 annually, will receive over $200 000 in lost wages and damages, including compensation for losses he incurred when he was forced to sell his house. The other four complainants will each receive between $5781 and $30 587. In addition, Ramsauer will provide each complainant with a letter of apology and $8000 in damages. Other terms of the settlement require Majestic to hire qualified women and racial minorities in proportion to the percentage of applications they receive from those groups. The company will also hold twice-yearly human rights education programs, and must include visible minorities and women in any advertisement that features Majestic employees.[4]

Religion

The Canadian Human Rights Act prohibits discrimination in an employer's employment policies and practices against an individual on the basis of his or her religion, unless the individual's religious practices would impose undue hardship on the employer. The employer is, however, obliged to make every reasonable attempt to accommodate an individual's religious practices. Failure to do so by the employer is a violation of the Act. The case shown in Human Resource Management in Action (p. 46) illustrates the consequence of discrimination on the basis of religion.

Sex

The Canadian Human Rights Act prohibits discrimination in an employer's employment policies and practices against an individual on the basis of his or her sex. Under the Act it is illegal for an employer to allow an individual's sex to influence its recruitment, selection, promotion, training, transfer, or termination policies and practices. It is illegal for an employer to use or promote tests, standards and/or criteria that are biased or discriminate against one sex, as the case below illustrates:

Three women complained that their employer, Canada Safeway Ltd., discriminated against them on the basis of sex, because the company provided medical benefits to employees who had to be absent from work for a medical reason, but excluded pregnancy from coverage. The company argued on the basis of an earlier Supreme Court decision that although it treated pregnant persons differently from non-pregnant persons, this was not sex discrimination because not all women are or become pregnant. The Court rejected this approach and held that since only women become pregnant, a denial of health benefits to "pregnant people" is tantamount to denying those benefits to women. The Court also noted that for too long society has allowed employment practices to impose all the costs of childbirth upon women.[5]

Marital Status

The Canadian Human Rights Act prohibits discrimination in an employer's employment policies and practices against an individual on the basis of his or her marital status. The following case illustrates the consequences of discrimination on the basis of marital status:

An airline pilot lost his job over the question of his marital status. He complained to the commission that he was released by the airline because he was married and because the company found it more convenient to employ single pilots. A Human Rights Tribunal concluded that he had indeed been fired for those reasons and ordered the company to pay him $24 487 in lost earnings and general damages.[6]

Age

The Canadian Human Rights Act prohibits discrimination in an employer's employment policies and practices against an individual on the basis of his or her age. The following case illustrates the consequences of discrimination on the basis of age:

A man, age 37, complained that he was refused employment by Greyhound Lines of Canada Ltd. on the basis of his age. The company which hired drivers only between the ages of 24 and 35 maintained that new drivers get the least favourable routes and must be young enough to cope with the stress. The Tribunal substantiated the complaint and ruled that there was not sufficient evidence to conclude that the inability to cope with stress was related to age.[7]

National or Ethnic Origin

The Canadian Human Rights Act prohibits discrimination in an employer's employment policies and practices against an individual on the basis of his or her national or ethnic origin. Therefore an employer cannot allow an individual's national or ethnic origin to influence its hiring and promotion decisions. The following case illustrates the fact that discrimination can be intentional or unintentional, direct or indirect, but regardless of the nature of discrimination it is a violation of the Act and is illegal.

A man and several other individuals, complained that Terry Long, Randy Johnson, and the Church of Jesus Christ Christian-Aryan Nations had been spreading hate propaganda against Jews and other minority groups by telephone in Alberta in late 1987 and 1988. The Tribunal ruled that the respondents were responsible for communicating messages likely to expose certain groups to hatred or contempt and ordered that they refrain from doing so in the future.

The Tribunal also considered whether the hate messages provision in the CHRA was a valid limitation on freedom of speech as protected by the Charter of Rights and Freedom. The Tribunal held that, although this provision did infringe upon freedom of speech, it amounted to a reasonable limitation on that right and did not violate the Charter.[8]

Physical Handicap

The Canadian Human Rights Act prohibits discrimination in an employer's employment policies and practices against an individual on the basis of his or her being disabled, unless the individual's disability would impose undue hardship on the employer. A board of inquiry could order an employer to change existing employment conditions to accommodate the special needs of handicapped individuals as long as such accommodation might be done without imposing undue hardship on the employer's business operations. This is known as the principle of reasonable accommodation, however, there are exceptions. An employer is not expected to hire a deaf individual as a telephone switchboard operator, or a blind individual to drive a bus or a truck. The following case illustrates the consequences of discrimination on the basis of physical handicap:

> A man lost his job as a cook and part-time watchman at Canadian Pacific after he confided to a co-worker that he had tested positive for HIV. He complained to the Canadian Human Rights Commission that he was discriminated against on this basis of his handicap. The Commission ruled that the company had indeed discriminated against the individual and ordered the company to pay him $25 000 for lost wages and for injury to his self-esteem.[9] This decision was appealed and was upheld by the Federal Court of Appeal in 1990.[10]

Pardoned Convicts

The Canadian Human Rights Act prohibits discrimination in an employer's employment policies and practices against an individual convicted for an offence for which a pardon has been granted.

> A man convicted and pardoned on a drug offence applied for a job as a counsellor at a community correctional centre. He had extensive experience working with ex-inmates and with the provincial commission on dependency. He was rated as the best candidate for the position. However, Correctional Services rejected him for the position because of his criminal record. They argued that he was a security risk, pardoned or not. He appealed to the Canadian Human Rights Commission. During the CHRC investigation, Correctional Services decided that the applicant's pardoned conviction would not, in fact, inhibit his ability to meet the requirements for the job, and satisfied that he was suitable, offered him the position.[11]

Exceptions

Under the Act an employer is permitted to make an exception to the preceding provisions when a bona fide occupational requirement (BFOR)[12] exists. This means that an employer may legally discriminate when it can demonstrate that it is absolutely justified in order that the duties of the job may be performed safely and when it is essential to do so to prevent the operation of the business from being undermined.

In *Maureen Stanley et al.* v. *RCMP (1987)*, the CHRC ruled an RCMP policy to be BFOR which requires that prison guards must be of the same sex as the inmates in police cells. The Tribunal found that there was no alternative or non-discriminatory method available of protecting prisoners' privacy since guards are required to watch inmates undress and use the toilet. However, it is common for the courts and human rights tribunals to rule against discriminatory requirements that employers establish as bona fide. In 1987 the Federal Court of Appeal upheld a CHRC tribunal decision that found that a bus company's policy of refusing to employ new drivers over the age of 35 was not a BFOR and was therefore illegal discrimination on the basis of age. In another case the CHRC ruled that visual acuity standards established by VIA Rail were not BFORs because VIA was unable to justify the objectivity of such standards.[13]

Enforcement[14]

The provisions of the Canadian Human Rights Act are administered by the **Canadian Human Rights Commission**. Figure 2.2 illustrates the CHRC enforcement process. The Commission comprises the Chief Commissioner, a Deputy Commissioner, and anywhere from three to six part-time members, all appointed by the Governor-in-Council. The Chief Commissioner and his or her Deputy are full-time members appointed for a term of not more than seven years. Part-time members are appointed for a term of not more than three years. The purposes of the Commission are to

- receive and act upon complaints filed by individuals concerning allegations of discrimination
- issue guidelines clarifying or interpreting the Act
- initiate investigative actions when the commission perceives discriminatory practices in the workplace
- appoint a tribunal

Once the Commission receives a complaint it reviews the complaint to determine whether it falls under the Commission's jurisdiction or under another jurisdiction. The Commission may refuse to deal with a complaint that falls within its jurisdiction if it considers the complaint to be trivial or frivolous, or if an unreasonable length of time has elapsed before the complaint was filed, or if the complaint is based on bad faith, or if the Commission believes there is a more appropriate procedure available for dealing with the complaint.

Following the acceptance of a complaint, the Commission appoints a human rights officer to conduct an impartial investigation to determine the facts of the case. The human rights officer may enter the employer's business premises, examine its records, and interview witnesses. The obstruction of the human rights officer's investigation is illegal. Therefore, if an employer refuses to allow the human rights officer entry or refuses to provide documents, then the Commission may seek a warrant to enter the premises and search for relevant documents. Individuals who file complaints, act as witnesses, or otherwise participate in human rights proceedings are protected from reprisals by employers. If the complaint is valid and substantiated during the investigation, it is not uncommon for the human rights officer to attempt to bring about a settlement between the parties. If this effort is unsuccessful then the Commission may appoint a conciliator to try through conciliation and persuasion to resolve the complaint in a manner satisfactory to the parties and the Commission. If the conciliator is unable to resolve the matter then the Commission may appoint a human rights tribunal to render a decision on the complaint. The human rights tribunal is an independent adjudicative body with wide-ranging powers to

- order an employer to compensate for pain and humiliation suffered by the complainant, as well as wages lost and any other expenses that the victim incurred as a result of the discriminatory practices of the employer

Canadian Human Rights Commission

FIGURE 2.2
The CHRC
Enforcement Process

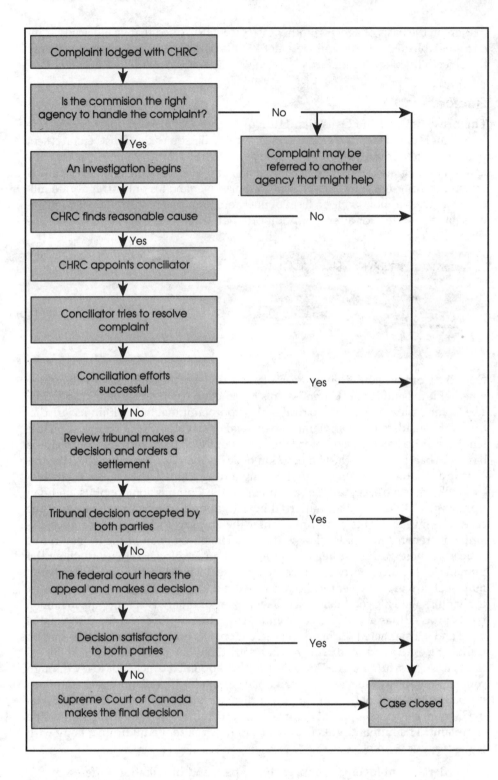

Complaint lodged with CHRC

Is the commision the right agency to handle the complaint? — No

Complaint may be referred to another agency that might help

Yes

An investigation begins

CHRC finds reasonable cause — No

Yes

CHRC appoints conciliator

Conciliator tries to resolve complaint

Conciliation efforts successful — Yes

No

Review tribunal makes a decision and orders a settlement

Tribunal decision accepted by both parties — Yes

No

The federal court hears the appeal and makes a decision

Decision satisfactory to both parties — Yes

No

Supreme Court of Canada makes the final decision

Case closed

- order the employer to change its policies and practices to prevent discrimination in the future
- order an employer to develop and implement special programs designed to equalize opportunities for previously discriminated against groups such as women and visible minorities
- order an employer to reinstate a discharged complainant
- order an employer to restore any rights, privileges, or opportunities that were lost or denied the complainant
- order the employer to write a letter of apology to the complainant and/or to the relevant human rights commission
- order the employer to attend workshops conducted by the human rights commission.

The decisions of the Canadian Human Rights Commission are enforceable in a similar manner to an order of the Federal Court of Canada. The decision of the Commission may be appealed to the courts, but if an appeal is not filed, the violator is required to comply with the decision. Failure to do so is a contravention of the Act and is subject to a fine.

Guide to Screening and Selection in Employment

The Canadian Human Rights Commission's guide to screening and selection in employment is illustrated in Figure 2.3. The purposes of the guide are to promote equal employment opportunities for all Canadians regardless of race, colour, religion, ethnic origin, sex, age, record of offenses, marital status, family status, or handicap. And it ensures that employment decisions are based on merit, and not on standards or criteria that are unrelated to the job and job performance.

Sexual Harassment

Sexual harassment is illegal under the provisions of the human rights acts of the federal government and most of the provinces. It is defined as unsolicited or unwelcome sexual conduct that has adverse employment consequences for the complainant.[15] It also includes unwanted sexual advances made by a person who is able to grant or deny a benefit (for example, an advance from a professor to a student, or from a supervisor to a subordinate) and unwelcome sexual advances by a person who is in a position to grant or deny a benefit who threatens or penalizes in any way the individual who rejects the sexual advance. Examples would include a manager who threatens not to hire a job candidate unless the individual agrees to his or her advances, or a supervisor who denies a subordinate a promotion because the subordinate rejected his or her advances. Recent court and tribunal rulings have held that organizations are responsible for the consequences of sexual harassment unless the organizations take appropriate steps to prevent and discourage such incidents. (For a comprehensive discussion of sexual harassment including recent human rights commission cases, see Chapter 16.) Illustrated below is a case showing the consequences of sexual harassment:

> A woman who put up with 14 years of sexual harassment before quitting her job has been awarded nearly $50 000 in damages by an Ontario Human Rights Board of Inquiry. The decision sends a warning to employers who are aware of

sexual harassment

FIGURE 2.3   A Guide to Screening and Selection in Employment

Subject	Do not ask	May ask	Comment
Name	• about the reason behind a name change • for maiden name • for 'Christian' name		If needed for a reference, to check on previously held jobs or on educational credentials, ask after selection.
Address	• for addresses outside Canada	• place and duration of current or recent address	
Age	• for birth certificates, baptismal records, or age or birth date	• applicants if they have reached age (minimum or maximum) for work as defined by law	If precise age is required for benefits plans or other legitimate purposes it can be determined after selection.
Sex	• Mr./Mrs./Miss/Ms • males or females to fill in different or coded applications • about pregnancy, childbirth, or child care arrangements (this includes asking whether birth control is used or what child bearing plans are)	• applicant if the attendance requirements or minimum service commitment can be met	Any applicants can be addressed during interviews or in correspondence without using courtesy titles such as Mr./Mrs./Miss/Ms.
Marital Status	• whether applicant is single, married, divorced, engaged, separated, widowed or living common-law • whether an applicant's spouse is subject to transfer • about spouse's employment	• whether there are any known circumstances that might prevent completion of a minimum service commitment, for example	If transfer or travel is part of the job, the applicant can be asked if this would cause a problem. Information on dependents for benefits can be determined after selection.
Family Status	• number of children or dependents • about arrangements for child care	• if the employer has a policy against the hiring of close relatives, an applicant can be asked about kinship to other employees	Contacts for emergencies and/or details on dependents can be determined after selection.
National or Ethnic Origin	• about birthplace, nationality of ancestors, spouse or other relatives • whether born in Canada • if naturalized or landed immigrant • for proof of citizenship	• since those who are entitled to work in Canada must be citizens, landed immigrants or holders of valid work permits, applicants can be asked if they are legally entitled to work in Canada	
Military Service	• about military service in other countries	• about Canadian military service where employment preference is given to veterans, by law	
Language	• mother tongue • where language skills obtained	• if applicant understands, reads, writes or speaks languages which are required for job	Testing or scoring applicants for language proficiency is not permitted unless fluency is job-related.
Race or Colour	• any inquiry which indicates race or colour, including colour of eyes, skin, or hair colour		Information required for security clearances can be obtained after selection.
Photographs	• for photo to be attached to applications or sent to interviewer before interview		Photos for security passes or company files can be taken after selection.
Religion	• about religious affiliation, church membership, or frequency of church attendance • whether applicant will work a specific religious holiday • for references from clergy or religious leader	• explain the required work shifts, asking if such a schedule poses problems for applicant	Employers are to reasonably accommodate religious needs of workers.

(continued)

FIGURE 2.3 (continued)

Height and Weight			No inquiry is permissible unless there is evidence that they are bona fide occupational requirements.
Disability	• for listing of all disabilities, limitations, or health problems • whether applicant drinks or uses drugs • whether applicant has ever received psychiatric care or been hospitalized for emotional problems	• whether applicant has any condition that could affect ability to do the job • whether the applicant has any condition that should be considered in selection	A disability is only relevant to job ability if it threatens the safety or property of others or if it prevents the applicant from safe and adequate job performance even if reasonable efforts were made to accommodate the disability.
Medical Information	• if currently under physician's care • name of family doctor • if receiving counselling or therapy		Medical exams should be preferably conducted after selection and only if an employee's condition is related to the job duties. Offers of employment can be made conditional on successful completion of a medical.
Affiliations	• for list of club or organizational memberships	• membership in professional associations or occupational groups can be asked if a job requirement	Applicants can decline to list any affiliation that might indicate a prohibited ground.
Pardoned Conviction	• whether an applicant has ever been convicted • if an applicant has ever been arrested • does applicant have a criminal record	• if bonding is a job requirement ask if applicant is eligible	Inquiries about criminal record/convictions – even those which have been pardoned – are discouraged unless related to job duties.
References			The same restrictions that apply to questions asked of applicants apply when asking for employment references.

SOURCE: Canadian Human Rights Commission, November 1984 (Ottawa: Minister of Supply and Services Canada, 1985).

harassment in their workplace but do nothing to stop it. The case involved a woman, who began working as a bookkeeper for Levac Supply Ltd. in 1973, sharing a general office area with the office manager. Both individuals got along well initially, but after a few months he became "less friendly" and uncommunicative, and began whistling particular tunes, and making noises and comments aimed at her, implying that she was working slowly or incompetently. He also began making personal comments about her size, referring to her and another female employee as "fridge sisters," and making snide comments about her behind her back. The comments that the woman found particularly demeaning were "waddle, waddle" or "swish, swish," when she was wearing nylons. She would sometimes yell at the office manager to "get off her back" but his behaviour continued. While he admitted to "bugging" and "teasing," he insisted that it was done simply to "get more productivity" out of her and he wasn't aware that his comments were upsetting to her. However, the board found it was not his job to monitor her productivity and that his "digs" at times drove her to tears and he was well aware of this. The complainant says she complained to the head of company operations, about three or four times a year about the harassment, but no one tried to remedy the situation.

In his written decision, board chairman H. A. Hubbard said, "Whether the harasser says "you are attractive and I want to have sex with you," or says "you are unattractive and no one is likely to want to have sex with you," the reference is sexual. It is verbal conduct of a sexual nature, and it is sexual harassment in the workplace if it is repetitive and has the effect of creating an offensive working environment." Thus, the comments, especially "waddle, waddle" and "swish, swish" imply sexual unattractiveness and as such are harassment because of sex. Since the head of operations did nothing to stop the harassment, he, the office manager and the company were order to pay her a total of $48 273 in damages.[16]

Pay Equity

pay equity

Pay equity is a very important aspect of equal opportunity and compensation. Pay equity became law in 1978 as an amendment to the Canadian Human Rights Act. It makes it illegal for employers to discriminate against individuals on the basis of job content. The focus of pay equity is to eliminate the historical gap between the income of men and women and ensure that the salary ranges correspond to the value of work performed. The federal pay equity applies to that section of the work force under its jurisdiction. Coverage is complete in that is no organization is exempted regardless of size (number of employees). The federal pay equity system is complaint-based, that is it is activated by a complaint, usually from an employee, group of employees, or a bargaining agent.[17]

The Province of Ontario has the most comprehensive pay equity system in Canada. It is a system-wide, proactive, regulatory approach, requiring employers to conduct job evaluations and implement pay equity whether or not there is direct or systemic evidence of discrimination. This system applies to the provincial civil service and the private sector. The Ontario system exempts fully organizations with fewer than 10 employees, and does not require organizations with 10-99 employees to conduct formal job evaluations.[18] For a comprehensive discussion of the implications of pay equity on compensation management and on collective bargaining see Chapters 13 and 20.

Systemic Discrimination

systemic discrimination

Systemic discrimination,[19] also known as indirect discrimination, constructive discrimination, or unintentional discrimination, is illegal under the Canadian Human Rights Act as well as under the human rights acts of other jurisdictions. Systemic discrimination is the consequences of an employer's policies, practices, or actions which are not openly discriminatory but are *indirectly* discriminatory by their impact or effect on some individuals. This form of discrimination occurs even though the employer's intent is not to discriminate and even among employment activities that are not motivated by prejudice or malice.

The concept of systemic discrimination was perhaps best articulated by the U.S. Supreme Court in *Griggs* v. *Duke Power Co. (1971)*.[20] The U.S. Supreme Court found that Griggs, a black employee, was discriminated against because the company used employment tests and educational requirements that effectively screened out a much larger proportion of black applicants than white applicants. According to the Court the tests and qualifications requirements were set too high for satisfactory performance in the janitorial job to which Griggs had applied. The Power employment practices were not deliberately established to discriminate against members of the designated group. Nevertheless, they had built-in biases that effectively restricted certain applicants from holding some jobs although they could perform them satisfactorily if given the opportunity. The court ruled that conscious attempt or intent does not matter; it is the consequences of an employer's action that determine whether the employer had discriminated against an individual. The approach adopted in the Griggs case of focusing on impact or consequences and not on intent has been adopted in Canada.

Various Canadian court and tribunal decisions have reinforced this prevailing view. In *Ishar Singh* v. *Security and Investigation (1977)*,[21] Singh complained that he was denied a job as a security guard because of his insistence on the right to wear a turban and a beard on religious grounds. The tribunal ruled that the employer's employment policy discriminated against Sikh males who are required by their religious faith to wear a turban and a beard. The tribunal also stated that it found that the "employer bore no ill will towards Sikh people ... had no intention to insult or act with malice ... and did not have the intention or motive of discrimination." However, it found that the impact of the employer's employment policy was to refuse employment to Sikhs. The tribunal ruled that the employer's intention was not necessary to establish a contravention of the human rights act. In *Colfer* v. *Ottawa Board of Commissioners of Police (1979)*, the tribunal ruled that the policy of a minimum height requirement of 5 feet, 10 inches (1.75m) and weight of 160 lbs (72.5kg) held by the board of commissioners of police "virtually eliminated women as police constables" because only 5% of females in Canada are that height or taller. According to the tribunal the height and weight requirement had an adverse impact on women and had a disproportionate effect upon women relative to men. Figure 2.4 outlines some examples of, and possible solutions to, systematically discriminatory employment practices.

EMPLOYMENT EQUITY[23]

Employment equity aims to remove those workplace barriers that prevent women, visible minorities, disabled persons, and native people from achieving their full potential. Its goal is to hire and promote people on the basis of competence only. This principle acknowledges the changing work force and provides a work setting of equal opportunity. Undeniably, the work force has undergone a profound transformation in recent years, with a rapid influx of women representing a sizeable pool of talent, education, and skills. The shrewd employer will take advantage of this resource and tap its enormous potential. By providing equal opportunity for all employees, organizations not only respond to modern trends—they benefit from them.

In 1983 the federal government appointed a royal commission (Abella) to examine the problem of under-utilization and under-representation of women and vis-

FIGURE 2.4
Examples of Systemic
Discrimination

Examples of Systemic Discrimination	Examples of Possible Solutions
1. Recruitment practices that limit applications from designated groups, e.g., word-of-mouth, internal hiring policies.	Word-of-mouth could be supplemented by contacting community organizations representing designated groups or the local Canada Employment Centre.
2. Job descriptions, performance appraisals, and job evaluation systems that undervalue the work of positions traditionally held by women.	Job descriptions can be rewritten, evaluation systems can be fine-tuned, and special training may be offered to make them aware of how to eliminate gender bias.
3. A workplace environment that does not expressly discourage sexual harassment.	A Company policy against sexual harassment with guidelines can be issued and followed-up through appraisal and discipline procedures; complaint and problem-solving mechanisms can be developed for all employees.
4. Written material that always uses male gender references.	Written material should be reviewed to eliminate gender-biased language in policies, job descriptions, etc. Policies and guidlines instructing that all organization communications acknowledge a male and female audience should be issued.[22]

ible minorities in employment. The Abella Commission submitted its recommendations in 1984 which resulted in the Employment Equity Act 1986.

employment equity

The relationship between the human resource management process and employment equity is simple and straightforward. **Employment equity** will ensure that organization's human resource management system runs fairly and efficiently. Employment equity programs will vary from company to company depending on such things as its size, location, industrial sector, management style, economic health, and work force composition. Like any human resource management activity, employment equity programs must fit the needs and culture of the organization. Each organization can develop a distinct approach to meet its particular objectives. Nevertheless, employment equity management processes have certain important elements in common.

Organizations implement employment equity because the program produces a human resource management system that is fairer and more efficient. Employment equity broadens the pool of candidates for jobs, strengthens internal recruitment and hiring methods by eliminating biases, and takes full advantage of all available human resources—not just a portion of them.

Employment equity can produce a more stable, productive, and committed labour force. Staff turnover often drops significantly. The special measures included in an employment equity program—such as work-sharing, flexible working hours, and special parental benefits—have a positive impact on both the morale and the productivity of employees.

All of these benefits combine to improve both the internal and external corporate image of an organization. They also sharpen the organization's competitive edge.

Employment equity should be tackled like any other management issue—with a comprehensive set of practical action steps. Developing a strategy to put the program into place will allow employers to manage actively the process of change, instead of reacting to it passively.

Application of the Employment Equity Act

The federal Employment Equity Act requires federally regulated companies with 100 or more employees to review employment policies and practices, institute positive policies and practices to ensure equal representation, and to implement employment equity programs for target groups.[24] The government has identified and designated four target groups as having been traditionally disadvantaged: women, visible minorities, disabled persons, and native people.[25] To accomplish this, the Act requires employers to develop annual plans detailing specific goals to be achieved in the implementation of employment equity, and to set out timetables for the implementation of the goals. The legislation also requires employers to report annually on the representation of members of designated groups by occupational groups and salary ranges as well as to provide information on those hired, promoted, and terminated.

Employers are required to retain each plan and all records used to prepare their annual reports for a period of at least three years. Upon receipt of each employer's report, CEIC make them available to the public and a copy is sent to the Canadian Human Rights Commission. The CHRC has the authority to initiate investigations of any company if it has reasonable grounds to believe that discrimination is indicated by the information in the reports. Firms that fail to comply the provisions of the Employment Equity Act are subject to fines of up to $50 000.

Employment Equity and the Federal Contract Compliance Program

Under the **Federal Contract Compliance Program**, companies who employ 100 or more employees and wish to bid on federal contracts of $200 000 or more to provide goods and services to the federal government are required to implement employment equity programs and to certify in writing their commitment to implement employment equity as a condition of the bid. Companies who have won government contracts are subject to random on-site compliance reviews by CEIC. If these reviews indicate that an employer failed to implement employment equity, then sanctions will be applied, including the exclusion of the employer from future government contracts.[26] The compliance criteria are listed in Figure 2.5.

Federal Contract Compliance Program

IMPLEMENTING EMPLOYMENT EQUITY[27]

An employment equity program is much more than a formal document prepared by a human resource management specialist. It is a deliberately structured process that involves planning, analysis, and a system to monitor and evaluate progress in all aspects of the employment equity program. The implementation of an employment equity program by an organization represents an exercise in the management of change. Success will depend on top management's commitment to the program and cooperation from division managers and employees.

Different groups within an organization will play a role in implementing the employment equity plan. They include senior management, line or divisional managers, human resource specialists, and all supervisory staff.

FIGURE 2.5
Federal Contractor's
Program for
Employment Equity

Compliance Criteria

1. Communication by the organization's Chief Executive Officer to employees, unions, and/or employee associations of the commitment to achieve equality in employment through the design and implementation of an employment equity plan.

2. Assignment of senior personnel with responsibility for employment equity.

3. Collection and maintenance of information on the employment status of designated group employees, by occupation and salary levels and in terms of hiring, promotion, and termination in relation to all other employees.

4. Analysis of designated group representation within the organization in relation to their representation in the supply of qualified workers from which the supplier may reasonably be expected to recruit employees.

5. Elimination or modification of those human resource policies, practices and systems, whether formal or informal, shown to have or likely to have an unfavourable effect on the employment status of designated group employees.

6. Establishment of goals for the hiring, training, and promotion of designated group employees. Such goals will consider projections for hiring, promotions, terminations, lay-offs, recalls, retirements and, where possible, the projected availability of qualified designated group employees.

7. Establishment of a work plan for reaching each of the goals in 6 above.

8. Adoption of special measures that are necessary to ensure that goals are achieved, including the provision of reasonable accommodation as required.

9. Establishment of a climate favourable to the successful integration of designated group members within the organization.

10. Adoption of procedures to monitor the progress and results achieved in implementing employment equity.

11. Authorization to allow representatives of the Canada Employment and Immigration Commission access to the business premises and to the records noted in 3 above, in order to conduct on-site compliance reviews for the purpose of measuring the progress achieved in implementing employment equity.

SOURCE: Employment and Immigration Canada, Federal Contractors Program, *Information for Suppliers* Used with permission.

Many people within the organization may not completely understand employment equity. It may challenge their traditional attitudes and beliefs about the roles of women and men, which may in turn affect both personal and professional relationships. It may make them apprehensive about how the program will affect their own careers.

The implementation strategy will help staff work effectively in the same direction. It will consider the probable impact of the program and respond to it. At the same time, it will offer support and incentives to employees to encourage them to carry out the changes that will be necessary if the program is to be effective.

In general terms, the purpose of an employment equity implementation strategy is to clarify the roles, responsibilities, and rewards attached to the employment equity program; to promote mutual responsibility for the program and its goals; and to further an understanding of the process as part of the organization's corporate ethics.

In order for the plan to be effective it must be designed to fit the unique needs of each employer. Nevertheless, there are certain basic steps that each employer should follow.

Step One: Obtaining Senior Management's Commitment and Support

Senior management's level of commitment to employment equity is essential to the program's success. This commitment is made explicit in the organization's policy statement and in supporting documentation. Throughout the entire implementation process, however, management must continue to be responsible and accountable for the employment position of the organization, and must make its role clear to the employees.

Written Policy

A written policy endorsed by the top management of the organization is an essential first step. Manulife Financial's policy statement is shown in Figure 2.6.

FIGURE 2.6
Corporate Policy
Statements—
Employment Equity

Manulife Financial

An integral part of the management philosophy at Manulife Financial is to provide employment equity for all persons currently employed, and those seeking employment. With that in mind, it is our practice to recruit and administer hiring, working conditions, benefits, and privileges of employment, compensation, training, advancement, transfers, and terminations of all employees without discrimination because of race, ancestry, place of origin, colour ethnic origin, citizenship, creed, sex, sexual orientation, age, record of offenses, marital status, family status, or disability.

We are therefore committed to maintaining a workplace where the terms and conditions of employment are equitable and nondiscriminatory, and we will actively remove barriers to provide each person with equal access to the benefits of employment. We believe it is the right of every employee to be treated with dignity and respect, within a work environment conducive to productivity, selfdevelopment, and career advancement based on demonstrated performance and individual ability.

At Manulife Financial we consider the equal treatment of all human beings to be a moral duty, a legal obligation, and a company commitment. The company strives to be progressive and committed in meeting the needs of our employees. We expect our employees to treat each other with dignity and respect and, in cooperation with each other, to help the company realize its employment equity objectives.

SOURCE: Reproduced by permission of Manulife Financial.

As can be seen, policy statements communicate to employees senior management's approval of and commitment to the development and successful implementation of the program. For example, the City of Ottawa has developed an effective method to ensure management responsibility. As part of its performance appraisal system, all managers have to measure the progress of employment equity activities in their particular areas of operation. Organizations such as Ontario Hydro have adopted a similar approach. The inclusion of employment equity initiatives within an organization's standard performance measurement system directly integrates employment equity into the corporate planning and accountability cycle. Although direction for employment equity comes from senior management, responsibility for program implementation rests with line management. Managers and supervisors hire, promote, evaluate, and train employees—so their role in employment equity is pivotal. It is essential, therefore, that the employment equity program acknowledges their role and makes them accountable.

Appointment of a Senior Official (Employment Equity Coordinator)

An organization should appoint a senior official and assign to that person the responsibility and authority for developing, implementing, and directing its employment equity program. This is important to ensure that the individual has the status and authority required to obtain the cooperation and trust of division managers, supervisors, employees, and labour. The employment equity coordinator assists management, supervisors, and staff in developing the various components of the plan. It is the coordinator's responsibility to support the managers in meeting their program objectives. The staff role, while often performed by the human resource department, is most effective when it can have direct access to the chief executive officer (CEO) of the organization. For example, The Royal Bank has appointed a manager of employment equity who reports to the vice-president.[28] Canadian National has appointed a vice-president of employment equity who reports to the President.[29] Brock University has appointed a coordinator of employment who has access to the president of the university.

Communication

Good communication is an essential aspect of an effective employment equity program. It is important that all managers are informed that employment equity has been added to their existing areas. The managers should also be persuaded of the importance of the program and the commitment it will take from each individual manager as well as the human resource department for it to succeed. It is important that the organization provide continuous reinforcement of its commitment to employment equity through such sources as the company newsletter, staff meetings, and special progress reports. For example, The Royal Bank communicates its policy internally by the following methods: a statement of its policy placed in its HRM manual; annual statements and periodic updates provided to staff; videotape presentations at staff meetings; newsletters sent to each employee; and orientation packages given to new hires. It communicates its policy externally through methods such as annual financial reports; addresses to community groups and civic organizations; and in publications of men and women.[30]

Assessing the Corporate Environment

As discussed in Chapter 1, each organization's written and unwritten rules, traditions, attitudes, beliefs, and structures create that company's culture and climate (environment). The organization's prevailing environment has a direct impact on its employment equity policy and program.

Various internal factors affect an organization's approach to employment equity. These include its size, its industrial sector, its economic health, the composition of its workplace, and whether the organization is unionized or not. A unionized environment, for example, may encourage an organization to approach employment equity in a joint or consultative manner. The current and projected economic health of an organization will affect both the resources allocated to the program and the priority and commitment assigned to it.

Employee's attitudes are an important part of an organization's environment. Therefore it is important to get their views on employment equity and to compare male and female points of view on their respective futures within the organization. Consultation with unions also helps to identify both support and potential problems early in the process.

Organizations could use an employee survey to learn more about their own environments and how employment equity can be applied to them. This provides valuable feedback on employee attitudes and encourages employees to become involved in the process. For example, Manulife Financial conducted a company-wide survey on employees' perceptions and attitudes regarding equal opportunity for women. The survey allowed the company to identify the range of support and opposition to the issue. It also helped to pinpoint obstacles that would require special attention. The survey found, for example, that older males, even some among senior management, were more inclined to oppose the advancement of women and to stereotype their roles. The company responded with training seminars, geared to specific groups in the organization, that focused on increasing employees' awareness of women's potential.

Step Two: Data Collection and Analysis

The organization should undertake comprehensive data collection of internal human resources and analyze these data to pinpoint areas of under-utilization and under-representation of females, visible minorities, and other designated group members. The organization should also collect data of availability of external resources to gain information on the availability of qualified job candidates in the labour market. Another purpose of this approach is to determine whether it is more economical to train existing members of the designated groups for future positions or to recruit externally.

Collection of an Internal Work Force Profile

To create such a profile requires assembling and analyzing data on:

- Current work force
- Job categories and departments
- Salary levels
- Length of time in position
- Attrition patterns
- Promotion eligibility lists
- Education and skill levels among current employees
- Composition of work force by gender, race, disability status

Collection of External Labour Force Availability Data

To gather this type of information requires collecting data on:

- Number of designated group members available in labour market
- Profile of available talents
- Demographics of available talents

Utilization analysis

The comparison of the internal work force profile with external work force availability is called a *utilization analysis*. Information on the availability of members of designated groups may be obtained from provincial women's directorates, Statistics Canada, Employment and Immigration Canada, and Canada Employment Offices and Training Centres. This information is available by SOC Code or Abella Groups.

This type of comparison is necessary in order to determine the underutilization or concentration of target group members. Underutilization exists when members of the target group are not equally utilized and represented in the employer's work force. It is the consequence of overt and/or systemic discrimination. Concentration means that a higher percentage of the designated group members are employed in a particular occupation or specialty than are represented in the labour market.

Analysis of availability establishes a standard of comparison for an organization's employment of designated group members. It also establishes realistic goals for an employment equity program and determines strategies to increase the pool of designated group candidates for specific jobs.

Step Three: Reviewing Employment Policies and Practices

It is essential that the organization undertake a comprehensive review of its corporate employment policies, procedures, and practices to determine their impact on designated group members and to eliminate any existing overt or systemic employment barriers. The evaluation should focus on various human resource management processes such as job analysis, recruitment and selection, performance appraisal, working conditions, training and development programs, promotion and transfer, and compensation.

Job Analysis

An assessment should be made of the organization's job analysis program to ensure that it is gender neutral, free of any biases, and accurate. This is important since job analysis forms the foundation for recruitment, selection, compensation, performance appraisal, and training and development, and has an impact on many other human resource management functions.

Recruitment and Selection

These two criteria should be reviewed to correct employment patterns or barriers which have been responsible for the under-utilization or concentration of the designated groups. They should also be reviewed to ensure that all selection instruments comply with the human rights guidelines, and to ensure compliance with the organization's employment equity obligations.

Performance Appraisal

These criteria should be carefully reviewed to ensure that their design and application are fair and objective.

Working Conditions

These criteria should be assessed to ensure that the work environment is free from sexual, racial, or other forms of harassment, that employees' rights are respected, and that work rules including disciplinary measures are applied on an equitable basis.

Training and Development Programs

A review of this category is needed to ensure that training and development opportunities are being made available to all employees, and that the eligibility requirements and nomination procedures are fair and objective and do not have an adverse impact on the designated group.

Promotion and Transfer

A review of these criteria is needed to ensure that the organization's formal and informal policies and practices on training and development provide the same promotion opportunities and career path opportunities for designated group and non-designated group members.

Compensation

A review of this category is necessary to ensure that the organization is complying with employment standards legislation, pay equity legislation, and all other relevant government legislation. Another reason for conducting this review is to ensure internal and external equity.

Step Four: Plan Development

Once an organization has completed the data collection process and an assessment of its corporate employment policies, procedures, and practices, it may commence the plan development stage of employment equity.

Goals and Timetables

Goals and timetables are the core of an employment equity program. They ensure that tangible changes and improvements are actually made—not just talked about. Goals should be flexible and tied to reasonable timeframes. Short-, medium-, and long-range goals are advisable. They make it much easier to assess the impact that different activities are having at specific times and allow the organization to pinpoint areas where adjustments are necessary. Goals are not quotas. They are estimates of the results that an organization can expect knowing its work force, the availability of the external work force, and the special measures that it is contemplating.

The organization should establish numeric goals specifying the number or percentage of qualified designated group members to be hired, trained, or promoted into each occupational group over a specified period of time. The goals will represent the targets that the organization believes are achievable through the elimination of discriminatory practices and the implementation of employment equity programs to increase the employment, upgrading, and retention of members of the designated group. Timetables represent the approaches used for achieving the targets established by the goals. Both the goals and timetables must be realistic. The goals may be quantitative as well as qualitative. To illustrate, a quantitative goal might be to hire five individuals of visible minorities over the next two years, while a qualitative goal might be to provide improved training opportunities for women to groom them for middle- and upper-level management positions.

Strategies

The organization should determine the type of strategies that it should pursue in order to get measurable and visible results in the short-, medium-, and long-term. These strategies should be both corrective and innovative. Corrective strategies are intended to eliminate employment barriers, eliminate discriminatory practices, change prejudiced attitudes and beliefs, and modify traditional human resource practices. They also include measures required to eliminate direct or indirect inequities. Innovative strategies represent new and creative measures designed to achieve equity in the work environment.

Step Five: Implementation

Implementation is the process that transforms goals and timetables into reality. Once an organization has completed the preceding steps it may implement the necessary changes and specific measures required to implement employment equity so as to increase employment and advancement opportunities for the designated groups found to be under-utilized and concentrated in particular job categories. An implementation plan, for example, may include the following:

- The use of traditional and nontraditional recruitment media to search for qualified and qualifiable designated group members
- Job rotation programs designed to increase the breadth of experience of promotable designated group members, thereby augmenting their skills
- Job restructuring, enrichment, and reclassification
- Establishment of support measures in such an area as career counselling for designated group members
- Organization of workshops for designated group members to encourage greater self-awareness of career opportunities.
- Revision of all selection instruments
- Revision of all communication media
- Establishment of special initiatives in training and development to broaden opportunities for designated group members

Step Six: Monitoring, Reviewing, and Revising

An effective employment equity program requires a control system to monitor and evaluate its progress and success. The vice-president, director, or employment equity coordinator will need periodic benchmarks to evaluate the degree to which the program is on target and is effective. Reviews, in turn, may lead to new goals and timetables based on the requirements of the program. The program may have to be revised to reflect changing circumstances. It is important that all relevant data, both internal and external, are updated on a continuing basis. Progress on the attainment of employment equity goals should be reviewed regularly, preferably on a quarterly basis. This might include the following:

- Review of flow data on job applications, hiring, promotions, training, and terminations to determine the progress being made by designated group members
- Personal interviews of managers, as well as designated group members
- Committee reviews of field representative reports, and management reports
- Statistical summaries of estimated versus actual goals and timetables achieved

THE CHARTER OF RIGHTS AND FREEDOMS

The Canadian **Charter of Rights and Freedoms** came into effect on April 17, 1982. It applies to individuals who deal with the federal government, the provincial governments, and their agencies.

Charter of Rights and Freedoms

The Charter of Rights and Freedoms provides the following fundamental rights to every Canadian:

- Freedom of conscience and religion
- Freedom of thought, belief, opinion, and expression, including freedom of the press and other media of communication
- Freedom of peaceful assembly; and
- Freedom of association

The charter also provides protection to every Canadian for the right to live and seek employment anywhere in Canada, and for minority language education rights, Canadian multicultural heritage rights, and native people's rights.[31]

The Charter's provisions regarding equality have the most dramatic and direct impact on employment and correspondingly on HRM.[32] This section 15(1) guarantees "equal protection and equal benefit of the law without discrimination based on race, national or ethnic origin, colour, religion, sex, age, mental or physical disability." The only exception to the preceding equality rights is provided in section 15(2) wherein an employer is allowed to implement programs and activities designed to remedy past discrimination.

At the time when the Charter was enacted it created high hopes and expectations for various interest groups, particularly regarding union management. It was generally expected by both parties that the Charter would work to their advantage and thus strengthen their respective bargaining positions. However, the high expectations have not been fulfilled for either side. The overall impact of the Charter on the industrial relations scene has been rather modest. One of the reasons for the disappointing results is due to the long period of time that cases take to reach the final arbiter of the Charter, the Supreme Court of Canada.[33]

Application of the Charter

Since the Charter came into effect a variety of issues have been before the courts for consideration. Some of the issues include mandatory retirement, the right of employees to bargain collectively and to strike, and the right of public servants to engage in partisan activities. The Supreme Court recently ruled on these challenges, and they are discussed below.

Mandatory Retirement

The Supreme Court of Canada has ruled that mandatory retirement at age 65 is justified in a free and democratic society, although it violates the equality provisions in the Charter. In a five-two majority decision the Court said that abolishing mandatory retirement would create "monumental social upheaval," especially for the human resource function.

The Supreme Court ruling was based on four cases—one from Ontario and three from British Columbia. The case from Ontario involved a challenge by several professors and a librarian to the mandatory retirement policies at four universities. The B.C. cases involved 14 doctors whose admitting privileges were not renewed at Vancouver General Hospital, an Administrator at UBC, and two instructors at Douglas College in New Westminster. All 22 individuals were forced to retire at 65, and all argued that they were discriminated against on the basis of age. The implication of this ruling is that it shifts the mandatory retirement issue from the legal arena to the political arena, because provincial governments can abolish mandatory retirement by amending their human rights codes. The provinces of Alberta, Manitoba, and Quebec have abolished mandatory retirement as has the federal government for civil servants.[34]

Restriction of Public Servant's Political Activities

Recently the Supreme Court ruled that public servants may be reasonably restricted from engaging in partisan political activities. Even though this restriction constitutes a denial of freedom of speech, it was nevertheless considered a reasonable and justifiable limitation under Section 1 of the Charter.

HUMAN RESOURCE MANAGEMENT

On the Front Line

One of the first problems Jennifer faced at Carter Cleaning Centres concerned the inadequacies of the firm's current human resource management practices and procedures.

One thing that particularly concerned her was the lack of attention that had been given to equal employment matters. Virtually all hiring was handled independently by each store manager, and the managers themselves had received no training regarding such fundamental matters as the types of questions that should not be asked of job applicants. It was therefore not unusual—in fact was even routine—for female applicants to be asked questions such as "Who's going to take care of your children while you are at work?" and for minority applicants to be asked questions about arrest records. Non-minority applicants—three stores managers were white males, by the way, and three were white females—were not asked questions such as these, Jennifer discerned from her interviews with the managers.

Based on discussions with her father, Jennifer deduced that part of the reason for the laid-back attitude toward equal employment stemmed from (1) her father's lack of sophistication regarding the human rights requirements and (2) the practical fact that, as Jack put it, "Virtually all our workers are women or minority members anyway, so no one can really come in here and accuse us of being discriminatory, can they?"

Jennifer decided to mull that question over, but before she could, she was faced with two serious human rights problems. Two women in one of her stores privately confided to her that their manager was making unwelcome sexual advances toward them, and one claimed he had threatened to fire her unless she "socialized" with him after hours. And on a fact-finding trip to another store, an elderly gentleman—he was 63 years old—complained that although he had almost 50 years' experience in the business, he was being paid less than people half of his age who were doing the very same job. Her review of the stores resulted in the following questions:

1. Is it true, as Jack Carter claims, that they "can't be accused of being discriminatory because we hire mostly women and minorities anyway?"

2. How should Jennifer and her company address the sexual harassment charges and problems?

3. How should she and her company address the possible problems of age discrimination?

4. Given the fact that each of their stores has only a handful of employees, is her company in fact covered by human rights legislation?

5. And finally, aside from the specific problems, what other human resource management matters (application forms, training, etc.) have to be reviewed given the need to bring them into compliance with human rights laws?

The Right to Bargain Collectively and to Strike

The Supreme Court ruled recently in a series of decisions on the impact of the Charter of Rights and Freedoms on both federal and provincial collective bargaining laws and regulations. In its first decision on this matter, the Court ruled that the Charter does not include the right to bargain collectively or to strike. The Court held that whereas Section 2 of the Charter protects the individual's right to work for the establishment of an association, to join an association, and to maintain such membership, this right does not extend to bargain collectively and to strike. According to the Court the rights to bargain collectively and strike are not fundamental freedoms. Instead they are statutory rights created and regulated by the federal parliament and provincial legislature.

The implications of this ruling are that a collective agreement is a private agreement that falls outside the scope of the Charter, and that a strike does not constitute freedom of expression and so it also falls outside the scope of the Charter.[35]

Other implications of this ruling are that the federal and provincial governments may restrict the collective bargaining process by restraining wage and salary increases (e.g., the wage restraints imposed in the 1991 budgets by the finance minister of the federal government, and the provincial governments of Quebec and Newfoundland), legislating strikers back to work, and imposing compulsory arbitration on both bargaining parties. Evidently this ruling, with its far-ranging implications, is a severe blow to the union movement.

SUMMARY

1. This chapter discussed the network of federal and provincial laws that are designed to assure equal opportunity for all Canadians and to secure special provisions for members of designated groups. These laws prohibit discrimination on the basis of race, colour, religion, sex, marital status, age, national or ethnic origins, physical handicaps, or for a conviction for which a pardon has been granted.

2. The human rights commission of each jurisdiction administers the network of federal and provincial equal opportunity legislation. The commissions have the authority to receive complaints, investigate the complaints, determine the validity of the complaints, try to achieve a settlement between the parties, and proceed with the complaints before boards, tribunals, or the courts.

3. Developing and implementing an employment equity program involves six elements: a strong commitment and support of top management, data collection and analysis, a review of employment policies and practices, plan development, implementation, and evaluation.

4. The Charter of Rights and Freedoms guarantees all Canadians certain fundamental rights. The Charter also provides protection to every Canadian in certain specific areas. Most other provisions of the Charter are open-ended and its full impact is presently unknown. The Supreme Court is the ultimate interpreter of the provisions of the Charter. The Charter applies to federal, provincial and municipal laws and statutes, and to the actions of public officials.

KEY TERMS

Canadian Human Rights Act

Canadian Human Rights Commission

sexual harassment

pay equity

systemic discrimination

employment equity

Federal Contract Compliance Program

Charter of Rights and Freedoms

DISCUSSION QUESTIONS

1. Discuss the major prohibitions of the Canadian Human Rights Act.
2. Define systemic discrimination. How does it come about and what steps should an organization take to remove it?
3. Describe how to develop an employment equity program for an organization.
4. What specific steps should an organization take to prevent or eliminate discrimination?
5. Describe the steps involved in a human rights complaint process.

CASE INCIDENT: Is the Restaurant Owner Guilty of Discrimination?

When it opened, a restaurant employed a woman of Chinese ancestry in its kitchen area. She was well-groomed, poised, well-spoken, and presented an attractive appearance. She had management aspirations and accepted a kitchen job in order to learn the restaurant trade from the ground up. After working in different capacities in the kitchen she eventually became a baker and proved to be an excellent one. Next to the kitchen manager, the baker was the highest paid "back" employee.

Some restaurant employees worked in "the front of the house" and others worked in the "back of the house." "Back" employees primarily worked in the kitchen and were involved in the preparation of food that "front" employees served to the customers. Working in the front was regarded as more prestigious. Because of gratuities, front employees earned more money than those in the back.

The baker soon applied for a front job with the hope of becoming a waitress. Management promised her a front job but adopted delaying tactics whenever she asked them when one would become available. Eventually the baker became discouraged and resigned. She believed that racial prejudice stood in her way. In all, she had worked for the restaurant for more than three and a half years.

The restaurant owner tried to persuade the baker to stay and asked her why she was leaving. The baker did not tell the owner that racial feelings played a role in her decision but said that she had studied art and wanted to be employed in that field. She subsequently became manager of a Toronto picture store but at a lower wage. Later she moved to Vancouver where her family lived and after working for some time as a baker, she was hired by a securities firm.

The baker eventually filed a complaint with the Ontario Human Rights Commission alleging that the failure to advance her to the front of the restaurant was due to racial prejudice.

A Board of Inquiry was convened to hear the baker's complaint. At the hearing the baker claimed that the atmosphere at the restaurant was "poisoned" racially. She contended that non-white employees were verbally insulted and that white employees were treated preferentially. She pointed to the fact that front workers were predominantly white.

The evidence confirmed that the front staff was overwhelmingly white. In the kitchen the majority of the day staff was non-white.

Several employees testified that racial slurs were common in the kitchen although none were directed specifically at the baker. These slurs came mainly from the kitchen managers who were both white. The restaurant's general manager had also, on at least one occasion, showed racial prejudice but he had apologized to the staff.

The baker and other employees regarded the general manager "as the hub of racial problems" because he failed to control the racist language of his subordinates and had been guilty of using such language himself.

The employees testified that remarks were expressed about Chinese workers being "cheap" and that on occasion Chinese accents were imitated. The kitchen managers often used profanities calling employees "niggers" and asking them to "move their fat asses." One of the Chinese employees did speak to the general manager about these slurs. The manager had brought this to the attention of the kitchen managers on two occasions but according to the employees, "did not follow this up."

The baker, while admitting that she had never been the target of racial remarks, said that they bothered her "because they demeaned people who deserved better by their supervisors."

The general manager denied the claim that there was a "poisoned atmosphere" in the restaurant. However, he admitted that "racial slurs and stereotypical disparagement of non-whites" occurred at the restaurant. He testified that the kitchen managers were well liked by the staff and that, in general, the employee-employer relationship was harmonious. The general manager also admitted uttering a racial slur on one occasion but termed it a "slip." He pointed out that when he became aware that the slur had produced "grave discontent," he had called the black staff into his office on an individual basis and apologized to each of them.

The general manager argued that he had a logical business reason for not giving the baker a job in the front part of the restaurant. He denied that the failure to promote her was racially motivated. The general manager said that she was an excellent baker who was hard to replace but that she would have been promoted to the front of the restaurant as soon as a replacement was found.

The general manager also disputed the baker's allegation that whites were given preferential treatment in hiring for front positions. He pointed out that the person who was in charge of the restaurant on weekends was of East Indian ancestry. He also testified that two other non-whites had been moved from the back of the restaurant to the front adding that "he simply could not get non-whites to apply" for waiting jobs. The general manager also claimed that he had asked another employee of Chinese ancestry to invite his friends to apply for waiting jobs.

SOURCE: *The Employment Law Report*, Vol. 11, no. 4 (April 1990), pp. 27-31. Reproduced by permission of Concord Publishing Ltd., 14 Prince Arthur Avenue, Toronto, Ontario M5R 1A9.

Questions

1. Assume the role of the human rights commission investigator. Decide the following and explain your answer:

   a) Did the restaurant directly discriminate against the baker?

   b) Did the restaurant indirectly discriminate against the baker?

   c) Did the baker resign because of discrimination?

   d) Did the preponderance of whites in front jobs result from discriminatory practices by the employer?

   e) What steps, if any, should the employer take to change the work environment?

NOTES

1. Walter S. Tarnopolsky, *Discrimination and the Law in Canada*. (Toronto: Richard DeBoo Limited 1982), p. 40; see also John G. Kelly, *Human Resource Management and the Human Rights Process* (Toronto: CCH Canadian Limited 1985), p. 7.

2. Canadian Human Rights Commission, *The Canadian Human Rights Act*, Paragraph 2, Subsection (a).

3. Tarnopolsky, p. 32.

4. "Firm Pays $300,000 in Racial Harassment Settlements," *Human Resources Management in Canada*, Report Bulletin no. 72. (Scarborough, Ont.: Prentice-Hall Canada Inc., February 1989), pp. 1-2.

5. Canadian Human Rights Commission, *Annual Report*, 1989, p. 42 (see *Brooks, Allen and Dixon v. Canada Safeway Ltd.*).

6. Canadian Human Rights Commission, *Annual Report*, 1988, p. 40 (see *Rinn and Russel v. Keewatin Air Ltd.*).

7. Canadian Human Rights Commission, *Annual Report*, 1985, p. 25 (see *McGreary v. Greyhound Lines of Canada*).

8. Canadian Human Rights Commission, *Annual Report*, 1989, p. 53 (see *Nealy v. Terry Long, Randy Johnson, and the Church of Jesus Christ Christian-Aryan Nations.*)

9. Canadian Human Rights Commission, *Annual Report*, 1989, p. 51.

10. *Human Resources Management in Canada*, Report Bulletin 95. (Scarborough, Ont.: Prentice-Hall Canada Inc., Jan. 1991), pp. 6-7.

11. Canadian Human Rights Commission, *Annual Report*, 1981, p. 29.

12. Bona-fide Occupational Requirements (BFOR) and Bona-fide Occupational Qualifications (BFOQ) are used interchangeably. BFOR is more used in most Canadian jurisdictions. BFOQ is more commonly used in the U.S. However, decisions of Canadian Courts and Human Rights Tribunals appear to confer the same meaning to both terms.

13. Many of these cases are listed in *Human Resources Management in Canada*.

14. For details of the enforcement procedures see The Canadian Human Rights Commission, *Annual Report*, 1985.

15. Canadian Human Rights Commission, Harassment: Commission Policy (Ottawa: CHRC, 1985); see also Harish C. Jain and P. Andippan, "Sexual Harassment in Employment in Canada," *Relations Industrielles*, 41, no. 4 (1986), pp. 758-76; Canadian Human Rights Commission, *Unwanted Sexual Attention and Sexual Harassment: Results of a Survey of Canadians* (Ottawa: CHRC, 1983).

16. *Human Resources Management in Canada*, Report Bulletin no. 95. (Scarborough, Ont.: Prentice-Hall Canada Inc., January 1991), pp. 7-8.

17. Morley Gunderson and Roberta Edgecombe Robb, "Equal Pay for Work of Equal Value: Canada Experience." *Advances in Industrial and Labour Relations*, Vol. 5, 1991, pp. 151-168. See also John G. Kelly, *Pay Equity Management*, (Toronto: CCH Canadian Ltd., 1988), pp. 45-54.

18. Gunderson and Robb, pp. 151-168.

19. For an excellent discussion of systemic discrimination see the Canadian Human Rights Commission, *Report of the Commission of Equality in Employment*, Chapter 1.

20. See *Griggs v. Duke Power Co.*, 401 U.S. 424, 1971.

21. See *Sing v. Security and Investigation Services Ltd.*, Ontario Board of Inquiry, May 31, 1977.

22. Ontario Women's Directorate, *Managing Employment Equity: Organizational Change and Organizational Impact*. Minister Responsible for Women's Issues 1989, p. 7.

    For further information on managing employment equity contact The Consultative Services Branch, Ontario Women's Directorate, 480 University Ave., 2nd Floor, Toronto, Ont. M5G 1V2.

23. The material in this section is drawn from (i) Ontario Women's Directorate, Used with permission. (ii) John H. Blakely and Edward B. Harvey, "Socioeconomic Change and Lack of Change: Employment Equity Policies in the Canadian Context" in *Journal of Business Ethics*, Vol. 7 (1988), pp. 133-150. (iii) P. Scott "Equality in Employment: A Royal Commission Report," *Current Readings in Race Relations*, Vol. 2, no. 4 (Toronto: Urban Alliance on Race Relations,Winter 1984/85). (iv) John G. Kelly, *Equal Opportunity Management: Understanding Affirmative Action and Employment Equity*. (Toronto: CCH Canadian Ltd., 1986). (v) I. A. Hunter, "Human Rights Legislation in Canada: Its Origin, Development, and Interpretation" *University of Western Ontario Law Review* 1976, Vol. 21, p. 25. (vi) Harish C. Jain, "Human Rights: Issues in Employment," in *Human Resources Management in Canada* (Scarborough, Ont.: Prentice-Hall Canada), pp. 50,011-50,103.

24. Edward B. Harvey and others, *Computing for Equity: Computer Applications for Employment Equity* (Toronto: CCH Canadian Ltd. 1990), p. 11.

25. *Employment Equity Act and Reporting Requirements* (Ottawa: Employment and Immigration Canada, 1986).

26. Employment Equity Act and Reporting Requirements. See also Harvey and others; Jain pp. 50,011-50,103.

27. Parts of this section are drawn from (i) Employment and Immigration Canada, Consultative Services, Employment Equity Branch, "Employment Equity: A Guide for Employers" in *Employment Equity Act and Reporting Requirements* (Ottawa: Ministry of Supply and Services Canada, 1986); (ii) *Report of the Commission on Equality in Employment (Ottawa: Ministry of Supply and Services Canada, 1984) (iii) D. Rhys Phillips, "Equity in the Labour Market: The Potential of Affirmative Action" in *Research Studies of the Commission on Equality in Employment* (Ottawa: Ministry of Supply and Services Canada, 1985), pp. 51-110; (iv) Treasury Board of Canada Secretariat, Human Resources Division, Personnel Policy Branch, *Employment Equity for Crown Corporations: Policy and Reference Guide* (Ottawa: Ministry of Supply and Services Canada, 1986); (v) *Ontario Women's Directorate*. Used with permission.

28. For an excellent discussion of employment equity in practice, see Linda White, "Equal Employment Opportunities—Challenges and Practices for Canadian Companies: The Royal Bank Experience," in *Canadian Readings in Personnel and Human Resource Management* (St. Paul: West Publishing, 1987), pp. 142-153.

29. For another excellent discussion of employment equity in practice, see Louise Piche, "Employment Equity at Canadian National Railway: Initiatives and Proactive Measures" in *Canadian Readings in Personnel and Human Resource Management* (St. Paul: West Publishing, 1987), pp. 112-119.

30. White, p. 147; see also the Royal Bank of Canada, 1989 *Annual Financial Statement*.

31. *The Charter of Rights and Freedoms*, Section 15(1) and 15(2).

32. John G. Kelly, *Human Resource Management and the Charter* (Toronto: CCH Canadian Limited, 1990), p. 23.

33. For a more comprehensive discussion of the impact of the Charter see Kelly, p. 23; S. D. Carter "Canadian Labour Relations Under the Chater," *Relations Industrielles*, 1988, Vol. 43, no. 2, pp. 305-321; H. Bayefsky and M. Ebert (eds), *Equality of Rights and the Canadian Charter of Rights and Freedoms* (Toronto: Carswell Publishers, 1985).

34. "Supreme Court Upholds Mandatory Retirement," *Human Resources Management in Canada* Report Bulletin no. 95 (January 1991), pp. 1-2.

35. For ongoing development in the legal environment see: (i) *The Employment Law Report*, (ii) Human Resources Management in Canada, and (iii) Industrial Relations Centre, *The Current Industrial Relations Scene in Canada* Queen's University, (Kingston, Ont.: Queen's University, 1989)

SUGGESTED READINGS

Baker, Janice. "Ending Discrimination in Hiring: Recruitment and Human Rights Legislation" in *Human Resources Management in Canada*. Toronto: Prentice-Hall Canada Inc., 1988, pp. 25,511-25,515.

Bayefsky, Ann F., and Mary Eberts, *Equality Rights and The Canadian Charter of Rights*. Toronto: Carswell, 1985.

Belcourt, Monica, H. Lee-Gosselin, and Ronald J. Burke. "Discriminatory Treatment of Women Entrepreneurs." Administrative Sciences Association of Canada (Personnel and Human Resources Division) *Proceedings of the Annual Conference Meeting*, June 1991, pp. 31-39.

The Employment Law Report. Toronto: Concord Publishing Ltd., 1991.

Fogarty, Kenneth H. *Equality Rights and Their Limitations in the Charter*. Toronto: Carswell, 1987.

Harvey, Edward B., Eric J. Severn, and John H. Blakely. *Computing for Equity: Computer Applications for Employment Equity*. Toronto: CCH Canadian Limited, 1990.

Jain, Harish C. "Human Rights: Issues in Employment" in *Human Resources Management in Canada*. Toronto: Prentice-Hall Canada Inc., 1989, pp. 50,011-50, 103.

Kelly, John G. *Human Resource Management and The Charter*. Toronto: CCH Canadian Limited, 1990.

——— *Human Resource Management and the Human Rights Process*, 2nd ed. Toronto: CCH Canadian Limited, 1991.

Royal Commission on Equality in Employment (Abella Commission), *Equality in Employment*. Ottawa: Minister of Supply and Services Canada, 1984.

CHAPTER THREE

HUMAN RESOURCE PLANNING

After studying this chapter you should be able to

1. Explain the purposes and importance of human resource planning (HRP) to the organization.
2. Define the major steps involved in the human resource planning process.
3. Explain the differences between strategic planning and operational planning.
4. Explain human resource planning forecasting techniques.
5. Discuss human resource information systems.
6. Explain the different approaches to human resource accounting.
7. Describe human resource evaluation.

OVERVIEW

This chapter examines the human resource planning process, emphasizing its purposes and importance. We also emphasize how essential it is to determine human resource supply and demand in view of the organization's goals, mission, operating and strategic plans, and the external labour market and industry conditions. We further identify the steps involved in the forecasting process, and discuss different approaches to forecasting the organization's human resource needs.

INTRODUCTION TO HUMAN RESOURCE PLANNING

human resource planning

Human resource planning (HRP) is the process of forecasting an organization's human resource needs (demand). HRP outlines the intended courses of action that the organization should take to ensure that it has the right number of individuals with the right mix of skills at the right time in the right occupations[1] so that the organization may accomplish its present and future objectives efficiently and effectively. Human resource planning is a proactive, or forward looking, process that actively anticipates and influences an organization's future.

Human resource planning may also be defined as the process of analyzing an organization's human resource needs under changing conditions and developing the activities necessary to satisfy these needs.[2] An important benefit of HRP is that it results in the coordination of all human resource management polices. Recruitment, training, promotion, layoff, and transfer policies all affect human resource requirements and supply. They must be properly integrated with each other if organizational objectives are to be achieved. HRP offers a framework for this to happen.[3] For example, by estimating the number of individuals needed and the necessary skills, knowledge, and abilities required, human resource specialists can better manage their staffing and development activities. HRP, which is sometimes called employment planning, can assist organizations to meet their employment equity commitments.

As a proactive process, HRP may also be characterized as a process of anticipating changes and assisting the organization to adapt to the changes on a timely basis. The changes we speak of include demographic, industrial, and technological changes, as well as the major shifts in international trading patterns[4] resulting from the Canada-U.S. Free Trade Agreement. This means that in order for many Canadian firms to survive and prosper they must become competitive and strive to gain and maintain a competitive advantage in their industry. Competitive advantage grows fundamentally out of improvement, innovation, and change.[5]

Human resource planning uses a variety of methods and techniques to establish the human resource requirements needed by the organization to achieve its goals and objectives. These techniques range from operational planning, strategic planning, and human resource forecasting to program planning and implementation. These techniques are used to forecast and plan present and future needs, surpluses and shortages, and to select the right mix of individuals to meet these needs. They are also used to manage internal shifts such as promotions, transfers, and terminations, and to respond to changes in the external environment.

Purposes and Importance of Human Resource Planning

The purposes and importance of human resource planning are to

- Provide management with the tools to help control and reduce labour costs by anticipating shortages and surpluses of human resources, to adjust these fluctuations before they have negative impacts on the organization, and to identify future trends and their likely results and impact on the organizations

- Project the quantity and quality of individuals and positions required by the organization to facilitate the attainment of the organization's plans, goals, and objectives

- Provide management with the means to forecast future supply and demand for human resources, including the projection of future human resources mobility, attrition, expansion, and type of skill utilization
- Provide the tools for evaluating the present availability of talent in the organization including an inventory of each employee's qualifications, expressed career interest, and future development potential
- Assist the organization to develop policies and procedures as well as logical paths/systems to meet mandated employment equity for women, minorities, and other groups
- Provide a better basis for planning recruitment and selection, and for coordinating and integrating different human resource management programs
- Provide the tools to identify, design, develop, and implement policies and programs that help management to optimize the organization's return on its investments in its human resources, and to facilitate the optimum use of employees' capabilities for increased performance and productivity
- Develop and install objective criteria for analysis of human resource costs, including turnover, relocation, attrition, training, payroll, and development costs

Strategic Planning

Strategic planning is the process of setting organizational objectives and deciding on comprehensive programs of action that will achieve these objectives.[6] Strategic planning is also concerned with the formulation of an organization's corporate policies aimed at accomplishing long-term goals or a major change in growth over a period of one to five years. It involves the commitment of major financial, human, and physical resources to enable the achievement of planned change in direction.

strategic planning

The strategic planning process involves the following:[7]

1. *Definition of the corporate philosophy and mission*. This is an essential first step. It is important to determine the answer to questions such as "What is the basic nature and purpose for which this organization exists?" and "What are the underlying motives and values of the organization?"

2. *Scanning of the environmental conditions*. It is important to scan the environment to determine changes, uncertainties, disturbances, and emerging economic, government, social, technological, political, geographical, demographic, and labour market trends. This must be done so that the organization can adapt to the changing environment as well as take proactive measures to better accomplish the organization's overall mission.

3. *Evaluation of the organization's strengths and weaknesses*. In this step it is important to carefully assess the organization's strengths or advantages and its weaknesses or disadvantages and determine what factors or influences may have a positive impact or negative impact on the future courses of action of the organization. Factors to be assessed include work-force demographics, skills levels, and development potential.

4. *Development of goals and objectives*. In this step the organization determines the goals and objectives needed to fulfil its corporate mission. Specific goals include projected sales, profits, and return on investments.

5. *Development of strategies.* Once the proceeding four steps are complete, the next step is the development of strategies to achieve the corporate mission goals and objectives.

An organization's strategic plan always seeks to balance two sets of forces: the company's external opportunities and threats, on the one hand, and its internal strengths and weaknesses, on the other. Companies that successfully balance these external and internal forces succeed. McDonald's Canada is a case in point: it has succeeded by diversifying its product line, by extending store hours, and by expanding overseas (it opened the first burger place in the former USSR).

HRM's Role in Strategic Planning

There are three ways the human resource management department helps top management formulate and execute the company's strategic plan: first, by helping supply intelligence regarding the company's external opportunities and threats; second, by supplying intelligence about the company's internal strengths and weaknesses; and third, by helping execute the plan, for instance, by eliminating a weakness that could be an impediment to the plan.

External Opportunities and Threats

Let's look at a few examples. The HRM manager can, first, help the CEO formulate the strategic plan by supplying intelligence about the company's external opportunities and threats. For example, labour projections regarding labour availability are crucial to firms like McDonald's Canada and Burger King Canada (and others) that depend heavily on entry-level labour. For companies like these the strategic implications of a diminishing entry-level labour pool include the need for increased automation of facilities and possibly the need to reduce the growing dependence on company-owned stores by shifting the recruiting burden to local franchises. Installing smaller, less labour-intensive drive-through locations is another strategic possibility that could emerge from such strategic input.

HRM is in a unique position to supply other data on external opportunities and threats as well. Details regarding advanced incentive plans being used by competitors, opinion survey data from employees that elicits suggestions about customer complaints, and information about pending legislation like labour laws or increased mandatory benefits are some other examples.

Internal Strengths and Weaknesses

Second, HRM specialists can also help top management formulate strategy by supplying information regarding the company's internal strengths and weaknesses.

The whole area of mergers and acquisitions is ripe for HRM's input. While financial and business considerations will usually prevail here, it is usually useful (and often essential) for the CEO to also know about matters like morale problems in the acquired firm, incompatibility of corporate cultures, and potential problems in merging compensation, seniority, and benefit plans. For example, if Bell Canada were to acquire and merge with AT & T, it would be beneficial for Bell to survey its AT & T employees to make sure that if there were a problem they knew about it as quickly as possible. Two researchers[8] found recently that although there were no substantial differences between Canadians and Americans in areas such as overall satisfaction with their jobs and with their companies, differences nevertheless exist in four broad categories: level of cohesiveness with the company, level of job stress, identification with the company, and organization involvement in employee development.

HRM, therefore, should be a source of strategic input regarding the company's strengths and weaknesses. This certainly applies to obvious areas like management talent and competitiveness of the firm's compensation plan. But increasingly it must include less obvious matters such as the attractiveness of a merger candidate in human resource terms, the potential people problems likely to occur as a result of introducing a new technology, and the human resource benefits and drawbacks of pursuing one strategic plan or another.

Successful Execution

Finally, HRM should be heavily involved in the successful execution of the company's strategic plan, for instance, by helping to eliminate weaknesses that could inhibit the plan. Today, HRM specialists are already heavily involved in the execution of most firms' downsizing and restructuring strategies, in terms of outplacing employees, instituting pay for performance plans, reducing health-care costs, and retraining employees. However, these activities are probably just the tip of the iceberg, considering the trends evolving today. Intensifying domestic and international competition, the changing nature of the work force, jobs that are increasingly complex and based on information technology, and continuing merger and divestiture activities mean that management will have to base strategic decisions more than ever on human resources considerations. Creating the right company culture, keeping key human resources after a merger, matching training needs and people with jobs, and solving the human problems (stress and low morale, for example) that can arise when employees' jobs are put in jeopardy are a few examples of the sorts of activities the human resource manager will play in helping execute the strategic plan.[9]

Operational Planning

Operational planning is concerned with the normal ongoing short-term operation of the organization. It involves the determination of the organization's short-term needs, human resources, and human resource programs and policies that are required to achieve these objectives. With operational planning the organization decides how, when, and where their demands can be met either through recruiting, training and development, transfers, promotions, or a combination of these activities.

operational planning

Operational planning also involves other resources required by the organization and usually covers operational activities over a one to 12 month period. Its aim is to meet the calibre of human resources needed to achieve consumer and customer demands, product modifications, production efficiency, and changes in the organization's processes and practices.

THE HUMAN RESOURCE PLANNING PROCESS

Human resource planning involves six distinct processes:
1. Establishing organizational goals and objectives.
2. Forecasting future human resource needs (demand).
3. Forecasting future human resource supplies (availability).
4. Planning human resource programs.

5. Implementing programs.

6. Monitoring and evaluating human resource planning results.

Figure 3.1 illustrates two of the major components of the human resource planning process, needs forecasting and program planning. (These will be discussed in detail later.)

FIGURE 3.1
The Human Resource Planning Process

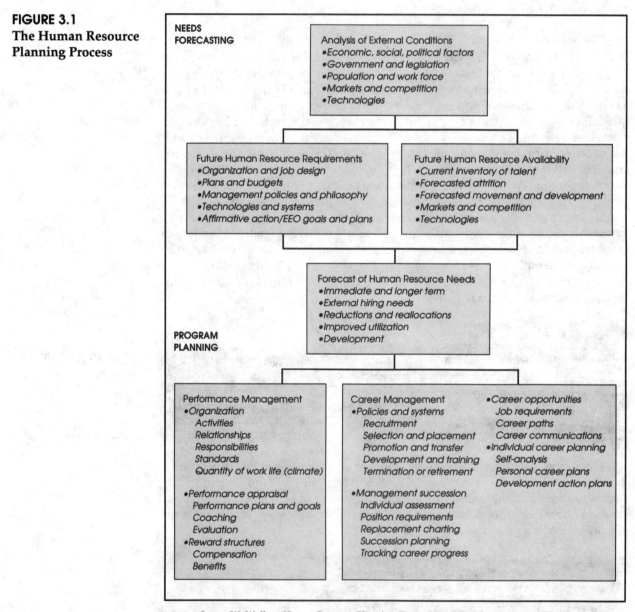

SOURCE: James W. Walker, *Human Resource Planning.* Copyright © 1980 by McGraw-Hill, Inc. Used with the permission of McGraw-Hill, Inc.

Human Resource Information System

Human resource information system (HRIS) is a computerized[10] data base process that may be used to facilitate the collection and analysis of a variety of information on human resources within an organization. It may be used to gather and assess very detailed information on individuals such as personal data, skill inventories, employee record keeping, (e.g. absenteeism report, job history, wage history, earnings and benefits, etc.), promotability data, safety and accident data, and many other attributes of individual employees. HRIS may be used for a variety of other purposes such as career planning, succession planning, projecting attrition, and calculating productivity ratios; collecting data on employment equity, performance appraisal, pay increases, compensation, and labour relations; and evaluating the effectiveness of the human resource department or a human resource activity.

According to one expert, the basic ingredients of such a computerized human resource skills inventory should include the following:

- *Work experience codes*. A list of work experience descriptions, titles, or codes that describe jobs within the company so that the individual's present, previous, and desired jobs can be coded.

- *Product knowledge*. The employee's level of familiarity with each of the employer's product lines or services as an indication of where the person might be transferred or promoted.

- *Industry experience*. The person's industry experiences should be coded, since for certain positions the employee's knowledge of key related industries is very useful.

- *Formal education*. The name of each post-secondary educational institution attended, the field of study, degree granted, and year granted should be entered.

- *Training courses*. Training courses conducted by the employer and, possibly, training courses taught by outside agents may be indicated.

- *Foreign language skills*. Level of proficiency in other languages as well the employee's native tongue should be on record.

- *Relocation limitations*. Information regarding the employee's willingness to relocate and the locales to which the person would prefer to be relocated should be compiled.

- *Career interests*. Using the same work experience codes used in the first section above, the employee should indicate what he or she would like to be doing for the employer in the future. Space can be provided for a brief priority of choices, and a code should be included indicating whether the employee's main qualification for the work he or she wants to do is experience, knowledge, or interests.

- *Performance appraisals*. These should be entered into the employee's skill bank and updated periodically to indicate the employee's achievement on each dimension appraised (leadership ability, motivation, communication skills, etc.), along with a summary of the employee's strengths and deficiencies.[11]

human resource information system (HRIS)

TABLE 3.1 Typical Data Elements in a Human Resource Information System

Address (work)	Garnishments	Salary change type
Address (home)	Grievance (type)	Salary
Birthdate	Grievance (outcome)	Salary range
Birthplace	Grievance (filing date)	Schools attended
Child support deductions	Handicap status	Service date
Citizenship	Health plan coverage	Service branch
Claim pending (description)	Health plan (no. dependents)	Service discharge type
Claim pending (outcome)	Injury date	Service ending rank
Claim pending (court)	Injury type	Service discharge date
Claim pending (date)	Job location	Sex
Date on current job	Job preference	Sick leave used
Department	Job position number	Sick leave available
Dependent (sex)	Job title	Skill function (type)
Dependent (number of)	Job location	Skill sub-function (type)
Dependent (relationship)	Leave of absence start date	Skill (number of years)
Dependent (birthdate)	Leave of absence end date	Skill (proficiency level)
Dependent (name)	Leave of absence type	Skill (date last used)
Discipline (appeal date)	Life insurance coverage	Skill (location)
Discipline (type of charge)	Marital status	Skill (supervisory)
Discipline (appeal outcome)	Marriage date	Social Security number
Discipline (date of charge)	Medical exam (date)	Spouse's employment
Discipline (outcome)	Medical exam (restrictions)	Spouse's date of death
Discipline (hearing date)	Medical exam (blood type)	Spouse's name
Division	Medical exam (outcome)	Spouse's birthdate
Driver's license (number)	Miscellaneous deductions	Spouse's sex
Driver's license (state)	Name	Spouse's Social Security number
Driver's license (exp. date)	Organizational property	Start date
Education in progress (date)	Pay status	Stock plan membership
Education in progress (type)	Pension plan membership	Supervisor's name
Educational degree (date)	Performance rating	Supervisor's work address
Educational degree (type)	Performance increase ($)	Supervisor's work phone
Educational minor (minor)	Performance increase (%)	Supervisor's title
Educational level attained	Phone number (work)	Termination date
Educational field (major)	Phone number (home)	Termination reason
EEO-1 code	Prior service (term. date)	Training schools attended
Emergency contact (phone)	Prior service (hire date)	Training schools (date)
Emergency contact (name)	Prior service (term. reason)	Training schools (field)
Emergency contact (relation)	Professional license (type)	Training schools completed
Emergency contact (address)	Professional license (date)	Transfer date
Employee weight	Race	Transfer reason
Employee number	Rehire code	Union code
Emergency code	Religious preference	Union deductions
Employee status	Salary points	United Way deductions
Employee height	Salary compa ratio	Vacation leave available
Employee date of death	Salary (previous)	Vacation leave used
Federal job code	Salary change date	Veteran status
Full-time/part-time code	Salary change reason	

SOURCE: Donald Harris, "A Matter of Privacy: Managing Personal Data in Company Computers," *Personnel* (February 1987), p. 37.

Table 3.1 illustrates some typical data elements in an HRIS. It is in effect an inventory of all employees, HRM policies and procedures, and other HRM activities of the organization. By computerizing its HRIS, an organization greatly improves its information retrieval, storage accessibility, and analysis capabilities. HRIS also simplifies an organization's administrative duties.

Establishing Organizational Objectives

Organizational objectives are broad statements of the organization's mission and purpose for existence, values, and philosophy. Organization objectives establish a common purpose that guides the conduct and behaviour of human resources and provides some consistency to the style of management in the organization. The objectives define outcomes that the organization desires and serve as standards against which to measure organizational efficiency and effectiveness. Examples of such objectives might include increasing productivity by 10% or increasing the company's profit margin by 15%.

organizational objectives

    Human resource objectives provide a sense of direction to employees, communicate to them the organization's expectations, reduce uncertainty, establish standards against which to measure performance or productivity, and establish the priorities by which they can operate. Objectives also specify employee responsibilities.

human resource objectives

    Figure 3.2 is an example of Ontario Hydro's corporate policy on HRP.

FORECASTING FUTURE HUMAN RESOURCE NEEDS (DEMANDS)

Changes in human resource requirements influence both short- and long-term forecasts of human resource requirements.[12] There are a variety of forecasting techniques an organization may use to predict its future human resource requirements.

The Forecasting

The forecasting process consists of six fundamental sequences or steps[13] illustrated in Figure 3.3. The first step requires the human resource specialist to develop a sound understanding of the internal and external environments and to carefully assess the impact of these conditions on the organization's future needs (demands). The second step is to take inventory of the available skills of employees in the organization. This may be accomplished through an examination of personal data on file, performance appraisals and employee career goals as well as through succession and replacement plans. The third step is to analyze present human resource needs (demands). This may be done by examining recruiting needs, training and development needs, and succession plans. The fourth step is to project future human resource supply. The fifth step is to project future requirements through an examination of the number of present positions, the desired mix of occupations as well as an examination of the organization structure. The sixth step requires the human resource specialist to compare human resource supply and demand and to project the organization's future human resource needs.

Factors in Forecasting Human Resource Needs

Most managers consider several factors when forecasting human resource requirements.[14] From a practical point of view, the demand for the organization's product or service is paramount.[15] Thus, in a manufacturing firm, sales are pro-

FIGURE 3.2
Ontario Hydro's Corporate Policy— Human Resource Planning

1. The corporation shall forecast its human resource requirements as a necessary part of other forecasts.

2. Managers at all levels shall engage in human resources planning as an integrated and supporting part of work program planning.

3. The corporation shall consider future as well as present requirements when filling positions.

4. Managers at level X+1 shall recommend succession plans for level X and shall provide assistance to prepare candidates to meet position requirements.

5. Human resources planning for senior management positions at levels 2 and 3 shall be conducted and monitored by a policy and administration comittee appointed by the president.

6. The policy and administration committee shall establish policy and procedures for forecasting of needs, identification of target jobs, nomination, assessment, succession planning, development, and selection of candidates for positions at levels 2 and 3 as part of the senior management human resources plan.

7. Employees shall have the primary responsibility for their own career development.

8. The corporation shall provide assistance to employees in individual career planning to the extent permitted by work priorities.

9. The corporation shall include consideration of the identified career aspirations, interests, and personal constraints on career mobility of potential candidates for positions in planning for its human resources requirements.

SOURCE: James Rush and L. Bourne, *Human Resource Planning at Ontario Hydro: A Field Study* (London, Ont.: University of Western Ontario, 1983). Used with permission.

jected first. Then the volume of production required to meet these sales requirements is determined. Finally, the staff needed to maintain this volume of output is estimated. But in addition to this "basic requirement" for staff, the organization will also have to consider several other factors including

1. Projected turnover (as a result of resignations or terminations).

2. Quality and nature of employees (in relation to what management sees as the changing needs of the organization).

3. Decisions to upgrade the quality of products or services or to enter into new markets.

4. Technological and administrative changes resulting in an increased productivity level.

5. The financial resources available to each department.

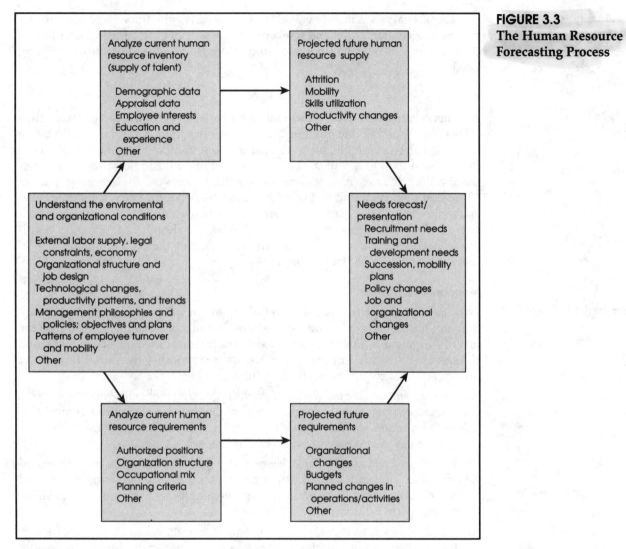

FIGURE 3.3
The Human Resource
Forecasting Process

Analyze current human
resource inventory
(supply of talent)

Demographic data
Appraisal data
Employee interests
Education and
    experience
Other

Projected future human
resource supply

Attrition
Mobility
Skills utilization
Productivity changes
Other

Understand the enviromental
and organizational conditions

External labor supply, legal
    constraints, economy
Organizational structure and
    job design
Technological changes,
    productivity patterns, and trends
Management philosophies and
    policies; objectives and plans
Patterns of employee turnover
    and mobility
Other

Needs forecast/
presentation
    Recruitment needs
    Training and
        development needs
    Succession, mobility
        plans
    Policy changes
    Job and
        organizational
        changes
    Other

Analyze current human
resource requirements

    Authorized positions
    Organization structure
    Occupational mix
    Planning criteria
    Other

Projected future
requirements

    Organizational
        changes
    Budgets
    Planned changes in
        operations/activities
    Other

SOURCE: James W. Walker, *Human Resource Planning* (New York: McGraw-Hill Inc., 1980). Reproduced with permission of McGraw-Hill, Inc.

Specific techniques for determining human resource requirements include trend analysis, ratio analysis, managerial judgment, computerized forecasting,[16] expert estimation, and statistical analysis.

Trend Analysis

A logical way to begin forecasting is by studying the firm's employment trends over the last five years or so. This may be done by computing the number of employees in the firm at the end of each of the last five years, or perhaps the number in each subgroup (like salespeople, production people, secretarial, and administrative) at the end of each of those years. The purpose is to identify employment trends that might continue into the future.

trend analysis
Trend analysis is mostly valuable as an initial, exploratory exercise since employment levels rarely depend solely on the passage of time. Instead, other factors (like changes in sales volume and productivity) will also affect future staffing needs.

Ratio Analysis

ratio analysis
Another approach is to do a **ratio analysis** between (1) some causal factor (like sales volume) and (2) the number of employees required (for instance, number of salespeople). For example, suppose a salesperson traditionally generates $500 000 in sales, and that in each of the last two years it required 10 salespeople to generate $5 million in sales. Also assume that the firm's plans call for increasing sales to $8 million next year, and to $10 million two years hence. Then, if the sales revenue-salespeople ratio remains the same, it would require six new salespeople next year (each of whom produces an extra $500 000 in sales). In the following year it would need an additional four salespeople to generate the extra $2 million in sales (between next year's $8 million and the following year's $10 million in sales).

Managerial Judgment

managerial judgment
Whichever approach is used, **managerial judgment** will play a large role. It is rare that any historical trend, ratio, or relationship will continue unchanged into the future. Judgment is thus needed to modify the forecast based on factors that could change in the future. Important factors that may modify the initial forecast of human resource requirements include the following:

1. *Decisions to upgrade the quality of products or services or enter into new markets*. These have implications for the nature of the employees required. It must also be determined whether the skills of current employees are compatible with the organization's new products or services.
2. *Technological and administrative changes resulting in increased productivity*. Increased efficiency (in terms of output per hour) could reduce personnel needs and might come about through installing new equipment or a new financial incentive plan, for instance.
3. *The financial resources available*. For example, a larger budget allows for the hiring of more people and higher wages, perhaps with an eye toward increasing the quality of products or services. Conversely, a projected budget crunch could mean fewer positions to recruit for and lower salary offers.

Computerized Forecasting

computerized forecasting
Some employers use computerized systems for developing human resources requirement forecasts. For example, one expert has developed a **computerized forecasting** package.[17] A human resource specialist, working in conjunction with line managers, compiles the necessary information in order to develop a computerized forecast of human resource requirements. The data to be supplied include direct manpower hours needed to produce one unit of product (a measure of productivity), and three sales projections—minimum, maximum, and probable—for the product line in question. Based on such inputs, the program generates figures on such things as "average staff levels required to meet product demands" as well as separate forecasts for direct manpower (such as assembly workers), indirect staff (like secretaries), and exempt staff (like executives).

With a computerized system like this, an employer can quickly translate estimates of projected productivity and sales levels into forecasts of human resource needs, and can easily check the effects of various levels of productivity and sales on human resource requirements.[18] There is a variety of computer software on the market. At this time, most successful products are *expert systems*. An expert system is software that contains a search process that links facts using programmed relationships or rules. It enables the user to match different items, such as jobs and people.

For example, an expert system may be used to ensure that the people scheduled to move up get first priority when a position becomes available. To do so, the user could program the following rules:

- If two candidates for a position have similar qualifications, preference should be given to ... (a gender, a minority, the handicapped, those having high potential, etc.).
- High-potential employees who are lacking in some important skill should be given preference for jobs that develop that particular skill.
- Employees with limited potential but good performance in jobs which are important development positions should be slotted for lateral transfers to non-developmental positions.

When a position opens up, the user may ask the system to suggest candidates for that particular job. Some of the individuals suggested may be obvious choices, some may come as a complete surprise, and some may seem clearly inappropriate. The system may be asked to show its "thinking" process in making the inappropriate suggestions. The results might show that the initial assumptions about a particular individual are incorrect or that the rules require some refinements.[19]

COMPUTER APPLICATIONS IN HUMAN RESOURCE PLANNING

In recent years computer systems have been developed to support human resource management specialists in performing activities such as HRP. These systems are known by many names, but can generally be called Human Resource Planning Decision Support Systems (HRPDS).

Every system differs in some respects, but there are a number of clearly identifiable functions that an HRPDS should perform for its users. These are:

- MODELLING & ANALYSIS. A model is a representation of reality that permits the exploration of alternatives and their associated decisions. Obviously it costs much less and is far less risky to develop a number of airplane models for testing in a wind tunnel than it is to build full-sized airplanes and then see which ones fly. In the same way, reorganizing a department several times to see which way works best is not a practical solution to an organizational problem.

Constructing different scenarios allows the HR planning to explore the implications of future decisions. For instance, building a model could show that a plan to eliminate several jobs at one level would lead to an unforseen blockage of positions at the level below. In terms of the HR planning process, modelling would help build the career development architecture by showing the path of current development along with possible alternatives. Also, modelling shows the impact of different chains of planned moves upon the organization.

The most important task in modelling is determining which elements of reality to represent. In HR planning, a model must represent two main elements: jobs and people. It can match and rematch different jobs with different people until the best career development architecture is found. Finally, an HR model should be easily understood by non-HR people. A sophisticated system is not much help if it communicates its findings in a way that is not easily understood by non-HR specialists. The movement of people through an organization must be both easy for the HR planner to represent and easy for others to follow.

- PROJECTION OF PLANNED EVENTS. The planned moves of people through positions can occur in the contexts of both succession planning and career planning.

In the past, succession planning in many organizations amounted to little more than a set of job replacement tables. Management simply looked at each job and determined who should move into it next. That kind of paternalism is becoming rare. Most organizations now use succession planning simply to identify replacement strength for critical positions. With today's emphasis on personal development, dynamic planned movement within an organization is more often expressed in the career planning process. In this context, the HRPDS should be able to identify and chart out the career moves of each person in the organization, in terms of what jobs they should move to and when to make the move.

The actual projection of career moves is not all that difficult with HRPDS. The real task is to discern whether the planned moves can actually be carried out. Problems can, and do, arise. Scheduling is often a conflict. A position will come open, but there may

be no one scheduled to fill it, or there may be more than one person, so that someone will lose out. Any number of such unforseen circumstances can thwart the orderly movement of people in an organization and it is vital that the HR planner recognize this and be ready to change plans on short notice.

HRPDS can be used not just for planning movement but also for planning training requirements. A planning system should be able to identify any lack of qualification among individuals moving into new jobs. If caught at the time of the move, a summary of training needs can be created to ease the transition into the new job.

- INFORMATION ENQUIRY AND RETRIEVAL. An HRPDS should provide information on employees' skills, performance ratings, potential ratings, age, gender, equal opportunity evaluation criteria, job level, mobility, and pretty well anything else necessary to know. On a daily basis this is probably the most useful function that a planning system provides. Furthermore, just it can be used for enquiries about people, so it can be used for enquiries about the positions in the organization. For example, if a high-potential employee is a bit weak in presentation skills, the HRPDS can provide information about which jobs will be coming available that will provide an opportunity for the employee to improve those skills. In terms of our planning model, employee enquiries are usually used to help determine who qualifies as a replacement for jobs coming open and can also be used to support HR planning. Job enquiries tend to be used in career planning to determine good development positions for employees.

SOURCE: Adapted from Andy Piebalgs, "The Use of Computers in Human Resource Planning," *Human Resources Management in Canada*, (Scarborough, Ont.: Prentice Hall Canada Inc., 1978), pp. 20,537-20,544. Used with permission.

Expert Estimation Techniques

The Delphi Technique

Periodically, top management in an organization is required to assess where the organization is going, the values that underlie its existence, and the steps needed to achieve its goals. Specific areas reassessed might include demand for present goods and services, product quality, product mix, and quality of the work force. An objective view requires outside experts who are better able to assess changes and challenges in economic, demographic, governmental, technological, and social conditions. The **delphi technique** is a judgmental forecasting method used to arrive at a group decision. The delphi technique involves the following steps:[20]

delphi technique

1. The problem is identified and each group member is requested to submit a potential solution by completing a carefully designed questionnaire (direct face-to-face contact is not permitted).

2. Each group member anonymously and independently completes the initial questionnaire. Someone at a centralized location compiles the results of the first questionnaire.

3. Each group member is given a copy of the results.

4. If viewing the results reveals that a consensus has not been reached, then each member is again asked to provide a solution.

5. Steps 3 and 4 are repeated as often as necessary until the group members reach a consensus.

The delphi technique is best suited for long-range forecasting (short-term forecasting is usually done by managers.) It allows for increased diversity of views since the group will critically evaluate a wider range of views in order to arrive at a solution acceptable to all group members. While the process is consistent with democratic ideals, it does have its drawbacks: it is time consuming, costly, and it may be difficult to integrate the diverse opinions of group members.

Nominal Grouping Technique

The **nominal group technique** is a method in which a group of individuals sit at a table and separately write their ideas on a sheet of paper on resolving a problem or an issue. When they have completed listing their ideas, each member take turns sharing their ideas with the group. The nominal group technique process is as follows:[21]

nominal group technique

1. Each member of the group independently writes down his or her ideas on the problem or issue.

2. The group sits in silence as each member takes turn presenting one set of ideas to the group. No discussion is allowed until all ideas have been presented and recorded either on a large chart or on the chalkboard.

3. The group then seeks clarifications where necessary and discusses and evaluates all the ideas.

4. In this, the final step, each member of the group ranks the ideas. This is done independently and in silence.

Statistical Analysis

Regression Analysis

Regression analysis is a method used for projecting future demands based on a past relationship between the organization's employment level (dependent variable) and some measurable factor of output (independent variable) such as revenues, sales, or production. When it is possible to determine or specify the past relationship between, say, the level of employment and a certain production rate, it is then possible to forecast future employment as well as future levels of production.

regression analysis

Multiple Regression Analysis

multiple regression analysis

Multiple regression analysis is a method used to handle complex or multiple dependent and independent variables. In other words human resource forecasters may wish to predict employment level demands with respect to the organization, production, product mix, and market share. Multiple regression may therefore incorporate several dependent and independent variables.

Stochastic Analysis

stochastic analysis

Stochastic analysis is a technique used to analyze employee career movements or mobility patterns of flow from one job to another within an organization. Two types of stochastic analysis which are frequently used are: 1) transition matrix, and 2) renewal model. Transition matrices show career path and exit ratios of individuals in certain jobs at given time intervals. These movement patterns are then used to project the expected years that an individual will spend in a given position, the internal talents available for promotions to higher level jobs, and when external recruits will be required.

The renewal model sees the movement or flow of human resources in the organization as being generated by vacancies. Whenever vacant positions are filled by individuals who came from the lower levels in the organization, they are considered to create a chain reaction which pull individuals through the system. In other words, the model argues that in many organizations an individual's career growth is dependent on other individuals' career growth.

FORECASTING FUTURE HUMAN RESOURCE SUPPLY

Forecasting human resource supply is the process of predicting future human resources available to the organization. This is done through careful assessment of current work force to determine those who are promotable, and those who possess potential. It involves analyzing estimated staffing changes and mobility patterns, and attrition due to retirement, turnover, and disability as well as forecasting the supply of external sources.

Forecasting the Supply of Inside Candidates

The human resource requirements forecast answers the question, "How many employees will we need?" However, before determining how many new outside candidates to recruit and hire, the organization must first know how many candidates for its projected job openings will come from within the organization and this determination is the purpose of forecasting the supply of inside candidates.

To tap this internal supply of candidates the skills of all employees must be assessed. This can be done through skill inventories as well as other methods such as replacement planning, succession planning, and human resource information systems.

Skill Inventories

skill inventories

Skill inventories provide important quantitative and qualitative data of the human resources in the organization. They provide a good foundation for planning future staffing requirements. Skill inventories contain data such as: employee name, present position, title, work site, previous positions, education/training, career goals, salary history, and professional affiliations.

Skill inventories are useful in identifying individuals who possess the capability to handle more challenging and demanding responsibilities and are therefore immediately promotable. It also indicates individuals who possess the potential to grow and assume greater responsibilities in the future.

Effective skill inventories allow employers to assess easily and speedily the types of individuals, and their specific skills, that are available in the organization. Skill inventories are especially useful to organizations that are considering expansion, changing strategies, or taking on additional or larger contracts. Some of the other purposes skill inventories may be used for include employment equity compliance, promotion, training, management development, and transfers.

There are various skill inventory software systems available in Canada. For example, Swiftsure Data Systems of Vancouver has developed a system called "Microprospect" that organizations may use to identify human resource surpluses or shortfalls in advance. This allows organizations to take proactive measures to address these emerging imbalances.[22] Office Data Systems of Toronto has developed a software package called "Recruiters." This is an automated skill inventory filing system that organizations use to store and rapidly retrieve their skills inventories.[23]

Replacement Planning

Replacement planning is the process of identifying when each position will be vacant and identifying individuals with the potential to replace the incumbent. Replacement planning is also known as replacement analysis. It is closely related to succession planning, but the primary difference is that replacement planning focuses on short-term needs. Using information from skill inventories and demonstrated employee performance, a replacement analysis is completed and the results are summarized and documented on an organizational chart. The chart presents a picture of who is most likely to move, when, and where. It also indicates each individual's strengths and weaknesses and any other important characteristics. Figure 3.4 presents a simplified replacement planning chart.

It should be noted that replacement planning may not fulfilled as charted, due to internal and external changes. These include employee resignations, employees who do not develop as expected, product failures, cutbacks in production/operations, and economic recessions.

Replacement planning has several shortcomings. Identification of backups or replacement candidates is largely subjective, based on the personal knowledge of the nominating managers. A high potential candidate may be qualified for more than one management position, but may be "boxed in" by vertical line oriented replacement planning or, alternatively, may be named as a backup for several positions, giving false impression of managerial depth.[24] Notwithstanding these limitations replacement planning is a useful planning tool as long as the constraints are taken into account.

replacement planning

Succession Planning

Succession planning is the process of making long-range management developmental plans to fill future human resource needs in management.

succession planning

The succession planning process represents an integrated set of activities that includes current performance information and future potential.

The succession planning process comprises the following key steps.[25]

1. Assessment of the background of prospective managerial candidates including biographical data, skills, knowledge and abilities, personality, interests, and preferences concerning future career aspirations.

2. Evaluation of feedback on the individuals' performances on previous challenging positions. This will provide a good indication of future performance capabilities and development potential.

3. Determination of the organization's future managerial human resources demands through forecasting, operational planning, and strategic planning.

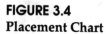
Placement Chart

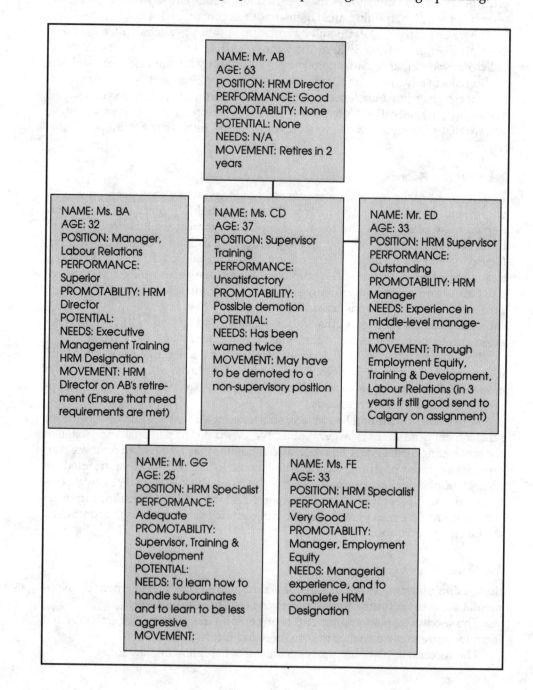

NAME: Mr. AB
AGE: 63
POSITION: HRM Director
PERFORMANCE: Good
PROMOTABILITY: None
POTENTIAL: None
NEEDS: N/A
MOVEMENT: Retires in 2 years

NAME: Ms. BA
AGE: 32
POSITION: Manager, Labour Relations
PERFORMANCE: Superior
PROMOTABILITY: HRM Director
POTENTIAL:
NEEDS: Executive Management Training HRM Designation
MOVEMENT: HRM Director on AB's retirement (Ensure that need requirements are met)

NAME: Ms. CD
AGE: 37
POSITION: Supervisor Training
PERFORMANCE: Unsatisfactory
PROMOTABILITY: Possible demotion
POTENTIAL:
NEEDS: Has been warned twice
MOVEMENT: May have to be demoted to a non-supervisory position

NAME: Mr. ED
AGE: 33
POSITION: HRM Supervisor
PERFORMANCE: Outstanding
PROMOTABILITY: HRM Manager
NEEDS: Experience in middle-level management
MOVEMENT: Through Employment Equity, Training & Development, Labour Relations (in 3 years if still good send to Calgary on assignment)

NAME: Mr. GG
AGE: 25
POSITION: HRM Specialist
PERFORMANCE: Adequate
PROMOTABILITY: Supervisor, Training & Development
POTENTIAL:
NEEDS: To learn how to handle subordinates and to learn to be less aggressive
MOVEMENT:

NAME: Ms. FE
AGE: 33
POSITION: HRM Specialist
PERFORMANCE: Very Good
PROMOTABILITY: Manager, Employment Equity
NEEDS: Managerial experience, and to complete HRM Designation

4. Establishment of a "position profile" that will indicate the type of future organization managerial position to be filled. This is an important guide for establishing the development criteria of prospective successors.

5. Obtaining the input of managers at all levels of the organization's hierarchy.

6. Definition of the method by which each succession candidate will be trained or developed. (For example, on-the-job development such as job rotation, lateral promotion, coaching, understudy assignments, or off-the-job development such as case study, sensitivity training, assessment centres, in-basket exercise, and so on.)

7. Planning of progressive paths for "fast-track" succession candidates to facilitate movement at an accelerated pace.

8. Preparation of summaries of succession candidates' availability and readiness.

9. Development of plans to balance any identified shortages or surpluses for managerial human resources. (e.g. recruitment, temporary assignments, lay-offs or terminations.)

10. Development of results-oriented programs, policies, goals, and processes to implement succession planning as an integral aspect of the organization's ongoing management.

Ontario's Ministry of Transportation and Communication (MTC) uses computerized succession planning for its 1300 middle and senior level management employees. Its computer can prepare separate analyses of forecasting for each of five primary and eight secondary operational functions. The following are descriptions of the data used by the forecasting model for each level of operational function.

- *Current strength*, determined from the personnel inventory.

- *Losses*, comprising resignations, dismissals, transfers, and retirements. These items are assessed from historical data and then modified according to current and future trends.

- *Backup*, which is determined from two sources: (1) as part of the formal annual appraisal process, managers identify employees considered promotable within the next one-year planning cycle, and (2) as part of a separate annual process, management identifies high potential employees whose ability suggests progress—in more than one function—to two responsibility levels higher during a five-year forecast period.

- *Future demand*, forecast on the basis of current as well as future business plans, as determined by MTC's strategic policy committee.

Next, MTC processes these data by a computerized forecasting model.[26]

Forecasting the Supply of Outside Candidates

Assuming there are not enough inside candidates to fill vacant positions, the organization next focuses on outside candidates—those not currently employed by the organization. Forecasting the supply of outside candidates will involve assessing market conditions, and using techniques such as the Markov analysis.

Labour Market Conditions

The human resource specialist must assess current as well as emerging trends in the labour market. The quality and quantity of human resources that the organization will be able to attract and recruit will depend on its state. The nature of the labour market information available from government and private sources is described below.[27]

Statistics Canada publishes reports on the labour force on a monthly, quarterly, occasional, and annual basis. This information is available by the following categories: labour force projections by geographic, demographic, and occupational specialty; labour income; population projections by sex and province; and census.

Canada Employment and Immigration Council (CEIC) publishes both short- and long-term labour force projections. The short-term projection is published in a report entitled *Forward Occupational Imbalance Listing* (FOIL). This is a quarterly publication that estimates both labour market demand and supply. The long-term projection is published in a report entitled *Canada Occupational Forecast Program* (COFOR).[28] This report forecasts data on a national and provincial basis. It covers over 500 occupational groups. Until recently, this report was the major tool used by the federal government to forecast labour market trends in Canada.

Another of CEIC's publications is entitled *Canada Occupational Projection System* (COPS).[29] This report projects both domestic occupational requirements and supply in Canada and the provinces for periods of one to 10 years. This report is useful for determining whether the imbalances may be self-correcting or whether they will require specific intervention on the part of the government and/or the private sector.

The Economic Council of Canada has developed a model called the Canadian Disaggregated Interdepartmental Econometric Model (CANDIDE).[30] This model is useful for forecasting medium-term trends in the economy. The model uses over 1500 regression equations to forecast unemployment and real domestic product (the value of all goods and services produced in Canada, less any increases due to inflation).

Microelectronics Simulation Model (MESIM)[31] is a computer based model that integrates the impact of technological change on the occupational composition in Canada. By incorporating shifts in the labour market it is able to forecast the occupational composition in Canada.

Markov Analysis

Markov analysis

The **Markov analysis** is a method for forecasting an organization's future supply of human resources by specific categories such as position and sex. Markov analysis is based on the development and use of transitional probability matrices. The process for applying Markov analysis is as follows:[32]

1. Specify the employee groups to be analyzed. This may be a selected group, selected department, or the whole organization.

2. Specify the classifications or grouping of employees from which the human resources flow is to be analyzed. It is usually the case that classifications are organized on the basis of job functions, levels, age, sex, education, and length of time on the job.

3. Calculate and summarize information from one time period to another. It is important that the time interval selected between period 1 and period 2 is long enough for movement (such as promotion) to take place, but not so long that multiple changes by individual employees have taken place. A one year time interval is a good time period.

4. Develop a transitional probabilities matrix. This requires converting the data gathered in step 3 into proportions (probabilities). It is important to note that it is these proportions that are used to forecast human resource supply.

5. Forecast projections of future human resource supply using the transitional probability matrix.

The Markov analysis is also useful for analyzing employee career paths within the organization. It may also be used to assess the effectiveness of various human resource activities.

PLANNING HUMAN RESOURCE PROGRAMS

Once the process for establishing objectives and forecasting human resource supply and demand is complete then program planning may commence. As Figure 3.1 indicated, program planning is done in two areas: performance management and career management. Performance management planning focuses on enhancing the performance of employees as well as the organization. Career management planning focuses on policies, selection, training, development, and career growth.

THE IMPLEMENTATION OF EFFECTIVE HUMAN RESOURCE PLANNING

Effective implementation of human resource planning is very important to corporate success. In order to ensure such success the human resource specialist must develop close cooperation with corporate planners, line managers, and major decision-makers. The HR specialist must share information with them and seek their input on all plans that will affect each of them in particular and the organization in general. It is necessary to get their input in identifying their short-, medium-, and long-term human resource needs. The human resource specialist must ensure that accurate, reliable human resource planning becomes an integral part of human resource management in order to serve the needs of the organization. The human resource specialist must take action to improve the accuracy of human resource operational and strategic planning assessment and ensure that all forecasts are based on reasonably reliable assessments of the present and future human resource needs of the organization. Developing an analysis of the implications of human resources on overall business plans may facilitate this process. Figure 3.5 provides a comprehensive checklist.

Barriers to Implementation of Effective Human Resource Planning

The implementation of human resource planning is often hindered by obstacles or barriers created by management and/or HRM specialists.[33]

Management Imposed Barriers

1. Top management is usually concerned more with short-term goals, short-term profitability, and other factors associated with short-term business results.

2. Management usually actively resists change, and often is reluctant or may even avoid conceding to the need for change.

3. Human resource management specialists are perceived as "personnel experts" and not experts in the operation of business.

Identify below those strategic plans having human resource implications	Possible areas for action: What could be done?
A. BUSINESS NEEDS	
1. Expansion of existing business activities?	– Recruitment – Training/development – Organization changes
2. Addition of new capacity (new plants, distribution facilities, etc.)?	– Recruitment – Training/development – Organization changes
3. De-emphasis or discontinuance of any business activities?	– Reassignments – Terminations – Retraining
4. Ventures, acquisitions, or divestitures?	– Management reassignments – Recruitment – Organization/position changes – Training/development
5. New products or services?	– Training/development – Recruitment – Organization/position changes
6. New technologies or applications?	– Training/development – Recruitment – New specializations – Organization/position changes
7. Changes in operating methods or productivity improvements?	– Organization/position changes – Training/development – Reassignments
8. Changes in administrative, information, or control systems?	– Organization/position changes – Organization/position changes – Staffing changes
9. Changes in management or organizational structure (matrix management)?	– Reassignments – Communications/training – Staffing changes – Recruitment – Terminations – Reassignments
10. Other:	
B. EXTERNAL FACTORS	
1. Are qualified (competent) recruits available in the market?	– Modify recruitment approach – Modify staffing requirements – Develop more talent from within
2. Are you able to competitively recruit the desired talent?	– Modify compensation/job evaluation – Modify recruitment approach – Modify job requirements
3. Are there changes in the personnel relations climate?	– Employee communications – Management orentation/training – Fact finding

(continued)

4. Are there new employment equity requirements?

- Modify recruitment
- Training/development
- Modify job requirements
- Performance appraisals

5. Are there other regulatory requirements affecting human resources?

- Management orientation/training
- New systems/procedures
- Additional staffing
- Fact finding

6. Are there new international business demands?

- Management orientation/training
- Recruitment
- Adapt management systems
- Fact finding

7. Other:

C. INTERNAL ANALYSIS

1. Do we have excessive turnover in any group?

- Modify recruitment/selection
- Accelerate career advancement
- Organization/position changes
- Reassignment/lateral moves

2. Is there too little turnover or mobility in any group

- Terminations
- Reassignment of work
- Organization/position changes
- Improved employee appraisals

3. Are age patterns imbalanced in any group, suggesting high future attrition or career path blockage?

- Modify recruitment/selection
- Reassignments
- Accelerate career advancement
- Terminations

4. Is there a proper balance (employee mix) of managerial, professional/ technical, and support staff?

- Organization/position changes
- Reassignment of work
- Modify recruitment/selection

5. Are there noteworthy performances in any group (or appraisal results signaling significant problems)?

- Organization/position changes
- Reassignments
- Improved employee appraisals
- Modify job requirements

6. In what areas are levels of technical competency potential shortcomings?

- Modify recruitment/selection
- Reassignments
- Career counselling
- Training/development

7. Are employment equity requirements being met?

- Modify recruitment/selection
- Modify job requirements
- Career counselling
- Training/development

8. Other:

D. MANAGEMENT IMPLICATIONS

1. Are there enough employees who become general managers? (pool of successors)

- Modify recruitment/selection
- Improved employee evaluation
- Special career development plans
- Organization changes for future

(continued)

2. Do the present managers have adequate technical competence in the face of changing demands?	– Training/development – Reassignments – Specialized recruitment – Specialization – Career counselling
3. Do they have adequate managerial skills to meet the changing demands of a growing company? (leading, planning, decision making, etc.)	– Training/development – Organization/position changes – Reassignments – Recruitment of managerial talent
4. Do key managers and successors have adequate management experience (multiple function exposure)?	– Training/development programs – Job rotation among functions – Recruitment of management talent – Evaluation of successors
5. Is the management structure and staffing appropriate for the achievement of our business objectives?	– Organization/position changes – Reduce/increase staffing levels – Accelerate management development – Study of strategy implications
6. Other:	

SOURCE: James W. Walker, *Human Resource Planning* (New York: McGraw-Hill, Inc., 1980). Reproduced with permission of McGraw-Hill, Inc.

4. Human resource information is often not compatible with other resources information used in the organization.

5. Top management may not recognize that human resources are its most important asset and are important means of increasing organizational effectiveness. This may lead management to merely pay lip service to human resource issues facing the organization.

6. Top management has traditionally been more concerned with productivity, material resources, financial resources, and profitability than with human resources.

7. Management often views human resource issues as overhead expenses rather than as investments with future returns.

8. The nature, size, design, structure, and complexity of many large organizations often do not allow management the time or desire to seriously focus on important human resource issues confronting the organization.

9. The more organizations grow, prosper, and diversify the greater the forces to maintain the administrative status quo. (That is, the more things change the more things stay the same.)

10. Top management does not see or is not aware of the need for HRP.

HRP Specialists (Staff) Imposed Barriers

In addition to management imposed barriers, the following obstacles created by human resource specialists themselves often hinder the effective implementation of HRP.

1. HRP specialists often are too concerned with the sophistication of the type of system implemented. As a result their zeal for overspecialization, concern for precision and accuracy, and passion for state-of-the art systems and approaches create unnecessary problems for themselves as well as management. These overspecialized systems may intimidate line managers.

2. HRP specialists often overwhelm managers with unnecessarily complicated data, unnecessarily detailed and elaborate forms, wordy procedures, and complex manuals.

3. HRP specialists often get "carried away" with the design of the system as well as with trying to impress their colleagues. That is, HRP specialists are often so concerned with their marvellous methods and systems and getting their colleagues' approval that they lose sight of the real purpose of their tasks and the organizational and human resources problems that they are supposed to solve.

4. HRP specialists often do not undertake proper planning, research, analysis, groundwork, feasibility studies, and cost benefit analysis. As a result hastily conceived ideas, concepts, and changes in human resource practices are often rushed into implementation.

5. HRP specialists often allow their objectivity to be influenced by organizational politics and may design a system that is not in the organization's overall best interest.

6. HRP specialists may provide management with inaccurate information or information that overhypes the system's capabilities. This may end up discrediting the need for HRP and discouraging management from implementing the program.

Essential Steps for Overcoming Barriers

There are steps that can be taken to overcome the barriers created by both management and HRP specialists:

1. *Top management commitment and support should be secured.* This will increase the chances of line manager's full cooperation, and acceptance of the change, and reduce the likelihood of their resistance as well as reduce the risk of failure.

2. *Management should be involved in the problem definition, problem analysis, and problem solving process.* Individuals are more willing to implement changes that they have had a hand in formulating.

3. *Workable, practical, rational, and cost-effective recommendations for implementations should be developed.* Only those recommendations that meet the organization's needs, that can be implemented with minimum inconvenience and disruptions, and that will be beneficial to the organization in the short-, medium-, and long-term should be concentrated on. It is also important to focus on a limited number of essential recommendations (probably three or four) rather than a long wish list of items which may end up being filed in the trash can.

4. *Effective communication is essential to reduce the risk of resistance.* The logic of the change, the type of resources required, the goals and benefits of the change, the administrative mechanism needed to integrate and operate the system, and the impact that it will have on existing resources and structures must all be communicated clearly.

5. *The project should be commenced when and where top management wants to start.* This approach is intended to facilitate adjustments and provide support to ease fear and anxiety. If the program recommended for implementation is beyond the type and level that management can accommodate, or if it involves too much risk or too drastic a change, then frustration and increased resistance are likely to occur.

HUMAN RESOURCE MANAGEMENT IN ACTION

Globalization and the Changing Nature of HRIS

Globalization means that "we all have to meet world standards," says Mark J. Daniel, Vice-president of Management Functions/Research at the Conference Board of Canada. The structural, technological, and financial changes globalization is bringing forces organizations to increase competitiveness and "we're going to need more from our employees if we're going to compete in the world market," Daniel says. He says that in this time of rapid change, organizations must realize their systems will need re-tooling every three to five years. Since it's impossible to predict change or anticipate new technology, it is no longer good enough to build systems on a "one size fits all" basis.

Alfred J. Walker, a principal with TPF&C in New York, says the focus for the 1990s will be less on data and more on how the data is used in the context of the new competitive demands. "The job is making the organization more effective" using HRIS, says Walker. To help improve efficiency and boost competitiveness, Walker recommends using technology to eliminate or reduce certain tasks performed by the human resource department. He says HR practitioners need to become advisors and consultants rather than record keepers, and can use automation and "out-sourcing" to reduce their administrative tasks and support staff. As well, Walker notes a trend toward computer-based training and job design, using HR systems to create "productivity models" as opposed to the traditional (and only marginally useful) performance evaluations and skills inventories functions. Walker adds that such models should include competitive analysis, historical views, "equivalent employees," and work needs analysis.

Selecting Software Only Part of the Evaluation Process

When evaluating HRIS software, human resource systems professionals should pay more attention to process innovation, or "re-engineering," than compiling and sending detailed requests for proposals (RFPs) to vendors, says Al Enzweiler, President of Enzweiler Consulting Group. He stresses that "evaluating software is a means to an end, not an end unto itself." He emphasizes that software alone is not the total solution to an organization's HRIS problems, but an integral part that must be in harmony with the overall plan. The difficulty with relying on RFPs is that most vendors sell pre-packaged solutions, and while packaged products have a certain amount of built-in-flexibility, the software is not made to specification. The built-in flexibility allows salespeople to answer "yes" to most requirements, so evaluators have to be keenly aware of what their ultimate HRIS goals are when comparing products, Enzweiler says.

He also cautions that there is a difference between "strategic" and "supported" products. A strategic product is one that will continue to be upgraded in the future, while a supported product is one that will merely be supported as long as maintenance revenues exceed costs. According to Enzweiler, the following is the critical factor analysis approach to HRIS software selection:

- Recognize the software vendor as a business partner.
- Evaluate critical vendor factors. These include the vendor's hardware platform(s), target markets, stability, and scope.

- Evaluate critical HR software factors. These include architecture, database flexibility, features, and constraints.
- Do detailed HR software analysis.
- Do detailed vendor analysis.

Goals Important When Planning HRIS Conceptual Design

In order to move ahead, HRIS systems must not only meet current needs, but be able to evolve smoothly to meet future needs while supporting the objectives and purposes of strategic importance to the organization. These goals should be kept in mind when preparing the conceptual design for a system, says George Eckhert, President and Associate Consultant of Consulting Dimension.

The conceptual design is a document that describes the business system to be automated and the kinds of technology to be used in the process. It helps users to determine the potential benefits of the proposed system, implementors to estimate costs, and managers to judge the project's advisability. Eckhert says a good design should be guided by the organization's goals, purposes and policies, and that "looking up" from the technology to these purposes and policies will help solve problems during the design phase. Some of the other basic principals for planning a successful conceptual design include:

- planning for consistency and logical integration of data;
- making the system service-and performance-oriented;
- making the system easy to use;
- securing the information;
- keeping the system compatible with the corporate technology direction.

SOURCE: *Human Resources Management in Canada*, Report Bulletin no. 43 (Scarborough, Ont.: Prentice-Hall Canada Inc., 1990), pp. 9-10. Used with permission

EVALUATION

Human resource planning should be assessed on an annual basis to determine its effectiveness to the organization in terms of management's expectations. It should be determined how certain goals were reached and the reasons that others were not. HRP should also be assessed to determine those areas that are in need of change to reflect changing internal and external conditions.

Special emphasis may be focused on assessing specific criteria such as:

- Achievement of employment equity plans versus set goals and objectives.
- Ratio of internal placement to external hiring.
- Actual staffing levels versus established staffing requirements.
- Internal mobility flow versus career development.
- Internal mobility flow versus turnover.

As James Walker points out, human resource planning is itself a process of anticipating needs for change in an organization and of monitoring responses to these needs. Yet the organization also requires a method to assure that HRP is having its desired impact. Since HRP links an organization's HRM activities with other objectives and other specific programs, a necessary measure of effectiveness must be a test of the strength and adequacy of these linkages.[34] This may be done by answering questions such as those in Figure 3.6.

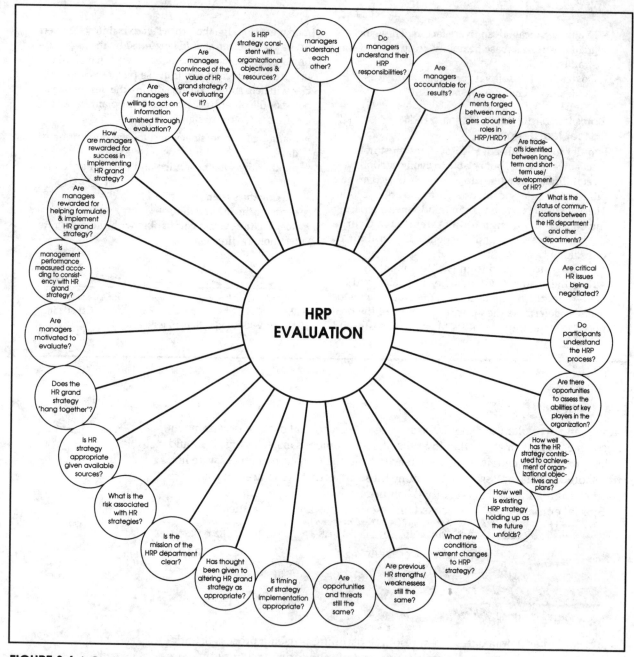

FIGURE 3.6 A Summary of Reasons for Conducting HRP Evaluation

SOURCE: William J. Rothwell and H.C. Kazanas, *Strategic Human Resources Planning and Management*, © 1988, p. 422. Reprinted by permission of Prentice-Hall, Inc., Englewood Cliffs, New Jersey.

Human Resource Accounting

Human resource accounting is a process designed to measure the present cost and value of human resources as well as their future worth to the organization.[35] Human resource accounting is also the process of measuring the worth of the organization's most important asset. As previously noted, it is through human resources that all other resources are generated and utilized. The right mix of human resources needed to produce the organization's objectives does not come easily. It is therefore important for the organization to know the present and future worth of its human resources.

human resource
accounting

There are at least three methods available to measure and forecast the worth of human resources. These are historical cost, replacement cost, and present value of future productivity.

The *historical cost* concept of human resource accounting is based on computing all the costs associated with the organization's investment in its human resources. This means all the costs incurred to identify, acquire, train, develop, recruit, place, and maintain employees. The total of all of these costs represents the historical costs of the organization's investment in its human resources.

The *replacement cost* concept of human resource accounting is based on computing all the costs that the organization would incur to replace its present work force on the open labour market. The total of the costs to recruit, select, place, train, and service new employees; the vacation pay and other severance pays for departing employees; and the costs associated with replacing an experienced work force with an inexperienced work force represent the replacement cost.

The *present value of future productivity* is a concept based on computing the present value of the expected value or contribution of the work force in an organization. The present value of future worth or output may be assessed by the present value of future compensation to be paid to the work force.

Human resource accounting is a very useful input into areas such as human resource planning, compensation and benefits, and training and development. Human resource accounting provides useful information to management by evaluating the overall effectiveness of the organization's human resources.

SUMMARY

1. Human resource planning is the process of analyzing the organization's human resources needs under changing conditions and developing programs required to satisfy these needs. HRP is also the process of forecasting an organization's human resources needs in light of the company's strategic goals, staffing needs, employment equity programs, and external market conditions.

2. HRP influences other HRM functions such as recruitment, selection, career management, training and development, and compensation.

3. Human resource planning involves six processes: establishing organizational goals and objectives; forecasting human resource needs; forecasting human resource supply; planning human resource policies, programs, and procedures; implementing programs; and monitoring and evaluating the results.

4. There are various HRP forecasting techniques available for estimating human resource demand and supply. Techniques that may be used to forecast the demand of human resources include: trend analysis, ratio analysis, managerial judgment, computerized forecasting, expert estimation, and statistical analysis.

Techniques that may be used to forecast the supply of human resources include: skill inventories, replacement planning, succession planning, labour market condition analysis, and market analysis.

5. Human resource planning should be evaluated annually to determine which goals were met, which were missed, and where improvement is needed.

6. Human resources accounting is designed to measure the present cost and value of human resources as well as their future worth to the organization. It evaluates the overall effectiveness of the organization's human resources.

KEY TERMS

human resource planning	trend analysis	multiple regression analysis
strategic planning	ratio analysis	stochastic analysis
operational planning	managerial judgment	skill inventories
human resource information system (HRIS)	computerized forecasting	replacement planning
organizational objectives	delphi technique	succession planning
human resource objectives	nominal group technique	Markov analysis
	regression analysis	human resource accounting

DISCUSSION QUESTIONS

1. Distinguish between demand forecasting and supply forecasting.
2. Define human resource planning.
3. Compare and contrast operational planning and strategic planning.
4. What type of information goes into human resource accounting?
5. Why is an evaluation of human resource planning important?
6. What is a human resource information system?

CASE INCIDENT: Human Resource Planning at Nova Scotia Engineering

Keir Burnstein was very happy when informed by the director of human resources that he was the successful candidate to become the new human resource planning specialist for the Nova Scotia Engineering and Construction International Company. One of Keir's first assignments is to decide whether the company should develop and implement a human resource planning program. Though the company has been in business for over 12 years, it has never undertaken any human resource planning activities. The director told Keir that both the president and top management feel that such a policy may not be necessary since the company has been operating successfully without one, but will look at his report with open minds.

The company has over 500 employees. It operates in Canada, the U.S., and in the Middle East. During the 1991 recession the company suffered substantial losses, but saw its business rebound after the Gulf War.

Over the years the company has hired employees for specific jobs and reduced its work force when the demand for many special contracts was reduced. More than half of its work force was hired on specific term contracts. Often the firm was unable to hire the type of skilled employees it needed to fill key positions for local and overseas commitments. More than once it was unable to fulfil its contractual commitments and had to ask its competitors to assume some portions of contracts that it had won through the bidding process.

Over the past 12 years the company has experienced substantial voluntary and involuntary turnover. Many employees claimed that they left the company because of a lack of job security. Others mentioned privately that they were only staying until they could find a secure job elsewhere. Yet others felt that the company hired many of its employees for a limited term. Since they were under no illusions about job security when they joined the company, these employees also stated that it was unfair to blame the company for lack of job security and the large turnover in the firm.

Questions

1. What are the pros and cons of developing and implementing a human resource planning policy for the firm?
2. What are the different factors Keir should examine when analyzing and developing a human resource planning policy for the firm?

NOTES

1. Naresh C. Agarwal, "Human Resources Planning," *Human Resources Management in Canada* (Toronto: Prentice-Hall Canada Inc., 1983), p. 20,011.
2. James W. Walker, *Human Resource Planning* (New York: McGraw-Hill Book Company, 1980), p. 10.
3. Agarwal, p. 20,011.
4. P. B. Fay, "Why Human Resource Planning is Important," *Human Resources Management in Canada* (Toronto: Prentice-Hall Canada Inc., 1983), p. 21,011.
5. Michael E. Porter, *The Competitive Advantage of Nations* (New York: The Free Press, 1990), p. 578.
6. Walker, p. 78.
7. Walker, p. 79. See also William J. Rothewell and H. C. Kazanas, *Strategic Human Resources Planning and Management* (Englewood Cliffs, N. J.: Prentice-Hall Inc., 1988), p. 10.
8. Ronald J. Grey and Gail Cook Johnson, "Differences between Canadian and American Workers," *Canadian Business Review* (Winter 1988), pp. 24-27.
9. Two writers point out that it is important not to fall into the trap of assuming that HRM is involved only in strategic planning to the extent of matching personnel activities with strategies, forecasting labour power requirements and supplies, and presenting means for integrating HRM into the overall effort to match corporate strategy. Instead, they say, there is a "reciprocal interdependence between a firm's business strategy and its human resources strategy." In other words, the company's human resources (and therefore human resource management department) can be among other things a way to gain an improved competition position. See Cynthia Lengnick-Hall and Mark Lengnick-Hall, "Strategic Human Resources Management, A Review of the Literature and a Proposed Typology," *Academy of Management Review* (July 1988), pp. 454-470.
10. Michael N. Wolf, "Computerization—It Can Bring Sophistication to Personnel," *Personnel Journal* (June 1978), pp. 325-326; Sidney H. Simon "Personnel's Role in Developing an Information System," *Personnel Journal* (November 1978), pp. 622-625, 640.

11. Alfred Walker, "Management Selection Systems That Meet the Challenge of the 80s," *Personnel Journal*, Vol. 60, no. 10 (Oct. 1981), pp. 775-780.

12. Guvenc G. Alpander, *Human Resources Management Planning* (New York: AMACOM Book Division, 1982), p. 98.

13. Walker, p. 10.

14. Herbert G. Heneman, Jr. and George Seitzer, "Manpower Planning and Forecasting in the Firm: An Exploratory Probe," in Elmer Burack and James Walker, *Manpower Planning and Programming* (Boston: Allyn and Bacon, 1972), pp. 102-120; Sheldon Zedeck and Milton Blood, "Selection and Placement," from *Foundations of Behavioral Science Research in Organizations* (Monterey, Calif.: Brooks/Cole Publishing, 1974) in J. Richard Hackman, Edward Lawler III, and Lyman Porter, *Perspectives on Behavior in Organizations* (New York: McGraw-Hill, 1977), pp. 103-119. For a discussion of equal employment implications of manpower planning, see James Ledvinka, "Technical Implications of Equal Employment Law for Manpower Planning," *Personnel Psychology*, Vol. 28 (Autumn 1975).

15. Roger Hawk, *The Recruitment Function* (New York: American Management Association, 1967). See also Paul Pakchar, "Effective Manpower Planning," *Personnel Journal*, Vol. 62, no. 10 (Oct. 1983), pp. 826-830.

16. Richard B. Frantzreb, "Human Resource Planning: Forecasting Manpower Needs," *Personnel Journal*, Vol. 60, no. 11 (Nov. 1981), pp. 850-857. See also John Gridley, "Who Will Be Where When? Forecast the Easy Way," *Personnel Journal*, Vol. 65 (May 1986), pp. 50-58.

17. Glenn Bassett, "Elements of Manpower Forecasting and Scheduling," *Human Resource Management*, Vol. 12, no. 3 (Fall 1973), pp. 35-43; reprinted in Richard Peterson, Lane Tracy, and Allan Cabelly, *Systematic Management of Human Resources* (Reading, Mass.: Addison-Wesley, 1979), pp. 135-146.

18. For an example of a computerized system in use at Citibank, see Paul Sheiber, "A Simple Selection System called Job Match," *Personnel Journal*, Vol. 58, no. 1 (Jan. 1979), pp. 26-54.

19. Andy Piebalgs, "The Use of Computers in Human Resource Planning," *Human Resources Management in Canada* (Toronto: Prentice-Hall Canada Inc., 1987), pp. 20,541-20,542.

20. G. Milkovich, A. J. Annoni, and T. A. Mahoney, "The Use of Delphi Procedures in Manpower Forecasting" *Management Science*, Vol. 19, no. 4 (1972), pp. 381-388.

21. A. L. Delbecq, A. H. Van DelVen, and D. H. Gustafson, *Group Techniques for Program Planning: A Guide to Nominal and Delphi Processes* (Glenview IL: Scott Foresman, 1975).

22. Gunter Ott, "A Variety of Personnel Software Solutions" *The Human Resource* (February-March 1986), pp. 12-13.

23. Robert M. Cohen and Jennifer Garland, "Computerizing the Personnel Department" *The Human Resource* (February-March 1986), pp. 13-14.

24. Walker, pp. 283-284.

25. Walker p. 276. See also Dave Jackson "Making Succession Planning Work," in *Human Resources Management in Canada* (Scarborough, Ont.: Prentice-Hall Canada, Inc. 1987), pp. 20,545-20,553.

26. L. J. Reypert, "Succession Planning in the Ministry of Transportation and Communication, Province of Ontario," *Human Resource Planning* 4 (1981), pp. 151-56.

27. Naresh C. Agarwal, p. 20,039.

28. Pierre Paul Prouly, Luce Bourqault, and Jean-Francois Manegre, "CANDIDE-COFOR and Forecasting Manpower Needs by Occupation and Industry in Canada" in Larry F. More and Larry Charack (eds), *Manpower Planning for Canadians*, 2nd ed. (Vancouver, BC: Institute of Industrial Relations, University of British Columbia, 1979.)

29. See (1) *Innovation and Jobs in Canada, A Research Report Prepared for the Economic Council of Canada* (Ottawa: Ministry of Supply and Services, 1987); Cat. no. EC22-141/1987#; (2) *The Canadian Occupational Projections Systems Issues and Approaches* (Ottawa: Employment and Immigration Canada, January 1983), WH-3-335E.

30. Prouly and others, *Ibid.*

31. *Human Resource Planning: A Challenge for the 1980s* (Ottawa: Ministry of Supply and Services, 1983), Cat. No. MP 43-125/83. See "Innovations and Jobs in Canada," ch. 4.

32. Naresh C. Agarwal, "Human Resource Planning" in *Human Resources Management in Canada* (Scarborough, Ont.: Prentice-Hall Canada, Inc. 1983), p. 20,029-20,031.

33. Walker, pp. 66-68, Rothwell and Kanzanas, pp. 15-17.

34. James Walker, pp. 355-356.

35. For a comprehensive discussion of human resource accounting see E. G. Famholtz, *Human Resource Accounting* (San Francisco: Jossey-Bass 1985); H. Das and M. Das, "One More Time: How do we Place a Value Tag on our Employees? Some Issues in Human Resource Accounting," in *Human Resource Planning*, 2, (1979), pp. 91-101, G.M.N. Baker "The Feasibility and Utility of Human Resource Accounting" in *California Management Review* 16(4) (1974), pp. 17-23. W. F. Cascio *Costing Human Resources: The Financial Impact of Behavior in Organizations* (Boston: Kent Publishing 1985).

SUGGESTED READINGS

Agarwal, Naresh C. "Human Resources Planning" in *Human Resources Management in Canada*. Toronto: Prentice-Hall Canada Inc., 1983, pp. 20,011-20,046.

Burack, Elmer H. *Creative Human Resource Planning & Applications: A Strategic Approach*. Englewood Cliffs, NJ: Prentice Hall Inc., 1988.

Fay, P. B. "Why Human Resource Planning is Important" in *Human Resources Management in Canada*. Toronto: Prentice-Hall Canada Inc., 1983, pp. 21,011-21,014.

Godkewitsch, Michael and Wayne Lamon. "Internal Selection of Managers: A Value-Added Method for Succession Planning" in *Human Resources Management in Canada*. Toronto: Prentice-Hall Canada Inc., 1991, pp. 20,551-20,555.

Hathaway, Donald B. "Computers and Human Resources: Determining Your HRIS Requirements" in *Human Resources Management in Canada*. Toronto: Prentice-Hall Canada Inc., 1991, pp. 70,587-70,591.

Jackson, Dave. "Making Succession Planning Work" in *Human Resources Management in Canada*. Toronto: Prentice-Hall Canada Inc., 1987, pp. 20545-20,550.

Rothwell, William J. and H. C. Kazanas. *Strategic Human Resources Planning and Management*. Englewood Cliffs, NJ: Prentice Hall Inc., 1988.

Walker, James W. *Human Resource Planning*, New York: McGraw-Hill Book Company, 1980.

CHAPTER FOUR JOB ANALYSIS

After studying this chapter you should be able to

1. Explain how to perform a job analysis.
2. Explain the relationship of job analysis to other HRM functions.
3. State the major steps in job analysis.
4. Identify the methods for collecting job analysis information.
5. Explain how to prepare job descriptions and job specifications.
6. Identify the purposes and uses of job descriptions and job specifications.

OVERVIEW

The main purpose of this chapter is to explain how to analyze—determine the specific duties and responsibilities of—a job. First, we discuss some basics of organizing, including organization charts and what kind of people should be hired for the job. Next, we explain job analysis and discuss its relationship to other HRM functions. We discuss several techniques for analyzing jobs and for writing job descriptions. Job analysis is in many ways one of the most important functions performed by HRM specialists. It provides information crucial for the preparation of job descriptions and job specifications. Job analysis must be carefully and accurately done in order to ensure the right fit between the position and the job holder.

FUNDAMENTALS OF ORGANIZING

One of the purposes of organization is to give each person a separate, distinct job and to insure that these jobs are coordinated in such a way that the organization accomplishes its goals. Organizations are never ends in themselves but are means to an end—that "end" being the accomplishment of the organization's goals. Thus an organization consists of people who carry out different jobs that are coordinated to contribute to the organization's goals.

Organization Charts

The usual way of depicting an organization is with an organization chart, as shown in Figure 4.1. An **organization chart** is a "snapshot" of the organization at a particular point in time and shows the skeleton of the organization's structure in chart form. It provides the title of each manager's position and, by means of connecting lines, shows who is accountable to whom and who is in charge of what department.

organization chart

The organization chart does not show everything about the organization, any more than a road map shows everything about the towns along its routes. Organization charts do not provide job descriptions, which describe the specifics of each job in terms of the actual day-to-day activities and responsibilities the person is expected to perform. (Job analysis, which we will discuss in the next section, provides these job descriptions.) Nor does the organization chart show the actual patterns of communication in the organization. It also does not show how closely employees are supervised or the actual level of authority and power that each position holder in the organization has. What it does show are the position titles and the "chain of command" from the top of the organization to the bottom.

Most organizations have, or should have, organization charts because they are helpful in informing employees of what their jobs are and how these jobs relate to others in the organization. However, many organizations have been quite successful without organization charts, while others have failed in spite of them.

In summary, organization charts are useful because they

1. Show the title of each manager's job.
2. Show who is accountable to whom.
3. Show who is in charge of what department.
4. Show what sorts of departments have been established.
5. Show the "chain of command."
6. Let each employee know his or her title and "place" in the organization.

But organization charts do *not* show

1. Job descriptions of specific day-to-day duties and responsibilities.
2. Actual patterns of communication in the organization.
3. How closely employees are supervised.
4. The actual level of authority and power each position holder has.

FIGURE 4.1
Organization Chart

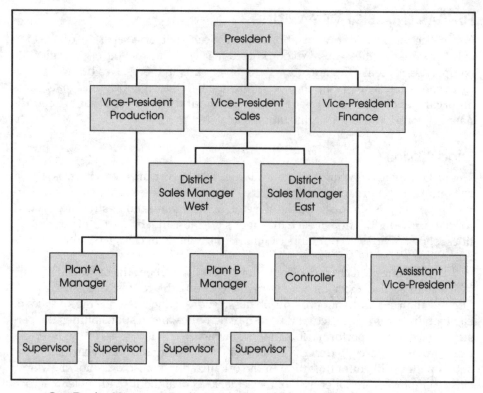

SOURCE: Gary Dessler, *Management Fundamentals*, 4th ed. (Englewood Cliffs, N. J.: Prentice-Hall, 1985), p. 106.

THE NATURE OF JOB ANALYSIS

Job Analysis Defined

job analysis

Developing an organization structure results in jobs that have to be staffed. **Job analysis** is the procedure through which the human resource management specialist determines the duties and nature of the jobs and the kinds of people (in terms of skills and experience) who should be hired for them.[1] It provides data on job requirements, which are then used for developing a **job description** (what the job entails) and a **job specification** (what kind of people to hire for the job).

job description
job specification

The HRM specialist normally collects one or more of the following types of information by doing the job analysis:[2]

Job activities.   First, information is usually collected on the actual work activities performed, such a cleaning, sewing, galvanizing, coding, or painting. Sometimes such a list of activities also indicates how, why, and when a worker performs each activity.

Human behaviours.   Information on human behaviours like sensing, communicating, decision making, and writing may also be compiled. Included here would be information regarding personal job demands in terms of human energy expenditure, walking long distances, and so on.

Machines, tools, equipment, and work aids used. Included here would be information regarding products made, materials processed, knowledge dealt with or applied (such as physics or law), and services rendered (such as counselling or repairing).

Performance standards. Information is also collected regarding the performance standards (in terms of quantity, quality, or time taken for each aspect of the job, for instance) by which an employee in this job will be evaluated.

Job context. Included would be information concerning such matters as physical working conditions, work schedule, and the organizational and social context—for instance, in terms of people with whom the employee would normally be expected to interact. Also included here might be information regarding financial and nonfinancial incentives the job entails.

Human resources requirements. Finally, information is usually compiled regarding such human requirements of the job as job-related knowledge or skills (education, training, work experience, etc.) and personal attributes (aptitudes, physical characteristics, personality, interest, etc.) required.

Purposes and Importance of Job Analysis

The purposes and importance of job analysis are to

- Provide the essential characteristics to enable the design and development of job descriptions and job specifications
- Provide clear and concise information of the job to be performed and of the skills, knowledge, and abilities which must be possessed by individuals who will fill these jobs
- Define the essential characteristics required to perform the job effectively. This way the organization can accurately match the job demand and requirements with the job holder's skills, knowledge, abilities, interests, and personality
- Enable the organization to obtain pertinent job information so that it may divide all of its work into specific jobs at all levels throughout the organization
- Study and analyze work processes, simplify methods, and measure and evaluate work to enable the establishment of performance standards
- Determine what responsibilities, duties and tasks the job will entail, and how much autonomy the job may entail
- Enable the organization to establish valid and objective compensation systems, so as to provide equitable pay and equal treatment to all employees. It also facilitates the design of a pay system based on the relative value of each job to the organization, and ensures internal and external equity
- Determine appropriate job characteristics needed to ensure compliance with prevailing pay equity laws
- Provide proper documentation to facilitate the coordinating of the human and nonhuman resources and activities of the organization

FIGURE 4.2
Job Analysis
Information Flow

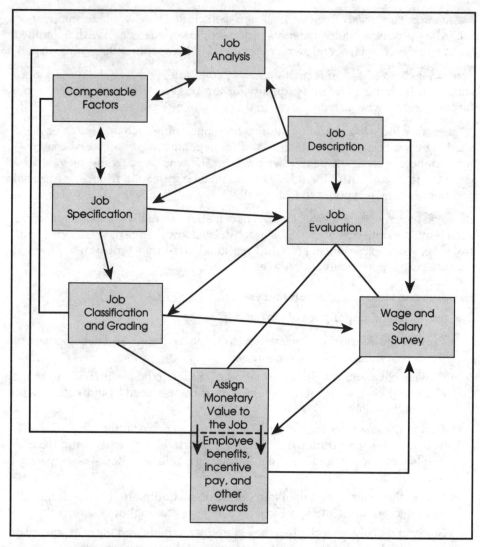

SOURCE: Richard J. Henderson, *Compensation Management: Rewarding Performance*, 4th ed., copyright 1985, p. 147. Reprinted by permission of Prentice-Hall, Englewood Cliffs, N.J.

The Relationship of Job Analysis to Other Human Resource Management Functions

Job analysis is interrelated to various human resource management functions. These include legal considerations, human resource planning, recruitment, selection, training and development, performance appraisal, compensation, employee health and safety, and labour relations. Figure 4.2 illustrates some other interrelated functions and activities of job analysis.

Legal Considerations

Job analysis information influences various HRM activities such as hiring, promotion, compensation, and compliance with human rights legislation, pay equity acts, and federal and provincial Employment Equity Acts. Employers must ensure that their job analysis information is free of systemic discriminatory biases, free of gender biases, and free of any information that would have an equal effect on job applicants and present employees. Thus the accuracy of job analysis information is vital since it forms the foundation of HRM activities such as pay equity. Various human rights tribunals have held that employers must show that their screening tools (such as tests) are accurate for measuring job performance (see discussion in Chapter 2). The reason is that an employer must be able to show that its screening tools are related to the performance of the job.

Human Resource Planning

Job analysis provides a clear description of the performance standards jobholders need to achieve to ensure job success. This description allows the organization's human resource planning specialist to identify what types of job candidates are needed, when, and where.

Recruitment

Job analysis provides information on what the job entails and what qualifications are required to carry out these activities. It supports recruitment by providing recruiters with the essential characteristics needed for optimum performance, thereby enabling recruiters to properly "fit" the organization's requirements and the individual's needs. Job analysis information is the basis upon which the organization decides what sort of people to recruit and hire.

Selection

Job analysis provides recruiters with the criteria of job descriptions and job specifications. A job description usually contains clear and unbiased facts that explain what the job is, and what specific tasks, duties, and responsibilities are involved. Job analysis identifies the specific skills, knowledge abilities, and other work characteristics required of the jobholder.

Training and Development

Job analysis is a valuable tool for identifying training and development needs and correcting employee performance deficiencies. Job analysis information is also used for designing training and development programs because it reveals what sorts of skills—and therefore training—are required.

Performance Appraisal

Performance appraisal involves comparing each employee's actual performance with his or her desired performance. It is through job analysis that the organization determines the standards to be achieved and specific activities to be performed.

Compensation

Job analysis provides job content data which is used to determine the value of and appropriate compensation for each job. Compensation (such as salary and bonus) is usually tied to the job's required skills and education level, safety hazards, and so on, and these are all factors that are identified through job analysis. Many organizations classify jobs into categories, and job analysis provides data for determining the relative worth of each job so that each job can be classified.

Employee Health and Safety

The performance of some jobs can be hazardous to workers' health and safety. Accurate job analysis can pinpoint areas where the organization needs to take steps to control physical hazards to employees' health, limit risk to employee safety, and implement safety rules and regulations to provide for safe working conditions.

Labour Relations

As noted previously, job analysis affects job classification—a subject of great importance to unions. Job descriptions, prepared from job analyses, are used in bargaining over wages, performance criteria, and working conditions. The Ontario Supreme Court[3] has held that job descriptions can be a subject of negotiation. It is usually the case that unions prefer the scope of job descriptions to be narrowly defined, whereas management prefers that they be broadly defined to provide them with maximum flexibility.

STEPS IN THE JOB ANALYSIS PROCESS

The six steps in doing a job analysis are as follows.

Step 1.

Determine the use of the job analysis information. Start by identifying the use to which the information will be put, since this will determine the type of data that should be collected and the technique used to collect them.

As explained later in this chapter, there are many methods for collecting job analysis data; they range from qualitative interviews to highly quantified questionnaires. Some techniques—such as interviewing an employee and asking the person what the job entails and what his or her responsibilities are—are uniquely suited for uses like writing job descriptions and selecting candidates for the job. Other job analysis techniques (like the position analysis questionnaire described later) do not provide appropriate information for job descriptions, but do provide numerical ratings for each job; these can then be used to compare jobs for compensation purposes. The first step should therefore be to determine the use of the job analysis information.

Step 2.

Collect background information. Review available background information such as organization charts, process charts, and job descriptions.[4] Organization charts show how the job in question relates to other jobs and where it fits in the overall organization. The organization chart should identify the title of each position and, by means of its interconnecting lines, show who reports to whom and with whom the jobholder is expected to communicate.

process chart

A **process chart** provides more detailed understanding of the flow of work than can be obtained from the organization chart alone. In its simplest form a process chart, such as the one in Figure 4.3, shows the flow of inputs to and outputs from the job under study; in this case, for instance, the inventory control clerk is expected to receive inventory from suppliers, take requests for inventory from the two plant managers, provide requested inventory to these managers, and provide information to the managers on the status of in-stock inventories. Finally, the existing job description, if there is one, can provide a good starting point from which to build a revised job description.

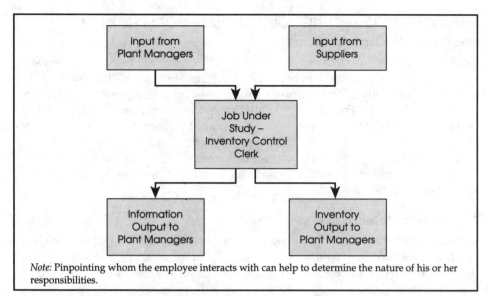

FIGURE 4.3
Process Chart for
Analyzing a Job's
Work Flow

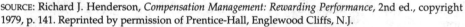

Note: Pinpointing whom the employee interacts with can help to determine the nature of his or her responsibilities.

SOURCE: Richard J. Henderson, *Compensation Management: Rewarding Performance*, 2nd ed., copyright 1979, p. 141. Reprinted by permission of Prentice-Hall, Englewood Cliffs, N.J.

Step 3.

Select representative positions to be analyzed. This is necessary where many similar jobs are to be analyzed and where it is too time-consuming to analyze, say, the jobs of all assembly workers.

Step 4.

Collect job analysis information. Analyze the job by collecting data on job activities, required employee behaviour, working conditions, and human requirements (the traits and abilities needed to perform the job). For this, use one or more of the job analysis techniques described later in this chapter.

Step 5.

Review the information with the participants. The analysis provides information on the nature and functions of the job, and this information should be verified with the worker performing the job and the worker's immediate supervisor. Verifying the information will help to determine if it is factually correct, complete, and easily understood by all concerned. Also, this "review" step can help gain the person's acceptance of the job analysis data collected by giving that person a chance to modify the description of the activities he or she performs.

Step 6.

Develop a job description and job specification. In most cases, a job description and a job specification are two concrete outcomes of the job analysis, and are typically developed next. The job description (as defined earlier) is a written statement that describes the activities and responsibilities of the job, as well as important features of the job such as working conditions and safety hazards. The job specification summarizes the personal qualities, traits, skills, and background required for getting the job done, and it may be either a separate document or in the same document as the job description.

METHODS OF COLLECTING JOB ANALYSIS INFORMATION

Who Collects the Job Information?

Collecting job analysis data usually involves a human resource management specialist, the worker, and the worker's supervisor. The HRM specialist (like the HRM manager, a job analyst, or a consultant) may be asked to observe and analyze the work being done and then develop a job description and job specification. The supervisor and worker will also get involved, perhaps by filling out questionnaires listing the subordinate's activities. Both the supervisor and worker may then be asked to review and verify the job analyst's conclusions regarding the job's activities and duties. Job analysis thus usually involves an integrated effort by the specialist, the supervisor, and the worker.

Procedures for Collecting Job Information

Once background information has been collected and the job to be analyzed has been identified, the next step is to actually collect information on the duties, responsibilities, and activities of the job. There are various techniques that can be used for collecting these data.

In practice, organizations use one or several techniques that best fit their purposes; thus, an interview might be appropriate for developing a job description, whereas the position analysis questionnaire is more appropriate for determining the worth of a job for compensation purposes. Some of the most popularly used methods are the interview, questionnaires, observation, participant diary/logs, and quantitative techniques.

The Interview

There are three types of interviews that can be used to collect job analysis data: individual interviews with each employee; group interviews with groups of employees having the same job; and supervisor interviews with one or more supervisors who are thoroughly knowledgeable about the job being analyzed. The group interview is used when a large number of employees are performing similar or identical work, since this can be a quick and inexpensive way of learning about the job. As a rule the worker's immediate supervisor would attend the group session; the supervisor is interviewed separately to get his or her perspective on the duties and responsibilities of the job.

Whichever interview method is used, it is important that the interviewee fully understand the reason for the interview, since there is a tendency for interviews like these to be misconstrued as "efficiency evaluations." When they are, interviewees may not be willing to accurately describe their jobs or those of their subordinates.

Pros and Cons

The interview is probably the most widely used method for determining the duties and responsibilities of a job, and its wide use reflects its many advantages. Most importantly, an interview allows the worker to report activities and behaviour that might not otherwise come to light. For example, important activities that only occur occasionally or informal communication (between, say, a production supervisor and the sales manager) that would not appear on the organization chart could be unearthed by a skilled interviewer. In addition, an interview can provide an opportunity to explain the need for and functions of the job analysis, as well as allow the interviewee to vent frustrations or views that might otherwise go unnoticed by management. An interview is also a relatively simple and quick way of collecting information.

The major problem with this technique is distortion of information, whether due to outright falsification or an honest misunderstanding.[5] A job analysis is often used as a prelude to changing a job's pay rate. Employees therefore sometimes view them as efficiency evaluations that may (and often will) affect their pay. Employees thus tend to exaggerate certain responsibilities while minimizing others. Consequently, obtaining valid information can be a slow and painstaking process.

Typical Questions

Despite their drawbacks, interviews are widely used. The following are typical questions:

- What is the job being performed?
- What are the major duties of your position? What exactly do you do?
- What different physical locations do you work in?
- What are the education, experience, skill, and (where applicable) certification and licensing requirements?
- What activities do you participate in?
- What are the responsibilities and duties of the job?
- What are the basic accountabilities or performance standards that typify your work?
- What exactly do the activities you participate in involve?
- What are your responsibilities? What are the environmental and working conditions involved?
- What are the physical demands of the job? The emotional and mental demands?
- What are the health and safety conditions?
- Are there any hazards or unusual working conditions you are exposed to?

These questions notwithstanding, it is generally agreed that the most fruitful interviews follow a structured or checklist format. One such job analysis information format is presented in the appendix to this chapter; it includes a series of 17 detailed questions regarding such matters as the general purpose of the job, supervisory responsibilities, job duties, and education, experience, and skills required. A form like this can also be used by a job analyst who has opted for collecting information by observing the work being done or by administering a questionnaire, two methods that will be explained below.[6]

Interview Guidelines

There are several things a job analyst must keep in mind when conducting a job analysis interview. First, it is important that the job analyst and the supervisor work together to identify the workers who know most about the job as well as workers who might be expected to be the most objective in describing their duties and responsibilities.

Second, the job analyst should establish rapport quickly with the interviewee, by knowing the person's name, speaking in easily understood language, briefly reviewing the purpose of the interview, and explaining how the person came to be chosen for the interview.

Third, the analyst should follow a structured guide or checklist, one that lists questions and provides space for answers. This ensures that crucial questions are identified ahead of time and that all interviewers (if there are more than one) cover all the required questions. However, it is important that workers be allowed some leeway in answering questions, and so some open-ended questions, such as "Was there anything we didn't cover with our questions?", should be provided.

Fourth, when duties are not performed in a regular manner—for instance, when the worker does not perform the same job repeatedly many times a day, the worker should be asked to list his or her duties in order of importance and frequency of occurrence. This will ensure that crucial activities that only occur infrequently—like a nurse's occasional emergency room duties—are not overlooked.

Finally, after the interview is completed the data should be reviewed and verified. This is normally done by the analyst, who reviews the information with the worker's immediate supervisor and with the interviewee.

Questionnaires

Having employees fill out questionnaires in which they describe their job-related duties and responsibilities is another good method for obtaining job analysis information.

The main issue to decide here is how structured the questionnaire should be and what questions to include. At one extreme, some questionnaires are very structured checklists. Each employee is presented with an inventory of perhaps hundreds of specific duties or tasks (like "change and splice wire") and is asked to indicate whether or not he or she performs each task and, if so, how much time is normally spent on each. At the other extreme, the questionnaire can be open-ended and simply ask the employee to "describe the major duties of your job." In practice, the best questionnaire often falls between these two extremes. As illustrated in Figure 4.4, a typical job analysis questionnaire might have several open-ended questions (like "Describe the major duties of your job"), as well as structured questions (concerning, for instance, experience required).

Whether structured or unstructured, any questionnaire has advantages and disadvantages. A questionnaire is, first, a quick and efficient way of obtaining information from a large number of employees—it is less costly than interviewing hundreds of workers, for instance. On the other hand, developing the questionnaire and testing it (perhaps by making sure the workers understand the questions) can be an expensive and time-consuming process. Therefore, the potentially higher development costs have to weighed against the time and expense saved by not having to interview as many workers.

Observation

Direct observation is especially useful in jobs that consist mainly of observable physical activity. Jobs like those of janitor, assembly line worker, and accounting clerk are examples. On the other hand, observation is usually not appropriate where the job entails a lot of unmeasurable mental activity (lawyer, design engineer)

FIGURE 4.4
Job Analysis
Questionnaire for
Developing Job
Descriptions

Employee Questionnaire

JOB DESCRIPTION QUESTIONNAIRE

Date _____

Company _____ Present Job Title and Grade _____

Department _____ Section or Group _____

Supervisor's Name _____

Home Office ☐ Branch or Area Service Office _____

---

1. Describe major duties of your job: _____

_____

_____

_____

_____

_____

_____

_____

_____

_____

_____

_____

_____

(Attach additional sheets if needed)

2. Other, less important job duties:

_____

_____

_____

_____

_____

_____

(Attach additional sheets if needed)

FIGURE 4.4
(continued)

3. List machines or equipment you use:

	Continually	Frequently	Occasionally
_____	❑	❑	❑
_____	❑	❑	❑
_____	❑	❑	❑

4. How much formal education is necessary to do this job (check one):

❑ Less than High School   ❑ High School plus 2-3 yrs of other schooling
❑ High School   ❑ College Degree (4 yrs) Major _____
❑ High School plus 1 yr. of   ❑ College Degree plus other schooling
     other schooling

List additional specialized courses, subjects or training which are *necessary* but which
are NOT easily available in High School or College:_____

5. How much previous similar or related work experience is *necessary* for a person
starting this job?

❑ None   ❑ 1 to 3 years
❑ Less than 3 months   ❑ 3 to 5 years   ❑ _____
❑ 3 months to 1 year   ❑ 5 to 10 years

6. How long should it take an employee with the *necessary* education and previous experience (as shown above) to become generally familiar with details and to do this job reasonably well?

❑ Two weeks or less   ❑ Six months   ❑ Two years
❑ Three months   ❑ One year   ❑ _____

7. What amount of supervision does this job ordinarly require? Check one:

❑ Frequent; all but minor variations are referred to supervisor.

❑ Several times daily, to report or to get advice and/or assignments. Follow established methods and procedures; refer exceptions.

❑ Occasional, since most duties are repetitive and related, with standard instructions and procedures as guides. Unusual problems are referred, frequently with suggestions for correction.

❑ Limited supervision. The nature of the work is such that it is performed to a large extent on own responsibility after assignment, with some choice of method. Occasionally develop own methods.

❑ Broad objectives are outlined. Work is judged primarily on overall results with much choice of method. Frequently develop methods to achieve desired results.

❑ Little or no direct supervision. Have wide choice in selection, development and coordination of methods within broad framework of general policies

8. What are the nature and scope of any *independent* decisions you make?

_____

_____

Are your decisions to approve usually reviewed before becoming effective? ❑
If so, by whom?_____

Are your decisions to reject usually reviewed before becoming effective? ❑
If so, by whom?_____

FIGURE 4.4
(continued)

9. In what ways does this job require resourcefulness, orginality and/or initiative? Examples:

_____

_____

10. What kinds of errors are likely to occur on this job?

_____

_____

    How are such errors ordinarily checked or discovered?

_____

_____

    What would be the effect of such errors, if not caught?

_____

_____

_____

11. Check the extent of contacts you have regarding Company business:

	Continually	Frequently	Occasionally	Never	Method (Phone, Letters, in person)
Employees in other units of the Company	❏	❏	❏	❏	_____
Policyholders and/or Agents	❏	❏	❏	❏	_____
General public; community or trade and professional assns.	❏	❏	❏	❏	_____
Federal and State Govt Agencies	❏	❏	❏	❏	_____
Other (specify)_____	❏	❏	❏	❏	_____

Example and purpose of such contacts:

_____

12. If the mental and visual alertness required is more than normal: check *one* in *each* column:

                    ❏ Occasional; periods of short duration

    ❏ Close   ❏ Frequent, but with occasional "breaks"

    ❏ Highly concentrated   ❏ Steady and sustained

13. Describe any muscular action, body movement, working positions or posture changes occuring while performing duties which result in unusual fatigue, Estimate percentage of time in each:

_____

14. Indicate any disagreeable job conditions to which you are exposed, such as dirt, noise, water, fumes, heat, outside weather, monotony, accident hazards, etc.

_____

    If you travel overnight on the job, indicate approximate times per month and method.

_____

    Approximately how many miles per month do you drive in doing this job?

_____

FIGURE 4.4
(continued)

ANSWER ONLY IF YOU ARE RESPONSIBLE FOR THE WORK OF OTHERS

15. Check below those supervisory responsibilities which are a part of this job:

❑ Instructing   ❑ Allocating personnel
❑ Assigning work   ❑ Acting on employee problems
❑ Reviewing work   ❑ Selecting new employees
❑ Planning work of others   ❑ Transferring/promoting
❑ Maintaining Standards   (Recommend?__ Approve?__)
❑ Coordinating activities   ❑ Disciplining
❑ Transferring/promoting   (Recommend?__ Approve?__)
    (Recommend?__ Approve?__) ❑ Discharge
                                  (Recommend?__ Approve?__)

List job titles which are under your *direct* supervision and the number of employees in each:

_____   _____
_____   _____
_____   _____
_____   _____
_____   _____

Show TOTAL number of employees (including those just above) over which you have supervisory authority: _____

COMMENTS: (Attach additional sheets if needed):

_____
_____
_____
_____
_____
_____
_____
_____
_____

                              Form completed by: _____

NOTE TO SUPERVISOR: Your signature below indicates that you have reviewed the above job description. If you desire to make revisions, please enter them in RED pencil in the appropriate spaces. If needed, use additional sheets, numbering your comments to match the items in question. These items will be reviewed with you before a final job description is prepared.

How many employees under your supervisiondo the job described above? _____

Reviewed by _____

Title _____

SOURCE: Prentice-Hall, *Personnel Management, Policies, and Practices*, 1966.

or if the employee is normally expected to engage in important activities that might occur only occasionally, such as a nurse handling emergencies.

Direct observation is often used in conjunction with interviewing. One approach is to observe the worker on the job during a complete work cycle. (The cycle is the time it takes to complete the job; it could be a minute for an assembly line worker or an hour, a day, or more for more complex jobs.) Here note is taken of all the job activities observed. Then, after as much information as possible is accumulated, the worker is interviewed; the person is encouraged to clarify points not understood and explain what additional activities he or she performs that were not observed. Another approach is to observe and interview simultaneously, while the worker performs his or her task. It is often best that questions be withheld until after observations are made. This helps to reduce the chance that the employee will become anxious or in some way distort his or her usual routine.

Participant Diary/Logs

Workers can be asked to keep daily **participant diary/logs** or lists of things they do during the day. For every activity he or she engages in, the employee records the activity (along with the time) in a log. This can provide a very comprehensive picture of the job, especially when it is supplemented with subsequent interviews with the worker and his or her supervisor. The employee might, of course, try to exaggerate some activities and underplay others. However, the detailed, chronological nature of the log tends to mediate against this.

participant diary/logs

Quantitative Job Analysis Techniques

While most employers use interviews, questionnaires, observations, or diary/logs for collecting job analysis data, there are many times when these narrative approaches are not entirely appropriate. For example, when the aim is to assign a quantitative value to each job, so the jobs can be compared for pay purposes, a more quantitative job analysis approach may be best. Two popular quantitative methods are the position analysis questionnaire and functional job analysis.

Position Analysis Questionnaire

Researchers at Purdue University have developed what they consider to be a sure-fire procedure for quantitatively describing jobs.[7] Their **position analysis questionnaire (PAQ)** is a very structured job analysis questionnaire. The PAQ itself is filled in by a job analyst, who should already be acquainted with the particular job to be analyzed. The PAQ contains 194 items. As in Figure 4.5, each of these 194 items (such as "written materials") represents a basic item that may or may not play an important role on the job. The job analyst decides if the item plays a role on the job and, if so, to what extent. In Figure 4.5, for example, "written materials" received a rating of 4, indicating that such materials (books, reports, office notes, etc.) play a considerable role on the job. On the other hand, "quantitative materials" play only an occasional role on the job. The advantage of the PAQ is that it provides a quantitative score or profile of any job in terms of how that job rates on five basic dimensions: (1) having decision making/communications/social responsibilities; (2) performing skilled activities; (3) being physically active; (4) operating vehicles/equipment; and (5) processing information. As a result, the PAQ's real strength is in classifying jobs. In other words, the PAQ allows the assignment of a quantitative

position analysis questionnaire (PAQ)

FIGURE 4.5
Portions of a Completed Page from the Position Analysis Questionnaire

INFORMATION INPUT

1 INFORMATION INPUT

1.1 Sources of Job Information

Rate each of the following items in terms of the extent to which it is used by the worker as a source of information in performing his or her job.

	Extent of Use (U)
NA	Does not apply
1	Nominal/very infrequent
2	Occasional
3	Moderate
4	Considerable
5	Very substantial

1.1.1 Visual Sources of Job Information

1 | 4 Written materials (books, reports, office notes, articles, job instructions, signs. etc)

2 | 2 Quantitative materials (materials which deal with quantities or amounts, such as graphs accounts, specifications, tables of numbers, etc.)

3 | 1 Pictorial materials (pictures or picturelike materials used as *sources* of information, for example, drawings, blueprints, diagrams, maps, tracings, photographic films, x-ray films, TV pictures, etc.)

4 | 1 Patterns/related devices (templates, stencils, patterns, etc., used as *sources* of information when *observed* during use; do *not* include here materials described in item 3 above)

5 | 2 Visual displays (dials, gauges, signal lights, radar scopes, speedometers, clocks, etc.)

6 | 5 Measuring devices (rulers, calipers, tire pressure gauges, scales, thickness gauges, pipettes, thermometers, protractors, etc., used to obtain visual information about physical measurements; do *not* include here devices described in item 5 above)

7 | 4 Mechanical devices (tools, equipment, machinery, and other mechanical devices which are *sources* of information when *observed* during use or operation)

8 | 3 Materials in process (parts, materials, objects, etc., which are *sources* of information when being modified, worked on. or otherwise processed, such as bread dough being mixed, workpiece being turned in a lathe, fabric being cut, shoe being resoled, etc.)

9 | 4 Materials *not* in process (parts, materials, objects, etc., not in the process of being changed or modified, which are *sources* of information when being inspected, handled, packaged, distributed, or selected, etc., such as items or materials in inventory, storage, or distribution channels, items being inspected, etc.)

10 | 3 Features of nature (landscapes, fields, geological samples, vegetation, cloud formations, and other features of nature which are observed or inspected to provide information)

11 | 2 Man-made features of environment (structures, buildings, dams, highways, bridges, docks, railroads, and other "man-made" or altered aspects of the indoor or outdoor environment which are observed or inspected to provide job information; do not consider equipment, machines, etc., that an individual uses in his work, as covered by item 7).

Note: This exhibits 11 of the "information input" questions or elements. Other PAQ pages contain questions regarding mental processes, work output, relationships with others, job context, and other job characteristics.

SOURCE: E.J. McCormick, P.R. Jeanneret, and R.D. Mecham, *Position Analysis Questionnaire*. Copyright 1969 by Purdue Research Foundation, West Lafayette, Ind. Reprinted with permission.

score to each job based on its decision making, skilled activities, physical activity, vehicle/equipment operation, and information-processing characteristics. The results of the PAQ can be used to compare jobs to one another and to decide, for instance, which jobs are more challenging;[8] this information can then be used to determine salary or wage levels for each job.[9]

Functional Job Analysis

Functional job analysis is a method used for classifying jobs by taking into account the extent to which instructions, reasoning, judgment, and verbal facility are necessary for performing job tasks, and by identifying objectives and training requirements.[10]

functional job analysis

Functional analysis rates the job not only on data, people, and things, but also on the following four dimensions: the extent to which specific instructions are necessary to perform the task; the extent to which reasoning and judgment are required to perform the task; the mathematical ability required to perform the task; and the verbal and language faculties required to perform the task. Second, functional job analysis also identifies performance standards and training requirements. Performing a job analysis using functional job analysis therefore allows the HRM specialist to answer the following question: To do this task and meet these standards, what training does the worker require?

An example of a completed functional job analysis summary sheet is presented in Figure 4.6. In this case the job is that of grader (an operator of heavy equipment used in road building). As illustrated, the functional job analysis provides information on things, data, people, instructions, reasoning, math, and language. All this is quantitatively rated. Also, the summary sheet lists the main tasks involved in the job, performance standards, and training required.

Canadian Classification and Dictionary of Occupations

The Canadian Classification and Dictionary of Occupations (CCDO) is an excellent source of standardized occupational information. The CCDO describes and classifies jobs by occupation. An aim of the CCDO is to provide a standardized method by which different jobs can be quantitatively rated, classified, and compared. The CCDO classification is a comprehensive system that provides useful information such as

- Coded job characteristics
- Occupational code number
- Occupational title
- Industry designation
- Statement of job duties
- Occupational groups

The CCDO classification system is divided into four distinct categories: (1) major group; (2) minor group; (3) unit group; and (4) individual unique occupations. Each occupational categorization in the CCDO is identified by a seven-digit code number. This code is based on the type of work performed, required performance standards, and other situational factors.

Each method available to collect job analysis information has unique advantages and disadvantages. Summarized in Table 4.1 are the advantages and disadvantages of six different methods.

CHAPTER FOUR Job Analysis **125**

FIGURE 4.6
Functional Job
Analysis Task
Statement

TASK CODE: GR-08									
WORKER FUNCTION AND ORIENTATION						**WORKER INSTRUCTIONS**	**GENERAL EDUCATIONAL DEVELOPMENT**		
THINGS	%	DATA	%	PEOPLE	%		REASONING	MATH	LANGUAGE
3C	65	3B	25	1A	10	3	2	1	3

GOAL:
  Operates Grader–Output Basic

OBJECTIVE :
  Backfilling, scarifying, windrowing, cutting firebreak, maintaining haul road, snow removal

TASK: Operates grader manipulating controls to travel forward/back, turn, raise/lower blade, position wheels and blade at current angles; follows work order, drawing on knowledge and experience, monitoring the performance of the equipment and adapting to the changing situation, constantly alert to the presence and safety of other workers/equipment, in order to perform routine grader tasks such as backfilling, haul road maintenance, snow removal.

(To Perform This Task)

PERFORMANCE STANDARDS

TRAING CONTENT

DESCRIPTIVE:
  – Operates equipment properly.
  – Is alert and attentive.

NUMERICAL:
  – All work meets work order requirements
  – No accidents/damage due to improper operating techniques.

FUNCTIONAL:
  – How to operate grader.
  – How to do routine grader tasks, such as backfilling, scarifying, windrowing, cutting firebreak, maintaining road, snow removal.

SPECIFIC:
  – Knowledge of specific grader.
  – Knowledge of work requirements.
  – Knowledge of specific job site (i.e., layout, soil condition, environment).

(To These Standards) ——————→ *(Worker Needs This Training)*

SOURCE: Howard Olson, Sidney A. Fine, David C. Myers, and Margarette C. Jennings, "The Use of Functional Job Analysis in Establishing Performance for Heavy Equipment Operators," *Personnel Psychology*, Summer 1981, p. 354.

TABLE 4.1 A Summary of General Data Collection Methods for Job Analysis

Method	Variations	Brief Description	Advantages	Disadvantages
Observations	Structured	• Watch people go about their work; record frequency of behaviors or nature of performance on forms prepared in advance	• Third-party observer has more credibility than job incumbents, who may have reasons for distorting information • Focuses more on reality than on perceptions	• Observation can influence behavior of job incumbents • Meaningless for jobs requiring mental effort (in that case, use information processing method) • Not useful for jobs with a long job cycle
	Unstructured	• Watch people go about their work; describe behaviors/tasks performed		
	Combination	• Part of the form is prepared in advance and is structured; part is unstructured.		
Surveys	Structured	• Ask job incumbents/ supervisors about work performed using fixed responses	• Relatively inexpensive • Structured surveys lend themselves easily to computer analyses • Good method when survey sample is widely scattered	• Depends on verbal skills of respondents • Does not allow for probing • Tends to focus on perceptions of the job
	Unstructured	• Ask job incumbents/ supervisors to write essays to describe work performed		
	Combination	• Part of the survey is structured; part is unstructured		
Diaries	Structured	• Ask people to record their activities over several days or weeks in a booklet with time increments provided	• Highly detailed information can be collected over the entire job cycle • Quite appropriate for jobs with a long job cycle	• Requires the job incumbent's participation and cooperation • Tends to focus on perceptions of the job
	Unstructured	• Ask people to indicate in a booklet over how long a period they work on a task or activity		
	Combination	• Part of the diary is structured; part is unstructured		
Individual interviews	Structured	• Read questions and/or fixed response choices to job incumbent and supervisor; must be face to face	• More flexible than surveys • Allows for probing to extract information	• Depends heavily on rapport between interviewer and respondent • May suffer from validity/reliability problems
	Unstructured	• Ask questions and/or provide general response choices to job incumbent and supervisor; must be face to face		
	Combination	• Part of the interview is structured; part is unstructured		

Method	Variations	Brief Description	Advantages	Disadvantages
Group interviews	Structured	• Same as structured individual interviews except that more than one job incumbent/supervisor is interviewed	• Groups tend to do better than individuals with open-ended problem solving • Chance that reliability/validity higher than with individuals because group members cross check each other	• Cost more because more people are taken away from their jobs to participate • Like individual interviews, tends to focus on perceptions of the job
	Unstructured	• Same as unstructured individual interviews except that more than one job incumbent/supervisor is interviewed		
	Combination	• Same as combination individual interview except more than one job incumbent/supervisor is interviewed		
Content analysis	Structured	• Use a form, created through unstructured content analysis, to record frequency of mention of tasks or activities in a job	• Avoids influencing behavior of job incumbents (as observation is prone to do) • Minimizes reliance on perceptions of job incumbents	• Depends heavily on choice of documents, previous descriptions • Tends to focus on norms rather than on reality
	Unstructured	• Identify common duties/tasks/activities of a job through examination of documents; create a form		
	Combination	• Use a form created through unstructured content analysis for same activities associated with a job; create a form for other activities		

SOURCE: William J. Rothewell and H. C. Kazanas, *Strategic Human Resource Planning and Management,* © 1988, pp. 66–68. Reprinted by permission of Prentice Hall, Inc., Englewood Cliffs, New Jersey.

COMPUTER APPLICATION IN JOB ANALYSIS AND STAFFING

Skills Inventory

Most managers lack complete, accurate information about their employees' capabilities. When vacancies occur, either due to attrition or to new opportunities, simply posting the opening on a company bulletin board does not guarantee that every employee will see the posting or will interpret the information appropriately. One way to improve the likelihood that qualified internal candidates will be introduced into the selection process is to have a skills inventory completed and updated regularly by employees.

Both the development of the inventory content and the updating of inventories requires significant input from employees. They must believe in the validity of the instrument, and this will happen only if they participate in the development process. If employees have ready access to computers, the inventory can be developed and updated from their workstations. Otherwise, hard copy memos should invite every employee to describe themselves in terms of the range of skills to be listed, the standards that differentiate various skill levels, and how skills should be categorized.

Inventories should be regularly updated, when an employee has completed a course, seminar, workshop, or assignment that is applicable. If computers are not generally available, employees should be allowed time (20 to 30 minutes) each quarter to update the inventory. Time spent on the updating may be minimized by periodically providing each employee with a hard copy of his or her inventory to mark up before the actual data entry. Skills should be reassessed at least annually at the time of performance appraisals. If an employee has questions about interpretations of skill levels or categories, supervisors or HRM specialists should offer assistance. Periodic review of the inventory and the process should occur, and all employees should receive regular training to maintain the validity of the system.

When a vacancy occurs, interviewers (either in HRM or, in small businesses, managers) would specify the parameters of the job in terms of the skill categories and levels. (This would be based on the job analysis.) The computer program would then produce a list of employees who qualify according to these parameters.

This list would be modified based on other factors, such as attendance, quality of performance, time in position, or interest of the candidate. Employees otherwise qualified could receive a letter informing them of the opening and inviting them to apply if interested, with a copy to the employee's supervisor.

Expressing interest in a position that offers greater responsibility should be encouraged by a company that is interested in retention. Employees who see company behaviours that encourage growth and development are more likely to stay with the company. Developing a skills inventory system with significant employee input, active encouragement to update, and results that keep employees informed of promotional possibilities will enhance retention.

Another aspect of developing a skills appraisal process as described above is straightforward communication with employees. If an employee is otherwise qualified, is invited to apply, does so, and is then found to have either performance or attendance problems, those hindrances to promotion will be addressed because the process encourages informational supervision. Most employees accept constructive criticism if it is offered in a manner designed to help them progress. Further, with employee participation in establishing the content and standards of the inventory, employees should have a better understanding of what is expected of them in order to qualify at specified levels, and should be able to provide valuable job analysis data based on what they actually know about their jobs.

WRITING JOB DESCRIPTIONS

A job description is a written statement of what the job holder actually does, how he or she does it, and under what conditions the job is performed. This information is in turn used to write a job specification, which lists the knowledge, abilities, and skills needed to perform the job satisfactorily. A job description also lists a job's duties, responsibilities, reporting relationships, working conditions, and supervisory responsibilities.

While there is no standard format used in writing a job description, most descriptions contain at least the following sections:

1. Job identification
2. Job summary
3. Relationships, responsibilities, and duties
4. Authority and job standards
5. Working conditions
6. Job specifications

An example of a job description is presented in Figure 4.7.

Job Identification

The job identification section (the top portion of Figure 4.7) contains several types of information.[11] The *job title* specifies the title of the job, such as supervisor of data-processing operations, sales manager, or inventory control clerk. The job *status* section of the job description permits quick identification of the exempt (e.g., exempt from overtime pay) or nonexempt status of the job. The *job code* permits easy referencing of all jobs: each job in the organization should be identified with a code; this code represents important characteristics of the job, such as the wage class to which it belongs. The *date* refers to the date the job description was actually written, and *written by* indicates the person who wrote it. There is also space to indicate who the description was *approved by* and space that indicates the location of the job in terms of its *plant/division* and *department/section*. The *title of the immediate supervisor* is also shown in the identification section.

The identification section also often contains information regarding the job's salary and/or pay scale. The space *grade/level* indicates the grade or level of the job if there is such a category; for example, a firm may classify secretaries as Secretary II, Secretary III, and so on. Finally, the *pay range* space provides for the specific pay or pay range of the job.

Job Summary

The job summary should describe the general nature of the job, listing only its major functions or activities. Thus (as in Figure 4.7) the supervisor of data processing "directs the operation of all data processing, data control, and data preparation requirements. Performs other assignments as required." For the job of materials manager, the summary might state that "the materials manager purchases economically, regulates deliveries of, stores, and distributes all material necessary on the production line." For the job of mailroom supervisor, "the mailroom supervisor receives, sorts, and delivers all incoming mail properly, and he or she handles all outgoing mail including the accurate and timely posting of such mail."[12]

FIGURE 4.7
Sample Job
Description

SAMPLE JOB DESCRIPTION

Supervisor of Data Processing Operations	Exempt 012.168
Job Title	**Status Job Code**
July 3, 1978	Olympia, Inc.—Main Office
Date	**Plant/Division**
Arthur Allen	Data Processing—Information Systems
Written By	**Department/Section**
Juanita Montgomery	12 736
Approved By	**Grade/Level Points**
Manager of Information Systems	14,800 – Mid 17,760–20,720
Title of Immediate Supervisor	**Pay Range**

SUMMARY

Directs the operation of all data processing, data control, and data preparation requirements. Performs other assignments as required

JOB DUTIES*

1. Follows broadly-based directives.
   (a) Operates independently.
   (b) Informs Manager of Information Systems of activities through weekly, monthly, and/or quarterly schedules.
2. Selects, trains, and develops subordinate personnel.
   (a) Develops spirit of cooperation and understanding among work group members.
   (b) Ensures that work group members receive specialized training as necessary in the proper functioning or execution of machines, equipment, systems, procedures, processes, and/ or methods.
   (c) Directs training involving teaching, demonstrating, and/or advising users in productive work methods and effective communications with data processing.
3. Reads and analyzes wide variety of instructional and training information.
   (a) Applies latest concepts and ideas to changing organization requirements.
   (b) Assists in developing and/or updating manuals, procedures, specifications, etc., relative to organizational requirements and needs.
   (c) Assists in the preparation of specifications and related evaluations of supporting software and hardware.
4. Plans, directs, and controls a wide variety of operational assignments by 5 to 7 subordinates; works closely with other managers, specialists, and technicians within Information Systems as well as with managers in other departments with data needs and with vendors.
   (a) Receives, interprets, develops, and distributes directives ranging from the very simple to the highly complex and technological in nature.
   (b) Establishes and implements annual budget for department.
5. Interacts and communicates with people representing a wide variety of units and organizations.
   (a) Communicates both personally and impersonally, through oral or written directives and memoranda, with all involved parties.
   (b) Attends local meetings of professional organizations in the field of data processing.

*This section should also include description of uncomfortable, dirty, or dangerous assignments.

EMPLOYMENT STANDARDS

In this example, the job specifications section lists employment standards. If there is no job specification section, then the Employment Standards section follows the Job Duties section.

ACCOUNTABILITIES

Successful completion of scheduled activities. Increased use of facility services through expansion of user understanding and satisfaction with delivered product.

SOURCE: Richard I. Henderson, *Compensation Management: Rewarding Performance*, 2nd ed., copyright 1979, p. 176. Reprinted by permission of Prentice-Hall, Inc., Englewood Cliffs, N.J.

General statements, such as "performs other assignments as required," should be avoided. On the one hand, such a statement can give supervisors more flexibility in assigning duties. On the other hand, some experts state unequivocally that "one item frequently found that should never be included in a job description is a 'cop-out clause' like 'other duties, as assigned,' "[13] since this leaves open the nature of the job—and the people needed to staff it. A job description should be as specific as possible in order to help identify the right type of individual that should be hired for the job, the job's training requirements, and how the job incumbent is to be appraised.

Relationships

The relationships statement shows the jobholder's relationships with others inside and outside the organization, and might look like this for a human resource manager:[14]

Reports to: vice-president of employee relations.

Supervises: human resources specialist, test administrator, labour relations director, and one secretary.

Works with: all department managers and executive management.

Outside the company: human resource management agencies, executive recruiting firms, union representatives, Canada Employment Centres, and various vendors.[15]

Responsibilities and Duties

Another section should present a detailed list of the actual responsibilities and duties of the job. As in Figure 4.7, each of the job's major duties should be listed separately, with one or two sentences describing each. In the figure, for instance, the duty "selects, trains, and develops subordinate human resources" is further defined as follows: "develops a spirit of cooperation and understanding," "ensures that work group members receive specialized training as necessary," and "directs training involving teaching, demonstrating, and/or advising." Other typical duties for different jobs might include maintaining balanced and controlled inventories, accurate posting of accounts payable, maintaining favourable purchase price variances, and repairing production line tools and equipment.

Authority

Another section should define the limits of the jobholder's authority, including his or her decision-making limitations, direct supervision of other personnel, and budgetary limitations. For example, the jobholder might have authority to approve purchase requests up to $500, grant time off or leaves of absence, discipline department personnel, recommend salary increases, and interview and hire new employees.[16]

Standards of Performance

Some job descriptions also contain a standards of performance section. This basically states the level the employee is expected to achieve for each of the main duties and responsibilities shown in the job description.

Setting standards is never an easy matter. However, most managers soon learn that just telling subordinates to "do their best" does not provide enough guidance to ensure top performance. One straightforward way of setting standards is to finish the statement "I will be completely satisfied with your work when..." This sentence, if completed for each responsibility listed in the job description, should result in a usable set of performance standards.[17] Some examples would include the following:

DUTY: ACCURATE POSTING OF ACCOUNTS PAYABLE

1. All invoices received are posted within the same working day.
2. All invoices are routed to proper department managers for approval no later than the day following receipt.
3. An average of no more than three posting errors per month occurs.
4. Posting ledger is balanced by the end of the third working day of each month.

DUTY: MEETING DAILY PRODUCTION SCHEDULE

1. Work group produces no less than 426 units per working day.
2. No more than an average of 2% of units is rejected at the next workstation.
3. Work is completed with no more than an average of 5% overtime per week.

Working Conditions and Physical Environment

The job description will also list any special working conditions involved on the job. These might include things like noise level, hazardous conditions, or heat.

Guidelines for Writing a Job Description

Here are some guidelines for writing a job description:[18]

Be clear. The job description should portray the work of the position so well that the duties are clear without reference to other job descriptions.

Indicate scope. In defining the position, be sure to indicate the scope and nature of the work by using phrases such as "for the department" or "as requested by the manager." Include all important relationships.

Be specific. Select the most specific words to show (1) the kind of work, (2) the degree of complexity, (3) the degree of skill required, (4) the extent to which problems are standardized, (5) the extent of the worker's responsibility for each phase of work, and (6) the degree and type of accountability. Use action words such as analyze, gather, assemble, plan, devise, infer, deliver, transmit, maintain, supervise, and recommend. Positions at the lower levels of an organization generally have the most detailed duties or tasks, while higher-level positions deal with broader aspects.

Be brief. Brief accurate statements usually best accomplish the purpose.

Recheck. Finally, to check whether the description fulfills the basic requirements, ask yourself the question, "Will a new employee understand the job if he or she reads the job description?"

JOB SPECIFICATIONS

Job specifications set forth the qualifications required of the jobholder to perform the job. These qualifications include education, training, experience, and any specific professional designation and/or certification required for the job. These qualifications are usually grouped under categories such as skills, knowledge, and abilities. The job specification takes the job description and answers the question, "What human traits and experience are necessary to do this job well?" It shows what kind of person to recruit and what qualities that person should be tested for. The job specification may be a separate section on the job description or a separate document entirely; often it is presented on the back of the job description.

JOB DESIGN

The design of jobs, that is, their content, structural environment, and physical demands, affects both productivity and workers' motivation and morale. Job design is the process of defining and arranging tasks, roles, and other work processes to achieve employees' goals and organizational objectives. Effective job design takes into consideration the social, physiological, and psychological characteristics of workers as well as the needs of the organization. It also considers the technical aspects of equipment, tools, lifting requirements, the way workers must sit to do their jobs, working conditions, and other task requirements. Some of the more common approaches to job design include job enrichment, job enlargement, job rotation, and ergonomics. (Job design is discussed in greater detail in Chapter 11.)

Job Enrichment

Job enrichment techniques are designed to change the nature of the relationship between the worker and the job. Job enrichment involves vertical job loading, meaning that changes are made to both the scope and the depth of the job. With this technique, employees are given a greater variety of tasks, greater work autonomy, and self-regulation—a greater say in how the job is planned, performed, and controlled. Job enrichment techniques are intended to activate employees' upper-level needs, particularly self-actualization, achievement, and responsibility.

Job Enlargement

Job enlargement entails adding more duties and tasks of similar characteristics to a given job. This process is also known as horizontal job loading as well as horizontal job enlargement. The intent of this process is to add interest to the employee's job by reducing boredom and monotony. One critic of this technique has argued that job enlargement is merely "adding zero to zero."[19] The implication here is that the process merely adds more boring and monotonous tasks (zero) to the already existing boring and monotonous tasks (zero).

Job Rotation

Job rotation entails moving workers from one job to another on a regular basis (e.g., every few days, weeks, or months.) Job rotation is in essence a horizontal change in job in which workers perform different jobs of a similar nature. The aim of this technique is to increase employee job satisfaction, motivation, and productivity. Another aim is to relieve employee boredom and job monotony.

On the Front Line

Based on her review of the stores Jennifer concluded that one of the first matters she had to attend to was developing job descriptions for her store managers.

As Jennifer tells it, the lectures on job descriptions in her basic management and human resource management courses helped to convince her of the pivotal role that accurate job descriptions play in the smooth functioning of an enterprise. Many times during her first few weeks on the job Jennifer found herself asking one of her store managers why he was violating what Jennifer knew to be recommended company policies and procedures, and repeatedly the answers were either "Because I didn't know it was my job" or "Because I didn't know that was the way we were supposed to do it." The job description, Jennifer knew, along with a set of standards and procedures that specified what was to be done and how, would go a long way toward alleviating this problem.

In general, the store manager is responsible for directing all store activities in such a way that quality work is produced, customer relations and sales are maximized, and profitability is maintained though effective control of labour, supply, and energy costs. In accomplishing that general aim, specific store manager's duties and responsibilities include quality control, store appearance and cleanliness, customer relations, bookkeeping and cash management, cost control and productivity, damage control, pricing, inventory control, spotting and cleaning, machine maintenance, employee safety and hazardous waste, human resource administration, and pest control.

The questions that Jennifer had to address were these:

1. What should be the format and final form of the store manager's job description?

2. Is it practical to specify standards and procedures in the body of the job description, or should these be kept separate?

3. How should she go about collecting the information required for the standards, procedures, and job description?

Ergonomics

Ergonomics seeks to accommodate and integrate the physical needs of workers into the design of jobs. It aims to break down physical barriers that could conceivably contribute to poor performance, low morale, and frustration on the part of workers. Ergonomics is also based on the premise that in order for organizations to increase job satisfaction and morale, and to attain optimal productivity and lower costs, they must take into account the physiology of workers in designing jobs. In essence ergonomics seeks to blend workers' physical needs with the organizational job design requirements in order to achieve compatibility. In other words, the focus of ergonomics is to decrease the negative physiological effects employees may expect.

SUMMARY

1. One of the purposes of an organization is to give each person a separate, distinct job and to ensure that these jobs are coordinated in such a way that the organization accomplishes its goals. The usual way of depicting an organization is with an organization chart. An organization chart shows the title of each manager's position and, by means of connecting lines, shows who is accountable to whom and who is in charge of what department.

2. Developing an organization structure results in jobs that have to be staffed. Job analysis is the procedure through which organizations determine what the

job entails, and what kind of person should be hired for the job. It involves six steps: (1) determining the use of the job analysis information; (2) collecting background information; (3) selecting the positions to be analyzed; (4) collecting job analysis data; (5) reviewing information with participants; and (6) developing a job description and job specification.

3. There are four basic techniques one can use to gather job analysis data: interviews, direct observation, questionnaires, and participant logs. These are good for developing job descriptions and specifications. The functional job analysis and PAQ approaches result in quantitative ratings of each job and are therefore useful in classifying jobs for pay purposes.

4. The job description should portray the work of the position so well that the duties are clear without reference to other job descriptions. The question one should ask is, "Will the new employee understand the job if he or she reads the job description?"

5. The job specification takes the job description and answers the question, "What human traits and experience are necessary to do this job well?" It tells what kind of person to recruit for and what qualities that person should be tested for.

6. Job analysis is in many ways the first HRM activity that affects motivation. Most people cannot perform a job when they do not have the ability and skills to do the job. Job analysis determines what the job entails and what skills and abilities job candidates should possess.

KEY TERMS

organization chart
job analysis
job description

job specification
process chart
participant diary/logs

position analysis questionnaire (PAQ)
functional job analysis

DISCUSSION QUESTIONS

1. What items are typically included in the organization chart? What items are not shown on the chart?

2. What is job analysis? How can you make use of the information it provides?

3. We discussed several methods for collecting job analysis data—interviews, the position analysis questionnaire, and so on. Compare and contrast these methods, explaining what each is useful for and listing the pros and cons of each.

4. Describe the types of information typically found in a job description.

5. Explain how you would conduct a job analysis.

CASE INCIDENT: Must We Always Follow Job Descriptions?

Gisele Lane, Manager, Product Development, is troubled by the number of complaints she has received from her two supervisors. They have complained more than once about problems they are experiencing with the work production and attitudes of some of their subordinates.

One supervisor told Gisele that more than once she noticed that the performance of five of her subordinates was at variance with the duties and responsibilities outlined in their job description. She noticed that "they were deliberately ignoring the performance standard defined in the job description and were in effect doing their own thing." When this variance occurred initially she decided to ignore it, but since the practice had not stopped she believed that something should be done. She indicated that she was concerned that other employees might decide to follow their example, and asked, "what good are the job descriptions if they are not followed?" She was also concerned that if she insisted they follow the job description this might stifle their creativity and innovation. Although she has recently received various compliments about the improved quality of the finished products from some sales and marketing teams, she has also heard negative feedback from one sales team.

The second supervisor told Gisele that various employees have complained recently that the performance standards in the recently revised job descriptions are too high. Some employees feel that the standards are meant for superhumans, not normal human beings.

Questions

1. What should Gisele do?
2. What, if anything, is responsible for the variation between employee performance and the standard defined in the job descriptions?

EXPERIENTIAL EXERCISE

Purpose: The purpose of this exercise is to give you experience in developing a job description, by developing one for your instructor.

Required Understanding: You should understand the mechanics of job analysis and be thoroughly familiar with the job analysis questionnaire (Figure 4.4) and the job analysis format (in the appendix to this chapter).

How to Set Up the Exercise/Instructions: Set up groups of four to six students for this exercise. As in all exercises in this book, the groups should be separated and should not converse with each other. Half the groups in the class will develop the job description using the job analysis questionnaire, while the other half of the groups will develop it using the job analysis format. Each student should review the questionnaire or format (as appropriate) before joining his or her group.

1. Each group should do a job analysis of their instructor's job: half the groups (to repeat) will use the job analysis questionnaire for this purpose, and half will use the job analysis format.
2. Based on this information, each group will develop its own job description and job specification for the instructor.
3. Next, each group should choose a partner group, one that developed the job description and job specification using the alternate method. (A group that used the job analysis questionnaire should be paired with a group that used the job analysis format.)
4. Finally, within each of these new combined groups, compare, contrast, and criticize each of the two sets of job descriptions and job specifications. Did each job analysis method provide different types of information? Which seems superior? Does one seem more advantageous for some types of jobs than others?

NOTES

1. Wayne Cascio, *Applied Psychology in Personnel Management* (Reston, Va.: Reston, 1978), p. 132.

2. Ernest J. McCormick, "Job and Task Analysis," in Marvin D. Dunnette, ed., *Handbook of Industrial and Organizational Psychology* (Chicago: Rand McNally, 1976), pp. 651-696.

3. See the Scarborough firefighter case, *Labour Law News,* Vol. 5, No. 9 (September 1979).

4. Richard Henderson, *Compensation Management* (Reston, Va.: Reston, 1979), pp. 139-150. See also Patrick Wright and Kenneth Wexley, "How to Choose the Kind of Job Analysis You Really Need," *Personnel,* Vol. 62, no. 5 (May 1985), pp. 51-55.

5. Cascio, *Applied Psychology,* p. 140.

6. Appendix from Henderson, *Compensation Management,* pp. 148-152.

7. Note that the PAQ (and other quantitative techniques) can also be used for job evaluation, which is explained in Chapter 12.

8. Again, we will see that job evaluation is the process through which jobs are compared to one another and their values determined. While usually viewed as a job analysis technique, the PAQ is, in practice, as much or more of a job evaluation technique and could therefore be discussed in either this chapter or in Chapter 12. For a discussion of how to use PAQ for classifying jobs, see Edwin Cornelius III, Theodore Carron, and Marianne Collins, "Job Analysis Models and Job Classification," *Personnel Psychology,* Vol. 32 (Winter 1979), pp. 693-708. See also Edwin Cornelius III, Frank Schmidt, and Theodore Carron, "Job Classification Approaches and the Implementation of Validity Generalization Results," *Personnel Psychology,* Vol. 37, no. 2 (Summer 1984), pp. 247-260.

9. Jack Smith and Milton Hakel, "Comparisons Among Data Sources, Response Bias, and Reliability and Validity of a Structured Job Analysis Questionnaire," *Personnel Psychology,* Vol. 32 (Winter 1979), pp. 677-692. See also Edwin Cornelius III, Angelo Denisi, and Allyn Blencoe, "Expert and Naive Raters Using the PAQ: Does It Matter?" *Personnel Psychology,* Vol. 37, no. 3 (Autumn 1984), pp. 453-464; Lee Friedman and Robert Harvey, "Can Raters with Reduced Job Description Information Provide Accurate Position Analysis Questionnaire (PAQ) Ratings?" *Personnel Psychology,* Vol. 34 (Winter 1986), pp. 779-789.

10. This discussion is based on Howard Olsen et al., "The Use of Functional Job Analysis in Establishing Performance Standards for Heavy Equipment Operators," *Personnel Psychology,* Vol. 34 (Summer 1981), pp. 351-364.

11. Regarding this discussion, see Henderson, *Compensation Management,* pp. 175-184.

12. James Evered, "How to Write a Good Job Description," *Supervisory Management* (April 1981), pp. 14-19.

13. Ibid., p. 16.

14. This discussion is based on ibid.

15. Ibid., p. 16.

16. Ibid., p. 17.

17. Ibid., p. 18.

18. Ernest Dale, *Organizations* (New York: American Management Association, 1967).

19. Frederick Herzberg, "One More Time: How do You Motivate Employees?" *Harvard Business Review* (January-February 1968), p. 89.

SUGGESTED READINGS

McCormick, Ernest J. *Job Analysis: Methods and Applications.* New York: AMACOM, 1979.

Sparks, C. Paul. "Job Analysis." *Canadian Readings in Personnel and Human Resource Management,* eds. Dolan and Schuler. St. Paul, MN: West Publishing Company, 1987.

Job Analysis Format

JOB ANALYSIS INFORMATION FORMAT

Your Job Title_____ Code _____ Date _____

Class Title _____ Department_____

Your Name _____ Facility _____

Superior's Title _____ Prepared by _____

Superior's Name _____

Hours Worked _____ AM/PM _____ to AM/PM _____

1. What is the general purpose of your job?

2. What was your last job? If it was in another organization, please name it.

3. To what job would you normally expect to be promoted?

4. If you regularly supervise others, list them by name and job title.

5. If you supervise others, please check those activities that are part of your supervisory duties:

    ____Hiring   ____Coaching   ____Promoting

    ____Orienting   ____Counseling   ____Compensating

    ____Training   ____Budgeting   ____Disciplining

    ____Scheduling   ____Directing   ____Terminating

    ____Developing   ____Measuring Performance   ____Other_____

6. How would you describe the successful completion and results of your work?

7. *Job Duties*—Please briefly describe WHAT you do and, if possible, HOW you do it. Indicate those duties you consider to be most important and/or most difficult.

    (a) *Daily Duties*—

    (b) *Periodic Duties*—(Please indicate whether weekly, monthly, quarterly etc.)—

    (c) *Duties Performed at Irregular Intervals*—

Signature _____**Date**_____

JOB ANALYSIS INFORMATION FORMAT (continued)

    (d) How long have you been performing these duties?

    (e) Are you now performing unnecessary duties? If yes, please describe.

    (f) Should you be performing duties not now included in your job? If yes, please describe.

8. *Education.* Please check the blank that indicates the educational *requirements* for the job, not your *own* educational background.

    (a)___ No formal education required   (e) ____ 4-Yr college degree

    (b)___ Less than high school diploma. (f) ____ Education beyond under-graduate

    (c)___ High school diploma or equivalent   degree and/or professional license

    (d)___ 2-Yr. college certificate or equivalent

List advanced degrees or specific professional license or certificate required.

Please indicate the education you had when you were placed on this job.

9. *Experience.* Please check the amount needed to perform your job.

    (a)___None   (e) ____More than one year to three years

    (b)___Less than one month   (f) ____Three to five years

    (c)___One month to less than six months (g) ____Five to ten years

    (d)___Six months to one year   (h) ____Over ten years

Please indicate the experience you had when you were placed on this job.

10. *Skill.* Please list any skills required in the performance of your job. (For example, amount of accuracy, alertness, precision in working with described tools, methods, systems, etc.)

Please list skills you possessed when you were placed on this job.

11. *Equipment.* Does your work require the use of any equipment? Yes___ No___.
If Yes, please list the equipment and check whether you use it rarely, occasionally, or frequently.

Equipment	Rarely	Occasionally	Frequently
(a)			
(b)			
(c)			
(d)			

JOB ANALYSIS INFORMATION FORMAT (continued)

12. *Physical Demands.* Please check all undesirable physical demands required on your job and whether you are required to do so rarely, occasionally, or frequently.

	Rarely	Occasionally	Frequently
(a)_____Handling heavy material			
(b)_____Awkward or cramped positions			
(c)_____Excessive working speeds			
(d)_____Excessive sensory requirements (seeing, hearing, touching, smelling, speaking)			
(e)_____Vibrating equipment			
(f) _____Others: _____			

13. *Emotional Demands.* Please check all undesirable emotional demands placed on you by your job whether it is rarely, occasionally, or frequently.

	Rarely	Occasionally	Frequently
(a)_____Contacts with general public	____	____	____
(b)_____Customer contact	____	____	____
(c)_____Close supervision	____	____	____
(d)_____Deadlines under pressure	____	____	____
(e)_____Irrecular activity schedules	____	____	____
(f) _____Working alone	____	____	____
(g)_____Excessive travelling	____	____	____
(h) _____Others:	____	____	____

14. *Work Place Location.* Check type of location of your job and if you consider it to be unsatisfactory or satisfactory.

	Unsatisfactory	Satisfactory
(a)_____Outdoor	____	____
(b)_____Indoor	____	____
(c)_____Underground	____	____
(d)_____Pit	____	____
(e)_____Scaffold	____	____

JOB ANALYSIS INFORMATION FORMAT (continued)

15. *Physical Surroundings.* Please check whether you consider the following physical conditions of your job to be poor, good, or excellent.

	Poor	Good	Excellent
(a)_____Lighting	___	___	___
(b)_____Ventilation	___	___	___
(c)_____Sudden temperature change	___	___	___
(d)_____Vibration	___	___	___
(e)_____Comfort of furnishings	___	___	___

16 *Environmental Conditions.* Please check the objectionable conditions under which you must perform your job and check whether the condition exists rarely, occasionally, or frequently.

	Rarely	Occasionally	Frequently
(a)_____Dust	___	___	___
(b)_____Dirt	___	___	___
(c)_____Heat	___	___	___
(d)_____Cold	___	___	___
(e)_____Fumes	___	___	___
(f)_____Odors	___	___	___
(g)_____Noise	___	___	___
(h)_____Wetness	___	___	___
(i)_____Humidity	___	___	___
(j)_____Others:_____	___	___	

17. *Health and Safety.* Please check all undesirable health and safety factors under which you must perform your job and whether you are required to do so rarely, occasionally, or frequently.

	Rarely	Occasionally	Frequently
(a)_____Height of elevated workplace	___	___	___
(b)_____Radiation	___	___	___
(c)_____Mechanical hazards	___	___	___
(d)_____Moving objects	___	___	___
(e)_____Explosives	___	___	___
(f)_____Electrical hazards	___	___	___
(g)_____Fire	___	___	___
(h)_____Others:_____	___	___	___

SUPERVISORY REVIEW

Do the incumbent's responses to the questionnaire accurately describe the work requirements and the work performed in meeting the responsibilities of the job?

Yes___ No___ . If No, please explain and list any significant omissions or additions.

Date	Title	Signature

SOURCE: Richard Henderson, *Compensation Management: Rewarding Performance*, 2nd ed., copyright 1979, pp. 148-152. Reprinted by permission of Prentice-Hall, Englewood Cliffs, N.J.

CHAPTER
FIVE RECRUITMENT OF HUMAN RESOURCES

After studying this chapter, you should be able to

1. Explain the recruitment process.
2. Describe the internal and external factors that affect recruitment practices.
3. Identify the sources and methods of obtaining both internal and external job candidates.
4. Discuss the main features in recruiting human resources.

OVERVIEW

The main purpose of this chapter is to explain how an organization develops a pool of qualified job candidates. We discuss the factors involved in recruiting human resources, such as recruitment planning, organizational recruiting policies, employment equity, and labour market considerations. We also discuss the methods used to recruit from internal and external sources, from job posting to televised advertising, and weigh the pros and cons of each method. We conclude with a section on the stages in the individual choice process.

INTRODUCTION: WHAT IS RECRUITMENT?

The **recruitment** of human resources is the process of searching for and locating potential job candidates of high quality and in adequate numbers so that the organization may select the most appropriate individuals to staff its job requirements.

recruitment

The Purposes and Importance of Recruitment

Recruitment represents a very important coordinating link between the organization and the environment in which the organization aims to thrive and prosper. The purposes of recruitment are to

- Increase the pool of job applicants at a minimum cost
- Meet the organization's legal and social obligations regarding the demographic composition of its work force
- Help increase the success rate of the selection process by reducing the number of applicants who are either poorly qualified or have the wrong skills[1]
- Bring the organization and qualified potential job candidates together to enable the optimal fit between the organization, the individual, the job, and the environment

FACTORS AFFECTING THE RECRUITMENT OF HUMAN RESOURCES

An organization's recruiting efforts and strategies are influenced by a variety of factors. These include recruitment planning, organizational recruiting policies, employment equity, and labour market considerations.

Recruitment Planning

The recruiting plan is a course of action designed to achieve recruiting goals and objectives. The design, development, and implementation of the plan is an essential process for selecting the appropriate methods for identifying and attracting available job prospects. An important consideration in planning a company's recruitment process is the development of sources that demonstrate good retention after employment (low turnover) and avoidance of sources that demonstrate higher turnover.[2] Recruiting plans must include strategies aimed at attracting the best qualified applicants. However, recruitment planning involves much more. Knowledge of the labour market conditions, competitor requirements, and excessive recruitment demands imposed by poor retention of hires are essential factors that should be incorporated into human resource planning as a context for recruitment.[3] Another important aspect of the recruiting plan is the preparation of a recruiting budget. This covers cost estimates of the funds required and allowed for recruiting efforts. These costs include advertising, travel, telephone calls, etc.

Recruitment planning can be aided by an organization's recruitment efforts in the past. Two concepts are relevant in this regard: recruiting yield and time-lapse data.[4] An organization may use *recruiting yield* to determine the number of applicants it must generate to hire the required number of new employees.[5] Figure 5.1 illustrates a pyramid that graphically displays the number of new leads that must be generated through recruiting efforts to hire the required number of new employees. In this case, the Ross Accounting Company knows it must hire 50 new entry-level accountants next year. From its experience it also knows that the ratio

FIGURE 5.1
Recruiting Yield
Pyramid

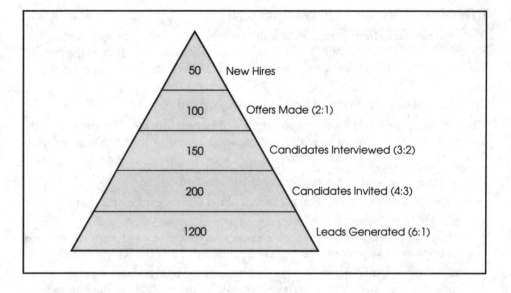

of offers made to actual new hires is two to one (about half the people to whom they make offers accept those offers). Similarly, the firm knows that the ratio of candidates interviewed to offers made is three to two, while the ratio of candidates invited for interviews to candidates actually interviewed has been four to three. Finally, the firm knows that the ratio of new leads generated to candidates actually invited has been six to one; in other words, of six leads that come in from the firm's advertising, college recruiting, and other recruiting efforts, only one typically gets an invitation to come in for an interview. Given these ratios, the firm knows it must generate 1200 leads in order to be able to invite 200 viable candidates to its offices for interviews. It will then get to interview about 150 of those it invites, and from these it will make 100 offers. Of those 100 offers, half (or 50 new CAs) will be hired. (a ratio of 2:1)

The average number of days that the records show it takes a company to generate the yield ratios is the *time-lapse data*. The record indicates that in the case of The Ross Company it took the following: six days from application (and the submission of resumes) to invitation, five days from interview to job offer, six days from job offer to acceptance, and 23 days from acceptance of job offer to commencement of work by the individual. This indicates that the organization must initiate recruitment efforts 45 days prior to the anticipated time that job openings will occur. The remaining 195 days may be used for planning and coordinating recruitment strategies.

Organizational Recruiting Policies

One of the most important reasons for recruiting quality job candidates is that the calibre of organization's labour force significantly determines its strength and success. In order to ensure success with its recruitment programs, the organization usually establishes formal or informal, carefully worked-out, and stable recruitment policies, also called employment policies.

These policies outline the organization's statements of intent and serve as a guide to action. Employment policies provide appropriate administrative guidelines to govern the conduct of the human resource specialists and line managers who must administer the recruitment, selection, placement, orientation, and socialization programs. Employment policies serve to ensure consistency, fairness, and equality in treatment. They also present the organization's aim in terms of meeting its employment equity goals and time-tables.

Employment Equity

An organization's recruiting efforts are affected by employment equity legislation enacted by Parliament and by the provincial legislatures. Employment equity requires that recruitment practices enable individuals in designated groups to be considered for employment. The legislations of the federal government and two provinces, Saskatchewan and Quebec, impose mandatory employment equity programs. The legislations of the other provinces call only for voluntary Employment Equity Programs. The federal government's legislation affects federally regulated employers with more than 100 employees, as well as companies bidding on contracts to supply goods and services to the federal government. These employers are required to incorporate into their recruiting plans, methods, and activities instruments to attract qualified job applicants from designated groups. In order to meet this objective, employers are urged to use non-traditional methods in their recruiting process. One such non-traditional method is to advertise in newspapers serving ethnic communities. (See Chapter 2 for a comprehensive discussion of employment equity.)

Labour Market Considerations

The **labour market** environment exerts strong influences on recruitment. An employer may adopt a policy of promote-from-within, fill all vacancies externally, or a combination of both. Regardless of the policy followed, the employer must go to the labour market in order to make net additions to its work force. The labour market may be defined as the geographical and demographical area within which an organization recruits employees and individuals seek employment. It is the environment where the forces of supply and demand meet and interact.

labour market

Conditions in the labour market affect the availability of workers, the scope of the recruiting effort, the methods to be used, and both monetary and non-monetary compensation to be paid in order to attract applicants for jobs.[6] Organizations must take a variety of factors into consideration when determining the quantity of labour that is available for recruiting. It is usually the case that the supply of labour is influenced by the population in the market, the reputation of the organization, the attractiveness of job, commuting patterns, and the levels of unemployment. The composition of the labour market is not fixed and unchanging in size and demographics. The labour market expands and contracts in proportion to the intensity of the demand for labour. Labour markets may be national or international, regional or local.[7] A tight labour market, with low levels of unemployment, is favourable to a job applicant, since there are more jobs than applicants.[8] Conversely a loose labour market benefits an employer as there are more applicants to choose from.[9]

An organization can find out about the state of the labour market and supply of certain types of labour through various publications of Employment and Immigration Canada, Canada Employment Centres at the local and provincial departments of labour, industry associations' newsletters, and journals of crafts, unions, or professional organizations.[10] Information regarding labour force characteristics on a national, provincial and in some cases by a large city basis is contained in the monthly labour force survey published by Statistics Canada.[11]

Whenever an employer decides to go to the labour market to recruit new employees, it must be prepared to operate in a labour market environment that is unorganized and unstructured for the most part. The procedures by which an employers recruit workers and the manner by which job candidates seek and obtain jobs is characterized by a variety of methods and approaches. At times pure chance pays a significant role in determining whether Jane Doe gets a job in company A or in company B. Many job applicants obtain employment through mutual friends, acquaintances, and relatives (referrals); others through unsolicited methods such as direct visit (walk-ins) to the employer, or direct application (write-ins) to the employment office; others through trade unions, professional associations, and trade journals; and still others through employment agencies. The process is also channelled through public agencies, as well as through media advertising.

A labour market is influenced by various factors. These include a divergent wage rate for similar or the same type of jobs. This variation in wage rates for similar jobs is caused by a variety of factors. Among these are the company's ability to pay, supply and demand for labour, productivity, organized labour, and the organization's attitude towards employee compensation, as well as nonwage factors as organizational climate, job security, and seniority.

Other characteristics of a labour market are labour mobility and lack of mobility. Labour mobility is characterized by employees who are willing to relocate to different areas to obtain a job. Lack of labour mobility is characterized by current workers' unwillingness to be transferred to a new location and by new recruits' unwillingness to relocate to a different area to obtain employment. There are many reasons for workers' reluctance to relocate. One might be the existence of seniority systems or employee benefits that accrue to long-service employees in some companies. Another might be new recruits possessing inaccurate information and incomplete knowledge about the job, working conditions, and the area where the new job is located.

INTERNAL RECRUITING SOURCES AND METHODS

There are two primary sources available to an organization for recruiting job candidates. These are: internal sources (current employees), and external sources (external prospects). There are many methods that the organization may use to recruit job candidates. The sources and methods used depend on whether the organization employs internal or external sources or a combination of both to fill job vacancies.

Internal recruiting serves to provide opportunities for employee advancement, career growth, and development as well as contributing to the enhancement of employee morale. Filling open positions with inside job candidates is fulfilling

FIGURE 5.2
Advantages and
Disadvantages of
Promote-From-Within-
Policy

Advantages

- Rewards successful performance
- Increases morale
- Boosts employee loyalty
- Enhances employee commitment to organization goals
- Eliminates the need to experiment with unknown people
- Requires less orientation and training
- Reduces risk in selection and placement

Disadvantages

- Prevents the infusion of new blood, new ideas, new skills, new knowledge, and new abilities to the organization.
- The process may be unnecessarily long, time consuming, and costly. This often occurs when the organization's policies dictate that all applicants must be interviewed. Yet the manager often knows ahead of time exactly who he or she wants to hire, and requiring the person to interview a stream of unsuspecting inside candidates is therefore a waste of time for all concerned.
- Groups may not be as satisfied when their new boss is appointed from within their own ranks as when he or she is a new comer.
- It is difficult for the newly chosen leader to shake off the reputation of being "one of the gang".

what is called a promote-from-within policy. A promote-from-within policy has many advantages and disadvantages. Figure 5.2 lists the pros and cons.

Perhaps the biggest disadvantage of the promote-from-within policy is inbreeding. When an entire management team has been brought up through the ranks, there may be a tendency to make decisions "by the book" and to maintain the status quo, when an innovative and new direction is what is called for. Balancing the benefits of morale and loyalty with the drawback of inbreeding is thus a problem. Promotion from within, to be effective, requires using job posting, human resources records, and skill banks.[13]

Job Posting

job posting

Essentially **job posting** is written notification to all current employees of job vacancies. Such notifications is usually posted on company bulletin boards and company publications including newsletters. Job posting has a number of advantages. Figure 5.3 illustrates the advantages and disadvantages of job posting.

Many companies have established policies to govern job posting. A statement of one firm's job-posting policies is presented in Figure 5.4.

Skill Inventories

skill inventories

Another approach to internal recruiting is the use of **skill inventories** (skill banks). With this method, the organization searches through its skill inventories to uncover employees who are qualified for available job vacancies. These individuals are contacted to determine whether they want to apply for any of the vacancies. The use of skill inventories may be coordinated with job postings to ensure that all qualified job candidates are aware of the vacancies. (See also our discussion on HRIS in Chapter 3.)

FIGURE 5.3
Advantages and Disadvantages of Job Posting

Advantages

- Provides equal opportunity for all qualified employees
- Provides every qualified employee with an opportunity to obtain a better job
- Reduces the likelihood of special deals and favouritism
- Demonstrates the organization's commitment to employee career growth and development
- Communicates to employees the organization's policies and guidelines regarding promotions and transfers

Disadvantages

- Unsuccessful job candidates may become demotivated, demoralized, discontented, and unhappy if feedback is not communicated in a timely and sensitive manner.
- Tensions may rise if it appears that a qualified internal job candidate was passed over for an equallly qualified or less qualified external candidate.
- The decision on which candidate to select may be more difficult if there is more than one equally qualified candidate.

FIGURE 5.4
One Firm's Job Posting Policies

Eligibility

- All permanent employees who have completed their probationary period are eligible to use the open position listing policy in order to request consideration for a position that would constitute a growth opportunity.
- Employees who have been promoted or transferred, or who have changed jobs for any reason, must wait a six-month period before applying for a different position.

Policy

- A list of open positions will be communicated to all employees in all facilities. Notices will include information on job title, salary grade, department, supervisor's name and title, location, brief description of the job content, qualifications, and instructions concerning whether or not candidates will be expected to demonstrate their skills during the interview process.
- Basic job qualifications and experience needed to fill the job will be listed on the sheet. Employees should consult with the human resource department if there are questions concerning the promotional opportunities associated with the job.
- Open position lists will remain on bulletin boards for five working days.
- Forms for use in requesting consideration for an open position may be obtained from the human resource department
- The human resource department will review requests to substantiate the employee's qualifications for the position.
- The hiring manager will review requests for employees inside the company before going outside the company to fill the position.
- It is the responsibility of the employees to notify their managers of their intent to interview for an open position.
- The hiring manager makes the final decision when filling the position; however, the guidelines for filling any open position are based on the employees' ability, qualifications, experience, background, and the skills they possess that will allow them to

(continued)

carry out the job successfully. It is the responsibility of the hiring manager to notify the previous manager of the intent to hire the employee.

- Employees who are aware of a pending opening, and who will be on vacation when the opening occurs, may leave a request with the human resource department for consideration.

- It is the manager's responsibility to ensure that the human resource department has notified all internal applicants that they did or did not get the job before general announcement by the manager of the person who did get the job.

- "Blanket" applications will not be accepted. Employees should apply each time a position they are interested in becomes available.

- Since preselection often occurs, employees should be planning for their career growth by scheduling time with potential managers before posting, to become acquainted with them, and to secure developmental information to be used in acquiring appropriate skills for future consideration.

- There are occasions when jobs will not be listed. Two such examples might include (1) when a job can be filled best by natural progression or is a logical career path for an employee, and (2) when a job is created to provide a development opportunity for a specific high-performance employee.

- In keeping with this policy, managers are encouraged to work with employees in career development in order to assist them in pursuing upward movement in a particular career path or job ladder.

What the Human Resource Department Does

- Reviews applications for open positions, and checks to see if applicants meet minimum time-on-the-job requirements.

- Reviews background material of applicants with hiring manager. Hiring manager selects the employees qualified for interviews.

- Notifies all applicants who will not be interviewed, and gives them the reasons why.

- Provides counselling to applicants who will not be interviewed.

- Answers questions from interviewed candidates concerning selection, if the interviewing extends beyond the normal three-week period.

What the Manager Does

- Selects employees to be interviewed for the position.

- Contacts employees selected and arranges for interviews.

- Screens interview applicants (may contact previous manager for reference).

- Decides who is the best-qualified candidate.

- Informs the human resource department of the selection and provides reasons for rejecting unsuccessful applicants.

- Notifies the successful applicant and his or her current manager.

- Arranges release dates with the current manager (normally two weeks).

- Completes application forms in full, at the bottom of the form, and answers all appropriate question blocks as necessary.

- Notifies the unsuccessful candidates, advising them of reasons for rejection.

- Makes sure that the interview process does not extend more than three weeks beyond the date the notice comes off the bulletin board.

SOURCE: Mary E. Cook, *Human Resource Director's Handbook* (Englewood Cliffs, N.J.: Prentice-Hall, Inc., 1984), pp. 77–78.

EXTERNAL RECRUITING SOURCES AND METHODS

Regardless of the recruiting policy followed by an employer, it must go to the external market from time to time to make net additions to its labour force. External recruiting brings to the organization people with new ideas, creative problem-solving approaches, and new attitudes. Other advantages are as follows:

- A larger pool of qualified job candidates is made available.
- Internal political infighting by employees jockeying for promotion is eliminated.
- New production methods, work techniques, and innovation may be brought to the organization.
- It is usually more economical to hire already trained and skilled job candidates.
- Job candidates from non-traditional sources may be available to help the organization meet its employment equity mandated goals and time-tables.

Walk-ins

Individuals who voluntarily go to organizations to apply for jobs without having been invited by the organization and without referral are called **walk-ins**. These unsolicited individuals constitute a relatively inexpensive source of job applicants for organizations. Walk-ins are often asked to complete an application to determine their skills, knowledge, abilities, and interests. The applications are then screened and those considered suitable are kept on file and are pulled when a vacancy becomes available and external sources are being considered. It is the practice of some organizations to interview all walk-ins as a public relations courtesy even though no jobs are open. Walk-ins' applications are often kept on file for a period of three to six months.

walk-ins

Write-ins

People who voluntarily submit unsolicited resumes to organizations are called **write-ins**. These unsolicitated resumes are a valuable source of applicants at relatively no cost to organizations. People who submit unsolicited resumes to organizations are usually seeking managerial, professional, sales, and technical positions. A common practice of many organizations is to have their recruiters review the unsolicited resumes to determine whether there are any applicants who are suitable match for any existing recruitment needs. Desirable applicants would be given further considerations. Applicants who are considered unsuitable are often sent a brief thank-you letter for their interest in the organization.

write-ins

Employee Referrals

These applicants are generally referred by present employees who may be their friends or relatives. Some organizations encourage such applicants by mounting an **employee referrals** campaign. Announcements of openings and requests for referrals are made in the organization's bulletins and posted on bulletin boards. Prizes are offered for referrals that culminate in hirings. This sort of campaign can cut recruiting costs by eliminating advertising and agency fees. It can result in higher quality candidates (since many people are reluctant to refer less qualified can-

employee referrals

didates). But the success of the campaign depends largely on the morale of the employees.[14]

Forty percent of the firms responding to one survey said they use some sort of employee referral system and actually hire about 15% of their people directly through such referrals by current workers. A cash award for referring candidates who are hired is the most common type of referral incentive. Naturally, the total amount a firm spends on its referral program will depend on its size. The cost per hire, however, is the important consideration and was uniformly low—far below the comparable cost of an employment service.[15] There are many disadvantages of employee referrals. These include:

- The potential of inbreeding and nepotism to cause morale problems.
- The friends of an employee who was rejected for a promotion may also feel rejected.
- Employees who recommend job candidates are usually dissatisfied when their job candidates are not hired. They could show their unhappiness by being uncooperative with the new employee.
- The applicants may not be the right mix that the employer needs to meet employment equity requirements.

Perhaps one of the biggest drawbacks is that employees are likely to recommend their friends or acquaintances who possess backgrounds similar to their own in such areas as age, race, sex, education, religion, aptitude, interest, personality, and preferences. This sameness or similarity in background often creates problems for the organization in terms of meeting its affirmative action and employment equity objectives and goals.

Employment Agencies

employment agency

The term **employment agency** includes a broad category of recruitment organizations and activities.[16] There are several reasons to use an employment agency for some or all of an organization's recruiting needs.[17] Some specific situations in which the organization might want to turn to employment agencies include the following:

1. The employer does not have its own human resource department and is therefore not geared up to do the necessary recruiting and screening.
2. The employer has found it difficult in the past to generate a pool of qualified applicants.
3. The employer's need for only a few people or an irregular demand for new employees makes it inefficient to maintain an elaborate recruiting office.
4. A particular opening must be filled quickly.
5. There is a perceived need to attract a greater number of minority or female applicants.
6. The recruitment effort is aimed at reaching individuals who are currently employed and who might therefore feel more comfortable answering ads from and dealing with employment agencies rather than competing companies.

There are many advantages of employment agencies. They provide prescreened and in many cases well screened applicants, and save the organization time by finding, interviewing, and selecting only the most qualified candidates for the organization's final hiring process. They cut down the number of people for the employer to interview, and ensure that the employer interviews only the right people. To match the employer's job specifications with the abilities and interests of potential job applicants, employment agencies perform a variety of services including advertising; interviewing; testing for skills, aptitudes and interests; and reviewing credentials and work experience.[18]

One of the main advantages of an employment agency is that it prescreens applicants for job, but this advantage can also backfire.[19] For example, the employment agency's screening may allow poor applicants to bypass the preliminary stages of the organization's own selection process. Unqualified applicants may thus be sent directly to the supervisors responsible for the hiring, who may in turn naively hire them. Such errors may in turn show up in high turnover and absenteeism rates, morale problems, and low quality and productivity. To help avoid such problems, two experts suggest the following:

1. An organization should give the agency an accurate and complete job description. The better the employment agency understands the job or jobs to be filled, the greater the likelihood that a reasonable pool of applicants will be generated.

2. An organization should specify the devices or tools that the employment agency should use in screening potential applicants. Tests, application blanks, and interviews should be a proven part of the employer's selection process. At the very least, the employer should know which devices the agency uses and consider their relevance to the selection process. Of particular concern would be any subjective decision-making procedures used by the agency.

3. Where possible, the organization should periodically review data on accepted or rejected candidates. This will serve as a check on the screening process and provide valuable information if there is a legal challenge to the fairness of the selection process.

4. If feasible, the organization should develop a long-term relationship with one or two agencies. It may also be advantageous to designate one person to serve as the liaison between the employer and agency. Similarly, a specific contact on the agency's staff to coordinate the employer's recruiting needs can be advantageous.

Public Employment Agencies (Canada Employment Centres)

The federal government of Canada operates over 800 **Canada Employment Centres** (CEC) throughout Canada. The purpose of these centres is to assist employers in finding suitable job candidates in the labour market to meet their labour force needs, and to assist job seekers to find suitable employment at no cost to either the employer or the job seeker.[20]

The process of matching employers to job seekers works in the following manner. When employers have job vacancies, they notify the CEC about the jobs and their requirements. The information about these vacancies is then posted on openly displayed cards or listings at the CEC's job information centre. Prospective employees are then contacted and interviewed by the Centre's counsellors. Applicants who are considered to be qualified are referred to the employers. In larger metropolitan regions such as Toronto, Montreal, and Vancouver, a *metropolitan order pro-*

Canada Employment
Centres

cessing system is available to the users. This is a computerized system which automatically conveys job information about vacancies listed at one centre to all other centres in that region. This system enables employers to have their job vacancies posted easily and quickly in multiple centres in the regions, thus enabling recruitment from a larger labour market. The CEC also maintains a computerized national job bank that links centres in all provinces. This system enables employers to recruit nationally.

The CEC also provides a variety of other services including aptitude and skill assessments, career and vocational counselling, and training referrals.

Private Employment Agencies

Private employment agencies provide two basic functions: they expand the pool of job applicants available to the hiring employers and they perform preliminary interviewing and screening. The basic difference between public and private agencies is that the majority of private agencies bill employers for their services. Private employment agencies are quite widespread throughout Canada. They are particularly good sources of white collar, blue collar, clerical, professional, technical, and managerial applicants.

Many private employment agencies concentrate in a particular field (e.g. computer specialists, accounting, operations managers, executives). Many agencies do a careful job of interviewing, testing, counselling, and screening in order to match employer's demands and specifications with the skills, knowledge, and abilities of job applicants, but some private employment agencies merely provide a pool of applicants for the employers to do their own screening.

Employers understandably contact those agencies with good reputations and those that are well-respected to meet their labour force needs. Private employment agencies earn bad reputations when they fail to screen the job applicants thoroughly. Some human resource specialists and line managers complain that a major problem is that agencies not only fail to screen applicants thoroughly but make some applicants appear to be more qualified than they actually are by embellishing their resumes and coaching them for employment interviews with hiring employers.

Temporary Help Agencies

These agencies—such as Office Overload—exist in all major cities in Canada. They help employers cope with seasonal work, peak work loads, vacation fill-ins, temporary replacements for sick employees, and a variety of short-term assignments which a company's own employees may be unable to perform.[21] These agencies are a very good source of supplemental workers. They do not provide job candidates for hiring employers, although it is not uncommon for the occasional help to be recruited and hired as full-time employees. Some temporary help workers actually work for the agencies, and are "hired-out" or "on loan" to requesting employers. Payment for their services is made directly to the agencies.

Executive Search Firms and Management Consultants

executive recruiters

These firms operate in substantially the same way as private agencies. **Executive recruiters** (also known as "head hunters") are retained by employers to seek out top management talent for their clients. They fill jobs in the $40 000 and up category, although $50 000 is often the lower limit. The percentage of a firm's positions filled by these services might be small, but these jobs would include the most crucial executive and technical positions. Head hunters may be the only source for an employer's executive positions. Their fees are always paid by the employer.

These firms can be very useful. They have many contacts and are especially adept at contacting qualified candidates who are employed and not actively looking to change jobs. They can also keep the firm's name confidential until late into the search process. The recruiter can also save top management time by doing the preliminary work of advertising for the position and screening what could turn out to be hundreds of applicants. The recruiter's fee could actually turn out to be insignificant compared to the cost of the time the executive saves.

But there are some pitfalls. It is essential for employers to explain completely what sort of candidate is required—and why. Some recruiters are also more salespeople than professionals. They may be more interested in persuading the employer to hire a candidate than in finding one that will really do the job. Recruiters also claim that what their client says he or she wants is often not really what is wanted. In choosing a recruiter, one expert suggests following these guidelines:[22]

1. *The agency chosen must be capable of conducting a thorough search.* Under the code of the Association of Executive Recruiting Consultants, a head hunter cannot approach the executive talent of a former client for a vacancy with a new client for a period of two years after completing a search for the former client. Former clients are thus off-limits to the recruiter for this period and the recruiter must thus make his or her search from a constantly diminishing market. It could turn out to be particularly difficult for the largest executive recruiting firms to deliver a top-notch candidate since their best potential candidates may already be working for their former clients.

2. *The HR representative should meet the recruiter.* The person handling the search will determine the fate of the search. If this person does not have the ability to aggressively seek out top-notch candidates and sell them on the employer's firm, it is unlikely that the firm will get to see the best candidates. Therefore the person who will be handling the assignment must be assessed by the firm.

3. *The agency's charges should be clarified.* Search firm's fees range from 25% to 35% of the guaranteed annual income of the position being filled. They are often payable one-third as a retainer at the outset, one-third at the end of 30 days, and one-third after 60 days, and are not necessarily only paid on a contingency basis. Often, a fee is payable whether or not the search is terminated for any reason.

4. *A recruiter the organization can trust must be chosen.* This is essential because this person will not only find the firm's strengths, but its weaknesses too. It is therefore important that someone is found who that can be trusted with what may be privileged information.

5. *The firm should talk to a couple of the agency's clients.* Finally, it may be helpful to request the names of two or three companies for whom the search firm has recently completed assignments. Questions like, "Did their appraisal of the candidate seem accurate?" "Did they really conduct a search, or was the job simply filled from their files?" And, "were time and care taken in developing the job specification?" are good choices.[23]

It is worth noting that there are also several things for job candidates to keep in mind when dealing with executive search firms. First, most of these firms pay little

FIGURE 5.5
Traits Sought by
College Recruiters

Intellectual ability

Good presentation skills

Self confidence, humility, poise

Good personal appearance

Evidence of initiative, enthusiasm

Good diction, good speech habits and expression

Maturity, leadership potential

Established career goals, ambition, decisiveness

Realistic wage expectations—more interest in the job opportunity than its monetary rewards

Good preparation for the interview

Motivation

heed to unsolicited resumes, preferring instead to ferret out their own candidates. Some firms have also been known to present an unpromising candidate to a client simply to make their other one or two proposed candidates look that much better. Also, executive recruiters and their clients are usually much more impressed with candidates who are obviously "not looking" for jobs. That eagerness to get a job has actually been the downfall of many candidates.[24]

There are many advantages to the use of executive search firms. These firms can provide a fairly comprehensive survey of available applicants in the target industry. Their screening of candidates can be consistent and thorough and can lead to a better match between the company's job requirements and an individual's needs. Finally, since they ensure a high degree of confidentiality, they attract candidates who are reluctant to deal directly with the hiring company.[25]

Educational Institutions

Universities and colleges are excellent sources of applicants for a variety of positions in organizations. These include entry-level sales, technical, professional, and management trainee positions in small, medium, and large organizations. Each year a large number of companies throughout Canada visit selected campuses at least once per year to conduct on-campus recruitment activities. These activities also include visits to classrooms and lectures to seek out promising students and to provide career counselling.

Most Canadian universities and community colleges have placement and counselling centres. Placement is usually carried out by a branch of Canada Employment Centre.[26] These centres keep a list of job openings with major companies. Placement centres on campuses also assist employers and students by holding job fairs on campuses: these programs make employers familiar with the programs offered by the institutions and facilitate recruiting. The placement centres also provide pre-screening services to hiring employers. Under this service students submit their applications and resumes to the placement centres, which match them with employers' staffing needs. The employers select those applicants they consider appropriate and arrange for interviews through the placement centres.

The counselling centres help students, individually or in groups, with preparation of resumes, covering letters, and application forms. Counsellors also administer skill assessment tests to the students.

Recruiters on the campus seek to accomplish two main jobs: the main function is *screening* or determining whether candidates are worthy of further consideration. Exactly which traits to look for will of course be a function of the employer's specific recruiting needs. However, the checklist presented in Figure 5.5 is a typical list of traits sought by college recruiters.

While the main function is to find and screen good candidates, the other aim is to attract them to the firm. The recruiter must help to sell the employer to the interviewee.

As summarized in Figure 5.6, employers choose their college recruiters largely on the basis of who can do the best job of identifying good applicants and filling all vacancies. Factors in selecting the schools in which to recruit are noted in Figure 5.7. They include reputation and performance of previous hires from the school.

There are two main problems with on-campus recruiting. First, it is usually both expensive and time-consuming from the point of view of the people doing the recruiting. To be done correctly, schedules have to be set well in advance, company brochures have to be printed, records of interviews have to be kept, and much recruiting time has to be spent on campus. A second problem is that recruiters themselves are sometimes ineffective (or worse). Many recruiters do not effectively screen their student candidates. For example, students' physical attractiveness has often been found to outweigh other, more valid, traits and skill.[27] Some recruiters also tend to assign females to "female-type" jobs and males to "male-type" jobs.[28] One suggestion is to train recruiters before sending them to the college campus.[29]

FIGURE 5.6
Factors in Selecting College Recruiters

Recruiting Aspect	Strength (1–7)	
Identification of high-quality applicants		5.8
Professionalism of recruiters		5.6
Filling all vacancies	5.5	
Generating the right number of applicants		5.5
High performance of new recruits	5.4	
High retention of new recruits	5.3	
High job acceptance rates	5.0	
Administrative procedures	4.7	
Turn-around times		4.5
Planning and goal setting	4.5	
Meeting EEO/AA targets		4.4
Program evaluation	4.3	
Cost control	4.2	

SOURCE: Reprinted with permission from Personnel Administrator (March 1987), The American Society for Personnel Administration, 606 North Washington Street, Alexandria, VA 22314

FIGURE 5.7
Factors in Selecting
Schools in which to
Recruit

Topic	Importance (1–7)
Reputation in critical skill areas	6.5
General school reputation	5.8
Performance of previous hires from the school	5.7
Location	5.1
Reputation of faculty in critical skill areas	5.1
Previous job offer and acceptance rates	4.6
Past practice	4.5
Number of potential recruits	4.5
Ability to meet EEO targets	4.3
Cost	3.9
Familiarity with faculty members	3.8
SAT or GRE scores	3.0
Alma mater of CEO or other executives	3.0

SOURCE: Reprinted with permission from Personnel Administrator (March 1987), The American Society for Personnel Administration, 606 North Washington Street, Alexandria, VA 22314

Professional and Trade Associations

Professional and trade associations are very good, major sources of experienced job candidates. Many professional and trade associations conduct ongoing placement activities on behalf of their members in order to assist recently graduated or experienced professionals get jobs. Many organizations place classified advertisements in the journals, magazines, and newsletters of various associations. There are many different professional and trade associations in Canada. These organizations, by virtue of their diversity, enable hiring employers to key in on desired specialties. Members of these associations are considered to be well-informed and up to date on new ideas and technology that have an impact on their field.

Labour Organizations

Recruiters of many skilled trades are commonly required to hire recruits through the local union hiring halls. This is especially prevalent in the construction trade. It is usually more convenient for recruiters to hire plumbers, electricians, and longshoremen through union hiring halls because the unions maintain a roster of job seekers in their respective industries and many contractors often recruit skilled labour on a per-project basis.

Advertising

Recruitment advertising is one of the most often used recruiting methods used by hiring employers. It includes newspapers, radio, T.V., and professional journal advertising. Newspaper advertising seems to be the most popular of the several advertising methods used.[30] Depending on the needs of the hiring employer, advertisements convey specific information about the employer and specific job-related information to almost any potential job applicant in any desired labour market.

For advertising to bring desired results, there are two issues that must be addressed: the media to be used, and the construction of the ad. The selection of the best medium—whether it be the local paper, the national paper, or a technical journal—depends on the type of positions for which the organization is recruiting.

The advertising media selected by the organization and the construction of the ad are very important. Selecting the type of medium and the content of the recruitment ad is a process that is often undertaken by human resource professionals sometimes in conjunction with an ad agency. To achieve optimum results from an advertisement, an organization should use the following four-point guide called AIDA to construct their advertisements:

- *The ad should attract attention*. Those ads using wide borders or lots of empty space stand out. For the same reason, key positions should be advertised in display ads, where they will not get lost in the columns of classified ads.

- *The ad should develop interest in the job*. Interest may be created by the nature of the job itself, such as, "you will thrive on challenging work." Sometimes, other aspects of the job, such as its location or working conditions or the company's reputation, can be used to create interest.

- *The ad should create desire for the job*. This may be done by capitalizing on the interest factors plus the extras of the job in terms of job satisfaction, career development, travel, or similar advantages. The ad should be written with the target audience in mind.

- *The ad should instigate action*. Pick up almost any ad and it will contain some statement like "Call today," "Fax your resume," "Write today for more information," or "Go to the site of our next job fair."

If done properly, advertisements can be an effective instrument for recruiting as well as for communicating the organization's corporate image to the general public. Figures 5.8 and 5.9 show two recruiting ads that incorporate most of the four-point AIDA guidelines discussed above.

There are two general types of advertisements: **want ads** and **blind ads**. Want ads describe the job, specifications and compensation, the hiring employer and the recruitment office to which to submit applications and/or resumes. Blind ads are similar to want ads. The only difference is the omission of the identity and street address of the hiring employer. Potential job candidates are instructed to forward their responses to a post office box number or a newspaper box number.

There are many factors which make advertising a very useful recruiting method. Hiring employers can use advertisements to reach and attract potential job applicants from a diverse labour market in as wide or as narrow a geographical location as they desire. In order to meet employment equity mandated goals and timetables hiring employers may need to recruit from nontraditional sources; one way this can be done is to place advertisements in designated minority newspapers. The advantages and disadvantages of advertisements in major types of media are shown in Table 5.1.

want ads
blind ads

Pros and Cons of Various Recruiting Sources

Which sources provide the best candidates? One study suggests that employee referrals are perhaps the best source of employees, while newspaper ads and employment agencies are among the worst.[31] Another study compared four recruiting sources (convention/journal ads, newspapers, college placement, and self-initiated

FIGURE 5.8
Newspaper
Recruitment
Advertisement

WE CARE ABOUT KIDS

at the Dr. Everett Chalmers Hospital
in Fredericton, New Brunswick

We want to continue to give our kids

THE BEST NURSING CARE POSSIBLE.

That's why we need

A HEAD NURSE WITH VISION

who can lead our Paediatrics Department
into the Year 2000.
We want a "People Person".
A leader who will challenge
our staff to be the best they can be.
And, one who will help us to
enhance our "Family Approach" to care.

Qualifications:
Must have Bachelor of Nursing Degree
Must be eligible for Registration with Nurses Association of N.B.
Must have a minimum of 3 years experience in Paediatrics
Must have a proven leadership/teaching skills

If you want to be part of

A DYNAMIC AND CHALLENGING REGIONAL HOSPITAL

Call or write by August 30, 1991:

Dawn Muzzerall-Foran
Recruitment Officer
Dr. Everett Chalmers Hospital
P.O. Box 9000
Fredericton, New Brunswick
E3B 5N5

(506) 452-5400

SOURCE: Dr. Everett Chalmers Hospital, Fredericton, New Brunswick. Reproduced by permission.

FIGURE 5.9
Newspaper
Recruitment
Advertisement

Valuing diversity
... recognizing service

Manager
Human Resources
$54,800 - $63,900

If you are an experienced, skilled professional who thrives in a challenging, constantly changing environment, consider joining the **Ministry of Community and Social Services'** CPRI, to provide leadership in the delivery of human resources services. With approximately 500 employees, CPRI provides services to developmentally handicapped and emotionally disturbed children and their families. As a member of the management team, your responsibilities will include recruitment, employee relations, employment equity, human resources planning, pension/benefits administration, organizational design and position analysis, classification and administration. **Location: London.**

Qualifications: Sound, practical, human resources management experience; thorough knowledge of all areas of human resources; excellent leadership, communication, interpersonal, analytical, problem-solving, organization and administrative skills; innovation; creativity; knowledge of human resources information systems.

Please send application or resume, quoting file CPRI-21/91, by Aug. 2, 1991 to: Administrator, CPRI, 600 Sanatorium Road, London, Ontario, N6H 3W7.

Ontario
Public Service
DEDICATED TO EMPLOYMENT EQUITY

SOURCE: CPRI, Ministry of Community and Social Services, 600 Sanatorium Road, London, Ontario. Reproduced by permission.

TABLE 5.1 Advantages and Disadvantages of the Major Types of Media

Type of Medium	Advantages	Disadvantages	When to Use
Newspapers	Short deadlines Ad size flexibility Circulation concentrated in specific geographic areas Classified sections well organized for easy access by active job seekers	Easy for prospects to ignore Considerable competitive clutter Circulation not specialized—you must pay for great amount of unwanted readers Poor printing quality	When you want to limit recruiting to a specific area When sufficient numbers of prospects are clustered in a specific area When enough prospects are reading help-wanted ads to fill hiring needs
Magazines	Specialized magazines reach pinpointed occupation categories Ad size flexibility High quality printing Prestigious editorial environment Long life—prospects keep magazines and reread them	Wide geographic circulation—usually cannot be used to limit recruiting to specific area Long lead time for ad placement	When job is specialized When time and geographic limitations are not of utmost importance When involved in ongoing recruiting programs
Directories	Specialized audiences Long life	Not timely Often have competitive clutter	Only appropriate for ongoing recruiting programs
Direct mail	Most personal form of advertising Unlimited number of formats and amount of space By selecting names by zip code, mailing can be pinpointed to precise geographic area	Difficult to find mailing list of prospects by occupation at home addresses Cost for reaching each prospect is high	If the right mailing list can be found, this is potentially the most effective medium—no other medium gives the prospect as much a feeling of being specially selected Particularly valuable in competitive situations
Radio and Television	Difficult to ignore Can reach prospects who are not actively looking for a job better than newspapers and magazines Can be limited to specific geographic areas Creatively flexible. Can dramatize employment story more effectively than printed ads Little competitive recruitment clutter	Only brief, uncomplicated messages are possible Lack of permanence; prospects cannot refer back to it. (Repeated airings necessary to make impression.) Creation and production of commercials—particularly TV—can be time-consuming and costly Lack of special interest selectivity; paying for waste circulation	In competitive situations when not enough prospects are reading your printed ads When there are multiple job openings and there are enough prospects in specific geographic area When a large impact is needed quickly. A "blitz" campaign can saturate an area in two weeks or less Useful to call attention to printed ads

TABLE 5.1 *(continued)*

Type of Medium	Advantages	Disadvantages	When to Use
Outdoor (roadside billboards) and Transit (posters on buses & subways)	Difficult to ignore. Can reach prospects as they are literally traveling to their current jobs Precise geographic selectivity Reaches large numbers of people many times at a low cost	Only very brief message is possible Requires long lead for preparation and must be in place for long period of time. (Usually one to three months.)	When there is a steady hiring need for large numbers of people that is expected to remain constant over a long period of time
"Point-of-Purchase" (Promotional materials at recruiting location)	Calls attention to employment story at time when prospects can take some type of immediate action Creative flexibility	Limited usefulness; prospects must visit a recruiting location before it can be effective	Posters, banners, brochures, audio-visual presentations at special events such as job fairs, open houses, conventions, as part of an employee referral program, at placement offices or whenever prospects visit at organization facilities.

SOURCE: Bernard S. Hodes, "Planning for Recruitment Advertising: Part II," *Personnel Journal*, Vol. 28, no. 5 (June 1983), p. 499. Reprinted with the permission of *Personnel Journal*, Costa Mesa, Calif. All rights reserved.

walk-ins) in terms of their effectiveness as measured by the following characteristics of the candidates they generated: quality of performance, quantity of performance, dependability, job knowledge, absenteeism, work satisfaction, and job involvement.[32] This study (which focused on research scientists) showed applicants recruited though college placement offices and newspaper ads were inferior in performance (quality and dependability) to those who made contact based on their own initiative or in response to a professional journal/convention advertisement. In terms of absenteeism, those recruited though newspaper ads missed almost twice as many days as did those referred by any of the other sources. College placement office recruits reported significantly lower levels of job involvement and satisfaction with supervision than did employees recruited in other ways.

These findings notwithstanding, some sources are more appropriate for recruiting some types of jobs than are others. This is illustrated by a recent study of the recruiting practices of 188 companies. For managerial positions, 80% of the companies used newspaper ads, 75% used employment agencies, and 65% relied on employee referrals. For professional and technical jobs, 75% used college recruiting, 75% also used ads in newspapers and technical journals, and 70% used private employment agencies. For recruiting sales personnel, 80% of the firms used newspaper ads, 75% used referrals, and 65% also used private employment agencies. For office and plant human resources on the other hand, referrals and walk-ins were relied on by 90% of the firms, while 80% of the firms used newspaper ads, and 70% used public employment agencies.[33]

ORGANIZATIONAL CHOICE: STAGES IN THE INDIVIDUAL CHOICE PROCESS[34]

organizational choice

Organizational choice is a process that involves a series of decisions that an individual makes about joining an organization. The concept of organizational choice is based on expectancy theory. How an individual decides depends on three primary factors: the attractiveness of an organization, the effort that the individual makes to gain employment in the organization, and the final choice that the individual makes of an organization from among those that offer employment. Therefore, attractiveness, effort, and choice refer to the stages in the individual choice process regarding entry into an organization.

Stage 1: Attractiveness

In stage 1, the relative attractiveness of an organization to an individual is determined by a combination of beliefs about certain essential characteristics of each organization and the importance attached to each of these characteristics. During this stage, the individual gathers information about the organization and generally asks himself or herself questions such as:

- What is the reputation of the organization?
- How large is the organization?
- What is the nature of the industry?
- What are the compensation practices? What are the opportunities for advancement in that organization?
- How secure are employees' jobs in the organization? How does the organization treat its employees?
- Will a job in this organization help my career?
- Is the organization an equal opportunity employer?

Individuals tend to find organizations attractive that provide the greatest potential for providing a good fit for need satisfaction. Wanous developed a formula that clearly explains the attractiveness stage. It is shown in Figure 5.10.

As can be seen the attractiveness of an organization to an individual is equal to the total belief about certain rewards to be gained from joining that organization multiplied by the importance of each outcome.

Stage 2: Effort

In stage 2, the individual's determination to join the organization is based on the attractiveness of the organization, and on an assessment of other alternatives. Once the individual has keyed in on the organization then he or she makes an intensive effort to gain entrance into or obtain employment with that organization.

For instance, when it is time to attend university a student does not apply to all universities in Canada, but rather to a limited number of universities. The decision to apply to these universities is based on the attractiveness of those universities to the individual. When an individual is seeking a job, he or she does not apply to all companies in Canada, but rather selects a certain number based on the attractiveness of those firms. This attractiveness equals the sum belief about each outcome times the importance of each of each outcome.

Once the person has narrowed the field, he or she develops a plan of action to gain admittance to the preferred university or to gain employment at the preferred firm. Wanous has developed another formula that explains this stage. It is shown below in Figure 5.11.

As can be seen an individual's total motivation (amount of effort) to join or gain admittance to an organization will be based on a realistic expectation of being admitted to the organization multiplied by the attractiveness of the organization. Thus an individual through self-selection will not apply to organizations to which he or she is unlikely to gain admittance.

Stage 3: Choice among Job Offers

As a consequence of the individual's effort, organizations make their selections and offer positions to their preferred job candidates. Once job offers have been

FIGURE 5.10

$$\text{Attractiveness of an organization} = \sum \quad \text{Belief about each outcome} \quad \times \quad \text{Importance of each outcome}$$

SOURCE: John P. Wanous, *Organizational Entry*, p. 93. © 1980 by Addison-Wesley Publishing Co. Reprinted by permission of Addison-Wesley Publishing Co., Inc. Reading, MA.

FIGURE 5.11

$$\text{Total motivation to join an organization} = \text{Expectancy of being admitted to the organization} \quad \times \quad \text{Attractiveness of the organization}$$

SOURCE: John P. Wanous, *Organizational Entry*, p. 93. © 1980 by Addison-Wesley Publishing Co. Reprinted by permission of Addison-Wesley Publishing Co., Inc. Reading, MA.

HUMAN RESOURCE MANAGEMENT

On the Front Line

If you were to ask Jennifer and her father what the main problem was in running their firm their answer would be quick and short: hiring good people. Originally begun as a string of coin-operated laundromats requiring virtually no skilled help, the chain grew to six stores, each heavily dependent on skilled managers, cleaner-spotters, and pressers. Employees generally have no more than a high school education (often less) and the market for them is very competitive. Over a typical weekend literally dozens of want ads for experienced pressers, or cleaner-spotters generally can be found in area newspapers. All of these people are usually paid minimum wage and they change jobs frequently. Jennifer and her father are thus faced with the continuing task of recruiting and hiring qualified workers out of a pool of individuals that they feel are almost nomadic in their propensity to move from area to area and job to job. Turnover in their stores (as in the stores of many of their competitors) often approaches 400%. "Don't talk to me about

human resources planning and trend analysis," says Jennifer. "We're fighting an economic war and I'm happy just to be able to round up enough live applicants to be able to keep my trenches filled."

In light of this problem, Jennifer's father gave her the following assignment:

1. Develop a set of recommendations for me concerning two main issues: First, how would you recommend we go about reducing the turnover in our stores? Next, provide me with a detailed list of recommendations concerning how we should go about increasing our pool of acceptable job applicants so we are no longer faced with the need of hiring almost anyone who walks in the door. Your recommendations regarding the latter should include completely worded advertisements and recommendations regarding any other recruiting strategies you would suggest we use.

made then individuals must select from among the various offers. Most individuals will choose the organization that offers the greatest likelihood of providing valued rewards.

It is important to note that expectancy theory does not say that individuals will write down or calculate the attractiveness of organizations in exactly the manner noted above. What it states is that this is the way most people make decisions whether or not they are consciously aware that all of these factors are taken into account. (Obviously if the individual receives only one offer then there is no choice to be made.)

SUMMARY

1. Recruitment is the process of seeking and obtaining qualified job candidates. In order to survive and prosper an organization must develop and utilize appropriate recruiting strategies to attract an adequate pool of job candidates with the required skills, knowledge, and abilities to meet its job requirements. In administering the organization's recruitment program the HRM specialists must be sensitive to the internal and external constraints that affect the organization. These constraints include organization recruiting strategy, recruiting plans, job requirements, affirmative action programs, and labour market conditions.

2. An organization's recruitment process includes a variety of methods and sources for attracting and obtaining viable job candidates. They include internal job posting and skill inventories as well as recruiting external sources through walk-ins, write-ins, employee referrals, private and public employment agencies, advertising, educational institutions, and trade associations.

3. The series of decisions that an individual makes about joining an organization is known as organizational choice. This expectancy theory recognizes three stages: attractiveness, effort, and choice.

KEY TERMS

recruitment	write-ins	want ads
labour market	employee referrals	blind ads
job posting	employment agency	organizational choice
skill inventories	Canada Employment Centres	
walk-ins	executive recruiters	

DISCUSSION QUESTIONS

1. What impact does the labour market have on recruitment?
2. What is the difference between recruiting methods and recruiting sources?
3. What are the advantages and disadvantages of job posting?
4. Explain the differences in effectiveness between walk-ins and write-ins.
5. What are the differences between Canada Employment Centres and private employment centres?
6. Explain the organizational choice process.

CASE INCIDENT: Large Turnovers Are Healthy?

Each year, for the past five years, Excellent Transmission Company (ETC) has been experiencing difficulty recruiting qualified job candidates for its design and production departments. Management operates on the philosophy that the best job candidates are recently graduated automotive engineers from community colleges and universities. The company feels that these individuals are much better prospects than seasoned workers because they offer various advantages that experienced workers do not possess.

New graduates, the company argues, are usually more innovative, and have newer ideas to offer. They are up-to-date on the latest developments in technology, are more energetic and productive, and are usually less costly to hire. Further, the company feels that new graduates are usually more loyal to the company. They are less concerned about internal politics and are less likely to engage in the type of behaviour that will disrupt production.

The ETC organization thinks that large turnover is healthy for the organization. They usually attempt to recruit all job candidates externally. If they are unsuccessful, they will recruit internally.

The company often receives many applicants each year but often it is unable to find the right type of job applicants that it needs.

Questions

1. What are the strengths and weaknesses of the organization's recruitment policy?

2. What are some of the barriers that have limited employment and advancement in the organization?

3. How would you change the organization's recruitment policies and practices?

NOTES

1. Robert D. Gatewood and Hubert S. Field, *Human Resource Selection* (Chicago: The Dryden Press 1990), p. 8.

2. James W. Walker, *Human Resource Planning* (New York: McGraw-Hill Books Inc., 1980) p. 28.

3. Ibid., p. 256.

4. Harris C. Jain, "Staffing: Recruitment and Selection" in *Human Resources Management in Canada* (Toronto: Prentice-Hall Canada Inc., 1984), p. 25, 013.

5. Roger Hawk, *The Recruitment Function* (New York: American Management Association, 1967), p. 28.

6. Jain, p. 25,011.

7. Ibid.

8. Ibid.

9. Ibid.

10. Ibid., p. 25,012.

11. Ibid.

12. Jeffery Daum, "Internal Promotion—Psychological Asset or Debit? A study of the Effects of Leader Origin," *Organizational Behaviour and Human Performance*, Vol. 13 (1975), pp. 404-413.

13. Arthur R. Pell, *Recruiting and Selecting Personnel* (New York: Regents Publishing, 1969), pp. 10-12.

14. Ibid., p. 13.

15. The study of employment referrals was published by Bernard Hodes Advertising Dept., 100-555 Madison Ave., New York, N.Y. 10022.

16. Jain, p. 25,021.

17. Stephen Rubenfeld and Michael Crino, "Are Employment Agencies Jeopardizing Your Selection Process?" *Personnel*, Vol. 58, (September-October 1981), pp. 70-77.

18. As quoted in Jain, p. 25,021.

19. Rubenfeld and Crino, pp. 70-77.

20. Employment and Immigration Canada, *Employment Programs and Services for Canadians*, Catalogue no. WH-7-092 (Ottawa: Minister of Supply and Services Canada, 1981), p. 1.

21. Jain, p. 25,021.

22. John Warcham, *Secrets of a Corporate Headhunter* (New York: Playboy Press 1981), pp. 213-225.

23. Pell, pp. 56-63; David L. Chicci and Carl Knapp, "College Recruitment from Start to Finish," *Personnel Journal*, Vol. 59 no. 8 (August 1980), pp. 653-657.

24. Alan J. Cox, *Confessions of a Corporate Headhunter* (New York: Trident Press, 1973.)

25. Jain, p. 25,023.

26. Jain, p. 25,021-24.

27. Robert Dipboye, Howard Frankin, and Ken Wiback, "Relative Importance of Applicant Sex, Attractiveness, and Scholastic Standing in Evaluation of Job Applicant Resumes," *Journal of Applied Psychology*, Vol. 61 (1975), pp. 39-48. See also Laura M. Graves, "College Recruitment: Removing the Personnel Bias from Selection Decisions," *Personnel* (March, 1989), pp. 48-52.

28. Dipboye, Franklin, and Wiback, pp. 39-48.

29. Dipboye, Franklin, and Wiback, pp. 29-48. See also "College Recruiting" in *Personnel Journal*, (May/June, 1980).

30. Ibid, pp. 16-34; see also Barbara Hunger "How to Choose a Recruitment Advertising Agency," *Personnel Journal*, Vol 64, no. 12 (December 1985), pp. 60-62. For an excellent review of ads, see Margaret Magnus, *Personnel Journal*, Vol. 64 and 65, no. 8 (August 1985 and 1986), and Bob Martin, "Recruitment Ad Ventures," *Personnel Journal*, Vol. 66 (August 1987), pp. 46-63.

31. P. J. Decker, and E. T. Cornelius, "A Note on Recruiting Sources and Job Survival Rates," *Journal of Applied Psychology*, Vol. 64 (1979), pp. 463-464.

32. James A. Breaugh "Relations Between Sources and Employee Performance, Absenteeism, and Work Attitudes," *Academy of Management Journal*, Vol. 24 (March 1981), pp. 142-147; R. Wayne Mondy, Robert Noe, and Robert Edwards, "Successful Recruitment: Matching Sources and Methods," *Personnel* (September 1987), pp. 42-46.

33. *Recruiting Practices*, Personnel Policy Form, Survey No. 462 (Washington D.C.: Bureau of National Affairs, August 1979), p. 114; reprinted in Stephen P. Robbins, "Personnel: The Management of Human Resources" (Englewood Cliffs, N.J.: Prentice Hall, 1982), p. 115. For another view of this see Phillip Swarott, Alan Bass, and Lizabeth Barclay,

"Recruiting Sources: Another Look," *Journal of Applied Psychology*, Vol. 70, no. 4 (1985), pp. 720-728. See also, David Caldwell and W. Austin Stivey, "The Relationship Between Recruiting Source and Employee Success: An Analysis by Race," *Personnel Psychology*, Vol. 36, no. 1 (Spring 1983), pp. 67-72.

34. This is based on John P. Wanous, *Organizational Entry* (Reading, Ma.: Addison-Wesley Publishing Co., 1980), pp. 86-95; see also, V. Vroom "Organizational Choice: A Study of Pre- and Post-Decision Process," *Organizational Behaviour and Human Performance*, I (1966), pp. 212-225. See also E. E. Lawler, *Motivation in Work Organization* (Monterey, Calif: Brook/Cole 1973); Richard M. Steers, Introduction to *Organizational Behavior*, 4th ed. (New York: Harper Collins Publishing Inc. 1991), pp. 584-587.

SUGGESTED READINGS

Hill, Jeff. "Avoiding the `Bent Truth' in Hiring" in *Human Resources Management in Canada*. Toronto: Prentice-Hall Canada Inc., 1991, pp. 25,565-25,568.

Jain, Harish C. "Staffing: Recruitment and Selection" in *Human Resources Management in Canada*. Toronto: Prentice-Hall Canada Inc., 1983, pp. 25,011-25,061.

Perry Douglas. "The New Recruiting Realities" in *Human Resources Management in Canada*. Toronto: Prentice-Hall Canada Inc., 1990, pp. 25,545-25,549.

CHAPTER SIX
THE SELECTION PROCESS

After studying this chapter, you should be able to

1. Define the selection process.
2. Explain the purposes and importance of interviews.
3. Define different types of interviewing techniques.
4. Discuss common pitfalls in interviewing.
5. Effectively interview job candidates.
6. Define validity and reliability and demonstrate how they relate to the selection process.
7. Discuss different types of psychological testing used in the selection process.

OVERVIEW

The main purpose of this chapter is to explain the basic assumptions underlying the selection process. We first present the key steps in the selection process. Next we discuss the interviewing process. Interviews are an important way to screen job candidates and to find those who have the skills, knowledge, abilities and therefore motivation to do the job. We talk about different types of psychological tests used in the selection process, including cognitive abilities tests, achievement tests, physical abilities tests, and personality, interest, and preference tests.

THE SELECTION PROCESS

Selection is the process of collecting and evaluating information about an individual in order to extend an offer of employment. Such employment could be either a first position for a new employee or a different position for an existing employee. The selection process is performed under legal and environmental constraints to protect the future interest of the organization and the individual.[1]

The majority of selection programs used by organizations are based on the successive-hurdles approach. This means that in order to be hired, job candidates must successively pass each and every screening mechanism that the organization uses in its selection process. These instruments include interviews, tests, application blanks, and background checks. In order for an individual to stay in contention for the position, he or she must meet or exceed the minimum requirements established for each hurdle. Of course some applicants are rejected at each step.

The types of selection instruments and screening devices commonly used by organizations vary from one organization to another. The mix of instruments depends on many factors. These may include the nature of the organization, the complexity of the job, the organization's employment policy, and the sources and methods of recruitment.

Purposes and Importance of Selection

The purposes and importance of selection are to

- select qualified job candidates who possesses the necessary skills, knowledge, abilities, personality, interests, and preferences to successfully fill the specific job opening in the organization.
- differentiate between those applicants who will be able to perform well from those job candidates who will not.
- evaluate how applicants' abilities fit the organization's requirements.
- find out as much as possible about the individual's background, training, experience, skills, and abilities so that the matching process may be completed accurately, at the same time balancing the applicant's right to privacy and the organization's right to know.
- facilitate the fulfillment of mandated goals and timetables specified in employment equity programs.
- ensure that all selection screening devices and instruments comply fully with all legal and ethical requirements.

Essential Steps in the Selection Process

Figure 6.1 illustrates the essential steps in the selection process. These steps or hurdles may change from one organization to another, however, all of the steps identified are normally completed at one time or another. The sequence may vary within different organizations according to the size of the organization and the nature of the business. The dotted lines indicate the failure of an applicant to successfully negotiate a hurdle that would result in him or her being rejected.

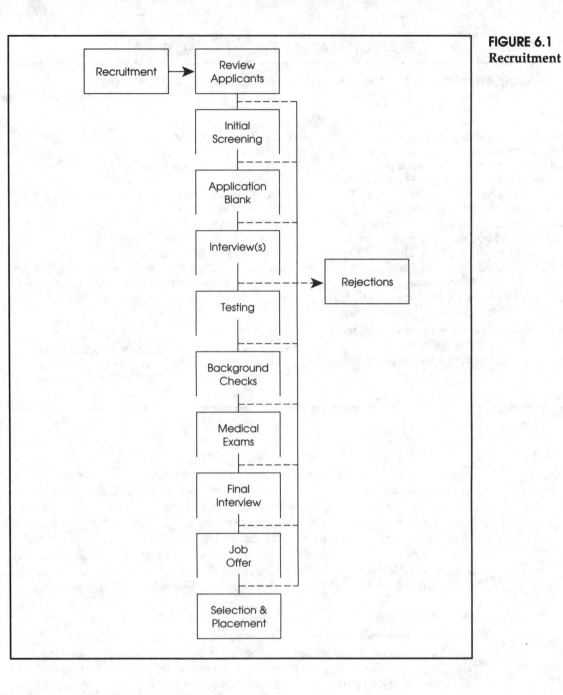

FIGURE 6.1
Recruitment

Review of Applicants

The sequential steps in the selection process begins with a review of the pool of applications which results from the organization's internal and/or external recruitment of job candidates. A review of job applicants is intended to determine which applicants meet the minimum qualifications for the job. Those applicants deemed not to deserve serious considerations are eliminated from the process.

Women, Minorities Make Slight Gains, Equity Report Shows

OTTAWA—The second Employment Equity Act annual report shows that the representation of all designated minority groups in the work force increased slightly in 1988. Under the Employment Equity Act, federally regulated employers with 100 or more employees must eliminate employment barriers, implement programs to achieve a representative work force, and report annually on their results. Failure to report could result in penalties up to $50 000. The 1989 report, tabled by Employment and Immigration Minister Monique Vezina, is based on results from 374 companies, representing 600 000 employees across Canada. The report also shows that:

- Women increased their representation in the work force from 40.9% in 1987 to 42.1% in 1988.
- Aboriginal peoples increased their representation from .66% to .73%.

- Persons with disabilities increased from 1.59% to 1.71%
- Visible minorities increased from 4.99% to 5.69%.
- Each designated group had an increased share of full-time hirings.
- Women and members of visible minorities had an increased share of full-time promotions.
- Women are paid 28.74% less than men.
- More than half (53.02%) of women working full-time and only 13.42% of men earned less than $25,000 in 1988.

SOURCE: *Human Resources Management in Canada*, Report Bulletin no. 84 (Scarborough, Ont.: Prentice-Hall Canada Inc., February 1990), pp. 1-2. Used with permission.

Initial Screening

The initial screening process is often used by those organizations that, on an ongoing basis, receive applications or inquires from interested job seekers. The initial screening may be done through a variety of strategies. It may be done by direct contact with a human resources specialist, or by the exchange of some basic information about the company through the receptionist. The type of information exchanged at this stage include the nature of the job, pay, and hours of work. Some applicants may become disinterested and self-select themselves out of the process, or their departure may be expedited, if they are determined to be undesirable or unsuitable.

Application Blank

This is an important step in the selection process. It is a formal record of the job candidate's application for employment opportunities with the organization. This document provides important information on the individual that is used to determine the suitability of the applicant and to check on the applicant's credibility. An application blank requests information such as the applicant's name, address, work history, and positions for which the individual has applied. (We discuss this instrument in more detail later.)

Interview(s)

The interview is a face-to-face conversation or verbal interaction between the applicant and a representative of the employer. This process enables the interviewer to seek and obtain information about the applicant to determine whether the applicant possesses the appropriate skills, knowledge, and abilities required by the employer. The process also provides the applicant with an opportunity to choose the organization.

Testing

Selection testing is a common screening device used by organizations to assess an applicant's general intelligence, personality characteristics, mental abilities, interests, and preferences. The test can be a written exercise, a simulation exercise, or any other testing device that the organization chooses to use which is job related. The use of valid selection tests can significantly assist in the hiring of the better qualified job candidate.

Background Checks

Almost all employers try to check and verify the background information and references of job applicants.[2] Estimates of the number of firms checking references range from 93% and up, with about 80% using telephone inquiries and the remainder using other background sources like reference letters.

Medical Examination

Many organizations require that job applicants submit to a medical examination. This is usually one of the final hurdles that an applicant must negotiate. A medical examination plays an important part in the selection process. It is used to ensure that the applicant is in good physical health and is capable of undertaking any physical demands of the job. It is also used to prevent the hiring of individuals who have an existing medical condition that could cause a financial burden on the organization. However, under Canadian human rights acts, medical examinations may only be required where they are job related.

Final Interview

The immediate supervisor usually conducts the final interview to determine the competence and suitability of the applicant, as well as the applicant's overall "fit" with the organization's requirements and the individual's needs. At this stage only the best candidates remain in contention.

Job Offer

The applicant(s) who possesses all the required technical abilities and personality characteristics as well as potential for growth usually receives the job offer.

Selection and Placement

This step marks the end of the selection process. It indicates that the job candidate has successfully negotiated all of the preceding hurdles. It also indicates that there has been a successful match between the candidate's expectations and the organization's requirements. The success of the selection decision depends on the effectiveness of all of the preceding steps in the process.

SELECTION INSTRUMENTS

Organizations use a variety of selection instruments to choose the job applicants that meet their requirements. It is essential that the selections are administered equally, consistently, and that they comply with the relevant human rights guidelines and charter of rights provisions. Some of the most common selection instruments and procedures include application forms, selection interviews, and tests.

APPLICATION FORMS

The application form is a good means of quickly collecting verifiable and therefore fairly accurate historical data from the candidate usually including information on such things as education, prior work history, and hobbies.

A filled-in blank or form can provide four types of information.[3] First, it allows the interviewer to make judgments on substantive matters such as whether the applicant has the education and experience to do the job. Second, the interviewer can draw conclusions about the applicant's previous progress and growth, a trait that is especially important for management candidates. Third, the interviewer can also draw some tentative conclusions regarding the applicant's stability based on the person's previous work record. (Here, however, the interviewer should be careful not to assume that an unusual number of job changes necessarily reflects on the applicant's ability; for example, the person's last two employers may have had to lay off large numbers of employees.) Fourth, the interviewer may be able to use the data in the application to predict which candidates will succeed on the job and which will not, a point we return to below.

In practice, most organizations use several different application forms. For technical and managerial human resources, for example, the form may require detailed answers to questions concerning the applicant's education and so on. The form for hourly factory workers might focus on the tools and equipment the applicant has used and the like. The application form(s) that organizations use must comply with human rights guidelines. These guidelines specify the type of questions that are non-discriminatory and are appropriate to include in an application blank. Figure 6.2 illustrates a sample application developed by the Ontario Human Rights Commission (see also our discussion in Chapter 2).

Using Job Applications

The application blank contains a wealth of information the interviewer can use for evaluating candidates. Some practical review guidelines for sorting out this information include the following:

1. Applications should be used as a guide to hiring. Job seekers reveal what they think are their strong points on applications and inadvertently reveal their weak ones, too, by playing them down. An interviewer can therefore use the application to help identify the candidate's strong and weak points.
2. The applicant's employment records should be studied. The application blank provides information as a starting point on what kinds of jobs they have held, how frequently they have changed jobs, and how ambitious they seem to be.
3. The quality of the applicant's writing should be checked. For example, an applicant who turns in a hastily scrawled sloppy application may have characteristics that the firm does not want in the particular kind of job the organization is recruiting for.
4. The way applicants reply to questions should be considered. Clear, accurate answers probably reflect clear thought process, just as disorganized answers may indicate the opposite.[4]

FIGURE 6.2
Sample Application
for Employment

Position being applied for	Date available to begin work

PERSONAL DATA

Last name	Given name(s)	

Address	Street	Apt. No.	Home Telephone Number

City	Province	Postal Code	Business Telephone Number

Are you legally eligible to work in Canada?   ❏ Yes   ❏ No

Are you willing to relocate in Ontario? ❏ Yes ❏ No	Preferred location	Category

To determine your qualification for employment, please provide information related to your academic and other achievements including voluntary work, as well as employment history. Additional information may be attached on a separate sheet.

EDUCATION

ELEMENTARY OR SECONDARY SCHOOL	BUSINESS, TRADE, OR TECHNICAL SCHOOL	
Highest grade or level completed	Name of course	Length of course
Type of certificate or diploma obtained	Licence, certificate or diploma awarded? ❏ Yes ❏ No	

COMMUNITY COLLEGE		UNIVERSITY		
Name of Program	Length of Program	Length of course	Degree awarded ❏ Yes ❏ No	❏ Pass ❏ Honours
Diploma received ❏ Yes ❏ No		Major subject		
Other courses, workshops, seminars		Licences, Certificates, Degrees		

Work related skills

Describe any of your work related skills, experience, or training that relate to the position being applied for.

FIGURE 6.2
(continued)

Name and Address of present/ last employer	Present/Last job title	
	Period of employment From To	Present/Last salary
	Name of Supervisor	Telephone
Type of Business	Reason for leaving	

Duties/Responsibilities

Name and Address of previous employer	Previous job title	
	Period of employment From To	Final salary
	Name of Supervisor	Telephone
Type of Business	Reason for leaving	

Duties/Responsibilities

Name and Address of previous employer	Previous job title	
	Period of employment From To	Final salary
	Name of Supervisor	Telephone
Type of Business	Reason for leaving	

Duties/Responsibilities

For employment references, may we approach:

Your present/last employer?   ❏ Yes   ❏ No

Your former employer(s)?   ❏ Yes   ❏ No

List references if different than above on a separate sheet.

Activities (civic, athletic, etc.)

I hereby declare that the foregoing information is true and complete to my knowledge. I understand that a false statement may disqualify me from employment, or cause my dismissal.

Have you attached an additional sheet?

❏ Yes   ❏ No

_____   _____
Signature   Date

SOURCE: Excerpts of the Ontario Human Rights Commission's *Employment Application Forms, Interviews*, 1991.

Weighted Application Blank

Application blanks are sometimes weighted. This process basically involves determining the relationship between (1) an application blank item (like age or geographical location) and (2) job performance. The "weight" to be applied to various degrees of that item is then determined. For instance, if it is known that suburbanites tend to have a lower turnover rate than people who live downtown, suburbanites would get a higher desirability rating, or greater weight ranking, for their response on the "address" blank than would urbanites. According to two experts, **weighted application blanks (WABs)** present an attractive alternative to the use of tests for employment decisions, and this attractiveness stems from several sources:

weighted application blank (WAB)

1. Most applicatants expect to be asked to complete an application form.

2. The weighted application form does not need to have distinguishable differences from an unscored form.

3. Filling in a blank with verifiable information about one's personal history is less noxious (to most people) than taking a test in which it is usually presumed that the test score will have something, perhaps everything, to do with whether one is offered employment.

4. Finally, weighted applications are developed on the basis of their statistically proven relationship to performance and should therefore be permissible from a human rights standpoint.

A WAB is very useful for predicting which candidates will be successful and which will not, in much the same way as test results may be used by employers for screening. A WAB may be used to predict job performance, job tenure, and motivation to work.

Although a WAB is easy to develop it is used by relatively few organizations.

SELECTION INTERVIEW

The selection interview is one of the most common and popular devices used for selecting job applicants. It is a process of providing and receiving information between the interviewee(s) and the interviewer(s). The selection interview is used virtually in all organizations for most jobs. The success of organizations depends upon their employees' performances. Thus it is critical that the "right individuals are hired and supported throughout their careers with the organization. The interview is one of the most critical management functions. It literally controls the quality of organizations, by determining the people who work for the organizations."[5]

Interviews are considered one of the most important aspects of the selection process and are likely to have an important impact on job applicants and on interviewers. Interviews significantly influence job applicants' views of the job and the organization. Interviews assist the organization in filling gaps in information provided by application forms and tests. Interviews may lead to entirely new types of information about applicants and organizations. A major reason for the selection interview's popularity is that it meets several objectives of both the interviewer and the applicant.

The interviewer's objectives include assessing applicants' qualifications; observing certain aspects of applicants' behaviour (such as communication skills, physical appearance and mannerisms, self-confidence, interpersonal skills, and motivation to work); gathering information about applicants so as to assist in the prediction of future performance (i.e., how well the applicants will perform and how long they will remain in the organization); communicating to the applicants information about the job; promoting the organization and attracting the applicants to the organization; and determining how well the applicants would fit into the organization.

The applicants' objectives include presenting a positive image of themselves, selling their skills, and marketing their positive attributes to the interviewer(s); and collecting information about the job and the organization so that they can make an informed decision about the job, the work environment, and career opportunities at the organization.[6]

The Effective Interview

The selection interview, to achieve the desired and/or expected outcome, ideally contains a series of steps designed to ensure the effectiveness and success of the interview process. Effective interviews require good note taking. According to two researchers, the taking of notes during the interview should reduce the likelihood of the interviewer forgetting the job-relevant information collected in the interview. Consequently the likelihood that the interviewer will reconstruct forgotten information in accordance with his or her biases and stereotypes should be reduced. Thus good note taking should increase interview validity.[7]

Planning the Interview

First, the interview should be planned in advance. The candidate's application and resume should be reviewed, and any areas that are vague or that may indicate strengths or weaknesses should be noted so that questions may be asked about them. The job specifications should be noted next to establish the traits an ideal candidate should possess.

The location in which the interview will take place should be planned. Ideally, it should be a private room. Telephone calls should not be put through, and other interruptions should be kept to a minimum.

Establishing Rapport

The candidate should be greeted and put at ease. The interviewing room itself should be conducive to reducing tensions and establishing rapport, and be private, quiet, and lacking in distractions. General questions may be used to start the interview—perhaps about the weather or the traffic conditions that day. A few minutes spent on questions like these can go far toward reducing the applicant's tension.

Questions

1. *Structured forms should be used.* Interviews based on structured guidelines usually result in the best interviews.[8] By forcing the interviewer to adhere to a preset sequence of questions, they help reduce the potential to let unfavourable information bias his or her opinions. They also help the interviewer to more accurately recall the information produced in the interview, and help to ensure that all interviewers ask all candidates the same questions. Research findings show that the structured interviews have greater validity and reliability than unstructured interviews.[9]

2. *The decision should be delayed.* Interviewers often make their decisions before they ever see the candidate—on the basis of his or her application blank, for instance—or during the first few minutes of the interview. Another principle of good interviewing is thus to delay the decision as long into the interview as possible. A record of the interview should be kept and later reviewed—the decision should be made then.[10] The quality of the applicant will influence how long it takes to make a decision, with the quickest decisions being made on the worst candidates—those that get off to the worst start, in terms of their answers to the interviewers questions.[11] The time allotted for the interview is another important factor; allotting more time for an interview will make it less likely to make a premature decision.[12]

3. *Traits that are more accurately assessed in the interview should be those focused upon.* Some traits are more accurately assessed during interviews than others. These include the candidate's intelligence, ability to get along with others, and motivation to work. As two researchers conclude:

> the results rather consistently indicate two areas which both contribute heavily to interview decisions and show greatest evidence of validity ... personal relations, and motivation to work. In other words, perhaps the interviewer should seek information on two questions: "What is the applicant's motivation to work?" and "Would he or she adjust to the social context of the job?" Such an approach would leave the assessment of abilities, aptitudes, and biographical data to other, and in all likelihood, more reliable and valid sources.[13]

4. *The interviewee must be encouraged to talk.* The main reason for the interview is to find out about the applicant and to do this the interviewer must get the person to talk. The interviewer must make the applicant feel at ease early in the interview, perhaps by making some general comment about the firm and the job, by avoiding asking too many direct questions; and by drawing out the applicant's opinions and feelings by repeating the person's last comment as a question (such as "You didn't like your last job?").

Common Interviewing Mistakes (Problems)

The usefulness of interviews depends mostly on how they are carried out. There are several common interviewing mistakes that undermine the interview's usefulness.

Poor Planning

Many selection interviews are simply not carefully planned. With their hectic schedules, many human resource specialists find themselves facing an applicant before they had time to think carefully about the interview they are about to conduct. Because they see job applicants infrequently, supervisors or line managers may also take little time to plan a selection interview.[14]

The interview is likely to fail if interviewers do not know their objectives and do not develop a plan to meet those objectives. Lack of planning usually leads to a relatively unstructured interview in which whatever comes up automatically becomes the content. Lack of structure creates problems because the less structured the interview is, the less reliable it will be.[15]

Snap Judgment

Interviewers usually make up their minds about candidates during the first few minutes of the interview; prolonging the interview past this point usually adds little to change the decisions. One researcher even found that in 85% of the cases the interviewer had already made up his or her mind about the candidate before the interview even began, on the basis of the applicant's application form and personal appearance!

This problem is especially acute when the interviewer gets negative feedback about the candidate before the interview. In one study, for instance, the researchers found that interviewers who received unfavourable reference letters about applicants were likely to give the applicant less credit for past successes and to hold the person more personally responsible for past failures. Furthermore, the final decision to accept or reject an applicant was always tied to what the interviewer expected of the person, based on the reference.[16]

Negative Emphasis

Interviewers are also influenced more by unfavourable than favourable information about or from the candidate. Similarly, interviewers' impressions are much more likely to change from favourable to unfavourable than unfavourable to favourable; in fact, the interview itself is often mostly a search for negative information.

The combination of the negative emphasis with the fact that interviewers tend to make snap judgments early in the interview, shows why most interviews tend to be loaded against the applicant. An applicant who is initially highly rated could easily end up with a low rating, given the fact that unfavourable information tends to carry more weight in the interview. And an interviewee who begins with a poor rating will find it very difficult to overcome that first bad impression during the interview.[17]

Not Knowing the Job

Interviewers who do not know precisely what the job entails and what sort of candidate is best suited for it usually develop incorrect stereotypes about what a good applicant is. They then erroneously match interviewees with their incorrect stereotypes.

Candidate-Order-Error

The order in which applicants are seen can also affect how they are rated. In one study, managers were asked to evaluate a candidate who was "just average" after first evaluating several "unfavourable" candidates. The average candidate was evaluated much more favourably than he might otherwise have been, since in contrast to the unfavourable candidates the average one looked much better than he actually was. This *candidate-order error* can be a major problem; in some studies, only a small part of the applicant's rating was based on his or her actual potential. Most of the applicant's rating was based on the effect of having followed very favourable or unfavourable candidates.[18] This is an error of judgment on the part of the interviewer.

Nonverbal Behaviour

Another problem is that an interviewer may be unconsciously influenced by the applicant's nonverbal behaviour. Often, in other words, it is not what the applicant says, but how the person says it that determines whether the person is rated high or low. For example, several studies have shown that applicants who demonstrate greater amounts of eye contact, head moving, smiling, and other similar nonverbal behaviours are rated higher, and that these nonverbal behaviours often account for more than 80% of the applicant's rating.[19]

Psychiatric Approach

One of the greatest weakness in the selection interview is the way in which human beings evaluate each other. All too often interviewers try to assess an applicant's basic character in half an hour. Judgments are made about the applicant's personality characteristics as well as his or her skills and knowledge.[20] It is very common for interviewers to place emphasis on assessment of traits such as maturity, aggressiveness, confidence, and initiative. The problem is that these traits are often generally poorly defined. This evaluation of traits has become institutionalized in many organizations through the use of interview rating forms that require interviewers to evaluate the personalities of applicants.[21] This evaluation scheme puts interviewers in the realm of the unseen and undefined—they act as amateur psychiatrists, judging the basic character of the applicants. Most interviewers are not trained to make these kind of assessments.[22] For instance, a student of one of the authors mentioned at one class that she was asked at an interview the following question, "If you were a tree what kind of tree would you be?"

Pressure to Hire

Often recruiters are under pressure to hire, resulting in the lowering of employment standards. In one study a group of managers were told to assume that they were behind in their recruiting quota, while a second group of managers were told that they were already ahead of their quota. Those who were told they were behind evaluated the same recruits much more highly than did the other group of managers.[23]

Major Types of Interviews

There are nine major types of interviews that are commonly used. They are structured, unstructured, mixed, serialized, stress, panel, problem-solving, behaviour description, and videotaped interviews.

Structured Interview

Structured interviews rely on a series of predetermined job-related questions. In some instances the interviewers focus on and probe certain selected aspects of the job candidate's background. These questions are consistently asked of all interviewees for a particular job. This method imposes constraints on both the interviewer and the interviewee. Neither party may deviate from the "structured format" to seek or provide clarification and/or elaboration on areas of interest. However, the structured interview method substantially increases the reliability of the interview process.

structured interview

Unstructured Interview

The **unstructured interview** is a conversational-style interview. The interviewer pursues points of interest as they come up in response to question. There is no spe-

unstructured interview

cial format to follow, and the conversation can wander off in various directions. Often, each applicant's interview starts off about the same, but the unstructured nature of the interview lets the interviewer wander far afield, asking questions based on the candidate's last statements.

Mixed (Semi-Structured) Interview

mixed interview

The **mixed interview** format is a combination of structured and unstructured interviews. This method allows both the interviewer and the interviewee the flexibility to focus on, elaborate on, and probe into those areas which deserve in-depth discussion.

Serialized (Sequential) Interview

Most employers require that applicants be interviewed by several persons before reaching a decision, but this process is usually nondirective and informal: each interviewer looks at the applicant from his or her own point of view, asks different questions, and forms an independent opinion of the candidate.

serialized interview

A more formal version of this is the **serialized interview**.[24] Here an applicant is interviewed by several people. Each interviewer then rates the candidate on a standard structured evaluation form, and the ratings are compared before a hiring decision is made. Assuming that the structured form focuses on skills and traits that are required for satisfactory job performance, the serialized interview should result in more reliable and valid interviews than would a purely nondirective approach.

Stress Interview

stress interview

The **stress interview** format is an approach in which the applicant is asked a series of rapid-fire, sometimes harsh and rude questions. This technique helps identify hypersensitive applicants and those with high or low stress tolerance. The objective of the stress interview is to determine how an applicant will react to stress on the job. To use this approach, the interviewer should be skilled in its use, and should be sure that stress is, in fact, an important characteristic of the job.

In the typical stress interview, the applicant is made uncomfortable by being put on the defensive by a series of frank (and often discourteous) questions from the interviewer. What the interviewer usually does is probe for weaknesses in the applicant's background. Having identified these, the interviewer then focuses on them, hoping to get the candidate to lose his or her composure. Thus, a candidate for customer-relations manager who obligingly mentions that she has had four jobs in the past two years might be told that frequent job changes reflect irresponsible and immature behaviour, behaviour that probably reflects the woman's upbringing. If the applicant then responds with a reasonable explanation of why the job changes were necessary, another topic might be pursued. On the other hand, if the person reacts with anger and disbelief, this might be taken as a symptom of low tolerance for stress.

This approach has its advantages and disadvantages. On one hand, it can be a good way of identifying applicants who are hypersensitive and who might be expected to overreact to mild criticism with anger and abuse. On the other hand, the interviewer who uses this approach should be sure that a thick skin and an ability to handle stress are really required for the job, and that he or she has the skills to keep the interview (and defensive or angry interviewee) under control.

Panel (Board) Interview

The **panel interview** format is an interview in which a group of interviewers question the applicant. The panel interview is widely used by various levels of government, school boards, military, and police departments.

This approach has several advantages. The typical interview process often involves having the candidate go over basically the same ground over and over again with each interviewer. The panel interview, on the other hand, lets each interviewer pick up on the candidate's answers to questions posed by different interviewers, much as reporters do in press conferences. Since the panel brings more points of view to bear, it's more likely that new and incisive questions will be prompted by the panel arrangement. This approach can thus elicit deeper and more meaningful responses than are normally produced by a series of one-to-one interviews. One variant is the *mass interview* in which several candidates are interviewed at once by a panel; the panel poses a problem to be solved, and then sits back and watches which of the candidates takes the lead in formulating an answer, organizing the candidates, and so forth.

panel interview

Problem-Solving Interview

The focus of **problem-solving interviews** is on simulation exercises or hypothetical situations which the job candidate is expected to analyze and solve. The job candidate is assessed by the approach which he/she uses to solve the problem as well as on the solution. This method is useful for understanding the job candidate's reasoning and analytical abilities.

problem-solving interview

Behaviour Description Interview

The **behaviour description interview** bases the hiring decision on behavioural skills instead of "personality." The basic approach involves identifying important behavioural dimensions of the job and then assessing the job applicants against those dimensions. The process also involves probing into the applicant's past behaviour.

behaviour description interview

A Behavioural Interview Program

The behaviour description interview method was developed by Professor Tom Janz[25] of the University of Calgary. The behaviour description interview is based on the assumption that "the best predictor of future performance is past performance in similar circumstances." According to Professor Janz in the past interviewers often fell in the "experience equals excellence fallacy" by assuming that if a candidate had performed a task at all, he or she had performed it well. Behaviour description interviewing overcomes this problem by requiring candidates to give specific examples of how they have performed job duties or handled job problems in the past.

The behaviour description interviewing questions are derived from the critical incidents techniques of job analysis. Suppose that, using this technique, one dimension of a sales job is identified as "establishing new client contacts." Then, based on this particular dimension, a behaviour description interview question for experienced candidates might be as follows, "Tell me about the most difficult new client contact you have made in the last six months." After the candidate has described a specific incident, the interviewer's next questions would be, "What

The Behaviour Dimension: Communicates clearly, handles delicate situations with sensitivity...

Human resource personnel are continually communicating with people in both good and bad situations, What do you feel is your most effective method of communication? Why?

Tell me about the last time you had a really good idea and had to persuade your supervisor to accept it.

- What was your idea?
- How did you present your idea to your supervisor?
- What did he or she find difficult to accept about your idea?
- What made the situation especially difficult for you?
- What was the outcome?

When a group of people work closely together, it is inevetable that conflict will arise. Tell me about the most serious disagreement you have had with a co-worker.

- When did this happen?
- What led to the disagreement?
- How did you attempt to solve the problem?
- What was your co-worker's reaction?
- How was the situation resolved?
- What is your relationship with that person today?
- How often over a period of 6 months did you find yourself in this type of situation?

Job Behaviour Dimension: Check work thoroughly; organization skills...

Sometimes, when we are pressed for time, we neglect to check our work to make sure that it is complete as well as correct. Tell me about a time when you were in this situation.

- What were the circumstances that caused you to neglect this task?
- What was the effect of this incident?
- How do you normally go about checking your work for completeness?
- How did you handle any problems that arose from this incident?
- What did you do the next time this situation arose?

Describe for me the last time you were asked to prepare a presentation on short notice and were given very sketchy details as to required content.

- What was the presentation?
- How did you gather the necessary information to prepare?
- What steps did you go through in organizing the task?
- Whom did you get to help you with the task?
- How did you work around the time constraint?
- What sort of feedback did you receive from those who attended the presentation? From your supervisor?
- How would you have organized the presentation if you had more time?

Job Behaviour Dimension: Assist employees...

Tell me about a time when you aided an employee in understanding a difficult policy.

- What was the policy?
- How did you know that the employee was having trouble understanding?
- What did you do or say that helped?
- How did you know that you had been successful in your attempt?
- What was it about the policy that was difficult?
- What steps did you take to change the policy so that it would be easier for others to understand?

Job Behavior Dimension: Time management; takes initiative to suggest new programs...

Some days it seems that everyone has a problem they need solved or a question they need answered. Tell me about a time when you had people waiting to see you because your appointment calendar was overbooked.

- What were the circumstances that led to your being overbooked?
- How did you handle the situation?
- What were the reactions of the people waiting to see you?
- What was your response to them?
- How satisfied was each individual with the time you spent with him or her and the way you resolved his or her problems?
- What steps did you take to reduce the occurence of this type of situation in the future?

Describe a time when you implemented a procedure to help make your job run more smoothly.

- What was the procedure?
- How did you go about organizing it?
- What was the reaction of your co-workers to this new procedure?
- How did it make the running of your job smoother?
- How did it affect the jobs of others in your department?

SOURCE: Tom Janz, Lowell Hellervik, and David C. Gilmore, *Behavior Description Interviewing* (Boston: Allyn and Bacon Inc., 1986), pp. 178–185. Reprinted with permission.

were the circumstances surrounding this event?" "What did you do to overcome the difficulty?" and "What were the consequences for the firm?"[26] Research has shown that behaviour description interviews are much more valid than the traditional interview methods. Recently the Royal Bank of Canada and the Canadian Imperial Bank of Commerce adopted the behaviour description interviewing method. Figure 6.3 illustrates some sample questions from a behaviour description interview for the position of a human resources manager.

The behaviour description interview may be implemented by performing the following steps:

1. *Conducting a skill analysis.* The job description must be studied and reviewed for the kinds of skills the job may require such as typing, scheduling, or negotiating.

2. *Selecting skill dimensions.* Next, specific skill dimensions such as the ability to deal with deadline pressures or making decisions on a available information should be precisely defined so as to help the interviewer know what qualities to look for in a job candidate.

3. *Preparing interview questions.* Next, tailor-made questions should be prepared for the job to maximize the chances of obtaining information about the selected skills. For example, the interviewee may be asked to provide specific examples of past work that illustrate how some skill—like making decisions under pressure—was used.

4. *Conducting the interview.* Every effort should be made to put the applicant at ease. Notes should be taken throughout the interview as the interviewer is on the lookout for nonverbal behaviour cues.

5. *Evaluating behaviour.* Finally, after the interview, the candidate should be rated when the interviewer has reread the skill dimensions previously cited for the job.[27]

Videotaped Interviewing

videotaped interview

The **videotaped interview** is conducted in two stages. First, the traditional face-to-face interview is conducted and is videotaped (with the consent of the interviewee of course). At the completion of the interview the job candidate is assessed by the interviewer. The videotape is then taken to the company for viewing by the hiring line managers and/or other interviewers. The applicant is also assessed by the viewer(s) of the videotape. The initial assessment of the applicant is then pooled with the subsequent assessment.

Guidelines for Interviewees

Here are some hints for excelling in interviews.

The first thing for applicants to understand is that interviews are used primarily to help employers determine what the applicant is like as a person.[28] In other words, information regarding interpersonal skills and the desire to work is of prime importance in the interview, since skills and technical expertise are usually best determined through tests and a careful study of educational and work history. Interviewers will look first for crisp, articulate answers. Specifically, concise responses, full cooperation in answering questions, statements of relevant personal opinions, and the ability to keep to the subject at hand are by far the most important elements in influencing the interviewer's decision. Additionally, there are seven things the applicant should know to get that extra edge in the interview.

First, preparation is essential. Before the interview, the applicant should learn as much as possible about the employer, the job, and the people doing the recruiting. Business periodicals should be consulted regarding what is happening in the employer's field, who the competition is, and how they are doing.

Second, the interviewer's real needs must be uncovered. The applicant should spend as little time as possible answering the interviewer's first questions and as much time as possible getting him or her to describe his or her needs: what the person is looking to get accomplished, and the type of person he or she feels is needed. Open-ended questions such as, "Could you tell me more about that?" may be used.

Third, the applicant should relate him- or herself to the interviewer's needs. Once it is known what type of person the interviewer is looking for and the sorts of problems he or she wants solved, the applicant should describe personal accomplishments in terms of the interviewer's needs. He or she may start by saying something like "one of the problem areas you've indicated is important to you is similar to a problem I once faced." He or she should then state the problem, describe the solution, and reveal the results.[29]

Fourth, answering a question should be a three-step process: Pause—think—speak.[30] The applicant should pause to make sure that what the interviewer is driving at is understood, think about how to structure the answer, and then speak.

The Computer-Aided Interview

Computer-aided interviews are built on the principles of patterned and structured interviews. The basic idea is to present the applicant with a series of questions regarding his or her background, experience, education, skills, knowledge, and work attitudes, questions that relate to a specific job for which the person has applied.[1] The questions are presented in a multiple-choice format, one at a time, and the applicant is expected to respond to the questions on the computer screen by pressing a key corresponding to desired responses. Here are some sample interview questions for a person applying for a job in a retail store:[2]

Are you applying to work part time or full time?

    A. Part-time (less than 40 hours per week).
    B. Full-time (40 hours per week).
    C. Whatever is available.

The position for which you are applying may require you to lift boxes that weight 25 to 30 pounds. Will this be a problem for you?

    A. It will definitely be a problem.
    B. It might be a problem.
    C. It will not be a problem.

Have you ever had a job where you worked directly with customers?

    A. Yes
    B. No.
    C. If yes, ...

How would your supervisor rate your customer service skills?

    A. Outstanding.
    B. Above average.
    C. Average.
    D. Below average.
    E. Poor.

Note that the last question would be asked only if the applicant answered yes to the previous question.

Computer-aided interviews usually precede and supplement the face-to-face interview. At the end of the computer-aided interview a printed report is produced that lists all interview questions, applicant responses, and follow-up comments and questions to be asked, such as "give me some examples of why your supervisor would rate your customer services skills as outstanding." The typical computer-aided interview involves about 100 questions and is completed in under 20 minutes.

Computer aided interviews can have some enormous benefits. Their ability to branch to follow-up questions allows topics to be pursued as they might be in a face-to-face interview; a lot of information can thus be obtained quickly without the interviewers' services. Several of the interpersonal interview problems we discuss in this chapter (such as making a snap judgment about the interviewee based on his or her appearance) are also obviously avoided with this nonpersonal approach to interviewing. Particularly for larger companies with the resources to develop job-specific, computer-aided interviews the savings in interviewer time and in avoiding hiring mistakes can be considerable.[3]

---

[1] This is based on Douglas D. Roders, "Computer-Aided Interviewing Overcomes First Impressions," *Personal Journal* (April 1987), pp. 148-152.

[2] These are based on, and quoted from, Rodgers, pp. 148-152.

[3] For additional information on the benefits of computer-aided interviewing see, for example, Christopher Martin and Denise Nagao, "Some Effects of Computerized Interviewing on Job Applicant Responses," *Journal of Applied Psychology*, Vol. 74, no. 1 (February 1989), pp. 72-80.

Fifth, appearance and enthusiasm are important. Appropriate clothing, good grooming, a firm handshake, and the appearance of controlled energy are important.

Sixth, first impressions are important. Applicants should remember that studies of interviews show that in most cases interviewers make up their minds about the applicant during the first minutes of the interview. A good first impression may turn to bad during the interview, but it is unlikely. Bad first impressions are almost impossible to overcome. In fact once individuals have formed an overall evaluation of another person it is difficult to alter that impression.[31]

Seventh, nonverbal behaviour will communicate more than the actual verbal content of what is said. Here, maintaining eye contact is very important; as is speaking with enthusiasm, nodding agreement, and remembering to take a moment to frame answers so that they come across as articulate and fluent.

THE VALIDATION PROCESS

The key to the success of an organization's selection program is the use of valid selection predictors. In order to find the right mix of selection instruments that will predict the applicants with the greatest potential to successfully perform the job, organizations have relied on a variety of screening devices and instruments. These screening devices and instruments range from the face-to-face interviews already discussed to psychological tests. A selection test is valid if it accurately predicts the criterion of job success. The test of selection accuracy is criterion-related validity.

A test is basically a sample of a person's behaviour. However, with some tests, the behaviour being sampled is more clearly recognizable than it is with others. Thus, in some cases the behaviour being sampled is obvious from the test itself. A typing test is an example. Here the test clearly corresponds to some on-the-job behaviour, in this case, typing. At the other extreme, there may be no apparent relationship between the items on the test and the behaviour. This is the case with projective personality tests, for example. Thus, in the *thematic apperception* test illustrated in Figure 6.4, the person is asked to explain how he or she interprets the blurred picture. That interpretation is then used to draw conclusions about the person's personality and behaviour.

In summary, some tests are more clearly representative of the behaviour they are supposed to be measuring than others. Because of this, it is much harder to "prove" that some tests are measuring what they are purported to measure—that they are *valid*.

Validity

validity

A test's **validity** is the accuracy with which the test measures what it is supposed to measure. A test's validity answers the question, "What does this test measure?"[32] With respect to testing for employee selection, the term validity often refers to evidence that the test is job related, in other words, that performance on the test is a *valid predictor* of subsequent performance on the job. A selection test must above all be valid since, without proof of its validity, there is no logical or legally permissible reason to continue using it to screen job applicants.

There are three distinct types of validity (1) criterion validity, (2) content validity, and (3) construct validity.

JUST LOOK AT THE PICTURE BRIEFLY (10 TO 15 SECONDS), TURN THE PAGE, AND WRITE THE STORY IT SUGGESTS.

FIGURE 6.4
Example of a TAT card

SOURCE: John Atkinson, ed., *Motives in Fantasy, Action, and Society* (New York: Van Nostrand Reinhold, 1958)

Criterion Validity

Demonstrating **criterion validity** basically involves demonstrating that those who do well on the test also do well on the job, and that those who do poorly on the test do poorly on the job.[33] Thus, the test has validity to the extent that the people with higher test scores perform better on the job. In psychological measurement, a *predictor* is the measurement (in the case, the test score) that one is trying to relate to a *criterion*, like performance on the job. The term *criterion validity* comes from that terminology.

There are two distinct types of criterion-related validity: *predictive validity* and *concurrent validity*. Predictive validity is used for making predictions about an individual's behaviour at some future date. This is determined by giving the test to all applicants. After those who have been employed have been working on the job for a long enough period, their applicant predictor scores are correlated with their subsequent (employee) criterion scores.

Concurrent validity is the extent to which the test scores of current employees relate to their performance. This approach is often referred to as the current employee method of test validation. This method involves administering the test to a group of current employees. Their test scores are then correlated with some gauge of their work performance. If those employees who receive high scores on the test

criterion validity

are also the most productive (best) employees then the test is considered valid. Concurrent validity yields an immediate estimate of test-criterion correlations.[34]

Content Validity

content validity

One demonstrates the **content validity** of a test by showing that the test constitutes a fair sample of the content of the job.[35] The basic procedure here is to identify the content of the job in terms of job behaviours that are critical to its performance, and then randomly to select and include a sample of those tasks and behaviours in the tests. A typing test used to hire a typist is an example. If the typing test is a representative sample of the typist's job, then the test is probably content valid.

Demonstrating content validity sounds easier than it is in practice. Demonstrating that the tasks the person performs on the test are in fact a comprehensive and random sample of the tasks performed on the job and demonstrating that the conditions under which the test is taken resemble the work situation is not always easy. For many jobs, other evidence of test's validity—such as its criterion validity—must therefore be demonstrated as well.

Construct Validity

construct validity

This process involves measuring the extent or degree to which a job candidate possesses the requisite ability, aptitudes, and qualities that are deemed necessary for performing the job successfully. These psychological traits or attributes are called constructs, and may include intelligence, verbal skills, analytical ability, and leadership ability. **Construct validity** involves two steps: to demonstrate that the predictor is validly related to the construct being measured, and to show that the construct is validly related to the criterion (performance).[36]

Reliability

reliability

A test has two important characteristics, *validity* and *reliability*. Validity is the more important characteristic since, if what the test is measuring cannot be ascertained, it is of little use. **Reliability** refers to the degree of dependability, consistency, or stability of a measure (either predictors, criteria, or other variables).[37] It is "the consistency of scores obtained by the same persons when retested with the identical tests or with an equivalent form of a test."[38] A test's reliability is very important; if a person scores 90 on an intelligence test on a Monday and 130 when retested on Tuesday, a firm probably would not have much faith in the test.

There are several ways to measure reliability. One way is to administer the same test to the same people at two different points in time and compare their test scores. Another way is to administer a test and then administer what experts believe to be an equivalent test at a later date.

A test's *internal consistency* is another measure of its reliability. For example, suppose there are 10 items on a test of vocational interests, all of which are supposed to measure, in one way or another, the person's interest in working out of doors. Here, one could administer the test and then statistically analyze the degree to which responses to these 10 items vary together. This would provide a measure of the internal reliability of the test. This is one reason one often finds questions that apparently are repetitive on some test questionnaires.

Figure 6.5 illustrates the major predictors used by various Canadian organizations in selecting employees for different positions. The findings resulted from a

	Management Staff	White Collar (Professional)	White Collar (Non-Professional)	Blue Collar
	All % Responding Firms Saying "Yes"			
Letters of reference	73.0–80.5	83.5	76.5	48.5
Weighted application blanks	60.9–73.9	91.3	78.2	69.6
Biographical blanks	65.2–79.2	81.9	83.3	70.1
Tests (personality)	68.4–82.5	54.4	50.0	23.7
Assessment centres	42.3–60.6	22.5	11.3	9.9

SOURCE: J.W. Thacker and R.J. Cattaneo, "Survey of Personnel Practices in Canadian Organizations," published in *ASAC Proceedings*, June 1987, pp. 56-66. Used by permission of the authors.

survey of 581 Canadian organizations conducted by James Thacker and Julian Cattaneo of the University of Windsor.

TESTING FOR EMPLOYEE SELECTION

In recent years selection tests, which are generally developed by psychologists, have become a well-accepted part of the selection process. Most organizations use tests for hiring as well as for promotion. There are very large scores of tests on the market that measure a variety of attributes. Testing techniques provide efficient, standardized procedures for screening large numbers of applicants for employment and promotion. The roots of psychological testing go back to the late 19th century when scientists interested in learning more about various aspects of human behaviour began to develop ways to compare people in terms of perceptual ability, physical skills, and mental capacity.[39] In addition many others tests were subsequently developed to assess other attributes of human behaviour such as personality, interests, and preferences as well as differences in motivation and emotional orientation. Psychological tests are commonly used as an important way to help match people with jobs. These tests can also add greatly to the accuracy of job candidates' job success. Therefore the utilization of valid tests can result significantly in the matching and hiring of better qualified applicants.

The use of tests for hiring, promotion, or both has been increasing in recent years after two decades of decline.[40] In one study, about 90% of companies responding in 1963 said they used tests for screening applicants; by 1975, another survey indicated that only about 42% of responding employers reported doing so.[41] By 1985 about 50% of U.S. employers again reported using tests. In Canada, studies have shown that approximately one-third of Canadian organizations use tests for hiring.[42]

In general, testing is more prevalent in larger organizations. For example, only about 30% of employers with fewer than 100 employees reported using tests for hiring, while almost 60% of employers with more than 25 000 employees reported doing so.[43] This reflects several things, including the larger firm's need for efficient, standardized procedures for screening high numbers of applicants and their ability to finance testing programs.

MAJOR TYPES OF TESTS

Cognitive Abilities Tests

Cognitive ability tests are designed to measure an individual's intellectual ability, namely knowledge and problem solving abilities. The two types of tests that are used to measure cognitive abilities are intelligence tests and aptitude tests.

Intelligence Tests

intelligence tests

Intelligence (IQ) **tests** are tests of general intellectual abilities. They measure not a single trait, but rather several abilities such as verbal comprehension, inductive reasoning, memory, numerical abilities, speed of perception, spatial visualization, and word fluency. They also may be used to measure learning speed, mental flexibility, and problem-solving ability.[44] Some of the popular tests include the Stanford-Binet test and the Wechsler test.

As it was originally used, IQ was literally a quotient. The procedure was to divide a child's mental age (as measured by the intelligence test) by his or her chronological age, and then multiply the results by 100. Thus, if an 8-year-old child answered questions as a 10-year-old might, his or her IQ would be 10 divided by 8, times 100, or 125.

For adults, of course, the notion of mental age divided by chronological age would not make much sense, since, for example, we would not necessarily expect a 30-year-old man to be more intelligent than a 25-year-old one. Therefore, an adult's IQ score is actually a derived score, reflecting the extent to which the person is above or below the "average" adult's intelligence score.

Aptitude Tests

aptitude tests

Aptitude tests measure an individual's aptitude or potential to perform an array of tasks, provided the individual is given proper training. In other words these tests measure an acquired knowledge or acquired skill. Although aptitude tests measure acquired learning, they are also used to predict the individual's likely level of learning capability. There are many multi-dimensional aptitude tests that are commonly used by organizations to aid in the selection of applicants. These include: the General Aptitude Test Battery (GATB), Employee Aptitude Survey (EAS), the Flanagan Aptitude Classification Test (FACT), and the Differential Aptitude Test (DAT).

Special Aptitude Tests

There are a number of special aptitude tests which are used to measure a variety of attributes. These include psychomotor tests, clerical aptitude tests, and tests of physical ability.

Psychomotor Tests

Psychomotor tests are used to evaluate a combination of factors including manual dexterity abilities, or motor skills. Commonly used psychomotor tests are the O'Connor Finger and Tweezers Dexterity Tests, the Minnesota Rate of Manipulation Tests, and the Stromberg Dexterity Test, illustrated in Figure 6.6.

FIGURE 6.6
Minnesota Rate of
Manipulation Test
(top) and Stromberg
Dexterity Test
(bottom)

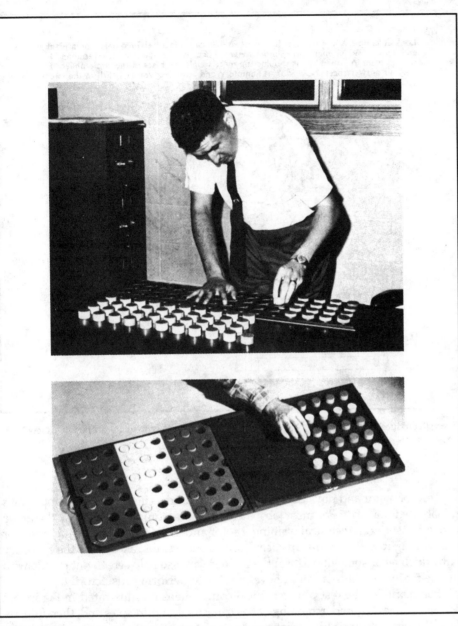

SOURCE: Educational Test Bureau and the Psychological Corporation

Clerical Aptitude Tests

These tests are used to predict specific capacities for performance in various office jobs, such as word processing and data entry.

Physical Ability Tests

Tests of physical abilities are also sometimes required.[45] Physical abilities includes static strength (lifting weights), dynamic strength (like pull-ups), body coordination (as in jumping rope), and stamina.

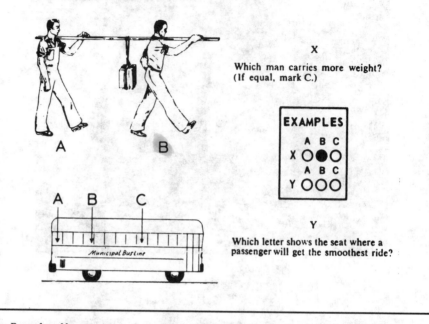

Look at Sample X on this page. It shows two men carrying a weighted object on a plank, and it asks, "Which man carries more weight?" Because the object is closer to man "B" than to man "A," man "B" is shouldering more weight; so blacken the circle under "B" on your answer sheet. Now look at Sample Y and answer it yourself. Fill in the circle under the correct answer on your answer sheet.

X

Which man carries more weight?
(If equal, mark C.)

EXAMPLES

Y

Which letter shows the seat where a passenger will get the smoothest ride?

Tests of motor and physical abilities are often used as indicators of an applicant's trainability for a job.[46] For most jobs, the minimum required physical skills can be developed through technical training. Motor and skills tests provide an indicator of how long it will take the applicant to learn the skills, as well as the accuracy with which he or she will perform them. They can also help screen out people who for one reason or another might never be able to perform satisfactorily.

For example, the test of mechanical comprehension illustrated in Figure 6.7 tests the applicant's understanding of basic mechanical principles and, therefore, reflects the person's aptitude for jobs—like that of machinist engineer—that require mechanical comprehension. Other tests of mechanical aptitude include the mechanical reasoning test and the SRA Tests of Mechanical Aptitude.

Medical Examinations

A medical examination is usually the last step in the selection process, although in some cases the examination takes place after the new employee starts work.[47] Under Canadian human rights laws, medical exams may only be required of job applicants when the medical exam is job related.

There are five main reasons for requiring pre-employment medical exams. The exam can be used to determine whether the applicant qualifies for the physical requirements of the position and to discover any medical limitations that should be taken into account in placing the applicant. The exam will also establish a record and baseline of the applicant's health for the purpose of future insurance or compensation claims. The examination can, by identifying health problems, also reduce absenteeism and accidents and, of course, detect communicable diseases that may be unknown to the applicant. The exam is usually performed by the employer's medical department (in the largest organizations), while smaller employers retain the services of consulting physicians to perform such exams, which are almost always paid for by the employer.

Achievement Tests

Achievement tests are used to measure knowledge and/or proficiency acquired through experience or educational learning. Achievement tests are basically a measure of what a person has learned. Achievement may be tested through such means as paper-and-pencil tests, recognition tests, work samples, and assessment centres. While *work samples* and *assessment centres* are considered tests, they differ from most of the other tests because they focus on measuring job performance directly.[48]

Paper And-Pencil Tests

These are tests which require written responses, either by placing marks on a coded answer sheet or by writing answers to written or orally presented questions.[49]

Recognition Tests

These tests are actual examples or displays of past performance. Recognition tests are commonly used in modelling and advertising agencies. For example, at the time of their interviews job applicants are asked to bring samples of their work with them to the interview site.

Work Samples

These test assess an individual's job skills under realistic work conditions. The *work sampling technique* is based on the assumption that the best way to determine how a candidate will do on the job is by measuring how that candidate actually performs some of the job's basic tasks.[50] "Why measure traits like intelligence or mechanical aptitude," say these experts, "in the hope that they will predict job performance, when it's simpler just to measure samples of that performance directly?"

There are several advantages to using work sampling. By measuring actual on-the-job tasks, it is harder for the applicant to fake answers. The work sample itself is more clearly relevant to the job the employer is recruiting for, so in terms of equal employment the employer may be on safer ground. Work sampling does not delve into the applicant's personality or psyche, so there is almost no chance of it being viewed as an invasion of privacy. And well-designed work samples almost always exhibit better validity than do tests designed to predict performance.

Assessment Centres

An assessment centre is an approach used to test management and executives. An assessment centre is usually a situation in which middle-management and upper-management candidates are asked to make decisions in hypothetical situations and are evaluated on their performance. It usually also involves testing and the use of management games. The term may be applied to the testing procedure itself.

Many organizations use management assessment centres for employee selection. A *management assessment centre* is a two- to three-day experience in which about a dozen management candidates perform realistic management tasks (like making presentations) under the watchful eye of expert appraisers. Each candidate's potential for management is thereby assessed or appraised.[51] The centre itself may be just a conference room, but it is often a special room with a one-way mirror to facilitate the assessor's observations.

Graphology

The use of graphology (handwriting analysis) is based on the assumption that the writer's basic personality traits will express themselves in his or her handwriting.[52] Handwriting analysis thus has some resemblance to projective personality tests.

In graphology, a complex technology and set of rules have evolved, through which the handwriting analyst studies an applicant's handwriting and signature in order to discover the person's needs, desires, and psychological makeup.[53] Figure 6.8, for instance, presents the handwriting of two candidates for a consultant position. According to Elaine Charal, Vice-President of C & M Consultants in Toronto, candidate A's writing specimen indicates that he believes in himself, feels he is competent, and is not afraid to stretch his talents and abilities. This candidate would excel in sales. Candidate B's writing specimen gives a picture of someone with a personable manner and good insight into people, however, Candidate B's manner is better suited for social work than the hard-driving, competitive, sales consulting environment.[54]

While some scientists doubt the validity of handwriting analysis, some writers estimate that many U.S. companies use handwriting analysis to assess applicants for certain strategic positions.[55] And the classified ads of some international newspapers like *The Economist* periodically run advertisements from graphologists offering to aid in an employer's selection process. According to Elaine Choral there are approximately 500 Canadian companies using handwriting analysis to assess job applicants.[56]

Honesty Tests

The use of honesty tests by organizations is growing in popularity. These tests are used to assess the credibility of the information provided by the applicants, and to help reduce theft at the workplace. According to the U.S. Chamber of Commerce, it is estimated that workplace theft amounts to $40 million annually. This means that $7125 is stolen per minute.[57] Honesty tests are psychological tests that measure an individual's attitude toward honest versus dishonest behaviours or actual lack of candour.[58] The underlying principle of honesty tests is that an individual's attitude is an accurate predictor of his or her behaviour.

Honesty in a work force is also important to consider because of the substantial and directly attributable damages that employers can suffer when employees break the rules.[59]

A formal test of honesty, in order to be useful, must first demonstrate that it is both valid and reliable. However, there is much variation in the definition of hon-

FIGURE 6.8
Handwriting Samples
of Two Job Candidates

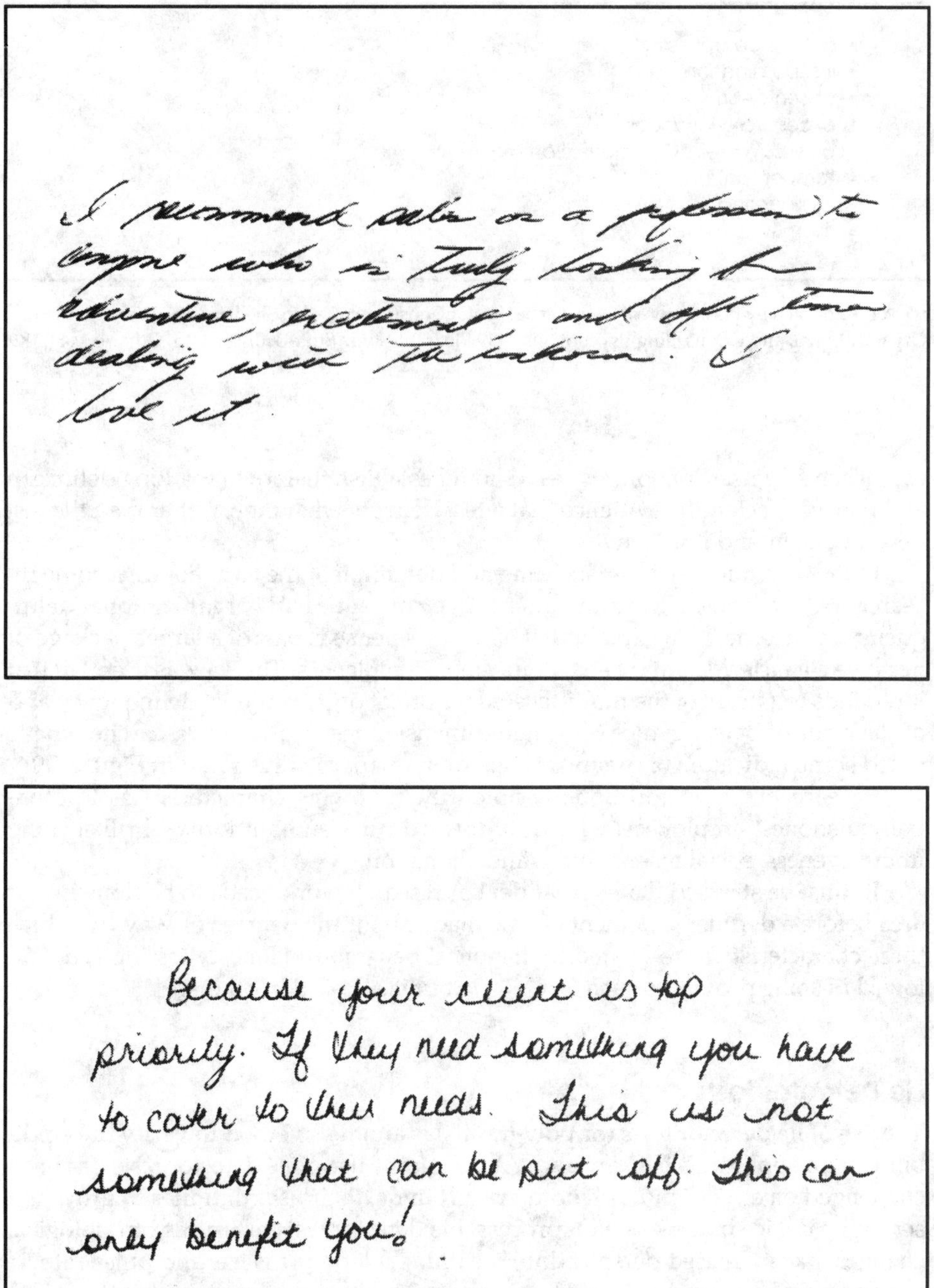

SOURCE: Elaine Charal, C & M. Consultants—Personnel Assessment and Screening, 1262 Don Mills Rd.
Don Mills, Ont. M3B 2W7. Used with permission.

FIGURE 6.9
Characteristics of
Organizational
Delinquency
Syndrome

- substance abuse
- insubordination
- absenteeism
- excessive grievances
- bogus Worker's Compensation claims
- temper tantrums
- malingering
- theft

SOURCE: Reprinted by permission of Glen Thede, Senior Consultant, Geller, Shedletsky & Weiss, Industrial, Organizational, and Counselling Psychologists, 39 Pleasant Blvd., Suite 300, Toronto, Ontario M4T 1K2

esty. Therefore users of honesty tests should establish their own working definition and then seek scientific evidence that a test delivers what they, rather than the test developers, intend it to deliver.

In the search for an understanding and definition of the term honesty, some researchers have put forward the alternative concept of an "organizational delinquency syndrome"[60] to explain that *dishonesty* per se is part of a larger package of negative characteristics and behaviours among employees. This view is useful in that it reminds test users of the multi-faceted nature of organizational delinquency and of the error of over-reliance on single-dimension testing. These researchers have noted some indicators of organizational delinquency,[61] illustrated in Figure 6.9.

Researchers have additionally noted the following characteristics of potentially dishonest employees:[62] hostility toward rules and authority, thrill-seeking impulsiveness, social insensitivity, and alienation.

It must be stressed that a great deal of research work needs to be done in this area before a definite statement can be made about the degrees or ways in which these characteristics are related to dishonest behaviour. Honesty testing is not allowed in some provinces such as Ontario but is allowed in others.[63]

Lie Detector Tests

The use of lie detector tests (or polygraphs) is another method to verify the credibility of an applicant's background. Although the use of lie detector tests has been challenged on ethical and psychometric grounds, their use continues to grow as a screening device in the selection process. Lie detector tests measures physiological changes, like increased perspiration, breathing, blood pressure, and pulse rate.

Several good arguments can be made against the use of polygraph testing. The experience of having one's private life probed in this way can be demeaning and embarrassing. Others argue that by forcing applicants to incriminate themselves the use of lie-detector tests may even be unconstitutional. Another argument is that the polygraph is not perfect in distinguishing between who is lying and who is not, with estimates of their accuracy ranging from about 70% to about 90%. The problem is that some emotional people will react stressfully under polygraph conditions even when they are telling the truth, while other accomplished actors can fool the examiner into thinking they are telling the truth, even when they are lying. Lie detector tests are illegal in Ontario and some other provinces.

Personality, Interest, and Preference Tests[64]

A person's mental and physical abilities are seldom enough to predict a person's job performance. Other factors like the person's motivation and interpersonal skills are important as well; therefore personality and interest inventories as well as preference tests are sometimes used as possible predictors of such intangibles.

Personality Tests

Personality tests are used to measure basic aspects of an applicant's personality, such as introversion, stability, motivation, neurotic tendency, self-sufficiency, self-confidence, and sociability.

    In many personality tests a projected or clouded picture is presented to the person taking the test, who is then asked to interpret or react to it. Since the pictures are ambiguous, the person's interpretation must come from within, or be projected. He or she supposedly projects into the picture his or her own emotional attitudes and ideas about life; thus, a security-oriented person might describe the man in Figure 6.7 as "worrying about what he'll do if he's fired from his job." Examples of personality tests (that are more properly called personality inventories) include the Thematic Apperception Test, Guilford-Zimmerman Temperament Survey, and the Minnesota Multiphasic Inventory. The Guilford-Zimmerman measures personality traits like emotional stability versus moodiness, and friendliness versus criticalness. The Minnesota Multiphasic Inventory, on the other hand, taps traits like hypochondria and paranoia.

    Personality tests—particularly the projective type—are the most difficult tests to evaluate and use. An expert has to assess the test taker's interpretations and reactions and infer from them the makeup of his or her personality. The usefulness of such tests for selection then assumes that it is possible to find a relationship between some measurable personality trait (like introversion) and success on the job.[65] In their study Thacker and Cattaneo found that personality tests were popular in Canada for selecting middle-management employees.[66]

personality tests

Interest Tests

Interest tests measure the relative strength of an applicant's interest in certain occupations or compare a candidate's interests with those of other people performing the same kind of work.[67]

    Interest inventories compare a person's interests with those of people in various occupations. Thus, if a person takes the Strong-Campbell Inventory, he or she would receive a report showing his or her interests in relation to those of people already in occupations such as accountant, engineer, manager, or medical technician. Interest inventories have many uses. They can be useful in career planning, since a person will likely do better on jobs that involve activities he or she is more interested in. These tests can also be useful as selection tools. Clearly, if the firm can select people whose interests are roughly the same as those of successful incumbents in the jobs it is recruiting for, it's more likely that the applicants will be successful on their new jobs.[68]

interest tests

Preference Tests

Preference tests are designed to assess a person's activity preferences. Once this is done the results are used to match with the job and other unique organizational characteristics.

preference tests

FIGURE 6.10
Selection Practices in
Canadian
Organizations (n=581)

Selection Tool	% of Respondents who use this Selection Tool in Organizations of		
	Small Size	Medium Size	Large Size
Application blank	93	94	100
Letters of reference	76	69	63
Weighted application blanks	4	3	5
Biographical information blanks	24	25	26
Personality tests	20	16	28
Aptitude tests	35	43	57
Honesty tests	2	0.4	0.8
Interests inventories	14	10	23

SOURCE: Adaped from J.W. Thacker, and R.J. Cattaneo, "Survey of Personnel Practices in Canadian Organizations," published in *ASAC Proceedings*, June 1987, pp. 56–66. Used by permission of the authors.

Validity of Various Selection Devices

Figure 6.10 summarizes the result of one study of the validity of various selection devices. Tests of actual performance—work samples, peer evaluations, and assessment centres—rate highest. Indirect evaluations, such as psychological tests or academic performance, rate lower. This suggests, again, that (1) predictors like these are best used in conjunction with other selection devices, and that (2) they must be employed properly to be of any use. The following chapter explains how to use interviews effectively.

ETHICAL AND LEGAL CONCERNS AND CRITICISMS IN PSYCHOLOGICAL TESTING

Psychological testing has been the subject of sustained criticisms on the ground that it has too significant an influence over the lives of people being tested, and on the ground that unethical and uninformed practices can potentially be undertaken by nonprofessionals who administer the test.

Criticisms of Tests

The following are some of the common criticisms of psychological testing.[69]

1. People without the appropriate knowledge and training are developing and selling tests. Such tests may be useless or even detrimental because they are neither reliable nor valid.

2. Even if the tests are well designed, they may be poorly administered or used for the wrong purpose.

3. There is a tendency among some employers to accept the results of tests as if they were carved in stone. These employers rely on the test score to point unerringly to a perfect candidate, thereby abdicating their own responsibility for making judgments.

4. The costs of not doing validity studies on these tests are not to be measured in dollars saved alone but in wasted human lives, goodwill, and public relations.

5. Tests in common use in Canada are U.S. designated and are not necessarily valid for assessing Canadians. (Psychologist Warren Shapell has been quoted as saying that on one standard sales aggressiveness test, the Canadian mean score is three points lower than the American standard. This means that Canadians whose scores fall on the borderline could be wrongly excluded from a job).[70]

6. Human resource directors in Canada are less likely than their counterparts in the United States to be college graduates. Lacking any theoretical grounding in testing, they can be sold a bill of goods.

Concerns about Reliability and Validity

Some factors that make a test less than reliable include:[71]

1. Improper test items that are readily misinterpreted (e.g. "True or False: I like reading and writing": note that an individual could like one but not the other, leading to the possibility that they regard true on one occasion and false on another. Out of frustration, they may also choose not to respond at all).

2. Lack of uniform testing conditions including variation in instructions, time limits, or rapport between the candidate and the administrator.

3. Improper selection of test items. These must be chosen in such a way as to lead the respondent through the test and encourage the development of some line of consistency. The reliability of a test can be called into question if test items confuse a respondent and affect the ability to reply consistently.

Some tests may try to measure something that cannot be measured due to the nature of the factor itself (e.g., no test could consistently measure or predict a respondent's "joy" level, since there is a lack of consistent understanding about what constitutes "joy").[72] In their study Thacker and Cattaneo found that most Canadian employers have little inclination to validate tests and that many Canadian human resource managers do not understand even basic validity concepts.[73]

Notwithstanding these criticisms, as Professor Harish Jain noted, there are a few examples of successful in-house research on employment testing. The Personnel Psychology Centres of the Public Service Commission Canada and the Canadian Armed Forces have done much work on test development and test validation and both have high quality human resources selection programs.[74] Individuals interested in the federal government in certain areas such as human resource management or foreign service are required to pass a cognitive ability test known as the Entry-Level Officer Selection Test. Additionally, Royal LePage (Canada) has developed an in-house recruitment program that uses a consistent and structured testing assessment approach to select the best possible candidates for its sales team. While testing is only one part of the procedure to attract, recruit, and hire the right people, Royal LePage has made a determined effort to use the most appropriate scientific methods to ensure that its testing procedures are valid and cost-efficient.[75]

The issue of validation played a significant part in the 1987 landmark decision by the Supreme Court of Canada. In the case of *Action Travail des Femmes* vs. *CN Rail* (1984), the Court upheld the findings of a CHRC tribunal that a mechanical aptitude test used by CN Rail was discriminatory. The Court ruled that CN must cease using the Bennet Mechanical Comprehension test because it had an adverse impact on hiring of women for entry-level blue-collar jobs.[76]

Fundamental Guidelines to Effective Testing

The Canadian Psychological Association has developed and published comprehensive testing standards, called Guidelines for Educational and Psychological Testing. They cover areas such as test instrumentation, test use and administration, scoring and reporting.[77]

The appropriate use of valid psychological tests can result in the hiring of better qualified job applicants. Because the field of selection testing involves so many different varieties of tests that purport to measure so many diverse attributes of an individual, it is important that organizations do a great deal of planning, analysis, and experimentations in order to develop the type of tests that best satisfy their needs.

The following are some basic guidelines for setting up a testing program.[78]

1. *Tests should be used as supplements.* Tests should not be used as the only selection technique; instead, they should be used to supplement other techniques like interviews and background checks. There are several reasons for this. First, tests are not infallible. Even in the best of cases the test score usually only accounts for about 25% of the variation in the measure of performance. In addition, tests are often better at telling which candidates will fail than which will succeed.

2. *Tests should be validated in the organization.* Both legal requirements and good testing practice demand that the test be validated in each organization. The fact that the same tests have been proven valid in similar organizations is not sufficient.

3. *All current hiring and promotion standards should be analyzed.* Questions like, "What proportion of aboriginal, handicapped, and non-target applicants are being rejected at each stage of the hiring process?" and "WHY are we using this standard—what does it mean in terms of actual behaviour on the job?" should be asked. The burden of proof is always on the organization to prove that the predictor (such as intelligence) is related to success or failure on the job.

4. *Accurate records of test results must be kept.* It is important to keep accurate records of why each applicant was rejected. For purposes of the Human Rights Commission, a general note such as "not sufficiently well qualified" would not be enough. It must be stated, as objectively as possible, why each candidate is rejected. The reasons for rejecting the candidate may be subject to validation at a later date.

5. *Employers should beware of certain tests.* Certain intelligence tests have been misused. The evidence the firm provides on their validity in the organization would have to be overwhelming to permit their use.

6. *Certified psychologists should be used.* The development, validation, and use of selection standards (including tests) generally requires the assistance of a qualified psychologist.

7. *Test conditions are important.* Administer tests in areas that are reasonably private, quiet, well lighted, and ventilated. All applicants should take the test under the same conditions. Once completed, test results should be held in the strictest confidence and only given to individuals who have a legitimate need for the information and who also have the ability to understand and interpret the scores.

On the Front Line

Jennifer and her father have what the latter describes as an easy but hard job when it comes to screening job applicants. The applicants are easily screened with about 20 minutes of on-the-job testing. As Jennifer points out, "a person either knows how to press clothes fast enough or how to use cleaning chemicals and machines, or he or she doesn't, and we find out very quickly by just trying them out on the job."

But, on the other hand, applicant screening for the stores can also be frustratingly hard because of the nature of things that Jennifer would like to screen for. Two of the most critical problems facing her company concern employee turnover. If there is a way to do this through employee testing and screening techniques Jennifer would like to know about it because of the management time and money that is now being wasted by the never-ending need to recruit and hire new employees.

Of even greater concern to Jennifer and her father is the need to institute new practices to screen out those employees who may be predisposed to steal from the company.

Employee theft is an enormous problem for the Carter Cleaning Centres, and one that is not just limited to employees who handle the cash. For example, the cleaner spotter and/or the presser often open the store themselves, without a manager (to get the day's work started), and it is not unusual to have one or more of these people steal supplies or "run a route." Running a route means that an employee canvases his neighbourhood to pick up people's clothes for cleaning and then secretly cleans and presses them in the Carter store, using the company's supplies, gas, and power. It would also not be unusual for an unsupervised person (or his or her supervisor, for that matter) to accept a one-hour rush order for cleaning or laundering, quickly clean and press the item, and return it to the customer for payment without making our a proper ticket for the item or posting the sale. The money, of course, goes into the person's pocket instead of into the cash register.

The more serious problem concerns the store manager and the counter people who actually have to handle the cash. According to Jack Carter, "you would not believe the creativity employees use to get around the management controls we set up to cut down on employee theft." As one extreme example of this felonious creativity, Jack tells the following story. "To cut down on the amount of money my employees were stealing, I had a small sign painted and placed in front of all our cash registers. The sign said: Your entire order free if we don't give you a cash register receipt when you pay.—Call 962-0734. It was my intention with this sign to force all our cash-handling employees to place their receipts into the cash register where they would be recorded for my accountants. After all, if all the cash that comes in is recorded in the cash register, then we should have a much better handle on stealing in our stores, right? Well, one of our managers found a diabolical way around this. I came into the store one night and noticed that the cash register that this particular manager was using just didn't look right although the sign was dutifully placed in front of it. It turned out that every afternoon at about 5:00 P.M. when the other employees left, this character would pull his own cash register out of a box that he hid underneath all our supplies. Customers coming in would notice the sign and of course the fact that he was meticulous in ringing up every sale. But unbeknown to them and to us, for about five months the sales that came in for about an hour every day went into his cash register, not mine. It took us that long to figure out where our cash for that store was going."

Given this and similar war stories, Jennifer now has the following questions:

1. What would be the advantages and disadvantages to her company of routinely administering polygraph exams to all its employees?

2. Specifically, what other screening techniques could the company use to screen out theft-prone employees, and how exactly could these be used?

SUMMARY

1. Selection is the process of selecting those employees who have the ability and potential required to successfully perform the duties of the job and to contribute to improved productivity. The primary objective of the selection process is to accurately predict a successful match or fit between the individual and the organization. An effective selection program must include sound human resource planning, proven job analysis, effective recruitment, and comprehensively valid and reliable screening devices and evaluative instruments.

2. The actual selection process includes a variety of screening devices, techniques, and instruments designed to evaluate the capabilities of applicants. In this chapter we discussed three major selection instruments: application forms, selection interviews, and selection testing. Application forms were recognized as providing a wealth of information to employers, weighted forms were also discussed. Several types of interviews were identified, including structured, unstructured, mixed (semistructured), serialized, stress, panel, sequential, problem-solving, behavior description, and videotaped. We discussed several factors and problems that can undermine the usefulness of an interview. These are poor planning, snap judgments, negative emphasis, not knowing the job, candidate-order-error, nonverbal behaviour, the psychiatric approach and pressure to hire. It was emphasized that understanding these common mistakes is the first step toward avoiding them.

4. Guidelines for interviewers include using a structured guide, knowing the requirements of the job, focusing on traits that can be accurately evaluated (like motivation): letting the interviewee do most of the talking, and remembering human rights commissions' guidelines. Effective interviewing can contribute directly to increasing the performance in an organization. First, it helps to select the best qualified candidates—ones who have the ability and potential to do the job. Second, a candidate's motivation is one of the traits most accurately measured during an interview.

5. We discussed several selection testing techniques and the importance of validity (including criterion validity and content validity.) We also discussed reliability and how to measure it.

6. There are many types of tests in use, including intelligence tests, tests of physical skills, tests of achievement, aptitude tests, interest inventories, and personality tests. For a selection test to be useful scores on the test should be validated in a predictable way to performance on the job.

7. Under human rights legislation, an employer may have to be able to prove that his or her tests are predictive of success or failure on the job. This usually involves a predictive validation study, although other means of validation are often acceptable.

8. Some basic testing guidelines include using tests as supplements, validating the tests for appropriate jobs, analyzing all current hiring and promotion standards, being wary of certain tests, using a certified psychologist, and maintaining good test conditions.

9. Other selection tools we discussed include the polygraph, and graphology.

KEY TERMS

weighted application blank
(WAB)
structured interview
unstructured interview
mixed interview
serialized interview
stress interview
panel interview

problem-solving interview
behaviour description interview
videotaped interview
validity
criterion validity
content validity
construct validity

reliability
intelligence tests
aptitude tests
personality tests
interest tests
preference tests

DISCUSSION QUESTIONS

1. Explain the selection process.

2. Do interviews have to be a waste of time? Why? Why not?

3. Explain at least six factors that affect the usefulness of interviews.

4. What steps should a recruiter take to become a more effective interviewer?

5. Write a short presentation entitled "How to Be Effective as an Interviewee."

6. Explain what is meant by reliability and validity. What is the difference between them? In what respect(s) are they similar?

7. What are the relationships among human resource planning, job analysis, recruitment, performance appraisal, and selection?

8. Explain the advantages and disadvantages of psychological testing.

9. Why is the selection process important to the organization and the individual?

CASE INCIDENT: The Painter and the Auto Body Shop

A Toronto company in the business of repairing vintage cars hired an employee to work in its paint department. The employee had grown up in Trinidad where he had spent two years working in a body shop learning how to prepare a car to be painted. He also learned how paint a car. After he became proficient, his mother opened a car repair shop and employed her son to paint cars. Two other employees were hired to paint cars.

The painter soon decided to move to Canada. Shortly after his arrival, he got a job in an auto collision shop "prepping" and painting cars at an hourly wage. After working in the auto collision shop for four years he worked for a car dealer for about a year. There he was paid 38% of the cost charged to a customer for painting a car. When the car dealership hired additional employees for the paint department, the painter's income was reduced. He then quit and was subsequently hired by the vintage car repair shop.

At the vintage car repair shop there were five employees in the shop's paint department. The employees were a head painter and an apprentice, both white, and three black painters including the one from Trinidad. About one month after the Trinidadian was hired, the head painter left and was not replaced. The car dealer's owner then promoted a body shop employee, who was white, to be the foreman of both the body shop and the paint department.

The owner soon became dissatisfied with the quality of work being performed in the paint department. He was in danger of losing his largest account. The owner then hired another painter, who happened to be white, but his work was unacceptable. The white employee left after four days on the job. The owner then decided that there should be a head painter in the paint department. He filled that position with a painter recommended to him by the foreman.

The Trinidadian was called into the owner's office and advised of the decision to hire a head painter. The owner told him that there was no one in the paint shop who was capable of holding that position. Therefore, he hired someone from the outside. The owner also told the Trinidadian that the head painter would be doing all the painting. The other employees in that department would only do "prepping."

The Trinidadian resented not being given an opportunity of being the head painter. He said that he would not stay if his work was limited to prepping. He ended up staying for a few days to finish some jobs and then quit. During those few days the new head painter arrived at the shop. Ironically, he proved to be unsatisfactory and eventually was replaced.

The Trinidadian, who had obtained another job two weeks after leaving the repair shop, filed a complaint with the Ontario Human Rights Commission. He claimed that the repair shop had contravened the Ontario Human Rights Code's prohibition against race discrimination alleging that he was not considered for the head painter position because of his race.

At the hearing of a Human Rights Board of Inquiry the repair shop's owner denied the accusation of race discrimination. The owner claimed that his conclusion that "none of [the repair shop's] current employees could handle the job" of head painter was a business decision "free of any improper considerations."

The owner insisted that he had not been "motivated by racist considerations" and said that he had employed "people with a variety of backgrounds." The owner supported his claim by pointing out that none of the other blacks in the paint department had complained.

The key witness at the hearing was a white auto body repairman who had previously been an employee of the repair shop. This ex-employee testified that when he was hired he noticed that the white and black employees ate their lunches in separate groups. The ex-employee said that the foreman had told him that he felt "uncomfortable about them black guys" and that "the black employees kept the place like a pigsty and behaved like pigs."

SOURCE: *The Employment Law Report*, Vol. 11, no. 4 (April 1990), pp. 31-32. Reproduced by permission of Concord Publishing Ltd., 14 Prince Arthur Avenue, Toronto, Ontario M5R 1A9.

Questions

1. Describe the staffing process at the auto body shop and discuss its implications for both the painter and the organization.

2. What are the human rights implications in this case?

3. As the organization's HRM specialist what steps would you take to enhance the company's staffing processes?

NOTES

1. Robert D. Gatewood and Hubert S. Field, *Human Resource Selection* (Chicago: The Dryden Press, 1990), p. 3.

2. See, for example, George Beason and John Belt, "Verifying the Job Applicant's Background," *Personnel Administration* (November-December, 1974), pp. 29-32; Bureau of National Affairs, "Selection Procedures and Personnel Records," *Personnel Policies Forum*, no. 114 (September 1976), p. 4. See also Paul Sackett and Michael M. Harris, "Honesty Testing for Personnel Selection: A Review and Critique," *Personnel Psychology*, Vol. 37, no. 2 (Summer 1985), pp. 221-245.

3. Arthur Pell, *Recruiting and Selecting Personnel* (New York: Regents Publishing, 1969), pp. 96-98; see also Wayne Cascio, "Accuracy of Variable Biographical information Blank Responses," Journal of Applied Psychology, Vol. 60, (December 1975), for a discussion of accuracy of bio-data.

4. This is based on "Evaluating Employment Applications" in *Personnel Journal*, Vol. 63, no. 1 (January 1984), pp. 22-24, and was reprinted from *Supervisor's Newsletter*, no. 276 (March 1983).

5. Ann McDonald, "Interviewing in Business and Industry," in John M. Dillard and Robert R. Reilly, eds., *Systemic Interviewing* (Columbia, Ohio: Merril Publishing Company, 1988), pp. 234-257.

6. James G. Goodale, *The Fine Art of Interviewing* (Englewood Cliffs, N.J.: Prentice-Hall Inc., 1982), p. 22. See also Robert L. Decker, "The Employment Interview," *Personnel Administrator* (26 November 1981), pp. 71-73.

7. Willi H. Wiesner and Robert J. Oppenheimer, "Note-Taking in the Selection Interview: Its Effect Upon Predictive Validity and Information Recall," Administrative Sciences Association of Canada (Personnel and Human Resources Division), *Proceedings of the Annual Conference Meeting*, Vol. 12, part 8, 1991, pp. 97-106.

8. Pell, p. 119.

9. M. M. Harris, "Reconstructing the Employment Interview: A Review of Recent Literature and Suggestions for Future Research," *Personnel Psychology*, 42 (1989), pp. 691-726; see also E. C. Webster, *The Interview: A Social Judgement Process*, (Schomberg, Ont.: SIP Publications, 1982).

10. William Tullar, Terry Mullins, and Sharon Caldwell, "Effects of Interview Length and Applicant Quality on Interview Decision Time," *Journal of Applied Psychology*, Vol. 64 (December 1979), pp. 669-674. See also Tracy McDonald and Milton Hakel, "Effects of Applicants Race, Sex, Suitability, and Answers on Interviewers Questioning Strategy and Ratings," *Personnel Psychology*, Vol. 38 (Summer 1985), pp. 321-334.

11. Tullar and others, "The Effects of Interview Length."

12. Ibid., p. 674. See also David Tucker and Patricia Rowe, "Consulting the Application Form Prior to the Interview: An Essential Step in the Selection Process," *Journal of Applied Psychology*, Vol. 63, no. 3 (1977), pp. 282-287.

13. Landy and Trumbo, *Psychology of Work Behaviour*.

14. Goodale, p. 26.

15. Ibid.

16. S. W. Constantin, "An Investigation of Information Favorability in the Employment Interview," *Journal of Applied Psychology*, Vol. 61 (1976), pp. 734-749. It should be noted that a number of the studies discussed in this chapter involve having interviewers eval-

uate interviews based on written transcripts (rather than face to face), and that a study suggests that this procedure may not be equivalent to having interviewers interview applicants directly. See Charles Gorman, William Grover, and Michael Doherty, "Can We Learn Anything about Interviewing Real People from `Interviews' of Paper People? A Study of the External Validity Paradigm," *Organizational Behaviour and Human Performance*, Vol. 22, no. 2 (October 1978), pp. 165-192.

17. David Tucker and Patricia Row, "Relationship between Expectancy, Casual Attribution, and Final Hiring Decisions in the Employment Interview," *Journal of Applied Psychology*, Vol. 64, no. 1 (February 1979), pp. 27-34. See also Robert Dipboye, Gail Fontenelle, and Kathleen Garner, "Effect of Previewing the Application on Interview Process and Outcomes," *Journal of Applied Psychology*, Vol. 69, no. 1 (February 1984), pp. 118-128.

18. R. E. Carlson, "Effects of Applicant Sample on Ratings of Valid Information in Employment Setting," *Journal of Applied Psychology*, Vol. 54 (1970), pp. 217-222.

19. See Richard Arvey and James Campion, "The Employment Interview: A Summary and Review of Recent Research," *Personnel Psychology*, Vol. 35 (Summer 1982), p. 305.

20. Goodale, p. 28.

21. Douglas T. Hall and James G. Goodale. *Human Resource Management* (Glenview, Ill: Scott, Foresman and Company 1986), pp. 260-261.

22. Goodale, p. 31.

23. R. E. Carlson, "Selection Interview Decisions: The Effects of Interviewer Experience, Relative Quota Situation, and Applicant Sample on Interview Decisions," *Personnel Psychology*, Vol. 20 (1967), pp. 259-280.

24. Pell, p. 119.

25. Tom Janz, Lowell Hellervik, and David C. Gilmore, *Behaviour Description Interviewing* (Boston: Allyn and Bacon Inc., 1986).

26. Janz, Hellervik, and Gilmore, pp. 64-65. Also see Tom Janz, "The Patterned Behaviour Description Interview: The Best Prophet of the Future Is the Past," R. W. Eder and G. R. Ferris, eds., *The Employment Interview: Theory, Research, and Practice* (Newbury Park, CA: Sage Publications, 1989), pp. 158-168; Cynthia D. Fisher, Lyle F. Schoenfeldt, and James B. Shaw, *Human Resource Management* (Boston: Houghton Mifflin Company, 1990), pp. 272-275; "Drake Personnel in Perspective: The Principles of Behaviour Description Interviewing." *Drake Business Review*, Vol. 4, No. 3 (1989), pp. 5-7.

27. From a speech by industrial psychologist Paul Green and contained in BNA Bulletin to Management, June 20, 1985, pp. 2-3.

28. James Hollandsworth, Jr. and others, "Relative Contributions of Verbal, Articulative, and Nonverbal Communication to Employment Decisions in the Job Interview Setting," *Personnel Psychology*, Vol. 32 (Summer 1979), pp. 359-367. See also Sara Rynes and Howard Miller, "Recruiter and Job Influences on Candidates for Employment," *Journal of Applied Psychology*, Vol. 68, no. 1 (1983), pp. 147-154.

29. Richard Payne, *How to Get a Better Job Quickly* (New York: New American Library, 1979).

30. J. G. Hollandsworth, R. C. Ladinski, and J. H. Russel, "Use of Social Skills Training in the Treatment of Extreme Anxiety of Deficient Verbal Skills," *Journal of Applied Behaviour Analysis*, Vol. 11 (1979), pp. 259-269.

31. Robert A. Barron, "Impression Management by Applicants During Employment Interviews: The `Too Much of a Good Thing' Effect" R. W. Eder and Gerald R. Ferris, eds., *The Employment Interview: Theory, Research, and Practice*, (Newburg Park, CA: Sage Publications, 1989), pp. 204-215.

32. Leona Tyler, *Test and Measurements* (Englewood Cliffs, N.J.: Prentice-Hall, 1971), p. 25.

33. *Primer of Equal Employment Opportunity* (Washington, D.C.: Bureau of National Affairs, 1978), p. 18. In practice, proving in court the criterion-related validity of paper and pen-

cil tests has been difficult. In a review of the subject, for instance, two experts conclude that "in general, most judges very carefully scrutinized these validation studies then were often found to be quite critical in their evaluations. In fact, the criterion-related validity of the predictor was upheld in only 5 of the 12 cases reported." See Kleiman and Faley. See also Ronald Pannone, "Predicting Test Performance: A Content Valid Approach to Screening Applicants," *Personnel Psychology*, Vol. 37, no. 3 (Autumn, 1984), pp. 507-514.

34. Laurence Siegel and Irving M. Lane, *Personnel and Organizational Psychology*, (Homwood Ill.: Richard D. Irwin Inc., 1987), p. 73.

35. See James Ledvinka, *Federal Regulation of Personnel and Human Resource Management* (Boston: Kent Publishing, 1982), p. 111.

36. Harris C. Jain, "Staffing: Recruitment and Selection" in *Human Resources Management in Canada* (Scarborough, Ontario: Prentice-Hall, 1983), p. 25,031.

37. Gatewood and Field, p. 89.

38. Ann Anastasi, *Psychological Patterns* (New York: Macmillan, 1968); reprinted in W. Clay Hamner and Fran Schmidt, *Contemporary Problems in Personnel* (Chicago: St. Claire Press., 1974), pp. 102-109. Discussion of reliability based on Marvin Dunnette, *Personnel Selection and Placement* (Belmont, CA: Wadsworth Publishing Inc., 1966), pp. 29-30.

39. Reginald T. Ellis, "The Use of Standardized Tests in Human Resources Management" in *Human Resources Management in Canada* (Scarborough, Ont.: Prentice-Hall Canada Inc., 1989), p. 25,517.

40. Tyler, p. 24.

41. Selection Procedure and Personnel Records, *Personnel Policies Forum Survey*, no. 114 (Washington, D.C.: Bureau of National Affairs, 1976), p. 7. Some surveys, however, indicate that pre-employment testing is losing favour. For example, see John Aberth, "Pre-employment Test is Losing Favour," *Personnel Journal*, Vol. 65, no. 9 (September 1986), pp. 96-99.

42. Steven Cranshaw, "The Status of Employment Testing in Canada: A Review and Evaluation of Theory and Professional Practice," *Canadian Psychology*, 27 (1986), pp. 183-195; James W. Thacker and R. Julian Cattaneo, "The Canadian Personnel Function: Status and Practices" Administrative Sciences Association of Canada (Personnel and Human Resources Division) *Proceedings of the Annual Conference Meeting*, 1987, pp. 56-66.

43. *Personnel Management: Policies and Practices Report*, no. 22, (Englewood Cliffs, N.J.: Prentice Hall, April 2, 1975.)

44. Reginald T. Ellis, "The Use of Standardized Tests in Human Resources Management" *Human Resources Management in Canada*, (Toronto: Prentice-Hall Canada Inc., 1989), pp. 25,517-25,524.

45. See, for example, Richard Reilly, Sheldon Zedeck, and Mary Tenopyr, "Validity and Fairness of Physical Ability Tests for Predicting Performance in Craft Jobs," *Journal of Applied Psychology*, Vol. 64, no. 3 (June 1970), pp. 262-274.

46. Siegel and Lane, *Personnel and Organizational Psychology*, p. 180. For an interesting example of use of the Minnesota Multiphastic Personality Inventory and other personality tests for detecting malingerers in the workplace, see Paul Lees-Haley, "How to Detect Malingerers in the Workplace," *Personnel Journal*, Vol. 65, no. 7 (July 1986).

47. Joseph Famularo, *Handbook of Modern Personnel Administration* (New York: McGraw-Hill, 1972), pp. 12-17, 18.

48. Emma D. Dunnette and W. D. Borman, "Personnel Selection and Classification Systems," *Annual Review of Psychology*, Vol. 30, (1970), pp. 477-525.

49. Siegel and Lane, pp. 182-183.

50. Paul Wernamont and John T. Campbell, "Signs, Samples, and Criteria," *Journal of Applied Psychology*, Vol. 52 (1968), pp. 372-376; James Campion, "Work Sampling for Personnel Selection," *Journal of Applied Psychology*, Vol. 56, (1972), pp. 40-44; reprinted in Hamner and Schmidt, *Contemporary Problems in Personnel*, pp. 168-180; Sidney Gael, Donald Grant, and Richard Ritchie, "Employment Test Validation for Minority and Nonminority Clerks with Work Sample Criteria," *Journal of Applied Psychology*, Vol. 60, no. 4 (August 1974); Fran Schmidt and others, "Job Sample vs. Paper and Pencil Trades and Technical Test: Adverse Impact and Examiner Attitudes," *Personnel Psychology*, Vol. 30 no. 7 (Summer 1977), pp. 187-198.

51. Ann Howard, "An Assessment of Assessment Centres," *Academy of Management Journal*, Vol. 17 (1974), pp. 115-134; see also Louis Olivas, "Using Assessment Centres for Individual and Organizational Development," Personnel, Vol. 57 (May-June 1980), pp. 63-67.

52. See for example, "Corporate Lie Detectors Under Fire," *Business Week*, January 13, 1973. For a discussion of how to improve the validity of the polygraph test, see Robert Forman and Clark McCauley, "Validity of a Positive Control Polygraph Test Using the Field to practice Model," *Journal of Applied Psychology*, Vol. 71, no. 4 (November 1986), pp. 691-698.

53. Ulrich Sonnemann, *Handwriting Analysis as a Psychodiagnostic Tool* (New York: Grune & Stratton, 1950), pp. 144-145.

54. Elaine Charal, "The Person Behind the Resume: Handwriting Analysis as a Precision Assessment Tool," *Human Resources Management in Canada* (Toronto: Prentice-Hall Canada Inc., 1991), pp. 25,559-25,564.

55. Jitendra Sharma and Harsh Vardham, "Graphology: What Handwriting Can Tell You about an Applicant," *Personnel*, Vol. 52, no. 2 (March-April 1975), pp. 57-63. Note that one recent empirical study resulted in the conclusion that "we find ourselves compelled to conclude that it is graphology, rather than just our small sample of graphologists, that is invalid." These researchers conclude that when graphology does seem to "work," it does so because the graphologist is reading a spontaneously written autobiography of the candidate and is thereby obtaining biographical information about the candidate from that essay. See Gershon Ben-Shakhar, Maya Bar-Hillel, Yoram Bilu, Edor Ben-Abba, and Anat Flug, "Can Graphology Predict Occupational Success? Two Empirical Studies and Some Methodological Ruminations," *Journal of Applied Psychology*, Vol. 71, no. 4 (November 1986), pp. 645-653.

56. C & M Consultants—Personnel Assessment and Screening, personal correspondence, June 1991.

57. Ron Zemke, "Employee Theft: How to Cut Your Losses," *Training* (May 1986), p. 74.

58. Michael A. McDaniel and John W. Jones, "A Meta-Analysis of the Employee Attitude Inventory Theft Scales" *Journal of Business and Psychology* (Fall 1986), p. 23. Quoted in Terry L. Leap and Michael D. Crino, *Personnel/Human Resource Management* (New York: Macmillan Publishing Company, 1989), p. 253.

59. This section is based on Glen Thede, "Building an Honest Workforce: Testing and Alternatives" *Human Resources Management in Canada* (Toronto: Prentice-Hall Canada Inc., 1990), pp. 25,539-25,544.

60. See Joyce Hogan and Robert Hogan, "How to Measure Employee Reliability," *Journal of Applied Psychology*, Vol. 74, no. 2, (1989), pp. 273-279.

61. Hogan and Hogan, p. 275; see also Glen Thede, pp. 25,539-25,544.

62. Hogan and Hogan, p. 273.

63. See Table 5 in James W. Thacker and R. J. Cattaneo, "The Canadian Personnel Function: Status and Practices," Administrative Sciences Association of Canada (Personnel and Human Resources Division), *Proceedings of the Annual Meeting* (June 1987).

64. Jain, p. 25,040.

65. Thacker and Cattaneo, pp. 56-66.

66. Jain, p. 25,040.

67. For a study describing how matching (1) task and working condition preferences of applicants with (2) actual job and working conditions can be achieved, see Ronald Ash, Edward Levine, and Steven Edgell, "Study of a Matching Approach: The Impact of Ethnicity," *Journal of Applied Psychology*, Vol. 64, no. 1 (February 1979), pp. 35-41. For a discussion of how a standard clerical test can be used to screen applicants who will have to use video display terminals, see Edward Silver and Corwin Bennett, "Modification of the Minnesota Clerical Test to Predict Performance on Video Display Terminals," *Journal of Applied Psychology*, Vol. 72, no., 1 (February 1987), pp. 153-155.

68. Thacker and Cattaneo, pp. 56-66.

69. M. Dewey, "Employers take a hard look at the validity and value of psychological screening," *Globe and Mail* (February 8, 1981), p. B1. See also M. Teff "Why more firms rely on psychological tests," *Financial Post* (December 12, 1981). See also V. Ross, "Psychological testing for successful workers" Maclean's (May 30, 1981), pp. 48-49.

70. Ross, pp. 48-94.

71. Glenn Thede, "Choosing the Right Tests for Employee Selection" *Human Resources Management in Canada* (Toronto: Prentice-Hall Canada Inc., 1989), pp. 25,527.

72. For a comprehensive discussion of research findings of concerns about validity see George F. Dreher and Steven D. Maurer, "Assessing the Employment Interview: Deficiencies Associated with the Existing Domain of Validity Coefficients" in Robert W. Eder and Gerald R. Ferris, eds., *The Employment Interview: Theory, Research, and Practice* (Newburg Park, Ca: Sage Publications 1989), pp. 249-268. See also Cranshaw Wiesner, pp. 269-281.

73. Thacker and Cattaneo, pp. 56-66.

74. Cranshaw, p. 183. See also Jain, p. 50,024-50,025.

75. Michael Godkewitsch, "Pre-Hiring Skills Assessment: How to Get the Right People in the Right Job at the Right Time," *Human Resources Management in Canada* (Toronto: Prentice-Hall Canada Inc., 1989), pp. 25,533.

76. Jain, pp. 50,024-50,025.

77. *Guidelines for Educational and Psychological Testing* (Old Chelsea, Que.: Canadian Psychological Association, 1987.)

78. See, for example, Floyd L. Ruch, "The Impact on Employment Procedures of the Supreme Court Decision in the Duke Power Case," *Personnel Journal*, Vol. 50, no. 4 (October 1971), pp. 777-783; Hubert Field, Gerald Bagley, and Susan Bagley, "Employment Test Validation for Minority and Non-Minority Production Workers," *Personnel Psychology*, Vol. 30, no. 1 (Spring 1977), pp. 37-46; Ledvinka, *Federal Regulations*, p. 110; M. K. Distefano, Jr., Margaret pryer, and Stella Craig, "Predictive Validity of General Ability Test with Black and White Psychiatric Attendants," *Personnel Psychology*, Vol. 29, no. 2 (Summer 1976). Also, see the Winter 1976 issue of *Personnel Psychology*, Vol. 2 no. 4. See also James Norborg, "A Warning Regarding the Simplified Approach to the Evaluation of Test Fairness and Employee Selection Procedures," *Personnel Psychology*, Vol. 37, no. 3 (Autumn 1984), pp. 483-386; Charles Johnson, Lawrence Messe, and William Crano, "Predicting Job performance of Low Income Workers: The Work Opinion Questionnaire," *Personnel Psychology*, Vol. 37. no. 2 (Summer 1984), pp. 291-299; Frank Schmidt, Benjamin Ocasio, Joseph Hillery, and John Hunter, "Further Within-Setting Empirical Tests of the Situational Specificity Hypothesis in Personnel Selection," *Personnel Psychology*, Vol. 38, no. 3 (Autumn 1985), pp. 509-524.

SUGGESTED READINGS

Canadian Psychological Association. *Guidelines for Educational and Psychological Testing*. Old Chelsea, Que., 1987.

Cranshaw, Steven F. "The State of Employment Testing in Canada: A Review and Evaluation of Theory and Professional Practice." *Canadian Psychology*, Vol. 27, no. 2, 1986, pp. 183-195.

Dillard, John M. and Robert R. Reilly. *Systematic Interviewing*. Columbus, Ohio: Merril Publishing Company, 1988.

Eder, Robert W. and Gerald R. Ferris, eds. *The Employment Interview: Theory, Research, and Practice*. Newbury Park, CA: Sage Publications, 1989.

Ellis, Reginald T. "The Use of Standardized Tests in Human Resources Management." *Human Resources Management in Canada*. Toronto: Prentice-Hall Canada Inc., 1989, pp. 25,517-25,524.

Fear, Richard A. *The Evaluation Interview*, 3rd ed. New York: McGraw-Hill Book Co., 1984.

Gatewood, Robert D. and Hubert S. Field. *Human Resource Selection*, 2nd ed. Chicago: The Dryden Press, 1990.

Godkewitsch, Michael. "Pre-Hiring Skills Assessment: How to Get the Right People in the Right Job at the Right Time." *Human Resources Management in Canada*. Toronto: Prentice-Hall Canada Inc., 1989, pp. 25,522-25,539.

Goodale, James G. *The Fine Art of Interviewing*. Englewood Cliffs, NJ: Prentice-Hall Inc., 1982.

Hill, Jeff. "Avoiding the `Bent Truth' in Hiring." *Human Resources Management in Canada*. Toronto: Prentice-Hall Canada Inc., 1991, pp. 25,565-25,568.

Jain, Harish C. "Human Rights: Issues in Employment." *Human Resources Management in Canada*. Toronto: Prentice-Hall Canada Inc., 1989, pp. 50,011-50,103.

Janz, Tom, Lowell Hellervik, and David C. Gilmore. *Behavior Description Interviewing*. Boston: Allyn and Bacon Inc., 1986.

Janz, Tom. "The Patterned Behaviour Description Interview: The Best Prophet of the Future Is the Past" in R. W. Eder and G. R. Ferris, eds., *The Employment Interview: Theory, Research, and Practice*. Newbury Park, CA: Sage Publications, 1989, pp. 158-168.

Thede, Glen. "Choosing the Right Tests for Employee Selection." *Human Resources Management in Canada*. Toronto: Prentice-Hall Canada Inc., 1989, pp. 25,525-25,532.

————. "Building an Honest Workforce: Testing and Alternatives." *Human Resources Management in Canada*. Toronto: Prentice-Hall Canada Inc., 1990, pp. 25,539-25,544.

Wanous, John P. *Organizational Entry: Recruitment, Selection, and Socialization of Newcomers*. Reading, Ma.: Addison Wesley Publishing, 1980.

Wiesner, Willi H. and Robert J. Oppenheimer. "Note-Taking in the Selection Interview: Its Effect Upon Predictive Validity and Information Recall" Administrative Sciences Association of Canada (Personnel and Human Resources Division), *Proceedings of the Annual Conference Meeting*, Vol 12, part 8, 1991, pp. 97-106.

PART TWO

TRAINING AND DEVELOPMENT

CHAPTER SEVEN
ORIENTATION, SOCIALIZATION, AND TRAINING

After studying this chapter, you should be able to

1. Describe the orientation process.
2. Explain the reasons for conducting orientation.
3. Explain the socialization process.
4. Describe the different stages of socialization.
5. Explain the purposes and benefits of training.
6. Explain different types of training programs.
7. Develop and implement a training program.
8. Prepare a job instruction training chart for a job.
9. Evaluate a training program.

OVERVIEW

The main purpose of this chapter is to explain the purposes and importance of orientation, socialization, and training. We define the orientation process, outline the reasons it is used, discuss the benefits of effective orientation, and refer to Canadian research findings on orientation programs. We also discuss various orientation techniques and approaches. We also define the socialization process, discuss stages of socialization, and describe how outsiders become insiders.

We further show how training may be used to improve employees' capabilities and performance and we explain how training programs are used to form or change employees' attitudes to obtain increased cooperation, loyalty, and productivity.

Finally, we explain how to use training programs to meet operational and human resource needs, and how training programs benefit employees. We also describe the major learning principles related to the various training techniques discussed.

ORIENTATION

Orientation is the process of introducing new employees to their colleagues, supervisors, and work groups, as well as to their departments, to the organization, to the organization's policies, and to the tasks to be performed. The orientation process may either be formal for informal. A *formal orientation* is planned in advance where groups of individuals go through the same process either sequentially or as a group, and where a human resource specialist may conduct the orientation.[1] An *informal orientation* is one in which the newcomer is introduced to his or her department and it is left to the supervisor and colleagues to provide any information that the newcomer may require.

Purposes and Importance of Orientation

The purposes and importance of orientation are to

- Familiarize new employees with the organization's policies, rules and procedures, physical facilities, and coworkers
- Reduce the newcomer's anxiety[2] and communicate a positive image of the organization
- Increase new employees' satisfaction, increase the level of new information they retain, and reduce the turnover rate

Why Use Orientation?

Orientation should be used because it can greatly enhance employee productivity, loyalty, and satisfaction. Effective orientation helps newcomers understand the physical, social, and organizational dimensions of the workplace. The expected result is that newcomers are able to make sense of the work environment faster and get on the job more quickly when necessary information is effectively communicated.[3] Orientation practices provide newcomers with a positive impression of the employer because the fact that these activities exist suggests to the newcomer that the organization is interested in the welfare of its employees.

Newcomers who undergo formalized orientation often believe that they are valued new employees and that they have been assigned meaningful tasks to perform. Formalized orientation may secure and sustain newcomers' loyalty to the organization. Although most newcomers are highly motivated as they begin to work toward organizational goals, their loyalty and commitment to the organization are often undermined if they do not feel particularly valued or if their work seems to be considered meaningless.

Newcomers often face the stress of wanting to do the "right thing" and are usually worried about how they are viewed by their coworkers. Effective orientation helps to reduce this stress and to develop newcomers' confidence in their performance.

Generally, newcomers are more likely to quit during the first few months of employment. Employers usually experience the highest rate of turnover among new recruits.[4] Effective orientation reduces employee turnover. Large turnovers in organizations can be costly. IBM's annual turnover averages 3% of its North American work force. Its domestic work force is approximately 242 000. This means that over 7000 employees leave IBM annually.[5] When organizations experience a high turnover rate this can result in substantial cost in terms of replacement cost—recruiting, selecting, training, and loss of important skills and knowledge. Organizations must therefore take all available steps to constrain turnover costs.

Two Canadian researchers,[6] McShane and Baal, surveyed the human resource managers in 85 of British Columbia's largest firms and found that most companies had overlooked the potentially powerful and beneficial human resource management activity of orientation. They found that 35% of the firms had no formal orientation at all for newcomers and another 27% provided only basic orientation. While the remaining 32 firms offered more advanced orientation, only six of these had a truly comprehensive orientation process. This Canadian study also revealed that approximately 10% of orientations lasted one hour, although 51% took a day or longer. And two-thirds of the firms conducted orientation immediately after employees commenced employment.

ORIENTATION TECHNIQUES

Orientation involves giving new employees the information they need to perform their jobs satisfactorily. This basic information includes facts like how to get on the payroll, how to obtain identification cards, what the working hours are, and who they will be working with. It is very important that newcomers are provided with information about the organization's culture and climate. For example:

At Digital Equipment of Canada Limited, new employees often hear stories that highlight the first rule in the company, namely, "When dealing with a customer or an employee, do what is 'right.' " "Doing right" often may mean turning down business that is profitable for the company but that is not right for the customer.[7]

Various Canadian researchers[8] argue that for orientations to be effective a variety of techniques should be used. These include the use of small groups, the opportunity to participate, group contact, top management's involvement, orientation before the first day, many short sessions (rather than one long one), and the presentation of material on a need-to-know basis. Orientations should be well-organized and professionally done, because they form an important part of a person's first impression of the organization.

Small Groups

Small groups should be used for at least part of the orientation process to increase the opportunity for active participation.

Opportunity to Participate

Orientation sessions should provide several opportunities for questions and answers. It is useful to encourage discussions.

Group Contact

Effective orientation identifies and encourages contact with the individuals who have the answers; i.e., by providing the names and phone or office numbers to be contacted with various questions.

Top Management Involvement

Involving top management in the orientation process is very important. An audience with a vice president, president, or CEO can have a lasting beneficial effect on new recruits. It humanizes corporate actions and increases the individual's identification with the company. The fact that top management take time out of their busy schedules to meet with newcomers communicates to the newcomers that the organization values its human resources. Top management is generally seen as a credible source of information and thus newcomers are more likely to remember and believe information presented by its members.

Orientation Before the First Day

Many employers, for example banks, hire employees months before their first day of work. This provides an opportunity for additional orientation. Failure to contact newcomers during this time may convey to the new recruits that individuals are not important to the organization and may weaken their attachment to the organization. The longer the time between acceptance and the starting date, the more often the organization should make contact with the newcomers. In their surveys, McShane and Baal found that organizations use a variety of approaches in conducting orientation before the first day. Examples from three companies[9] as provided below:

- When individuals accept employment with us, they start to receive the company newsletter and the immediate supervisor sends a personal letter of welcome. The idea is to assure recruits that the job is waiting for them. (government agency)
- Upon confirmation of job acceptance, we send recruits an information package and invite them to come in whenever possible. The purpose of this is to show that we really mean: "Welcome to (the company)!" (hotel chain)
- When the individual accepts the job, a letter is sent out confirming the starting date. A couple of weeks before the recruit starts, the orientation schedule is sent out. The purpose is to let them know that we're thinking of them. (energy company)

Short Sessions

Orientation procedures should be simple, clear, and brief. Ideally, orientation should last no more than two to three hours at a time. This provides the newcomers sufficient time to absorb the information and organize the material presented.

Multiple Sessions

Spreading out the orientation over several sessions decreases the chance of information overload.

Presentation of Material On A Need-To-Know Basis

The information provided to newcomers should not be overwhelming. Therefore information on matters such as benefits should be discussed in general terms, and detailed information should be provided later. It is usually the case that newcomers are less attentive to such matters, because they are usually more concerned about matters such as proper dress code and supervisor's performance expectations.

Orientation programs range from brief, informal introductions to lengthy, formal programs. In the latter, the new employee is usually given a handbook or printed materials that cover matters like working hours, performance reviews, getting on the payroll, and vacations, as well as a tour of the facilities. As illustrated in the orientation handbook presented in Figure 7.1, other information typically includes employee benefits, human resource management policies, the employee's daily routine, company organization and operations, and safety measures and regulations.[10]

FIGURE 7.1
Contents of an
Orientation Handbook

Employee's Name: _____   Discussion Completed
                                                                  (please check each
                                                                  individual item)

    I. Word of welcome   _____

   II. Explain overall departmental organization and its relationship
to other activities of the company

  III. Explain employee's individual contribution to the objectives
of the department and his or her starting assignment in
broad terms   _____

  IV. Discuss job content with employee and give him or her a
copy of job description (if available)   _____

   V. Explain departmental training program (s) and salary increase
practices and procedures   _____

  VI. Discuss where the employee lives and transportation facilities _____

 VII. Explain working conditions:

     a. Hours of work, time sheets
     b. Use of employee entrance and elevators
     c. Lunch hours
     d. Coffee breaks, rest periods
     e. Personal telephone calls and mail
     f. Overtime policy and requirements
     g. Paydays and procedure for being paid
     h. Lockers
     i. Other   _____

VIII. Requirements for continuance of employment—explain company standards as to:

     a. Performance of duties
     b. Attendance and punctuality
     c. Handling confidential information
     d. Behaviour
     e. General appearance
     f. Wearing of uniform   _____

  IX. Introduce new staff member to manager(s) and other supervisors.
Special attention should be paid to the person to whom the
new employee will be assigned.   _____

   X. Release employee to immediate supervisor who will:
     a. Introduce new staff member to fellow workers
     b. Familiarize the employee with his or her workplace
     c. Begin on-the-job-training   _____

If not applicable, insert N/A in space provided.

_____   _____
Employee's Signature   Supervisor's Signature

_____   _____
Date   Division

Form examined for filing:

_____   _____
Date   Personnel Department

SOURCE: Joseph Famularo, *Handbook of Modern Personnel Administration*, New York: (McGraw-Hill Book Company, 1972). Used with permission.

CONDUCTING THE ORIENTATION

The orientation activities themselves are usually split between the person's new supervisor and the human resource department. The supervisor often gets an orientation checklist similar to that in Figure 7.2. This helps to ensure that the supervisor has covered all the necessary orientation steps.

In most firms, though, the first part of the orientation is performed by the human resource management specialist who explains such matters as working hours and vacation. The employee is then introduced to his or her new supervisor, who continues the orientation by explaining the exact nature of the job, introducing the person to his or her new colleagues, and familiarizing the person with the workplace.

A more detailed listing of what the human resource management department and supervisor each might be expected to cover during orientation is summarized in Figure 7.3. The human resource management department performs the general company orientation, including overview of the organization's policies and procedures, compensation, and the like. The person's new supervisor then does the specific departmental orientation, including explaining department functions, and the employee's new job duties.

Even new executives can benefit from an orientation program. As one expert points out, "by the time a new executive has finished a year on the job, the company may have spent hundreds of thousands of dollars on him or her—including salary, bonus, and moving expenses. After committing that kind of money to finding and launching a new executive, it makes good business sense to human resource managers to make sure that everything possible is done to integrate the new man or woman into the company."

One suggestion is to assign the new executive to a senior "sponsor," preferably the person to whom he or she will be reporting. The sponsor should make sure that the new executive gets up-to-date information about the firm's goals and strategy in written form and should discuss the material with him or her to answer any questions that may arise. There should also be a series of confidential briefings by the key department heads.[11]

Some companies also provide new employees with special anxiety-reduction seminars. For example, when the Texas Instrument company found out how high the anxiety level of its new employees was, it initiated special full-day seminars. These focused on information about the company and the job and allowed many opportunities for questions and answers. The new employees were told what to expect in terms of rumours and hazing from old employees. They were also told that it was very likely they would succeed on their jobs. These special seminars proved to be very useful. By the end of the first month, the new employees who had participated in the seminar were performing much better than those who had not.[12] Orientation is one activity that contributes to the new employee's successful socialization into the firm.

Regardless of how well organized and well executed an orientation plan is, things can go wrong. Therefore it is important that organizations evaluate periodically the effectiveness of their orientation programs. For example, at Exxon Research and Engineering Division, 50 to 150 engineers have been hired each year for several years. Exxon had an action guide and reference manual developed for supervisors to help them do a better job with newcomers. The manual outlines actions the supervisor should take before the employee arrives, such as arranging

FIGURE 7.2
Areas Covered in a Comprehensive Orientation Program

1. **Overview of the company**
   - Welcoming speech
   - Founding, growth, trends, goals, priorities, and problems
   - Traditions, customs, norms, and standards
   - Current specific functions of the organization
   - Products/services and customers served
   - Steps in getting product/service to customers
   - Scope of diversity of activities
   - Organization, structure, and relationship of company and its branches
   - Facts on key managerial staff
   - Community relations, expectations, and activities

2. **Key policies and procedures review**

3. **Compensation**
   - Pay rates and ranges
   - Overtime
   - Holiday pay
   - Shift differential
   - How pay is received
   - Deductions; required and optional, with specific amounts
   - Option to buy damaged products and costs thereof
   - Discounts
   - Advances on pay
   - Loans from credit union
   - Reimbursement for job expenses
   - Tax shelter options

4. **Fringe benefits**
   - Insurance
   - Medical-dental
   - Life
   - Disability
   - Workers' compensation
   - Holidays and vacations (patriotic, religious, birthday)
   - Leave; personal illness, family illness, bereavement, maternity, military, jury duty, emergency, extended absense
   - Retirement plans and options
   - On-the-job training opportunities
   - Counselling services
   - Cafeteria
   - Recreation and social activities
   - Other company services to employees

5. **Safety and accident prevention**
   - Completion of emergency data card (if not done as part of employment process)
   - Health and first aid clinics
   - Exercise and recreation centres
   - Safety precautions
   - Reporting of hazards
   - Fire prevention and control
   - Accident procedures and reporting
   - WCB requirements (review of key sections)
   - Physical exam requirements
   - Use of alcohol and drugs on the job

6. **Employee and union relations**
   - Terms and conditions of employment review
   - Assignment, reassignment, and promotion
   - Probationary period and expected on-the-job conduct
   - Reporting of sickness and lateness to work
   - Employee rights and responsibilities
   - Manager and supervisor rights
   - Relations with supervisors and shop stewards
   - Employee organizations and options
   - Union contract provisions and/or company policy
   - Supervision and evaluation of performance
   - Discipline and reprimands
   - Grievance procedures
   - Termination of employment (resignation, layoff, discharge, retirement)
   - Content and examination of personnel record
   - Communications: channels of communication—upward and downward—suggestion system, posting materials on bulletin board, sharing new ideas
   - Sanitation and cleanliness
   - Wearing of safety equipment, badges, and uniforms
   - Bringing things on and removing things from company grounds
   - On-site political activity
   - Gambling
   - Handling of rumours

7. **Physical facilities**
   - Tour of facilities
   - Food services and cafeteria
   - Restricted areas for eating
   - Employee entrances
   - Restricted areas (e.g., cars)
   - Parking
   - First aid
   - Washrooms
   - Supplies and equipment

8. **Economic factors**
   - Costs of damage by select items with required sales to balance
   - Costs of theft with required sales to compensate
   - Profit margins
   - Labour costs
   - Cost of equipment
   - Costs of absenteeism, lateness, and accident

SOURCE: W. D. St. John, "The Complete Employee Orientation Program, " *Personnel Journal* (May 1980) pp. 376–77. Reprinted with the permission of *Personnel Journal*. Costa Mesa, California; all rights reserved.

FIGURE 7.3
Areas Covered in a
Job-Specific
Orientation Program

1. **Department functions**
   - Goals and current priorities
   - Organization and structure
   - Operational activities
   - Relationship of functions to other departments
   - Relationships of jobs within the department

2. **Job duties and responsibilities**
   - Detailed explanation of job based on current job description and expected results
   - Explanation of why the job is important, how the specific job relates to others in the department and company
   - Discussion of common problems and how to avoid and overcome them
   - Performance standards and basis of performance evaluation
   - Number of daily work hours and times
   - Overtime needs and requirements
   - Extra duty assignments (such as changing duties to cover for an absent worker)
   - Required records and reports
   - Checkout on equipment to be used
   - Explanation of where and how to get tools, have equipment maintained and repaired
   - Types of assistance available; when and how to ask for help
   - Relations with provincial and federal inspectors

3. **Policies, procedures, rules, and regulations**
   - Rules unique to the job and/or department
   - Handling emergencies
   - Safety precautions and accident prevention
   - Reporting of hazards and accidents
   - Cleanliness standards and sanitation (such as cleanup)
   - Security, theft problems and costs
   - Relations with outside people (e.g. drivers)
   - Eating, smoking and chewing gum etc., in department area
   - Removal of things from department
   - Damage control (e.g. smoking restrictions)
   - Time clock and time sheets
   - Breaks/rest periods
   - Lunch duration and time
   - Making and receiving personal telephone calls
   - Requisitioning supplies and equipment
   - Monitoring and evaluating of employee performance
   - Job bidding and requesting reassignment
   - Going to cars during work hours

4. **Tour of department**
   - Washrooms and showers
   - Fire-alarm box and fire extinguisher stations
   - Time clocks
   - Lockers
   - Approved entrances and exits
   - Water fountains and eye-wash systems
   - Supervisors's quarters
   - Supply room and maintenance department
   - Sanitation and security offices
   - Smoking areas
   - Locations of services to employees related to department
   - First aid kit

5. **Introduction to department employees**

SOURCE: W. D. St. John, "The Complete Employee Orientation Program, " *Personnel Journal* (May 1980) pp. 376–77. Reprinted with the permission of *Personnel Journal*. Costa Mesa, California; all rights reserved.

for work space, telephones, office supplies, and the like. It also describes the actions a supervisor should take after the new employee arrives, such as follow-up meetings with the supervisors and new engineers. These sessions are called "How's it Going" meetings. They are intended to open up communications between the newcomer and the supervisor. Information is shared, concern is shown, and matters of interest are discussed. To make these sessions as effective as possible, they are held separately from meetings that give work assignments or review performance. Supervisors also are trained to conduct these meetings. The objectives of the training are to increase the supervisor's awareness of the new employee's needs, introduce the newcomers to the company's socialization procedures, and improve the supervisor's skills at communicating with new employees.

Internal company research showed that after the training, supervisors were 40% more likely to hold initial orientation discussions with newcomers and were 20% more likely to hold follow-up sessions at the end of three months.[13]

SOCIALIZATION

socialization

Socialization is the process through which employees learn the basic responsibilities of the job, the required behaviour patterns for effective performance, and organizational norms and values.[14] Further, it is the process by which newcomers acquire the skills, knowledge, and the type of behaviour required to make the transition effective and to succeed in the organization. Effective socialization means changing the newcomers' basic beliefs and attitudes to create internal commitment to the organization, rather than just compliance with the organization's policies.[15] It means transforming newcomers from "outsiders" to "insiders," participating and effective team members.[16] There are three stages of socialization: anticipatory socialization, accommodation, and role management.[17]

Anticipatory Socialization: "Getting In"

anticipatory socialization

Anticipatory socialization is the process in which individuals develop certain attitudes, values, and expectations about what it will be like working and succeeding in their chosen organizations. What this indicates is that the socialization process usually starts before newcomers actually join organizations. It begins with such activities as occupational choice, attraction to organizations, and the selection process.[18] During the selection process interviewers often ask job candidates probing questions to determine whether there is a good fit between the individual's skills and needs and the organization's demands and opportunities.[19] "Indeed, the ability of the individual to present the appropriate face during the selection process determines his ability to move into the organization in the first place. Thus, success depends on the degree to which the aspiring member has correctly anticipated the expectations and desires of those in the organization in charge of selection."[20]

Accommodation: "Breaking In"

accommodation

Accommodation is the process by which the newcomer, upon entering (joining) the organization, attempts to become a functioning member of it. This is the stage of the newcomers initial encounter of organizational life as a full-fledged member. At this stage the "honeymoon" of the recruiting and selection process is over, and the day-to-day realities of the job begin to sink in.[21]

It is at this stage that the newcomers must confront the clash between their initial expectations and experiences, i.e., the contrast between their expectations—about their jobs, their colleagues, their supervisors, and the organization in general—and reality. This is called reality shock. **Reality shock** is defined as the process by which newcomers' prior expectations are not fulfilled in their actual job experiences.[22]

reality shock

If reality differs from the newcomers' expectations then the newcomers must undergo socialization to replace their previously held assumptions and perceptions with the organization's norms and values. This may require a change from idealism to realism, and an increase in awareness and understanding of the interpersonal aspects of organizational life. It may also require a shift from enthusiasm to patience regarding change, and a move from anticipating an exciting and challenging job to an actual underutilization of their skills. For example a new-comer with an MBA may be required to work four to six weeks as a teller in order to familiarize himself or herself with that aspect of banking.

When newcomers are unable to handle the actualities of their jobs, they be-come frustrated, less committed to their jobs, less optimistic about their chances of success, and may even resign. It is important for organizations to use proper selection procedures, including realistic job previews, to eliminate the likelihood of newcomers quitting. When an organization's realities meet a newcomer's expec-tations the accommodation stage serves to confirm previously held assumptions.

Four processes enable newcomers to progress through the accommodation stage. First, proper initiation to the task entails mastering a job and becoming a productive work partner. Second, initiation to the group is the social aspect of be-coming integrated in the organization. Here, newcomers acquire good interper-sonal relationships, and become accepted and trusted by their colleagues. Third, role definition is achieved, which involves learning the new work role and reaching agreement with others about one's task activities, priorities, and behaviour. Fourth, the provision of timely and consistent feedback to newcomers is important, to let them know how well they are doing in their "breaking in" efforts. The absence of feedback may be interpreted by newcomers as organizational indifference, disin-terest, or disappointment with their performance.[23]

Role Management: "Settling In"

Role management is the third stage of the socialization process. It is at this stage that newcomers must come to grips with, cope, and resolve any problems discovered during the accommodation stage. Newcomers must also resolve conflicts between their job demands (supervisors' expectations of a high level of productivity) and their co-workers' expectations that newcomers will acquire group norms and will not at-tempt to "show off" by trying to outperform group members.[24]

According to one researcher, two important outcomes result from successful so-cialization. These are *mutual influence* (the amount of control newcomers have over their work) and *general satisfaction* (the levels of satisfaction with work that new-comers experience).[25] According to Feldman and Arnold, organizational social-ization is a two-way process between newcomers and organizations. Some negotiation and modification of job expectations takes place, regardless of how in-stitutionalized the new recruit's role might be. When newcomers join organiza-tions they must make a variety of changes in order to fit into their new settings. But they do not change completely to meet the demands of the organization; the or-ganization also changes its expectations and behaviours toward newcomers. Organizations often reassess newcomers to see how well they are adjusting. They often redefine jobs to take advantage of special strengths of newcomers; and they may also change training and orientation.[26] The absence of individual influence may lead to socialization that is ineffective. Schein distinguishes between three basic responses to socialization: rebellion (the rejection of all behaviours, values, and norms), conformity (the acceptance of all behaviours, values and norms), and cre-ative individualism (the acceptance of only pivotal behaviours, values and norms and the rejection of others). According to Schein, creative individualism is health-ier both for newcomers and their organizations.[27] Over-conformity too often leads to sterile, bureaucratic behaviour.[28]

role management

HUMAN RESOURCE MANAGEMENT IN ACTION

Students and Full-time Employees

There are seven major ways in which the environment of a student and that of a full-time employee differ. The adjustment required by these differences is what causes new entrants into the work force to feel such discomfort in the "real world."

1. *Supervisors.* Students, at any point in time, will have four or five supervisors (teachers). These teachers usually change every four months and are often selected by the students themselves. In contrast, an employee usually has one manager, sometimes for years, with little (perhaps no) influence over the choice of that superior. Newcomers often treat their supervisors as they treated their professors, with unfortunate results.

2. *Feedback.* Students learn to expect brief, quantitative performance evaluations (grades) on numerous specific occasions throughout the year. An employee, on the other hand, may never get any concrete feedback from superiors outside of pay raises or promotions. It is not unusual for new workers to feel that they are working in a vacuum and to become angry that they are not receiving more feedback. Many young managers detest being treated as "average."

3. *Time horizons.* Students learn to think in terms of time cycles of one or two hours (a class), a week (after which a sequence of classes repeats itself), or four months (a semester, when classes and professors change). Time horizons in the working world are much more likely to be either very short (as short as a few hours in some production/operating jobs) or very long (as long as several years in some planning jobs). These changes in time cycles can leave new employees feeling disoriented.

4. *Magnitude of decisions.* Business students often get used to making a number of major decisions (hy-

pothetically) every day. At least at first, the new employee will rarely make any major decisions in his or her job. This often leads to feelings of being underused or ignored.

5. *Speed of change.* Because students are encouraged to think about planning and implementing innovative programs, they often develop highly unrealistic expectations concerning the ease and quickness of making changes in the real world. Organizations often move more slowly, and changes are often based on political, rather than on technical or business, considerations. Very little change can be effected by one person alone, especially a newcomer.

6. *Promotions.* A student with a master's degree and no full-time work has lived in an environment where promotions occur once every twelve months—eighteen promotions in eighteen years. It is not surprising that students are frustrated that they are not moving up the corporate hierarchy as quickly. Moreover, students are frustrated that movement through an organization can depend on nothing more than luck or having the right connections.

7. *The nature of problems.* Professors typically assign problems that can be solved in a short period of time, using some specific method or theory that is currently being taught. Such a process is efficient by many educational standards. However, new workers often find it incredibly frustrating when the problems they are given are not neat and easily solvable.

SOURCE: Hugh J. Arnold and Daniel Feldman, *Organizational Behavior* (New York: McGraw-Hill, Inc., 1986), pp. 550-551. Reproduced with permission of McGraw-Hill, Inc.

The socialization process is complete when newcomers have moved through all three stages (i.e., getting in, breaking in, and settling in). In order to ensure that the socialization process is effective, companies must take the initiative to create conditions for successful organizational socialization. There are two primary reasons for employers, through the immediate supervisors, to get involved in the early socialization of newcomers: cost and competing norms.[29]

Cost

Employees are more likely to quit during the first year of employment than at any subsequent time. Early turnover varies substantially from one organization to another. Some organizations lose up to a third of their new employees in the first month and by the end of three months retain only half of the people who had accepted employment. This is not typical, but even lower rates represent substantial costs to the employer, as discussed earlier.

Competing Norms

New employees want to fit in and get along not only with the boss, but also with coworkers. The attitudes and norms of this peer group may not necessarily support the organization's goals. In some organizational settings, informal groups have a way of "protecting" individuals from what they experience as undesirable and/or unfair organizational expectations. An organization will not *eliminate* the effect of group pressures by getting managers to invest time and effort in new members, but failing to articulate and reinforce the organization's expectations creates a situation in which the newcomer will look to other sources to determine which values should govern behaviour.

TRAINING

Employee training is the process of teaching new or current employees new skills designed to improve their skills, knowledge, abilities, attitudes, and competencies in order to meet the organization's requirements of maintaining and increasing productivity and the individual's need for further growth. Training is used to improve the individual and has a short-term focus. Effective employee training is essential for the organization to maintain a qualified work force that will enable the organization to easily adopt and integrate new technological advancements into its operations. Organizations use training to achieve a variety of purposes. Employee training has a variety of benefits for organizations and the individuals. Management development (explained in Chapter 8) is training of a more long-term nature: its aims are to develop employees for future jobs in the organization, such as supervisors, managers, and executives. It is also aimed at solving some organizational problems concerning, for instance, poor interdepartmental communication and poor interpersonal relationships.

employee training

Purposes and Importance of Training

Benefits to the Organization

- Leads to improved profitability and/or more positive attitudes toward profit orientation.
- Improves job knowledge and skills at all levels of the organization.
- Improves the morale of the work force.
- Helps people identify with organizational goals.
- Helps create a better corporate image.
- Fosters authenticity, openness, and trust.
- Improves the relationship between boss and subordinate.
- Aids in organizational development.

- Learns from the trainee.
- Helps prepare guidelines for work.
- Aids in understanding and carrying out organizational policies.
- Provides information for future needs in all areas of the organization.
- Promotes more effective decision making and problem solving.
- Aids in developing promotions from within.
- Aids in developing leadership skill, motivation, loyalty, positive attitudes, and other traits that successful workers and managers usually display.
- Aids in increasing productivity and/or quality of work.
- Helps keep costs down in many areas, e.g., production, personnel, administration, etc.
- Develops in employees a sense of responsibility for being competent and knowledgeable.
- Improves labour-management relations.
- Reduces outside consulting costs by utilizing competent internal consulting.
- Stimulates preventive management, as opposed to "putting out fires."
- Eliminates suboptimal behaviour.
- Creates an appropriate climate for growth and communication.
- Aids in improving organizational communication.
- Helps employees adjust to change.
- Aids in handling conflict, thereby helping to prevent stress and tension.

Benefits to the Individual, which in Turn Benefit the Organization

- Helps the individual toward better decision making and effective problem solving.
- Fosters a sense of recognition, achievement, growth, responsibility, and desire for advancement.
- Aids in encouraging and achieving self-development and self-confidence.
- Helps in handling stress, tension, frustration, and conflict.
- Provides information for improving leadership knowledge, communication skills, and attitudes.
- Increases job satisfaction and recognition.
- Moves the individual toward personal goals while improving interaction skills.
- Satisfies personal needs of the trainer (and trainee!).
- Provides trainee an avenue for growth and a say in his/her own future.
- Develops a sense of growth in learning.
- Helps a person develop speaking and listening skills—and writing skills when exercises are required.
- Helps eliminate fear of attempting new tasks.

On the Front Line

At present Carter Cleaning Centers have no formal orientation programs. Jennifer feels that the absence of orientation programs serves to explain some of the problems that exist at the company.

For example, two new employees became very upset last month when they discovered that they were not paid at the end of the week, on Friday, but instead were paid (as are all Carter employees) on the following Tuesday. The Carters take the extra two days in part to give them time to obtain everyone's hours and compute their pay. The other reason they do it, according to Jack is that "frankly, when we stay a few days behind in paying employees it helps to ensure they at least give us a few days notice before quitting on us. While we are certainly obligated to pay them anything they earn, we find that psychologically they seem to be less likely to just walk out on us Friday evening and not show up Monday morning if they still haven't gotten their pay from the previous week. This way they at least give us a few days' notice so we can find a replacement."

Other matters that could be covered during an orientation, says Jennifer, include company policy regarding paid holidays, lateness and absences, health and hospitalization benefits and general matters like maintaining a clean and safe work area, personal appearance and cleanliness, filling time sheets, personal telephone calls and mail, company policies regarding matters like substance abuse, and eating or smoking on the job.

Jennifer believes that implementing orientation and training programs would help to ensure that employees know how to do their jobs the right way. And she and her father further believe that it is only when employees understand the right way to do their jobs that there is any hope that their jobs will in fact be accomplished the way the Carters want them to be accomplished. She therefore has the following questions:

1. Specifically what should we cover in our new employee orientation program and how should we cover this information?

2. What orientation techniques should be used?

Benefits in Personnel and Human Relations, Intra- and Intergroup Relations, and Policy Implementation

- Improves communication between groups and individuals.
- Aids in orientation for new employees and those taking new jobs through transfer or promotion.
- Provides information on equal opportunity and affirmative action.
- Provides information on other governmental laws and administrative policies.
- Improves interpersonal skills.
- Makes organizational policies, rules, and regulations viable.
- Improves morale.
- Builds cohesiveness in groups.
- Provides a good climate for learning, growth, and coordination.
- Makes the organization a better place in which to work.[30]

Companies spend millions of dollars annually on training in order to get their work done in a smooth, efficient manner.[31] For example, one survey concluded that companies subscribing to *Personnel Journal* spent over $5.3 billion on training and development in 1988: this represents a 38% increase in training and development expenditures from the 1986 Figure.[32]

In a recent study conducted by the Conference Board of Canada of mid- to large-size Canadian companies it was found that Canadian companies are spending more on training than was previously thought. The survey, based on 440 responses from a random selection of 2500 organizations in all sectors, estimates that Canadian companies spend roughly $474 per employee on training and development. About half this amount is spent on the training staff's salaries. Companies also expect to increase their training budgets, perhaps by as much as 11%.

Significantly, the study found that the fear of "poaching," often touted as the reason for not undertaking training, seems to be exaggerated in larger companies. Eighty-nine percent of respondents reported the degree of fear that poaching might inhibit training as "low," while only 2% said it was "high." The study also found:

- There is an increasing focus on training. Nearly 60% of respondents expect to spend more on this "critical challenge."

- Training is carried out at all levels, but there is more time invested in training executives and managers than production and trades people. The former group got an average of 28 hours of training while the latter received about 14.

- Canadian companies tend to rely more on internal resources while their American counterparts are more likely to use external training. At the same time, 23% of respondents indicated "lack of resources" as the most critical challenge to improved training.

The Basic Training Process

Any training program ideally consists of four steps, which are summarized in Figure 7.4. The purpose of the assessment step is to determine whether there is a performance deficiency that can be rectified by training. Then, if one or more deficiencies that can be eliminated through training are identified, training objectives should be set; specifying in observable, measurable terms the performance expected to be obtained from the employees who are to be trained. In the third step the actual training techniques are chosen and the training takes place. Finally, in the evaluation step, the trainees' pre and post-training performances are compared, and the effectiveness of the training program is thus evaluated.

ASSESSMENT: DETERMINING TRAINING NEEDS

The first step in training is to determine what training, if any, is required. Assessing the training needs of employees who are new to their jobs is a fairly straightforward manner. The main task is to determine what the job entails and to break it down into subtasks, each of which is then taught to the new employee. But assessing the training needs of *present* employees can be more complex. The need for training is usually prompted by problems so there is the added task of deciding whether training is, in fact, the solution. Often, for instance, performance is down because the standards are not clear or because the person is just not motivated.

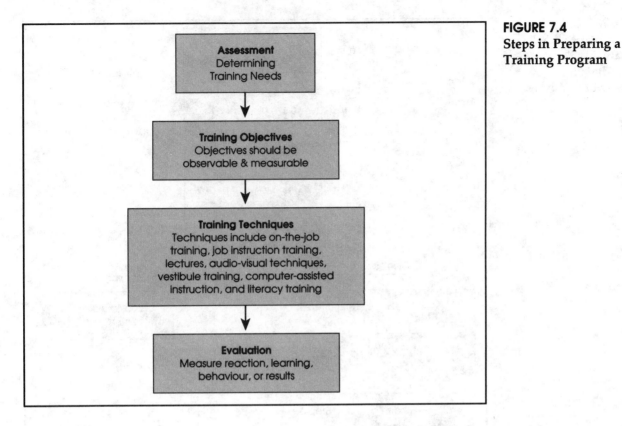

FIGURE 7.4
Steps in Preparing a
Training Program

Performance Analysis: Determining the Training Needs of Current Employees

Performance analysis basically involves verifying the fact that there is a significant performance deficiency, and then determining whether that deficiency should be rectified through training or by some other means (such as changing the machinery or transferring the employee). The performance analysis procedure consists of ten steps,[33] as summarized in Figure 7.5.

performance analysis

1. The first step is to identify the performance discrepancy. In other words, if the aim is to improve the employee's performance, current performance must be assessed and compared with what it ought to be (i.e., John averages six new contacts per week, but each salesperson is expected to make 10 new contacts per week.)

2. The second step is to determine whether rectifying the problem is worth the time and effort that will have to be put into doing so. Sometimes not solving the problem is cheaper than setting up a training program to rectify it.

3. This step is the heart of analysis, involving three sets of questions: (1) Does the person know what to do, and what is expected in terms of performance? (2) Could the person do the job if he or she wanted to? and (3) Does the person want to do the job, and what are the consequences of performing well? Once the problem is identified as either a can't do or a won't do problem, the following steps are taken.

FIGURE 7.5
Performance Analysis:
Analyzing the
Training Needs of
Current Employees

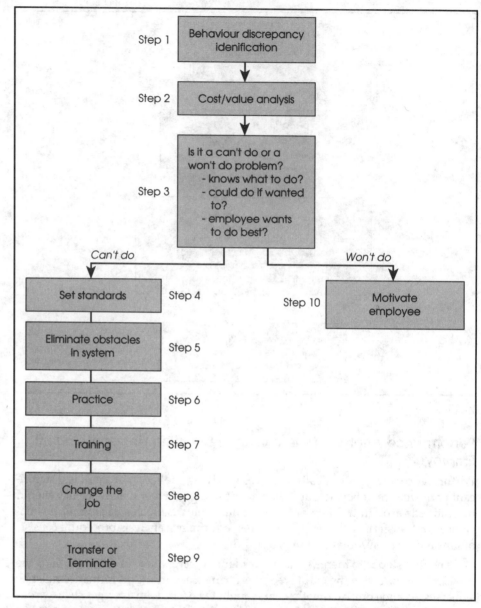

SOURCE: Adapted from Donald F. Michalak and Edwin G. Yage, *Making the Training Process Work*. Copyright © 1979 by Donald F. Michalak and Edwin G. Yager. Reprinted by permission of Harper & Row, Publishers, Inc.

4. Sometimes employees do not perform up to par either because they do not know what par is, or because they think they are already performing up to standard. It is necessary to review performance standards and the employees' understanding of what is expected of them. It must also be determined if they know that they are not performing up to par.

5. This step is to identify and eliminate any obstacles to performance that are present. This involves, for instance, "finding out whether the right material

arrives at a person's work station on time." Sometimes an easy solution is to use a job aid. For example, one firm found that its electronic assemblers were having trouble remembering which wire was to be welded to which junction. The job aid in this case involved colour coding all wires and junctions. The assemblers can now see at a glance which wire goes where.

6. Sometimes employees lose a skill or knowledge they once had because of a lack of practice. Hotel fire drills are an example of practice being used to make sure employees maintain satisfactory skill and knowledge levels.

7. As we have seen, training is not always the best solution: in fact, it can sometimes be the most expensive one.

8. Sometimes the best way to handle can't do problems is to change the job. For example, most sales jobs consist of three parts: prospecting, demonstrating, and closing. Training someone who is good at prospecting and demonstrating to also close a deal is often difficult. On the other hand, some hot-shot closers are best off not wasting their time prospecting and demonstrating. The solution here is to change the sales job by subdividing it and have one person prospect and demonstrate and another close.

9. Finally, if after all the steps above have been taken, the person obviously wants to do the job but can't, transfer or termination may be required.

10. The root of a won't do problem is a lack of motivation. It is then necessary to select the appropriate rewards or punishments to motivate the employee.

TRAINING OBJECTIVES

After determining training needs the next step should be setting concrete, measurable training objectives. For example, a concrete training objective for a Xerox machine technician might be as follows:

Given a tool kit and a service manual, the technical representative will be able to adjust the registration (black line along paper edges) on this Xerox duplicator within 20 minutes according to the specifications stated in the manual.[34]

Well-written behavioural objectives specify what the trainee will be able to accomplish after successfully completing the training program.[35] They thus provide a focus for the efforts of both the trainee and the trainer, as well as a benchmark for evaluating the success of the training program.

Learning Principles

Training is essentially a learning process. Effective training programs require the incorporation of ten **learning principles**. These principles are discussed below.[36]

learning principles

1. *Trainees should be provided with an overview of the material to be presented.* Knowing the overall picture in advance helps the trainees to anticipate and understand each step in the training and to integrate the parts into a meaningful whole. One example of this approach is the overview that precedes each chapter in a textbook.

2. *The material presented should make use of a variety of familiar examples.* Just as a picture is "worth a thousand words," often a familiar example that illustrates what the trainer is getting at can help crystallize the concept for the trainees.

3. *The material should be split into meaningful chunks rather than presented all at once.* Trainees can only absorb a limited amount of information at a time; that is why textbooks whose chapters are 80 pages each do not sell.

4. *Terms and concepts that are already familiar to the trainees should be used.*

5. *The training situation should resemble the work situation.* Thus, if the person is being trained off the job and will eventually have to work in a noisy environment, he or she should get some practice under noisy conditions during training.

6. *Important features of the task must be labelled or identified.* Training a machine operator would involve giving each important part of the machine a label (e.g., "starter switch"), and labelling each step of the procedure (e.g., "start machine," and "place tube in press").

7. *Trainees learn best by doing.* As much real-life practice as possible should be made available since practice and repetition are important for learning new skills. Skills that are practised often are better learned and less easily forgotten.

8. *Reinforcement should be provided as quickly and frequently as possible.* Praise should not be withheld until the end of the day. Instead, good performance must be reinforced often—whenever the trainees do something right.

9. *Trainees learn best when they learn at their own pace.* No one likes having someone look over their shoulder as he or she tries to learn a new subject.

10. *The trainees must be motivated to learn.* Explanations of how training will affect their performance and rewards can facilitate the motivation to learn. Adhering to the principles above may also foster and increase motivation.

TRAINING TECHNIQUES

After determining employees' training needs—in particular the tasks and skills for which they need training and the knowledge they require—and setting training objectives, the actual training can take place. The actual training technique that is used—whether on-the-job training, programmed learning, or some other—will depend on several things, including the nature of the tasks and skills to be learned, the number of employees to be trained, and the employer's resources. The advantages and disadvantages of the most popular training techniques are explained below.

On-the-Job Training

on-the-job training (OJT)

On-the-job training (OJT) involves having a person learn a skill by actually performing it on the job. Virtually every employee, from mailroom clerk to company president, gets some on-the-job training when he or she joins a firm. This is why William Tracey calls it "the most common, the most widely accepted, and the most necessary method of training employees in the skills essential for acceptable job performance." In many companies, OJT is the only type of training available to employees and usually involves assigning new employees to experienced workers or supervisors who then do the actual training.[37]

There are several types of on-the-job training. Probably the most familiar is the coaching or understudy method, in which the employee is trained on the job by an experienced worker or the trainee's supervisor. At lower levels the coaching may just involve having trainees acquire the skills for running the machine by observing the supervisor. But this technique is also widely used at top management levels.

OJT has several advantages. It is relatively inexpensive—trainees learn while producing—and there is no need for expensive off-job facilities like classrooms or programmed learning devices. The method also facilitates learning since trainees learn by actually doing the job and get quick feedback about the correctness of their performance.

However there are several trainer-related factors to keep in mind when designing an OJT program.[38] The trainers themselves must be carefully trained and given the necessary training materials. (Often, instead, an experienced worker is simply told to "go train John.") Employees who will function as trainers should also be convinced that training new employees will not jeopardize their own job security, and that their added training responsibility will be instrumental in obtaining rewards for themselves. Trainers and trainees should be paired so as to minimize differences in background, language, or age, and the choice of trainers should be based upon their ability and desire to teach. Experienced workers who are chosen as trainers should be thoroughly trained in the proper methods of instruction—in particular the principles of learning, explained previously, and perhaps the job instruction technique that we address next. Trainees should also be rotated to capitalize on the strengths of various trainers: John may be especially good at teaching new trainees how to weld for instance, while Ruth is especially good at showing them how to paint the finished circuit board. Trainers should also understand the importance of close supervision in preventing training injuries. A useful step-by-step approach for giving a new employee on-the-job training can be summarized as follows:

Step 1: Preparation of the Learner

1. The trainer should put the learner at ease—relieve the tension—and explain why he or she is being taught.
2. The trainer should create interest, encourage questions, and find out what the learner already knows about his or her job or other jobs.
3. The "why" of the whole job should be explained and related to some job the worker already knows.

Step 2: Presentation of the Operation

1. Quantity and quality requirements should be explained.
2. The trainer should go through the job at the normal work pace.
3. The trainer should then go through the job at a slow pace several times, explaining each step. Between operations, the difficult parts, or those in which errors are likely to be made, should be explained.

Step 3: Performance Tryout

1. The learner should go through the job several times, slowly, explaining his or her understanding of each step. The trainer should correct mistakes, and if necessary, do some of the complicated steps the first few times.
2. The trainer should run the job at the normal pace.

3. He or she should then have the learner do the job, gradually building up skill and speed.

4. As soon as the learner demonstrates ability to do the job, the work should begin in earnest, but the trainer should not abandon the learner.

Step 4: Follow-up

1. A person to whom the learner should go for help if he or she needs it should be delegated.

2. Supervision should be gradually decreased. Work should be checked from time to time against quality and quantity standards.

3. Faulty work patterns that begin to creep into the work should be corrected before they become a habit. The ways in which learned method is superior should be demonstrated.

4. Good work should be complimented, and the worker should be encouraged until he or she is able to meet the quality/quantity standards.

Job Instruction Training

job instruction training (JIT)

Many jobs consist of a logical sequence of steps and are best taught in this manner—step-by-step. This step-by-step learning is called **job instruction training (JIT)**. It involves listing all necessary steps in the job, each in its proper sequence. Alongside each step also list a corresponding "key point" (if any). The steps show what is to be done, while the key points show how it's to be done—and why. Figure 7.6 is

FIGURE 7.6
Example of a Job Instruction Training Sheet

	Steps	Key Points
1.	Start motor	None
2.	Set cutting distance	Carefully read scale—to prevent wrong-sized cut
3.	Place paper on cutting-table	Make sure paper is even—to prevent uneven cut
4.	Push paper up to cutter	Make sure paper is tight—to prevent uneven cut
5.	Grasp safety release with left hand	Do not release left hand—to prevent hand from being caught in cutter
6.	Grasp cutter release with right hand	Do not release right hand—to prevent hand from being caught in the cutter
7.	Simultaneously pull cutter safety releases	Keep both hands on corresponding releases—to avoid hands being on cutting table
8.	Wait for cutter to retract	Keep both hands on releases—to avoid having hands on cutting table
9.	Retract paper	Make sure cutter is retracted; keep both hands away from releases
10.	Shut off motor	None

an example of a job instruction training sheet for teaching a trainee how to operate a large motorized paper cutter.

Lectures

Just lecturing to new trainees can have several advantages. It is a quick and simple way of providing knowledge to large groups of trainees, as when the sales force must be taught the special features of some new product. While written material like books and manuals can also be used here, they may involve considerable printing expense, and do not permit the give and take of questioning that lectures do. Therefore lectures may be used as an integral part of a training program, with the actual practice required for learning the new skills provided by a training technique like on-the-job training.

Audiovisual Techniques

Presenting information to trainees via audiovisual techniques like films, closed-circuit TV, audiotapes, or videotapes can be very effective, and today this technique is widely used.[39] At Weyerhaeuser Company, for instance, portions of entertainment films like "Bridge on the River Kwai" have been used as a basis for discussing interpersonal relationships in the company's management school. The Ford Motor Company uses films in its dealer training sessions to simulate problems and reactions to handling various customer complaints.

Audiovisuals are more expensive than conventional lectures, but they offer some unique advantages. First, when there is a need to illustrate how a certain sequence should be followed over time, such as when teaching welding or telephone repair, the stop action, instant replay, and fast- or slow-motion capabilities of audiovisuals can be useful. Second, they may be used when there is a need to expose trainees to events not easily demonstrable in live lectures, such as a visual tour of a factory or open-heart surgery. Third, they may be used when the training is going to be used organization-wide and it is too costly to move the trainers from place to place.

Teletraining

Companies today are also experimenting with *teletraining*, through which a trainer in a central location can train groups of employees at remote locations via television hookups.[40]

Programmed Learning

Whether the programmed instruction device is a textbook or machine, **programmed learning** always consists of three functions: (1) presenting questions, facts, or problems to the learner; (2) allowing the person to respond; and (3) providing feedback on the accuracy of his or her answers.

programmed learning

Programmed instruction can facilitate learning since it lets trainees learn at their own pace, provides immediate feedback, and reduces the risk of error. On the other hand, trainees do not learn much more with programmed learning than they would with a conventional textbook approach. Therefore, the cost of developing the manuals, books, and machinery for programmed instruction (which can be high) has to be weighed against the accelerated but not better learning that should occur.

Vestibule or Simulated Training

vestibule or simulated training

Vestibule or **simulated training** is a technique in which trainees learn on the actual or simulated equipment they will use on the job, but are actually trained off the job. Vestibule training therefore aims to obtain the advantages of on-the-job training without actually putting the trainee on the job. Vestibule training is virtually a necessity on jobs where it is too costly or dangerous to train employees on the job. It is therefore useful for training new assembly-line workers where putting them right to work could slow production. Similarly, where safety is concerned—as with pilots—it may be the only practical alternative.

Vestibule training may just involve setting up in a separate room the equipment the trainees will actually be using on the job. However, it often involves the use of equipment simulators, as in pilot training.

Computer-Assisted Instruction

computer-assisted instruction (CAI)

Many firms are now using computers to facilitate the training process. **Computer-assisted instruction (CAI)** systems like Control Data's PLATO have several advantages. They provide self-paced individualized instruction that is one-on-one and easy to use, and trainees get immediate feedback on their input. CAI also provides accountability in that tests are taken on the computer so that management can monitor each trainee's progress and needs. A CAI training program can also be easily modified to reflect technological innovations in the equipment for which the employee is being trained. This training also tends to be more flexible in that trainees can usually use the computer almost any time they want, and thus get their training when they prefer. Computer-assisted instruction systems like PLATO can also provide simulation capabilities. Specifically, the system can be designed to simulate complex or difficult tasks and to challenge trainees with "what if" questions like, "If wind velocity on the ground is 80 knots, then what will happened if you decrease your aircraft velocity below its stall speed?"

Some examples of how systems like PLATO are being used can help to illustrate the usefulness of CAIs. In some schools, security analyst trainees are able to learn and manipulate various stock valuation models, by programming in various assumptions about economic growth rates and risks; they can thus assess how changes in these factors will influence the price of these stocks.

PLATO is also being used to train airline pilots. Part of a pilot's training includes time in a cockpit trainer, in a flight simulator, and in an actual airplane—all expensive pieces of equipment. The PLATO system minimizes the amount of time spend in the simulator and thus reduces training costs. By using this computerized system, pilots familiarize themselves with the complicated instrument panel before working with the actual equipment in a simulator or airplane. This is illustrated in the accompanying photograph.[41] While a textbook, film, or lecture could present photos of the same instruments, neither could provide the almost realistic reactions and problems supplied by the CAI system.[42]

Literacy Training Techniques

Functional illiteracy is an increasingly serious problem for many employers. It is estimated that four million Canadians are functionally illiterate.[43] Of this number approximately 40% all younger than forty-five years. This is having an adverse impact on the overall levels of productivity in organizations. It also may be a major

Computer-Assisted Instruction

One of Canada's most successful examples of computer-based training is the program developed by the Edmonton Police Department (EPD).

The program, referred to as Decentralized, Individualized, Inservice Training (DIIT), uses modern forms of training delivery: a powerful combination of video-based training, for realism and accuracy, plus computer-based training for efficiency, cost effectiveness, and record-keeping.

The EPD implemented CBT (computer-based training) in 1983 following dissatisfaction with other training methods. Thirty-two CBT modules were developed in the areas of criminal law and specialized investigations, such as landing bomb threats, vehicle thefts, and high-risk incidents. The courseware was developed using Control Data's PLATO Learning Management and the OMNISIM's Authoring Systems. Officers are required to achieve 100% mastery of all topics.

"Not only was the department dissatisfied with conventional training methods, but it realized that training a large group of 1100 people was not possible with those methods," says William Wosar of the Learning Resources Unit, Training Section, EPD. The department's commitment to CBT appears to be years ahead of most Canadian organizations.

Efficient Results

In on-the-job performance measures (for the first six months after CBT was implemented, compared to the previous six-month period), the number of scenes attended by the canine unit increased by 27%, and the number of apprehensions by the canine unit rose by 45%. In the area of criminal law, the number of incorrectly written warrant notices decreased by 49.8% after the first year CBT was implemented, saving four worker-months of paperwork.

The previously used method of instruction consisted of a two-week classroom course offered every five years and lasting eighty hours. DIIT training now requires only sixty hours and provides training on a monthly basis.

The net training cost to the EPD has been reduced by $70 000 per year for five years due to reduction in student hours devoted to training, reduced delivery costs, improved job performance, a decrease in the number of failures on promotional exams for upgrades, and an increase in the average score of participants.

In addition to its record-keeping abilities, CBT is considered by the EPD to be an effective means of increasing retention, improving motivation, and providing standardized information.

How DIIT Works

The first part of DIIT is individually administered and scored diagnostic tests, determining which objectives have been mastered and which require further training. The computer handles all details of testing, including recording the performance of each trainee.

Once the set of mastered objectives for each trainee is known, they are given a list of study assignments to prepare them to meet their objectives. The trainees then study the materials until they are confident of mastery.

At this point, trainees are retested by the computer and the cycle is repeated until all objectives are mastered. The time spent testing is more than made up in time saved by not having trainees study assignments they already know. Testing time is brief because retesting is done only on the unmastered objectives, and each retest is terminated as soon as mastery is or is not possible.

Since the lessons, video, and testing components of DIIT are self-contained, the program is highly individualized and interactive and can be delivered in a decentralized fashion.

The instructor can examine the extensive performance records of each trainee with the push of a few buttons. This information enables the instructor to provide further assistance or motivation if needed.

A learning station consists of a terminal (or microcomputer), modem, and videotape player. One learning station is required for 100 to 150 trainees and another is recommended for the instructor.

Trainees learn to sign on in less than three minutes. Computer-managed training automatically routes or directs trainees through the correct lesson sequence.

SOURCE: "CBT a Success with Edmonton Police Department," *The Human Resource*, April–May 1987, p.9. Used with permission.

PHOTO 7.1
Pilot Training with
PLATO

Note: The PLATO System (left) is used to train pilots in the use of complicated instrument panels. (Reprinted by permission of Control Data Corporation.)

contributor to safety violations and accidents in organizations.[44] Yet as the Canadian economy shifts from goods to services, there is a corresponding need for workers who are more skilled and more literate. There is a widening gap between the job skills of the unemployed and those required to fill job vacancies, according to a recent Canadian labour market and productivity centre report. Estimates place the 1987 national job-vacancy rate (the number of job openings expressed as a percentage of the labour force) at 3.8%, while the unemployment rate over the same period was 8.9%. The employment-vacancy gap (the difference between the unemployment rate and the job-vacancy rate) was 5.1%, which means that for half of the unemployed in Canada in 1987 there was no job available of any kind. Occupational and regional shifts in the demand for labour are the chief causes of the growing disparity, according to the report. The introduction of new technologies and occupations can render obsolete certain traditional skills and create a demand for new skills that few workers possess. For example, while the growth of management and professional jobs in Canada accounted for 86% of the total employment growth between 1981 and 1987, only 14% of the unemployed were formerly from these fields.[45] To help alleviate this problem, the federal government of Canada recently established the Canadian Labour Force Development Board to focus on means to retrain workers who have been displaced by the rapidly changing economy.[46]

There are various techniques that organizations may use to train employees. One approach gaining wider acceptance is based on a device called an interactive video disk (IVD). This technique combines the drama of video with the power of microcomputers.[47] One such program is Principles of Alphabet Literacy (PALS). It uses animated video and a computer-stored voice to enable nonreaders to associate sounds with letters and letters with words, and to use the words to create sentences.[48] A second IVD program is called SKILLPAC. This program, subtitled English for Industry, was designed primarily for non-native English speakers and combines video, audio, and computer technologies to teach language skills in the context of the specific workplace situation in which those skills will be used.[49]

EVALUATING THE TRAINING EFFORT

After trainees have completed their training programs (or perhaps at planned intervals during the training), the program should be evaluated to see how well its objectives have been met. Thus, if assemblers should be able to weld a junction in 30 seconds, or a Xerox technician repair a machine in 30 minutes, then the program's effectiveness should be measured based on whether these goals are met. It is unfortunate (but true) that most managers do not spend much time appraising the effects of their training programs.

There are two basic issues to address when evaluating a training program. The first is the design of the evaluation study and, in particular, whether controlled experimentation will be used. The second is determining what training effect to measure.

Controlled Experimentation

Ideally, the best method to use in evaluating a training program involves **controlled experimentation**. In such an experiment both a training group and a control (no training) group are used. Relevant data (for instance, on the quantity or quality of production) should be obtained both before and after the training effort in the group exposed to training and before and after a corresponding work period in the control group. In this way, it is possible to determine to what extent any change in performance in the training group resulted from the training itself, rather than from some organization-wide change like a raise in pay; the latter, one assumes, would have affected employees in both the training and control groups. In terms of current practices, however, one survey found that something less than half of the companies responding attempted to obtain before and after measures from trainees; the number of organizations using control groups was negligible.[50]

controlled experimentation

What Training Effects to Measure

There are four basic categories of training outcomes or effects that may be measured:

1. *Reaction*. First, the trainees' reactions to the program should be evaluated. Did they like the program? Did they think it worthwhile?

2. *Learning*. Second, the trainees should be tested to determine if they learned the principles, skills, and facts they were to learn from the objectives

3. *Behaviour*. Third, it should be determined whether any measurable changes in the trainees' behaviour on the job occurred because of the training program. For example, are employees in the store's complaint department more courteous toward disgruntled customers than previously?

4. *Results*. Last, but probably most importantly, the following questions should be asked: "What final results were achieved in terms of the training objectives previously set? Did the number of customer complaints about employees drop? Did the reject rate improve? Did scrappage cost decrease? Was turnover reduced? Are production quotas now being met?" And so forth. Improved results are, of course, especially important.[51]

The training program may succeed in terms of the reactions from trainees, increased learning, and even changes in behaviour. But if the results are not achieved, then, in the final analysis, the training has not achieved its goals. If so, the problem may lie in the training program. It is also always possible that the results may be inadequate because the problem was not amenable to training in the first place.

On the Front Line

At the present time the Carter Cleaning Centres have no formal training policies or procedures, and Jennifer believes this is one reason why the standards that she and her father would like employees to adhere to are generally not adhered to.

Several examples can illustrate this. In dealing with the customers at the front counters the Carters would prefer that certain practices and procedures be used. For example, all customers should be greeted with what Jack refers to as a "big hello." And any garments they drop off should immediately be inspected for any damage or unusual stains so these can be brought to the customer's attention, lest the customer later return to pick up the garment and erroneously blame the store for the damage or an unusual stain. The garments are then supposed to be immediately placed together in a nylon sack to separate them from other customer's garments. The ticket also has to be carefully written up with the customer's name, telephone number, and the date precisely and clearly noted on all copies. The counterperson is also supposed to take the opportunity to try to sell the customer some additional services, such as waterproofing, if a raincoat has been dropped off, or simply notifying the customer that the centre is "having a special on drapery cleaning all this month." Finally, as the customer leaves, the counterperson is supposed to make some courteous comment like "have a nice day," or "drive safely." Each of the other jobs in the stores—pressing, cleaning and spotting, periodically maintaining the coin laundry equipment, and so forth—similarly contain certain steps, procedures, and most importantly, standards which the Carters would prefer to see adhered to.

1. Having previously developed a job description for a store manager's job Jennifer would now like to develop a job inventory for store managers. How should she go about doing this?

2. Which specific training techniques should she use to train her pressers, her cleaner-spotters, her managers, and her counterpeople, and why?

SUMMARY

1. Orientation is the process of introducing newcomers to organizations, to departments, and to work groups. It also involves familiarizing newcomers to the policies, rules, and procedures of organizations.

2. Socialization is the process through which newcomers learn the attitudes, standards, values, and patterns of behaviour that are expected of them by organizations. It helps to make newcomers feel that they are "part of the family," and to increase their commitment to the organization. As a result, it helps to reduce anxiety, boost morale, reduce turnover, and lead to higher performance than might be expected without an effective socialization process in place. Socialization, therefore, is an important human resource management process.

3. In this chapter we focused on training for new employees and for present employees whose performance is deficient. For either, uncovering training requirements involves analyzing the cause of the problem and determining what (if any) training is needed.

4. We discussed some principles of learning that should be understood by all trainers. The guidelines include making the material meaningful by providing a bird's-eye view and familiar examples, organizing the material, splitting it into meaningful chunks, and using familiar terms and visual aids.

5. We discussed several training techniques. Job instruction training is useful for training on jobs that consist of a logical sequence of steps. Vestibule training combines the advantages of on- and off-the-job training.

6. On-the-job training is a third training technique. It might involve the understudy method, job rotation, or special assignments and committees. In any case, it should involve four steps: preparing the learner; presenting the operation (or nature of the job); performance tryouts; and a follow-up. Other training methods include audiovisual techniques, lectures, and computer assisted instruction.

7. Most managers do not spend time evaluating the effect of their training program although they should. In measuring the effectiveness of a training program there are four categories of outcomes to measure: reaction, learning, behaviour, and results. In some cases where training seems to have failed, it may be because training was not the appropriate solution.

KEY TERMS

orientation

socialization

anticipatory socialization

accommodation

reality shock

role management

employee training

performance analysis

learning principles

on-the-job training (OJT)

job instruction training (JIT)

programmed learning

vestibule or simulated training

computer-assisted instruction (CAI)

controlled experimentation

DISCUSSION QUESTIONS

1. What benefits can orientation provides for newcomers?

2. Compare and contrast socialization with realistic job previews.

3. Why is socialization important to organizations?

4. Think of two jobs you have held. What type of orientation and socialization did your employers provide for you?

5. Explain how to apply our "principles of learning" in developing a lecture, say, on "orientation and training."

6. Pick out some task with which you are familiar—mowing the lawn, tuning a car—and develop a job instruction training sheet for it.

EXPERIENTIAL EXERCISE

Purpose. The purpose of this exercise is to give you practice in developing a training program.

Required Understanding. Familiarity with the training methods we discussed in this chapter, and a thorough understanding of the following description of a directory assistance operator's duties:

Customers contact directory assistance operators to obtain the telephone numbers of persons whose numbers are not yet listed, whose listings have changed, or whose numbers are unknown to the customer. These operators check the requested number via a computerized video display, which then transmits the numbers to the customers. If more than one number is requested, the operator reports the first number, and the system then transmits the second to the caller. A number must be found quickly so that the customer is not kept waiting. It is often necessary to check various spellings of the same name since customers frequently give incorrect spellings.

Next, imagine you are the supervisor of ten directory assistance operators in a small regional phone company that has no formal training program for new operators. Since you get one or two new operators every few months you think it would raise efficiency for to develop a "new directory assistance operator's training program" for your own use in your department. Consider what such a program would consist of before proceeding to your assigned group.

The class should be divided into groups of four or five students. Each group should go through the following steps:

1. List the duties and responsibilities of the job (of directory assistance operator) using the description provided.

2. List some assumed standards of work performance for the job.

3. Within your group, develop some assumptions about what parts of the job give new employees the most trouble (you would normally be able to do this based on your experience as the operators' supervisor).

4. Determine what kind of training is needed to overcome these difficulties.

5. Develop a "new directory assistance operator's training package." In this you will provide two things. First, you will provide a one-page outline showing the type(s) of training each new operator in your unit will go through. (For example, you might indicate that the first two hours on the job will involve the new operator observing existing operators; then four hours of lectures; and so on.) Second, in this package, if you are going to use job instruction training, show the steps to be included; if you're going to use lectures, provide an outline of what you'll discuss; and so on.

If time permits, a spokesperson from each group can put his or her group's training program outline on the board, and the class can discuss the relative merits of each group's proposal.

CASE INCIDENT: Why Are the Others Happy?

It is not unusual to hear both new and long serving employees of the Calgary division of Houston Magnetics express satisfaction with the general quality of work life and job security. They also often express satisfaction with compensation, organizational culture, and climate of their firm. Similar sentiments are commonly heard at the firm's head office in Edmonton. But, at the firm's Edmonton South division employees feelings are the opposite and the turnover rate is unusually high.

Houston Magnetics, a medium-sized electronic magnetics firm operates two divisions. The Calgary division is responsible for the design of the units. The Edmonton South division is responsible for the production of the units and head office is responsible for administration, marketing, and sales of finished products.

The company has a uniform orientation and socialization program that they administer to all employees at the time they join the firm. Employees at the Edmonton

South division feel that their work is more valuable than that of those at head office and at the other division. Yet they feel underpaid and unappreciated.

Questions

1. What orientation and socialization problems exist?
2. How can the organization deal with the issues raised by employees at the Edmonton South division?

NOTES

1. Douglas T. Hall and James G. Goodale, *Human Resource Management* (Glenview, Ill.: Scott, Foresman and Company, 1986), p. 285.

2. David A. DeCenzo and Stephen P. Robbins, *Personnel/Human Resource Management* (Englewood Cliffs, N.J.: Prentice Hall, 1988), p. 213.

3. Parts of the material in this section are drawn from: (i) Steven L. McShane and Trudy Baal, "Rediscovering the Employee Orientation Process," *The Human Resource* (December-January 1988), pp. 11-14. Used with permission. (ii) Steven L. McShane, "The Impact of Orientation Practices on the Socialization of New Employees: A Longitudinal Study" in T. H. Stone, ed., *Personnel and Human Resources Division Proceedings* (Halifax: St. Mary's University, June 1988), pp. 52-61. (iii) David E. Dimick, "Human Resources Development" in *Human Resources Management in Canada* (Toronto: Prentice-Hall Canada Inc., 1989), p. 35,026.

4. John P. Wanous, *Organizational Entry: Recruitment, Selection and Socialization of Newcomers* (Reading, Massachusetts: Addison-Wesley Publishing Co., 1980).

5. Carl J. Loomis, "IBM's Big Blues: A Legend Tries to Remake Itself," *Fortune* (January 1987), p. 52.

6. McShane and Baal, pp. 11-14.

7. M. Lubliner, "Employee Orientation," *Personnel Journal* (April 1978), pp. 207-208.

8. See McShane and Baal pp. 11-14, and Dimick, p. 35,026.

9. McShane and Baal, p. 12.

10. Joseph Famularo, *Handbook of Modern Personnel Administration* (New York: McGraw-Hill, 1972), pp. 23-7, 23-8. See also Ronald Smith, "Employee Orientation: Ten Steps to Success," *Personnel Journal*, Vol. 63, no. 12 (December 1984), pp. 46-49.

11. Charles Durakis, "Making the New Executive a Team Member," *Personnel*, Vol. 62, no. 10 (1985), pp. 58-60.

12. See also Walter St. John, "The Complete Employee Orientation Program," *Personnel Journal*, Vol. 59 (May 1980), pp. 373-378.

13. Thomas K. Meier and Susan Hough, "Beyond Orientation: Assimilating New Employees," *Human Resource Management* (Spring 1982), pp. 27-29.

14. Daniel C. Feldman and Hugh J. Arnold, *Managing Individual and Group Behaviour in Organizations* (New York: McGraw-Hill Book Company, 1983), p. 80.

15. John P. Wanous, *Organizational Entry* (Reading, Mass.: Addison-Wesley Publishing Company, 1980), p. 171.

16. Feldman and Arnold, p. 78.

17. The material in this section is drawn from: Daniel C. Feldman, "A Contingency Theory of Socialization" in *Administrative Science Quarterly*, Vol. 21, (1976); Hall and Goodale, pp. 275-278; Wanous, *Organizational Entry*, pp. 174-175; and Feldman and Arnold, pp. 79-85.

18. Feldman and Arnold, p. 80.

19. Ibid., p. 67.

20. John Van Maanen and Edgar H. Schein, "Career Development" in *Improving Life at Work*, J. Richard Hackman and J. Lloyd Suttle, eds. (Santa Monica, Calif.: Goodyear, 1977), p. 59, as quoted in DeCenzo and Robbins, p. 222.

21. Hall and Goodale, p. 276.

22. Hall and Goodale, p. 274.

23. Feldman, p. 435, and Hall and Goodale, p. 278.

24. Hall and Goodale, p. 278; Feldman and Arnold, p. 80.

25. Feldman and Arnold, p. 81.

26. Feldman and Arnold, p. 81.

27. Edgar H. Schein, "Organizational Socialization and the Profession of Management," *Industrial Management Review*, 9 (1968), pp. 1-16 (as quoted in Feldman and Arnold, p. 81).

28. William H. Whyte Jr., *The Organization Man* (Garden City, New York: Anchor, 1957) as quoted in Feldman and Arnold.

29. This section is drawn from the writings of David E. Dimick, "Human Resources Development," in *Human Resources Management in Canada* (Scarborough, Ont.: Prentice-Hall Canada Inc., 1989), p. 35,031.

30. M. J. Tessin, "Once Again: Why Training?" *Training* (February 1978), p. 7. Used with permission.

31. Albert Alan, "Training," in *Human Resources Management in Canada* (Toronto: Prentice-Hall Canada Inc., 1990), p. 30,011.

32. Morton E. Grossman, "The $5.3 Billion Bill for Training," *Personnel Journal* (July 1986), p. 54.

33. These steps are adapted and abridged from Donald F. Michalak and Edwin G. Yager, *Making the Training Process Work* (New York: Harper & Row, 1979). Copyright 1979 by Donald F. Michalak and Edwin G. Yager. Reprinted by permission of Harper & Row, Publishers, Inc. See also Kenneth R. Kramm, "Productivity: A Training Issue?" *Personnel Journal*, Vol. 67, no. 11 (November 1988), pp. 117-121.

34. J. P. Cicero, "Behavioral Objectives for Technical Training Systems," *Training and Development Journal*, Vol. 28 (1973), pp. 14-17. See also Larry D. Hales, "Training: A Product of Business Planning," *Training and Development Journal*, Vol. 40, no. 7 (July 1986), pp. 87-92, and Arnold H. Wensky and Robert Legendre, "Training incentives," *Personnel Journal*, Vol. 68, no. 4 (April 1989), pp. 102-108.

35. I. L. Goldstein, *Training: Program Development and Evaluation* (Monterey, Calif: Wadsworth, 1974). See also Stephen B. Wehrenberg, "Learning Contracts," *Personnel Journal*, Vol. 67, no. 9 (September 1988), pp. 100-103, and Murray B. Heibert and Norman Smallwood, "Now for a Completely Different Look at Needs Analysis," *Training and Development Journal*, Vol. 41, no. 5 (May 1987), pp. 75-79.

36. Kenneth Wexley and Gary Yukl, *Organizational Behaviour and Personnel Psychology* (Homewood, Ill.; Irwin, 1977), pp. 289-295.

37. Wexley and Latham, *Developing and Training*, p. 107.

38. Ibid., pp. 107-112. Four Steps in On-the-Job Training based on William Berliner and William McLarney, *Management Practice and Training* (Homewood, Ill.: Irwin, 1974), pp. 442-443. See also Robert Sullivan and Donald Miklas, "On-the-Job Training that Works," *Training and Development Journal*, Vol. 39, no. 5 (May 1985), pp. 118-120, and Stephen B. Wehrenberg, "Supervisors as Trainers: The Long-Term Gains of OJT," *Personnel Journal*, Vol. 66, no. 4 (April 1987), pp. 48-51.

39. Wexley and Latham, *Developing and Training*, pp. 131-133. See also Terri O. Grady and Mike Matthews, "Video ... through the Eyes of the Trainee," *Training*, Vol. 24, no. 7 (July 1987), pp. 57-62.

40. Mary Boone and Susan Schulman, "Teletraining: A High-tech Alternative," *Personnel*, Vol. 62, no. 5 (May 1985), pp. 4-9. See also Ron Zemke, "The Rediscovery of Video Teleconferencing," *Training*, Vol. 23, no. 9 (September 1986), pp. 28-36; and Carol Haig, "Clinics Fill Training Niche," *Personnel Journal*, Vol. 66, no. 9 (September 1987), pp. 134-140.

41. Control Data Corporation sales brochure, *Plato: A New Way to Solve Training Problems*.

42. Ibid. See also Nancy Madlin, "Computer-Based Training Comes of Age," *Personnel*, Vol. 64, no. 11 (November 1987), pp. 64-65; Marilyn Gist and others, "The Influence of Training Method and Trainee Age on the Acquisition of Computer Skills," *Personnel Psychology*, Vol. 41., no. 2 (Summer 1988), pp. 255-266; and Ralph E. Ganger, "Computer-Based Training," *Personnel Journal*, Vol. 68, no. 6 (June 1989), pp. 116-123.

43. Morton Ritts "What if Johnny Still Can't Read," *Canadian Business* (May 1986), p. 12, 54-57.

44. Ibid.

45. "Unemployed Lack Required Job Skills, Report Says" *Human Resources Management in Canada*. Report Bulletin no. 67. (Scarborough, Ont.: Prentice-Hall Canada Inc., September 1988),. p. 7.

46. "Ottawa Sets Up Skills Development Board," *Human Resources Management in Canada*. Report Bulletin no. 96. (Scarborough, Ont.: Prentice-Hall Canada Inc., February 1991), p. 2.

47. Nancy Lynn Bernardon, "Let's Erase Illiteracy from the Workplace," *Personnel* (January 1989), pp. 29-32.

48. Ibid. The PALS course was developed by educator Dr. John Henry Martin.

49. Ibid., p. 32. SKILLPAC was created by the Centre for Applied Linguistics and Dr. Arnold Packer, senior research fellow at the Hudson Institute in Indianapolis, Indiana.

50. R. E. Catalano and D. L. Kirkpatrick, "Evaluating Training Programs—The State of the Art," *Training and Development Journal*, Vol. 22, no. 5 (May 1968), pp. 2-9. See also J. Kevin Ford and Steven Wroten, "Introducing New Methods for Conducting Training Evaluation and for Linking Training Evaluation to Program Redesign," *Personnel Psychology*, Vol. 37, no. 4 (Winter, 1984), pp. 651-666. See also Basil Paquet and others, "The Bottom Line," *Training and Development Journal*, Vol. 41, no. 5 (May 1987), pp. 27-33; Harold E. Fisher and Ronald Weinberg, "Make Training Accountable: Assess Its Impact," *Personnel Journal*, Vol. 67, no. 1 (January 1988), pp. 73-75; and Timothy Baldwin and J. Kevin Ford, "Transfer of Training: A Review and Directions for Future Research," *Personnel Psychology*, Vol. 41, no. 1 (Spring 1988), pp. 63-105.

51. Donald Kirkpatrick, Effective Supervisory Training and Development. Part 3: "Outside Programs," *Personnel*, Vol. 62, no. 2 (February 1985), pp. 39-42. See also James Bell and Deborah Kerr, "Measuring Training Results: Key to Managerial Commitment," *Training and Development Journal*, Vol. 41. no. 1 (January 1987), pp. 70-73. Among the reasons training might not pay off on the job are a mismatching of courses and trainee's needs, supervisory slip ups (with supervisors signing up trainees and then forgetting to have them attend the sessions when the training session is actually given), and no help applying skills back on the job. For a discussion, see Ruth Colvin Clark, "Nine Ways to Make Training Pay Off on the Job," *Training*, Vol. 23, no. 11 (November 1986), pp. 83-87. See also Herman Birnbrauer, "Troubleshooting Your Training Program," *Training and Development Journal*, Vol. 41, no. 9 (September 1987), pp. 18-20.

SUGGESTED READINGS

Alon, Albert. "Developing A Context for Training" in *Human Resources Management in Canada*. Toronto: Prentice-Hall Canada, 1990. pp. 30,011-30,047.

Blake, R. William. "The Role of the Senior Human Resource Executive: Orientation and Influence." *Administrative Sciences Association of Canada* (Personnel and Human Resources Division), Proceedings of Annual Meeting, 1988. pp. 62-71.

DeSouza, Jackie. "Training: The Key Human Resources Issues for the 1990s," in *Human Resources in Canada*. Toronto: Prentice-Hall Canada, 1990. pp. 30,511-30,515.

Laird, Dugan. *Approaches to Training and Development*, 2nd ed., Reading, Mass: Addison-Wesley Publishing Company, 1985.

McShane, Steven L. "The Impact of Orientation Practices on the Socialization of New Employees: A Longitudinal Study." *Administrative Sciences Association of Canada* (Personnel and Human Resources Division), Proceeding of Annual Meeting, 1988. pp 52-61.

Schein, Edgar H. "Socialization and Learning to Work." Joe Kelly and others, eds. *Organizational Behaviour*, 2nd ed. Toronto: Prentice-Hall Canada Inc, 1991. pp. 167-174.

Wanous, John P. *Organizational Entry: Recruitment, Selection and Socialization of Newcomers*. Reading, Mass.: Addison-Wesley, 1980.

Wesley, Kenneth N. and Gary P. Latham. *Developing and Training Human Resources in Organizations*. Dallas, Texas: Scott, Foresman and Company, 1981.

Wynberg, Jack. "Computer Based Training" in *Human Resources in Canada*. Toronto: Prentice-Hall Canada Inc., 1990. pp. 30,523-30,529.

CHAPTER EIGHT
MANAGEMENT DEVELOPMENT

After studying this chapter you should be able to

1. Define management development.
2. Explain the relationship of management development to other HRM functions.
3. Explain the most frequent management development needs.
4. Identify the steps in a typical management development program.
5. Describe the different techniques used in management development.
6. Discuss the different types of leadership training models.

OVERVIEW

Management development is similar to technical training and is, in a sense, training for managers, since it is aimed at providing managers with the leadership skills they need to do their job. In this chapter we explain the purposes of management development, the management development process, various managerial on-the-job training techniques, and basic off-the-job development techniques. We also discuss various contemporary leadership training models.

INTRODUCTION TO MANAGEMENT DEVELOPMENT

management development

Management development is any attempt to improve current or future managerial performance by imparting knowledge, changing attitudes, or increasing skills. It includes in-house programs and executive MBA programs, such as those offered by the University of Toronto,[1] the University of Western Ontario, Queen's University, and the Certified in Management (CIM) designation offered by the Canadian Institute of Management. The necessity of having managers who are not only capable of dealing with their specialties but who can also manage complex organizations tends to stimulate interest in broad development programs for such areas as administration, human relations, organization theory, and other specialties.[2] Formal management development programs that are specifically designed to groom candidates for managerial positions are both popular and widespread.[3]

Management development is important for several reasons. The main reason is that promotion from within is a major source of management talent. One survey[4] of 84 employers reported that about 90% of supervisors, 73% of middle-level managers, and 51% of executives were promoted from within; virtually all these managers, in turn, required some development to prepare them for their new or prospective job. Similarly, management development facilitates organizational continuity by preparing employees and current managers to smoothly assume higher-level positions. It also helps to socialize management trainees by developing in them the right values and attitudes for working in the firm. Companies today are upgrading their corporate education and training and development programs, even if they have recently cut their work force.

Purposes and Importance of Management Development

The purposes and importance of management development are to

- Provide systematic and comprehensive management education programs to managers to improve the company's current and future ability to meet its goals
- Provide formal programs specifically designed for high-potential management candidates so that they may acquire the skills, knowledge, and abilities to effectively lead and manage the organization in the future
- Ensure that all managers have the requisite skills and expertise to manage effectively in today's highly competitive business environment and rapidly changing technological environment
- Develop managerial talent to ensure continuous availability of skilled managers
- Provide career-growth opportunities to meet managers' career aspirations and higher-order level needs
- Ensure that the organization has the talent to be able to improve its internal process and rapidly adapt to environmental changes, challenges, and disturbances
- Help the organization avoid managerial obsolescence
- Cultivate and groom young, well-educated management prospects
- Maintain and nurture designed organizational culture, climate, and norms
- Ensure the most effective utilization of human resources and organizational resources to accomplish organizational objectives

- Expand the capabilities of managers and allow the organization to engage in replacement and succession planning

Relationship of Management Development to Other Human Resource Management Functions

Management development is interrelated with many human resource management functions, including human resource planning, job analysis, selection, and performance appraisal. These are discussed below.

Human Resource Planning

Human resource planning (HRP) is one of the essential aspects of management development. Through HRP the organization is able to determine future management staffing requirements; anticipate retirements and resignations; forecast organization changes (expansions, reductions); manage inventory data; and analyze the availability of management candidates and their readiness to undertake various management assignments. Management development is also aided by two other HRP techniques, namely replacement planning and succession planning. Replacement planning is used to focus on short-term availability of management candidates and is a very useful source for identification of potential succession candidates. Succession planning's scope is broader, longer-range, and much more development-focused.

Job Analysis

Job analysis is a key component of management development. Once organizations have determined their future management staffing needs, the next step is to develop a "position profile." This is done through job analysis, which defines the skills, knowledge, abilities, and other job-related criteria required for the management position. (For a comprehensive discussion of job analysis see Chapter 4.)

Selection

Organizations often must hire competent managers away from competitors to fill a critical shortage of specialized management talent. However, the common practice in organizations is to hire from the external labour market to fill lower-level positions, and to groom and promote from within to upper-level management positions. Regardless of the source of management candidates, the candidates need management development training. The management development activities that may be implemented for these candidates will be dependent upon the calibre of human resources that the selection process provides, the capabilities and management development needs of the candidates, and the qualitative requirements of the management positions.

Performance Appraisal

Performance appraisal is another essential ingredient of an organization's management development program. Effective performance appraisal identifies an organization's management development needs and potential management candidates. Performance appraisal also provides feedback on the effectiveness of the management development program. (For a comprehensive discussion of performance appraisal see Chapter 9.)

FIGURE 8.1
Human Resource
Planning Replacement
Chart

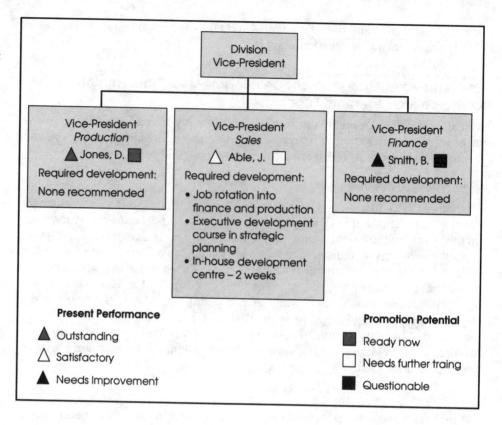

The Management Development Process

The typical management development program involves several steps. First, an organization projection is made, such as the department's management needs based on factors like planned expansion or contraction. Next the human resource department reviews its management skill inventories to determine the management talent currently employed. These inventories contain data on things like educational and work experience, career preferences, and performance appraisals. Next management replacement charts are developed. These summarize potential candidates for each management slot, as well as each person's development needs. As shown in Figure 8.1, the development needs of a future division vice-president might include job rotation (to obtain more experience in the firm's finance and production division), executive development programs (to provide training in strategic planning), and assignment for two weeks to the employer's in-house management development centre.

The Most Frequent Management Development Needs

As illustrated in Table 8.1, different levels of management have different development needs.[5] For example, 15 high-ranked needs as expressed by those at the supervisory and middle-management levels stress technical skills like evaluating and appraising employees, setting objectives, communicating, and disciplining. At the executive level the development needs stress general business skills like financial management, budgeting, and labour relations. Note especially the increased

TABLE 8.1 Most Frequent Development Needs at Each Level of Management

Executive Level	Middle Level	Supervisory Level
1. Managing time Team building	1. Evaluating and appraising employees	1. Motivating others
3. Organizing and planning Evaluating and appraising employees	2. Motivating others	2. Evaluating and appraising others
	3. Setting objectives and priorities	3. Leadership
5. Coping with stress Understanding human behavior	4. Oral communication	4. Oral communication
	5. Organizing and planning	5. Understanding human behavior
7. Self-analysis Motivating others	6. Understanding human behavior	6. Developing and training subordinates Role of the manager
	7. Written communication Managing time	
9. Financial management Budgeting	9. Team building Leadership Decision making	7. Setting objectives and priorities Written communication
11. Setting objectives and priorities Holding effective meetings	10. Holding effective meetings Delegation Developing and training subordinates	10. Discipline Organizing and planning
13. Oral communication		11. Managing time Counseling and coaching
14. Labor/management relations	15. Selecting employees	14. Selecting employees
15. Decision making Developing strategies and policies		15. Decision making

SOURCE: Reprinted, by permission of the publisher, from Lester Digman, "Management Development: Needs and Practices," *Personnel* (July-August 1980), p. 53. © 1980 American Management Association, New York. All rights reserved.

need for team-building skills at higher management levels; "team building" was ranked eighteenth for supervisors, ninth for middle managers, and first for executives.

Popularity of Various Development Techniques

On-the-job experiences (supplemented by coaching, rotational assignments, and other in-house training) are, by far, the most popular form of management development. This is illustrated by the following table, which shows the percentages for techniques reported by human resource managers as being the "most important means of development" in their firms:

Means of Development	Percentage Reporting Most Important (%)
On-the-job experience	68.2
Coaching by superiors	20.9
In-house classroom	4.7
Rotational assignment	2.4
University programs	2.3
Consultant programs	1.1
Other	1.1

While job rotation is the primary development method in most firms, other methods are used as well. For example, one survey found that 93% of companies responding used on-the-job management training but that 89% also used special projects or task forces to develop managers, 57% used mentoring, and 40% used job rotation. Thus, while on-the-job experiences are generally the most important means of developing managers, most firms use several other methods as well.[6]

Furthermore, different techniques are favoured for different levels of management, as summarized in Table 8.2. In-house workshops—that teach, for instance, interviewing or leadership skills—coaching plus on-the-job workshops, and external conferences and seminars are favoured for middle managers. For executives, external conferences and seminars are the most important type of development.

TABLE 8.2 Type of Development Received

Type of Development	PERCENT RECEIVING		
	Executive	Middle	Supervisory
External conference/seminars	27.7%	26.1%	17.3%
In-house workshops	22.9	21.6	34.7
Coaching plus on-the-job experience	13.3	29.5	33.4
Participation in university programs	10.8	10.2	4.0
Association/professional conferences and workshops	16.8	4.5	0
Consultant programs	7.2	5.7	5.3
Self-study courses	1.2	2.3	5.3

SOURCE: Reprinted, by permission of the publisher, from Lester Digman, "Management Development: Needs and Practices," *Personnel* (July-August 1980), p. 56. © 1980 American Management Association, New York. All rights reserved.

MANAGERIAL ON-THE-JOB TRAINING

On-the-job training is one of the most popular development methods. Important techniques include job rotation, coaching and understudy assignments, and action learning.

Job Rotation

job rotation

Job rotation entails moving workers from one job to another on a regular basis (e.g. every few days, weeks, or months), and has several advantages for management development programs.[7] In addition to providing a well-rounded training experience for each person, job rotation helps avoid stagnation through the constant introduction of new points of view in each department. Also, it tests the management trainee and helps identify the person's strong and weak points. Periodic job changing can also improve interdepartmental cooperation: managers become more understanding of each other's problems, while rotation widens the trainee's acquaintances among management.

Rotation does have disadvantages. It encourages "generalization" and tends to be more appropriate for developing general line managers than functional staff experts.

There are several things that can be done to improve a rotation program's success.[8] The program should be tailored to the needs and capabilities of the individual trainee. The trainee's interests, aptitudes, and career preferences should be considered, along with the employer's needs; the length of time the trainee stays in a job should then be determined by how fast he or she learns. Furthermore, the managers to whom these people are assigned should themselves be specially trained to provide feedback and to monitor performance in an interested and competent way.

Coaching/Understudy Approach

In the coaching/understudy approach, the trainee works directly with the person he or she is to replace; the latter is in turn responsible for the trainee's coaching. Normally, the understudy relieves the executive of certain responsibilities, thereby giving the trainee a chance to learn the job.[9] This helps ensure that the employer will have trained managers to assume key positions when they become vacated due to retirement, promotions, transfers, or terminations. It also helps guarantee the long-run development of company-bred top managers.

To be effective, the executive has to be a good coach and mentor. Moreover, this person's motivation to train the replacement will depend on the quality of the relationship between them. Some executives are better than others at delegating responsibility, providing reinforcement, and communicating, and this too will affect the results.

Action Learning

Action learning[10] involves releasing middle-management trainees to work full time on projects, such as analyzing and solving problems in departments other than their own. The trainees meet periodically with a four- or five-person project group, where their findings and progress are discussed and debated.

action learning

Action learning is similar to giving a management trainee a special assignment or project; however, with action learning several trainees meet once a week as a project group to compare notes and discuss each other's projects. It gives trainees real experience with actual problems, and to that extent can develop skills such as problems analysis and planning. Furthermore, the trainees (working with the others in the group) can and do find solutions to major problems.

BASIC OFF-THE-JOB DEVELOPMENT TECHNIQUES

There are many techniques that are used to develop managers off the job, perhaps in a conference room at headquarters or off the premises entirely at a university or special seminar. These techniques include (1) the case study method; (2) management games; (3) outside seminars; (4) role playing; (5) behaviour modelling; and (6) in-house development centres.

The Case Study Method

The case study method[11] involves presenting a trainee with a written description of an organizational problem; the person then analyzes and diagnoses the problem, and presents his or her findings and solutions in a discussion with other trainees.[12] The case method approach is aimed at giving trainees realistic experience in identifying and analyzing complex problems in an environment in which their progress can be subtly guided by a trained discussion leader. Through the class discussion of the case, the trainee learns that there are usually many ways to approach and solve complex organizational problems and that the trainee's own solution is often influenced by his or her needs and values.

The case method has five main features:[13] (1) the use of actual organizational problems; (2) the maximum possible involvement of participants in stating their view, inquiring into others' views, confronting different views, and making decisions, resulting in (3) a minimal degree of dependence on the faculty members who, in turn (4) hold the position that there are rarely any right or wrong answers, that cases are incomplete and so is reality, and (5) who strive nonetheless to make the case method as engaging as possible through the creation of appropriate levels of drama. The instructor plays (or should play) a crucial role;[14] the person should be not a lecturer or expounder of principles lifted from books, but rather a catalyst and coach. The instructor should also be a helpful source of information, at the same time asking probing questions to elicit lively debate among trainees.

Problems to Avoid

Unfortunately, according to Argyris the case approach often falls far short of this mark.[15] In practice, he says, faculty often dominate classroom discussions by asking students questions that they then proceed to answer themselves, by answering specific questions asked by students, and by presenting statements of the facts about the case. Faculty, he found, also use "mystery to achieve mastery" by intentionally withholding information (for instance, regarding what the company actually did and what its competitors were doing at the time the case was written), with the aim of maintaining control of the classroom discussion. In his study of the case method, Argyris also found that there were inconsistencies between the approach the faculty espoused and what they actually did. For example, faculty say there are no right or wrong answers, yet some faculty members do take positions and give answers; faculty say there are many different points of view possible, yet faculty members seem to select viewpoints and organize them in a way to suggest that they have a preferred route. Finally, few attempts were made by the faculty to relate the trainees' behaviour in the classroom to their behaviour at work. For example, faculty members missed several opportunities to relate the problems experienced by the company in the case to problems faced by the trainees' own employer.

There are several ways the case approach can be made more effective. Where possible, cases should be actual cases from the trainees' own firm. This helps ensure that trainees understand the background of the case and makes it easier for them to transfer what is learned to their own job and situation. Argyris also contends that instructors have to guard against dominating the case analysis and make sure that they remain no more than a catalyst or coach. Finally, instructors must carefully prepare the case discussion, and let the students discuss the case in small groups before class.[16]

Management Games

In a computerized management game trainees are divided into five- or six-person companies, each of which has to compete with the others in a simulated marketplace. Each company sets a goal (such as "maximize sales") and is told it can make several decisions. For example, the group may be allowed to decide (1) how much to spend on advertising, (2) how much to produce, (3) how much inventory to maintain, and (4) how many of which product to produce. Usually the game compresses a two- or three-year period into days, weeks, or months. As in the real world, each company usually cannot see what decisions the other firms have made, although these decisions do affect their own sales. For example, if a competitor decides to increase its advertising expenditures, that firm may end up increasing its sales at the expense of another.

Management games[17] can be good development tools. People learn best by getting actively involved in an activity, and the games can be useful for establishing such involvement. Games are almost always interesting and exciting for the trainees because of their realism and competitiveness. They help trainees develop their problem-solving skills, as well as focus their attention on the need for planning, rather than on just "putting out fires." The companies also usually elect their own officers and develop their own divisions of work; the games can thus be useful for developing leadership skills and for fostering cooperation and teamwork.

Management games also have their drawbacks. One problem is that the game can be expensive to develop and implement, particularly when (as is usually the case) it is computerized. Games also usually force the decision makers to choose alternatives from a closed list (for instance, they might have choices of only three levels of production); in real life managers are more often rewarded for creating new, innovative alternatives. On the whole, though, trainees almost always react favourably to a well run game, and it is a good technique for developing problem-solving and leadership skills. Computerized management games are available at many Canadian universities, such as York University's Atkinson College and Brock University's Faculty of Business.

Outside Seminars

Earlier in this chapter we listed the most important development needs at each level of management, including the need to develop specific skills like motivating others, appraising employees, leadership, communication, setting objectives, budgeting, and decision making.

Many organizations hold special seminars and conferences aimed at providing this sort of skill-building training for managers. Canadian universities and community colleges, for instance, provide thousands of courses in areas such as the following:

- General management
- Human resources
- Sales and marketing
- International management
- Finance
- Information systems and technology

- Manufacturing and operations management
- Purchasing, transportation, and physical distribution
- Packaging
- Research and technology management
- General and administrative services
- Insurance and employee benefits

The courses range from "how to sharpen your business writing skills" to "strategic planning" and "assertiveness training for managers."[18] Topics covered include review of management and organization concepts, developing effective interpersonal skills, communication, motivation, and developing leadership skills. These seminars may be attended at institutions such as the University of Western Ontario.

Role Playing

role playing

Role playing is a training technique that has trainees act out the parts of people in a realistic management situation. Role playing had its origin in psychotherapy, but it has found wide use in industry for improving sales, leadership, and interviewing skills, as well as other skills. The aim of role playing is to create a realistic situation and then have the trainees assume the parts (or roles) of specific persons in that situation.[19]

One such role—that of Walt Marshall, supervisor—from a famous role-playing exercise called the "New Truck Dilemma" is presented in Figure 8.2. Roles like these for each of the participants (when combined with the general instructions for the role-playing exercise) can lead to a spirited discussion among the role players, particularly when each throws himself or herself into the role, rather than merely acting. The idea of the exercise is to solve the problem at hand and thereby develop trainees' skills in areas like leadership and delegating.

Role playing can be an enjoyable and inexpensive way to develop many new skills. With the "New Truck Dilemma" exercise, for instance, participants learn the importance of fairness in bringing about acceptance of resource allocation de-

FIGURE 8.2
Typical Role in a Role-Playing Exercise

Walt Marshall—Supervisor of Repair Crew

You are the head of a crew of telephone maintenance workers, each of whom drives a small service truck to and from the various jobs. Every so often you get a new truck to exchange for an old one, and you have the problem of deciding to which of your crew members you should give the new truck. Often there are hard feelings, since each seems to feel entitled to the new truck, so you have a tough time being fair. As a matter of fact, it usually turns out that whatever you decide is considered wrong by most of the crew. You now have to face the issue again because a new truck, a Chevrolet, has just been allocated to you for assignment.

In order to handle this problem you have decided to put the decision up to the crew. You will tell them about the new truck and will put the problem in terms of what would be the fairest way to assign the truck. Do not take a position yourself, because you want to do what they think is most fair.

SOURCE: Norman R.F. Maier and Gertrude Casselman Verser, *Psychology in Industrial Organizations*, 5th ed., p. 190. Copyright © 1982 by Houghton Mifflin Company. Used by permission of the publishers.

cisions. The role players can also give up their inhibitions and experiment with new ways of acting. For example, a supervisor could experiment with both a considerate and autocratic leadership style; in the real world the person might not have this harmless way of experimenting. According to Maier, role playing also trains a person to be aware of and sensitive to the feelings of others.[20]

Role playing has some drawbacks. An exercise can take an hour or more to complete, only to be deemed a waste of time by participants if the instructor does not prepare a wrap-up explanation of what the participants were to learn. Some trainees also feel that role playing is childish, while others, having had a bad experience with the technique, are reluctant to participate at all.

Behaviour Modelling

Behaviour modelling is a relatively new development technique. It involves (1) showing trainees the right (or "model") way of doing something, (2) letting the person practise the right way to do it, and then (3) providing feedback regarding his or her performance.[21] It has been used, for example, to

behaviour modelling

1. Train first-line supervisors to better handle common supervisor-employee interactions, including giving recognition, disciplining, introducing changes, and improving poor performance.
2. Train middle managers to better handle interpersonal situations involving, for example, giving directions, discussing performance problems, discussing undesirable work habits, reviewing performance, and discussing salary problems.
3. Train employees (and their supervisors) to take and give criticism, ask and give help, and establish mutual trust and respect.

The basic behaviour modelling procedure can be outlined as follows:

1. *Modelling*. First, trainees watch films or videotapes that show model persons behaving effectively in a problem situation. In other words, trainees are shown the right way to behave in a simulated but realistic situation. The firm might thus show a supervisor disciplining a subordinate, if teaching how to discipline is the aim of the training program.
2. *Role playing*. Next the trainees are given roles to play in a simulated situation; here they practise and rehearse the effective behaviours demonstrated by the models.
3. *Social reinforcement*. The trainer provides reinforcement in the form of praise and constructive feedback based on how the trainee performs in the role-playing situation.
4. *Transfer of training*. Finally, trainees are encouraged to apply their new skills when they are back on their job.

Examples

An example can help illustrate the basic behaviour modelling technique.[22] The training group (which consisted of first-line supervisors) was divided into two groups of 10, with each group meeting for two hours each week for nine weeks. The sessions focused on management skills such as orienting new employees, giving recognition, motivating poor performers, and correcting poor work habits.

CHAPTER EIGHT Management Development **261**

Each training session followed the same format. First, the topic (such as handling a complaining employee) was introduced by two trainers. Next a film was presented that depicted a supervisor "model" effectively handling a complaining employee, by following several guidelines that were shown in a film immediately before and after the "model film" was presented. (In the case of handling a complaining employee, these guidelines included (1) avoiding responding with hostility or defensiveness; (2) asking for and listening openly to the employee's complaint; (3) restating the complaint for thorough understanding; and (4) recognizing and acknowledging his or her viewpoint.) Next there was a group discussion of the model supervisor's effectiveness in demonstrating the desired behaviours, such as, "Did the person avoid responding with hostility or defensiveness?" Next the trainees practised (via role playing) the desired behaviours in front of the class and got feedback from the class on their effectiveness in demonstrating the desired behaviours. In each practice session one trainee took the role of supervisor and another assumed the role of employee. No prepared scripts were used, and trainees were simply asked to recreate an incident that had happened to one of them in the past 12 months.

Another behaviour modelling program involved training sales associates who sold large appliances, radios, and television sets for a chain of retail stores in one metropolitan area. The supervisors of the sales associates were trained as instructors and the program focused on specific aspects of sales situations, such "approaching the customer," "explaining features, advantages, and benefits," and "closing the sale." Guidelines or "learning points" for handling each of these aspects of the sales interaction were presented first, followed by a videotape situation where a "model" sales associate followed the guidelines to carry out an aspect of the sales interaction with a customer. The trainees then practised the same situation in role-playing rehearsals, and their performance was reinforced by their supervisors.

The behaviour modelling program apparently had a significant impact on both the sales associates' sales effectiveness and commissions, as well as on their turnover. Sales associates who were trained saw their per hour commission rise from $9.27 to $9.95, or by 7%. During the same period, sales associates who did not receive the behaviour modelling training experienced a 3% decline in average earnings. Perhaps as a result of this, only about 7% of the trained sales associates left the firm during the ensuing year, whereas about 22% of the sales associates in the untrained control group left the company during that same period.[23]

In-House Development Centres

in-house development
centres

Some employers have established **in-house development centres** in which prospective managers and executives are exposed to realistic problems and tasks, evaluated on their performance, and encouraged to develop improved management skills. These centres usually combine classroom learning (lectures and seminars, for instance) with other techniques like assessment centres, in-basket exercises, and role playing.

SPECIAL MANAGEMENT DEVELOPMENT TECHNIQUES

There are also various special development techniques that are aimed at developing leadership ability and reducing interdepartmental conflict.

Leader Match Training

Fred Fiedler developed the first comprehensive situational model for leadership.[24] Fiedler's model proposes that effective group performance depends upon the proper match between the leader's style of interaction with his or her subordinates and the degree to which the situation gives control and influence to the leader. **Fiedler leader match training** is aimed at teaching managers how to match their leadership style to the situation. Fiedler developed an instrument, which he called the least preferred co-worker (LPC) questionnaire, that measures whether a person is task or relationship oriented. Further, Fiedler isolated three situational criteria—leader-member relations, task structure, and position power—that he believes can be mixed so as to create the proper match with the behavioural orientation of the leader.

Fiedler leader match training

Fiedler believes a key factor in leadership success is an individual's basic leadership style. He created the LPC questionnaire to find out what a leader's basic style is. The questionnaire contains 16 contrasting adjectives (such as pleasant-unpleasant, efficient-inefficient, open-guarded, supportive-hostile). Next the questionnaire asks respondents to think of all the co-workers they have ever had and to describe the one person they least enjoyed working with by rating him or her on a scale of one to eight for each of the 16 sets of contrasting adjectives. Fiedler argues that based on the respondents' answers to this LPC questionnaire, he can determine their basic leadership style. If the least preferred co-worker is described in relatively positive terms (a high LPC score), then the respondent is primarily interested in good personal relations with this co-worker. This respondent is relationship oriented. In contrast, if the least preferred co-worker is described in relatively unfavourable terms (a low LPC score), the respondent is primarily interested in productivity and thus would be labelled task oriented.

Fiedler argues that an individual's leadership style is fixed. This is important because it means that if a situation requires a task-oriented leader and the person in that leadership position is relationship oriented, either the situation has to be modified or the leader removed and replaced if optimum effectiveness is to be achieved. Fiedler believes that leadership style is innate to a person—therefore an individual cannot change his or her style to fit changing situations.

After an individual's basic leadership style has been assessed through the LPC, it is necessary to match the leader with the situation. Fiedler has identified three measures that, he argues, define the key situational factors that determine leadership effectiveness. These are leader-member relations, task structure, and position power. They are defined as follows:

1. *Leader-member relations* is a measure reflecting the extent to which a leader has the respect, trust, and confidence of his or her subordinates.

2. *Task structure* is the degree to which the job assignments are clearly specified by job descriptions, rules, regulations, and policies.

3. *Position power* is the extent to which a leader has power and authority over such factors as hiring, firing, discipline, promotions, and salary increases.

Fiedler argues that the better the leader-member relations, the more highly structured the job, and the stronger the position power, the more control or influence the leader has. For example, a very favourable situation (where the leader would have a great deal of control) might involve a new car manager who is well respected and whose subordinates have confidence in him or her (good leader-member relations), where the activities to be done—such as selling and leasing cars—are spe-

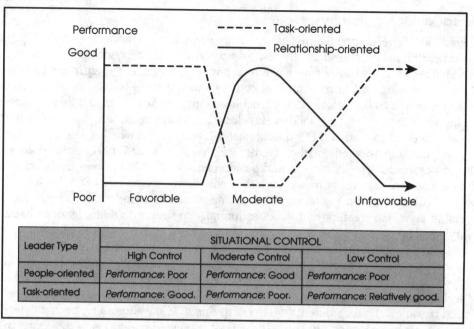

SOURCE: Fred Fiedler, Martin Chemers, and Linda Mahar, *Improving Leadership Effectiveness: The Leader Match Concept* (New York: John Wiley, 1977).

cific and clear (high task structure), and the job provides considerable freedom for him or her to reward and punish his or her subordinates (strong position power). By contrast, an unfavourable situation might involve the disliked chairman of a voluntary fund-raising team. In this job, the leader has very little control and lacks any real base of power to reward or punish followers.

After an individual's LPC has been assessed and an assessment has been made of the three contingency variables, the Fiedler model proposes matching them up to achieve maximum leadership effectiveness.[25] Fiedler's study of over twelve hundred groups, including service station crews, basketball teams, and laboratory groups, compared relationship versus task-oriented leadership styles in each of the eight situational categories. From the results Fiedler concluded that task-oriented leaders tend to perform better in situations that are very favourable to them and in situations that are very unfavourable (see Figure 8.3). Thus Fiedler predicts that when faced with a category I, II, III, VII, or VIII situation, task-oriented leaders perform better. Relationship-oriented leaders, however, perform better in moderately favourable situations—categories IV through VI.

The best way to apply Fiedler's model is to match leaders and situations. Individuals' LPC scores would determine the type of situation for which they were best suited. That "situation" would be defined by evaluating the three contingency factors of leader-member relations, task structure, and position power.[26] But since, according to Fiedler, leadership style is fixed, there are really only two ways in which to improve leader effectiveness. The first would be to change the leader to fit the situation. This would be similar to a hockey game, where the coach can go to the bench and put a hard-hitting forward or defenceman on the ice, depending on the situational characteristics of the other team on the ice. So, for example, if a group situation rates as highly unfavourable but is currently led by a relationship-oriented manager, the group's performance could be improved by replacing that manager with one who is task oriented. The second alternative would be to change the situation to fit the leader. That could be done by restructuring tasks or increasing or decreasing the power that the leader has to control factors such as salary increases, promotions, and disciplinary actions.

Vroom-Yetton Leadership Training

The **Vroom-Yetton leadership training** model is a development program for management trainees that focuses on decision making and on developing the trainees' ability to determine the degree to which their subordinates should be allowed to participate in decisions that must be made. Vroom and Yetton say, first, that there are five degrees of participation (as summarized in Figure 8.4), ranging from no par-

Vroom-Yetton leadership training

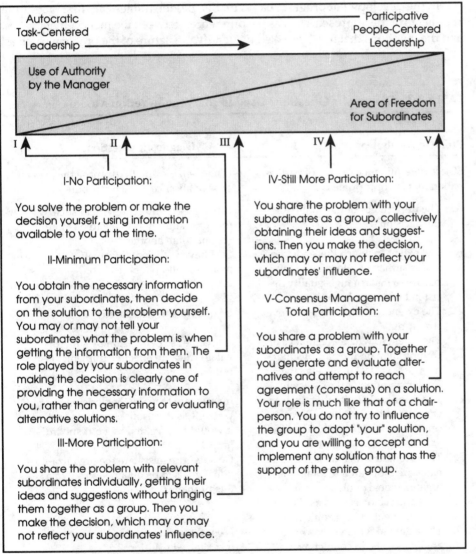

FIGURE 8.4
Five Degrees of Participative Leadership

Autocratic Task-Centered Leadership → ← Participative People-Centered Leadership

Use of Authority by the Manager

Area of Freedom for Subordinates

I   II   III   IV   V

I-No Participation:

You solve the problem or make the decision yourself, using information available to you at the time.

II-Minimum Participation:

You obtain the necessary information from your subordinates, then decide on the solution to the problem yourself. You may or may not tell your subordinates what the problem is when getting the information from them. The role played by your subordinates in making the decision is clearly one of providing the necessary information to you, rather than generating or evaluating alternative solutions.

III-More Participation:

You share the problem with relevant subordinates individually, getting their ideas and suggestions without bringing them together as a group. Then you make the decision, which may or may not reflect your subordinates' influence.

IV-Still More Participation:

You share the problem with your subordinates as a group, collectively obtaining their ideas and suggestions. Then you make the decision, which may or may not reflect your subordinates' influence.

V-Consensus Management Total Participation:

You share a problem with your subordinates as a group. Together you generate and evaluate alternatives and attempt to reach agreement (consensus) on a solution. Your role is much like that of a chairperson. You do not try to influence the group to adopt "your" solution, and you are willing to accept and implement any solution that has the support of the entire group.

SOURCE: R.H. George Field, "A Test of Vroom-Yetton Normative Model of Leadership," *Journal of Applied Psychology*, vol. 67, no. 5 (October 1982), pp. 523-532. Copyright © 1982 by the American Psychological Association. Reprinted by permission of author.

ticipation to total participation. Next, Vroom and Yetton say that the right degree of participation depends on seven attributes of the situation, including the importance of the quality of the decision, the extent to which the individual possesses sufficient information to make a high-quality decision, and whether the problem is routine and structured or unclear and complicated. (These seven attributes are summarized in Table 8.3.) Finally, Vroom and Yetton present a chart for determining the appropriateness of employee participation in the form of a decision tree, as presented in Figure 8.5. To use this model, trainees are taught to work from left to right. First, they must determine whether the quality of the decision is important, then determine if sufficient information exists to make a high-quality decision, and so forth. By starting on the left of the model and answering each question "yes" or "no," the trainee can work his or her way across the decision tree and thereby determine the degree of participation that is best, given the nature of the decision that must be made.

In the development program based on this model, trainees are first taught the rudiments of the approach, such as the differences between the management styles, and the questions that must be asked to identify the nature of the problem (such as,

TABLE 8.3 Diagnostic Questions Used in the Vroom-Yetton Model

Problem Attributes	Diagnostic Questions
(These determine the degree of participation that is appropriate.)	(These enable you to diagnose the presence or absence of each attribute.)
A. The importance of the quality of the decision	Is there a quality requirement such that one solution is likely to be more rational than another?
B. The extent to which the leader possesses sufficient information/expertise to make a high-quality decision by him- or herself	Do I have sufficient information to make a high-quality decision?
C. The extent to which the problem is structured	Is the problem structured?
D. The extent to which acceptance or commitment on the part of subordinates is critical to the effective implementation of the decision	Is acceptance of decision by subordinates critical to effective implementation?
E. The prior probability that the leader's autocratic decision will receive acceptance by subordinates	If you were to make the decision by yourself, is it reasonably certain that it would be accepted by your subordinates?
F. The extent to which the subordinates are motivated to attain the organizational goals as represented in the objectives explicit in the statement of the problem	Do subordinates share the organizational goals to be obtained in solving this problem?
G. The extent to which subordinates are likely to be in conflict over preferred solutions	Is conflict among subordinates likely in preferred solutions?

"How important is the quality of the decision?"). Next they are given a series of written case incident problems that briefly summarize a difficult situation. For example, "Suppose you are the captain of a submarine that is being shelled by enemy torpedo boats. You must decide whether to sink to the bottom and wait for them to pass, or to surface and make a run for it in open waters. Which management style would you choose?" Trainees then use the decision tree to determine the best style, starting with the first column on the left. (This particular example is presented as a discussion question at the end of this chapter.) The results of training managers in the use of the Vroom-Yetton model indicate that the training is effective.[27]

Hersey-Blanchard's Situational Leadership Theory

One of the most widely practised leadership models is Paul Hersey and Ken Blanchard's situational leadership theory.[28] It has been used as a major training device at such Fortune 500 companies as Caterpillar, IBM, Imperial Oil, and Xerox, and has been widely accepted in all the military services.[29] It is also widely used at places like the Niagara Institute, in Niagara Falls, and the Personal Development Institute in Toronto. Both institutes offer a variety of leadership development and other management development programs.

The **Hersey-Blanchard situational leadership theory** is a contingency theory that focuses on the followers. Hersey and Blanchard argue that successful leadership is achieved by selecting the right leadership style to match the maturity of

Hersey-Blanchard situational leadership theory

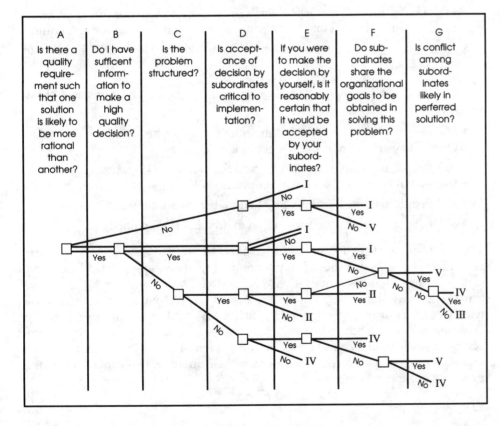

FIGURE 8.5
The Vroom-Yetton Model: Deciding How Much Employees Participate in the Decisions

the followers. They believe that emphasis should be placed on the followers in assessing leadership effectiveness, to reflect the reality that it is the followers who accept or reject the leader. Regardless of what the leader does, his or her effectiveness depends on the actions of his or her followers.

Hersey and Blanchard defined maturity as the ability and willingness of individuals to take responsibility for directing their own behaviour. Hersey and Blanchard stated that it has two components: job maturity and psychological maturity. The first, job maturity, encompasses one's knowledge and skills. Individuals who are high in job maturity have the knowledge, ability, and experience to perform their job tasks without direction from others. Psychological maturity is the extent to which people are willing or motivated to do something. Individuals high in psychological maturity do not need much external encouragement—they are already intrinsically motivated.

The Hersey-Blanchard situational leadership model uses the same two leadership dimensions that Fiedler identified: task behaviour and relationship behaviour. However, the situational leadership model goes a step further by considering each behaviour as either high or low, and then combining them into four specific leadership styles: telling, selling, participating, and delegating. The four styles are described as follows:

- *Telling (high task–low relationship).* The leader defines roles and tells people what, how, when, and where to do various tasks. It emphasizes directive behaviour.
- *Selling (high task–high relationship).* The leader provides both directive behaviour and supportive behaviour.
- *Participating (low task–high relationship).* The leader and follower share in decision making, with the main role of the leader being facilitating and communicating.
- *Delegating (low task–low relationship).* The leader provides little direction or support.

The final component in Hersey and Blanchard's theory is defining four stages of maturity:

- *M1.* People are both unable and unwilling to take responsibility to do something. They are neither competent nor confident.
- *M2.* People are unable but willing to do the necessary job tasks. They are motivated but currently lack the appropriate skills.
- *M3.* People are able but unwilling to do what the leader wants.
- *M4.* People are both able and willing to do what is asked of them.

The implications of the Hersey-Blanchard model are that as followers' maturity level increases, a leader should rely more on a relationship-oriented leadership style and less on a task-oriented style. Thus with followers who are highly immature (M1), the leader should emphasize a telling (directive) style. With subordinates whose maturity level is low (M2), the leader should emphasize a selling style. With subordinates whose maturity level is medium (M3), the leader should emphasize a participating style. With subordinates whose maturity level is high (M4) and who are considered self-motivated and self-directed, the leader should emphasize a delegating style.

Transactional Analysis

Transactional analysis is aimed at analyzing the interpersonal "transactions" or communications between a manager and his or her subordinates. It provides an effective analysis of any interpersonal situation.

The Three Ego States

To use transactional analysis (TA), a person has to be able to analyze the particular ego state that he or she is in, and also that of the person being addressed. There are three ego states: parent, adult, and child.

When a person is in a particular ego state, he or she behaves in characteristic ways. Characteristics of a person acting in the parent state include being over protective, distant, dogmatic, indispensable, and upright. A person in this state tends to argue not on the basis of logical facts, but on the basis of rules, or ways that were successful in the past. The person thus argues and explains much like his or her parent might have, all the while wagging a finger to show displeasure. A person operating in this mode is usually not an O.K. manager.

A person in the child ego state reflects all those behaviours that we normally attribute to childishness. For example, this person tends to take illogical, precipitous actions that provide him or her with immediate satisfaction. In an argument or discussion, this person's actions may include temper tantrums, silent compliance, coyness, and giggling.

A person in the adult state takes a rational, logical approach. He or she processes new data, carefully seeks out new information, thoughtfully considers these data, and then bases the argument on the facts. An adult manager is usually an O.K. manager: he or she is not out to "get" his subordinates, or to manoeuvre them into embarrassing positions. Instead, an adult manager is interested in confronting and solving problems in a straightforward, sensible manner by considering all points of view and arriving at a solution.

Types of Transactions

The aim of transactional analysis is to help the two people involved in a transaction to communicate and interact more effectively. Being able to identify one's own and the other person's ego state can be useful because it can help one to understand what is prompting the other person's behaviour and, therefore, how to frame an argument or response to the other person's statements.

In TA jargon, two main types of transactions are possible: complementary, and noncomplementary or crossed (see Figure 8.6). With complementary transactions the lines of communication are parallel since the employee's ego state complements that of the supervisor; each therefore gets an expected response (a "positive stroke") to what he or she says. Some complementary transactions would be as follows:

Adult (supervisor)–adult (employee). If both the supervisor and employee are in the adult state, the supervisor might say, "Sales increased 10% last year because of our improved sales incentive program." To this the employee might respond, "Yes, and our studies show that the incentive plan works especially well for those salespeople in the urban areas."

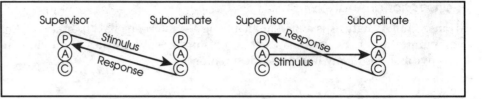

SOURCE: U.P. Luchsinger and L.L. Luchsinger, "Transactional Analysis for Managers, or How to be More O.K. with O.K. Organizations," *MSU Business Topics* (Spring 1974), pp. 5-12. Reprinted by permission.

Child–child. Here the supervisor might say, "I'll show them I won't work with those people. Stop the machines." And the employee might respond, "Great! Let's take a coffee break."

Child–parent. Here the supervisor might say, "I'll show them I won't work with those people. Stop the machines," to which the employee might respond, "It's against the rules to stop the machines. The plant manager will be mad at you if you stop the machines."

By contrast, in a noncomplementary or crossed transaction, one does not get an expected response. Because the person is interacting with someone who is not in a complementary state, both get a response that they neither want nor expect (a "negative stroke"). This is also illustrated in Figure 8.6. For example, a supervisor in the adult state might say that by increasing sales by 10% the salesperson could boost his or her commission correspondingly, to which the salesperson might respond, "Stop picking on me." In this case, the manager was in the adult state and expected the subordinate to be as well. Instead, the salesperson was in the child state and answered as if the manager was in the parent state. Notice again that the thing that distinguishes a crossed or noncomplementary transaction from a complementary one is that in a crossed transaction neither person gets the hoped for response.

Managerial Grid

grid training

managerial grid

Grid training is a formal approach to team building designed by Blake and Mouton.[30] As summarized in Table 8.4, grid training is based on a device called the **managerial grid**, which represents different possible leadership styles (specifically, whether the leader is more concerned with people or production).

TABLE 8.4 Managerial Grid Leadership Styles

TYPE OF LEADER AS RANKED ON GRID	TYPE OF CONCERN FOR PEOPLE	TYPE OF CONCERN FOR PRODUCTION
(1-1)	Low	Low
(1-9)	High	Low
(9-1)	Low	High
(9-9)	High	High

SOURCE: Based on material in Robert R. Blake and Jane S. Mouton, *The Managerial Grid* (Houston: Gulf Publishing, 1964).

A Computerized Managerial Assessment and Development Program

There are a number of computerized management assessment and development programs that can facilitate an employer's development process. One particularly useful example of such a management development tool is called ACUMEN.

ACUMEN[1] is a sophisticated managerial assessment and development program. The educational version of ACUMEN consists of three elements: instructions, a self-assessment, and an assessment report. After spending approximately 20 minutes interacting with ACUMEN'S IBM-compatible program, an individual will receive a visual display or hard-output "management profile" that focuses on 12 basic management traits:

1. Humanistic-helpful. Measures an individual's inclination to see the best in others, to encourage their growth and development, and to be supportive.

2. *Affiliation*. Measures the degree of friendliness, sociability, and outgoing tendencies the individual is likely to exhibit.

3. *Approval*. Measures a person's need to seek others' approval and support in order to feel secure and worthwhile as a person.

4. *Conventional*. Measures a person's need to conform, follow the rules, and meet the expectations of those in authority.

5. *Dependence*. Measures an individual's tendency to be compliant, passive, and dependent on others.

6. *Apprehension*. Measures a person's tendency to experience anxiety and self-blame.

7. *Oppositional*. Measures a person's tendency to take a critical, questioning, and somewhat cynical attitude.

8. *Power*. Measures a person's tendency to be authoritarian and controlling.

9. *Competition*. Measures a person's need to be seen as the best and, to some extent, to maintain a self-centered attitude.

10. *Perfectionism*. Measures a person's need to seek perfection, and his or her tendency to base self-worth on his or her own performance.

11. *Achievement*. Measures a person's need to achieve and have an impact on things.

12. *Self-actualization*. Measures an individual's level of self-esteem, interest in self-development, and general drive to learn about and experience life to the fullest extent.

When an individual completes the self-assessment, ACUMEN analyzes his or her responses and generates scores on 12 major scales. Each scale represents a particular attitude, or thinking style. The way the individual thinks (thinking style) affects

• What a person strives to achieve (goals).
• The individual's effectiveness as a leader.
• How the individual relates to and communicates with other people.
• Whether the individual views change as positive or negative.
• How an individual responds to crises and stress.

The major aim of ACUMEN is to help individuals develop a fuller understanding and appreciation of how their own thinking styles and personal dispositions play a role in productivity and management effectiveness. ACUMEN's analysis of a person's assessment responses, presented in graphic or textual form, provides this information.

When an individual views a graphic profile display, he or she will notice that each scale's extension is of varying length. On the circular graph, some scales extend a long way from the centre of the circle while other segments are relatively short. Similarly, scales on the bar graph will vary in length. The longer extensions indicate styles that are more prominent in a profile. By comparing the extensions the individual will be able to find the thinking styles that have the most impact on his or her own behaviour.

The text printout on each scale provides a detailed assessment and development information for each scale. For example, it might show a high score on the Humanistic Helpful Scale. This means that the person is likely to enjoy developing, helping, and teaching others, likes to motivate others, and attempts to see the best in others. So far so good. However, on the Oppositional Scale a low score indicates a fairly accepting, agreeable type of person. Up to a point, these may be laudable traits for managers. But in terms of development, "beware of being too reticent about making critical comments." In summary, a computerized management tool like ACUMEN can be very valuable, both for assessing management aptitudes (say, for future promotability) and for providing detailed development advice for the trainee.

---

[1]ACUMEN is a trademark of Human Factors Advanced Technology Group. This box is from "What Acumen is and How it Works," by HFATG.

HUMAN RESOURCE MANAGEMENT

On the Front Line

"Management development? Did you say management development? Jennifer, you're my daughter and I love you but I can't believe that with all the problems we're facing here—strong competition, softening economy, 400% turnover, employee theft, and supply and waste management cartage costs that are going through the roof—you actually want me to consider setting up some kind of a program that will turn that bunch of deadbeats that we have as managers into nice guys. I love you, Jenny, but please let's focus on the problems that we have to get solved today."

Jennifer was not altogether surprised with her father's reaction, but she did believe that he was being more than a little shortsighted. For example, she knew that some successful organizations, like Club Med, had a policy of rotating managers annually to help avoid their getting "stale," and she wondered whether such a program would make sense for Carter's. She also felt that some type of simulations might help managers do a better job of dealing with their customers and subordinates, and she further believed that periodic off-site meetings between her, her father, and the store managers might help to identify and solve problems with the stores. Outside seminars in areas like modern cleaning techniques might also help to boost the current store managers' interest and performance and, of course, there was also the possibility of scheduling potential managers (like a few of the current cleaner-spotters) for management development as well. The company really didn't have much money to spend on matters like this however, and Jennifer knew that to sell the idea to her father she would need a very concrete, tight set of recommendations. She contemplated the following questions:

1. Given a budget of $750, what type of management development program can I formulate for my current store managers? The proposal must include the specific activities (like job rotation) in which my managers should engage over the next four months.

2. Would it be worthwhile for us to administer an attitude survey of all our employees? I know we don't have a big company, but I am curious to know if employees would anonymously express to us their concerns, their likes, and their dislikes, and perhaps even help us identify problems like employee theft that they are encountering on their job. If we do go ahead with the survey, what questions should we ask?

The grid program is aimed, first, at developing **"9,9" managers**—managers who are interested in getting results by being high on both their concern for production and for people; they want to get results through committed, cooperative subordinates, say Blake and Mouton. The grid program assumes that possessing such a style makes it easier to work with subordinates, superiors, and peers in analyzing group, intergroup, and organizational problems and developing action steps to solve these problems.

The following is an outline of the program, which usually lasts three to five years:

Phase 1. This usually involves a one-week conference. Here trainees are taught the fundamentals of grid training.

Phase 2. Here trainees and their subordinates discuss, analyze, and solve their unit's practices and problems; teamwork is stressed.

Phase 3. Here the techniques developed in Phase 2 are used to discuss, analyze, and jointly solve problems between a trainee's unit and others in the organization.

Phase 4. Next, top management meets with various groups. Here the aims are to work out company-wide problems and to set some development targets for the company as a whole.

Phase 5. In this step, specific procedures are outlined for accomplishing the company's development targets.

Phase 6. Here the unit's and the company's accomplishments are evaluated and work begins on any remaining (or new) problems.

SUMMARY

1. Management development is aimed at preparing employees for some future job with the organization, or at solving organization-wide problems concerning, for instance, inadequate interdepartmental communication.

2. On-the-job experience is by far the most popular form of management development. However, the preferred techniques differ by organizational level, with in-house programs being preferred for first-line supervisors, and external conferences and seminars more widely used for top executives.

3. Managerial on-the-job training includes job rotation, coaching, and action learning. Basic off-the-job techniques include case studies, management games, outside seminars, role playing, behaviour modelling, and in-house development centres. Special management development techniques include Fiedler's leader match training, Vroom-Yetton training, Hersey-Blanchard's situational leadership model, and transactional analysis.

4. Grid programs aim at developing better problem solving and more cooperativeness at work through action research. Each work group analyzes work team problems and generates action plans for solving them. This same approach is then used by special intergroup teams to solve company-wide problems.

KEY TERMS

management development

job rotation

action learning

role playing

behaviour modelling

in-house development centres

Fiedler leader match training

Vroom-Yetton leadership training

Hersey-Blanchard situational
leadership theory

transactional analysis

grid training

managerial grid

"9,9" managers

DISCUSSION QUESTIONS

1. Describe the pros and cons of five management development methods.

2. Review the "submarine captain" example in our discussion of the Vroom-Yetton development method, and use their chart and technique to determine what approach the captain should use.

3. List the key factors in a typical management development program.

4. Compare and contrast the different leadership training techniques.

CASE INCIDENT: What's Wrong at the Bank?

The Maximum Return Bank has a policy of promote-from-within. All its managers and senior level employees were once tellers. The bank's motto is "Maximum return of savings, and progressive opportunity for employees." The bank is not automated. In 20 years of operations, only tellers have been recruited externally. Promotions are based on seniority. Most employees at the bank, particularly the older ones, are very pleased with the policy. They feel that the bank is a very good place to work, and that this policy contributes to a very good work environment, motivates, and provides recognition of employees' contributions to the company's success.

Once employees are hired, they progress through the ranks as follows: teller, customer service, accounting, credit, assistant manager, and manager. Recently, various employees expressed dissatisfaction with the bank's policy. They feel that some individuals are undeserving of their promotions to the assistant manager and manager ranks because they do not have any managerial abilities and were only promoted because of long service to the bank. Others argued that performance does not count since everyone is promoted when there is a vacancy. Another group of employees argued that the bank does not encourage employees to upgrade their skills and thus they do not have the talent required to set up and manage rapidly changing technology. Finally, they feel that the bank's policy frustrates capable employees and is unfair to outstanding performers.

Questions

1. What problems do you see with the bank's management development program?

2. Develop a management development program for the bank.

EXPERIENTIAL EXERCISE

Purpose: The purpose of this exercise is to give you some experience in dealing with some problems encountered in implementing a change.

Required Understanding: You should be familiar with the contents of Chapter 8, although this exercise can precede reading of the chapter.

How to Set Up the Exercise: Divide the class into groups of four persons and assign a name to each person. The same four names will be used in each group. The instructor can assign extra persons to various groups as observers.

Once the class is divided into groups all students should read the "general instructions" and should assign roles to each group member. Each person should read his or her instructions only. (Roles are presented at the end of this exercise.)

It will help if, in each group, role players Jack, Walt, and Steve wear name tags so that Jane, the supervisor, can call them by name. (It also helps to have all Janes stand up when they have finished reading their role.) They may also continue to refer as needed to the data supplied with their instructions.

Instructions:

1. When all the Janes are standing, the instructor can remind the Jacks, Walts, and Steves that they are waiting for Jane in her office. When she sits down and greets them, this will indicate that she has entered her office, and each person should adopt his or her role.

2. At the instructor's signal, all Janes are seated. All groups should begin the role play simultaneously.

3. About 25 minutes should be given for the groups to reach a decision. If certain groups have trouble, the instructor may ask Jane, the supervisor, to do the best she can in the next minute or two.

4. While groups are role playing, the instructor will write a table on the chalk board with the following column headings: (1) Group Number, (2) Solution, (3) Problem Employees, (4) Expected Production, (5) Method Used by Supervisor, and (6) Sharing of Data.

5. Collecting results.

   a. Each group should report in turn, while remaining seated as a group. The instructor will enter in column 1 the number of the group called on to report.

   b. Each Jane reports the solution she intends to follow. The solutions may be of four types: (1) continuation of old method (i.e., rotation through all positions), (2) adoption of new method with each person working his best position, (3) a compromise (new method in the morning, old in the afternoon), or (4) integrative solution containing features of old and new solutions (e.g., each person spends more time on best position, two workers exchange positions and third works on his best position, all three exchange but confine changes to work their two best positions). The instructor will enter type of solution in column 2 and add notes to indicate whether a trial period is involved, a rest pause is added, and so on.

   c. Each Jane reports whether she had any special trouble with a particular employee. If so, the initial of the problem individual is entered in the third column.

   d. Jack, Walt, and Steve report whether production will stay the same, go up, or down, as a result of the conference. The estimates of Jack, Walt, and Steve should be recorded as "0," "+," and "-" signs in column 4.

e. Group observers report on the way Jane handled the group and how the group responded. Enter a descriptive term in column 5 for Jane's method (e.g., tried to sell her plan, used group decision, blamed group, was participative, was arbitrary and somewhat abusive). If no observers were present in a group, data should be supplied by the group itself. For leading questions about method, see "Instructions for Observers."

6. Class discussion. Discuss differences obtained and see if they can be related to the attitude and the method of Jane. What kinds of resistance were encountered? Classify them into fear, hostility, and so on. What are the proper methods of dealing with each of these kinds of resistance? What study that we discussed is this situation similar to?

The instructions and roles follow. Please be sure to read only the general instructions and the roles that you have been assigned.

1. *General Instructions* You work in a plant that does a large number of sub-assembly jobs, such as assembling fuel pumps, carburetors, and starters. Jane Thompson is supervisor of several groups, including the one with which we are concerned today. Jack, Walt, and Steve make up your particular group, which assembles fuel pumps. The assembly operation is divided into three positions or jobs. Since the three jobs are simple and each of you is familiar with all of the operations, you find it desirable to exchange jobs or positions. You have worked together this way for a long time. Pay is based on a team piece-rate and has been satisfactory to all of you. Presently, each of you will be asked to be one of the following: Jane Thompson, Jack, Walt, or Steve. In some instances an observer will be present in your group. Today, Jane, the supervisor, has asked Jack, Walt, and Steve to meet with her in her office. She said she wanted to talk about something.

2. *Instructions for Observers* (May be omitted if desired) Your job is to observe the method used by Jane in handling a problem with her workers. Pay special attention to the following:

a. *Method of presenting problem.* Does she criticize, suggest a remedy, request their help on a problem, or use some other approach?

b. *Initial reaction of members.* Do group members feel criticized or do they try to help Jane?

c. *Handling of discussion by Jane.* Does she listen or argue? Does she try to persuade? Does she use threats? Or does she let the group decide?

d. *Forms of resistance expressed by the group.* Did members express fear, hostility, satisfaction with present method, and so on?

e. What does Jane do with the time-study data? (1) Lets group examine the table, (2) mentions some of the results, or (3) makes little or no reference to the data.

Best results are obtained if Jane uses the data to pose the problem of how they might be used to increase production.

3. *Roles for Participants* (Read only your own role, please.)

ROLE FOR JANE THOMPSON, SUPERVISOR You supervise the work of about 20 people in a shop. Most of the jobs are piece-rate jobs, and some of the employees work in teams and are paid on a team piece-rate basis. In one of the teams,

Jack, Walt, and Steve work together. Each one of them does one of the operations for an hour and then they exchange, so that all employees perform each of the operations at different times. The workers themselves decided to operate that way and you have never given the plan any thought.

Lately, Jim Clark, the methods expert, has been around and studied conditions in your shop. He timed Jack, Walt, and Steve on each the operations and came up with the following facts:

TIME PER OPERATION (MIN.)

	Position 1	Position 2	Position 3	Total
Jack	3	4	4 1/2	11 1/2
Walt	3 1/2	3 1/2	3	10
Steve	5	3 1/2	4 1/2	13
				34 1/2

He observed that with the men rotating, the average time for all three operations would be one-third of the total time of 11 1/2 minutes per complete unit. If, however, Jack worked in the No. 1 spot, Steve in the No. 2 spot, and Walt in the No. 3 spot, the time would be 9 1/2 minutes, a reduction of over 17%. Such a reduction in time would amount to saving more than 80 minutes. In other words the lost production would be about the same as that which would occur if the men goofed off for 80 minutes in an eight-hour day. If the time were used for productive effort, production would be increased more than 20%.

This time study makes pretty good sense to you so you have decided to take up the problem with the team. You feel that they should go along with any change in operation that is made.

ROLE FOR JACK You are one of three team members on an assembly operation. Walt and Steve are your teammates and you enjoy working with them. You get paid on a team basis and you are making wages that are entirely satisfactory. Steve isn't quite as fast as Walt and you, but when you feel he is holding things up too much each of you can help out.

The work is very monotonous. The saving thing about it is that every hour you all change positions. In this way you get to do three operations. You are best on the No. 1 position so when you get in that spot you turn out some extra work and so make the job easier for Steve who follows you in that position.

You have been on this job for two years and you have never run out of work. Apparently your group can make pretty good pay without running yourselves out of a job. Lately, however, the company has had some of its experts hanging around. It looks like the company is trying to work out some speedup methods. If they make these jobs any more simple you won't be able to stand the monotony. Jane Thompson, your supervisor, is a fair person and has never critizized your team's work.

ROLE FOR STEVE You work with Jack and Walt on an assembly job and get paid on a team piece-rate. The three of you work very well together and make a pretty good wage. Jack and Walt like to make a little more than you think is necessary, but you go along with them and work as hard as you can so as to keep the production up where they want it. They are good fellows, often help you out if you fall behind, and so you feel it is only fair to try and go along with the pace they set.

The three of you exchange positions every hour. In this way you get to work all positions. You like the No. 2 position the best because it is easiest. When you get in the No. 3 position you can't keep up and then you feel Jane Thompson, the supervisor, watching you. Sometimes Walt and Jack slow down when you are on the No. 3 spot and then the supervisor seems satisfied.

Lately the methods man has been hanging around watching the job. You wonder what he is up to. Can't they leave guys alone who are doing all right?

ROLE FOR WALT   You work with Jack and Steve on a job that requires three separate operations. Each of you works on each of the three operations by rotating positions once every hour. This makes the work more interesting and you can always help out the other fellow by running the job ahead in case one of you doesn't feel well. It's all right to help out because you get paid on a team piece-rate basis. You could actually earn more if Steve were a faster worker, but he is a swell guy and you would rather have him in the group than someone else who might do a little bit more.

You find all three positions about equally desirable. They are all simple and purely routine. The monotony doesn't bother you much because you can talk, daydream, and change your pace. By working slow for a while and then fast you can sort of set your pace to music you hum to yourself. Jack and Steve like the idea of changing jobs, and even though Steve is slow on some positions, the changing around has its good points. You feel you get to a stopping place every time you change positions and this kind of takes the place of a rest pause.

Lately some kind of efficiency expert has been hanging around. He stands some distance away with a stopwatch in his hand. The company could get more for its money if it put some of those guys to work. You say to yourself, "I'd like to see one of these guys try and tell me how to do this job. I'd sure give him an earful."

If Jane Thompson, your supervisor, doesn't get him out of the shop pretty soon, you're going to tell her what you think of her dragging in company spies.

SOURCE: Norman R. F. Maier, *Psychology in Industrial Organizations*, 4th ed. (Boston: Houghton Mifflin, 1973), pp. 295-299.

NOTES

1. See Executive MBA, Faculty of Management, University of Toronto, 1991.

2. Wendell L. French, *The Personnel Management Process* (Boston: Houghton Mifflin Company, 1987), p. 379.

3. Ibid.

4. "Trends in Corporate Education and Training," Report no. 870 (1986), The Conference Board, 845 Third Avenue, New York, NY, 10022.

5. Lester A. Digman, "Management Development: Needs and Practices," *Personnel*, Vol. 57 (July-August 1980), pp. 45-57.

6. Lise Saari et al., "A Survey of Management Training and Education Practices in U.S. Companies," *Personnel Psychology* (Winter 1988), pp. 731-743.

7. See also Jack Phillips, "Training Supervisors Outside the Classroom," *Training and Development Journal*, Vol. 40, no. 2 (February 1986), pp. 46-49.

8. Kenneth Wexley and Gary Latham, *Developing and Training Resources in Organizations* (Glenview, Ill.; Scott, Foresman, 1981), p. 118.

9. Ibid., p. 207.

10. This is based on Nancy Foy, "Action Learning Comes to Industry," *Harvard Business Review*, Vol. 56 (September-October 1977), pp. 158-168.

11. For a discussion of the advantages of case studies over traditional methods, see, for example, Eugene Andrews and James Noel, "Adding Life to the Case Study," Training and Development Journal, Vol. 40, no. 2 (February 1986), pp. 28-33.

12. Wexley and Latham, *Developing and Training Resources in Organizations*, p. 193.

13. Chris Argyris, "Some Limitations of the Case Method: Experiences in a Management Development Program," *Academy of Management Review*, Vol. 5, no. 2 (1980), pp. 291-298.

14. David Rogers, *Business Policy and Planning* (Englewood Cliffs, N.J.: Prentice-Hall, 1977), pp. 532-533.

15. Argyris, "Some Limitations of the Case Method," pp. 292-295.

16. Rogers, *Business Policy and Planning*, p. 533.

17. For an interesting discussion of how to design a management game that is both educational and stimulating, see Beverly Loy Taylor, "Around the World in 80 Questions," *Training and Development Journal*, Vol. 40, no. 3 (March 1986), pp. 67-70.

18. Mona Pintkowski, "Evaluating the Seminar Marketplace," *Training and Development Journal*, Vol. 40, no. 1 (January 1986), pp. 74-77.

19. John Hinrichs, "Personnel Training," in Marvin Dunnette, ed., *Handbook of Industrial and Organizational Psychology* (Chicago: Rand McNally, 1976), p. 855.

20. Norman Maier, Allen Solem, and Ayesha Maier, *The Role Play Technique* (San Diego, Calif.: University Associates, 1975), pp. 2-3.

21. This section based is on Allen Kraut, "Developing Managerial Skills via Modeling Techniques: Some Positive Research Findings—A Symposium," *Personnel Psychology*, Vol. 29, no. 3 (Autumn 1976), pp. 325-361.

22. Gary Latham and Lise Saari, "Application of Social-Learning Theory to Training Supervisors Through Behavioral Modeling," *Journal of Applied Psychology*, Vol. 64, no. 3 (June 1979), pp. 239-246. Note that in one study in which managers were substituted for professional trainers, the researchers concluded that while behaviour-modelling resulted in favourable reactions and an increase in learning, it did not produce behaviour change on the job or improved performance results. The researchers here conclude that behaviour-modelling could be improved by such techniques as persuading supervisors that the new behaviours they are asked to learn are more effective than their current behaviours. See also James Russell, Kenneth Wexley, and John Hunter, "Questioning the Effectiveness of Behaviour-Modelling Training in an Industrial Setting," *Personnel Psychology*, Vol. 37, no. 3 (Autumn, 1984), pp. 465-481.

23. Herbert Meyer and Michael Raich, "An Objective Evaluation of a Behavior-Modeling Training Program," *Personnel Psychology*, Vol. 36, no. 4 (Winter 1983), pp. 755-761.

24. Parts of this section were drawn from Fred E. Fiedler, *A Theory of Leadership Effectiveness* (New York: McGraw Hill, 1967); Fred Fiedler and Linda Mahar, *Improving Leadership Effectiveness: The Leader Match Concept* (New York: John Wiley, 1977); Stephen P. Robbins, *Organizational Behavior*, 5th ed. (Englewood Cliffs, N.J.: Prentice-Hall Inc., 1991), pp. 361-364; John R. Schermerhorn Jr., James G. Hunt, and Richard N. Osborn, *Managing Organizational Behavior*, (New York: John Wiley & Sons Inc., 1991), pp. 469-472.

25. F. E. Fiedler, M. M. Chemers, and L. Mahar, *Improving Leadership Effectiveness: The Leader Match Concept* (New York: John Wiley, 1977).

26. Fred Fiedler and Linda Mahar, "The Effectiveness of Contingency Model Training: A Review of the Validation of Leader Match," *Personnel Psychology*, Vol. 32 (Spring 1979), pp. 45-62; Lewis Csoka and Paul Bons, "Manipulating the Situation to Fit the Leader Style: Two Validation Studies to Leader Match," *Journal of Applied Psychology*, Vol. 53 (June 1978), pp. 295-300; Boris Kabanoff, "A Critique of Leader Match and Its Implications for Leadership Research," *Personnel Psychology*, Vol. 34 (Winter 1981), pp. 765-769; Arthur Jago and James Ragan, "The Trouble with Leader Match Is that It Doesn't Match Fielder's Contingency Model," *Journal of Applied Psychology*, Vol. 71, no. 4 (November 1986), pp. 555-559; Martin Chemers and Fred E. Fiedler, "The Trouble with Assumptions: A Reply to Jago and Ragan," *Journal of Applied Psychology*, Vol. 71, no. 4 (November 1986) pp. 560-563.

27. See, for example, R. H. George Field, "A Test of the Vroom-Yetton Normative Model of Leadership," *Journal of Applied Psychology*, Vol. 67, no. 5 (October 1982), pp. 523-532.

28. The material in this section is drawn from P. Hersey and K. H. Blanchard, "So You Know Your Leadership Style?" *Training and Development Journal* (February 1974), pp. 1-5; P. Hersey and K. Blanchard, *Management of Organizational Behavior: Utilizing Human Resources*, 4th ed. (Englewood Cliffs, N.J.: Prentice-Hall Inc.), pp. 150-161; Stephen P. Robbins, *Organizational Behavior*, 5th ed. (Englewood Cliffs, N.J.: Prentice-Hall Inc., 1991), pp. 365-368.

29. Hersey and Blanchard, *Management of Organizational Behavior*, p. 171.

30. Robert Blake and Jane Mouton, *The Managerial Grid* (Houston, Tex.: Gulf Publishing, 1964). For an interesting description of the effectiveness of team building in solving a management problem, see, for example, Barry Miller and Ronald Philips, "Team Building on a Deadline," *Training and Development Journal*, Vol. 40, no. 3 (March 1986), pp. 54-58.

SUGGESTED READINGS

Foulkes, Fred K. and E. Robert Livernash. *Human Resources Management: Cases and Text*, 2nd ed. Englewood Cliffs, NJ: Prentice-Hall, Inc., 1989.

Hersey, Paul and Kenneth H. Blanchard. *Management of Organizational Behavior: Utilizing Human Resources*, 5th ed. Englewood Cliffs, NJ: Prentice-Hall Inc., 1988.

Stevens, George E. *Cases and Exercises in Human Resource Management*, 5th ed. Boston: Irwin, 1991.

PART THREE

APPRAISAL AND CAREER MANAGEMENT

CHAPTER
NINE PERFORMANCE APPRAISAL

After studying this chapter you should be able to

1. Develop, evaluate, and administer at least four performance appraisal tools.

2. List and discuss the pros and cons of graphic rating scales, the alternation ranking method, the paired comparison method, the forced distribution method, the critical incident method, the essay method, the behaviourally anchored rating scale, management by objectives, and behavioural observation scales.

3. Explain the problems to be avoided in appraising performance.

4. Discuss the pros and cons of using different potential raters to appraise a person's performance.

5. Hold an effective appraisal interview.

OVERVIEW

This chapter starts a new section of this book. Once workers have been selected and trained, the next step is to appraise their performance; the purpose of this chapter is to present several techniques for doing so. We will explain how to use different appraisal techniques, how to avoid common performance appraisal problems, and how to review the appraisal with a subordinate. Performance appraisal is the step that reveals how well employees have been placed and motivated. Should any problems be identified, the next steps would involve communicating with the employee and taking remedial career action—topics we discuss in the following chapter.

INTRODUCTION TO PERFORMANCE APPRAISAL

Performance appraisal is the formal, systematic process of evaluating qualitatively and quantitatively employee job performance and potential for the future. Performance appraisal is also known as performance evaluation, performance review, merit evaluation, and employee evaluation.

performance appraisal

The Role of the Human Resource Department

The nature of performance appraisal is such that line managers and human resource specialists both play important roles in the process. Line managers play a central role because in almost all cases the supervisor does the actual appraising. As a result, supervisors have a responsibility to see to it that they are completely familiar with the appraisal techniques to be used, that they understand (and can avoid) the problems that can cripple an appraisal system, and that they perform their appraisal function fairly and objectively. The human resource department, on the other hand, serves a policy-making and advisory function with respect to performance appraisals. As explained in this chapter, there are many performance appraisal tools in use, and the human resource office should be able to assist line managers in choosing the most appropriate ones. In one recent survey, for example, about 80% of the companies responding said that the human resource office provides advice and assistance regarding appraisal but leaves final decisions on appraisal procedures to operating division heads; in the rest of the firms the human resource department prepares detailed forms and procedures and insists that they be used by all departments in the organization.[1] The human resource specialist is also responsible for making available "performance appraisal training" for supervisors, training aimed at improving supervisors' appraisal skills.

Finally, the human resource department is often responsible for monitoring the use of the appraisal system, particularly in regard to ensuring that the format and criteria being measured do not become outdated. (In fact, organizations rarely install an appraisal system without changing it gradually over the years. In the survey mentioned above, for example, one-third of the organizations surveyed had appraisal systems that had been in use for less than a year, and another third had systems that had been in use for one to five years. Half the organizations were currently in the process of revising their appraisal programs and several other organizations were conducting reviews to see how well their programs were working.)[2] Related to this, the human resource specialist plays an increasingly important role in ensuring that the employer's appraisal program complies with fair employment practice.

Purposes and Importance of Performance Appraisal

The purposes and importance of performance appraisal are to

- Improve organizational decision-making processes and ensure the efficient use of human resources
- Provide feedback to employees to let them know how well they have met performance standards and to warn them about unsatisfactory performance
- Provide coaching and counselling to employees on ways to improve their performance and develop their future potential

- Communicate to employees the organization's expectations
- Provide feedback to the organization on the quality of its recruitment, selection, training, and development programs
- Identify areas in which employees need coaching, counselling, training, and developing
- Provide employees with feedback on ways to improve their performance to enable them to meet the organization's goals and their own career goals

DEVELOPING A PERFORMANCE APPRAISAL SYSTEM

In developing a performance appraisal system, many decisions regarding its design, its implementation, and the intended uses of the appraisal information must be made. Decisions must also be made about the impact of government laws, guidelines, and other legal requirements, and the choice of appraiser.

It is important that the organization decide on the objectives of the performance appraisal system and the appropriate method to be used, and establish the appropriate policies and procedures to govern its administration. The organization must determine performance standards for employees to attain and against which employee performance can be measured. The organization must also communicate to employees the purpose and goals, standards and measurement criteria of the performance appraisal system for performance appraisal to be effective; employees' performance must be observed (monitored) and documented (recorded), then evaluated against established standards.

Legal Considerations

The Canadian Human Rights Act and the acts of other jurisdictions have an important impact on the design, development, and administration of performance appraisal systems. If a complaint is filed, the human rights acts require that an organization demonstrate that the selection procedures and processes used are valid. Performance appraisal is an important aspect of the selection procedures and processes because it is the criterion against which selection tests are validated. If the performance appraisal criterion is biased it will result in a biased selection procedure. Further, performance appraisal has an impact on other human resource management activities such as training and promotions, and may therefore be considered an extended selection procedure. As a result, performance appraisal has to comply with human rights guidelines, specifically with respect to being valid. While fair employment law with respect to performance appraisals is relatively new, a prudent organization should still take steps like the following to help ensure that its appraisal procedures are defensible.[3]

1. Appraisal of job performance must be based upon a thorough job analysis as reflected in specific performance standards. Graphically

    Job analysis—Performance standards—Performance appraisal

2. Performance standards should be communicated to and understood by employees; only then is an appraisal of job performance reasonable.

3. Clearly defined individual dimensions of job performance (like quantity or quality) should be rated, rather than undefined, global measures of job performance (like "overall performance").

4. Performance dimensions should be behaviourally based so that all ratings can be supported by objective, observable evidence.

5. When using graphic rating scales (discussed later in this chapter), avoid abstract trait names (for example, loyalty, honesty) unless they can be defined in terms of observable behaviours.

6. Appraisal systems should be validated. (Note that in a recent survey only one of 217 firms using performance appraisals said they were validating theirs. About 40% of these firms had not analyzed the jobs being rated.)

7. While they can be useful, subjective supervisory ratings should be used as only one component of the overall appraisal process.

8. Appraisers should be adequately trained in the use of appraisal techniques.

9. Appraisers should have substantial daily contact with the employee being evaluated.

10. Whenever possible, the appraisal should be conducted by more than one appraiser, and such appraisals should be conducted independently. As explained below, this process can help to "cancel out" individual errors and biases on the part of the individual appraisers.

11. A mechanism for appeal should be provided in case an employee disagrees with a supervisor's appraisal.

Administrative Considerations

The design and development of a performance appraisal system is shaped by a number of influences, including compensation, promotions and discharges, and staffing procedure. Performance appraisal assists decision makers to determine the most appropriate compensation reward for their employees, including merit increases, performance bonuses, and other forms of pay increases. Performance appraisal helps decision makers determine which employee to retain, promote, transfer, layoff, demote, and discharge. It also serves to warn an employee about unsatisfactory performance and the areas in need of improvement. Performance appraisal may be used to evaluate the success or failure, and strengths and weaknesses of the recruitment, selection, and placement functions of the organization. The effectiveness of these procedures may be assessed or validated by comparing an employee's job application score with his or her performance on the job as revealed on the performance appraisal report.

Employee Development Considerations

The second objective of performance appraisal is to improve and develop employee skills, to motivate and encourage employees, and to help employees achieve their career objectives. Developmental performance appraisals provide employees with feedback to let them know how well they are doing and where they stand; they also satisfy the employees' need to receive recognition for their accomplishments and thereby encourage improved performance. Appraisals serve to aid employees in their career planning and their career path. They also help employees understand the areas where improvement is needed and the steps or directions that must be followed to achieve that improvement. They also help managers and supervisors discover areas where the employees need coaching and counselling.

During the performance appraisal process the supervisor and the subordinate can develop specific plans to achieve desired levels of performance. This may include the joint setting of specific goals and performance targets.

Who Should Do the Appraising?

An important issue concerns who should rate an employee's performance. While rating by the person's supervisor is still the prevailing approach, several options are possible.

Supervisor Approach

A supervisor's rating is the heart of most appraisal systems, because getting a supervisor's appraisal is relatively easy and also makes a great deal of sense. The supervisor should be—and usually is—in the best position to observe and evaluate a subordinate's performance. Therefore, most appraisal systems rely heavily on the supervisor's evaluation.

Peer Appraisals

The appraisal of an employee by his or her peers has proven to be effective in predicting future management success. From a study of military officers, for example, we know that peer ratings were quite accurate in predicting which officers would be promoted and which would not.[4] In another study that involved more than two hundred industrial managers, peer ratings were similarly useful in predicting who would be promoted.[5] One potential problem here is "logrolling," in which all the peers simply get together to rate each other high.

Committee Appraisals

Many employers use rating committees to evaluate employees. These committees are often composed of the employee's immediate supervisor and three or four other supervisors; everyone on the committee should be able to intelligently evaluate the employee's performance.

There are a number of advantages to using several appraisers, or "multiple raters."[6] First, while there may be a discrepancy in the ratings made by the different supervisors, the composite ratings tend to be more valid than those of individual raters since they can help cancel out problems like bias and the halo effect that individual raters bring to the appraisal process. (Fair employment practice makes using multiple raters advisable.) Furthermore, where there are differences in raters' ratings, they usually stem from the fact that raters at different levels in the organization often observe different facets of an employee's performance; the appraisal ought to reflect these differences.[7] Even where a committee is not used, it is common to at least have the appraisal reviewed by the manager immediately above the one who makes the appraisal. This was found to be standard practice in 16 of 18 companies surveyed in one study.[8]

Self Appraisals

Some employers have experimented with using employees' self-rating of performance (usually in conjunction with supervisors' ratings), but this is generally not a recommended option. The basic problem is that most studies show that employees consistently rate themselves higher than they are rated by supervisors or peers.[9] In one study, for example, it was found that when asked to rate their own job performance, 40% of the employees in jobs of all types placed themselves in the top 10% ("one of the best"), while virtually all remaining employees rate themselves either in the top 25% ("well above average"), or at least in the top 50% ("above average"). Usually, no more than 1% or 2% will place themselves in a below-average category, and then those are almost invariably in the top below-average category.

Thus self-appraisals should be used quite carefully. Supervisors requesting self-appraisals (say, for work-planning and review purposes) should be forewarned that their appraisals and the self-appraisals of subordinates might be quite different, and that requiring written self-appraisals may tend to accentuate differences and rigidify positions.[10] And, of course, even if self-appraisals are not formally requested, each employee will undoubtedly enter the performance-review meeting with his or her own self-appraisal in mind, and this self-rating will almost invariably be higher than the supervisor's rating.

Higher-Level Supervisor Appraisals

Higher-level appraisals, although not that common, are used to evaluate and supplement the appraisals of employees' immediate supervisors. This method is particularly useful for controlling and eliminating many problems in performance appraisals such as bias. For example, it may be used to control supervisory influences when the supervisor and a subordinate have a close personal relationship or when there exists a personality conflict between the parties. The existence of either of these factors may have an adverse influence on the objectivity of the supervisor when appraising his or her subordinates.

Subordinate Appraisals

Performance appraisals by subordinates are designed to provide supervisors with feedback on their supervisory behaviour and their impact on subordinates. It is usually the case that subordinate appraisals are used in conjunction with other types of performance appraisal to assess superiors. Subordinate appraisals are commonly used at colleges and universities, and are used in companies such as IBM and RCA.

PERFORMANCE APPRAISAL METHODS

A variety of performance appraisal methods are available for evaluating the performance of employees. An organization must select from among them based on its needs and objectives, and the practicality of a performance appraisal method. Some of the more common methods are (1) graphic rating scale, (2) alternation ranking, (3) paired comparison, (4) forced distribution, (5) critical incident, (6) essay, (7) behaviourially anchored rating scales, (8) management by objectives, and (9) behavioural observation scales.

Graphic Rating Scale Technique

One of the simplest and most popular techniques for appraising performance is called a **graphic rating scale**. A typical graphic rating scale lists a number of traits and a range of performance for each (see Figure 9.1). The employee is then rated by identifying the score that best describes his or her level of performance for each trait. The assigned values for each trait are then added up and totalled.

graphic rating scale

FIGURE 9.1 Example of a Graphic Rating Scale

Employee: _____ Job title: _____ Date: _____

Department: _____ Job number: _____ Rate: _____

FACTOR	SCORE-RATING				
	UNSATIS-FACTORY So definitely inadequate that it justifies release	FAIR Minimal; barely adequate to justify retention	GOOD Meets basic requirement for retention	SUPERIOR Definitely above norm and basic requirements	EXCEP-TIONAL Distinctly and consistently outstanding
QUALITY Accuracy, thoroughness, appearance and acceptance of output					
QUANTITY Volume of output and contribution					
REQUIRED SUPERVISION Need for advice, direction or correction					
ATTENDANCE Regularity, dependability and promptness					
CONSERVATION Prevention of waste, spoilage; protection of equipment					
CONSERVATION Prevention of waste, spoilage; protection of equipment					

Reviewed by: _____ (Reviewer comments on reverse)

Employee comment: _____

Date: _____ Signature or initial _____

SOURCE: Dale Yoder, *Personnel Management*, 6th ed. (Englewood Cliffs, N.J.: Prentice-Hall, 1970), p. 240. Reprinted by permission.

FIGURE 9.2
Rating-Ranking Scale
Using Alternation
Ranking Technique

RATING-RANKING SCALE

Consider all those on your list in terms of their (quality). Cross out the names of any you cannot rate on this quality. Then select the one you would regard as having most of the quality. Put this name in Column I, below, on the first line, numbered 1. Cross out this name on your list. Consult the list again and pick out the person having least of this quality. Put this name at the bottom of Column II, on the line numbered 20. Cross out this name. Now, from the remaining names on your list, select the one having most of the quality. Put this name in the first column on line 2. Keep up this process until all names have been placed in the scale.

Column I (Most)

1. _____
2. _____
3. _____
4. _____
5. _____
6. _____
7. _____
8. _____
9. _____
10. _____

Column II (Least)

11. _____
12. _____
13. _____
14. _____
15. _____
16. _____
17. _____
18. _____
19. _____
20. _____

SOURCE: Dale Yoder, *Personnel Management*, 6th ed. (Englewood Cliffs, N.J.: Prentice-Hall, 1970), p.237. Reprinted by permission.

Alternation Ranking Method

Another popular and simple method for evaluating employees is to rank them from best to worst on some trait. Since it is usually easier to distinguish between the worst and best employees than to simply rank them, an **alternation ranking method** is most popular. First, all subordinates to be rated are listed. Then, on a form like the one in Figure 9.2 the employee who is the highest on the characteristic being measured is indicated along with the one who is the lowest. Then the next highest and the next lowest are chosen, and so on, until all the employees to be rated have been ranked.

alternation ranking method

Paired Comparison Method

The **paired comparison method** helps to make the ranking method more effective. For every trait (quantity of work, quality of work, and so on), every subordinate is compared to every other subordinate in pairs.

Suppose there are five employees to be rated using the paired comparison method. First a chart, as in Figure 9.3, is drawn up showing all possible pairs of employees for each trait. Then for each trait the better employee of the pair is indicated (with a + or -). Finally, the number of times an employee is rated better is added up. In Figure 9.3 employee Bob ranked highest for quality of work, while Art was ranked highest for creativity.

paired comparison method

FIGURE 9.3
Ranking Employees
by the Paired
Comparison Method

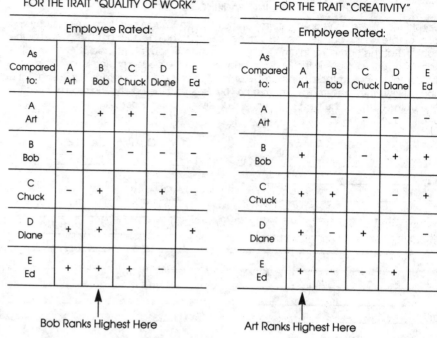

FOR THE TRAIT "QUALITY OF WORK"					
Employee Rated:					
As Compared to:	A Art	B Bob	C Chuck	D Diane	E Ed
A Art		+	+	−	−
B Bob	−		−	−	−
C Chuck	−	+		+	−
D Diane	+	+	−		+
E Ed	+	+	+	−	

↑ Bob Ranks Highest Here

FOR THE TRAIT "CREATIVITY"					
Employee Rated:					
As Compared to:	A Art	B Bob	C Chuck	D Diane	E Ed
A Art		−	−	−	−
B Bob	+			+	+
C Chuck	+	+		−	+
D Diane	+	−	+		−
E Ed	+		−	+	

↑ Art Ranks Highest Here

Note: + means "better than," — means "worse than." For each chart, add up the number of +'s in each column to get the highest ranked employee.

SOURCE: Dale Yoder, *Personnel Management*, 6th ed. (Englewood Cliffs, N.J.: Prentice-Hall, 1970), p. 242. Used by permission.

Forced Distribution Method

forced distribution method

The **forced distribution method** is similar to "grading on a curve." With this method, predetermined percentages of ratees are placed in various performance categories. For example, employees may be distributed as follows:

15% high performers

20% high-average performers

30% average performers

20% low-average performers

15% low performers

One practical way to use this method would be to have each employee's name written on an index card. Then for each trait being appraised (quality of work, creativity, and so on), the employee's card would be placed in the appropriate category.

Critical Incident Method

critical incident method

With the **critical incident method**, the supervisor keeps for each subordinate a record of uncommonly good or undesirable examples (or "incidents") of the person's work-related behaviour. Then every six months or so the supervisor and subordinate meet and discuss the latter's performance using the specific incidents as examples.

This method can be used to supplement the primary appraisal technique and as such has several advantages. For one thing, it provides some specific hard facts for explaining the appraisal. It ensures that the appraiser thinks about the subordinate's appraisal all during the year (because the incidents must be accumulated) and that the rating therefore does not just reflect the employee's most recent performance. Ideally, a running list of critical incidents also provides some concrete examples to subordinates of what they can specifically do to eliminate any performance deficiencies.

The critical incident method should be geared directly to the specific job expectations laid out for the subordinate at the beginning of the appraisal. Thus, in the example presented in Table 9.1, one of the assistant plant manager's continuing duties was to supervise procurement and to minimize inventory costs. The critical incident shows that he let inventory storage costs rise 15%, and this would provide a specific example of what performance he must improve in the future.

A subjective approach like the critical incident method may not be effective for comparing employees and making salary or promotion decisions, so it is often used together with a rating-ranking technique. However, it is useful for identifying specific examples of good and poor performance in terms of the specific activities a subordinate is expected to perform, and for planning how deficiencies can be corrected.

TABLE 9.1 Examples of Critical Incidents for an Assistant Plant Manager

CONTINUING DUTIES	TARGETS	CRITICAL INCIDENTS
Schedule production for plant	Full utilization of personnel and machinery in plant; orders delivered on time	Instituted new production scheduling system; decreased late orders by 10% last month; increased machine utilization in plant by 20% last month
Supervise procurement of raw materials and inventory control	Minimize inventory costs while keeping adequate supplies on hand	Let inventory storage costs rise 15% last month; overordered parts "A" and "B" by 20%, underordered part "C" by 30%
Supervise machinery maintenance	No shutdowns due to faulty machinery	Instituted new preventive maintenance system for plant; prevented a machine breakdown by discovering faulty part

Essay Method

In the **essay method** the appraiser describes the employee's performance within a number of broad categories. These include (1) the appraiser's overall assessment of the employee's performance; (2) the promotability of the employee; (3) the jobs that the employee is presently qualified to perform; (4) the employee's strengths and weaknesses; and (5) the type of training and development programs required by the employee to improve performance and to aid career development.[11]

Behaviourally Anchored Rating Scales (BARS)

behaviourally anchored rating scale (BARS)

A **behaviourally anchored rating scale (BARS)** aims at combining the benefits of narrative critical incidents and quantified ratings by anchoring a quantified scale with specific narrative examples of good or poor performance, as in Figure 9.4. Its proponents claim that it provides better, more equitable appraisals than do the other tools we have discussed.[12]

Developing a BARS typically requires five steps:[13]

1. *Generate critical incidents.* Persons who know the job being appraised (job holders and/or supervisors) are asked to describe specific illustrations (critical incidents) of effective and ineffective performance.

2. *Develop performance dimensions.* These people then cluster these incidents into a smaller set (say, five or ten) of performance dimensions. Each cluster (dimension) is then defined.

3. *Reallocate incidents.* Another group of people who also know the job then reallocate the original critical incidents. They are given the clusters' definitions and the critical incidents and are asked to reassign each incident to the cluster they think fits best. Typically, a critical incident is retained if some percentage (usually 50% to 80%) of this second group assigns it to the same cluster as did the group in step 2.

4. *Scale the incidents.* This second group is generally asked to rate (seven- or nine-point scales are typical) the behaviour described in the incident as to how effectively or ineffectively it represents performance on the appropriate cluster's dimension.

5. *Develop final instrument.* A subset of the incidents (usually six or seven per cluster) are used as "behaviourial anchors" for each dimension.

Example

Here is an example of how this works in practice. Three researchers developed a BARS for grocery checkout clerks who were working in a large western grocery chain.[14] They collected a number of critical incidents and then clustered them into eight performance dimensions:

- Knowledge and judgment
- Conscientiousness
- Skill in human relations
- Skill in operation of register
- Skill in bagging
- Organizational ability of checkstand work

FIGURE 9.4

A Behaviorally Anchored Rating Scale for the Performance Dimension "Knowledge and Judgment" for Grocery Checkout Clerks

Extremely good performance	7	By knowing the price of items, this checker would be expected to look for mismarked and unmarked items.
Good performance	6	You can expect this checker to be aware of items that constantly fluctuate in price.
		You can expect this checker to know the various sizes of cans—No. 303, No. 2, No. 2 1/2.
Slightly good performance	5	When in doubt, this checker would ask the other clerk if the item is taxable.
		This checker can be expected to verify with another checker a discrepancy between the shelf and the marked price before ringing up that item.
Neither poor nor good performance	4	When operating the quick check, the lights are flashing, this checker can be expected to check out a customer with 15 items.
Slightly poor performance	3	You could expect this checker to ask the customer the price of an item that he does not know.
		In the daily course of personal relationships, may be expected to linger in long conversations with a customer or another checker.
Poor performance	2	In order to take a break, this checker can be expected to block off the checkstand with people in line.
Extremely poor performance	1	

SOURCE: Lawrence Fogli, Charles Hulin, and Milton Blood, "Development of First Level Behavioral Job Criteria," *Journal of Applied Psychology*, Vol. 55 (1971), p.6. Copyright © 1971 by the American Psychological Association. Reprinted by permission of the authors.

- Skill in monetary transactions
- Observational ability

Figure 9.4 shows the behaviourally anchored rating scale for one of these dimensions, "knowledge and judgment." There is a scale (ranging from 1 to 7) for rating performance from "extremely poor" to "extremely good," and the BARS is behaviourally anchored with specific critical incidents. For example, there is a specific critical incident ("by knowing the price of items, this checker would be expected to look for mismarked and unmarked items") that helps anchor or specify what is meant by "extremely good" performance. Similarly, there are other critical incident anchors all along the scale.

Advantages

Developing a BARS can be more time-consuming than developing other appraisal tools, such as graphic rating scales. But BARS are felt to have some important advantages:[15]

1. *A more accurate gauge.* People who know the job and its requirements better than anyone else develop BARS. The resulting BARS should therefore be a very good gauge of performance on that job.

2. *Clearer standards.* The critical incidents along the scale help to clarify what is meant by "extremely good" performance, "average" performance, and so forth.

3. *Feedback.* The use of the critical incidents may be more useful in providing feedback to the people being appraised.

4. *Independent dimensions.* Systematically clustering the critical incidents into five or six performance dimensions (such as "knowledge and judgment") should help to make the dimensions more independent of one another. For example, a rater should be less likely to rate an employee high on all dimensions simply because he or she was rated high in "conscientiousness."

5. *Consistency.*[16] BARS evaluations seem to be relatively consistent and reliable, in that different raters' appraisals of a person tend to be similar.

Management by Objectives (MBO)

management by objectives (MBO)

Management by objectives (MBO) is a form of performance appraisal designed to overcome many of the limitations of traditional appraisal techniques. MBO is a participative goal-setting process that entails the setting of specific goals for selected tasks for a specified period of time. The MBO process begins with a meeting between the supervisor and the employee during which they mutually agree on the objectives to be attained by the employee within the agreed upon time period, and that periodic reviews will be held to assess the employee's progress and to make needed adjustments.

The main processes of management by objectives are as follows:

1. The supervisor and the subordinate jointly agree on the primary duties and areas of responsibility of the employee's job.

2. The supervisor and the subordinate jointly establish the subordinate's specific goals for a predetermined period of time (usually six months or one year). It is generally the case that the supervisor guides the goal-setting process to ensure that it is in harmony with the corporate direction of the organization.

3. The supervisor and the subordinate jointly agree on the criteria to be used to evaluate performance.

4. The supervisor and the subordinate periodically review the subordinate's progress and modify goals if necessary to reflect changing conditions.

5. The appraisal process focuses more on accomplishments than on the employee's personal traits. During this process new goals and performance objectives are jointly established for the next period.

MBO has many advantages. For instance, by participating in the setting of specific goals employees are likely to be more committed to the process. MBO also serves to enhance the supervisor-subordinate relationship, provides employees with an opportunity for greater self-control over their work environment, improves the motivational climate, and furthers employees' growth and development.

MBO also has many disadvantages. For example, a subordinate may try to set easily achievable goals in order to look good. Goals may be attained, but they may be so easy that very little effort or motivation was involved. One solution is perhaps to use different criteria to evaluate each goal (e.g., excellent, very good, good, etc).

MBO sometimes lead to distortions in behaviour; that is, individuals may focus on those parts of their job where goals are established over those parts of the job where goals are not set. For example, in a case study of a financial institution with a new MBO program it was discovered that when some managers were given the goal of obtaining a specified number of new customers, they neglected old customers to such a degree that their gain in new customers was more than offset by their loss of old customers. Studies of salespeople indicate that specific sales goals can create alienation of customers because of the "hard sell" approach, inadequate servicing of accounts, and neglect of long-term sales prospects. One solution would be to ensure that goals include a requirement that existing levels of performance must be maintained.

MBO systems tend to require the completion and maintenance of a large amount of paper work, because the goals and the action plan must be written in detail. Copies are usually sent to the human resources department, and to other relevant sections or departments. One solution here is to make the system requirements as simple as possible.[17]

Behavioural Observation Scales (BOS)

Behaviourial observation scales are based on carefully developed job analyses. Once important dimensions of a given job are established, scales are determined. Various scales may be used for major performance dimensions such as reliability, dependability, and interpersonal skills. Next an employee is carefully observed and assessed against these specific job behaviours.

BOS[18] is similar to BARS, but also differs in some respects. With the BARS method, appraisers are given a behavioural statement and asked to state what degree or level of performance the employee exhibits. With the BOS method, appraisers are asked to indicate the frequency with which the ratee engages in the behaviour using a scale (e.g., very frequently, often, seldom, never).

The rater is asked to obtain scores for each ratee by assigning a numerical value to the frequency judgments. The scores in each scale are totalled and translated to an overall performance appraisal score. Behavioural items are eliminated if their observed frequency is either too high or too low for the group of jobholders, because their inclusion would not make it possible to distinguish between high and low performers.

BOS is an effective performance appraisal technique. Its strengths lies in its clarity, thoroughness, and specificity in assessing a subordinate's job behaviour. It provides specific feedback to ratees and allows users to participate in its development and implementation. One of the weaknesses of BOS lies in its cost, and the fact that it takes a long time to develop.

behavioural observation scales (BOS)

Mixing the Methods

In practice, most firms combine several appraisal tools. An example of one such mixed method is illustrated in Figure 9.5. This figure presents a rating form used to appraise the performance of managers at a large airline. It is basically a graphic rating scale, with descriptive phrases included to define the traits being measured. But, in addition, there is a "comments" section below each trait. This allows the rater to jot down several relevant critical incidents.

The practice of using both critical incidents and rating-ranking tools to appraise performance mostly results from the fact that both serve a different purpose. Quantifiable rating-ranking methods permit comparisons of employees and are therefore useful for making salary, transfer, and promotion decisions. Critical incidents, on the other hand, are useful for providing specific examples of good or poor performance.

IMPLEMENTING A PERFORMANCE APPRAISAL SYSTEM

The planning, design, and implementation of a performance appraisal system must be done jointly by the human resource specialist and line managers. The input and involvement of line managers is important to ensure their commitment to the successful implementation and administration of the system. It is also important to communicate to all employees the policies and procedures that will govern the administration of the system. This may be done through orientation meetings. The performance appraisal forms should be shown to employees at the implementation stage.

Problems in Performance Appraisal

Problems may arise at each of three steps. Some appraisals fail because subordinates are not informed ahead of time of exactly what is expected of them in terms of good performance. Other appraisals fail because of the problems built into the forms or procedures used to appraise the performance; a lenient supervisor might rate all subordinates "high," for instance, although many are actually unsatisfactory. Still other problems arise during the interview-feedback session, such as arguing and poor communications. Figure 9.6 summarizes these common evaluation problems. We address these problems and how to avoid them on the following pages.

Halo Effect

halo effect

The **halo effect** is the tendency of appraisers to allow a rating they assign to one aspect of an employee's performance to excessively influence the rating they assign to other aspects of the employee's performance evaluation. This means that the employee would be rated either high or low (good or poor) on all categories. Appraisers can minimize the halo effect by providing an opportunity for subordinates to review and correct any inaccuracies that may exist in their evaluation.

Central Tendency Effect

central tendency effect

The **central tendency effect** occurs when appraisers rate employees as average or around the middle point for all performance qualities of the rating scale. This is a very common type of error. By rating all employees as average, appraisers are being unfair to superior performers, and are giving poor or mediocre performers higher performance ratings than they have earned or deserve. This problem often occurs because the appraisers are not properly trained, are unfamiliar with an employee's job, and lack good evaluative skills.

FIGURE 9.5 One Page from a Typical Management Appraisal Form

Read the definitions of each management factor below and choose the ranking which most accurately describes the employee. If, after reading the definition, it is determined that the skill area was not demonstrated because of the nature of the employee's position, indicate as Non-Applicable (N/A). Your evaluation on each of the management factors below should relate directly to the employee's actual performance on the job.

PLANNING SKILL — Degree to which incumbent:	Ranking Code	(CHECK ONE)
- Assessed and established priorities of result area. - Designed realistic short and long range plans. - Formulated feasible timetables. - Anticipated possible problems and obstacles toward reaching required results.	1 2 3 4	Far exceeds requirements Usually exceeds requirements Fully meets requirements Usually meets requirements

Comments:
_____
_____
_____

ORGANIZING SKILL — Degree to which incumbent:	Ranking Code	(CHECK ONE)
- Grouped activities for optimal use of personnel and material resources in order to achieve goals. - Clearly defined responsibilities and authority limits of subordinates - Minimized confusion and inefficiencies in work operations.	1 2 3 4 5	Far exceeds requirements Usually exceeds requirements Fully meets requirements Usually meets requirements Fails to meet requirements

Comments:
_____
_____
_____

CONTROLLING SKILL — Degree to which incumbent:	Ranking Code	(CHECK ONE)
- Established appropriate procedures to be kept informed of subordinate's work progress. - Identified deviations in work goals progress. - Adjusted to deviations in work to ensure that established goals were met.	1 2 3 4 5	Far exceeds requirements Usually exceeds requirements Fully meets requirements Usually meet requirements Fails to meet requirements

Comments:
_____
_____
_____

FIGURE 9.6
Common Performance Evaluation Problems

Problems can occur at any stage in the evaluation process. Some of the pitfalls to avoid in performance appraisals are:

1) Lack of standards. Without standards, there can be no objective evaluation of results, only a subjective guess or feeling about performance.

2) Irrelevant or subjective standards. Standards should be established by analyzing the job output to ensure that standards are job related.

3) Unrealistic standards. Standards are goals with motivating potential. Those that are reasonable but challenging have the most potential to motivate.

4) Poor measures of performance. Objectivity and comparison require that progress toward standards or accomplishment of standards be measurable. Examples of measurable standards include quantifiable measures such as 10 rejects per 1000 units or 10 sales per 100 calls, as well as qualitative measures, such as projects completed or not completed.

5) Rater errors. Rater errors include rater bias or prejudice, halo effect, constant error, central tendency, and fear of confrontation.

6) Poor feedback to employee. Standards and/or ratings must be communicated to the employee in order for the performance evaluation to be effective.

7) Negative communications. The evaluation process in hindered by communication of negative attitudes, such as inflexibility, defensiveness, and a non-developmental approach.

8) Failure to apply evaluation data. Failure to use evaluations in personnel decision making and personnel development negates the primary purpose of performance evaluations. The use and weighting of multiple criteria as well as the frequency of evaluation also present problems.

SOURCE: John E. Oliver, "Performance Appraisals That Fit," *Personnel Journal*, Vol. 64, no. 6 (June 1985), p. 69. Reprinted by permission.

Leniency Effect

leniency effect

The **leniency effect** occurs when appraisers give employees high evaluations on all aspects of performance regardless of their actual performance, or higher evaluations than they actually deserve. The leniency problem is especially serious with graphic rating scales because the supervisor can conceivably rate all subordinates either high or low. However, it is not a problem with the ranking or forced distribution approach because of the requirement to distinguish between high and low performers.

Strictness Effect

strictness effect

The **strictness effect** occurs when appraisers evaluate employee performance standards too harshly and give employees low ratings, although some employees may have performed at average and above-average levels and deserved higher ratings. This problem is common when performance standards are unclear or nonexistent. It also occurs when evaluators are not trained.

Recency Effect

recency effect

The **recency effect** occurs when appraisers evaluate an employee's total performance based on the employee's last or most recent performance. The recency effect is most likely to occur when appraisers use subjective measures to evaluate performance. This problem could have significantly adverse consequences for employees who have superior or above-average performance for six to eight months but unintentionally make a few mistakes immediately preceding their performance evaluation.

Similarity Effect

The **similarity effect** occurs when appraisers evaluate an employee's performance based on the characteristics they perceive in themselves. This means that evaluators who perceive themselves as cooperative, knowledgeable, and aggressive may assess their employees by looking for evidence of these characteristics. Employees who exhibit these characteristics would be evaluated positively and those who do not would be evaluated negatively.

similarity effect

Supervisory Bias

Supervisory bias occurs when appraisers evaluate their subordinates based on individual differences among ratees, such as age, race, and sex. This bias affects the rating an employee gets, often quite apart from the employee's actual performance.[19] In one study, for instance, researchers found a systematic tendency to evaluate ratees over 60 years of age lower on "performance capacity" and "potential for development" than younger employees.[20] The ratee's race and sex may also affect the person's rating, although here the bias is not necessarily consistently against a minority or women, as it seems to be in the case of older workers. In one study in which objective performance measures (such as graphic rating scales) were used, high-performing females were often rated significantly higher than high-performing males. Similarly, low-performing blacks were often rated significantly higher than low-performing whites.[21]

supervisory bias

An interesting picture of how an employee's age can distort his or her evaluation emerges from a study of registered nurses. Where the nurses were 30 to 39 years of age, supervisors and nurses exhibited perfect average agreement in performance ratings, indicating that the nurses and their supervisors each rated the nurses' performance virtually the same. In the 21 to 29 category, on the other hand, supervisors rated subordinates higher than the subordinates rated themselves. However, for the 40 to 61 subordinate age category, the supervisors rated the subordinates' performance lower than the subordinates rated their own performance. The conclusion here may be that supervisors are tougher in appraising older subordinates; they do not give them as much credit for their success, while attributing low performance to their lack of ability.[22]

An employee's previous performance can also affect the supervisor's evaluation of his or her current performance. In one study, for instance, the researchers concluded that "raters who develop systematic expectations regarding the performance of a specific ratee may find it difficult to accurately evaluate that ratee's performance if he or she departs from a previous pattern of performance."[23] The inaccurate evaluation can take several forms. Sometimes the rater may systematically overestimate improvement on the part of a poor worker or may overestimate declines on the part of a good worker. In some situations—especially when the change in behaviour is more gradual—the rater may simply be insensitive to changes in the ratee's behaviour. In any case, objectivity is important when rating a performance.

How to Avoid Appraisal Problems

First, appraisers should be thoroughly familiar with the problems just discussed. Understanding a problem is a big step toward avoiding it.

Second, the right appraisal technique must be chosen. Each of the techniques, such as the graphic rating scale or critical incident method, has its own advantages and disadvantages. For example, as summarized in Table 9.2, the ranking method avoids central tendency but can cause ill feelings among employees whose performance is in fact very similar—as when all are actually "high." Similarly, both graphic ratings and ranking methods are good for comparing employees for salary and promotion decisions.

TABLE 9.2 Important Advantages and Disadvantages of Appraisal Tools

	ADVANTAGES	DISADVANTAGES
Graphic rating scales	Simple to use; provides a quantitative rating for each employee.	Standards may be unclear; halo effect, central tendency, leniency, bias can also be problems.
Alternation ranking	Simple to use (but not as simple as graphic rating scales). Avoids central tendency and other problems of rating scales.	Can cause disagreements among employees and may be unfair if all employees are, say, excellent.
Forced distribution method	End up with a predetermined number of people in each group.	Appraisal results depend on the adequacy of your original choice of cutoff points.
Critical incident method	Helps specify what is "right" and "wrong" about the employee's performance; forces supervisor to evaluate subordinates on an ongoing basis.	Difficult to rate or rank employees relative to one another.
Behaviourally anchored rating scale	Provides behavioural "anchors." BARS is very accurate.	Difficult to develop.
MBO	Tied to jointly agreed upon performance objectives.	Time-consuming.

Training Raters

The human resource specialist should ensure that supervisors are trained to eliminate rating errors, such as halo, leniency, and central tendency, to improve their effectiveness as appraisers.[24] In the traditional method, raters are shown a videotape of jobs being performed and are asked to rate the worker. Ratings made by each participant are then placed on a flip chart and the various errors (such as leniency and halo) are explained. For example, if a trainee rated all criteria (such as quality, quantity, etc.) about the same, the trainer might explain that halo error had occurred; if a trainee rated all videotaped workers very high, this might be explained as leniency error. Typically, the trainer gives the correct rating and then illustrates the rating errors the participants made.[25] According to one study, computer-assisted instruction training improved managers' abilities to conduct performance appraisal discussions with their subordinates.[26]

Rater training is no remedy for reducing rating errors or improving the accuracy of appraisals. From a practical point of view, several factors, including the extent to which pay is tied to performance ratings, union pressure, turnover rates, time constraints, and the need to justify ratings, may be more important than training in influencing the ratings appraisers give. This means that improving an appraisal procedure's accuracy involves not only training but also considering outside factors such as union pressure. To be effective, rater training should address real-life problems, such as the fact that union representatives will try to pressure supervisors to rate everyone high.[27]

How to Ensure the Subordinate Views the Appraisal as a Fair One[28]

There are five things that can be done. First, the subordinate's performance should be evaluated frequently, even if the formal appraisal takes place only once a year. If the person is doing well, this feedback will provide reinforcement. If the person is not doing well, the feedback will give him or her an opportunity to improve and means there will not be any surprises when the formal appraisal rolls around.

Second, appraisers should be familiar with the performance of the person being appraised—this is when critical incidents can be useful. Third, there should be agreement between the appraiser and subordinate concerning the latter's job duties. Fourth, the subordinate's help should be elicited when plans are formulated for eliminating performance weaknesses. (These plans are usually developed as part of the appraisal interview, which we will explain in the following section.) Finally, it should be remembered that subordinates who participate in developing the appraisal tool react more favourably to the resulting appraisal interview.[29]

THE APPRAISAL INTERVIEW
Main Types of Interviews

The **appraisal interview** is a process of communicating to employees the outcome of their performance assessment for the past appraisal period. The performance appraisal may have one or more purposes, such as communicating decisions concerning salary, promotion, demotion, or transfers. It is being used for an administrative purpose whenever it is used for any of these activities. The performance appraisal interview is being used for development purposes whenever it is used to encourage desired behaviour, communicate performance deficiencies, and explain future planning changes. The three main types of performance appraisal interviews[30] are the "tell and sell," "tell and listen," and "problem-solving." These are presented in Table 9.3.

The *tell and sell* method uses a directive approach to communicate to employees where they stand and how well they are performing. With this method the appraiser sells the subordinate on the benefits of taking appropriate steps to improve performance. The *tell and listen* interview approach provides an opportunity for the subordinate to participate in the appraisal interview. With this approach the appraiser communicates his or her assessment of the subordinate's performance to the subordinate. Next the subordinate is given a chance to comment on each dimension

appraisal interviews

TABLE 9.3   The Characteristics of the Three Main Types of Appraisal Interviews

Characteristic	Tell and Sell	Tell and Listen	Problem-solving
Objectives	Communicate evaluation Persuade employee to improve	Communicate evaluation Release defensive feelings	Stimulate growth and development in employee
Psychological Assumptions	Employee desires to correct weaknesses if known Any person who desires to do so can improve A superior is qualified to evaluate a subordinate	People will change if defensive feelings are removed leads to improved performance	Growth can occur without correcting faults Discussing job problems
Role of interviewer	Judge	Judge	Helper
Attitude of interviewer	People profit from criticism and appreciate help	One can respect the feelings of others if one understands them	Discussion develops new ideas and mutual interests
Skills of interviewer	Sales ability Patience	Listening and reflecting feelings Summarizing	Listening and reflecting feelings Reflecting ideas Using exploratory questions Summarizing
Reactions of Employee	Suppresses defensive behaviour Attempts to cover hostility	Expresses defensive behaviour Feels accepted	Problem-solving behaviour
Employee's Motivation for Change	Use of positive or negative incentives or both Extrinsic: motivation is added to the job	Resistance to change reduced Positive incentive Extrinsic and some intrinsic motivation	Increased freedom Increased responsibility Intrinsic: motivation is inherent in the task
Possible Gains	Success most probable when employee respects interviewer	Develops favourable attitude toward superior, which increases probability of success	Almost assured of improvement in some respect
Risks of Interviewer	Loss of loyalty Inhibition of independent judgment Creates face-saving scenes	Need for change may not be developed	Employee may lack ideas Change may be other than what superior had in mind

SOURCE: Norman R.F. Maier, *Three Types of Appraisal Interview: Three Basic Approaches* (San Diego, CA: University Associates, 1976). Used with permission.

of the appraiser's evaluation. The *problem-solving* interview method uses a participative approach in which there is active two-way communication between the appraiser and the subordinate. During this process both the appraiser and the subordinate explore alternate solutions to problems. They also establish joint goals for the employee's growth and development.

Other Types of Interviews

There are three other types of appraisal interviews, each with its own objectives. These are summarized next:[31]

Summary-of-Performance	Appraisal Appraisal Interview Objective
(1) Satisfactory—Promotable	(1) Make development plans
(2) Satisfactory—Not promotable	(2) Maintain performance
(3) Unsatisfactory—Correctable	(3) Plan correction
Unsatisfactory—Uncorrectable	Fire or tolerate (no interview needed)

Satisfactory—Promotable

In this type of interview the person's performance is satisfactory and there is a promotion ahead. This is an easy type of appraisal interview. The objective is to discuss the person's career plans and to develop a specific action plan for the educational and professional development the person needs to move on to his or her next job.

Satisfactory—Not Promotable

This interview is for employees whose performance is satisfactory but for whom promotion is not possible. There may be no promotion ahead because the person has reached his or her level of competence or because there is no more room in the company or because of some educational barrier. Furthermore, some employees are happy where they are and do not want to receive a promotion. The objective here should be not to improve or develop the person but to maintain satisfactory performance.

Unsatisfactory—Correctable

When the person's performance is deemed unsatisfactory but correctable, the objective of the interview is to develop plans (as explained later) for correcting the unsatisfactory performance. It is never easy to tell someone that his or her performance is unsatisfactory, and this is usually the most difficult type of appraisal interview.

How to Prepare for the Appraisal Interview

There are three things for appraisers to do.[32] First, they must *assemble the data*. They must study the person's job description, compare the employee's performance to the standards, and review the files of the employee's previous performance appraisals. Next, they must *prepare the employee*. Employees should be given at least a week's notice to review their work, read over their job description, analyze problems, and gather their questions and comments. It should be stressed that the appraisal review is mainly to help them know where they stand. Finally, appraisers must *choose the time and place*. A mutually agreeable time for the interview should be established that allows enough time for the entire interview. Interviews with lower-level human resources like clerical workers and maintenance staff will probably take no more than an hour. Appraising management employees often takes two or three hours. Illustrated in Figure 9.7 are other factors contributing to the effectiveness of the performance appraisal session.

How to Conduct the Interview

There are four things appraisers should keep in mind.[33] First, they must *set the tone at the start of the interview*, by explaining how the interview will proceed and emphasizing that it is a two-way conversation. Second, they should *be as positive as they can in assessing the employee's strong and weak points*. They should not talk about past mistakes or faults; rehashing past events and becoming mired in trivial examples of what the person has done wrong will get the employee defensive. Instead, solving problems should be stressed. If necessary appraisers should criticize an act rather than the subordinate. (For example, they might emphasize that "sales are down" rather than "you aren't selling enough.") Third, they must *summarize and clarify areas in which they and the employee agree and differ* and try to resolve the differences by emphasizing why the employee should improve. The employee may disagree; the important point is that both understand each other's reasons and points of view. Finally, the appraiser and the employee should develop an action plan. The appraiser should work with the person to set improvement goals that are specific and practical, along with a timetable for achieving them.

The action plan might look like this:

ACTION PLAN

Date: May 18

For: John, Assistant Plant Manager
Problem: Parts inventory too high
Objective: Reduce plant parts inventory by 10% in June

Action Steps	When	Expected Results
Determine average monthly parts inventory	6/2	Establish a base from which to measure progress
Review ordering quantities and parts usage	6/15	Identify overstock items
Ship excess parts to regional warehouse and scrap obsolete parts	6/20	Clear stock space
Set new ordering quantities for all parts	6/25	Avoid future overstocking
Check records to measure where we are now	7/1	See how close we are to objective

---

Then the appraiser should conclude the interview, thanking the employee for his or her time and effort and summarizing the main points once more.[34]

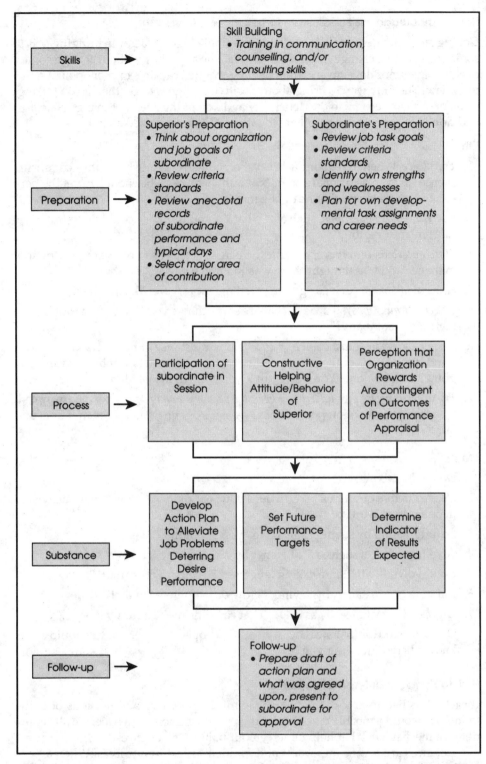

Skills →

Skill Building
- *Training in communication, counselling, and/or consulting skills*

Preparation →

Superior's Preparation
- *Think about organization and job goals of subordinate*
- *Review criteria standards*
- *Review anecdotal records of subordinate performance and typical days*
- *Select major area of contribution*

Subordinate's Preparation
- *Review job task goals*
- *Review criteria standards*
- *Identify own strengths and weaknesses*
- *Plan for own developmental task assignments and career needs*

Process →

Participation of subordinate in Session

Constructive Helping Attitude/Behavior of Superior

Perception that Organization Rewards Are contingent on Outcomes of Performance Appraisal

Substance →

Develop Action Plan to Alleviate Job Problems Deterring Desire Performance

Set Future Performance Targets

Determine Indicator of Results Expected

Follow-up →

Follow-up
- *Prepare draft of action plan and what was agreed upon, present to subordinate for approval*

SOURCE: Craig E. Schneier and Richard W. Beatty, "Combining BARS and MBO: Using an Appraisal System Diagnose Performance Problems," *Personnel Administrator*, Vol. 24 (September 1979) p.57. Reprinted by permission of HR Magazine (formerly Personnel Administrator) published by the Society for Human Resource Management, Alexandria, VA.

How to Encourage the Subordinate to Talk in the Interview[35]

Getting subordinates to talk is probably the single biggest factor in bringing about some constructive change in their behaviour. The appraiser will not change someone's behaviour or develop an action plan by arguing, cajoling, or monopolizing the interview. The only way to bring about positive change is to get the person talking so he or she can recognize the deficiency and accept the need for change. The dos and don'ts of getting a subordinate to talk can be summarized as follows:

Do

1. *Try silence.* When the subordinate says something, don't rush in with a comment; silence (plus an occasional nod or "uh-huh") will often be enough to get the person to elaborate on what he or she means.

2. *Use open-ended questions,* such as "What do you think we could do to improve sales in your region?"

3. *State questions in terms of a problem,* such as "Suppose you were production manager and you thought there was too much waste?"

4. *Use a command,*[36] such as "go on," "tell me more," and "keep talking."

5. *Use choice questions,* such as "What are some things you don't like about working for the company?"

6. *Restate the person's last point as a question.* For instance, if he or she says, "I just don't think I can get the job done," try to draw him or her out by restating the point as a question, "You don't think you can get the job done?"

7. *Try to get at the feelings underlying what the person is saying.* Is the person frustrated by a lack of promotion possibilities? Does he or she think the treatment is unfair?

Don't

1. Do all the talking.

2. Use restrictive questions (like "would you" or "did you") that can be answered in one or two words.

3. Be judgmental by saying things like "you shouldn't have."

4. Give free advice, such as "If I were you ..."

5. Get involved with name calling (such as "Boy, that was stupid!").

6. Ridicule (for instance, by saying, "How did you manage that?").

7. Digress (for instance, by saying, "That reminds me of a funny story ...").

8. Use sarcasm (for instance, by saying, "I'd hoped for more but I should have known better knowing you").

How to Handle a Defensive Subordinate

If each of us had to absorb the full impact of the problems and tensions of daily living, we would probably crack under the pressure. In order to cope, we all set up defence mechanisms that help us screen out painful experiences.

Defences are a very important and familiar aspect of our lives. When a person is confronted with a poor performance appraisal, the first reaction will often be denial. By denying the fault, the person avoids having to question his or her own competence. Some others react to criticism with anger and aggression. This helps them let off steam and postpones confronting the immediate problem until they are able to cope with it. Still others react to criticism by retreating into a shell.

In any event, understanding and dealing with defensiveness is an important appraisal skill. Psychologist Mortimer Feinberg suggests the following:

1. *Recognize that defensive behaviour is normal.*

2. *Never attack a person's defences.* Don't try to "explain someone to themselves" by saying things like "you know the real reason you're using that excuse is because you can't bear to be blamed for anything." Instead, try to concentrate on the act itself ("sales are down") rather than on the person ("you're not selling enough").

3. *Postpone action.* Sometimes the best thing to do is to do nothing at all. People frequently react to sudden threats by instinctively hiding behind their "masks," but, given sufficient time, a more rational reaction takes over.

COMPUTER APPLICATION IN PERFORMANCE APPRAISAL

Performance Analysis

One measure of the performance of HRM interviewers is how long the people they place stay with the company. This retention measure can be quantified, which makes it suitable for computerization. HRM professionals often begin their careers interviewing applicants, sometimes without adequate training in interviewing techniques. One purpose of an effective performance appraisal system is to pinpoint areas in which an employee needs further training.

If company research shows a high turnover rate of employees within the first six months of employment, for example, this implies mismatches between the employees and the position. The problem may be an inadequate job analysis (or its outcome, a poor job description), inaccurate job specifications, or a poorly trained interviewer. The first step is to establish what the retention rates are, both for interviewer and by the supervisor. (The supervisors are recorded because of their significant impact on retention, regardless of the input of HRM in the hiring process.)

Retention rates can be calculated by capturing the name, race, sex, position code of job applied for, department code where referred, and supervisor's code (a unique number or letters assigned to each supervisor who has hiring responsibilities). By linking this spreadsheet to one that lists new hires and one that lists terminations, retention rates can be calculated regularly. A macro (which combines several keystrokes into one set of directions taking two keystrokes) can link the spreadsheets, complete the calculations, and print the report.

A table can be constructed in which supervisors who have hired someone in the specified time frame are identified by a unique number or a two- or three-letter abbreviation. Each time a new employee is hired, one column of data would include the supervisor's identification. Through a database count or extraction, the total the number of employees hired by each supervisor in that time period can be totalled. Only those supervisors to whom a given interviewer referred applicants can be counted by adjusting the formula to perform that discrimination of data. This is particularly helpful if the interviewer feels that one supervisor significantly impacted the retention rate negatively. This is an example of "What if ...?" which allows managers to see how a change in facts affects the outcome—and possibly the manager's decision.

While retention rates should not be used as the sole measure of the effectiveness of an interviewer, it offers one objective performance measure on which to base decisions about future goals and/or training.

On the Front Line

After spending several weeks on the job, Jennifer was surprised to discover that her father had not formally evaluated any employee's performance for all the years that he had owned the business. Jack's position was that he had "a hundred higher priority things to attend to," such as boosting sales and lowering costs, and, in any case, many employees didn't stick around long enough to be appraisable anyway. Furthermore, contended Jack, manual workers such as those doing the pressing and the cleaning did periodically get positive feedback in terms of praise from Jack for a job well done or criticism, also from Jack, if things did not look right during one of his swings through the stores. Similarly, Jack was never shy about telling his managers about store problems so that they, too, got some feedback on where they stood.

This informal feedback notwithstanding, Jennifer believes that a more formal appraisal approach is needed. She believes that there are criteria such as quality, quantity, attendance, and punctuality that should be evaluated periodically even if a worker is paid on piece rate. Furthermore, she feels quite strongly that the managers need to have a list of quality standards for matters such as store cleanliness, efficiency, safety, and adherence to budget on which they know they are to be formally evaluated.

1. Is Jennifer right about the need to formally evaluate the workers? The managers? Why or why not?

2. Develop a performance appraisal method for the workers and managers in each store.

---

4. *Recognize your own limitations.* Don't expect to be able to solve every problem that comes up, especially the human ones. More important, remember that a supervisor should not try to be a psychologist. Offering people understanding is one thing; trying to deal with deep psychological problems is another matter entirely.

How to Criticize a Subordinate

When some criticism is required, it should be done in a manner that helps the person maintain his or her dignity and sense of worth. Specifically, criticism should be done privately and constructively, and should provide examples of critical incidents and specific suggestions of what could be done and why. Once-a-year "critical broadsides" should be avoided; subordinates should be praised often, on a daily basis, so that at the formal review there are no surprises. Finally, criticism should be objective and free from any personal feelings on the appraiser's part.

How to Ensure that the Appraisal Interview Leads to Improved Performance[37]

The appraiser should clear up job-related problems and set improvement goals and a schedule for achieving them. In one study researchers found that whether or not subordinates expressed satisfaction with their appraisal interview depended mostly on three things: not feeling threatened during the interview; having an opportunity to present their ideas and feelings and to influence the course of the interview; and having a helpful and constructive supervisor conduct the interview. The researchers found that clearing up job-related problems with the appraisee and setting measurable performance targets and a schedule for achieving them—an action plan—were the two actions that consistently led to improved employee performance.

SUMMARY

1. Performance appraisal plays a crucial role in improving motivation at work. People want and need feedback regarding how they are doing, and appraisal provides an opportunity for the organization to give them that feedback. And if performance is not up to par, the appraisal conference provides an opportunity to review a subordinate's progress and map out a plan for rectifying any performance deficiencies that might be identified.

2. Before the appraisal, it must be clear what performance is expected so that the employee knows the standards against which he or she will be assessed.

3. There are several types of performance appraisal tools. They include the graphic rating scale, alternation ranking, paired comparison, forced distribution, essays, BARS, BOS, MOB, and critical incidents.

4. Each performance appraisal technique has its own advantages and disadvantages. Appraisal problems to beware of include the halo effect, the central tendency effect, the leniency or strictness problem, the recency effect, the similarity effect, and supervisory bias.

5. Most subordinates probably want some specific explanation or examples regarding why they were appraised high or low and, for this, compiling critical incidents can be useful. Here, a running record of uncommonly good or undesirable examples of each person's work-related behaviour is maintained.

6. It is important that the subordinate view the appraisal as fair, and in this regard there are four things an appraiser can do: evaluate the subordinate's performance frequently; be familiar with the person's performance; ensure that there is agreement on what the job duties are; and finally, solicit the person's help when plans are formulated for eliminating performance weaknesses.

7. There are three main types of performance appraisal interviews. The tell and sell method uses a directive approach to communicate to employees where they stand and how well they are performing. The tell and listen approach allows the subordinate to participate in the appraisal interview by commenting on each dimension of the appraiser's evaluation. Finally, the problem-solving method is an active, two-way communication process that allows both the appraiser and the subordinate to explore alternate solutions to problems.

8. There are three other types of appraisal interviews, each with its own objectives. The first is for performance that is unsatisfactory but correctable. Here, the objective of the interview is to lay out an action plan for correcting the unsatisfactory performance. The second type of interview is for employees whose performance is satisfactory but for whom promotion is not possible. The objective here is not to improve or develop the person but to maintain satisfactory performance. Finally, there is the satisfactory-promotable interview in which the main objective is to discuss the person's career plans and to develop a specific action plan for the educational and professional development the person needs to move on to the next job.

9. To prepare for the appraisal interview there are three things an appraiser must do: assemble the data, prepare the employee, and choose the time and place.

10. To bring about some constructive change in a subordinate's behaviour it is important to get the person to talk in the interview. Dos for encouraging the person to talk include the following: try silence, use open-ended questions, state questions in terms of a problem, use a command question, use choice questions to try to understand the feelings underlying what the person is saying, and restate the person's last point as a question. On the other hand, *don't* do all the talking, use restrictive questions, be judgmental, give free advice, get involved with name calling, ridicule, digress, or use sarcasm.

11. The best way for an appraiser to handle a defensive subordinate is to proceed very carefully. Specifically, the appraiser should recognize that defensive behaviour is normal, never attack a person's defences, postpone actions, and recognize his or her own limitations.

12. One of the objectives of the appraisal interview is to improve a subordinate's performance, and this is accomplished by clearing up job-related problems, and setting improvement goals and a schedule for achieving them.

KEY TERMS

performance appraisal
graphic rating scale
alternation ranking method
paired comparison method
forced distribution method
critical incident method
essay method

behaviourally anchored rating scale (BARS)
management by objectives (MBO)
behavioural observation scales (BOS)
halo effect
central tendency effect

leniency effect
strictness effect
recency effect
similarity effect
supervisory bias
appraisal interviews

DISCUSSION QUESTIONS

1. Discuss the pros and cons of at least four performance appraisal tools.
2. Develop a graphic rating scale for the following jobs: secretary, engineer, directory assistance operator.
3. Explain how to use the alternation ranking method, the paired comparison method, and the forced distribution method.
4. Over the period of a week, develop a set of critical incidents covering the classroom performance of one of your instructors.
5. Explain in your own words how you would go about developing a behaviourally anchored rating scale.
6. Explain the problems to be avoided in appraising performance.
7. Discuss the pros and cons of using different potential raters to appraise a person's performance.

8. Explain how to conduct an appraisal interview.
9. Answer the question: "How would you get the interviewee to talk during an appraisal interview?"

CASE INCIDENT: From Superior to Mediocre

It was common for the performance evaluation of most employees at Courtesy Store to range from excellent to superior. Performance evaluation has traditionally been used to justify pay increases and promotions. It is the practice of top management to review all performance appraisals before employees receive them. All performance appraisals are conducted together and once a year, despite an employee's starting date. Based on the results of the performance appraisals, all employees receive their annual pay increases. This has been the case until this year, when the new appraisal system came into effect.

For many years employees expressed dissatisfaction with the old form because they felt that some employees whose performances were below theirs were receiving similar or higher ratings. Upper management also was unhappy with the ratings because they could not understand how employees could be receiving such high ratings when the employees were making so many errors in packing and shipping, and when total employee performance seemed to be declining. It was based on their observations and employee input that management decided to adopt the new appraisal form.

After the performance appraisals were complete, using the new and improved form, they were sent to top management for review. The results showed that most employees were rated between fair and good, and no one received a rating higher than good. The average rating was satisfactory. Based on these results no employees would be entitled to receive a pay increase.

Questions

1. What factors do you believe contributed to the high ratings that resulted from the old performance appraisal system?
2. What factors do you believe contributed to the low ratings that resulted from the new performance appraisal system?
3. What should management do with the results of the performance appraisals?

EXPERIENTIAL EXERCISE

Purpose: The purpose of this exercise is to give you practice in developing and using a performance appraisal form.

Required Understanding: You are going to develop a performance appraisal form for an instructor and should therefore be thoroughly familiar with the discussion of performance appraisal in this chapter.

How to Set Up the Exercise: Divide the class into groups of four or five students.

Instructions for the Exercise

1. Your group should develop a tool for appraising the performance of an instructor. Decide which of the appraisal tools (graphic rating scales, alternation ranking, and so on) you are going to use and then design the instrument itself.

2. Next, have a spokesperson from each group put his or her group's appraisal tool on the board. How similar are the tools? Do they all measure the same factors? Which factor appears most often? Which do you think is the most effective tool on the board? Can you think of any way of combining the best points of several of the tools into a superior performance appraisal tool?

NOTES

1. Kenneth Teel, "Performance Appraisal: Current Trends, Persistent Progress," *Personnel Journal* (April 1980), p. 301. See also Christina Banks and Kevin Murphy, "Toward Narrowing the Research-Practice Gap in Performance Appraisals," *Personnel Psychology*, Vol. 38, no. 2 (Summer 1985), pp. 335-346. For a description of how to implement an improved performance appraisal system, see, for example, Ted Cocheu, "Performance Appraisal: A Case in Point," *Personnel Journal*, Vol. 65, no. 9 (September 1986), pp. 48-53; Weitzel, "How to Improve Performance Through Successful Appraisals," *Personnel*, Vol. 64, no. 10 (October 1987), pp. 18-23; William H. Wagel, "Performance Appraisal with a Difference," *Personnel*, Vol. 64, no. 2 (February 1987), pp. 4-6; and Jeanette Cleveland et al. "Multiple Uses of Performance Appraisal: Prevalence and Correlates," *Journal of Applied Psychology*, Vol, 74, no. 1 (February 1989), pp. 130-135.

2. Teel, "Performance Appraisal," p. 301.

3. Wayne Cascio and H. John Bernardin, "Implications of Performance Appraisal Litigation for Personnel Decisions," *Personnel Psychology* Vol. 34 (Summer 1981), pp. 211-212.

4. R. G. Downey, F. F. Medland, and L. G. Yates, "Evaluation of a Peer Rating System for Predicting Subsequent Promotion of Senior Military Officers," *Journal of Applied Psychology*, Vol. 61 (April 1976).

5. Allan Kraut, "Prediction of Managerial Success by Peer and Training Staff Ratings," *Journal of Applied Psychology*, Vol. 60 (February 1975). See also Michael Mount, "Psychometric Properties of Subordinate Ratings of Managerial Performance," *Personnel Psychology*, Vol. 37, no. 4 (Winter 1984), pp. 687-702.

6. Robert Libby and Robert Blashfield, "Performance of a Composite as a Function of the Number of Judges," *Organizational Behaviour and Human Performance*, Vol. 21 (April 1978), pp. 121-129; Walter Borman, "Exploring Upper Limits of Reliability and Validity in Job Performance Ratings," *Journal of Applied Psychology*, Vol. 63 (April 1978), pp. 135-144.

7. Walter C. Borman, "The Rating of Individuals in Organizations: An Alternate Approach," *Organizational Behaviour and Human Performance*, Vol. 12 (1974), pp. 105-124.

8. Teel, "Performance Appraisal," p. 301.

9. George Thornton III, "Psychometric Properties of Self Appraisal of Job Performance," *Personnel Psychology*, Vol. 33 (Summer 1980), p. 265; Cathy Anderson, Jack Warner, and Cassie Spencer, "Inflation Bias in Self-Assessment Examinations: Implications for Valid Employee Selection," *Journal of Applied Psychology*, Vol. 69, no. 4 (November 1984), pp. 574-580. See also Shaul Fox and Yossi Dinur, "Validity of Self-assessment: A Field

Evaluation," *Personnel Psychology*, Vol. 41, no. 3 (Autumn 1988), pp. 581-592; and John W. Lawrie, "Your Performance: Appraise It Yourself!" *Personnel*, Vol. 66, no. 1 (January 1989), pp. 21-33, a good explanation of how self-appraisals can be used at work.

10. Herbert Myer, "Self-Appraisal of Job Performance," *Personnel Psychology*, Vol. 33 (Summer 1980), pp. 291-293; Robert Holzbach, "Rater Bias in Performance Ratings: Superior, Self, and Peer Ratings," *Journal of Applied Psychology*, Vol. 63, no. 5 (October 1978), pp. 579-588; Herbert G. Heneman III, "Comparison of Self and Superior Ratings of Managerial Performance," *Journal of Applied Psychology*, Vol. 59 (1974), pp. 638-642; Richard J. Klimoski and Manuel London, "Role of the Rater in Performance Appraisal," *Journal of Applied Psychology*, Vol. 59 (1974), pp. 445-451; Hubert S. Field and William H. Holley, "Subordinates' Characteristics, Supervisors' Ratings, and Decisions to Discuss Appraisal Results," *Academy of Management Journal*, Vol. 20, no. 2 (1977), pp. 215-221. See also Robert Steel and Nestor Ovalle II, "Self-Appraisal Based Upon Supervisory Feedback," *Personnel Psychology*, Vol. 37, no. 4 (Winter 1984), pp. 667-685; Gloria Shapiro and Gary Dessler, "Are Self-Appraisals More Realistic Among Professionals or Nonprofessionals in Health Care?" *Public Personnel Management*, Vol. 14 (Fall 1985), pp. 285-291; James Russell and Dorothy Goode, "An Analysis of Managers' Reactions to Their Own Performance Appraisal Feedback," *Journal of Applied Psychology*, Vol. 73, no. 1 (February 1988), pp. 63-67; and Michael M. Harris and John Shaubroeck, "A Meta-Analysis of Self-Supervisor, Self-Peer, and Peer-Supervisor Ratings," *Personnel Psychology*, Vol. 41, no. 1 (Spring 1988), pp. 43-62.

11. Richard I. Henderson, *Compensation Management: Rewarding Performance* 4th ed. (Reston Virginia: Prentice-Hall Inc., 1985), p. 562.

12. See, for example, Timothy Keaveny and Anthony McGann, "A Comparison of Behavioral Expectation Scales and Graphic Rating Scales," *Journal of Applied Psychology*, Vol. 60 (1975), pp. 695-703. See also, John Ivancevich, "A Longitudinal Study of Behavioral Expectation Scales: Attitudes and Performance," *Journal of Applied Psychology* (April 1980), pp. 139-146.

13. Based on Donald Schwab, Herbert Heneman III, and Thomas DeCotiis, "Behaviorally Anchored Scales: A Review of the Literature," *Personnel Psychology*, Vol. 28 (1975), pp. 549-562. For a discussion, see also Uco Wiersma and Gary Latham, "The Practicality of Behavioral Observation Scales, Behavioral Expectations Scales, and Trait Scales," *Personnel Psychology*, Vol. 39, no. 3 (Autumn 1986), pp. 619-628.

14. Lawrence Fogli, Charles Hulin, and Milton Blood, "Development of First Level Behavioral Job Criteria," *Journal of Applied Psychology*, Vol. 55 (1971), pp. 3-8. See also Terry Dickenson and Peter Fellinger, "A Comparison of the Behaviorally Anchored Rating and Fixed Standard Scale Formats," *Journal of Applied Psychology* (April 1980), pp. 147-154.

15. Keaveny and McGann, "A Comparison of Behavioral Expectation Scales," pp. 695-703; Schwab, Heneman, and DeCotiis, "Behaviorally Anchored Rating Scales;" James Goodale and Ronald Burke, "Behaviorally Based Rating Scales Need Not Be Job Specific," *Journal of Applied Psychology*, Vol. 60 (June 1975).

16. Wayne Cascio and Enzo Valenzi, "Behaviorally Anchored Rating Scales: Effects of Education and Job Experience of Raters and Ratees," *Journal of Applied Psychology*, Vol. 62, no. 3 (1977), pp. 278-282. See also Gary P. Latham and Kenneth N. Wexley, "Behavioral Observation Scales for Performance Appraisal Purposes," *Personnel Psychology*, Vol. 30, no. 2 (Summer 1977), pp. 255-268; H. John Bernardin, Kenneth M. Alveres, and C. J. Cranny, "A Recomparison of Behavioral Expectation Scales to Summated Scales," *Journal of Applied Psychology*, Vol. 61, no. 5 (October 1976), p. 564; Frank E. Saal and Frank J. Landy, "The Mixed Standard Rating Scale: An Evaluation," *Organizational Behavior and Human Performance*, Vol. 18, no. 1 (February 1977), pp. 19-35; Frank J. Landy and others, "Behaviorally Anchored Scales for Rating the Performance of Police Officers," *Journal of Applied Psychology*, Vol. 61, no. 6 (December 1976), pp. 750-

758; and Kevin R. Murphy and Joseph Constans, "Behavioral Anchors as a Source of Bias in Rating," *Journal of Applied Psychology*, Vol. 72, no. 4 (November 1987), pp. 573-577.

17. Stephen J. Carroll and Craig E. Schneier, *Performance Appraisal and Review Systems* (Glenview, Illinois: Scott, Foresman and Company, 1982), pp. 149-151.

18. Ibid., p. 114. See also Kevin R. Murphy and Jeanette N. Cleveland, *Performance Appraisal* (Boston: Allyn and Bacon, 1991), p. 302.

19. For a discussion of this see, for example, Wayne Cascio, *Applied Psychology in Personnel Management* (Reston, Va: Reston Publishing Co., 1978), pp. 337-341.

20. B. Rosen and T. H. Gerdee, "The Nature of Job Related Age Stereotypes," *Journal of Applied Psychology*, Vol. 61 (1976), pp. 180-183.

21. William J. Bigoness, "Effect of Applicant's Sex, Race and Performance on Employer's Performance Ratings: Some Additional Findings," *Journal of Applied Psychology*, Vol. 61 (February 1976). See also Duane Thompson and Toni Thompson, "Task-Based Performance Appraisal for Blue Collar Jobs: Evaluation of Race and Sex Effects," *Journal of Applied Psychology*, Vol. 70, no. 4 (1985), pp. 747-753.

22. Gerald Ferris, Valerie Yates, David Gilmore, and Kendrith Rowland, "The Influence of Subordinate Age on Performance Ratings and Casual Attributions," *Personnel Psychology*, Vol. 38, no. 3 (Autumn 1985), pp. 545-557. As another example, see Gregory Dobbins and Jeanne Russell, "The Biasing Effects of Subordinate Likeableness on Leader's Responses to Poor Performers: A Laboratory and Field Study," *Personnel Psychology*, Vol. 39, no. 4 (Winter 1986), pp. 759-778. See also Michael E. Benedict and Edward Levine, "Delay and Distortion: Passive Influences on Performance Appraisal Effectiveness," *Journal of Applied Psychology*, Vol. 73, no. 3 (August 1988), pp. 507-514; and James Smither et al., "Effect of Prior Performance Information on Rating of Present Performance: Contrast Versus Assimilation Revisited," *Journal of Applied Psychology*, Vol. 73, no. 3 (August 1988), pp. 487-496.

23. Kevin Murphy, William Balzer, Maura Lockhart, and Elaine Eisenman, "Effects of Previous Performance on Evaluations of Present Performance," *Journal of Applied Psychology*, Vol. 70, no. 1 (1985), pp. 72-84. See also Kevin Williams, Angelo DeNisi, Bruce Meglino, and Thomas Cafferty, "Initial Decisions and Subsequent Performance Ratings," *Journal of Applied Psychology*, Vol. 71, no. 2 (May 1986), pp. 189-195.

24. W. C. Borman, "Effects of Instruction to Avoid Halo Error in Reliability and Validity of Performance Evaluation Ratings," *Journal of Applied Psychology*, Vol. 65 (1975), pp. 556-560. Borman points out that since no control group (a group of managers who did not undergo training) was available, it is possible that the observed effects were not due to the short five-minute training experience. G. P. Latham, K. N. Wexley, and E. D. Pursell, "Training Managers to Minimize Rating Errors in the Observation of Behavior," *Journal of Applied Psychology*, Vol. 60 (1975), pp. 550-555; John Ivancevich, "Longitudinal Study of the Effects of Rater Training on Psychometric Error in Ratings," *Journal of Applied Psychology*, Vol. 64 (1979), pp. 502-508. For a related discussion, see, for example Bryan Davis and Michael Mount, "Effectiveness of Performance Appraisal Training Using Computer Assistance Instruction and Behavior Modeling," *Personnel Psychology*, Vol. 37 (Fall 1984), pp. 439-452.

25. Walter Borman, "Format and Training Effects on Rating Accuracy and Rater Errors," *Journal of Applied Psychology*, Vol. 64 (August 1979), pp. 410-412; and Jerry Hedge and Michael Cavanagh, "Improving the Accuracy of Performance Evaluations: Comparison of Three Methods of Performance Appraiser Training," *Journal of Applied Psychology*, Vol. 73, no. 1 (February 1988), pp. 68-73.

26. Ryan Davis and Michael Mount, "The Effectiveness of Performance Appraisal Training Using Computer-Assisted Instruction and Behavior Modeling," *Personnel Psychology*, Vol. 37, no 3 (Autumn 1984), pp. 439-452.

27. Dennis Warnke and Robert Billings, "Comparison of Training Methods for Improving the Psychometric Quality of Experimental and Administrative Performance Ratings," *Journal of Applied Psychology*, Vol. 64 (April 1979), pp. 124-131. See also Timothy Athey and Robert McIntyre, "Effect of Rater Training on Rater Accuracy: Levels of Processing Theory and Social Facilitation Theory Perspectives," *Journal of Applied Psychology*, Vol. 72, no. 4 (November 1987), pp. 567-572.

28. Frank Landy, Janet Barnes, and Kevin Murphy, "Correlates of Perceived Fairness and Accuracy of Performance Evaluation," *Journal of Applied Psychology*, Vol. 63 (December 1978), pp. 751-754; Frank Landy, Janet Barnes-Farrell, and Jeanette Cleveland, "Perceived Fairness and Accuracy of Performance Evaluation: A Follow Up," *Journal of Applied Psychology*, Vol. 65 (June 1980), pp. 355-356; Jerald Greenberg, "Determinants of Perceived Fairness of Performance Evaluations," *Journal of Applied Psychology*, Vol. 71, no. 2 (May 1986), pp. 340-342.

29. Stanley Silverman and Kenneth Wexley, "Reaction of Employees to Performance Appraisal Interviews as a Function of Their Participation in Rating Scale Development," *Personnel Psychology*, Vol. 37, no. 4 (Winter 1984). For a discussion of the use of participative management for developing a more effective performance appraisal system, see David Cowfer and Joanne Sujansky, "Appraisal Development at Westinghouse," *Training and Development Journal*, Vol. 41, no. 7 (July 1987), pp. 40-45.

30. This is based on N.R.F. Maier, "Three Types of Interview" *Personnel Journal* Vol. 34 (March-April 1958), p. 29.

31. This is based on Robert Johnson, *The Appraisal Interview Guide* (New York: AMACOM, 1979), pp. 45-50. See also Michael E. Cavanagh, "Employee Problems: Prevention and Intervention," *Personnel Journal*, Vol. 66, no. 9 (September 1987), pp. 35-38; Includes a manager's problem counselling checklist for how to address employee problems.

32. Judy Block, *Performance Appraisal on the Job: Making It Work* (New York: Executive Enterprises Publications, 1981), pp. 58-62. See also Terry Lowe, "Eight Ways to Ruin a Performance Review," *Personnel Journal*, Vol. 65, no. 1 (January 1986).

33. Block, *Performance Appraisal on the Job.*

34. Johnson, *The Appraisal Interview*, p. 45. See also Paul Reed and Mark Kroll, "A Two-Perspective Approach to Performance Appraisal," Personnel, Vol. 62, no. 10 (October 1985), pp. 51-57.

35. George Thornton III, "Psychometric Properties of Self-Appraisals of Job Performance," *Personnel Psychology*, Vol. 33 (Summer 1980), p. 265

36. These are based on Johnson, *Appraisal Interview Guide*, Chapter 14.

37. Ronald Burke, William Witzel, and Tamara Weis, "Characteristics of Effective Employee Performance Review and Development Interviews: Replication and Extension," *Personnel Psychology*, Vol. 31 (Winter 1978), pp. 903-919. See also Joane Pearce and Lyman Porter, "Employee Response to Formal Performance Appraisal Feedback," *Journal of Applied Psychology*, Vol. 71, no. 2 (May 1986), pp. 211-218.

SUGGESTED READINGS

Bernardin, H.J. and R.W. Beatty. *Performance Appraisal: Assessing Human Behavior at Work.* Belmont, CA: Wadsworth, 1984.

Carroll, S.J. and C.E. Schneier. *Performance Appraisal and Review Systems.* Scotts, Foresman, 1982.

Elangovan, A.R. "An Artificial Intelligence Approach to Performance Appraisal in 1990's: Forging a Link with Fuzzy Logic and Expert Systems." Administrative

Sciences Association of Canada (Personnel and Human Resources Division) Proceedings of Annual Conference, June 1991.

Latham, Gary P. and Kenneth N. Wexley. *Increasing Productivity through Performance Appraisal*. Reading, Mass: Addison-Wesley Publishing Company, 1981.

Maier, Norman F. *The Appraisal Interview: Three Basic Approaches*. La Jolla, California: University Associates, 1976.

Murphy, Kevin R. and Jeanette N. Cleveland. *Performance Appraisal: An Organizational Perspective*. Boston: Allyn and Bacon, 1991.

Manage People, Not Personnel: Motivation and Performance Appraisal. Cambridge, MA: Harvard Business School Press, 1990.

CHAPTER
TEN CAREER MANAGEMENT

After studying this chapter, you should be able to

1. Describe each stage in a person's career cycle.
2. Identify the six types of occupational orientations.
3. Describe the three categories of occupational skills.
4. Identify career anchors.
5. Explain the employer's role in career management.
6. Understand and explain how to manage promotions, transfers, and retirement.

OVERVIEW

It often happens that after the appraisal of an employee's performance some new career decisions must be made. Perhaps the person should be directed toward a new career, for instance, or a decision must be made regarding that person's promotion, transfer, or separation. The main purpose of this chapter is to improve career-management skills. We will explain how to identify a person's occupational orientations (or interests) and a person's career anchors and skills. We will also explain how to manage promotions, transfers, and retirements. Effective performance is usually rewarded, perhaps with more pay or with a promotion. Ineffective performance, however, may require retraining or more attractive rewards, a transfer to a more suitable job, or termination.

INTRODUCTION TO CAREER MANAGEMENT

Career refers to all the jobs an individual occupies over the span of his or her life. The management of careers is a process that involves managers, human resource specialists, and the individuals themselves.[1] Career management, therefore, is an integrated process and is the responsibility of both organizations and their employees.

Some other concepts basic to understanding career management are defined as follows:

Career path is the sequential pattern of jobs that forms an individual career.

Career ladders illustrate the horizontal and vertical progression of an individual from one job to another within an organization. Career ladders are very useful for helping an individual visualize potential advancement with an organization and plan the sequence of learning, training, and work experience required to reach a particular career goal.

Career goals are specifically identified future positions or jobs that individuals target and aim to achieve.

Career planning is the process of choosing occupations, organizations, and goals, and includes the path that an individual selects and follows to achieve his or her career aspirations.

Career development comprises the personal improvement programs, training, and activities an individual undertakes to achieve his or her personal career plan.

Career counselling is the process by which individuals meet with their managers, supervisors, or guidance counsellors to assess their career aspirations.

Career management involves the integration of career planning and career goals. It is the process of designing and implementing goals, plans, and strategies to achieve organizational objectives and the individual's career aspirations.

Purposes and Importance of Career Management

The purposes and importance of career management are to

- Enable employees to get a better job, increase their responsibility, and make better use of their skills

- Foster in employees a better understanding of the need to plan and manage their careers

- Facilitate the coordination of career planning activities with other activities in human resource management, such as human resource planning, recruitment selection, performance appraisal, and retirement planning

- Encourage and motivate promotable individuals to grow and develop their potential

- Identify career opportunities available in organizations, and determine the degree to which employees' career aspirations realistically match up with the available opportunities

- Identify the development activities employees require to prepare themselves for further career growth

Who Is Responsible for Career Management?

For career management to be effective, it must be a shared responsibility.[2] All employees are influenced by an organization's policies and practices at each step of their career. This influence occurs before and after employees join an organization. An individual's choice of an organization is influenced by the company's reputation and recruiting programs; the choice of job assignment is influenced by internal placement, and promotion policies and practices; an individual's performance on the job is influenced by the design of the job and the performance standards, criteria, and objectives established.[3] In other words, the responsibility for inducements, administration, maintenance, and effective utilization of a career management program rests with the organization.

Nonetheless, the ultimate responsibility for career planning and development rests with individual employees.[4] Individuals have ultimate control over the choice of an organization. Finding a job does not just happen. Individuals have to make it happen. Individuals know which career they want to pursue and usually arrange their educational training to prepare themselves for their career.[5] It is therefore the responsibility of individual employees to decide whether to join or stay with the organization, whether to seek and accept job promotions, and whether to strive for high performance and personal growth on the job.[6] Organizations cannot dictate to individuals in matters of this nature. They cannot force employees to undertake career planning convenient to the firm or to develop abilities that correspond to career goals. Organizations can only try to identify and attract candidates, notify employees of opportunities and paths for advancement, design appropriate training and development programs, provide the necessary evaluation and feedback, and provide other systems and information that can influence personal career decisions.[7]

HUMAN RESOURCE MANAGEMENT AND HUMAN RESOURCE DEVELOPMENT

Activities like screening, training, and appraising serve two basic functions in an organization. First, their traditional function has been to staff the organization—to fill its open positions with employees who have the requisite interests, abilities, and skills. Increasingly, however, these activities are taking on a second role—that of ensuring that the long-term interests of the employees are protected by the organization and that, in particular, the employee is encouraged to grow and realize his or her full potential. Referring to staffing or human resource management as human resource planning and development reflects this second role. The basic, if implicit, assumption underlying the focus on human resource planning and development is that the organization has an *obligation* to utilize its employees' abilities to the fullest and to give every employee an opportunity to grow and to realize his or her full potential. To some experts, this means that the organization has an obligation to improve the quality of work life of its employees; notice again, though, that "quality of work life" refers not just to things like working conditions or pay but also to the extent to which each employee is able to utilize fully his or her abilities, engage in interesting jobs, and obtain the training and guidance that allows the person to move up to jobs that fully utilize his or her potential.[8]

Career Planning and Development

One way this trend is manifesting itself is in the increased emphasis many managers are placing on career planning and development, an emphasis, in other words, on giving employees the assistance and opportunities that will enable them to form realistic career goals and achieve them. Many experts believe that enabling employees to pursue expanded, more realistic career goals should be the major aim of an organization's human resource system, partly because they believe that organizations have a duty to help their employees realize their full potential and partly because they believe that by integrating the "careers" of both the individual and the organization, both will gain. For the employee, satisfaction, personal development, and quality of work life are the clearest benefits.[9] For the organization, increased productivity levels, creativity, and long-range effectiveness may occur, since the organization would be staffed by highly committed employees who are carefully trained and developed for their jobs.

Impact of Human Resource Management on Career Planning and Development

Activities like human resource planning, screening, and training play a big role in the career development process. Human resource planning, for example, can be used not just to forecast job openings but to identify potential internal candidates and the training they would need to fill those jobs. Similarly, an organization can use its periodic employee appraisals not just for salary decisions but for identifying the development needs of individual employees and for ensuring that those needs are met. All staffing activities, in other words, can be used to satisfy the needs of both the organization and the individual in such a way that both gain: the organization from improved performance from a more dedicated work force and the individual from a richer, more challenging career.

FACTORS THAT AFFECT CAREER CHOICES

The first step in planning a career (someone else's or one's own) is to learn as much as possible about the person's interests, aptitudes, and skills. People naturally seek out and excel in jobs in which they are interested and for which they have the requisite skills.

Stages in a Person's Career

career cycle

Each person's career goes through stages, so it is important to understand the nature of the **career cycle**. One reason it is important to understand how careers evolve is that it can enable a person to better plan his or her career and to deal with occasional career crises if and when they occur. Another reason is because it can improve the performance of a supervisor by giving him or her a better insight into employees' behaviour. (For example, many employees undergo a "midlife crisis," during which they agonize over the fact that their accomplishments have not kept pace with their expectations. The result of this introspection can be a period of prolonged disappointment for employees, during which their performance can be adversely affected.) The main stages of a career are summarized below.[10]

Growth Stage

The **growth stage** lasts roughly from birth to age 14 and is a period during which the person develops a self-concept by identifying and interacting with other people such as family, friends, and teachers. Near the beginning of this period, role playing is important, and children experiment with different ways of acting; this helps them to form impressions of how other people react to different behaviours and contributes to their development of a unique self-concept, or identity. Toward the end of this state, the adolescent (who by this time has developed some preliminary ideas of what his or her interest and abilities are) begins some realistic thinking about alternative occupations.

growth stage

Exploration Stage

The **exploration stage** is the period, roughly from age 15 to 24, during which a person seriously explores various occupational alternatives, attempting to match these alternatives with what he or she has learned about them (and about his or her own interests and abilities from school, leisure activities, and part-time work). Some tentative broad occupational choices are usually made during the beginning of this period. This choice is refined as the person learns more about the choice and about himself or herself until, toward the end of this period, a seemingly appropriate choice is made and the person pursues a specific job.

exploration stage

Probably the most important task the person has in this and the preceding stage is that of developing a realistic understanding of his or her abilities and talents. Similarly, the person must discover and develop his or her values, motives, and ambitions and make sound educational decisions based on reliable sources of information about occupational alternatives.

Establishment Stage

The **establishment stage** spans roughly ages 24 to 44 and is the heart of most people's work lives. Sometime during this period (hopefully, toward the beginning) a suitable occupation is found and the person engages in activities that help him or her to earn a permanent place in it. Often (particularly in the professions) the person locks onto a chosen occupation early. But in most cases this is a period during which the person is continually testing his or her capabilities and ambitions, and assessing and comparing them against the initial occupational choice.

establishment stage

The establishment stage is itself comprised of three substages. The **trial substage** lasts from about age 25 to 30. During this period the person determines whether or not the chosen field is suitable; if it is not, several changes might be attempted. (Jane Smith might have her heart set on a career in retailing, for example, but after several months of constant travel as a newly hired assistant buyer for a department store, she might decide that a less travel-oriented career such as one in market research is more in tune with her needs.) Roughly between the ages of 30 and 40, the person goes through a **stabilization substage** during which firm occupational goals are set and the person does more explicit career planning to determine the sequence of promotions, job changes, and/or educational activities that seem necessary to accomplish those goals. Finally, somewhere between the mid-thirties and mid-forties, the person may enter the **mid-career crisis substage**. During this period people often conduct a major reassessment of their progress relative to original ambitions and goals. They may find that they are not going to realize their dreams (such as being company president) or that, having accomplished what they

trial substage

stabilization substage

mid-career crisis substage

set out to do, their dreams are not what they imagined they would be. Also during this period, people have to decide how important work and career are to be in their life. It is often during this mid-career crisis substage that the person is, for the first time, faced with the difficult decisions of what he or she really wants, what can realistically be accomplished, and how much must be sacrificed to achieve this. It is usually during this crisis stage that some people first realize they have what Schein calls career anchors[11]—basic concerns for security or for independence and freedom, for instance—which they will not give up if a choice has to be made.

Maintenance Stage

maintenance stage

Between the ages of 45 and 65, many people simply slide from the stabilization substage into the **maintenance stage**. During this period the person has typically created for himself or herself a place in the world of work and most efforts are now directed to securing that place.

Decline Stage

decline stage

As retirement age approaches, there is often a deceleration period—the **decline stage**—during which many people are faced with the prospect of having to accept reduced levels of power and responsibility and have to learn to accept and develop new roles as mentor and confidante for those who are younger. There is then the more or less inevitable retirement, after which the person is faced with the prospect of finding alternative uses for the time and effort formerly expended on his or her occupation.

Identifying Occupational Orientations

occupational orientation

Career-counselling expert John Holland says that a person's personality (including values, motives, and needs) is one important determinant of career choices, and that there are six basic "personal orientations" (**occupational orientation**) that determine the sorts of careers to which people are drawn. For example, says Holland, a person with a strong social orientation might be attracted to careers that entail interpersonal rather than intellectual or physical activities, and thus to occupations such as social work. Based on research with his vocational preference test (VPT), Holland defines six basic personality types or orientations.[12]

1. *Realistic orientation.* These people are attracted to occupations that involve physical activities requiring skill, strength, and coordination. Some examples include forestry, farming, and agriculture.

2. *Investigative orientation.* These people are attracted to careers that involve cognitive (thinking, organizing, understanding) rather than affective (feeling, acting, or interpersonal and emotional) activities. Examples include biologist, chemist, and professor.

3. *Social orientation.* These people are attracted to careers that involve interpersonal rather than intellectual or physical activities. Examples include clinical psychology, foreign service, and social work.

4. *Conventional orientation.* These people prefer careers that involve structured, rule-regulated activities, as well as careers where it is expected that the employee subordinate his or her personal needs to those of the organization. Examples include accountants and bankers.

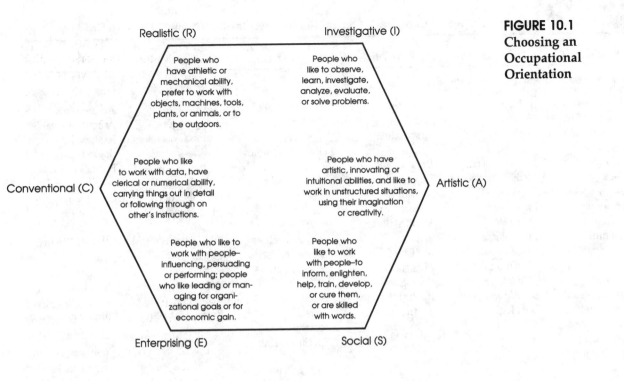

FIGURE 10.1
Choosing an
Occupational
Orientation

Realistic (R)

People who have athletic or mechanical ability, prefer to work with objects, machines, tools, plants, or animals, or to be outdoors.

Investigative (I)

People who like to observe, learn, investigate, analyze, evaluate, or solve problems.

Conventional (C)

People who like to work with data, have clerical or numerical ability, carrying things out in detail or following through on other's instructions.

Artistic (A)

People who have artistic, innovating or intuitional abilities, and like to work in unstructured situations, using their imagination or creativity.

Enterprising (E)

People who like to work with people–influencing, persuading or performing; people who like leading or managing for organizational goals or for economic gain.

Social (S)

People who like to work with people–to inform, enlighten, help, train, develop, or cure them, or are skilled with words.

5. *Enterprising orientation.* These people are attracted to careers that involve verbal activities aimed at influencing others. Examples include managers, lawyers, and public relations executives.

6. *Artistic orientation.* People here are attracted to careers that involve self-expression, artistic creation, expression of emotions, and individualistic activities. Examples include artists, advertising executives, and musicians.

Most people have more than one orientation (they might be both realistic and investigative, for example), and Holland believes that the more similar or comparable these orientations are, the less internal conflict or indecision a person will face in making a career choice. To help illustrate this, Holland suggests placing each orientation in one corner of a hexagon, as in Figure 10.1. As can be seen, the model has six corners, each of which represents one personal orientation (for example, enterprising). According to Holland's research, the closer two orientations are in this figure, the more compatible they are. Thus, adjacent categories (realistic-investigative, enterprising-social) are quite similar, while those diagonally opposite (enterprising-investigative, artistic-conventional) are quite dissimilar. Holland believes that if an individual's primary and secondary orientations fall side by side, that individual will have a relatively easy time choosing a career. However, if the orientations turn out to be opposite (such as realistic and social), the individual may experience a great deal of indecision in making a career choice because his or her interests are driving him or her toward very different types of careers.

In Table 10.1 we have summarized some of the occupations that have been found to be the best match for each of these six personal occupational orientations. For example, researchers have found that people with realistic orientations often

TABLE 10.1 Occupations Scoring High on Each Occupational Orientation Theme

Realistic	Investigative	Artistic	Social	Enterprising	Conventional
Consider these occupations if you score high here:					
Agribusiness managers	Biologists	Advertising executives	Auto sales dealers	Agribusiness managers	Accountants
Carpenters	Chemists	Art teachers	Guidance counselors	Auto sales dealers	Auto sales dealers
Electricians	Engineers	Artists	Home economics teachers	Business education teachers	Bankers
Engineers	Geologists	Broadcasters	Mental health workers	Buyers	Bookkeepers
Farmers	Mathematicians	English teachers	Ministers	Chamber of Commerce executives	Business education teachers
Foresters	Medical technologists	Interior decorators	Physical education teachers	Funeral directors	Credit managers
Highway patrol officers	Physicians	Medical illustrators	Recreation leaders	Life insurance agents	Executive housekeepers
Horticultural workers	Physicists	Ministers	School administrators	Purchasing agents	Food service managers
Industrial arts teachers	Psychologists	Musicians	Social science teachers	Realtors	IRS agents
Military enlisted personnel	Research and development managers	Photographers	Social workers	Restaurant managers	Mathematics teachers
Military officers	Science teachers	Public relations directors	Special education teachers	Retail clerks	Military enlisted personnel
Vocational agricultural teachers	Sociologists	Reporters	YMCA/YWCA directors	Store managers	Secretaries

Note: For example, if you score high on "realistic," consider a career as a carpenter, engineer, farmer, and so on.

SOURCE: Reproduced by special permission of the publisher, Consulting Psychologists Press, Inc., Palo Alto, CA 94306, from *Manual for the SVIV-SCII*, Fourth Edition, by Jo-Ida C. Hansen and David P. Campbell. © 1985 by the Board of Trustees of Leland Stanford Junior University.

gravitate toward occupations such as carpentry, engineering, farming, forestry, highway patrol, and machinist. Similarly, those with investigative orientations gravitate toward astronomy, biology, and chemistry.

Identifying Skills

Successful performance depends not just on motivation but on ability as well; even the most highly motivated hockey player is not going to play like Wayne Gretzky, for instance, nor will the most highly motivated singer sing like Anne Murray. The same applies to an individual's interests and occupational orientations; he or she may (for example) have a conventional orientation, but whether he or she has the skills to be an accountant, banker, credit manager, or police officer will largely determine which specific occupation is chosen in the end. Therefore, the next step is to identify an individual's occupational skills.

Occupational Skills

occupational skills

Before embarking on an assessment of **occupational skills**, one needs a list of important skills as a reference. *Canadian Classifications and Dictionary of Occupations*, published by Employment & Immigration Canada, can provide this list.

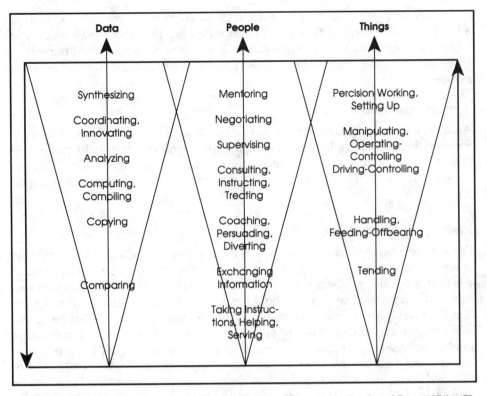

FIGURE 10.2
The Three Basic Skill
Categories

SOURCE: Richard N. Bolles, *What Color Is Your Parachute?* (Berkeley, Calif.: Ten Speed Press, 1976), p.73. Reprinted by permission.

According to one authoritative guide, occupational skills break down into three groups, depending on whether they are to be used with data, people, or things. As summarized in Figure 10.2, data-related skills range from low-level skills such as the skill of merely comparing items or copying them, to increasingly sophisticated data-related skills such as compiling, computing, analyzing, innovating, coordinating, and, finally, synthesizing. Similarly, there is a hierarchy of people-related skills, starting with helping/serving and ranging through supervising, negotiating, and mentoring. Finally, things-related skills range from tending, to operating, manipulating, and precision working.

An Exercise

One useful exercise for identifying your own occupational skills is as follows: take a blank piece of paper and write the heading "The Most Enjoyable Occupational Tasks I Have Had." Then write a short essay that describes the tasks. Make sure to go into as much detail as possible about previous duties and responsibilities and (especially) what it was about each task that was enjoyable. (In writing the essay, by the way, note that it is not necessarily the most enjoyable job that is important but rather the most enjoyable task previously performed; after all, you may have had jobs that you really did not like except for one of the specific duties or tasks in the job, which you really got a kick out of.) Next, on other sheets of paper, do the same thing for two other tasks previously performed. Now go through the three essays and underline the skills that are mentioned the most often. For example, did you get a big kick out of putting together and coordinating the school play when you worked in the principal's office one year? Did you especially enjoy the hours spent in the library doing research for the boss when you worked one summer as an office clerk?[13]

Aptitudes and Special Talents

aptitudes and special talents

An individual's **aptitudes and special talents** also play an important role in career decisions and have long been used by career counsellors to help guide their clients. Aptitudes include intelligence, numerical aptitude, mechanical comprehension, and manual dexterity. (For a more comprehensive discussion see Chapter 6.)

Identifying Career Anchors

career anchor

Edgar Schein says that career planning is a continuous process of discovery—one in which a person slowly develops a clearer occupational self-concept in terms of what his or her talents, abilities, motives, needs, attitudes, and values are. Schein also says that as a person learns more about himself or herself, it will become apparent that the person has a dominant **career anchor**, a concern or value that he or she will not give up if a choice has to be made. These career anchors, as their name implies, are the pivots around which a person's career swings; a person becomes conscious of them as a result of learning about his or her talents and abilities, motives and needs, and attitudes and values. Based on his research at the Massachusetts Institute of Technology (MIT), Schein believes that these career anchors, while crucial in career decisions, are difficult to predict ahead of time because they are evolutionary and a product of a process of discovery. Some people, in fact, may never really find out what their career anchors are until they have to make a major choice—such as whether to accept the promotion to the headquarters staff or strike out on their own by starting a business. And it is at this point that all the person's past work experiences, interests, aptitudes, and orientations converge into a meaningful pattern (or career anchor) that helps show what is personally the most important. Based on his study of MIT graduates, Schein identified five career anchors.[14]

Technical/Functional Career Anchor

People who have a strong technical/functional career anchor seem to make career choices based on the technical or functional content of the work, such as engineering or financial analysis. They tend to avoid decisions that would drive them toward general management. Instead, they make decisions that will enable them to remain and grow in their chosen technical or functional field. Thus, they remain engineers or accountants instead of moving into management.

Managerial Competence as a Career Anchor

Other people show a strong motivation to become managers, "and their career experience enables them to believe that they have the skills and values necessary to rise to such general management positions." A management position of high responsibility is the ultimate goal of these people. When pressed to explain why they believed they had the skills necessary to gain such positions, many MIT graduates answered that they were qualified for these jobs because of what they saw as their competencies in a combination of three areas: (1) analytical competence (ability to identify, analyze, and solve problems under conditions of incomplete information and uncertainty); (2) interpersonal competence (ability to influence, supervise, lead, manipulate, and control people at all levels); (3) emotional competence (the capacity to be stimulated by emotional and interpersonal crises rather than exhausted or debilitated by them, and the capacity to bear high levels of responsibility without becoming paralyzed). Therefore, Schein concluded that "the person who wants to rise to higher levels of management and be given higher levels of responsibility must be simultaneously good at analyzing problems, handling people, and handling his or her own emotions in order to withstand the pressures and tensions of the executive suite."

Creativity as a Career Anchor

Some of the graduates had gone on to become successful entrepreneurs, and to Schein these people seemed to have an enveloping need "to build or to create something that was entirely their own product—a product or process that bears their name, a company of their own, or a personal fortune that reflects their accomplishments." For example, one graduate had become a successful purchaser, restorer, and renter of townhouses in a large city; another had built a successful consulting firm; and another had formed a new computer-based financial service organization.

Autonomy and Independence as Career Anchors

Some seemed driven by the need to be on their own, free from the kind of dependence that can arise when a person elects to work in a large organization where promotions, transfers, and salary decisions make them dependent on others. Many of these graduates also had a strong technical/functional orientation, but instead of pursuing this orientation in an organization, they had decided instead to become consultants, working either alone or as a part of a relatively small firm. Other members of this group had become a professor of business, a freelance writer, and a proprietor of a small retail business.

Security as a Career Anchor

A few of the graduates seemed to be mostly concerned with long-term career stability and job security. They seemed willing to do what was required to maintain job security, a decent income, and a stable future in the form of a good retirement program and benefits. They were therefore much more willing to let the organization they were working for decide what their career should be.

For those interested in geographical security, maintaining a stable, secure career in familiar surroundings was generally more important than was pursuing superior career choices, if choosing the latter meant injecting instability or insecurity into their lives by forcing them to pull up roots and move to another city. For others, security meant organizational security, and they might today opt for government jobs, where tenure still tends to be a way of life.

THE EMPLOYER'S ROLE IN CAREER MANAGEMENT

Career-Management Guidelines

An employer can use its human resource processes—its human resource planning, recruiting, screening, placement, training, and appraising activities—not just to satisfy the organization's staffing needs but also to ensure that its employees are given an opportunity to develop their potential and to formulate and accomplish realistic career goals. From this perspective, organizational career management involves more than occasional career-planning seminars and meetings; instead, it entails injecting a career development perspective into all human resource activities. The goal is to meld these activities into what today is often called, for reasons that should now be clearer, a human resource planning and development system.

An employer can inject a career-planning-and-development perspective into its human resource processes in a number of ways. We will look at some in the following sections.

Avoid Reality Shock

Perhaps at no other stage in the person's career is it more important for the organization to take career development issues into account than at the initial entry stage during which the person is recruited, hired, and given a first assignment and boss. For the employee this is a critical period, a period during which he or she has to develop a sense of confidence, learn to get along with the boss and with coworkers, learn how to accept responsibility, and, most importantly, quickly gain an insight into his or her talents, needs, and values as they relate to initial career goals. For the new employee, in other words, this is (or should be) a period of reality testing during which his or her initial hopes and goals confront for the first time the reality of organizational life and of the person's talents and needs.

For many first-time workers, this turns out to be a disastrous period, one in which their often naive expectations first confront the realities of organizational life (see Chapter 7). The young MBA, CA, or CGA graduate, for example, might come to the first job seeking a challenging, exciting assignment in which to apply the new techniques learned in school and to prove his or her abilities and gain a promotion. In reality, however, the trainee is often turned off by being relegated to an unimportant low-risk job where he or she "can't cause any trouble while we're trying him/her out," or by the harsh realities of interdepartmental conflict and politicking, or by a boss who is neither rewarded for nor trained in the unique mentoring tasks needed to properly supervise new employees.[15]

Provide Challenging Initial Jobs

Most experts therefore agree that one of the most important things an organization can do is to provide new employees with challenging first jobs. In one study of young managers at AT&T, for example, the researchers found that the more challenging a person's job was in his or her first year with the company, the more effective and successful the person was even five or six years later.[16] Based on his own research, Hall contends that challenging initial jobs provide "one of the most powerful yet uncomplicated means of aiding the career development of new employees ..."[17] In most organizations, however, providing such jobs seems more the exception than the rule. In one survey of research and development organizations, for example, only one out of 22 companies had a formal policy of giving challenging first assignments.[18] And this, as one expert has pointed out, is an example of "glaring mismanagement" when one considers the effort and money invested in recruiting, hiring, and training new employees.[19]

Provide Realistic Job Previews in Recruiting

Providing recruits with realistic previews of what to expect once they begin working in the organization can be an effective way of minimizing reality shock and improving their long-term performance. Schein points out that one of the biggest problems recruits (and management) encounter during the crucial entry stage involves obtaining accurate information in a "climate of mutual selling."[20] The recruiter (anxious to hook good candidates) and the candidate (anxious to present as favourable an impression as possible) often give and receive unrealistic information during the interview. The result is that the interviewer may not be able to form a realistic picture of the candidate's career goals, while at the same time the candidate forms an unrealistically favourable image of the organization.[21]

Realistic job previews can, we know, significantly improve the survival rate among employees who are being hired for relatively complex jobs like those of management trainee, salesperson, or life insurance agent,[22] although such realistic previews do not seem to make much difference in the survival rates of those[23] who have less complex jobs.[24]

Be Demanding

Management experts[25] know that there is a "Pygmalion effect"[26] in the relationship between a new employee and his or her boss.[27] In other words, the more organizations expect and the more confident and supportive organizations are of new employees, the better the employees will perform. Therefore, as two experts put it, "don't assign a new employee to a `dead wood,' undemanding, or unsupportive supervisor."[28] Instead, choose specially trained, high-performing, supportive supervisors who can set high standards for new employees during their critical exploratory first year.

Provide Periodic Job Rotation and Job Pathing

The best way new employees can test themselves and crystallize their career anchors is by trying out a variety of challenging jobs. By rotating the person to jobs in various specializations—from financial analysis to production to human resources, for example—the employee gets an opportunity to assess his or her aptitudes and preferences. At the same time, the organization obtains a manager with a broader multifunctional view of the organization.[29] One extension of this is called job pathing,[30] which assumes that carefully sequenced job assignments can have a big impact on personal development. Some companies have therefore laid out a sequence of carefully planned interdisciplinary job assignments leading to an executive job. The preliminary results indicate that job pathing can substantially reduce the amount of time and training usually required to bring a novice trainee to the point where he or she is ready for the executive position.

Improve Career-Oriented Performance Appraisals

Edgar Schein contends that supervisors must understand that valid performance appraisal information is in the long term more important than protecting the short-term interests of one's immediate subordinates.[31] Therefore, he says, supervisors need concrete information regarding the appraisee's career path—information, in other words, about the nature of the future work for which he or she is appraising the subordinate, or which the subordinate desires.[32]

Encourage Career-Planning Activities

Employers also have to take steps to increase employees' involvement in their own career planning and development. For example, some employers are experimenting with activities designed specifically to make employees aware of the need for career planning and of improving career decisions. Here, for example, employees might learn about the rudiments of career planning and the stages in one's career and engage in various activities aimed at crystallizing career anchors and formulating more realistic career goals.[33] Similarly, employers are increasingly engaging in career-counselling meetings (perhaps as part of the performance appraisal meeting) during which the employee and his or her supervisor (or perhaps a human resource director) assess the employee's progress in light of his or her career goals and identify development needs.[34]

What the Human Resource Department Can Do

There are two basic things that the human resource department can and should do to assist employees to improve their career decisions.[35] First, the department should help employees to take charge of their own career by helping them understanding that there are major decisions to be made and that making them requires considerable personal planning and effort. In other words, the human resources department should help employees to understand that they cannot leave their choices in the hands of others but must decide where they want to go in terms of a career and what job moves and education are required to get there. Related to this, the department should help them to become effective diagnosticians; it should assist them in determining (through career counselling, testing, self-diagnostic books, and so on) what talents or values they have and how they fit with the sorts of careers they are considering.[36] In summary, therefore, the key to career planning is insight—into what employees want out of a career, into their talents and limitations, and into their values and how they will fit in with the alternatives being considered. As Schein points out, "too many people never ask, much less attempt to answer, these kinds of questions. It was shocking to me when I conducted the interview for the MIT panel study and discovered how many respondents said that they had never in 10 years of their career asked themselves the kinds of questions which I was asking just to fill in the details of their job history."[37]

MANAGING PROMOTIONS AND TRANSFERS

Performance appraisal and career management often lead to concrete human resource actions such as promotion, transfer, layoff, and retirement. These matters are addressed in the following sections.

Making Promotion Decisions

There are three main promotion-related decisions employers have to make, and how these decisions are made will affect employees' motivation, performance, and morale.

Decision 1: Seniority or Competence?

Probably the most important decision concerns whether promotion will be based on seniority or competence, or some combination of the two. From the point of view of motivation, promotion based on competence is best. However, an organization's ability to use competence as a sole criterion depends on several things, most notably whether or not the firm is unionized or governed by employment equity requirements. Union agreements often contain a clause such as the following that emphasizes seniority in promotions: "In the advancement of employees to higher paid jobs when ability, merit, and capacity are equal, employees with the highest seniority will be given preference."[38] Although this might seem to leave the door open for giving a person with less seniority (but slightly better abilities) the inside track for a job, labour arbitrators have generally held that where clauses such as these are binding only substantial differences in abilities can be taken into account.

Decision 2: How is Competence Measured?

Where promotion is to be based on competence, employers must decide how competence will be defined and measured. As we explained in the previous chapter, defining and measuring past performance should not be difficult as long as the job is defined, standards are set, and one or more appraisal tools are used to record the employee's performance. But promotion also requires predicting the person's potential; thus, an employer must have some valid procedure for predicting a candidate's future performance.

Many employers simply use prior performance as a guide and extrapolate, or assume, that (based on the person's prior performance) he or she will perform well on the new job. This is the simplest procedure to use.

Some other employers use tests to evaluate promotable employees[39] and to identify those employees with executive potential.[40] Others use assessment centres to assess management potential.

Decision 3: Formal or Informal?

Next (particularly if the organization decides to promote based on competence) the employer must decide if the process will be a formal or informal one. Many employers still depend on an informal system. Here, the availability and requirements of open positions are kept secret, and the promotion decisions are made by key managers from among employees they know personally and also from among those who, for one reason or another, have impressed them with their activities or presence.[41] The problem is that when employers do not make employees aware of what jobs are available, what the criteria are for promotion, and how promotion decisions are made, the link between performance and promotion is cut and the effectiveness of promotion as a reward is diminished.

Many employers therefore do establish formal, published promotion policies and procedures. Here, employees are generally provided with a formal promotion policy statement that describes the criteria by which promotions are awarded. Formal systems often include a policy of open-posting jobs, which states that open positions and their requirements will be posted and circulated to all employees. Computerized information systems can be especially useful for maintaining qualifications inventories on hundreds or thousands of employees. The net effect of such actions is twofold: (1) an employer can ensure that all qualified employees are considered for openings; and (2) promotion becomes more closely linked with performance in the minds of employees and as a result its effectiveness as a reward increases.

Handling Transfers

Reasons for Transfers

A transfer involves a movement from one job to another, usually with no change in salary or grade. There are several reasons why such changes take place. Employees may seek transfers for personal enrichment, for more interesting jobs, for greater convenience—better hours, location of work, and so on—or for jobs offering greater possibilities for advancement.[42] Employers may transfer a worker from a position where he or she is no longer needed to one where he or she is needed, or to retain a senior employee (bumping where necessary a less senior person in another department), or (more generally) to find a better fit for the employee within the firm. Many employers choose to consider demotions as transfers, specifically transfers into a lower employment classification. Here it is important that they recognize employee rights, as discussed in Chapters 2 and 16.

Effect on Family Life

Many firms have had policies of routinely transferring employees from locale to locale, either to give their employees more exposure to a wide range of jobs or to fill open positions with trained employees. Such transfer policies have fallen into disfavour, though, partly because of the cost of relocating employees (paying moving expenses, buying back the employee's current home, and perhaps financing his or her next home, for instance) and partly because it was assumed that frequent transfers had a negative effect on an employee's family life.

But one study seems to indicate that the latter argument, at least, is without merit.[43] The study compared the experiences of "mobile" families who had moved on the average of once every two years with "stable" families who had lived in their communities for more than eight years.

In general, the stable families were not more satisfied with their marriages and family life or children's well-being than were the mobile families. In fact, mobile men and women believed their lives to be more interesting and their capabilities greater than did stable men and women. Likewise, they were more satisfied with their family lives and marriage than were stable men and women.

However, mobility was associated with dissatisfaction with social relationships among men and women (for instance, in terms of "opportunities to make friends at work and in the community"). Developing new social relationships was cited as a problem for children of mobile parents, with "missing old friends and making new friends" a bigger problem for teenagers than for younger children.

The major finding of this study, though, is that for these people there were few differences between mobile and stable families. Few families in the mobile group believed moving was easy. However, despite their mobility, these families were as satisfied with all aspects of their lives (except social relationships) as were stable families. Yet—this study notwithstanding—there is no doubt that employees do resist geographical transfers more today than they did even a few years ago. In one study, for instance, "the proportion of top executives who are `eager or willing' to make a geographic move has dropped ten percentage points to 51.5% since 1979, while 45% described themselves as reluctant."[44]

MANAGING LAYOFFS AND RETIREMENT

Employee separations are a fact of life in organizations and can be initiated by either the employer or employee. For the employer, reduced sales or profits may require layoffs, for instance, while employees may terminate their employment so as to retire or to seek better jobs.

Managing Layoffs

Layoff Defined

The term **layoff** refers to a situation in which three conditions are present: (1) there is no work available for the employee who is being sent home; (2) management expects the no-work situation to be temporary and probably short term; and (3) management intends to recall the employee when work is again available.45 (A layoff is therefore not a termination, which is a permanent severing of the employment relationship, although some employers do use "layoff" as a euphemism for discharge or termination.)

layoff

Bumping/Layoff Procedures

Employers who encounter frequent business slowdowns and layoffs usually draw up detailed procedures that allow employees to use their seniority to remain on the job. Most layoff procedures have these features in common:[46]

1. For the most part, seniority is the ultimate determiner of who will work.
2. Seniority can give way to merit or ability but usually only when none of the senior employees is qualified for a particular job.
3. Seniority is usually based on the date the employee joined the organization, not the date he or she took a particular job.
4. Because seniority is usually company-wide, an employee in one job is usually allowed to bump or displace an employee in another job provided a more senior employee is able to do the job in question without further training.

Alternatives to Layoffs

Many employers today recognize the enormous investments they have in their "human capital," investments they made in recruiting, screening, and training their employees and in developing their commitment and loyalty. As a result, many employers are hesitant to lay off employees at the first sign of business decline; instead, they are using new approaches to either blunt the effects of the layoffs or eliminate the layoffs entirely.

There are several alternatives to a layoff. With the **voluntary reduction in pay plan**, all employees agree to reductions in pay in order to keep everyone working. Other employers arrange to have all or most of their employees accumulate their vacation time and to concentrate their vacations during slow periods; temporary help thus does not have to be hired for vacationing employees during peak periods, and employment automatically falls off when business declines. Other employees agree to take **voluntary time off**, which again has the effect of reducing the employer's payroll and avoiding the need for a layoff. Control Data Corporation avoids layoffs with what it call its "rings of defence" approach. In its plan, temporary supplemental employees are hired with the specific understanding that their work is of a temporary nature and they may be laid off at any time or fired. Then when layoffs come, the first "ring of defence" is the group of supplemental workers. Control Data contends that because the temporary nature of their jobs is understood, hard feelings are avoided when these people are laid off, while permanent Control Data employees can be secure in the knowledge that they probably will never be laid off.[47]

voluntary reduction in pay plan

voluntary time off

Outplacement Counselling[48]

outplacement
counselling

Outplacement counselling is a systematic process by which a terminated person is trained and counselled in the techniques of (1) self-appraisal and (2) securing a new job that is appropriate to his or her needs and talents.[49] As the term is generally used, outplacement does not mean the employer takes responsibility for placing the terminated person in a new job. Instead, it is a counselling service whose purpose is to provide the person with advice, instructions, and a sounding board to help formulate career goals and successfully execute a job search. **Outplacement counselling** thus might more accurately (but more ponderously) be called "career counselling and job search skills for terminated employees." The counselling itself is done either by the employer's in-house specialist or by outside consultants. The outplacement counselling is considered part of the terminated employee's support or severance package.

In practice, outplacement counselling is aimed at providing a terminated employee with much the same knowledge and skills as contained in this chapter. As summarized in Figure 10.3, the first part of the counselling includes a personal debriefing aimed at reducing the trauma of the termination, and then vocational testing to identify the person's occupational orientations, skills, and aptitudes. The next step is to define the person's prior work accomplishments in order to identify not only the person's saleable skills but the key accomplishments, or "worth points," he or she can use to sell himself or herself for potential jobs. Specific job objectives (in terms of where the person would like to be five years hence, for instance) are then determined. Next, outplacement moves into its job search skills phase, in which the person is trained in basic job search skills like résumé preparation, writing direct-mail letters, and being interviewed. In one survey, 14 of the 41 employer respondents offered terminated employees both severance pay and outplacement services, while 17 of the 41 had severance pay plans alone.[50]

Retirement

Retirement for most employees is a bittersweet experience. For some it is the culmination of their careers, a time when they can relax and enjoy the fruits of their labour without worrying about the problems of work. For others, it is the retirement itself that is the trauma, as the once busy employee tries to cope with being suddenly "nonproductive" and with the strange (and not entirely pleasant) experience of being home every day with nothing to do. For many retirees, in fact, maintaining a sense of identity and self-worth without a full-time job is the single most important task they will face. And it is one that employers are increasingly trying to help their retirees cope with, as a logical last step in the career management process.

Preretirement Counselling

About 30% of the employers in one recent survey said they had formal preretirement programs aimed at easing the passage of their employees into retirement.[51] The most common preretirement practices were

- Explanation of pension benefits (reported by 97% of those with preretirement education programs)
- Leisure time counselling (86%)
- Financial and investment counselling (84%)

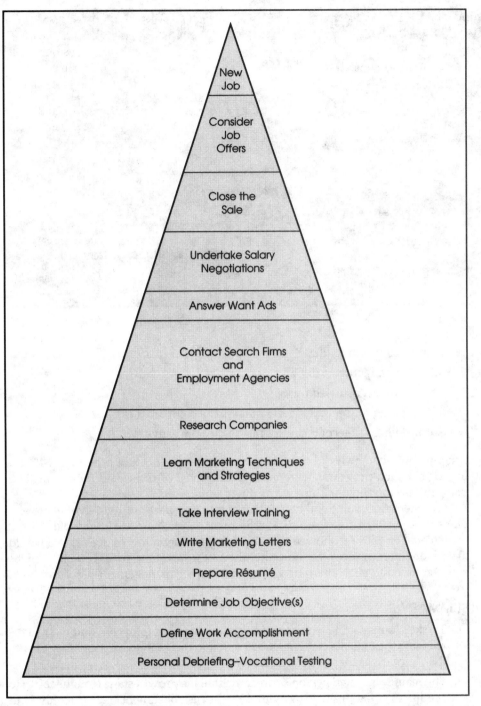

FIGURE 10.3
Outplacement
Counselling: Steps in
the Job Search

New
Job

Consider
Job
Offers

Close the
Sale

Undertake Salary
Negotiations

Answer Want Ads

Contact Search Firms
and
Employment Agencies

Research Companies

Learn Marketing Techniques
and Strategies

Take Interview Training

Write Marketing Letters

Prepare Résumé

Determine Job Objective(s)

Define Work Accomplishment

Personal Debriefing–Vocational Testing

SOURCE: F. Leigh Branham, "How to Evaluate Executive Outplacement Services," *Personnel Journal*,
April 1983, p. 325

On the Front Line

Career planning has always been a pretty low priority item for Carter Cleaning, since "just getting workers to come to work and then keeping them honest is enough of a problem," as Jack likes to say. Yet Jennifer thought it might not be a bad idea to give some thought to what a career planning program might involve for Carter. A lot of their employees had been with them for years in dead-end jobs, and she frankly felt a little bad for them. "Perhaps we could help them gain a better perspective on what they want to do," she thought. And she definitely believed that the store management group needed some better

career direction if Carter Cleaning was to develop and grow. Her questions were as follows:

1. What would be the advantages to Carter Cleaning of setting up such a career planning program?

2. Who should participate in the program? All employees? Selected employees?

3. Describe the program you would propose for injecting a career planning and development perspective into the Carter Cleaning Centres.

- Health counselling (82%)
- Living arrangements (59%)
- Psychological counselling (35%)
- Counselling for second careers outside the company (31%)
- Counselling for second careers inside the company (4%)

Among employers that did not have preretirement education programs, 64% believed that such programs were needed, and most of these said their firms had plans to develop them within two or three years.

Another important trend here is that of granting part-time employment to employees as an alternative to outright retirement. Several recent surveys of blue and white-collar employees showed that about half of all employees over age 55 would like to continue working part-time after they retire, and employers can probably be expected to build such alternatives into their career-management processes.

SUMMARY

1. The key to managing a career is insight into what employees want out of a career, into their talents and limitations, and into their values and how they fit with the alternatives they are considering.

2. The main stages in a person's career include the growth stage (roughly birth to age 14); exploration stage (roughly 15 to 24); establishment stage (roughly 24 to 44, and the heart of most people's work lives); maintenance stage (45 to 65); and decline stage (pre-retirement). The establishment stage itself may consist of a trial substage, a stabilization substage, and a midcareer crisis substage.

3. The first step in planning a career is to learn as much as possible about an employee's interest, aptitudes, and skills. The human resource specialist should

begin by identifying the employee's occupational orientation: realistic, investigative, social, conventional, enterprising, or artistic. The next step is to identify skills and rank them from high to low. Finally, the HR specialist should identify career anchors: technical/functional, managerial, creativity, autonomy, and security.

4. Supervisors play an important role in the career management process. Some important guidelines for supervisors include the following: avoid reality shock, be demanding, provide realistic job previews, conduct career-oriented performance appraisals, and encourage job rotation.

5. In making promotion decisions, an organization has to decide between seniority and competence, between a formal or informal system, and how to measure competence.

6. Transfers today are reportedly not as traumatic as they are popularly thought to be, but the proportion of top executives willing to transfer is still falling.

7. A layoff is a situation in which there is no work available for the employee being sent home, but management expects the situation to be temporary and the employee to be recalled. In most cases, formal bumping/layoff procedures are developed; these generally tie layoffs to seniority. Alternatives to layoffs include voluntary pay reductions, voluntary time off, and specially scheduled vacation time.

KEY TERMS

career	stabilization substage	aptitudes and special talents
career cycle	mid-career crisis substage	career anchors
growth stage	maintenance stage	layoff
exploration stage	decline stage	voluntary reduction in pay plan
establishment stage	occupational orientations	voluntary time off
trial substage	occupational skills	outplacement counselling

DISCUSSION QUESTIONS

1. Briefly describe each of the stages in a typical career.
2. What is a career anchor? What are the main types of career anchors discussed in this chapter?
3. What are the main types of occupational orientations discussed in this chapter?
4. Describe some important sources of information you could use to learn about careers of interest to you.
5. Write a one-page essay stating "Where I would like to be career-wise 10 years from today."
6. Explain career-related factors to keep in mind when making the employee's first assignments.
7. What are some of the important factors to consider when making promotion and transfer decisions?

CASE INCIDENT: Hard Work Does Not Always Pay Off?

Lori Nichols, a well educated, hard-working, energetic, and ambitious individual was passed over for a promotion in the human resources department for the second time recently. When the position became vacant, most of her co-workers thought Lori was the odds-on favourite to become Manager of Labour Relations. Lori holds an undergraduate degree in psychology and a master of arts in labour relations. She is currently pursuing the CPM designation. Lori did well on the psychological tests and did well during the interview.

Lori is very well respected by, and is popular with, her co-workers. She has worked with Extra Strength Auto Glass for over one year in two different positions and is currently the Employment Equity Co-ordinator.

Last Friday the decision was announced: the external candidate was chosen. When the Director spoke to Lori, she said, "While I am impressed with your educational qualifications I do not believe that you have the relevant experience required for the labour relations position. Four of our five union contracts expire shortly and I need someone with experience to handle that portfolio." Lori suggested that she was told the same story six months ago and felt that she was the best qualified candidate for the job. The Director said, "I believe that someday this may be the position for you, but I do not think that is the case now. By the way, you may be interested in knowing that I have added an Assistant Labour Relations Officer position to the department. If you are interested I would be happy to consider you for that position. This position will provide good exposure to anyone interested in that field."

Questions

1. What implications can be drawn from Lori's being passed over for promotion?
2. What should Lori do?
3. What responsibilities, if any, does the organization have in assisting Lori to meet her career aspirations?

EXPERIENTIAL EXERCISE

Because you are reading this book you are probably at a point in your career where you have already made some important choices, such as choice of an occupation or general field of work or choice of a degree program. However, there are always other issues to be resolved and decisions to be made throughout a career.

It sometimes aids the decision process to talk it over with someone else. In this exercise, you will be working in groups of three. Each person will have the opportunity to be interviewed about his or her career choices, to be a career interviewer (or counsellor), and to be an observer. Try to learn from each role—how to be a better career decision maker, how to be a better career counsellor, and how to be a more sensitive observer of interviewing and helping processes.

Instructions for the Exercise:

The class should split into groups of three. There will be three rounds to the exercise. In each round, there will be three roles: interviewer, interviewee, and observer. At the end of each round, you will switch roles and assume a role you haven't played yet. Therefore, at the end of the third round, each person in the trio should have had a chance to try every role.

Step 1. Round 1. Pick one person to act as interviewer, one as interviewee, and one as observer. For 15 minutes, the interviewer will conduct a counselling interview with the interviewee on the topic of career choice. Interview questions are provided as a guide; questions may be selected or the interviewer may make them up.

During the interview, the observer should be silent and should take notes on the process of the interview. The observer should also act as timekeeper, stopping the interview after 15 minutes.

For the next 5 minutes, the observer will feed back his or her observations and all three members will discuss the interview. Focus on the following two issues:

a. What did the interviewee learn?

b. What did the interviewer or interviewee do that helped or hindered the interview?

Step 2. Round 2. Switch roles (for example, interviewer becomes interviewee, interviewee becomes observer, observer becomes interviewer). Follow the same procedure as in Round 1.

Step 3. Round 3. Switch roles again, as in Round 2. Be sure that no one plays the same role twice. Follow the same procedure as in Round 1.

Step 4. Class Discussion. Meet again as a class. Discuss what the interviewees seemed to be learning. What career choice issues were discussed most frequently? What choices or solutions were considered?

Also discuss what people learned about the process of interviewing and helping. What did the interviewer do that helped or hindered the decision-making process? What did the interviewee do to help or hinder his or her own progress?

Interview Questions

1. How would you describe yourself as a person?

2. What are you best at doing? Worst?

3. What do you really enjoy doing most? Least?

4. What have been one or two of your best successes—times when you felt especially productive and proud of your capabilities and potential?

5. What would you stop doing if you could?

6. What would you like to do more?

7. What would you like to learn more about?

8. What aspects of yourself do you like most? Least?

9. Could you describe your ideal self?

10. Who are your heroes? What do you like about them?

11. If you could have any job at all, what would you do? What would be an ideal job for you?

12. What do you plan to do during the next five years? (If you haven't yet decided, pretend you had to decide *right now*. What would you choose to do?)

13. What are the pros and cons of the different career options you are considering right now?

14. What way are you leaning?

15. Pretend a person amazingly similar to you (background, interests, plans, and so on) came to you for advice on the same issue you're wrestling with now. What advice would you give this person?

SOURCE: Douglas Hall, *Careers in Organizations* (Pacific Palisades, Calif.: Goodyear, 1976), pp. 127-128.

NOTES

1. James W. Walker, *Human Resource Planning* (New York: McGraw-Hill Book Company, 1980), p. 251.

2. Lawrence A. Klatt, Robert G. Murdick, and Frederick E. Schuster, *Human Resource Management* (Columbus: Charles E. Merril Publishing Company, 1985), p. 383.

3. Walker, *Human Resource Planning*, p. 251.

4. Klatt and others, *Human Resource Management*, p. 383.

5. David J. Cherrington, *Organizational Behavior* (Boston: Allyn and Bacon, 1989), p. 350.

6. Walker, p. 253; see also Klatt and others, p. 383.

7. Ibid.

8. Except as noted, this section is based on J. Richard Hackman and J. Lloyd Suttle, *Improving Life at Work* (Santa Monica, Calif.: Goodyear, 1977); see also William Steiges, "Can We Legislate the Humanization of Work?" in W. Clay Hamner and Frank Schmidt, *Contemporary Problems in Personnel* (Chicago: St. Clair Press, 1974).

9. Suttle, *Improving Life at Work*, p. 4.

10. Donald Super and others, *Vocational Development: A Framework for Research* (New York: Teachers College Press, 1957); Edgar Schein, *Career Dynamics: Matching Individual and Organizational Needs* (Reading, Mass.: Addison-Wesley Publishing, 1978).

11. Schein, *Career Dynamics*, pp. 128-129.

12. John Holland, *Making Vocational Choices: A Theory of Careers* (Englewood Cliffs, N.J.: Prentice-Hall, 1973).

13. Richard Bolles, *The Quick Job Hunting Map* (Berkeley, Calif.: Ten Speed Press, 1979), pp. 5-6.

14. Schein, *Career Dynamics*, pp. 128-129.

15. Richard Bolles, *What Color Is Your Parachute?* (Berkeley, Calif.: Ten Speed Press, 1976), p. 86.

16. *The Guidance Information System*, Time Share Corporation, 630 Oakwood Avenue, West Hartford, Conn. 06110; described in Andrew Dubrin, *Human Relations: A Job-Oriented Approach* (Reston, Va.: Reston, 1982), p. 358.

17. Gail Martin, "The Job Hunters Guide to the Library," *Occupational Outlook Quarterly* (Fall 1980), p. 10.

18. Robert Jameson, *The Professional Job Changing System* (Verona, N.H.: Performance Dynamics, 1975).

19. Richard Payne, *How to Get a Better Job Quicker* (New York: New American Library, 1987).

20. Ibid.

21. Richard Reilly, Mary Tenopyr, and Steven Sperling, "The Effects of Job Previews on Job Acceptance and Survival Rates of Telephone Operator Candidates," *Journal of Applied Psychology*, Vol. 64 (1979).

22. Schein, *Career Dynamics*, p. 19.

23. For example, telephone operators or sewing machine operators.

24. D. W. Ilgen and W. Seely, "Realistic Expectations as an Aid in Reducing Voluntary Resignations," *Journal of Applied Psychology*, Vol. 59 (1974), pp. 452-455.

25. Douglas Bray, Richard Campbell, and Donald Grant, *Formative Years in Business* (New York: Wiley, 1974).

26. J. Sterling Livingston, "Pygmalion in Management," *Harvard Business Review*, Vol. 48 (July-August 1969), pp. 81-89.

27. Joel Ross, *Managing Productivity* (Reston, Va.: Reston Publishing Co., Inc., 1979).

28. Douglas Hall and Francine Hall, "What's New in Career Management?" *Organizational Dynamics*, Vol. 4 (Summer 1976).

29. H. G. Kaufman, *Obsolescence and Professional Career Development* (New York: AMACOM, 1974).

30. Hall and Hall, "What's New in Career Management?" p. 350.

31. For a discussion of the role played by the supervisor in appraisals, see Donald Hall, "Career Planning for Employee Development: A Primer for Managers," *California Management Review*, Vol. 20 (1977), pp. 23-25.

32. Schein, *Career Dynamics*, p. 19.

33. See, for example, D. B. Miller, *Personal Vitality* (Reading, Mass.: Addison-Wesley Publishing Co., 1977) and *Personal Vitality Workbook* (Reading, Mass.: Addison-Wesley, 1977).

34. Albert Griffith, "Career Development: What Organizations Are Doing About It," *Personnel*, Vol. 57 (1980), pp. 63-69; see also Richard Vosburgh, "The Annual Human Resource Review (A Career Planning System)," *Personnel Journal*, Vol. 59 (October 1980), pp. 830-837.

35. Schein, *Career Dynamics*, pp. 252-253, and Bowen and Hall, "Career Planning and Employee Development," p. 279.

36. For self-diagnosis books, see, for example, G. A. Ford and G. L. Lippitt, *A Life Planning Workbook* (Fairfax, Va.: NTL Learning Resources Corp., 1972).

37. Schein, *Career Dynamics* p. 253.

38. Pigors and Meyers, *Personnel Administration*, p. 283.

39. National Industrial Conference Board, *Personnel Practices in Factory and Office*, Studies in Personnel Policy No. 145 (1954), pp. 12-69.

40. Bureau of National Affairs, *Finding and Training Potential Executives*, Personnel Policies Form, Survey No. 58, September 1960, p. 4.

41. See, for example, Joseph Famularo, *Handbook of Modern Personnel Administration* (New York: McGraw-Hill, 1972), p. 17.

42. Commerce Clearing House, *Personnel Practices/Communications*, p. 1351.

43. Ibid.

44. Commerce Clearing House, "Top Executive Are Growing Reluctant to Relocate," *Ideas and Trends*, December 10, 1982, p. 218.

45. Commerce Clearing House, *Personnel Practices/Communications*, p. 1402.

46. Ibid. p. 1410.

47. Commerce Clearing House, "Ideas and Trends in Personnel," July 9, 1982, p. 131.

48. Ibid., pp. 132-146.

49. Ibid., p. 132.

50. Hermine Zagat Levine, "Outplacement and Severance Pay Practices," *Personnel*, Vol. 62, no. 9 (September 1985), pp. 13-21.

51. "Preretirement Education Programs," *Personnel*, Vol. 59 (May-June 1982), p. 47. For a discussion of why it is important for retiring employees to promote aspects of their lives aside from their careers, see Daniel Halloran, "The Retirement Identity Crisis—and How to Beat It," *Personnel Journal*, Vol. 64 (May 1985), pp. 38-40. For an example of a program aimed at training pre-retirees to prepare for the financial aspects of their retirement, see, for example, Silvia Odenwald, "Pre-Retirement Training Gathers Steam," *Training and Development Journal*, Vol. 40, no. 2 (February 1986), pp. 62-63.

SUGGESTED READINGS

Burack, Elmer H. and Nicholas J. Mathys. *Career Management in Organizations: A Practical Human Resource Planning Approach.* Brace-Park Press, 1980.

Greenhaus, Jeffrey H. *Career Management.* New York: The Dryden Press, 1987.

Hall, Douglas T. *Careers in Organizations.* Goodyear, 1976.

Levinson, Hary, ed. *Designing and Managing Your Career.* Cambridge, MA: Harvard Business School Press, 1989.

Schein, Edgar H. *Career Dynamics.* Reading, Mass: Addison-Wesley, 1978.

PART FOUR

COMPENSATION, PROTECTION, AND MOTIVATION

CHAPTER ELEVEN
FUNDAMENTALS OF MOTIVATION

After studying this chapter, you should be able to

1. Explain what motivation is.
2. Develop an expectancy model diagram of motivation.
3. Discuss the Maslow needs hierarchy.
4. Compare and contrast the Maslow and the Herzberg motivation theories.
5. Summarize what we know about "what people want."
6. Explain how human resource management activities influence motivation.

OVERVIEW

This chapter starts a new part of this book, on compensating, protecting, and motivating employees. People will be motivated if they think there is a good chance that effort on their part will lead to obtaining some desired reward. In Parts One, Two, and Three (Recruitment and Placement, Training and Development, and Appraisal and Career Management), we discussed techniques aimed at ensuring that employees have the skills and abilities to do their jobs, since it is only by being able to do their jobs that they will obtain their rewards and be motivated.

In Part Four, we turn to the second aspect of motivation—the rewards themselves. To reiterate, if employees do not find the rewards, salary, promotions, etc., attractive, they will not be motivated. We devote four chapters (12-15) to the question of rewards, but before going on to those chapters we thought it important to briefly review the fundamentals and mechanics of motivation—what it is, what rewards people find important, and how human resource management activities (like training) affect motivation.

INTRODUCTION: MOTIVATION AND HUMAN RESOURCE MANAGEMENT

The subject of motivation is central to everything one studies in human resource management. After all, the bottom line of recruiting, selecting, training, paying, and appraising workers is, largely, one of optimizing employee performance. To do this requires an understanding of what motivates people—what makes them "tick"—as well as what the motivational implications are of HR processes such as job analysis, selection, establishing pay plans, and performance appraisal. For instance, job analysis, selection, and training help ensure the person has the ability to do the job, while compensation helps ensure he or she has the desire; as we have noted, both ability and desire are needed for motivated performance to occur. This chapter briefly reviews some major theories of motivation, explains two applied motivation techniques (job enrichment and behaviour modification) that HR managers often use, and finally, summarizes how motivation affects and is affected by HR activities such as job analysis, selection, and compensation management.

Relationship of Motivation to Other HRM Functions

People are motivated to accomplish those tasks that they feel will lead to rewards. This is the essence of motivation, and it is an idea that has important implications for all human resource management activities. Specifically, here is how these activities directly affect employee motivation:

Job analysis: Job analysis is in many ways the first human resource activity that affects motivation. Most people are not too motivated to perform a job when they find they do not have the skills and abilities to do it, and it is through job analysis that one determines what the job entails, and what skills and abilities one should look for in candidates for the job.

Recruitment of human resources: Motivation depends on recruiting employees who have the aptitude to do the job well, and the more qualified applicants there are, the higher standards can be. Application blanks are the first step in screening out the best candidates for the job.

Selection process: In addition to application blanks, there are a variety of tools—tests, previous experience, assessment centres, and so on—that can help in choosing the best qualified, most highly motivated candidates: candidates with the ability to get the job done and get rewarded. One must keep in mind that the ability to do the job is one prerequisite to motivation. Effective interviewing is also an important tool in the selection process.

Orientation, socialization, and training: Effective orientation is an important motivating technique that can be used to strengthen employees' commitment to the organization and increase their productivity. Employee training provides employees with the basic knowledge and skills necessary to perform their jobs—and therefore be motivated.

Management development: Management development provides managers with the developmental activities they will need to function more effectively.

Performance appraisal: Performance appraisal evaluates employees' motivation and performance, and determines what rewards are appropriate.

Career management: Career management assists employees in career planning, establishing career goals, and career counselling to further increase their motivation—or, if necessary, to correct their mistakes—while providing them with career guidance.

Compensation management: Wages (or salaries) are the most widely used rewards for motivating performance, but to be effective they must be adequate and equitable, and it is job evaluation that helps make them so.

Financial incentives: Financial incentives, which tie rewards to performance, are powerful motivation tools.

Benefits and services: Benefits and services are important rewards, and therefore influence employees' motivation. Employees' preferences for different benefits vary—with the employees' age, marital status, and so on—and so it is important to "customize" the benefits package so it is used to its best advantage.

Quality of work life and nonfinancial motivation techniques: To motivate employees one also tries to tap their higher-level needs; through quality circles and other techniques, challenges—and thus rewards—are built into the job itself.

HUMAN NEEDS AND MOTIVATION

Most psychologists believe that all motivation is ultimately derived from a tension that results when one or more of our important needs are unsatisfied. Thus, a person who is hungry is motivated to find food; a person who needs security is motivated to find it; and a person with a compelling need to accomplish challenging tasks might try to conquer a mountain. The work of three psychologists—Abraham Maslow, John Atkinson, and Frederick Herzberg—is closely associated with human needs and motivation.

Abraham Maslow and the Needs Hierarchy

needs hierarchy

Maslow says that people have five basic categories of needs: physiological, safety, social, ego, and self-actualization needs. He says these needs form a **needs hierarchy** or ladder (as in Figure 11.1) and that (generally speaking) each need becomes active or aroused only when the lower needs are reasonably satisfied.

Physiological Needs

The lowest level in Maslow's hierarchy contains the physiological needs. These are the most basic needs everyone has, for food, drink, shelter, and rest.

Safety Needs

When the physiological needs are reasonably satisfied—when one is no longer thirsty, has enough to eat, has a roof overhead, and so forth—then the safety needs become activated. They become the needs that the person tries to satisfy, the needs that motivate him or her. These are the needs for protection against danger or deprivation, and the need for security.

Social Needs

Once a person's physiological and safety needs are satisfied, according to Maslow, they no longer motivate behaviour. Now the social needs become the active moti-

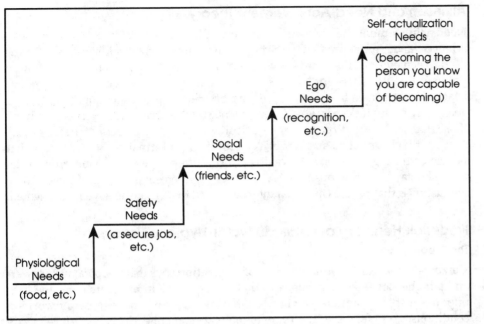

FIGURE 11.1
Maslow's Needs
Hierarchy

Note: Each higher-order need becomes active only when succeedingly lower-level needs are fairly well satisfied.

vators of behaviour—needs for affiliation, for giving and receiving affection, and for friendship.

Ego Needs

Next in the hierarchy are the ego needs, which Maslow has interpreted as

1. Those needs that relate to one's self-esteem—needs for self-confidence, for independence, for achievement, for knowledge
2. Those needs that relate to one's reputation—needs for status, for recognition, for appreciation, for the deserved respect of one's peers

One of the big differences between the ego needs and the physiological, safety, and social needs is that the ego needs (and the self-actualization needs discussed next) are rarely satisfied. Thus, according to Maslow, people have a constant, infinite need for more achievement, more knowledge, and more recognition. The physiological, safety, and social needs, however, are finite; they can be and often are fairly well satisfied. As with all needs, ego needs motivate behaviour, says Maslow, only when the lower-level needs are reasonably satisfied.

Self-Actualization

Finally, the highest-order need begins to dominate a person's behaviour once all lower-level needs are reasonably satisfied. This is the need for self-actualization or fulfillment, the need to become the person one feels one has the potential to become. This is the need that drives an artist to express herself on canvas, the need that motivates a student to work all day and then pursue a university degree in night school. This need, as with the ego needs, is rarely if ever satisfied.

Atkinson and Need Achievement Theory

need achievement theory

Need achievement theory focuses on one of Maslow's "ego" needs—the need to achieve—and aims at predicting the behaviour of those who rank high or low in the need to achieve. Atkinson says people who are high in the need to achieve have a predisposition to strive for success.[1] They are highly motivated to obtain the satisfaction that comes from accomplishing or achieving some challenging task or goal. They prefer tasks for which there is a reasonable chance for success and avoid those that are either too easy or too difficult. Relatedly, such people prefer getting specific, timely criticism and feedback about their performance. Studies show that people with a high need to achieve do perform better, especially on entrepreneurial tasks like starting a new business.[2] And one of the interesting aspects of achievement motivation is that people can apparently be trained to be more achievement-oriented.

Frederick Herzberg and the Motivator-Hygiene Theory
The Theory

motivator-hygiene theory of motivation

Herzberg's **motivator-hygiene theory of motivation** says that people have a lower- and a higher-level set of needs, and that the best way to motivate someone is to offer to satisfy the higher-level needs. Offering a person a raise or better working conditions, says Herzberg, is no way to motivate someone, since lower-level needs are quickly satisfied. And once they are satisfied (once the person has enough income, for instance), the only way to motivate the person is by offering even more money, or even better working conditions, in an endlessly escalating process. The right way to motivate someone, says Herzberg, is to arrange the job in such a way that the person gets a "charge" out of doing it. Then, by performing the job, the person is motivated to keep trying to satisfy his or her infinite craving to satisfy higher-level needs, for such things as achievement and recognition.

Hygienes and Motivators

hygiene factors

Based on his studies, Herzberg believes that the factors (which he calls hygienes) that can satisfy lower-level needs are different from those (which he calls motivators) that can satisfy (or partially satisfy) a person's higher-level needs. He says that if **hygiene factors** (like better working conditions, salary, and supervision) are inadequate, employees will become dissatisfied. But—and this is extremely important—adding more of these hygiene factors (like salary) to the job is not the way to try to motivate someone, since once the lower-level needs are satisfied, it is necessary to increase the incentive to further motivate the person. Hygienes like salary and working conditions, says Herzberg, will only prevent dissatisfaction (as when an employee thinks his or her salary is too low). Offering more hygienes is a very inefficient way to encourage motivation. Figure 11.2 illustrates Herzberg's two-factor motivator and hygiene theory.

motivator factors

On the other hand, says Herzberg, "job content" or **"motivator" factors** (like opportunities for achievement, recognition, responsibility, and more challenging jobs) can motivate employees, because they appeal to employees' higher-level needs for achievement and self-esteem. These are needs that are never completely satisfied and for which most people have an infinite craving. Thus, according to Herzberg, the best way to motivate employees is to build challenges and opportunities for achievement into their jobs. The method Herzberg recommends for applying his theory is called job enrichment.

FIGURE 11.2
Herzberg's Two Factor
Theory

MOTIVATORS	HYGIENES
Work itself	Company policies and administration
Recognition	Salary
Responsibility	Wroking conditions
Achievement	Relationship with supervisors
Growth	Relationship with subordinates
Advancement	Security
	Status

Job Enrichment Versus Job Enlargement and Job Rotation

Though the terms are sometimes used interchangeably, job enlargement and job enrichment are not exactly the same thing. Job enlargement usually involves the horizontal expansion of the worker's job, by increasing the number of similar tasks he or she is assigned. For example, if the work involves assembling chairs, the worker who previously only bolted the seat to the legs might take on the additional tasks of assembling the legs and attaching the back as well. **Job enrichment** usually involves a vertical expansion of the worker's job, in that tasks formerly carried out by his or her supervisor are now assigned to the worker. It involves redesigning jobs, for example, by letting workers schedule their own work and check their own results. The purpose is to increase the opportunities for experiencing a feeling of responsibility, achievement, growth, and recognition that result from doing the job well.

job enrichment

Job rotation involves systematically moving workers from one job to another. For instance, on an assembly line a worker might spend an hour fitting doors, the next hour installing headlamps, the next hour fitting bumpers, and so on.

Job enrichment is an important human resource management technique for several reasons. To a great extent job design—the determination of exactly what duties will comprise one job—concerns the question of how specialized versus broad the job will be. Thus, in producing a job description (as discussed in Chapter 4), the degree to which the job involves (1) repetitively performing one or two duties or (2) performing (less frequently) a wider range of duties is or should be a basic concern. Making that determination requires knowing the pros and cons of job enrichment.

Aside from its basic use in job analysis, job enrichment is an important motivation technique. Human resource managers in particular are often called upon for advice on how to improve worker performance, attendance, and morale; job enrichment is one technique they can use.

Pros and Cons of Job Enrichment

Job enrichment can improve employee performance and attendance. Few rewards are as powerful for a person as the sense of accomplishment and achievement that comes from doing a job that he or she genuinely wants to do, and doing it well. Thus, the person who collects stamps, builds a ham radio, or volunteers at a hospital generally does not have to be coerced or prodded into doing the job well since the job carries its own intrinsic rewards—in terms of challenge, achievement, and recognition. In other words, this sort of job—its content, functions, and specific duties—is designed in such a way that performing it makes the person feel good. Needless to say, therefore, designing jobs to provide such intrinsic rewards can substantially increase employee morale and performance.

These advantages notwithstanding, job enrichment also has two big drawbacks. First, job enrichment can be expensive. Specifically, it increases costs for exactly those reasons that specialization reduces them: it requires more time for learning; there is more waste of material during the training period; there is more time lost in switching from task to task; employees are not quite as proficient at each task; and hiring is made less efficient.

The other drawback is that not all employees react well to job enrichment. Given a choice between working on a routine, "boring" job on an assembly line and working on a more enriched job, many employees choose the anonymity and simplicity of the assembly-line job.

So how effective is job enrichment? It is difficult to say. Many programs have been successful while just as many have failed. Even where job enrichment programs have apparently been successful (at improving attendance or performance), it is impossible to say that it is the job enrichment that caused the improvement, since other changes are normally made as well. At the Volvo auto plant in Sweden, for instance, a job enrichment program seems to have caused improved attendance and performance. But while the jobs were being enriched, workers' wages were also being increased, better worker housing was being built near the plant by the company, and day care centres were established as well. It is therefore almost impossible to unscramble the effect of the job enrichment from the other changes that normally occur with the job enrichment. The bottom line seems to be that job enrichment can be effective. However, an employer has to diagnose the situation carefully to be sure that the benefits outweigh the costs and that the program is implemented properly.

Measuring How Enriched the Job Is Now

According to Herzberg, the more characteristics on the following checklist that the job contains, the more enriched it is.[3]

	Yes	No
Direct feedback: Does the employee get timely, direct feedback concerning performance?		
Client relationships: Does the worker have a customer or client to serve, either external to the organization or inside it? For example, instead of typing memos for everyone on a first-come, first-served basis, each secretary in the typing pool is assigned to a specific department.		
New learning: Does the person's job entail new learning? In one case, for example, laboratory technicians were previously responsible only for setting up the laboratory equipment for the research scientists. After job enrichment, they were given additional responsibility for the research reports, which created the opportunity for them to analyze and evaluate data and to learn to write scientific reports.		

	Yes	No

Scheduling: Can the person schedule his or her own work? In one plant, for instance, workers previously were told when they could take coffee, rest, and lunch breaks. After enrichment, workers were held accountable for meeting quotas and could schedule their own breaks.

Unique experience: Herzberg says that "in this day of mechanization and assembly intelligence when everyone is judged on sameness, there exists a countervailing need for some personal uniqueness at work—for providing aspects of jobs that the worker can consider as 'doing his own thing'." So, can the person "do his or her own thing"?

Control over resources: Does the person have some control over resources? Herzberg recommends giving employees or groups of employees their own "minibudget," and pushing costs and profit centres down as low as is organizationally feasible.

Direct communications with client: Does the worker have direct access to his or her customer or client?

Personal accountability: For example, inspectors should be eliminated and the employee allowed to both assemble and inspect his or her own product whenever possible. Is this the case on the job in question?

How to Enrich a Subordinate's Job

There are at least five specific actions that can be taken to enrich a job.[4]

1. *Form natural work groups.* Change the job in such a way that each group is responsible for, or "owns," an identifiable body of work. For example, instead of having a typist in a typing pool do work for all departments, make the work of one or two departments the continuing responsibility of each group of typists.

2. *Combine tasks.* Let one person assemble a product from start to finish, instead of having it go through several separate operations that are performed by different people.

3. *Establish client relationships.* Let the worker have contact as often as possible with the client. For example, let a secretary research and respond to customers' requests, instead of automatically referring all problems to the supervisor.

4. *Vertical loading.* Let the worker plan and control his or her own job, instead of having it controlled by outsiders. For example, let the worker set his or her own schedule, do his or her own trouble-shooting, and decide when to start and stop work.

5. *Open feedback channels.* Finally, find more and better ways for the worker to get quick feedback on his or her performance.

Here is an example of how these steps were used in a successful application at Traveler's Insurance Company. The work group chosen was a keypunching operation.

Formed natural work groups. Each keypunch operator was assigned full responsibility for certain accounts—for example, each worked only for particular departments.

Combined tasks. Keypunchers began doing more of their own verifying (inspecting) to see that the cards were punched correctly.

Established client relationships. Each operator was given several channels of direct contact with a client. The operators, not their assignment clerks, now inspect the documents for correctness and legibility. When problems arise, the operators, not the supervisor, take them up with the client.

Provided feedback. In addition to feedback from client contact, other channels of feedback were installed. For example, computer operators now return incorrect cards to the operators who punched them, and operators correct their own errors.

Vertically loaded jobs. For example, operators may now set their own schedule and plan their daily work as long as they meet the schedule.

Basic Questions to Ask When Implementing a Job Enrichment Program

Job enrichment is not for everyone. Employers thinking of implementing a job enrichment program should therefore first ask the following questions.[5]

1. *Is motivation central to the problem?* Employers should ensure that the low performance is not a result of some other problem, like a poorly designed production system or inadequate training.

2. *Is there an easier way?* Related to the first point, employers should ask, "Is there an easier way to improve the situation in question?" For example, sometimes improved human resources testing and training might eliminate the problem.

3. *Are salary and working conditions adequate?* Most job enrichment experts agree that enrichment will not reduce the problems caused by inadequate pay or working conditions. Employees usually have to be adequately satisfied with these for job enrichment to be effective. In other words, job enrichment cannot be used to improve a subordinate's morale or performance when the person is dissatisfied with his or her salary or working conditions.

4. *Is the job low in providing intrinsic rewards?* It is not worthwhile trying to enrich a job that is already sufficiently interesting and challenging.

5. *Is it technically and economically feasible to enrich the job?* In some cases there are simply too many costs involved in de-automating to make job enrichment pay for itself. The reason that highly specialized, routine jobs evolved in the first place was that manufacturers found them much more efficient.

6. *Is quality important?* It is usually the quality of the final product rather than its quantity that is the main beneficiary of job enrichment.

7. *Are workers ready for the change, and do they want it?* Some workers neither want nor need more challenging jobs. Not everyone is turned off by an apparently boring, routine job. Some people, in fact, seem to prefer the monotonous pace and derive their satisfaction from various nonwork interests.

EQUITABLE REWARDS AND HUMAN MOTIVATION

Equity Theory

The **equity theory of motivation** assumes that people are strongly motivated to maintain a balance between what they perceive as their inputs, or contributions, and their rewards. Basically, equity theory states that if a person perceives an inequity, a tension or drive will develop in the person's mind, and the person will be motivated to reduce or eliminate the tension and perceived inequity.

equity theory of motivation

Most human resource managers recognize that inequitable treatment does have profound effects on employee behaviour. Michel might be happy with his $20 000 salary and work hard to earn it, until he learns that Kristen down the hall earns $800 more for the same job. Michel's first reaction will very likely be to get a quick raise, but if that fails, his performance will probably diminish as he tries to reduce what he sees as an inequity, by reducing his contribution to the firm. The concept of equity thus plays a crucial role in salary management.

One of the tricky aspects of these inequities is that most people have an inflated view of their own performance and also tend to overestimate what other people are earning. Most people, in other words, have a sort of built-in predisposition toward viewing situations as inequitable.

Effect on Performance

According to equity theory, exactly how the person goes about reducing what is perceived as an inequity depends on whether he or she is paid on a piece-rate basis (by the piece) or on a straight salary basis (say, by the week).

1. If a person is paid on a piece-rate basis and thinks he or she is overpaid, the quantity the person produces should stay the same or may decrease, since producing more would simply increase the financial rewards to the person and therefore increase his or her perceived inequity even more. However, quality should increase, since this should allow an increase in the input a person sees himself or herself as providing, thus reducing the perceived inequity.

2. On the other hand, if the person is paid per piece and views himself or herself as underpaid, the quality of the person's work should go down, and the quantity he or she produces will probably increase, depending on how much the person is paid per piece.

3. If the person is paid a salary (regardless of his or her output), and views himself or herself as overpaid, then either the quantity or quality of his or her work should increase, since this will reduce the perceived inequity.

4. However, if the person is paid a salary and believes he or she is underpaid, then quality and quantity should both decrease.

These four points are summarized in Figure 11.3.

BEHAVIOUR MODIFICATION AND POSITIVE REINFORCEMENT AT WORK

Behaviour modification (a term that is often used synonymously with **operant conditioning**) involves changing (modifying) behaviour through the use of rewards or punishment. Behaviour modification is built on two principles: (1) be-

behaviour modification/operant conditioning

FIGURE 11.3
The Effects of a
Perceived Inequity on
Performance

	Employee thinks he or she is underpaid	Employee thinks he or she is overpaid
Piece-rate Basis	Quality down Quantity the same or up	Quantity the same or down Quality up
Salary Basis	Quantity or quality should go down	Quantity or quality should go up

haviour that appears to lead to a positive consequence (reward) tends to be repeated, whereas behaviour that appears to lead to a negative consequence tends not to be repeated;[6] and (2) therefore, by providing the properly scheduled rewards, it is possible to change a person's motivation and behaviour. The two important concepts in behaviour modification are the types of reinforcement and the schedules of reinforcement.

Types of Reinforcement

A manager whose employees are chronically late for work wants to use behaviour modification to train them to come in on time. There are four types of reinforcement that could be used: positive reinforcement, negative reinforcement, extinction, and punishment.

First, one could focus on reinforcing the *desired* behaviour (which in this case is coming to work on time). To do this, either positive or negative reinforcement could be used. Positive reinforcement might involve giving rewards like praise or raises each time the person comes to work on time. Negative reinforcement also focuses on reinforcing the desired behaviour—coming to work on time—but instead of providing a positive reward, the "reward" is that the employee avoids some negative consequence, such as being harassed or reprimanded for coming in late. The "reward" is thus a negative one: employees come in on time to avoid some negative consequence like harassment or a reprimand.

Alternatively, one might focus on reducing the *undesired* behaviour (coming in late) rather than on rewarding the desired behaviour. With behaviour modification, there are two types of reinforcement that can be used to reduce undesired behaviour: extinction and punishment. People tend to repeat behaviour that they have learned leads to positive consequences; with extinction, reinforcement is withheld, so that over time, the undesired behaviour (coming in late) disappears. For example, suppose an employee learns from experience that coming to work late invariably lead to a scolding by the supervisor, which in turns leads to much laughter and attention from the worker's peers. That laughter represents a positive reinforcement to the worker for coming in late. Extinction would involve the supervisor's ignoring the employee, thus removing the attention and laughter—the reinforcement—from the worker's friends.

Punishment is a second way to reduce undesired behaviour. Here, for instance, one might reprimand or harass late employees. Punishment is the most controversial method of modifying behaviour, and Skinner (who did much of the work in this area) recommends extinction rather than punishment for decreasing the frequency of undesired behaviour at work.[7] In fact, whenever possible, managers are advised to use positive reinforcement, since this focuses on improving the desired behaviour, rather than reducing the undesired behaviour.

The four types of reinforcement—positive reinforcement, negative reinforcement, extinction, and punishment—are summarized in Figure 11.4.

Schedules of Positive Reinforcement

The schedule with which positive reinforcement is applied is as important as the type of reinforcement used.[8] Basically, there are four schedules that may be used.

Fixed-Interval Schedule

A fixed-interval schedule is based on time. Here, the person gets reinforcement (a reward) only when the desired response occurs and only after the passage of a

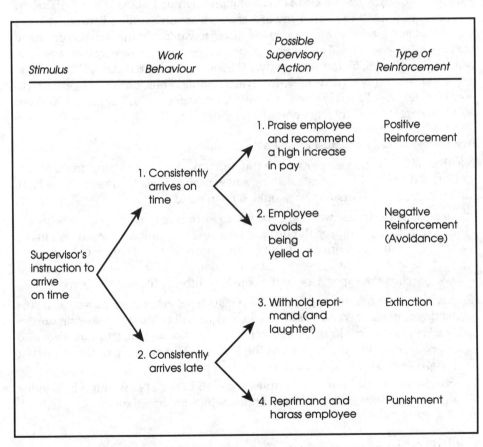

FIGURE 11.4
Types of
Reinforcement

SOURCE: Adapted from John Ivancevich, Andrew Szilagyi, Jr., and Marc Wallace, Jr., *Organizational Behavior and Performance*, 1977, Scott, Foresman and Company, Reprinted by permission.

specified fixed period of time since the preceding reinforcement. For example, at the end of each week, a supervisor might go around and praise each employee who came to work on time every day that week.

Variable-Interval Schedule

Variable-interval schedules are also based on time. However, the person is reinforced at some variable interval around some average. For example, suppose the intent is to provide reinforcement on the average of once a day for all employees who come to work on time. The supervisor can visit them on average once a day—once on Tuesday, skip Wednesday, three times on Thursday, and so on—in such a way that the praise averages out to about once a day.

Fixed-Ratio Schedule

A fixed-ratio schedule is based on units of output rather than on time. With a fixed-ratio schedule, rewards are delivered only when a fixed number of desired responses occur. Most piece-rate incentive pay plans are on a fixed-ratio schedule. The worker is rewarded every time he or she produces a fixed number of pieces.

Variable-Ratio Schedule

Variable-ratio schedules are also based on units of output, but the number of desired outcomes necessary to elicit a reward changes around some average. The Las Vegas-type slot machines are good examples of rewards administered according to variable-ratio schedules. The number of times a person can expect to hit a jackpot with such machines, on the average over the long term, is predictable. Yet the jackpots come randomly on a variable-interval schedule. Thus, one might get no jackpots five times and then hit two in a row; another individual might go 50 times without a jackpot and then get one.

Which Ratio Schedule Is Most Effective?

Whether reinforcing an employee in a training program, disciplining an employee for ineffective behaviour, or establishing a new incentive plan, there are three basic rules human resource managers should keep in mind:

1. In general, the fastest way to get people to learn is not to put them on schedule at all. Instead, reinforce the desired outcome continuously, each and every time it occurs. The drawback is that the desired behaviour also diminishes very rapidly once the supervisor stops reinforcing it. Training is accomplished fastest when the supervisor continuously reinforces the desired behaviour.

2. Variable-ratio reinforcement (the Las Vegas type) is the most powerful at sustaining behaviour. With this schedule, people will continue producing the desired response for a long time even without reinforcement, since they are also expecting to "hit the jackpot" on the next try. The example in the following section illustrates how to put this idea into practice.

3. Fixed- and variable-ratio schedules are both better at sustaining behaviour than are either of the interval schedules, which are based on time.

Example

An electronics manufacturer found that it had an acute absenteeism problem and that tardiness was a problem as well. Management concluded that a program should in initiated to reward the desired behaviour (prompt and regular attendance) and a program was initiated. Under this program the employees could qualify for a monthly drawing of a prize only if they had perfect attendance and punctuality records for the period. This eligibility for the monthly drawing was contingent upon the desired behaviour—good attendance. All absences of any kind precluded employee eligibility; the program was described in a company bulletin. A drawing was held on the last work day of each month in which a winner was selected at random from a basket containing the names of all employees who had maintained perfect attendance and punctuality records for that month. A small cash prize was awarded to the winner of each monthly lottery. In addition, to provide reinforcement to those not winning the lottery, the names of all employees who qualified were listed on the plant bulletin board and these people were praised by their supervisors.

The results of this program were fairly impressive: the average net monthly savings amounted to about $282 and the total yearly savings were in excess of $3000 for a program that involved almost no cost to the company.

MOTIVATION: AN OVERVIEW
An Expectancy Approach

It would be useful to summarize and integrate these motivation theories, and to do so we can draw on what is called the **expectancy theory of motivation**. This theory assumes that a person's motivation to exert effort is based on his or her expectations of success.[9] Expectancy theory as formulated by psychologist Victor Vroom assumes that to motivate someone, it is not enough to offer the person something to satisfy his or her important needs. The reason for this, says Vroom, is that in order for the person to be motivated, he or she must also be reasonably sure that he or she has the ability to obtain the reward. For example, telling someone you will appoint him or her sales manager if he or she increases sales in his or her district will probably not motivate the person if he or she knows the task is virtually impossible.

expectancy theory of motivation

Basically, Vroom contends that for motivation to take place, two things must occur:

1. The **valence** or value of the particular outcome (such as becoming sales manager) must be high for the person.

2. The person must feel he or she has a reasonably good chance of accomplishing the task and obtaining the outcome. That is, the person must be convinced that effort will be instrumental in obtaining the reward.

valence

A Model of Motivation

As illustrated in Figure 11.5, motivating someone can be thought of within an expectancy framework. Expectancy theory states that motivation will occur (1) if the incentive is of value to the person, and (2) if the person is reasonably sure that effort on his or her part will result in accomplishing the task and obtaining the incentive.

As Figure 11.5 shows, for motivation to take place, several things must occur. First, the incentive must be important to the person. (Theorists like Maslow, Herzberg, and Atkinson would suggest that certain needs—like those for recognition, esteem, and achievement—are the most important in our society.) Related to this, the incentive cannot just be important but must also be viewed as equi-

FIGURE 11.5
A Model of Motivation

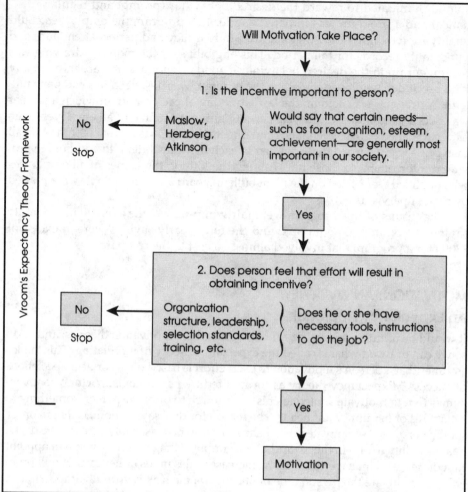

table if it is to elicit the desired motivation. (A inequitable reward can also elicit motivation if, for instance, a person paid a salary believes he or she is overpaid.) Second, the person must feel that effort will in fact lead to rewards. Here, other nonmotivational matters (including human factors like skills and work groups, and organizational factors like adequate plans, organization charts, and training) must be addressed, to ensure that there are no impediments to performing.

Principles of Motivation

The main principles of motivation can be summarized as follows:

- *Rewards should be tied to performance.* Theories we have studied show that motivation is greatest when obtaining the reward depends on performance. Tasks for which pay is the most obvious reward should employ incentive bonuses and piece-rate plans. For all jobs, tying nonfinancial rewards (like advancement, recognition, and praise) to performance can also be effective.

On the Front Line

As front-line managers, Jennifer and her father know perhaps better than anyone the wide disparity that often exists between the theories of motivation and their practical applications. In running her cleaning centres Jennifer finds she has many practical motivation problems that must be solved, but she is not sure that she sees the relevance of concepts like achievement-motivation or self-actualization.

This week, for instance, Jennifer had to come to grips with several of what she would consider to be "motivation problems." In this business productivity is always a problem. Each store's total labour bill should not exceed 28-30% of the store's revenues, but to maintain that ratio it is necessary for all employees to work industriously: pressers have to produce about 30 pieces per hour, for instance, and the spotter-cleaner has to clean at least 85 pounds of garments per hour. Other jobs in the store—bagging the clothes, for instance, and "tagging them in" (marking each item with an identification number so the items can later be reassembled into a single order)—have similar standards. Jennifer is also not sure that the problems she is having with employee theft and with counterpersons who are not as friendly or professional as they should be are not at least partly motivation problems rather than lack of ability or training problems.

Jennifer knows that sooner or later she will have to deal with the "motivation" aspect of the problems her firm is encountering and that some of the most immediate problems to be solved involve employees' salaries, possible incentive pay plans, and in general doing something to overcome what Jennifer considers to be the lethargic attitude on the part of most of her employees. This lethargy, Jennifer believes, is a product of the highly routine and unattractive nature of most of the jobs in each store, since most of these jobs involve performing the same short-cycle jobs over and over and over again under hot conditions and for little pay. Jennifer therefore wonders what can be done to improve the situation.

1. To what extent are jobs like presser, cleaner-spotter, and counter person amenable to job enrichment? To the extent that any of these jobs are subject to improvement through job enrichment, what exactly should Jennifer do to enrich them?

2. What are the implications of equity theory for Jennifer and her first-line supervisors?

3. To what extent do you think people performing routine jobs like that of presser are able to satisfy their higher-level needs at work and what, if any, are the implications of this?

- *Rewards should be equitable.* For example, salaried employees who feel they are underpaid will reduce the quality or quantity of their performance, whereas those who believe they are overpaid will improve their performance.

- *A person must have the ability to accomplish the task to be motivated to do so.* If a person believes there is little or no chance of successfully completing a task (and therefore obtaining the reward), that person would probably not be motivated to accomplish it. Thus always ask, "Could the employee do the job if he or she wanted to?" Job analysis, selection, and training play an important role here.

- *Lower-level needs and higher-level needs should be distinguished.* Lower-level needs are those for food, clothing, shelter, and security. Higher-level needs are those for recognition, achievement, and self-actualization. Wherever possible, motivation should be elicited by an appeal to the relatively infinite higher-level needs (for instance by using job enrichment, and the participative techniques described in Chapter 15). However, the lower-level needs must first be adequately satisfied by equitable pay and good supervision.

SUMMARY

1. Basically, people are motivated or driven to behave in a way that they feel leads to rewards. Thus there are two basic requirements for motivating someone: (1) the incentive or reward must be important to the person; and (2) he or she must feel that effort on his or her part will probably lead to obtaining the reward. This is the essence of Vroom's expectancy theory of motivation.

2. Abraham Maslow says that people's needs can be envisioned in a hierarchy. Each succeeding higher-level need does not become aroused until the next lower-level need is fairly well satisfied. Working up the hierarchy, the five Maslow needs are physiological, safety, social, ego, and self-actualization.

3. Herzberg says that the work factors involved in producing job satisfaction and motivation are separate and distinct from those that lead to job dissatisfaction. Those leading to job dissatisfaction (if they are absent) are the hygiene factors. These include "extrinsic" factors such as supervision, working conditions, and salary. The factors leading to satisfaction and motivation (if they are present) include intrinsic job factors such as achievement and challenge.

4. The equity theory of motivation assumes that people are strongly motivated to maintain a balance between what they perceive as their inputs or contributions and their rewards. The concept thus plays a crucial role in salary management.

5. Behaviour modification is built on two principles: (1) behaviour that appears to lead to a positive consequence (reward) tends to be repeated, whereas that which leads to a negative consequence tends not to be repeated; therefore, (2) behaviour can be changed by providing the properly scheduled rewards. By manipulating the types of reinforcement (positive, negative, extinction, and punishment), and the schedules of reinforcement (fixed and variable interval, and fixed and variable ratio), discipline, incentives, and many other human resource management methods can be more effectively employed.

KEY TERMS

needs hierarchy

need achievement theory

motivator-hygiene theory of motivation

hygiene factors

motivator factors

job enrichment

equity theory of motivation

behaviour modification/operant conditioning

expectancy theory of motivation

valence

DISCUSSION QUESTIONS

1. If you have not already done so, fill in the questionnaire in the experiential exercise to this chapter. What would you say this tells you about your important needs? About the tasks for which you would be best suited?

2. Explain what motivation is.

3. Develop an "expectancy model" diagram of motivation.

4. Discuss the Maslow needs hierarchy.

5. Compare and contrast the Maslow and Herzberg motivation theories.

6. Compare and contrast the Vroom and Herzberg theories of motivation. Are they compatible?

7. Summarize what we know about "what people want." How would you make use of this knowledge as a manager?

8. Explain how all the human resource management functions influence motivation.

9. "I don't need to know about any fancy motivation theories," your boss tells you. "What they all come down to is that you should practise the Golden Rule—do unto others as you would have them do unto you." Explain whether you agree or disagree with this statement, and why.

CASE INCIDENT: What's Wrong With Some of Our Workers?

Jupiter Bakery and Convenience Store employs more than 30 individuals. The firm has been experiencing a lack of productivity and satisfactory job performance among its work force for over four years. The company also has been experiencing increased labour costs due to excessive overtime. Some time ago the firm observed that low productivity and unsatisfactory job performance was prevalent among its part-time workers and its younger workers. The performance of long-serving workers, experienced, and older workers was the opposite. The firm felt that maybe younger workers and part-time workers did not feel like part of the Jupiter family. It decided that something had to be done.

Three years ago, management established a bonus system for all employees. The aim was to motivate employees to be more productive, increase morale, increase loyalty, and increase employee rewards. It was decided that all employees would be eligible for the bonus. The size of each employee's bonus was based on merit. Part-time and full-time younger workers were paid minimum wage. Full-time experienced workers were paid higher wages. However, their base pay did not factor into the determination of bonuses. Bonuses were paid in cash, and ranged from $250 to $5000.

Since the plan was established, the firm has noticed that the performance of its longer-serving workers and older workers decreased substantially, as has the performance of managerial employees. However, the results have improved marginally for its younger workers and its part-time workers.

Questions

1. Use Maslow's hierarchy of needs to explain the motivational aspects of the bonus system on employee performance.

2. How can equity theory be used to explain the low performance and lack of productivity of some of Jupiter's employees?

EXPERIENTIAL EXERCISE

Purpose: The purposes of this exercise are

1. To provide you with some information on what your needs are.
2. To give you information on what behaviours characterize people with different needs.

Required Understanding: This exercise can be used either prior to or after reading this chapter.

How to Set Up the Exercise: Readers should work on this exercise individually.

Instructions for the Exercise: First, fill in the following questionnaire:

	Yes	No
1. When you start a task, do you stick with it?	___	___
2. Do you try to find out how you are doing, and do you try to get as much feedback as possible?	___	___
3. Do you respond to difficult, challenging situations? Do you work better when there is a deadline or some other challenge involved?	___	___
4. Are you eager to accept responsibility? Do you set (and meet) measurable standards of high performance?	___	___
5. Do you seem to enjoy a good argument?	___	___
6. Do you seek positions of authority where you can give orders rather than take them? Do you try to take over?	___	___
7. Are status symbols especially important to you, and do you use them to gain influence over others?	___	___
8. Are you especially eager to be your own boss, even when you need assistance, or when joint effort is required?	___	___
9. Do you seem to be uncomfortable when you are forced to work alone?	___	___
10. Do you interact with other workers, and go out of your way to make friends with new workers?	___	___
11. Are you always getting involved in group projects, and are you sensitive to other people (especially when they are "mad" at you)?	___	___
12. Are you an "apple polisher," and do you try hard to get personally involved with your superiors?	___	___

Now score your answers. According to George Litwin and Robert Stringer, "Yes" answers to questions 1-4 mean that you have a high need to achieve. You prefer situations that have moderate risks, in which you can identify your own contribution, and in which you receive concrete feedback concerning your performance.

"Yes" answers to questions 5-8 mean that you have a high need for power. You prefer situations in which you can get and maintain control of the means for influencing others.

Finally, "Yes" answers to questions 9-12 mean that you have a high need for af-filiation. You have a strong desire to maintain close friendships and positive emotional relationships with others. (Keep in mind that a quick test like this can give you only the roughest guidelines about what your needs are.)

Next, if time permits, write down on a sheet of paper the number of questions you answered "Yes" to for each of the three needs (achievement, power, affiliation). It is not necessary to sign your names. Pass these sheets on to your instructor.

Your instructor can then list respondents vertically on the board (#1, #2, etc.) and the number of "Yes" answers (for each respondent) in each of three columns headed achievement, power, and affiliation. (Student 1, for example, might show 2, 2, and 4 in the respective columns.) Did the test appear to distinguish between students on the basis of their needs? Do you think you could identify people in your class who have high needs to achieve? For power? For affiliation? What does this exercise tell you about the factors that characterize people who are high (or low) on each of these three needs?

SOURCE: George Litwin and Robert Stringer, Jr., *Motivation and Organizational Climate* (Boston: Division of Research, Harvard Business School, 1968), pp. 173-174. Used with permission.

NOTES

1. John Campbell and Robert Pritchard, "Motivation Theory in Industrial and Organizational Psychology," in M. Dunnette, ed., *Handbook of Industrial and Organizational Psychology* (New York: Rand McNally, 1976), pp. 63-103. Based on Frederick Herzberg, "One More Time: How Do You Motivate Employees?" in *Harvard Business Review*, Human Relations Series, Part II (Boston: President and Fellows of Harvard College, 1969), pp. 115-124.

2. David McClelland, *The Achieving Society* (New York: Van Nostrand Reinhold, 1961); Edwin Cornelius II and Frank Lane, "The Power Motive and Managerial Success in a Professionally Oriented Service Industry Organization," *Journal of Applied Psychology*, Vol. 69 (February 1984), pp. 32-39.

3. Parts of this chapter are adapted from Gary Dessler, *Organization Theory* (Englewood Cliffs, N.J.; Prentice-Hall, 1986), pp. 332-341.

4. J. R. Hackman, Greg Oldham, Robert Johnson, and Kenneth Purdy, "A New Strategy for Job Enrichment," *California Management Review*, Vol 17, no. 4, pp. 51-71.

5. For a discussion, see Ramon Aldag and Arthur Brief, *Task Design and Employee Motivation* (Glenview, Ill.: Scott Foresman and Co., 1979), pp. 83-101.

6. W. Clay Hamner, "Reinforcement Theory and Motivation in Organizational Settings," in Henry Tosi and W. Clay Hamner, eds., *Organizational Behavior and Management: A Contingency Approach* (Chicago: St. Clair, 1974), pp. 86-112. This principle is also known as the law of effect.

7. Hamner, "Reinforcement Theory," p. 95.

8. Ibid., pp. 99-103.

9. David Nadler and Edward Lawler III, "Motivation: A Diagnostic Approach," in J. Richard Hackman, Edward Lawler III, and Lyman Porter, eds., *Perspectives on Behavior in Organizations* (New York: McGraw-Hill, 1977), pp. 26-38.

SUGGESTED READINGS

Alderfer, C.P. *Existence, Relatedness, and Growth: Human Needs in Organizational Settings.* New York: Free Press, 1972.

Evans, M.G. "Organizational Behavior: The Central Role of Motivation." *Yearly Review of Management of the Journal of Management* (Summer 1986), pp. 203-222.

Mowday, Richard T. "Equity Theory Predictions of Behavior in Organizations," in Richard M. Steers and Lyman W. Porter, eds., *Motivation and Work Behavior*, 5th ed. New York: McGraw-Hill Inc., 1991.

Nadler, David A. and Edward E. Lawler, III. "Motivation—A Diagnostic Approach," in Joe Kelly et al eds., *Organizational Behavior*, 2nd ed. Toronto: Prentice-Hall Canada Inc., 1991.

Pinder, C.C. *Work Motivation: Theory, Issues and Applications.* Glenview, Ill: Scott, Foresman, 1984.

Steers, Richard M. and Lyman W. Porter, eds. *Motivation and Work Behavior*, 5th ed. New York: McGraw-Hill, Inc., 1991.

CHAPTER TWELVE
COMPENSATION MANAGEMENT

After studying this chapter, you should be able to

1. Describe the internal and external environmental influences on compensation.
2. Describe the job evaluation process.
3. Explain what is meant by compensable factors.
4. Perform a job evaluation using the ranking method.
5. Price jobs using job evaluation results and a wage curve.
6. Discuss the concept of pay equity.

OVERVIEW

The main purpose of this chapter is to explain how to establish a pay plan. Developing a pay plan involves evaluating the relative worth of jobs (through the technique of job evaluation), and then pricing each job using wage curves and pay grades. In this chapter four evaluation methods (ranking, classification, point, and factor comparison) are explained, as is the process for developing wage curves and pay grades. Salaries or wages are the most widely used rewards for motivating performance, but to motivate they must be adequate and equitable—and job evaluation helps make them so.

BASIC ASPECTS OF COMPENSATION

compensation

Compensation refers to all financial rewards received by employees as a result of their employment relationship with an organization. Compensation management is a subset of the human resource management function of the organization.[1] Consequently, its goals are essentially drawn from the human resource management goals of the organization.[2] Compensation has three components. It includes direct financial payments in the form of wages, salaries, incentives, commissions, and bonuses; indirect payments in the form of financial fringe benefits like employer-paid insurance and vacations; and nonfinancial rewards that are not easily quantifiable, such as a more challenging job, flexible work hours, and a more prestigious office.

The Purposes and Importance of Compensation

The purposes and importance of compensation are to

- Ensure that employees are motivated to achieve desired levels of performance
- Demonstrate the organization's recognition that employees must feel that there is real or perceived fairness and equity in their compensation in comparison with other workers
- Attract qualified job applicants to the organization
- Ensure that the organization remains competitive with other organizations within its industry that provide similar products and services.
- Assist employees in meeting and maintaining their needs for financial and emotional security, self-esteem, social acceptance, and protection
- Stimulate employees to increase organizational productivity and achieve personal career aspirations
- Keep employees satisfied, minimize turnover, reduce employee complaints, and maintain overall stability in the organization's work force
- Provide equitable compensation to employees for services performed

INTERNAL ENVIRONMENTAL FACTORS AFFECTING COMPENSATION

There are many internal environmental factors that affect an organization's compensation system. These include

- The role of the human resource department
- The organization's ability to pay
- Compensation policies
- Equity

The Role of the Human Resource Department

The human resource department has a major influence on the compensation process. In conjunction with top management, the human resource department formulates compensation policies (regarding, for instance, whether the organization should be a pay leader, an average wage-payer, or a pay follower). In addition, the human resources department conducts wage surveys to find out prevailing wage rates, implements job evaluation programs to determine the comparable worth of each job in the firm, and works with benefits consultants, insurance firms, and the like to choose the benefits packages for the organization's employees. The human resource department is usually also responsible for monitoring and ensuring legal compliance with government legislation affecting the compensation system.

Line managers also play a major role in compensation management. Specifically, the line supervisor should[3]

1. Review all job descriptions to make sure that they are accurate statements of duties assigned and performed, since compensation is typically tied to the job's duties and responsibilities.

2. Report all changes in assignments to make sure that descriptions are current.

3. Review all job evaluation results to ensure that decisions regarding the relative worth of each job are accurate.

4. Recommend pay increases on the basis of the facts and equities of each case and within the framework of existing policy.

5. Carefully review work methods and work standards.

6. Administer the incentive program, including effective performance appraisal.

7. Control overtime work and pay by determining the need for it, and assure its equitable distribution among employees.

8. Control abuses of benefit programs including unemployment compensation and sick leave.

9. Report compensation needs and problems to the appropriate managers.

10. Communicate all aspects of the compensation program to subordinates, including answering questions and handling complaints.

The Organization's Ability to Pay

An organization's compensation structure is directly influenced by its ability to pay. If the organization is profitable and is able to maintain its profitability for several consecutive years, then the organization is in a better position to pay well above average compensation and to grant generous increases to its employees. However, if the organization is just breaking even or losing money, then there is a strong likelihood that it will grant small increases, if any, and may even seek reduction in existing wages, salaries, and benefit rates.

Compensation Policies

An organization's compensation policies influence the wages and benefits that it pays since these policies provide basic compensation guidelines in several important areas. One decision the organization must make is whether it wants to be a pay leader or a pay follower. For example, one hospital might have a policy of starting nurses at a wage at least 20% above the prevailing market wage and might pay even inexperienced nurses at least 10% more than they would receive for comparable work at other area hospitals.

Some important areas for which an organization needs compensation policies are presented in Table 12.1.[4] As the table indicates, some important areas usually covered by compensation policies include the basis for salary increases, promotion and demotion policies, overtime pay policies, and policies regarding probationary pay, leaves for jury duty, and holidays. Compensation policies are usually written by the human resource department in conjunction with top management and the compensation manager.[5]

TABLE 12.1 Topics Usually Covered by Compensation Policies

Hiring rates	Confidentiality
Levels compared with other employers	Relation to hourly rates
Breadth of salary ranges	Overtime
Basis for salary increases:	Vacations
Merit	Holidays
Tenure	Leave of absence
Age	Sick pay
Position in range	Exceptions
Period since last increase	Approval levels
Percent	Salary advances
Timing	Supervisory differentials
Market advances	Temporary assignments
Seniority	Separation pay, salary continuance, or
General versus individual	"notice pay"
Promotions	Probationary pay
Demotions	Learning pay
For cause	Military service
For company purposes	Jury duty
For personal reasons	Funeral leave
Transfers	Temporary hires
Red circles	Hours of work
Interruptions in service	School time off

SOURCE: Stanley B. Henrici, *Salary Management for the Nonspecialist* (New York: AMACOM, 1980), p. 20.

Equity

The need for equity is perhaps the most important factor in determining pay rates. Real and perceived equity in an organization's rewards system is important to employee job satisfaction and performance. Regardless of how scientifically sound a compensation system is, it will be ineffective if the employees perceive it to be inequitable and unreasonable.[6] There are two types of equity: internal equity and external equity.

Internal Equity

Internal equity consists of two components: job equity and employee equity. Job equity means that different jobs in the organization are paid according to their respective worth or value. The relative worth of jobs are determined by factors such as job content (responsibilities, duties, and function) and job requirements (skills, knowledge, and abilities). Employee equity means that individuals who hold the same or similar jobs within the organization are compensated according to their contribution measured by performance criteria and/or seniority. The concept of internal equity is based on two linkages. The first linkage exists between pay and job worth, and the second between pay and individual performance. In order for employees to feel that they are being fairly treated, they must feel that their personal contribution to the organization is at least equal to their personal rewards or outcomes received from the organization.

External Equity

External equity means that the organization's compensation levels should compare favourably with compensation in other organizations; if it does not, the organization will find it hard to attract and retain qualified employees. In order to establish external equity the organization must conduct a salary survey. Salary surveys play a central role in the pricing of jobs, and may be either formal or informal.

The process of establishing equitable pay rates involves five steps.

1. Conduct a salary survey of what other employers are paying for comparable jobs (to help ensure external equity).
2. Determine the worth of each job in the organization through job evaluation (to ensure internal equity).
3. Group similar jobs into pay grades.
4. Price each pay grade by using wage curves.
5. Fine tune pay rates.

EXTERNAL ENVIRONMENTAL FACTORS AFFECTING COMPENSATION

There are many external environmental factors that affect an organization's compensation system. These include

- Competitors' influences
- Government influences
- Union influences
- Labour market conditions

Competitors' Influences

External competitiveness has an important impact on an organization's compensation levels. Unless an employer's compensation levels are similar to and competitive with other, comparable employers in the same industry providing similar goods and services, then the employer will have difficulty attracting good job candidates and retaining desired employees. The employer must be aware that prospective employees, when deciding on the attractiveness of an employer, will almost certainly compare the relative compensation levels provided by different organizations. They will, of course, assess other factors such as job security, career prospects, organizational climate, and working conditions, but the amount of information available on these issues is likely to be limited. Therefore, the job candidate's decision on which organization to join is most likely to be based on which employer's compensation is most attractive.

Competitor's compensation levels also have an important effect on an organization's ability to retain present employees. If the current employer's compensation levels are not competitive with other organizations, then present employees, particularly the good ones, are likely to leave. However, these employees are also likely to be influenced by other factors such as job satisfaction, the nature of the job, interpersonal relationships with superiors and co-workers, and potential for advancement.

In order to remain competitive, an organization must find out what its competitors are paying as well as their planned increases. This may be done by conducting salary surveys (which we will discuss later). A survey conducted by the Conference Board of Canada found that there was little variation in pay plans for individual industries in 1991.[7] However, when the pay projections are examined on the basis of company size, it appears that larger organizations are planning to give slightly higher salary increases to satisfactory performers in 1991 than smaller firms, although there is little variation around the mean of 5.4%. Organizations with less than 500 employees plan the smallest average increases. Companies with more than 2500 employees plan the highest increases.

Increases in both the manufacturing and nonmanufacturing sectors were projected to be 5.5%. The largest increases were projected among industries such as chemicals, pharmaceuticals, and allied products, at 6.1%; oil and gas, 5.9%; and utilities, 5.8%. Information such as this provides valuable insight into pay trends.

Government Influences

Governments have an important impact on an organization's compensation system. Governments' interest in compensation is intended to further the greater good of society by ensuring that the allocation and distribution of financial compensation helps to support the social and economic interests of the general society. Governments influence an organization's compensation decisions through a network of legislations designed to provide a basic and essential safety level of security from poverty and to maintain or strengthen the society's social and economic vitality.

An employer's compensation system must comply with all government laws and legislations that regulate the employment relationship. These laws and legislations include the Canada Labour Code and provincial employment standards acts, which mandate and regulate the general employment contract between the employer and the employee; they cover such issues as the minimum wage rate, overtime, age of employment, hours of work, termination of employment, and vacation pay. Also included are income protection legislations such as Workers' Compensation, Unemployment Insurance, and the Canada Pension Plan, all of which were created and established to cushion the impact of monetary burdens of unemployment, long-term disability, retirement, and injury. Other legislations include income tax laws; labour relations and occupational health and safety legislation; public policy laws, including employment equity, affirmative action, and pay equity; and finally, wage and price legislation which is used during inflationary periods to regulate compensation practices in order to stem the erosion of the purchasing power of workers' income.

Union Influences

Labour unions have a major impact on the compensation systems of employers. In a unionized organization, labour unions influence the organization's compensation system directly through the collective bargaining process. Through this process unions have a direct input into the determination of wage rates, the composition of wage structures, and the rules of wage administration. Labour unions also have an indirect impact on nonunionized organizations. The wages, benefits, job security, and working conditions negotiated by unions for their members create pressure on nonunionized companies to provide similar packages to avoid dissatisfaction among their employees and prevent unionization. Nonunionized organizations must compete with unionized organizations for the services of prospective employees and the loyalty of existing employees.[8]

Union Attitudes Toward Compensation Decisions

Several studies shed some light on union attitudes toward compensation plans and underscore a number of commonly held union fears.[9] Many union leaders fear that any technical system (like time and motion study) used to evaluate the worth of a job and judge the relative value of a job can quickly become a tool for management malpractice. Union leaders tend to feel that no one can judge the relative value of jobs better than the workers themselves. They also feel that management's usual method of using several compensable factors (like "degree of responsibility") to evaluate and rank the worth of jobs can be a manipulative device for restricting or lowering the pay of workers. One implication seems to be that the best way to gain the cooperation of union members in job evaluation is to request their active involvement in the process of evaluating the relative worth of jobs and in assigning fair rates of pay to these jobs. However, management has the right to ensure that its prerogatives—such as the use of job evaluation techniques to assess the relative worth of jobs—are not surrendered.

Labour Market Conditions

An organization's compensation for certain jobs may be influenced by the supply and demand for individuals to perform these jobs. If the supply of certain skilled workers is limited and if the demand is great then the organization must be prepared to increase its compensation budget and pay more for the available workers than it would ordinarily pay if the supply were abundant and the demand were low.

THE ROLE OF MONEY IN WORK MOTIVATION[10]

According to psychologists people have many needs, only some of which can be satisfied directly with money. Other needs—for achievement, affiliation, power, or self-actualization, for instance—also motivate behaviour but can only be satisfied indirectly (if at all) by money.

Yet even with all our modern motivation techniques (like job enrichment), there is no doubt that money is still the most important motivator. As three researchers put it,

> Pay in one form or another is certainly one of the mainsprings of motivation in our society.... The most evangelical human relationist insists it is important, while protesting that other things are too (and are, perhaps in his view, nobler).

FIGURE 12.1
Consequences of Pay
Dissatisfaction

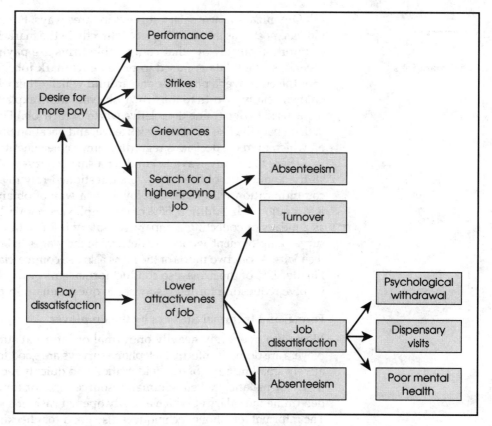

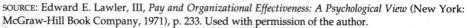

SOURCE: Edward E. Lawler, III, *Pay and Organizational Effectiveness: A Psychological View* (New York: McGraw-Hill Book Company, 1971), p. 233. Used with permission of the author.

It would be unnecessary to belabour the point if it were not for a tendency for money drives to slip out of focus in a miasma of other values and other practices. As it is, it must be repeated: Pay is the most important single motivator used in our organized society.[11]

Figure 12.1 illustrates the consequences of pay dissatisfaction. As can be seen, when employees are unhappy with their pay they become de-motivated and their behaviour may be adversely affected. The adverse change in behaviour may be manifested by reduced performance/productivity, reduced job satisfaction, increased absenteeism, increased turnover, and psychological withdrawal. Dissatisfaction with pay may occur when there is real or perceived inequities in pay,[12] or insufficient pay to allow individuals to meet their physiological[13] or existence needs.[14]

Figure 12.2 illustrates the consequences of employee satisfaction with pay. As can be seen, satisfaction with pay has a positive impact on job attitude and job behaviour—it leads to increased job satisfaction, increased motivation, and increased harmony in the work environment.

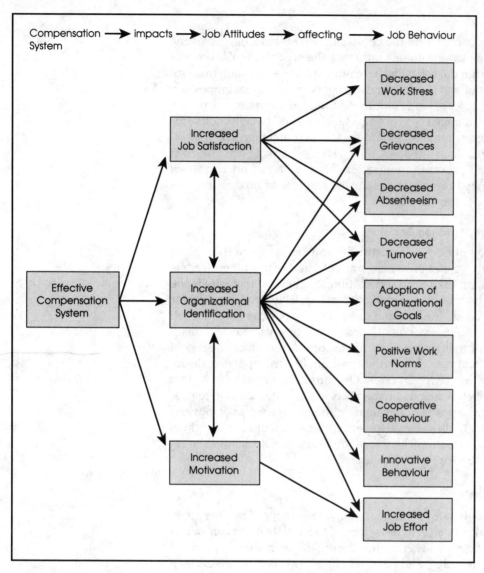

Compensation ⟶ impacts ⟶ Job Attitudes ⟶ affecting ⟶ Job Behaviour
System

SOURCE: Richard J. Long, "Reward and Compensation," in M. Srinivas Kalburgi, ed., *Human Resource Management: Contemporary Perspectives in Canada* (Toronto: McGraw-Hill Ryerson Limited, 1984), p. 338. Used with permission

ESTABLISHING PAY RATES

Step 1: Conduct the Salary Survey

Introduction

Compensation or **salary surveys** play a central role in the pricing of jobs, and virtually every employer (regardless of size) conducts such surveys for pricing one or more of its jobs.[15]

salary surveys

Organizations use salary surveys in three ways. First, 20% or more of any employers' positions are usually priced directly in the marketplace, based on a formal or informal survey of what comparable firms are paying for comparable jobs. Second, survey data are used to price **benchmark jobs**, jobs that are used to anchor the employer's pay scale and around which other jobs are then slotted based on their relative worth to the firm. (Job evaluation, explained in step 2, is the technique used to determine the relative worth of each job.) Finally, surveys also collect data on benefits like insurance, sick leave, and vacation time and so provide a basis on which to make decisions regarding employee benefits.

There are many ways to conduct a salary survey. According to one British study, about 71% of the employers questioned rely to some extent on informal communication with other employers as a way of obtaining comparative salary information.[16] In addition, 55% of the employers regularly review newspaper ads as a means of collecting comparative salary information, while 33% of the firms survey employment agencies to determine the wages to be paid for at least some of their jobs. About two thirds of the firms also use commercial or professional surveys. Finally, 22% of the firms also conduct formal surveys with other employers; these involve requesting formal responses to questionnaire-type surveys.

Formal and Informal Surveys by the Employer

Most employers rely heavily on formal or informal surveys of what other employers are doing.[17] Informal telephone surveys are good for collecting data on a relatively small number of easily identified and quickly recognized jobs, and can be used, for instance, when a human resource director for a bank wants to quickly determine the salary at which a newly opened cashier's job should be advertised. The informal telephone technique is also good for checking discrepancies, such as when the human resource director wants to confirm if some area banks are really paying tellers 10% more than is his or her bank. Informal discussions among human resource specialists at professional conferences (like local meetings of the Human Resources Professionals of Ontario) are other occasions that typify informal salary surveys.

Perhaps 20% to 25% of employers use formal questionnaire surveys to collect compensation information from other employers. A survey may be a one-page questionnaire that inquires about things like number of employees, overtime policies, starting salaries, and paid vacations. Formal surveys like this let respondents answer at their leisure, and are quite comprehensive. However, they are also time-consuming to complete, and some employers will object to completing them for competitive reasons.

For a salary survey to be useful, it must be sufficiently specific: 60% of the respondents in one study, for instance, claimed that job categories were too broad or imprecise, as were industry categories. Therefore, a survey should be constructed with enough detail to make it useful to the organization.[18]

Commercial, Professional, and Government Salary Surveys

Many organizations also rely on surveys that are published by various commercial firms, professional associations, or government agencies. Commercial firms that conduct pay surveys include Peat, Marwick, and Partners, and Hay Associates. Professional organizations that conduct pay surveys include the Administrative Management Society and the Engineers Joint Salary Survey. Finally, government agencies that conduct wage surveys include Statistics Canada; Labour Canada; the Pay Research Bureau; and the Conference Board of Canada (which publishes The Compensation Data Source).

Step 2: Determine the Worth of Each Job: Job Evaluation

Purpose of Job Evaluation

Job evaluation is aimed at determining the relative worth of a job. It involves a formal and systematic comparison of jobs in order to determine the worth of one job relative to another and eventually results in a wage or salary hierarchy. The basic procedure of job evaluation is to compare the content of jobs in relation to one another, for example, in terms of their effort, responsibility, and skills. If an organization knows (based on a salary survey and compensation policies) how to price key benchmark jobs and can use job evaluation to determine the relative worth of all the other jobs in the firm relative to these key jobs, then it is well on its way to being able to equitably price all the jobs in the organization.

Compensable Factors

Job evaluation involves comparing jobs to one another based on their content and it is the job's **compensable factors** that constitute what is meant by content.

    There are two basic approaches that are used for comparing several jobs. First, the organization can take an intuitive approach. For example, it might decide that one job is "more important" than another and not dig any deeper into why in terms of specific job-related factors.

    As an alternative, the organization can compare jobs by focusing on certain basic factors each of the jobs has in common. In compensation management, these basic factors are called compensable factors. They are the factors that determine the definition of job content and are the basic factors that help determine the compensation paid for each job.

    Some employers develop their own compensable factors; most use factors that have been popularized by packaged job evaluation systems or by government legislation. For example, in Ontario pay equity focuses on four compensable factors—skills, effort, responsibility, and working conditions—and holds that women in jobs that are about the same as men's (in terms of these factors) should be paid the same. As another example, the job evaluation method popularized by the Hay consulting firm focuses on three compensable factors: know-how, problem solving, and accountability.

    The compensable factors an organization focuses on depend on the nature of the job and the method of job evaluation to be used. For example, the organization might choose to focus on the compensable factor decision making for a manager's job, while that factor might be inappropriate for the job of assembler.

    Identifying compensable factors plays a pivotal role in job evaluation. In job evaluation each job is usually compared with all comparable jobs using the same compensable factors. Thus the same elemental components for each job are evaluated, making the jobs easier to compare to each other—for example, in terms of the degree of skill, effort, responsibility, and working conditions present in each job.[19]

Planning and Preparation for the Job Evaluation

Job evaluation is mostly a judgmental process, one that demands close cooperation among supervisors, human resource specialists, and the employees and their

compensable factor

union representatives. The main steps involved include identifying the need for the program, getting cooperation, and then choosing an evaluation committee; the latter then carries out the actual job evaluation.[20]

Identifying the need for job evaluation should not be a difficult task. For example, dissatisfaction reflected in high turnover, work stoppages, or arguments may result from the inequities of paying employees different rates for similar jobs.[21] Similarly, managers may express uneasiness with the current, informal way of assigning pay rates to jobs, accurately sensing that a more systematic means of assigning pay rates would be more equitable and manageable because rules, procedures, and an accepted method could be used for deciding how much to pay for each job.

Since employees may fear that a systematic evaluation of their jobs may actually reduce their wage rates, getting employee cooperation (for the evaluation) is the second important step. Employers can tell employees that, as a result of the impending job evaluation program, wage rate decisions will no longer be made just by management whim, that job evaluation will provide a mechanism for considering the complaints they have been expressing, and that no present employee's rate will be adversely affected as a result of the job evaluation.[22]

Next the organization has to establish a job evaluation committee, for two reasons. First, the committee should bring to bear the points of view of several people who are familiar with the jobs in question, each of whom may have a different perspective regarding the nature of the jobs to be evaluated. Second (assuming the committee is composed at least partly of employees), the committee approach can help ensure greater acceptance by employees of the results of the job evaluations.

The committee usually consists of about five members, most of whom are employees. While management has the right to serve on such a committee, its presence may be viewed with suspicion by employees and "it is probably best not to have managerial representatives involved in committee evaluation of nonmanagerial jobs...."[23] However, the inclusion of a human resource specialist can usually be justified on the grounds that he or she has a more impartial image than line managers and can provide expert assistance in the job evaluation. One approach is to have this person serve in a nonvoting capacity. Union representation is also possible; in most cases, though, the union's position is that it is only accepting job evaluation as an initial decision technique, and is reserving the right to appeal the actual job pricing decisions through grievance or bargaining channels.[24] Once constituted, each committee member receives a manual explaining the job evaluation process, and special instructions and training that explain how to conduct a job evaluation.

The evaluation committee serves three main functions. First, it usually identifies 10 or 15 key benchmark jobs. These will be the first jobs to be evaluated and will serve as the anchors or benchmark against which the relative importance or value of all other jobs can be compared and slotted into a hierarchy of jobs. Next, the committee may select compensable factors (although the human resource department will usually choose these themselves, as part of the process of determining the specific job evaluation technique to be used). Finally, the committee turns to its most important function, evaluating the worth of each job. For this the committee will probably use one of the following job evaluation methods, such as the ranking method, the job classification method, the point method, or the factor comparison method.

Ranking Method of Job Evaluation

The simplest job evaluation method is the **ranking method**. It involves ranking each job relative to all other jobs, usually based on some overall factor like "job difficulty." There are several steps involved in ranking jobs.

ranking method

1. *Obtain job information.* The first step is job analysis. Job descriptions for each job are prepared and these are (usually) the basis upon which the rankings are made. (Sometimes job specifications are also prepared, but the job ranking method usually ranks jobs according to "the whole job" rather than a number of compensable factors. Therefore, job specifications—which provide an indication of the demands of the job in terms of problem solving, decision making, and skills, for instance—are not quite as necessary with this method as they are for other job evaluation methods.)

2. *Select raters and jobs to be rated.* It is often not practical to make a single ranking of all jobs in an organization. The more standard procedure involves ranking jobs by department or in "clusters" (i.e., factory workers, clerical workers, etc.). This eliminates the need for having to compare directly, say, factory jobs and clerical jobs.

3. *Select compensable factors.* In the ranking method, it is common to use just one factor (such as job difficulty) and to rank jobs on the basis of "the whole job." Regardless of the number of factors chosen, it is advisable to carefully explain the definition of the factor(s) to the evaluators so that they evaluate the jobs consistently.

4. *Rank jobs.* Next, the jobs are ranked. The simplest way to do this involves giving each rater a set of index cards, each of which contains a brief description of a job. These cards are then ranked from lowest to highest. Some managers use an "alternation ranking method" for making the procedure more accurate: they take the cards and first choose the highest and then the lowest, then the next highest and next lowest and so on until all the cards have been ranked. Since it is usually easier to choose extremes, this approach facilitates the ranking procedure. A job ranking is illustrated in Table 12.2. Jobs in this small health facility are ranked from maid up to office manager. The corresponding pay scales are shown on the right.

5. *Combine ratings.* It is common to have several raters rank the jobs independently. After this is done, the rating committee can then simply average the rankings.

The advantages of the ranking method are that it is the simplest job evaluation method, as well as the easiest to explain. Also, it usually takes less time to accomplish than other methods.

It has some disadvantages too, but these derive more from how it is used than the method itself. For example, there is a tendency to rely too heavily on "guesstimates." Another drawback is that ranking provides no yardstick for measuring the value of one job relative to another. For example, job No. 4 may in fact be five times "more valuable" than job No. 5, but with the ranking system all that is known is that the one job ranks higher than the other. Ranking is usually more appropriate for small organizations that cannot afford the time or expense of developing a more elaborate system.

TABLE 12.2 Job Ranking by Olympia Health Care

Ranking Order	Annual Pay Scale
1. Office manager	$28 000
2. Chief nurse	27 500
3. Bookkeeper	19 000
4. Nurse	17 500
5. Cook	16 000
6. Nurse's aide	13 500
7. Maid	10 500

After ranking, it becomes possible to slot additional jobs between those already ranked and to assign an appropriate wage rate.

Job Classification (or Grading) Evaluation Method

classification (or grading) method

classes

grades

The **classification (or grading) method** is a simple, widely used method by which jobs are categorized into groups. The groups are called **classes** if they contain similar jobs (like all "administrative assistants"), or **grades** if they contain jobs that are similar in difficulty but are otherwise different (thus in the federal government's pay grade system a "press secretary" and a "fire chief" might both be graded "PM-2").

There are several ways to categorize jobs. One is to draw up class descriptions and place jobs into classes based on their correspondence to these descriptions. Another is to draw up a set of classifying rules for each class (e.g., "How much independent judgment, skill, physical effort, etc., does the class of jobs require?") and then categorize the jobs according to these rules.

The usual procedure is to choose compensable factors and then develop class or grade descriptions that describe each class in terms of the amount or level of compensable factor(s) in jobs.

The job classification method has several advantages. Its main advantage is that most employers usually end up classifying jobs anyway, regardless of the job evaluation method that they use. They do this to avoid having to work with and price an unmanageable number of jobs; with the job classification method all jobs are already grouped into several classes. The disadvantages are that it is difficult to write the class or grade descriptions, and considerable judgment is required in applying them. Yet many employers (including the Canadian government) use this method with success.

Point Method of Job Evaluation

point method

The **point method** is a more quantitative job evaluation technique. It involves identifying (1) several compensable factors, each having several degrees, as well as (2) the degree to which each of these factors is present in the job. A different number of points is usually assigned for each degree of each factor. Once it is determined to what degree each factor is present in the job, the corresponding number of points for each factor is then added up. The result is a quantitative point rating for each job. The point method is apparently the most widely used job evaluation method.

Factor Comparison Job Evaluation Method

The **factor comparison method** is also a quantitative technique and entails deciding which jobs have more of the chosen compensable factors than others. The method is actually a refinement of the ranking method. With the ranking method, the user generally looks at each job as an entity and ranks the job on some overall factor like job difficulty. With the factor comparison method, the user ranks each job several times—one for each compensable factor chosen. For example, jobs might be ranked first in terms of the compensable factor "skill." Then they would be ranked according to their "mental requirements," and so forth. Finally, these rankings would be combined for each job into an overall numerical rating for the job. This method is also widely used.

factor comparison method

Step 3: Group Similar Jobs Into Pay Grades

Once a job evaluation method has been used to determine the relative worth of each job, the committee can turn to the task of assigning pay rates to each job, but it will usually want to first group jobs into **pay grades**. If the committee used the ranking method, point method, or factor comparison method it could assign pay rates to each individual job.[25] But for a large employer such a pay plan would be difficult to administer, since there might be different pay rates for hundreds or even thousands of jobs. Even in small organizations there is a tendency to try to simplify wage and salary structures as much as possible. Therefore, the committee will probably want to group similar jobs (similar in terms of their ranking or number of points, for instance) into grades for pay purposes. Then, instead of having to deal with hundreds of pay rates, it might only have to focus on, say, 10 or 12 pay grades.[26]

pay grades

A pay grade comprises jobs of approximately equal difficulty or importance as determined by job evaluation. If the point method was used, the pay grade consists of jobs falling within a range of points. If the ranking plan was used, the grade consists of all jobs that fall within two or three ranks. If the classification system was used, then the jobs are already categorized into classes or grades. (If the factor comparison method is used, the grade will consist of a specified range of pay rates, as explained in the appendix to this chapter.) Ten to 16 grades per "job cluster" (factory jobs, clerical jobs, etc.) is common.

Step 4: Price Each Pay Grade—Wage Curves

The next step is to assign pay rates to each pay grade. (Of course, if the employer chooses not to slot jobs into pay grades, pay rates would instead have to be assigned to each individual job.) Assigning pay rates to each pay grade (or to each job) is usually accomplished with a **wage curve**.

wage curve

The wage curve depicts graphically the pay rates currently being paid for jobs in each pay grade relative to the points or rankings assigned to each job or grade (as determined by the job evaluation). An example of a wage curve is presented in Figure 12.3. Note that pay rates are shown on the vertical axis, while the pay grades (in terms of points) are shown along the horizontal axis. The purpose of the wage curve is to show the relationship between (1) the value of the job as determined by one of the job evaluation methods and (2) the current average pay rates for the grades.

The pay rates shown on the graph are traditionally those now paid by the organization; if there is reason to believe that the present pay rates are substantially

FIGURE 12.3
Plotting a Wage Curve

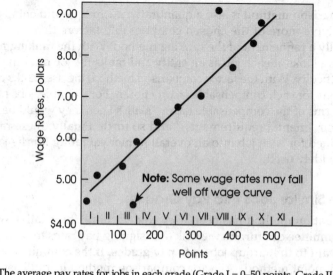

Note: The average pay rates for jobs in each grade (Grade I = 0–50 points, Grade II = 51–100 points, Grade III = 101–150 points, etc.) are plotted, and the wage curve fitted in.

out of step with the prevailing market pay rates for these jobs, benchmark jobs within each pay grade are chosen and priced via a compensation survey. These new market-based pay rates are then the wage rates plotted on the wage curve.

There are several steps in pricing jobs with a wage curve. First, the average pay for each pay grade must be determined, since each of the pay grades consists of several jobs. Next, the pay rates for each pay grade are plotted, as was done in Figure 12.3. Then a line (called a wage line) is fitted through the points just plotted. This is either done free hand or by the use of a statistical method. Finally, jobs are priced. Wages along the wage line are the target wages or salary rates for the jobs in each pay grade. If the current rate being paid for any job or grade falls well above or below the wage line, that rate may be "out of line"; raises or a pay freeze for that job may be in order. Fine tuning the pay rates, then, is the next step.

Step 5: Fine Tune Pay Rates

Finally, the pay rates for each pay grade are fine tuned. This involves correcting out-of-line rates and (usually) developing rate ranges.

Developing Rate Ranges

rate ranges

Most employers do not pay a single rate for all jobs in a particular pay grade; instead, they develop **rate ranges** for each grade so that there might, for instance, be 10 levels or "steps" and 10 corresponding pay rates within each pay grade. One way to depict the rate ranges for several grades is with a wage structure, as in Figure 12.4. The wage structure graphically depicts the range of pay rates (in this case, per hour) to be paid for each pay grade.

There are several benefits in using rate ranges for each pay grade. First, an employer can take a more flexible stance with respect to the labour market. For example, it makes it easier to attract experienced, higher-paid employees into a pay

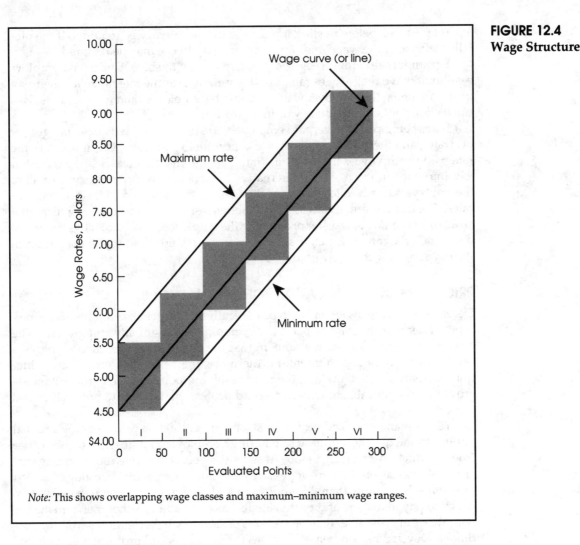

FIGURE 12.4
Wage Structure

Note: This shows overlapping wage classes and maximum–minimum wage ranges.

grade where the starting salary for the lowest step may be too low to attract such experienced personnel. Rate ranges also allow employers to provide for performance differences between employees within the same grade or between those with different seniorities. As in Figure 12.4, most employers structure their rate ranges to overlap a bit so that an employee with experience or seniority may earn more than an entry-level person in the next higher pay grade.

The rate range is usually built around the wage line or curve. One alternative is to arbitrarily decide on a maximum and minimum rate for each grade, such as 15% above and below the wage line. As another alternative, some employers allow the rate range for each grade to become wider for the higher pay ranges, reflecting the greater demands and performance variability inherent in these more complex jobs.

Correcting Out-of-Line Rates

It is possible (as in Figure 12.3) that the wage rate for a job may fall well off the wage line (or well outside the rate range for its grade). This means that the average pay for that job is currently too high or too low, relative to other jobs in the firm. If a point falls well below the line, a pay raise for the job may be required. If the plot falls well above the wage line, a pay cut or a pay freeze may be required.

For underpaid employees, the problem is easy to solve. Underpaid employees should have their wages raised to the minimum of the rate range for their pay grade, assuming the employer wants to retain the employees and has the funds. This can be done either immediately or in one or two steps.

Rates being paid to overpaid employees are often called red circle, flagged, or overrates, and there are several ways to cope with this problem. One is to freeze the rate paid to employees in this grade until general salary increases bring the other jobs into line with it. A second alternative is to transfer or promote some or all of the employees involved to jobs where they can legitimately be paid their current pay rates. The third alternative is to freeze the rate for six months, during which time an attempt is made to transfer or promote the employees involved; if this cannot be done, then the rate at which these employees are paid is cut to the maximum in the pay range for their pay grade.

PRICING MANAGERIAL AND PROFESSIONAL JOBS

Developing a compensation plan to pay executive, managerial, and professional personnel is similar in many respects to developing a plan for any employees.[27] The basic aims of the plan are the same in that the goal is to attract good employees and maintain their commitment. Furthermore, the basic methods of job evaluation—classifying jobs, ranking them, or assigning points to them, for instance—are about as applicable to managerial and professional jobs as to production and clerical ones.

Yet for managerial and professional jobs, job evaluation provides only a partial answer to the question of how to pay these employees because these jobs differ from production and clerical jobs in several respects. For one thing, managerial and professional jobs tend to emphasize nonquantifiable factors like judgment and problem solving more than do production and clerical jobs. Second, there is a tendency to pay managers and professionals based on ability—their performance or what they can do—rather than on the basis of "static" job demands like working conditions. Developing compensation plans for managers and professionals therefore tends to be a relatively complex matter, one in which job evaluation, while still important, usually plays a secondary role to nonsalary issues like bonuses, incentives, and benefits.

Compensating Managers
Basic Compensation Elements

There are five elements in a manager's compensation package: salary, benefits, short-term incentives, long-term incentives, and perquisites.[28]

The amount of salary managers are paid is usually a function of the value of the person's work to the organization and how well the person is discharging his or her responsibilities. As with other jobs, the value of the person's work is usually determined through job analysis and salary surveys and the resulting fine tuning of salary levels. Salary is the cornerstone of executive compensation, since it is on this element that the other four are layered, with benefits, incentives, and perquisites normally awarded in some proportion to the manager's base pay.

The other four elements are benefits, short- and long-term incentives, and perquisites. Benefits (including time off with pay, health care, employee services, survivors protection, and retirement coverage) are discussed in Chapter 14. Short-term incentives are designed to reward managers for attaining short-term (normally yearly) goals, while long-term incentives are aimed at rewarding the person for long-term performance (in terms of increased market share and the like). Incentives are discussed in Chapter 13. Perquisites (perks for short) begin where benefits leave off and are usually given to only a select few executives based on organizational level and (possibly) past performance.

Executive compensation tends to emphasize performance incentives more than do other employees' pay plans, since organizational results are more likely to directly reflect the contributions of executives than those of lower-echelon employees. In point of fact, there is considerable disagreement regarding what determines executive pay and therefore whether top executives are worth what they are paid. At the lower levels of management (like first-line supervisor), there is no debate; supervisors' pay grades are usually set so that their median salaries are 10% to 25% above those of the highest paid workers supervised.

Managerial Job Evaluation

Despite questions regarding the rationality of executive pay levels, job evaluation still plays an important role in pricing executive and managerial jobs, at least in most firms. According to one expert, "the basic approach used by most large companies to ensure some degree of equity among various divisions and departments is to classify all executive and management positions into a series of grades, to which a series of salary ranges is attached."[29]

As with nonmanagerial jobs, one alternative is to rank the executive and management positions in relation to each other, grouping those of equal value. However, the job classification and point evaluation methods are also used, with compensable factors like scope of the position, complexity, difficulty, and creative demands.

Compensating Professional Employees

Compensating nonsupervisory professional employees like engineers and scientists presents some unique problems.[30] Investigative work puts a heavy premium on creativity and problem solving, compensable factors that are not easily compared or measured. Furthermore, the professional's economic impact on the firm is often related only indirectly to the person's actual effort; for example, the success of an engineer's invention depends on many factors, such as how well it is produced and marketed.

The job evaluation methods we explained previously can be used for evaluating professional jobs.[31] The compensable factors here tend to focus on problem solving, creativity, job scope, and technical knowledge and expertise. Both the point method and factor comparison methods are used, although the job classification method seems most popular. Here a series of grade descriptions are written, and then a position is slotted into the grade having the most appropriate definition.

Yet, in practice, traditional methods of job evaluation are rarely used for professional jobs since "it is simply not possible to identify factors and degrees of factors which meaningfully differentiate among the values of professional work."[32]

Computerized Reports for Salary Administration

Because of the routine nature of many salary administration decisions, the payroll department is usually one of the first to be computerized in any organization. In terms of decisions, for example, weekly or biweekly cheques must be produced based on the number of hours (or salary) of each employee. From each person's gross pay, various deductions then must be routinely computed, deductions that include federal tax, and unemployment insurance and pension contributions. These are all routine decisions that lend themselves to computerization.

Computerization also facilitates producing salary administration reports, and there are several such reports that managers require.[1] The *Job Classification Listing* report in Table 12.3 ranks all jobs in the supervisor's department, arranging them by base pay in descending order. (The "Value" column might reflect points in a Hay plan, for instance, while "base" indicates the person's base pay as compared with the midpoints and maximum pay in the person's rate range.) The *Manpower Control Report* indicates, for each position in the manager's department, the extent to which that position classification is fully staffed: in this case, for instance, the department is missing one part-time electrician and is budgeted for (and has) no part-time painters.

In addition to these periodic departmental reports, it is not uncommon for many other pay reports to be produced on an ad hoc basis. For example, the *Base Pay by Job Classification Report* lists the base pay of each employee in each job classification, along with their position effective date (the day they moved into that position), their employment date, and months of prior experience. This report can be valuable for comparing employees' pay within a job classification. *The Pay Increase Report* shows at a glance each employee's current pay, proposed increase, and new pay. A computerized report can be produced showing the total cost of all increases, by job classification, and in total for the organization.

Other computerized reports are produced as well. The *Pay Comparison Report* is useful because it shows (across departments) the salary ranges, position effective date, date employed, and months of prior experience (before joining the company) of each employee in a job classification. This can help to eliminate inequities that might otherwise occur, say, between electricians in different departments. The *Compa-Ratio Report* indicates how each employee in a job classification is being paid relative to the midpoint in his or her rate range. The *Average Salary Data Report* is produced for a single job classification and provides salary data. In Table 12.3, for instance, there are a total of four electricians in this job classification, their maximum base pay is $8.86 per hour, their minimum base pay is $8.45 per hour, and their average base pay is $8.67 per hour.

---

[1]Michael P. Jaquish, "Reports for Salary Administration," *Personnel Journal* (December 1988), pp. 79-83.

"Knowledge and the skill of applying it," as one expert notes, "are extremely difficult to quantify and measure."[33]

As a result, most employers use a market-pricing approach in evaluating professional jobs. They price professional jobs in the marketplace to the best of their ability to establish the values for benchmark jobs; then these benchmark jobs and the employer's other professional jobs are slotted into a salary structure. Specifically, each professional discipline (like mechanical engineering or electrical engineering) usually ends up having four to six grade levels, each of which requires a fairly broad salary range. This somewhat more subjective approach to job evaluation helps ensure that the employer remains competitive when bidding for professionals whose attainments vary widely and whose potential employers are literally found worldwide.

TABLE 12.3 Job Classification Listing

Figure 1
JOB CLASSIFICATION LISTING

Dept	Job No	Title	Value	Base	Mid	Max
345	400	electrician	256	8.50	9.50	10.50
	350	painter	220	7.95	8.95	9.95
	326	secretary	197	7.50	8.50	9.50

Figure 2
MANPOWER CONTROL REPORT

Dept	Job No	Title	Budget/Actual FT	Budget/Actual PT	Budget/Actual Full-Time Equiv
345	400	electrician	12/12	2/1	13/12.5
	350	painter	1/1	0/0	1/1

Figure 3
BASE PAY BY JOB CLASSIFICATION

Dept	Job No	Title	Employee	Base Pay	Posn Date	Emp Date	MPE*
345	400	electrician	Williams, Bill	8.8	2/22/86	2/22/86	46
235	400	electrician	Johnson, Joe	8.8	1/15/86	1/15/86	50
321	400	electrician	Jones, Henry	8.52	6/12/83	5/23/79	0
345	400	electrician	Glass, George	8.45	3/15/83	3/15/83	2

*months of prior experience

Figure 4
PAY INCREASE REPORT

Curr Dept	Prop Job No	New Title	Employee	Pay	Inc	Pay
345	400	electrician	Williams, Bill	8.86	.35	9.21
235	400	electrician	Johnson, Joe	8.86	.35	9.21
321	400	electrician	Jones, Henry	8.52	.35	8.87
345	400	electrician	Glass, George	8.45	.35	8.80

TABLE 12.3 (continued)

Figure 5
PAY INCREASE REPORT SHOWING TOTAL COST

Dept	Job No	Title	Employee	Prev Pay	Inc	New Pay
345	400	electrician	Williams, Bill	8.86	.35	9.21
235	400	electrician	Johnson, Joe	8.86	.35	9.21
321	400	electrician	Jones, Henry	8.52	.35	8.87
345	400	electrician	Glass, George	8.45	.35	8.80

Total cost 1.40

Figure 6
JOB CLASS INCREASE REPORT

Job No	Title	FT	PT	FTE	Indiv' Incr	Total Cost
400	electrician	27	3	28.5	.35	9.98
326	secretary	11	1	11.5	.26	2.99
350	painter	3	0	3.0	.30	.90

Total cost per hour: $13.87

Annual cost: $28 849.60

Figure 7
PAY COMPARISON REPORT

Dept	Job No	Title	Employee	Base Pay	Posn Date	Emp Date	MPE*
345	400	electrician	Williams, Bill	8.8	2/22/86	2/22/86	46
235	400	electrician	Johnson, Joe	8.86	1/15/86	1/15/86	50
321	400	electrician	Jones, Henry	8.52	6/12/83	5/23/79	0
345	400	electrician	Glass, George	8.45	3/15/83	3/15/83	2

*months of prior experience

Figure 8
COMPA-RATIO REPORT

Dept	Job No	Title	Employe	Base Pay	Posn ate	Emp Date	MPE*	Compa-ratio
345	400	electrician	Williams, Bill	8.86	2/22/86	2/22/8	46	93.26
235	400	electrician	Johnson, Joe	8.86	1/15/86	1/15/8	50	93.26
321	400	electrician	Jones, Henry	8.52	6/12/83	5/23/7	0	89.68
345	400	electrician	Glass, George	8.45	3/15/83	3/15/8	2	88.94

*months of prior experience

Figure 9
AVERAGE SALARY DATA REPORT

Dept	Job No	Title	Employe	Base Pay	Posn Date	Emp Date	MPE*	Compa-ratio
345	400	electrician	Williams, Bill	8.86	2/22/86	2/22/8	46	93.26
235	400	electrician	Johnson, Joe	8.86	1/15/86	1/15/8	50	93.26
321	400	electrician	Jones, Henry	8.52	6/12/83	5/23/7	0	89.68
345	400	electrician	Glass, George	8.45	3/15/83	3/15/8	2	88.94

total employees: 4   **min base pay:** 8.45   **avg compa-ratio:** 91.29

max base pay: 8.86   **average base pay:** 8.67

SOURCE: Michael P. Jaquish, "Reports for Salary Administration," *Personnel Journal* (December 1988), pp. 80–81.

HUMAN RESOURCE MANAGEMENT IN ACTION

Canadian CEOs Rank Third in Compensation

Toronto—Chief executive officers of Canadian companies rank eighth in the world in salaries earned, but when taxes and purchasing power are figured in, move up to third spot overall. A recent survey by Towers Perrin Forster & Crosby shows that a typical Canadian CEO earns $234 000. Americans topped the list at $383 867 and Swiss executives were second at $322 267. After taxes and cost-of-living are taken into account, Americans rank first in net purchasing power and Venezuelans second. At the other end of the scale, Japanese CEOs rank third in net pay, but only sixteenth in net purchasing power.

The survey reveals that there is a bigger gap between the salaries of managers and labourers in countries with little union representation than in those with a large union membership. In Canada and the U.S., managers earn from five to nine times the salary of the typical production worker, but in Argentina, Brazil, and Venezuela, managers may earn 35 times as much. As for social security contributions, Canadians contribute the third-smallest percentage of covered earnings (4%) of the 20 countries surveyed, behind Hong Kong (which has no social security system) and Australia (1.25%).

SOURCE: *Human Resources Management in Canada*, Report Bulletin no. 70 (December 1988), p. 2. Used with permission.

CURRENT ISSUES IN COMPENSATION MANAGEMENT

Pay Equity

Pay equity is a concept that requires that specific measures be undertaken by employers to redress inequities in pay between men and women in the workplace. Pay equity means equal pay for work of equal value. It is based on two other concepts. The first is equal pay for equal work.[34] This concept requires that male and female workers be paid the same wage rate for doing identical work. The application of this principle requires organizations to pay waiters and waitresses the same

pay equity

levels of pay. The second concept is equal pay for similar or substantially similar work (equal pay for work of comparable worth). This concept requires that male and female workers be paid the same wage rate for jobs of a similar nature which may have different titles. The application of this principle requires organizations to pay nurses' aides the same as orderlies, and male janitors the same as female cleaners.

Pay equity is substantially broader in scope than these two fundamental concepts, in that it is intended to eliminate the historical wage gap between men and women.[35] The historical wage gap that has existed in Canada has resulted in female workers making substantially less than their male counterparts. The wage gap is partly explained by the fact that female workers have traditionally occupied certain low-paying jobs,[36] particularly secretarial, teaching, nursing, and retail sales. The application of pay equity requires organizations to pay male and female employees the same pay when their work is shown to be equal in value. This applies even though the female and male jobs may be dissimilar. For example, in 1985 the Canadian Human Rights Commission approved an interim settlement between the federal government and the Public Service of Canada for the payment of equal pay for dissimilar jobs. The approved settlement paid home economists and physical therapists the same as agriculture and forestry workers. What must be demonstrated is that the jobs performed by male and female workers are equal in composite skill, effort, responsibility, and working conditions.

According to the Canadian Human Rights Commission (CHRC), job value or job content is defined as follows:

> Value of work is the value which the work performed by an employee in a given establishment represents in relation to the work of another employee, or group of employees, the value being determined on the basis of approved criteria, without the wage market or negotiated wage rates being taken into account. The CHRC defines criteria as skill, effort, responsibility, and working conditions. These criteria form a composite measure to be used by employers to equalize the wage rates for female jobs in order to achieve and maintain pay equity between males and females. Under the Canadian Human Rights Act it is illegal for an employer to establish and maintain differences in wages between male and female employees working in the same organization who are performing work of equal value or content. However, the Act provides for exceptions where reasonable factors exist. In order for employers to make use of these factors they must demonstrate that the wage differences are not based on sex. These factors must be applied consistently, fairly, and equally. These exceptions are outlined in the Equal Wage Guidelines as follows:[37]

1. Seniority (based on length of service)
2. Different performance ratings (this is based on the ratings derived from a formal performance appraisal system which has been brought to the attention of each employee)
3. Red-circling (based on the results of job evaluation)
4. Rehabilitation assignment (re-entry into the workforce by an employee after lengthy absence due to illness)
5. Procedure of phased-in wage reductions
6. Demotion pay procedures (this is based on unsatisfactory job performance by an employee, or due to reassignment because of work force surplus)
7. Temporary training positions

One of the aims of pay equity is to eliminate gender discrimination from the wage-setting process. Pay equity requires employers to pay women and men the same for jobs that are of similar value. Pay equity legislation requires that employers evaluate jobs and search for inequities between male and female job classes.[38] A *job class* means that those positions in an establishment that have similar duties and responsibilities and require similar qualifications should be filled by similar recruiting procedures and have the same compensation schedule, salary grade, or range of salary rates.

One of the methods used to determine job classes is the *group of jobs* approach, defined as a series of job classes that bear a relationship to each other because of the nature of the work required to perform the job. Some comparison systems allow for factors to be weighed to reflect their relative importance in the organization. Weighing involves making judgments about how the organization values different aspects of job content. This is acceptable, provided that the judgments are free of gender bias.

The Pay Equity Act does not mention job evaluation specifically. It does, however, require employers to engage in a process of job comparison, and that the comparison be done in a way that is gender-neutral.[39] If the comparators are found to be of equal or similar value and the female job pays less, then an upward wage adjustment is made to the female job class. However, no wage reductions are allowed under the legislation.

The Pay Equity Act designates a specific sequence for identifying the appropriate male comparator job class for any particular job class. A male job class can serve as a comparator for more than one female job class.

Pay Equity Models

As we indicated in Chapter 2, the federal government uses a complaints-based system, whereas the Province of Ontario uses a system-wide, proactive model.

Under the complaint-based model, the legislation has to be activated by a complaint, usually from an employee (or group of employees), or a bargaining agent. A complaint may not go forward if the comparison is not being made between predominantly male and female jobs, or the jobs are not in the same establishment, or the jobs are exempt because the pay difference is based upon one of the "reasonable factors" recognized by the Human Rights Commission. If the complaint goes forward, then appropriate steps are taken to implement a job comparison (job evaluation) procedure that is gender-neutral. After the process is complete and the results are known, the commission may act as conciliator to bring about a voluntary settlement. But if a voluntary settlement is not achieved, then the commission appoints a tribunal to give a binding decision that may be challenged only in a federal court.

The complaint-based system has many drawbacks: from an employee's point of view it is time-consuming and could be costly because of the potential that exists for employer reprisal. The complainant may have to bear the burden of the costs involved in processing the complaint, while other groups may "piggy-back" on the outcome of the process if they too receive a wage adjustment. Because of these factors, few pay equity complaints have been filed in the federal sector.

The Ontario proactive model requires all employers (with more than 100 employees) to use a bona fide job evaluation plan, to develop and post a pay equity plan, and eventually to achieve pay equity by eliminating any wage disparities or differential between male- and female-dominated jobs of the same value as determined by the job evaluation plan.

The Ontario model solves many of the problems of the federal complaint-based model. However, it creates the potential for conflicts of efficiency. That is, it involves the substantial administrative cost of a job evaluation procedure that is required whether or not there is a complaint, or whether or not there is evidence of discrimination.[40]

In 1991 the Province of Ontario introduced amendments to the Pay Equity Act that included two additional ways of making job comparisons. These are proportional value comparisons in the private and public sectors, and proxy comparisons in the public sector.

Proportional value comparison is a method of comparing female and male job classes indirectly. It examines the relationship between the value of the work done and the pay received by male job classes and ensures that the same relationship is applied to female job classes. This method permits all female job classes in an organization to be compared with the male job classes in the organization, even if the number of male job classes is relatively small; for instance, a retail store with male managers and male janitors could use proportional value comparisons to determine raises for female retail clerks.

Proxy comparison is a method that applies to the public sector only where job-to-job comparison or proportional value comparison cannot be used because there are no male job classes or too few male job classes exist. A proxy comparison allows for comparison with job classes in another public sector organization that performs similar work.[41]

Pay Equity Legislation

A number of jurisdictions in Canada have introduced equal pay legislation designed to achieve fairness in the distribution of pay, and protection against discrimination in pay levels. These jurisdictions are the federal government, the provincial governments of Manitoba, New Brunswick, Newfoundland, Nova Scotia, Ontario, Prince Edward Island, and Quebec, and the Yukon territorial government. Table 12.4 lists the pay equity provisions of these jurisdictions. As Table 12.4 indicates, the pay equity legislations are frequently governed by similar composite criteria. The Canadian Human Rights Commission has the responsibility for enforcing the federal pay equity legislation.

The Issue of Pay Secrecy

There are basically two opposing points of view with respect to the question "Should employees know what other employees in the organization are being paid?" The basic argument for "open pay" is that it improves employee motivation, and the basic thinking here is as follows. According to the expectancy theory of motivation (explained in Chapter 11) an employee's perception of how (and if) pay depends on effort has a direct bearing on the person's motivation. In other words, if employees believe that greater effort does not result in greater rewards, then, generally speaking, greater effort (and therefore motivation) will not be forthcoming. On the other hand, if employees do believe that there is a direct relationship between effort and rewards, then greater effort should result. Proponents of "open pay" contend that where workers do not know each other's pay they cannot easily (or at all) assess how effort and rewards are related, and as a result of this uncertainty motivation tends to suffer. (They cannot, for example, say "Smith doesn't work hard, so is paid less than Jones, who works hard.") A related argument is based on equity

TABLE 12.4 Pay Equity at a Glance

	FEDERAL	MANITOBA	NEW BRUNSWICK	NEW-FOUNDLAND	NOVA SCOTIA	ONTARIO	PEI	QUEBEC	YUKON
Legislation	Canadian Human Rights Act (1978)	Pay Equity Act (1984)	Pay Equity Act (1989)	N/A (Collective Agreement)	Pay Equity Act (1988)	Pay Equity Act (1987)	Pay Equity Act (1988)	Charter of Rights & Freedoms (1976)	Yukon Human Rights Act (1987)
Model	Complaint-based	Pro-Active	Pro-Active	Collective Agreement-Civil Service	Pro-Active	Pro-Active	Pro-Active	Complaint-based	Complaint-based
Coverage	Federal Public Sector, Crown Corporations, Federally Regulated Industries	Public & Broader Public Sectors (except municipalities, school boards)	Public (Government employees-excludes hospitals and school boards)	Public Sector (Government employees only)	Government, Crown corporations, hospitals & school boards (universities, municipalities & other broader public sectors in 1990; Private sector coverage in 1992)	Public & Private Sectors	Public & Broader Public Sectors	Public & Private Sectors	Public Sector
Approach	Wage Line/ Job to Job	Wage Line	Wage Line	Wage Line	Job to Job	Job to Job	Job to Job	Not specific	Job to Job
Gender Predominance	Staggered percentages, equally applicable to female & male	70% female/male	60% female 70% male (historical incumbency)	60% female/male	60% female/male gender stereotypes	60% female 70% male (historical incumbency, gender stereotypes)	60% female/male (historical incumbency, gender stereotypes)	N/A	Not defined
Establishment	Functional definition	N/A	N/A	N/A	N/A	Geographic	N/A	Not specific	Functional

(continued)

TABLE 12.4 (Continued)

	FEDERAL	MANITOBA	NEW BRUNSWICK	NEW-FOUNDLAND	NOVA SCOTIA	ONTARIO	PEI	QUEBEC	YUKON
Incumbency Rule	No	10 employees in a job class	10 employees in a job class	5 employees in a job class	10 employees in a job class	No	No	N/A	N/A
Exceptions	Performance ratings seniority, red-circling, rehabilitation assignments, demotion pay or phased-in reduction of pay, training assignments	Factors justifying pay differences may be negotiated	Same as Ontario	Service, temp training, red-circling, skills shortage	Seniority, temporary training, merit pay, skills shortage	Seniority, Red-circling, temp training skills shortage	Performance appraisal, seniority, skills shortage	Difference based on the following criteria not discriminatory if applicable to all positions: experience, seniority, years of service, merit, productivity or overtime	Demotion procedures, seniority, training programs, skills shortage, regional rates, red-circling
Agency	Canadian Human Rights Commission	Pay Equity Bureau	Pay Equity Bureau	N/A	Pay Equity Commission	Pay Equity Commission	Pay Equity Bureau	Quebec Human Rights Commission	Yukon Human Rights Commission

SOURCE: Reproduced with permission from *Canadian Pay Equity Compliance Guide*. This table was prepared by Peat Marwick Thorne and is published by and copyright CCH Canadian Limited, Don Mills, ON.

theory. Specifically, Lawler contends that pay secrecy can and does result in misperceptions of salary levels and, consequently, in feelings of inequity. Lawler believes that by following an "open pay" policy, organizations can reduce such misperceptions by showing employees that they are in fact equitably paid. The opposing argument is that in practice there are usually real inequities in the pay scale, perhaps because of the need to hire someone "in a hurry," or because of the superior salesmanship of a particular applicant. Even if the employee in a similar job who is being paid more actually deserves the higher salary because of his or her effort, skill, or experience, it is possible that employee's lower-paid colleagues, viewing the world though their own point of view, may still convince themselves that they are underpaid relative to him or her.

The research findings to this point are sketchy. In one study a researcher found that managers' satisfaction with their pay increased following their firms' implementation of an open pay policy.[42] One survey found that less than half the firms responding gave employees access to salary schedules. Those not providing such information indicated, among other things, that "secrecy prevents much quibbling...," "salary is a delicate matter...," open pay "could well lead to unnecessary strain and dissatisfaction among managers...," and "open systems too often create misunderstandings and petty complaints." The author of this study notes that "whether the inequities result from a growth situation or some other factor, it is clear that some inequities and openness are incompatible."[43] The implication for compensation management seems to be that a policy of open pay can, under the best of conditions, improve employees' satisfaction with their pay and (possibly) their efforts as well. On the other hand, if conditions are not right—and especially if there are any lingering inequities in the employer's pay structure—moving to an open pay policy is not advisable.

The Issue of Inflation and Compensation Management

Inflation and how to cope with it has been another important issue in compensation management. According to one estimate, a family of four earning $21 000 in 1975 would have to earn $43 000 (over 60% more) by 1981 to maintain the same purchasing power because of inflation, and because the family would move to higher income tax brackets as their income increased.[44] With reduced inflation in the mid-1980s, though, this has become somewhat less of an issue.

A related problem—salary compression—was ranked as a major problem by 15% of the respondents in one study. Salary compression is a result of inflation. Its symptoms include (1) higher starting salaries, thereby compressing current employees' salaries; (2) unionized hourly pay increases that overtake supervisory and nonunion hourly rates; and (3) the recruitment of new college graduates at salaries above those of current jobholders.[45]

In the 1970s and early 1980s, employers tried to cope with inflation's impact in many ways. More employers granted across-the-board salary increases either in lieu of or in addition to performance-based merit increases. Others changed their pension plans to index them to inflation so that the value of the pension payments increased along with the rise in the price of goods.[46] Others changed the compensation mix to decrease the emphasis on taxable income like wages and salary and to substitute nontaxable benefits like flexible work hours, dental plans, day care centres, and group legal and auto insurance plans.[47]

The cost of living adjustment (or COLA) clause is another way employers tried to cope with inflation.[48] The COLA clause was first adopted by the United Auto Workers and the General Motors Corporation in 1950. The COLA escalator clause is designed to maintain the purchasing power of the wage rate and operates as follows. Specified increases in the Consumer Price Index trigger increases in the wage rate, with the magnitude of the increase depending on the negotiated COLA formula.[49] The most common formula provides a one cent per hour wage adjustment for each 0.3% or 0.4% change in consumer prices.[50] Nonunion employees often then receive a similar adjustment. Periodically, the employer then takes a portion of the dollar COLA and builds it into the employee's base salary, a procedure known as "baking in."[51] Again, though, COLAs have become less of a concern to unions as inflation has moderated.

The Issue of Cost of Living Differentials

Cost of living differences between localities have escalated from occasional inconveniences into serious compensation problems. For example, a family of four might live in Ottawa for just over $39 000 per year while the same family's annual expenditures in Toronto would be over $46 000. Deciding whether and how to have differential pay rates for employees living in different locales and how to handle employees moving from one area to another are thus important compensation issues today.

Employers are using several methods to handle cost of living differentials. The main approach is to give the transferred person a nonrecurring payment, usually in a lump sum, or perhaps spread over one to three years.[52] Other employers pay

HUMAN RESOURCE MANAGEMENT

On the Front Line

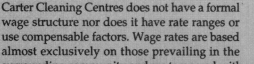

Carter Cleaning Centres does not have a formal wage structure nor does it have rate ranges or use compensable factors. Wage rates are based almost exclusively on those prevailing in the surrounding community and are tempered with an attempt on the part of Jack Carter to maintain some semblance of equity between what workers with different responsibilities in the stores are paid.

Needless to say, Carter does not make any formal surveys when determining what his company should pay. He peruses the want ads almost every day and conducts informal surveys among his friends in the local chapter of the laundry and cleaners trade association. While Jack has taken a "seat-of-the-pants" approach to paying employees, his salary schedule has been guided by several basic pay policies. While many of his colleagues adhere to a policy of paying absolutely minimum rates, Jack has always followed a pol-

icy of paying his employees about 10% above what he feels are the prevailing rates, a policy that he believes reduces turnover while fostering employee loyalty. Of somewhat more concern to Jennifer is her father's policy of paying men about 20% more than women for the same job. Her father's explanation is "They're stronger and can work harder for longer hours, and besides they all have families to support." Jennifer has several questions:

1. Is our company at the point where we should be setting up a formal salary structure, complete with a job evaluation? Why?

2. Is my father's policy of pay 10% more than the prevailing rates a sound one, and how could I determine whether or not it is?

3. Similarly, is his male-female differential wise and if not why not?

a differential for ongoing costs in addition to a one-time allocation. For example, one employer pays a differential of $6000 per year to people earning $35 000 to $45 000 who are transferred from Ottawa to Toronto; the first $6000 is a lump sum at the time of the move, and in the second year the employee gets another $6000 in quarterly increments. Employees already living in Toronto (or any other high-cost area) are not given any adjustment.[53] Other companies simply increase the employee's base salary rate. They give the person an automatic raise equal to the amount that living costs in the new locale exceed those in the old, in addition to any other promotion-based raise the employee may get.

SUMMARY

1. Compensation has three components: direct financial payments, indirect payments (financial fringe benefits), and nonfinancial rewards.

2. There are a number of internal and external environmental factors that affect compensation. Internal factors include the role of the human resource department; the organization's ability to pay; compensation policies; and equity. External factors include competitors' influences; government influences; union influences; and labour market conditions.

3. Establishing pay rates involves five steps, each of which are explained in this chapter: conducting salary surveys; evaluating jobs; developing pay grades; using wage curves; and fine-tuning pay rates.

4. Job evaluation is aimed at determining the relative worth of a job. It involves comparing jobs to one another based on their content, which is usually defined in terms of compensable factors like skills, effort, responsibility, and working conditions.

5. The ranking method of job evaluation involves five steps: (1) obtaining job information; (2) selecting clusters of jobs to be rated; (3) selecting compensable factors; (4) ranking jobs; and (5) combining ratings (of several raters). This is a simple method to use but there is a tendency to rely too heavily on guesstimates. The classification (or grading) method is a second qualitative approach that involves categorizing jobs based on a "class description" or "classification rules" for each class.

6. The point method of job evaluation requires identifying a number of compensable factors and then determining the degree to which each of these factors is present in the job. As explained in the appendix, it involves nine steps: (1) determining types of jobs to be evaluated; (2) collecting job information; (3) selecting compensable factors; (4) defining compensable factors; (5) defining factor degrees; (6) determining relative weights of factors; (7) assigning point values to factors and degrees; (8) developing a job evaluation manual; and (9) rating the jobs. This is a quantitative technique and many packaged plans are readily available.

7. The factor comparison method (as explained in the appendix) is a quantitative job evaluation technique that entails deciding which jobs have more of certain compensable factors than others. It is one of the most widely used job evaluation methods and entails eight steps: (1) obtaining job information; (2) selecting key jobs; (3) ranking key jobs by factors; (4) distributing wage rates by factors for each job; (5) ranking jobs by wage rates; (6) comparing the two sets of rankings to screen out unusable key jobs; (7) constructing the job compari-

son scale; and (8) using the job comparison scale. This is a systematic, quantifiable method. However, it is also a difficult method to implement. Steps 5 and 6 may be skipped.

8. Most managers group similar jobs into wage or pay grades for pay purposes. These comprise jobs of approximately equal difficulty or importance as determined by job evaluation.

9. The wage curve (or line) shows the average target wage for each pay grade (or job). It can help show what the average wage for each grade should be, and whether any present wages (or salaries) are out of line. Developing a wage curve involves four steps: (1) finding the average pay for each pay grade; (2) plotting these wage rates for each pay grade; (3) drawing the wage line; and (4) pricing jobs, after plotting present wage rates.

10. Developing a compensation plan for managerial and professional personnel is complicated by the fact that factors like performance and creativity must take precedence over "static" factors like working conditions. Market rates, performance, and incentives and benefits thus play a much greater role than does job evaluation for these employees.

11. Four current compensation issues we discussed were pay equity, pay secrecy, inflation, and cost of living differentials.

KEY TERMS

compensation
salary surveys
benchmark jobs
compensable factor
ranking method

classification (or grading) method
classes
grades
point method

factor comparison method
pay grades
wage curve
rate ranges
pay equity

DISCUSSION QUESTIONS

1. What is the difference between internal equity and external equity?
2. What external factors affect compensation?
3. What is (are) the purpose(s) of salary surveys? Why are they important?
4. Discuss the pros and cons of the following methods of job evaluation: ranking, classification, factor comparison, and point method.
5. In what respect is the factor comparison method similar to the ranking method? How do they differ?
6. What is the difference between the federal pay equity model and the Province of Ontario pay equity model?

CASE INCIDENT: How Much Are They Worth to You?

The Vice President of Atlantic Fishing International called a meeting to discuss the company's compensation system because there had been persistent complaints from employees about real or perceived inequities in pay.

Various employees complained that some of their fellow workers were making more than they were for doing the same or similar work. Others complained that the rate of pay at Atlantic was much lower that at other companies in the community.

The Vice President started the meeting by saying that though he was aware of the complaints of workers, it was not the policy of the company to be a pay leader, nor was the company prepared to match the rate of pay that more profitable and larger companies were paying. He also felt that the company should not pay all workers the same pay for the same job since each worker's performance varied according to his or her capabilities and motivation.

Atlantic has been in existence since 1965. It has never conducted a pay survey or a job evaluation. The company has generally paid workers what it believes they are worth and what it feels it can afford. The company employs 50 individuals. The average seniority in the company is about 15 years. Until the current wave of complaints, employees were happy with the company. They felt that Atlantic was a very good employer that cared about its workers and that often went out of its way to help employees in times of difficulty.

Sheldon Anderson, Compensation Manager, sat quietly during the Vice President's presentation. He was hesitant initially to respond to the Vice President. He is experienced with job evaluations and pay surveys as methods of establishing internal and external equities in pay rates. Yet, based on what he heard, it became clear to him that the Vice President might not be receptive to information gathered through pay surveys and job evaluations.

However, he told the Vice President that the company might benefit from the appearance of pursuing both methods. He said, "Just because you conduct a pay survey and job evaluation, it does not mean you have to change your pay structure. These methods generally provide information about where an organization stands in comparison to its competitors. They also assist in determining the fairness of a firm's compensation policies."

Questions

1. How can Sheldon convince the Vice President to authorize conducting a pay survey and job evaluation?

2. Assuming the Vice President gave Sheldon the authorization, what steps should Sheldon take to accomplish both tasks?

EXPERIENTIAL EXERCISE

Purpose: The purpose of this exercise is to give you experience in performing a job evaluation using either the ranking method or the point method.

Required Understanding: You should be thoroughly familiar with both the ranking and the point methods of job evaluation and with the five job descriptions presented in Figure 12.5.

How to Set Up the Exercise/Instructions

1. Divide the class into groups of four or five students. Half the groups will perform a job evaluation of the clerical positions described at the end of this exercise

using the ranking method; the other half will do so using the point method (as described in the appendix to this chapter).

2. *Groups using the ranking method.* Perform a job evaluation by ranking the jobs described at the end of this exercise. You may use one or more compensable factors.

3. *Groups using the point method.* Perform a job evaluation on the jobs described at the end of this exercise using the point method. This should include selecting compensable factors, defining these factors, defining factor degrees, determining the relative values of factors, assigning point values to factors and degrees, and rating the jobs. Since all the jobs you are evaluating are clerical they already comprise just one "cluster."

4. If time permits, a spokesperson from each point method group can put his or her group's factors, points, and ratings on the board. Did the "point method" groups end up with about the same results? How did they differ? Why do you think they differed? How did the point method groups' results differ from the ratings developed by the "ranking" groups?

5. The job descriptions for five secretarial jobs are presented in Figure 12.6. They are *not* necessarily in order of difficulty. The appropriate order of the jobs from lowest to highest is given below, but please do not read this until *after* you have completed this exercise.

(low) Job D; Job A; Job E; Job C; Job B

FIGURE 12.5 Job Description A

DISTINGUISHING CHARACTERISTICS OF WORK

This is responsible supervisory and/or technically varied and complex typing and clerical work involving the excercise of independent judgment and initiative in the development of specialized work methods and procedures and their application to the solution of technical problems.

An employee in a position allocated to this class independently performs varied and complex clerical functions that require the use of initiative and judgment in carrying assignments to completion; performs specialized technical clerical work of a complex nature; types a variety of materials and reports which frequently include specialized scientific or legal terminology; supervises a small group of employees performing relatively complex clerical and related assignments; or supervises a larger group in the performance of more routinized or less difficult assignments.

Work is performed under the general supervision of a higher-level employee. Assignments are restricted only by their subject content and its relation to the activities or functional unity with which the incumbent is connected. Where the work situation involves the performance of individually difficult and varied clerical duties, the number of subordinate personnel for whom the Clerk Typist III is responsible is ordinarily small.

EXAMPLES OF WORK PERFORMED

(Note: These examples are intended only as illustrations of the various types of work performed in positions allocated to this class. The omission of specific statements of duties does not exclude them from the position if the work is similar, related, or a logical assignment to the position.)

Plans, assigns, corrects, and generally reviews the work of a large group of secretarial and clerical employees performing routine uncomplicated clerical activities or a smaller number of subordinate personnel performing individually difficult and varied tasks.

Compiles and edits information for special reports concerning the operation of the agency in which the employee gathers various information from the agency and other sources, and separates the data into pre-arranged categories.

Verifies, checks, and examines technical and complex surveys and other types of reports for accuracy, completeness, compliance with agency standards and policies, and adequacy.

Types, with speed and accuracy, involved correspondence, reports, records, orders, and other documents from rough drafts, transcribing machines, notes, and oral instructions in rough and/or finished form.

Composes important correspondence without review and/or specific instructions.

May perform all clerical work related to a particular phase of a program for which the supervisor is responsible.

Performs related work as required.

MINIMUM TRAINING AND EXPERIENCE

Graduation from a standard high school and two years of clerical and/or typing experience.

Successful completion of post-high school training from an accredited college or university, or vocational or technical school may be substituted at the rate of 30 semester hours or 720 classroom hours on a year-for-year basis for the required experience.

NECESSARY SPECIAL REQUIREMENT

Ability to type at the rate of 35 correct words per minute.

FIGURE 12.5 Job Description B

DISTINGUISHING CHARACTERISTICS OR WORK

This is varied and highly responsible secretarial, clerical, and administrative work as the assistant to a high level administrator, an agency head, academic dean, major department head, or senior attorney.

An employee in a position allocated to this class performs a variety of secretarial, clerical and administrative duties requiring an extensive working knowledge of the organization and program under the supervisor's jurisdiction. Work involves performing functions that are varied in subject matter and level of difficulty and range from performance of standardized clerical assignments to performance of administrative duties which would otherwise require the administrator's attention. Work also includes relieving the supervisor the administrative detail and office management functions.

Work is performed under general supervision and only assigned projects which are highly technical or confidential are given close attention by the supervisor.

EXAMPLES OF WORK PERFORMED

(Note: These examples are intended only as illustrations of the various types of work performed in positions allocated to this class. The omission of specific statements of duties does not exclude them from the position if the work is similar, related, or a logical assignment to the position.)

Takes and transcribes dictation that may vary from simple correspondence to legal, medical, engineering, or other technical subject matter,

Serves as personal assistant to a high level administrative official by planning, initiating, and carrying to completion clerical, secretarial, and administrative activities.

Develops material for supervisor's use in public speaking engagements.

Attends conferences to take notes, or is briefed on meetings immediately after they take place in order to know what amendments were made and what developments have occurred in matters that concern the supervisor.

Makes arrangements for conferences including space, time, and place; and informs participants of topics to be discussed; and may provide them with background information.

Assists in and coordinates the preparation of operating and legislative budgets; examines budget documents to insure that they comply with state regulations.

Receives and routes telephone calls, answering questions which may involve the interpretation of policies and procedures.

Interviews and makes preliminary selection of clerical, stenographic, and secretarial employees, makes assignments, schedules hours of work, provides for office coverage, and reviews the work of subordinate employees.

Serves as office receptionist; greets, announces, and routes visitors.

Performs related work as required.

MINIMUM TRAINING AND EXPERIENCE

Graduation from a standard high school and four years of secretarial and/or clerical experience, two of which must have been at the Secretary II level or above.

Successfully completed classroom studies in secretarial science or commercial subjects beyond high school level may be substituted for the required non-specific experience at the rate of 710 classroom hours or 30 semester hours per year for up to a maximum of two years.

NECESSARY SPECIAL REQUIREMENT

Ability to take and transcribe dictation at a rate of 80 words per minute and to type at a rate of 35 correct words per minute.

FIGURE 12.5 Job Description C

DISTINGUISHING CHARACTERISTICS OF WORK

This is secretarial work of considerable variety and complexity.

An employee in a position allocated to this class performs duties which involve taking and transcribing dictation for a supervisor who is carrying out a moderately broad program; composing correspondence; and typing memoranda, reports and correspondence. Duties include making travel arrangements and keeping the supervisor's calendar. Assignments at this level involve relieving the supervisor of minor administrative and/or clerical functions and exercising considerable initiative in carrying out legal dictation of ordinary complexity and preparing and processing legal documents and records.

Work is performed under general or administrative supervision. Only projects which entail technical or confidential matters are given close attention by the immediate supervisor.

EXAMPLES OF WORK PERFORMED

(Note: These examples are intended only as illustrations of the various types of work performed in positions allocated to this class. The omission of specific statements of duties does not exclude them from the position if the work is similar, related, or a logical assignment to the position.)

Takes and transcribes dictation.

Receives and reads incoming mail. Screens items which she can handle herself, forwarding the rest to her supervisors or her subordinates, together with necessary background material.

Maintains alphabetical and chronological files and records of office correspondence, documents, reports, and other materials.

Acts as office receptionist; answers telephone, greets, announces and routes visitors.

Assists in expediting the work of the office including such matters as shifting clerical subordinates to take care of fluctuating work loads.

Assembles and summarizes information from files and documents in the office or other available sources for the supervisor's use on the basis of general instructions as to the nature of the information needed.

Performs all clerical work related to a particular phase of the supervisor's program, maintaining all records and composing correspondence relative to the project.

Composes and signs routine correspondence of a non-technical nature in her supervisor's name.

Keeps supervisor's calendar by scheduling appointments and conferences with or without prior clearance.

Performs related work as required.

MINIMUM TRAINING AND EXPERIENCE

Graduation from a standard high school and three years of secretarial and/or clerical experience.

Successfully completed classroom studies in secretarial science or commercial subjects beyond the high school level may be substituted at the rate of 720 classroom hours or 30 semester hours on a year-for-year basis.

NECESSARY SPECIAL REQUIREMENT

Ability to take and transcribe dictation at a rate of 80 words per minute and type at a rate of 35 correct words per minute.

FIGURE 12.5 Job Description D

DISTINGUISHING CHARACTERISTICS OF WORK

This is varied and moderately complex typing and clerical work requiring the exercise of some independent judgment in the use of relatively involved work methods and procedures.

An employee in a position allocated to this class is required to utilize the touch system in typing, from rough drafts and from transcription machine recordings, a variety of materials which may include specialized reports or tabular arrangements of numerical or statistical data. Work includes performing a variety of clerical duties which are individually of moderate complexity and difficulty, or where work is repetitive, there is some latitude for finality of decision or independence of action.

Work is performed under general supervision with detailed instructions given in cases involving new or unusually difficult problems. Assignments may be made through the operation of established unity procedures, and work is reviewed by a higher level clerical or administrative supervisor while in progress or upon completion.

EXAMPLES OF WORK PERFORMED

(Note: These examples are intended only as illustrations of the various types of work performed in positions allocated to this class. The omission of specific statements of duties does not exclude them from the position if the work is similar, related, or a logical assignment to the position.)

Types correspondence, memoranda, reports, records, orders, stencils, and other office documents from rough drafts, transcribing machines, notes, and oral instructions for rough and finalized copy work which is general, complex, and often technical or scientific in nature.

Verifies, codes, or classifies incoming materials and documents, and may be responsible for returning incorrect material to sender for correction and maintains follow-up procedures to be sure that corrected materials are returned; may make computations for reports and records or reduce information to a simple form for use by the agency.

Gathers a variety of information from various sources for use by others in answering correspondence, preparing reports, conducting interviews, or writing speeches, articles, or news releases; may prepare simple reports or draft routine correspondence.

Establishes and may be responsible for the complete maintenance of small files which would include responsibility for accurate filing and retrieval of materials.

Answers telephone, screens and routes calls, takes messages, and may answer routine questions.

May plan, assign, review, and correct work of lower level employees and train them in the performance of assigned duties.

May operate a variety of general office machines with such accuracy as can be acquired from their use on the job and not from any skills possessed before appointment.

Performs related work as required.

MINIMUM TRAINING AND EXPERIENCE

Graduation from a standard high school and one year of clerical and/or typing experience.

Successful completion of post-high school training from and accredited college or university, or vocational or technical school may be substituted at the rate of 30 semester hours or 720 classroom hours for the required experience.

NECESSARY SPECIAL REQUIREMENT

Ability to type at a rate of 35 correct words per minute.

FIGURE 12.5 Job Description E

DISTINGUISHING CHARACTERISTICS OF WORK

This is secretarial and clerical work of moderate variety and complexity.

An employee in a position allocated to this class performs duties which involve taking and transcribing dictation for a supervisor; composing routine correspondence; typing memoranda, reports, and correspondence; and making travel arrangements and keeping supervisor's calendar. Heavy emphasis is placed on relieving the supervisor of as much clerical detail as possible, and work varied widely both in subject matter and level of difficulty.

Work is performed under general supervision and only projects which entail technical or confidential matters are given close attention by the immediate supervisor.

EXAMPLES OF WORK PERFORMED

(Note: These examples are intended only as illustrations of the4 various types of work performed in positions allocate to this class. The omission of specific statements of duties does not exclude them from he position if the work is similar, related, or a logical assignment to the position.)

Takes and transcribes dictation.

Types correspondence, articles, reports, manuals, and other materials on general or technical subjects; drafts routine acknowledgments in response to inquiries not requiring a supervisor's attention.

Examines, checks, and verifies complex statistical and other reports for completeness, propriety, adequacy, and accuracy of computations; determines conformity to established requirements; and personally follows up the more complicated discrepancies.

Keeps supervisor's calendar by clearing requests for and reminding him of appointments.

Makes travel arrangements and arranges travel itineraries.

Prepares special reports as required and maintains files and records.

Performs related work as required.

MINIMUM TRAINING AND EXPERIENCE

Graduation from a standard high school and one year of secretarial and/or clerical experience.

Successfully completed course work in secretarial science or commercial subjects beyond the high school level may be substituted at the rate of 720 classroom hours or 30 semester hours per year for one year of the required experience.

NECESSARY SPECIAL REQUIREMENT

Ability to take and transcribe dictation at a rate of 80 words per minute and type at a rate of 35 correct words per minute.

NOTES

1. Naresh C. Agarwal, "Wage and Salary Administration," in *Human Resources Management in Canada* (Scarborough, Ont.: Prentice-Hall Canada, 1986), p. 40,013.

2. Thomas Patten, Jr., *Pay: Employee Compensation and Incentive Plans* (New York: Free Press, 1977), p. 1.

3. Robert Sibson, *Compensation* (New York: AMACOM, 1981), pp. 284-286.

4. Stanley Henrici, *Salary Management for the Nonspecialist* (New York: AMACOM, 1980), p. 20.

5. Joseph Famularo, *Handbook of Modern Personnel Administration* (New York: McGraw-Hill, 1972), pp. 27-29. See also Bruce Ellig, "Strategic Pay Planning," *Compensation and Benefits Review*, Vol. 19, no. 4 (July-August 1987), pp. 28-43; Thomas Robertson, "Fundamental Strategies for Wage and Salary Administration," *Personnel Journal*, Vol. 65, no. 11 (November 1986), pp. 120-132.

6. This section is based on Naresh C. Agarwal, "Wage and Salary Administration," in *Human Resources Management in Canada* (Scarborough, Ont.: Prentice-Hall Canada, 1986), pp. 40,013–40,014.

7. *Compensation Planning Outlook 1991*, 9th ed., Judith Lendvay-Zwickl, ed., Report SR25 (The Conference Board of Canada, 1990), pp. 4-5.

8. Ibid.

9. Edward Hay, "The Attitude of the American Federation of Labour on Job Evaluation," *Personnel Journal*, Vol. 26 (November 1947), pp. 163-169; Howard James, "Issues in Job Evaluation: The Union's View," *Personnel Journal*, Vol. 51 (September 1972), pp. 675-679; Henderson, *Compensation Management*, pp. 117-118; Harold Jones, "Union Views on Job Evaluations: 1971 vs. 1978," Personnel *Journal*, Vol. 58 (February 1979), pp. 80-85.

10. For a lively discussion on motivating individuals, see David A. Nadler and Edward E. Lawler, "Motivation: A Diagnostic Approach" in Joe Kelly, J. Bruce Prince, and Blake Ashford, *Organizational Behaviour*, 2nd ed. (Toronto: Prentice-Hall Canada Inc., 1991), pp. 112-120.

11. Orlando Behling and Chester Schriesheim, *Organizational Behavior* (Boston: Allyn & Bacon, 1976) p. 233.

12. See our discussion of equity theory in Chapter 11.

13. See our discussion of Maslow's three needs theory in Chapter 11.

14. For a comprehensive discussion of the literature on motivation and work behaviour, see Richard M. Steers and Lyman W. Porter, eds., *Motivation and Work Behavior*, 4th ed. (New York: McGraw-Hill Book Company, 1987).

15. "Use of Wage Surveys," *BNA Policy and Practice Series* (Washington, D.C: Bureau of National Affairs, 1976), pp. 313-314. In a recent survey of compensation professionals, uses of salary survey data were reported. The surveys were used most often to adjust the salary structure and ranges. Other uses included determining the merit budget, adjusting individual job rates, and maintaining pay leadership. D. W. Belcher, N. Bruce Ferris, and John O'Neill, "How Wage Surveys are Being Used," *Compensation and Benefits Review* (September-October 1985), pp. 34-51. For further discussion, see, for example, Kent Romanoff, Ken Boehm, and Edward Benson, "Pay Equity: Internal and External Considerations," *Compensation and Benefits Review*, Vol. 18, no. 3 (May-June 1986), pp. 17-25.

16. Helen Murlis, "Making Sense of Salary Surveys," *Personnel Management*, Vol. 17 (January 1981), pp. 30-33. For an explanation of how market analysis can be used to ensure fair and competitive pay for all jobs in the organization, see, for example, Peter Olney, Jr., "Meeting the Challenge of Comparable Worth: Part 2," *Compensation and Benefits Review*, Vol. 19, no. 3 (May-June 1987), pp. 45-53.

17. Richard I. Henderson, *Compensation Management: Rewarding Performance* (Englewood Cliff, N.J.: Prentice-Hall Inc. 1989), pp. 213-233.

18. Joan O'Brien and Robert Zawacki, "Salary Surveys: Are They Worth the Effort," *Personnel*, Vol. 62, no. 10 (October 1985), pp. 70-74.

19. You may have noticed that job analysis as discussed in Chapter 4 can be a useful source of information on compensable factors, as well as on job descriptions and job specifications. For example, a quantitative job analysis technique like the position analysis questionnaire generates quantitative information on the degree to which the following five basic factors are present in each job: having decision making/communication/social responsibilities; performing skilled activities; being physically active; operating vehicles or equipment; and processing information. As a result, a job analysis technique like the PAQ is actually as (or, some say, more) appropriate as a job evaluation technique in that jobs can be quantitatively compared to one another on those five dimensions and their relative worth thus ascertained. Another point worth noting is that a single set of compensable factors may not be adequate for describing all jobs. Many managers therefore divide their jobs into job clusters, such as a separate job cluster for factory workers, for clerical workers, and for managerial personnel. Similarly, there would probably be a somewhat different set of compensable factors for each job cluster.

20. A. N. Nash and F. J. Carroll, Jr., "Installation of a Job Evaluation Program," from *Management of Compensation* (Monterey, Calif.: Brooks/Cole, 1975); reprinted in Craig Schneier and Richard Beatty, *Personnel Administration Today: Readings and Commentary* (Readings, Mass.: Addison-Wesley, 1978), pp. 417-425; and Henderson, *Compensation Management*, pp. 231-239. According to one survey, about equal percentages of employers use individual interviews, employee questionnaires, or observations by personnel representatives to obtain the actual job evaluation information. See Mary Ellen Lobosco, "Job Analysis, Job Evaluation, and Job Classification," *Personnel*, Vol. 62, no. 5 (May 1985), pp. 70-75. See also Howard Risher, "Job Evaluation: Validity and Reliability," *Compensation and Benefits Review*, Vol. 21, no. 1 (January-February 1989), pp. 22-36; and David Hahn and Robert Dipboye, "Effects of Training and Information on the Accuracy and Reliability of Job Evaluations," *Journal of Applied Psychology*, Vol. 73, no. 2 (May 1988), pp. 146-153.

21. See, for example, Donald Petri, "Talking Pay Policy Pays Off," *Supervisory Management*, (May 1979), pp. 2-13.

22. As explained later, the practice of red circling is used to delay downward adjustments in pay rates that are presently too high given the newly evaluated jobs. See also E. James Brennan, "Everything You Need to Know About Salary Ranges," *Personnel Journal*, Vol. 63, no. 3 (March 1984), pp. 10-17.

23. Nash and Carroll, "Installation of a Job Evaluation," p. 419.

24. Ibid.

25. If the job classification method was used, then of course the jobs are already classified.

26. David Belcher, *Compensation Administration* (Englewood Cliffs, N. J.: Prentice-Hall, 1973), pp. 257-276.

27. Dale Yoder, *Personnel Management and Industrial Relations* (Englewood Cliffs, N.J.: Prentice-Hall, 1970), pp. 643-645; Joseph Famularo, *Handbook of Modern Personnel Administration* (New York: McGraw-Hill, 1972), pp. 32.1-32.6 and 30.1-30.8.

28. Bruce Ellig, *Executive Compensation—A Total Pay Perspective* (New York: McGraw-Hill, 1982), pp. 9-10.

29. Famularo, *Handbook of Modern Personnel Administration*, pp. 32.1-32.6. See also Peter Sherer, Donald Schwab, and Herbert Henneman, "Managerial Salary-Raise Decisions: A Policy-Capturing Approach," Personnel Psychology, Vol. 40, no. 1 (Spring 1987), pp. 27-38.

30. Ibid., pp. 30.1-30.15.

31. Ibid., pp. 30.1-30.5. See also Patrick Moran, "Equitable Salary Administration in High-Tech Companies," *Compensation and Benefits Review*, Vol. 18, no. 5 (September-October 1986), pp. 31-40.

32. Sibson, *Compensation*, p. 194.

33. Ibid.

34. Russel G. Juriansz, *Equal Pay Legislation and Ontario's New Pay Equity Act* (Toronto: Blake, Cassels & Graydon), pp. 3-5.

35. See *Equal Pay for Work of Equal Value*, Labour Canada, Ministry of Labour, Ministry of Supply and Services.

36. William W. Back, *Equality in Employment: A Systemic Approach* (Ottawa: Human Rights Research and Education Centre, University of Ottawa, 1985), p. 3.

37. "Equal Pay for Male and Female Employees Who Are Performing Work of Equal Value," Interpretation guide for Section 11 of the Canadian Human Rights Act, Canadian Human Rights Commission, Ottawa.

38. J. G. Kelly, *Pay Equity Management* (Toronto: CCH Canadian Ltd., 1988), pp. 20-21.

39. David Conklin and Paul Bergman, eds. *Pay Equity in Ontario: A Manager's Guide* (Halifax, N.S.: The Institute for Research on Public Policy, 1990), p. 32.

40. Morley Gunderson and Roberta Edgecombe Robb, "Equal Pay for Work of Equal Value: Canada's Experience," *Advances in Industrial and Labour Relations*, Vol. 5, JA1 Press Inc., 1991, pp. 151-168.

41. *Newsletter*, The Pay Equity Commission, Vol. 3, no. 1 (March 1991), p. 1.

42. Charles M. Futrell, "Effects of Pay Disclosure on Satisfaction for Sales Managers: A Longitudinal Study," *Academy of Management Journal*, Vol. 21. no. 1 (March 1978), pp. 140-144.

43. Mary G. Miner, "Pay Policies: Secret or Open? and Why?" *Personnel Journal*, Vol. 53 (February 1974), reprinted in Richard Peterson, Lane Tracy, and Alan Cabelly, *Readings in Systematic Management in Human Resources*, (Reading, Mass.: Addison-Wesley, 1979), pp. 233-239.

44. Margaret Yao, "Inflation Outruns Pay of Middle Managers, Increasing Frustration," *Wall Street Journal*, June 9, 1981, p. 1. See also "The Impact of Inflation on Wage and Salary Administration," *Personnel*, Vol. 58 (November-December 1981), p. 55.

45. This section is based on or quoted from "The Impact of Inflation on Wage and Salary Administration," p. 55.

46. Robert Dockson and Jack Vance, "Retirement In Peril: Inflation and the Executive Compensation Program," *California Management Review*, Vol. 24 (Summer 1981), pp. 87-94.

47. Joan Lindroth, "Inflation, Taxes, and Perks: How Compensation is Changing," *Personnel Journal*, Vol. 60 (December 1981), pp. 934-940.

48. Clearance Deitch and David Dilts, "The COLA Clause: An Employer Bargaining Weapon?" *Personnel Journal*, Vol. 61 (March 1982), pp. 220-223.

49. Patten, Pay, p. 181.

50. Deitch and Dilts, "The COLA Clause," p. 221.

51. Patten, Pay, p. 182.

52. Rufus Runzheimer, Jr., "How Corporations Are Handling Cost of Living Differentials," *Business Horizons*, Vol. 23 (August 1980), p. 39.

53. Ibid.

SUGGESTED READINGS

Agarwal, Naresh C. "Wage and Salary Administration," *Human Resources Management in Canada*. Toronto: Prentice-Hall Canada Inc., 1986, pp. 40,011 to 40,054.

Bratton, David A. "Pay Equity and Performance Appraisal," *Human Resources Management in Canada*. Toronto: Prentice-Hall Canada Inc., 1989, pp. 40,559 to 40,562.

Conklin, David, and Paul Bergman. *Pay Equity in Ontario: A Manager's Guide.* London, Ont.: The University of Western Ontario, 1990.

Henderson, Richard. *Compensation Management*, 5th ed. Englewood Cliffs, NJ: Prentice-Hall, Inc., 1989.

Kelly, John G. *Pay Equity Management*. Toronto: CCH Canadian Limited, 1988.

Milkovich, George T., and J.M. Newman. *Compensation*, 3rd ed. Homewood, Ill.: Richard D. Irwin, 1990.

Weiner, Nan, and Morley Gunderson. *Pay Equity*. Toronto: Butterworths, 1990.

Winter, Nadine. "Pay Equity and Job Evaluation: Selecting the Right Tool," *Human Resources Management in Canada*. Toronto: Prentice-Hall Canada Inc., 1988, pp. 40,531 to 40,534.

APPENDIX 12.1 Quantitative Job Evaluation Methods

THE FACTOR COMPARISON JOB EVALUATION METHOD

The factor comparison technique is a *quantitative* job evaluation method. It has many variations and appears to be one of the most widely used, most accurate, and most complex job evaluation methods.

It entails deciding which jobs have more of certain compensable factors than others and is actually a refinement of the ranking method. With the ranking method each job is looked at as an entity and ranked. With the factor comparison method each job is ranked *several times—once for each compensable factor chosen.* For example, jobs might be ranked first in terms of the factor "skill." Then they are ranked according to their "mental requirements." Next, they are ranked according to their "responsibility," and so forth. Then these rankings are combined for each job into an overall numerical rating for the job. The required steps are as follows.

Step 1. Obtain Job Information

This method requires a careful, complete job analysis. First, job descriptions are written. Then job specifications are developed, preferably in terms of the compensable factors the committee has decided to use. *For the factor comparison method, these compensable factors are usually* (1) *mental requirements,* (2) *physical requirements,* (3) *skill requirements,* (4) *responsibility, and* (5) *working conditions.* Typical definitions of each of these five factors are presented in Figure 12.6.

Step 2. Select Key "Benchmark" Jobs

Next, 15 to 25 key jobs are selected by the job evaluation committee. These jobs will have to be representative of the range of jobs under study. Thus, they have to select "benchmark jobs" that are acceptable reference points, ones that represent the full range of jobs to be evaluated.

Step 3. Rank Key Jobs by Factors

Here evaluators are asked to rank the key jobs on each of the five factors (mental requirements, physical requirements, skill requirements, responsibility, and working conditions). This ranking procedure is based on job descriptions and job specifications. Each committee member usually makes this ranking individually, and then a meeting is held to develop a consensus (among raters) on each job. The result of this process is a table, as in Table 12.5. This shows how each key job ranks on each of the five compensable factors.

TABLE 12.5 Ranking[1] Key Jobs by Factors

	Mental Requirements	Physical Requirements	Skill Requirements	Responsibility	Working Conditions
Welder	1	4	1	1	2
Crane operator	3	1	3	4	4
Punch press operator	2	3	2	2	3
Security guard	4	2	4	3	1

[1]1 is high, 4 is low.

FIGURE 12.6 Sample Definitions of Five Factors Typically Used in Factor Comparison Method

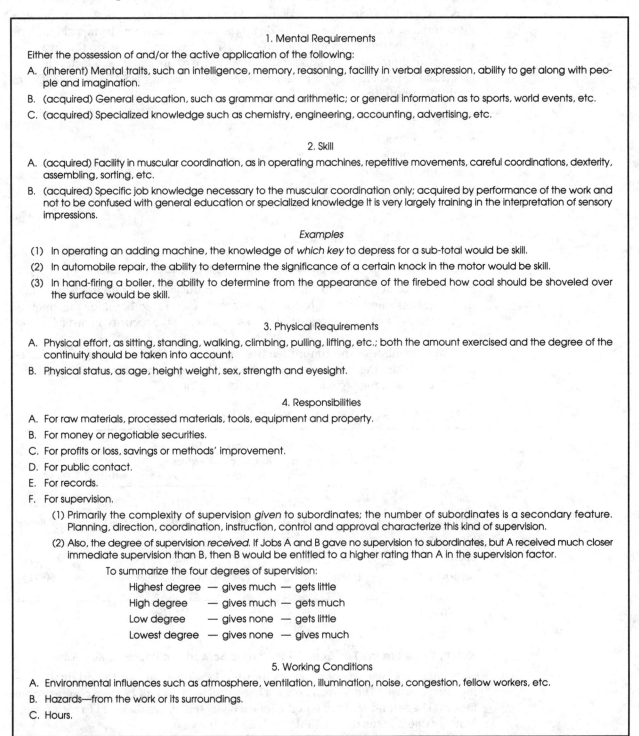

1. Mental Requirements

Either the possession of and/or the active application of the following:

A. (inherent) Mental traits, such an intelligence, memory, reasoning, facility in verbal expression, ability to get along with people and imagination.

B. (acquired) General education, such as grammar and arithmetic; or general information as to sports, world events, etc.

C. (acquired) Specialized knowledge such as chemistry, engineering, accounting, advertising, etc.

2. Skill

A. (acquired) Facility in muscular coordination, as in operating machines, repetitive movements, careful coordinations, dexterity, assembling, sorting, etc.

B. (acquired) Specific job knowledge necessary to the muscular coordination only; acquired by performance of the work and not to be confused with general education or specialized knowledge It is very largely training in the interpretation of sensory impressions.

Examples

(1) In operating an adding machine, the knowledge of *which key* to depress for a sub-total would be skill.

(2) In automobile repair, the ability to determine the significance of a certain knock in the motor would be skill.

(3) In hand-firing a boiler, the ability to determine from the appearance of the firebed how coal should be shoveled over the surface would be skill.

3. Physical Requirements

A. Physical effort, as sitting, standing, walking, climbing, pulling, lifting, etc.; both the amount exercised and the degree of the continuity should be taken into account.

B. Physical status, as age, height weight, sex, strength and eyesight.

4. Responsibilities

A. For raw materials, processed materials, tools, equipment and property.

B. For money or negotiable securities.

C. For profits or loss, savings or methods' improvement.

D. For public contact.

E. For records.

F. For supervision.

    (1) Primarily the complexity of supervision *given* to subordinates; the number of subordinates is a secondary feature. Planning, direction, coordination, instruction, control and approval characterize this kind of supervision.

    (2) Also, the degree of supervision *received*. If Jobs A and B gave no supervision to subordinates, but A received much closer immediate supervision than B, then B would be entitled to a higher rating than A in the supervision factor.

        To summarize the four degrees of supervision:

Highest degree	— gives much	— gets little
High degree	— gives much	— gets much
Low degree	— gives none	— gets little
Lowest degree	— gives none	— gives much

5. Working Conditions

A. Environmental influences such as atmosphere, ventilation, illumination, noise, congestion, fellow workers, etc.

B. Hazards—from the work or its surroundings.

C. Hours.

SOURCE: Jay L. Otis and Richard H. Leukart, *Job Evaluation: A Basis for Sound Wage Administration*, p. 181. © 1954, renewed 1983. Reprinted by permission of Prentice-Hall, Englewood Cliffs, N.J.

Step 4. Distribute Wage Rates by Factors

This is where the factor comparison method gets a bit more complicated. In this step the committee members have to divide up the present wage now being paid for *each key job*, distributing it among the five compensable factors. They do this in accordance with their judgments about the importance to the job of each factor. For example, if the present wage for the job of common labourer is $4.26, the evaluators might distribute this wage as follows:

Mental requirements	$0.36
Physical requirements	2.20
Skill requirements	0.42
Responsibility	0.28
Working conditions	1.00
Total	$4.26

Such a distribution is made for all key jobs.

Step 5. Rank Key Jobs According to Wages Assigned to Each Factor

Here again each job is ranked, factor by factor. But here the ranking is based on the wages assigned to each factor. For example (see Table 12.6), for the "mental requirements" factor, the welder job ranks first, while the security guard job ranks last.

Each member of the committee first makes this distribution working independently. Then the committee meets and arrives at a consensus concerning the money to be assigned to each factor for each key job.

TABLE 12.6 Ranking[1] Key Jobs by Wage Rates

	Hourly Wage	Mental Requirements	Physical Requirements	Skill Requirements	Responsibility	Working Conditions
Welder	$9.80	4.00(1)	0.40(4)	3.00(1)	2.00(1)	0.40(2)
Crane operator	5.60	1.40(3)	2.00(1)	1.80(3)	0.20(4)	.20(4)
Punch press operator	6.00	1.60(2)	1.30(3)	2.00(2)	0.80(2)	0.30(3)
Security guard	4.00	1.20(4)	1.40(2)	0.40(4)	0.40(3)	.60(1)

[1] 1 is high, 4 is low.

Step 6. Compare the Two Sets of Rankings to Screen Out Unusable Key Jobs

Now there are two sets of rankings for each key job. One was the original ranking (from step 3). This shows how each job ranks on each of the five compensable factors. The second ranking reflects, for each job, the wages assigned to each factor. Now a table like the one in Table 12.7 can be drawn up.

For each factor, this shows *both* rankings for each key job. On the left is the ranking from step 3. On the right is the ranking based on wages paid. For each factor, the ranking based on the amount of the factor (from step 3) should be about the same as the ranking based on the wages assigned to the job (step 5). If there is much of a discrepancy, it suggests that the key job might be a "fluke," and from this point on, such jobs are no longer used as key jobs. (Many managers do not bother to screen out "unusable" key jobs. To simplify things, they skip steps 5 and 6, going instead from step 4 to step 7; this is an acceptable alternative.)

TABLE 12.7 Comparison of Factor and Wage Rankings

	Mental Require-ments		Physical Require-ments		Skill Require-ments		Responsibility		Working Conditions	
	A[1]	$[2]	A[1]	$[2]	A[1]	$[2]	A[1]	$[2]	A[1]	$[2]
Welder	1	1	4	4	1	1	1	1	2	2
Crane operator	3	3	1	1	3	3	4	4	4	4
Punch press operator	2	2	3	3	2	2	2	2	3	3
Security guard	4	4	2	2	4	4	3	3	1	1

[1]Amount of each factor based on step 3.

[2]Ratings based on distribution of wages to each factor from step 4.

Step 7. Construct the Job-Comparison Scale

Once the usable, "true" key jobs have been identified, the next step is to set up the job-comparison scale (Table 12.8). (Note that there is a separate column for each of the five compensable factors.) To develop it, the assigned wage table from step 4 is needed.

For each of the factors (for all key jobs), the job is written next to the appropriate wage rate. Thus in the assigned wage table (Table 12.6), the welder job has $4.00 assigned to the factor "mental requirements." Therefore, on the job comparison scale (Table 12.8) "welder" is written in the "mental requirements" factor column, next to the "$4.00" row. The same is done for all factors for all key jobs.

Step 8. Use the Job-Comparison Scale

Now, all the other jobs to be evaluated can be slotted, factor by factor, into the job-comparison scale. For example, suppose a job of plater has to be slotted in. Where the "mental requirements" of the plater job would fit as compared with the mental requirements of all the other jobs listed has to be decided. It might, for example, fit between punch press operator and inspector. Similarly, where the "physical requirements" of the plater's job fit as compared with the other jobs listed would have to be determined. One might find that it fits just below crane operator. The same would be done for each of the remaining three factors.

An Example

Let us work through an example to clarify the factor comparison method. We will just use four key jobs to simplify the presentation—usually one would start with 15 to 25 key jobs.

Step 1. First, we do a job analysis.

Step 2. Here we select our four key jobs: welder, crane operator, punch press operator, and security guard.

TABLE 12.8 Job (Factor) Comparison Scale

	Mental Requirements	Physical Requirements	Skill Requirements	Responsibility	Working Conditions
.20				Crane Operator	Crane Operator
.30					Punch Press Operator
.40		Welder	Sec. Guard	Sec. Guard	Welder
.50					
.60					Sec. Guard
.70					
.80				Punch Press Operator	
.90					
1.00					
1.10				(Plater)	
1.20	Sec. Guard				
1.30		Punch Press Operator			
1.40	Crane Operator	Sec. Guard	(Inspector)	(Plater)	
1.50		(Inspector)			(Inspector)
1.60	Punch Press Operator				
1.70	(Plater)				
1.80			Crane Operator	(Inspector)	
1.90					
2.00		Crane Operator	Punch Press Operator	Welder	
2.20		(Plater)			
2.40	(Inspector)				(Plater)
2.60					
2.80					
3.00			Welder		
3.20					
3.40					
3.60					
3.80					
4.00	Welder				
4.20					
4.40					
4.60					
4.80					

Step 3. Here (based on the job descriptions and specifications) we rank key jobs by factor, as in Table 12.5.

Step 4. Here we distribute wage rates by factor, as in Table 12.6.

Step 5. Then we rank our key jobs according to wage rates assigned to each key factor. These rankings are shown in parentheses in Table 12.6.

Step 6. Next, we compare the two sets of rankings. In each left-hand column (marked A) is the job's ranking from step 3 based on the amount of the compensable factor. In each right-hand column (marked $) is the job's ranking from step 5, based on the wage assigned to that factor, as in Table 12.7.

In this case, there are no differences between any of the pairs of A (amount) and $ (wage) rankings, so *all* our key jobs are usable. If there had been any differences (for example, between the A and $ rankings for the welder job's mental requirement factor) we would have dropped that job as a key job.

Step 7. Now we construct our job comparison scale as in Table 12.8. For this, we use the wage distributions from step 4. For example, let us say that in steps 4 and 5 we assigned $4.00 to the mental requirement factor of the welder's job. Therefore, we now write "welder" on the $4.00 row under the "mental requirements" column in the exhibit.

Step 8. Now all our other jobs can be slotted, factor by factor, into our job-comparison scale. We do not distribute wages to each of the factors for our other jobs to do this. *We just decide where, factor by factor, each of our other jobs should be slotted.* We have done this for two other jobs in the factor comparison scale: they are shown in parentheses. Now we also know what the wages for these two jobs should be, and we can also do the same for *all* our jobs.

A Variation

There are several variations to this basic factor comparison method. One involves converting the dollar values on the factor comparison chart (Table 12.8) to points. (This can be done by multiplying each of the dollar values by 100, for example.) The main advantage in making this change is that the system would no longer be "locked in" to the present wage rates. Instead, each of the jobs would be compared with one another, factor by factor, in terms of a more "constant" point system.

Pros and Cons

We have presented the factor comparison method at some length because it is (in one form or another) a very widely used job evaluation method. Its wide use derives from several advantages. First, it is an accurate, systematic, quantifiable method for which detailed step by step instructions are available. Second, jobs are compared to other jobs to determine a *relative* value. Thus, in the job comparison scale one not only sees that the welder requires *more* mental ability than a plater; one can also determine about *how much more* mental ability is required—apparently about twice as much ($4.00 versus $1.70). (This type of calibration is not possible with the ranking or classification methods.) Third, this is also a fairly easy job evaluation system to explain to employees.

Probably the most serious *disadvantage* of the factor comparison method is its complexity. While it is fairly easy to explain the factor comparison scale and its rationale to employees, it is difficult to show them how to *build* one. In addition, the use of the five factors is an outgrowth of the technique developed by its originators. Yet, using the same five factors for all organizations and for all jobs in an organization may not always be appropriate.

THE POINT METHOD OF JOB EVALUATION

The point method is widely used. Basically, it requires identifying several compensable factors (like skills and responsibility), each with several degrees, and also the *degree* to which each of these factors is present in the job. A different number of points is usually assigned for each degree of each factor. So once the degree to which each factor is present in the job is determined, one need only add up the corresponding number of points for each factor to arrive at an overall point value for the job. Here are the steps.

Step 1. Determine Clusters of Jobs To Be Evaluated

Because jobs vary widely by department, usually more than one point rating plan is used in the organization. Therefore, the first step is usually to *cluster* jobs, for example, into shop jobs, clerical jobs, sales jobs, and so forth. Then the committee will generally develop a point plan for one group (or cluster) at a time.

Step 2. Collect Job Information

This involves job analysis and writing job descriptions and job specifications.

Step 3. Select Compensable Factors

Here select compensable factors, like education, physical requirements, or skills. (Often each cluster of jobs may require its own compensable factors.)

Step 4. Define Compensable Factors

Next, carefully define each compensable factor. This is to ensure that the evaluation committee members will each apply the factors with consistency. Some examples of definitions are presented in Figure 12.7. The definitions are often drawn up or obtained by the human resource specialist.

Step 5. Define Factor Degrees

Next, define each of several degrees for each factor so that raters may judge the amount or "degree" of a factor existing in a job. Thus, for the factor "complexity" there might be four degrees, ranging from "job is repetitive" through "requires initiative" (definitions for each degree are shown in Figure 12.7). The number of degrees usually does not exceed five or six, and the actual number depends mostly on judgment. Thus, if all employees either work in a quiet, air-conditioned office, or in a noisy, hot factory, then two degrees would probably suffice for the factor "working conditions." One need not have the same number of degrees for each factor, and should limit degrees to the number necessary to distinguish among jobs.

Step 6. Determine Relative Values of Factors

The next step is to decide how much weight (or how many total points) to assign to each factor. This is important because for each cluster of jobs some factors are bound to be more important than others. Thus, for executives the "mental requirements" factor would carry far more weight than would "physical requirements." The opposite might be true of factory jobs.

FACTOR 1: COMPLEXITY OF JOB

Refers to amount of judgment, planning, and initiative required. Consider the extent to which the job requires the exercise of discretion and the difficulty of the decisions that must be made. It is not necessary that all qualifications noted in a degree definition to present in order for a job to qualify for that degree. The best fit is used for assigning degrees.

1st Degree   35 points

Covers jobs that are so standardized as to require *little or no choice* of action including repetitive jobs that do not need close supervision.

2nd Degree   70 points

Follows detailed instructions and standard practices. Decisions are limited strictly to *indicated choices between prescribed alternatives* which *detail course of action.*

3rd Degree   105 points

Follows detailed instructions and standard practices, but, due to variety of factors to be considered, decisions require *some judgment, or planning to choose prescribed alternatives* which *detail course of action.*

4th Degree   140 points

General instructions and standard practices usually applicable. Due to variety and character of factors to be considered, decisions require some *initiative as well as judgment and planning to choose prescribed alternatives* which in turn require use of *resourcefulness or judgment to adapt to variations* in problems encountered.

FACTOR 2: RESPONSIBILITY FOR RELATIONSHIPS WITH OTHERS

This factor measures the degree to which the job requires the employee to get results by working with or through other people. Consider the extent to which the job involves responsibility for the work of others, and for contacts within and outside the company. The primary considderation is the nature of contact. Frequency of contact is contributory only.

1st Degree   15 points

Requires employee to get along harmoniously with fellow workers. Covers jobs with simple personal contacts within and outside own department involving little responsibility for working with or through other people, and simple telephone calls involving identification, referral of calls, taking or giving simple messages without discussion.

2nd Degree   30 points

Requires routine personal, telephone, or written contacts with others in or out of the company involving exchange and explanation of information calling for courtesy to avoid friction.

3rd Degree   45 points

Requires personal, telephone, or written contacts with others in or out of the company involving exchange and discussion of information calling for tact as well as courtesy to get cooperation or to create a favorable impression.

4th Degree   60 points

Requires personal, telephone, or written contacts with others in or out of the company involving the exercise of persuasion, discretion, and tact to get willing action or consent on a non-routine level.

SOURCE: Joseph Famularo, *Handbook of Modern Personnel Administration*, pp. 28-29. Copyright © 1972 by McGraw-Hill Inc. Used with permission.

So, the next step is to determine the relative values or "weights" that should be assigned to each of the factors. Assigning factor weights is generally done by the evaluation committee. The committee members carefully study factor and degree definitions, and then determine the relative value of the factors for the cluster of jobs under consideration. Here is one method for doing this.

First, assign a value of 100% to the highest-ranking factor. Then assign a value to the next highest factor *as a percentage of its importance to the first factor*, and so forth. For example,

Decision making	100%
Problem solving	85%
Knowledge	60%

Next, sum up the total percentage (in this case 100% + 85% + 60% = 245%). Then convert this 245% to a 100% system as follows:

Decision making:	100	÷	245	=	40.82	= 40.8%
Problem solving:	85	÷	245	=	34.69	= 34.7%
Knowledge:	60	÷	245	=	24.49	= 24.5%
Total						100.0%

Step 7. Assign Point Values to Factors and Degrees

In step 6 total weights were developed for each factor, in percentage terms. Now assign points to each factor as in Table 12.9. For example, suppose it is decided to use a total number of 500 points in the point plan. Then since the factor "decision making" had a weight of 40.8%, it would be assigned a total of 40.8% x 500 = 204 points.

Thus it was decided to assign 204 points to the "decision-making" factor. *This automatically means that the highest degree for the decision-making factor would also carry 204 points.* Then assign points to the other degrees for this factor, usually in equal amounts from the lowest to the highest degree. For example, divide 204 by the number of degrees (say, 5); this equals 40.8. Then the lowest degree here would carry about 41 points. The second degree would carry 41 plus 41, or 82 points. The third degree would carry 123 points. The fourth degree would carry 164 points. Finally, the fifth and highest degree would carry 204 points. Do this for each factor (as in Table 12.9).

TABLE 12.9 Evaluation Points Assigned to Factors and Degrees

	1st Degree Points	2nd Degree Points	3rd Degree Points	4th Degree Points	5th Degree Points
Decision making	41	82	123	164	204
Problem solving	35	70	105	140	174
Knowledge	24	48	72	96	123

Step 8. Write the Job Evaluation Manual

Developing a point plan like this usually culminates in a "point manual" or "job evaluation manual." This simply consolidates the factor and degree definitions and point values into one convenient manual.

Step 9. Rate the Jobs

Once the manual is complete, the actual evaluations can begin. Raters (usually the committee) use the manual to evaluate jobs. Each job, based on its job description and job specification, is evaluated factor by factor to determine the number of points that should be assigned to it. First, committee members determine the *degree* (1st degree, 2nd degree, etc.) to which each factor (like decision making) is present in the job. Then they note the corresponding *points* (see Table 12.9) that were previously assigned to each of these degrees (in step 7). Finally, they add up the points for all factors, arriving at a *total point value* for the job. Raters generally start with rating key jobs, obtaining consensus on these. Then they rate the rest of the jobs in the cluster.

"Packaged" Point Plans

Developing a point plan of one's own can obviously be a time-consuming process. For this reason a number of groups have developed standardized point plans. These have been used or adapted by thousands of organizations. They contain ready-made factor and degree definitions and point assignments for a wide range of jobs, and can often be used with little or no modification. One survey found that 93% of those using a ready-made plan rated it successful.

Pros and Cons

Point systems have their advantages, as their wide use suggests. This is a quantitative technique that is easily explained to and used by employees. On the other hand, it can be difficult to develop a point plan, and this is one reason many organizations have opted for ready-made plans. In fact, the availability of a number of ready-made plans probably accounts in part for the wide use of point plans in job evaluation.

CHAPTER THIRTEEN FINANCIAL INCENTIVES

After studying this chapter, you should be able to

1. Compare and contrast at least six types of incentive plans.
2. Explain at least five reasons why incentive plans fail.
3. Discuss when to use—and when not to use—incentive plans.
4. Establish and administer an effective incentive plan.

OVERVIEW

The main purpose of this chapter is to explain how to use financial incentive plans—plans that tie pay to performance—to motivate employees. Several types of incentive plans including piecework, the standard hour plan, commissions, and stock options are explained. We also discuss why incentive plans fail, and when to use them.

INCENTIVE COMPENSATION

Incentive compensation, which is also called performance-based pay or variable compensation, is a type of financial reward that ties and strengthens the link between pay and performance. Incentive compensation assumes that employees' performances can be measured and controlled by employees. It is a positive reinforcement system: for increasing their efforts and improving their performances, employees gain greater rewards.[1]

The concept of incentive compensation assumes that pay is valued highly by workers and that more entrepreneurial, achievement-oriented individuals are attracted to organizations where rewards are based on competency and performance. Because good performers expect and need more rewards in order to be as satisfied as lower performers, it follows that in order to retain them, organizations must pay them more than the lower performers.[2]

Incentive compensation assists the organization in developing a productive work environment by rewarding employees who contribute toward improving organizational productivity beyond established standards.[3] However, unions as well as many employees are usually opposed to performance-based pay because they fear that production standards will be set unfairly and that workers will be required to increase production by working harder for the same compensation. They also believe that performance-based pay will result in work speed-up, and that management will cheat workers of their rightful share of increased productivity.[4]

Linking pay to performance introduces both a risk and reward component, and has a positive incentive value. Performance-based compensation aims to attract, motivate, and retain outstanding employees. By offering incentive compensation, employers hope to encourage individuals to exert effort toward achieving organizational goals through increased productivity and profitability. At the same time, by tying parts of employee compensation to profitability indicators or performance objectives, employers are able to better control their labour costs in relation to revenue.[5]

Purposes and Importance of Incentive Compensation

The purposes and importance of incentive compensation are to

- Increase productivity, improve effectiveness, and improve employee job satisfaction
- Provide employees with a means of tying their rewards to their performance and competence
- Provide employees with appropriate positive reinforcement to encourage and maintain desired behaviour
- Attract individuals who are motivated, ambitious, and hard working to the organization
- Communicate to employees the importance of the relationship between rewards (pay) and their attitudes and behaviour

MONEY AND MOTIVATION: BACKGROUND

The ultimate aim of any incentive compensation is to increase corporate profitability. Incentives and bonus plans use the prospect of a financial gain to influence employees' behaviour: to get them to work smarter, harder, and better toward the overall accomplishment of corporate objectives. The motivation-reward theory on which this premise is based states that a person will increase performance in the belief that it will be rewarded.

For optimal effectiveness as a financial motivator the timing, size, and form of the reward must be carefully matched with the performance to be measured. An incentive's value is diminished if the payout occurs long after the performance, if the reward is too small or too large, or if the reward is in an inappropriate form.

Because the link between performance and reward plays a pivotal role in incentive compensation, it follows that the more control an employee has over performance the more effectively the reward will motivate. Control over performance also refers to the degree to which an employee has responsibility for making decisions.[6]

The use of financial incentives—financial rewards paid to workers whose production exceeds some predetermined standard—was popularized by Frederick Taylor in the late 1800s. As a supervisory employee of the Midvale Steel Company, he had become concerned with what he called "systematic soldiering"—the tendency of employees to work at the slowest pace possible and produce at the minimum acceptable level. One of Taylor's great insights was in seeing the need for a standardized, acceptable view of a **fair day's work**. As he saw it, this fair day's work should depend not on the vague estimates of supervisors but on a careful, formal, scientific process of inspection and observation. It was this need to scientifically evaluate each job that led to what became known as the **scientific management** movement. Taylor designed an incentive plan called differential piece rate. Under this plan workers were paid at one rate if they produced less than the standard amount of output and paid at a higher rate if their output exceeded the established

fair day's work

scientific management

standard. The aim of the plan was to encourage workers to equal or exceed the production standard.

With today's new interest in cutting costs, restructuring, and boosting performance, financial incentive or *pay for performance* plans are undergoing a major renaissance. Gainsharing plans (like the Scanlon plan discussed later in this chapter), in which groups of workers share in the fruits of their productivity improvements, are also increasingly popular. Pay for performance incentive plans like those explained in this chapter are thus sure to be of major importance throughout the 1990s.[7]

Shifting Compensation Environments and Practices[8]

According to the results of a survey conducted by the Conference Board of Canada, flexibility and the ability to control costs are mandatory in a fast-changing business environment. As firms continue to adjust to competitive pressures, changes are occurring in their competitive compensation orientation and the degree of employee participation in various forms of variable compensation.

Changing Organizational Structure and Decision Making

Over the last few years, a fundamental shift has occurred in the way firms are structured and managed. Changes in the social values, attitudes, and behaviour of employees have also taken place. The majority of the survey respondents reported that significant structural changes had occurred in their organizations.

Nearly 40% of those surveyed reported that decision making is largely decentralized in their organizations. This concentration on driving businesses through employees at lower levels in the organization has naturally led to changes in compensation approaches. For instance, some large corporations engaged in multiple businesses have abandoned their corporate-wide rewards approach and replaced it with individual unit reward strategies.

Employee Participation in Incentive and Bonus Plans

Incentive or bonus plan eligibility appears to be growing within organizations. Forty percent of survey respondents reported that the percentage of full-time and part-time employees in their organizations who were eligible for participation in some type of plan was higher than two years previously. Estimates provided by respondents of the actual percentage of employee eligibility within their organizations ranged from less than 1% to 100%.[9] (This wide-ranging distribution of responses is not unusual, as some organizations use incentive compensation as a management tool more strongly than others. Moreover, some companies employ large numbers of part-time employees who are often not eligible for these plans.)

THE HRM DEPARTMENT'S ROLE IN ADMINISTERING INCENTIVES

The human resource department plays a major role in developing and administering incentive plans. First, this department works with industrial engineers in the area of work measurement. Work measurement is the technique used to study each job and determine a normal or base-line production rate; it is the base rate that the incentives will be based on.[10] The human resource department also develops the details of the plans, including who will be eligible, what increases will be awarded for each level of performance, and how large a bonus can be awarded to persons in each grade level. The human resource department also develops and implements the performance appraisal tool used to appraise performance, and on which merit increases are usually based. Furthermore, the human resource department is responsible for providing the necessary supervisory training (regarding, for instance, how to appraise performance or how the incentive plan works). This department also develops the communiques through which workers are informed of the new plan. Finally, the human resource department should continually review pay differentials between employees, the company's pay relative to other firms, and any appeals and/or grievances from employees regarding the incentive plan. The human resource department's role in incentives is therefore a major one.

Supervisors also play an important role in administering the incentive plan.[11] They help to determine the proper work methods and help to develop and monitor the work standards that are set by industrial engineers. They must also make sure that employees follow the methods that have been established, which in itself involves both training and supervising the workers involved. Daily supervision is also required in terms of monitoring employee performance, correcting improper procedures, and appraising employees' performances.

Last (but not least), supervisors affect incentives through their effects on appraising performance. The basic aim of an incentive should be to encourage good performance by linking performance and rewards, and this in turn requires valid, accurate performance appraisals. When, as is sometimes the case, the supervisor undermines the appraisal system (for instance by indiscriminately scoring everyone high so they can all get a raise or by treating some employees unfairly), the result is to undermine the incentive plan as well. Line managers, too, therefore play a crucial role in administering the incentive system.

Types of Incentive Plans

There are many incentive plans in use and a number of ways to categorize them. Figure 13.1 illustrates the most commonly used incentive compensation plans found in businesses.

For simplicity we will discuss the following types of incentives: incentives for production employees, incentives for managers and executives, incentives for sales-

FIGURE 13.1
Summary of Incentive Plans

Individual Incentives	Group Incentives	Organization-wide Incentives
Piecework plans	Group incentive plans	Cash bonus
Standard hour plan	Executive incentives	Profit sharing
Attendance incentive plan	Manager incentives	Stock option
Employee suggestion plans		Scanlon plan
Recognition awards		
Incentive for salespeople		
Merit pay		

people, merit pay as an incentive (primarily for white-collar and professional employees), and organization-wide incentives.

INCENTIVES FOR PRODUCTION EMPLOYEES

Piecework Plans

Piecework is the oldest type of incentive plan, as well as the most commonly used. Earnings are tied directly to what the worker produces by paying the person a "piece rate" for each unit he or she produces. Thus, if Tom Smith gets 40 cents apiece for stamping out door jambs, then he would make $40 for stamping out 100 a day and $80 for stamping out 200.

Developing a workable piece-rate plan requires both job evaluation and (usually) industrial engineering. Job evaluation enables the assignment of an hourly wage rate to the job in question. But the crucial issue in piece-rate planning is the production standard, and this standard is usually developed by industrial engineers. The standard is usually stated in terms of a standard number of minutes per unit or a standard number of units per hour. In Tom Smith's case, the job evaluation indicated that his door jamb stamping job was worth $8 an hour. The industrial engineer determined that 20 jambs per hour was the standard production rate. Therefore, the piece rate (for each door jab) was $8.00 divided by 20 or 40 cents per door jamb.

Under a **straight piecework** plan, Tom Smith would simply be paid on the basis of the number of door jambs he produced; a minimum wage would not be guaranteed. However, under the Canada Labour Code and the Employment Standard Acts of the provinces, employers must pay their workers a minimum wage. Thus, under a **guaranteed piecework** plan, Mary Jones would be paid the hourly minimum wage regardless of her production rate, but as an incentive she would also be paid at a piece rate for each unit she produced in excess of 20 per hour.

Piecework (to most people) implies *straight piecework*, a strict proportionality between results and rewards regardless of the level of output. Thus, in Smith's case, he would continue to get 40 cents apiece for stamping out door jambs, even if he stamped out many more than planned, say 500 per day. On the other hand, certain types of piecework incentive plans call for a sharing of productivity gains between worker and employer such that the worker does not receive full credit for all production above normal.[12]

piecework

straight piecework

guaranteed piecework

Advantages and Disadvantages

Piecework incentive plans have several advantages. They are simple to calculate and easily understood by employees. Piece-rate plans appear equitable in principle, and their incentive value can be powerful since rewards are directly tied to performance.

Piecework also has some disadvantages. The main disadvantage is its somewhat unsavoury reputation among many employees, a reputation based on some employers' habit of arbitrarily raising production standards whenever they found their workers earning "excessive" wages. In addition, piece rates are stated in monetary terms (like 40 cents per piece), so when a new job evaluation results in a new hourly wage rate the piece rate must also be revised; this can be a big clerical chore. The other disadvantage is more subtle; since the piece rate is quoted on a per piece basis, in worker's mind production standards become tied inseparably to the amount of money earned. When an attempt is then made to revise production standards, it meets considerable worker resistance, even if the revision is fully justified.[13]

Standard Hour Plan

standard hour plan

The **standard hour plan** is very similar to the piece-rate plan, with one major difference. With a piece-rate plan the worker is paid a particular rate per piece that he or she produces. With the standard hour plan the worker is rewarded by a percent premium that equals the percent by which his or her performance is above standard. The plan assumes that the worker has a guaranteed base rate.

As an example, suppose the base rate for Smith's job is $8 per hour. (The base rate may, but need not, equal the hourly rate determined by the job evaluation.) And again assume that the production standard for Smith's job is 20 units per hour, or 3 minutes per unit. Suppose that in one day (8 hours) Smith produces 200 door jambs. According to the production standard, this should have taken Smith 10 hours (200 divided by 20 per hour); instead it took him 8 hours. He produced at a rate that is 25% (40 divided by 160) higher than the standard rate. The standard rate would be 8 hours times 20 (units per hour) = 160: Smith actually produced 40 more, or 200. He will therefore be paid at a rate that is 25% above his base rate for the day. His base rate was $8 per hour times 8 hours equals $64. So he'll be paid 1.25 times 64 or $80.00 for the day.

The standard hour plan has most of the advantages of the piecework plan and is fairly simple to compute and easy to understand. But the incentive is expressed in units of time instead of in monetary terms (as it is with the piece-rate system). Therefore, there is less tendency on the part of workers to link their production standard with their pay. Furthermore, the clerical job of recomputing piece rates whenever hourly wage rates are reevaluated is avoided.[14]

Group Incentive Plans

group incentive plan

Some employers use **group incentive plans,** and there are several ways to implement them.[15] One approach is to set work standards for each member of the group and maintain a count of the output of each member. Members are then paid based on one of three formulas: (1) all members receive the pay earned by the highest producer; (2) all members receive the pay earned by the lowest producer; or (3) all members receive payment equal to the average pay earned by the group. The second approach is to set a production standard based on the final output of the group as a whole; all members then receive the same pay, based on the piece rate that exists for the group's job. The group incentive can be based on either the piece rate or standard hour plan, but the latter is somewhat more prevalent.

There are several reasons to use a group plan. Sometimes several jobs are interrelated, as they are on assembly lines. Here one worker's performance reflects not only his or her own effort but that of co-workers as well, so group incentives make sense. One writer points out that in Japan "the first rule is never reward only one individual," instead, employees are rewarded as a group in order to reduce jealousy, make group members indebted to one another (as they would be to the group), and encourage a sense of cooperation.[16] There tends to be less bickering among group members as to who has "tight" production standards and who has loose ones. We also know that groups can bring pressure to bear on their members and keep shirkers in line, assuming the group as a whole agrees with the standards that are set. This in turn can help reduce the need for supervision. Group incentive plans also facilitate on-the-job training, since each member of the group has an interest in getting new members trained as quickly as possible.[17]

The chief disadvantage of group plans is that each worker's rewards are no longer based just on his or her own efforts. To the extent that the person does not see his or her effort leading to the desired reward, a group plan is usually not as effective as an individual plan. In one study, however (where the researchers arranged to pay the group based on the performance of its best member), the group incentive plan proved as effective as an individual incentive plan in improving performance.[18]

Attendance Incentive Plans

Another example of the use of incentives is to reduce employee absence. A typical **attendance incentive** program was implemented in a nonprofit hospital with about 3000 employees. At the end of the year eligible employees could convert up to 24 hours of unused sick leave into additional pay or vacation. To determine the size of the incentive, the number of hours absent was subtracted from 24. The surplus, if any, could either be added to the next year's vacation allowance or converted to additional pay at the employee's wage rate. In this case, absenteeism declined an average of 11.5 hours (32%) during the incentive period.[19]

attendance incentive plan

However, incentive plans like this have to be used with caution. In one case, for instance, the so-called attendance bonus plan instituted by a small manufacturer actually backfired. Here the rules for the plan were simple. Each employee with no more than three hours of lost time per quarter, excluding time off for jury duty and funerals, received a $25 bonus. An additional $25 bonus was paid to any employee who earned all four quarterly bonuses in a calendar year. The plan actually resulted in the company paying about $7500 in bonuses but getting an increase in hours absent of about 12.3%. The number of employees with perfect attendance did increase but this improvement was offset by reduced attendance of the remaining employees.

There were three possible reasons for these poor results. The reward itself was only about one day's pay, an amount that may have been too small to affect behaviour over a three-month span. Second, the three-month qualifying period was probably too long, given the size of the reward. Finally, the program provided only rewards, and the researchers suggest that plans that provide both punishments and rewards are considerably more effective than those that solely punish or reward.[20]

Employee Suggestion Plans

Promoting idea generation, creativity, and employee involvement are some of the objectives behind renewed corporate interest in **employee suggestion plans**. Employees are encouraged to submit suggestions on ways to improve some aspect of an organization's operations. Improvements can be tangible (cost reduction, productivity, or revenue gains) or intangible (aesthetics, quality of working environment, and so on).

employee suggestion plan

Some Canadian companies have allowed employees as much as 30% of the saving realized from the implementation of the suggestion plan in the first year. For instance IBM Canada paid out $680 000 in awards for savings of $2.5 million, and the Treasury Board of Canada awarded $250 000 in 1983 for savings realized of almost $11.5 million.[21]

According to a recent Conference Board of Canada survey, employee suggestion programs exist in a significant percentage of surveyed organizations (42%). Although more than one-third of these plans are fairly new (introduced since 1985) another third has been in existence for 20 years or more. The oldest plan was introduced in 1928 and has since become firmly embedded in the company's corporate culture.[22]

Recognition Awards

It is well known that financial rewards are not the only employee motivators. Programs that have recognition as their aim, rather than reward, are being used successfully by a growing number of Canadian organizations. A significant number of the firms surveyed by the Conference Board of Canada reported having introduced non-cash recognition programs for different employee groups. The majority (60 per cent) of non-cash award programs are fairly new, having been introduced in 1986 or later.

An example of one recognition program that is growing in use is the "spot bonus." Allocation of rewards is usually discretionary, with few guidelines regarding the form of the reward, its dollar value, timing, or eligible recipients. The aim of these programs is to recognize individual contribution and extra effort in an appropriate and immediate way.[23]

INCENTIVES FOR MANAGERS AND EXECUTIVES

Short-term Incentives: The Annual Bonus

Most firms have annual bonus plans that are aimed at motivating the short-term performance of their managers and executives. Unlike salaries (which are rarely reduced to reflect a fall-off in performance), **short-term incentive bonuses** can easily result in plus or minus adjustments of 25% or more in total pay. There are two popular types of annual bonus plans: the cash bonus plan and profit sharing.

short-term incentive bonuses

Cash Bonus Plans

cash bonus plan

The **cash bonus plan** is a popular type of incentive offered to employees by Canadian companies. Cash bonus plans provide employees with cash bonuses, in addition to regular compensation, based on the achievement of established performance goals.

In the survey conducted by the Conference Board of Canada 126 firms or 80% of the surveyed firms provided or intended to provide cash bonuses to their employees. The objective of cash bonus plans is to motivate employees to accomplish short-term objectives.[24] In another survey conducted by the Conference Board of Canada, respondents considered cash bonus plans to have the greatest incentive value. These plans tend to be directed primarily toward executives and management. The survey results showed that 93% of executives 78% of the managerial and professional group and only 20% of non-management employees are eligible to participate.[25]

Strengths and Weaknesses

Two themes were predominant among the strengths mentioned by respondents: employee involvement and teamwork. Cash bonus plans serve to foster a commonality of employee-employer goals. They also serve as a unifying force in developing teamwork.

The survey participants identified weaknesses in several areas. One complaint was that participating group eligibility was not extended far enough downward in the organization. Another was that eligibility was restricted to those with line responsibilities. Using the same performance evaluation tool in the determination of both individual merit and bonus increases was felt to be a weakness of one plan. Finally, the fact that the link between individual effort and corporate performance was often weak was frequently cited as a problem with this and with other incentive plans.[26]

Profit Sharing

Profit sharing plans are currently enjoying a resurgence of popularity in Canada. Under this type of plan, the dollar payout to an individual employee is directly linked to corporate financial results and is normally paid in cash on a current rather than deferred basis (as was the case in the past).[27]   profit sharing plan

Profit sharing plans provide for the distribution of company profits to employees, based on a predetermined formula, in addition to regular compensation. Profit sharing is an incentive plan which pays out to plan participants a portion of a firm's profits either in cash or stock. There are three types of plans: current distribution, deferred distribution, and a combination. Under a current distribution plan, profit sharing payouts are distributed to participants immediately following the earning of the profit and the determination of the proportionate shares for each participant. The deferred plan, as the name suggests, provides for setting aside and placing earned funds into some type of trust fund for distribution at a future date. A combined plan consists of features of both plans. Of the three, the current distribution plan is the most popularly used in Canada.

In the survey conducted by the Conference Board, 43 of the 157 firms surveyed offered or intended to offer profit sharing plans. According to these firms, the three major objectives of their plans, in order of importance, are to motivate employees to accomplish short-term goals, improve employee productivity, and provide competitive compensation.

Strengths and Weaknesses

According to survey participants, the major strength of profit sharing plans is that employees can share in the success of the firm in a meaningful way. Contributing to the bottom line, these respondents felt, leads to greater employee satisfaction.

The major weakness of profit sharing plans concerns the lack of relationship between the contribution of any one employee and overall company performance.[28]

How Much To Pay Out (Fund-Size)

A determination must be made regarding fund determination—the amount of bonus money that will be available—and there are several formulas used to do this. For example, some companies use a nondeductible formula. Here a straight percentage (usually of the company's net income) is used to create the short-term incentive fund.

In practice, what proportion of profits is usually paid out as bonuses? Here there are no hard and fast rules, and some firms don't even have a formula for developing the bonus fund.[29] One alternative is to reserve a minimum amount of the profits, say 10%, for safeguarding stockholders' investment, and then to establish a fund for bonuses equal to, say, 20% of the corporate operating profit before taxes in excess of this base amount.

Deciding Individual Awards

The third issue regarding short-term incentives is deciding the individual awards to be paid and here the main task is determining the amounts. Typically a target bonus is set for each eligible position and adjustments are then made for greater or less than targeted performance: a maximum amount, perhaps double the target bonus, may be set. Performance ratings are obtained for each manager and preliminary bonus estimates are computed.

Many experts argue that in most organizations managerial and executive-level bonuses should be tied to both organizational and individual performance, and there are several ways to do this.[30] Perhaps the simplest is the *split award method*, which breaks the bonus into two parts. Here the manager actually gets two separate bonuses, one based on his or her individual effort and one based on the organization's overall performance. Thus a manager might be eligible for an "individual performance" bonus of up to $10 000 but receive an individual performance bonus of only $8000 at the end of the year, based on his or her individual performance evaluation. In addition, though, the person also might receive a second bonus of $8000 based on the company's profits for the year. Even if there were no company profits, the high-performing manager would still get an individual performance bonus.

Long-Term Incentives

long-term incentive plans

Long-term incentive plans are intended to motivate and reward management for the corporation's long-term growth and prosperity and to inject a long-term perspective into the executive's decisions. If only short-term criteria were used, a manager could, for instance, increase profitability by reducing plant maintenance, a tactic that might, of course, catch up with the company over two or three years. Another purpose of these plans is to encourage executives to stay with the company by providing them with the opportunity to accumulate capital (like company stock) based on the firm's long-term success. Long-term incentives or capital accumulation programs are most often reserved for senior executives.[31] Two of the more popular long-term incentive plans are stock options and stock purchase plans.

Stock Options

stock option

A **stock option** is the right to purchase a stated number of shares of company stock at a stated price during a stated period of time; the executive thus hopes to profit by exercising his or her option in the future, but at today's price. Respondents to a survey conducted by the Conference Board of Canada believe that the three primary objectives of this plan are to: motivate employees to accomplish long-term goals, encourage identification with shareholder interests, and provide competitive compensation. The assumption is that the price of the stock will go up, rather than down or stay the same. Unfortunately, this depends partly on considerations outside the executive's control, such as general economic conditions. Stock price is, of course, affected by the firm's profitability and growth, and to the extent that the executive can affect these factors the stock option can be an incentive.

Strengths and Weaknesses of Stock Option Plans

The incentive value of stock option plans is the potential for an increase in the market price of the stock. Thus, a major strength of these plans is that they help ensure that shareholder and employee interests are the same: the accumulation of shareholder wealth.

Several respondents to the Conference Board of Canada survey cited as a weakness the often tenuous link between individual effort or performance and stock market price. Others noted that the stock price does not always reflect corporate performance. Another potential weakness is that although individual performance affects the number of shares granted, after the award is made there is no further differentiation between individuals. For example, two employees each awarded an option to buy the same number of shares would be able to exercise and get the same gain at the same time, regardless of differences in individual initiative, effort, or performance after receiving the option.[32]

Stock Purchase Plans

Stock purchase plans allows employees to buy company shares on a voluntary basis, usually with their own funds. Stock purchase plans are offered by various Canadian companies. In the survey conducted by the Conference Board of Canada, 61 firms provided or intended to provide stock purchase plans to their managers. According to these firms, the three major objectives of their stock purchase plans are to: encourage identification with shareholder interests, promote an entrepreneurial spirit among employees, and motivate employees to accomplish long-term goals.[33]

Currently, most stock purchase plans are broadly based, in contrast with earlier years when most were available only to executives. According to the Conference Board of Canada survey results, eligibility for participation ranges from 82% to 92% across the three employee groups. As was the case with the other stock-based plans, many of these plans are relatively new: more than a third have been introduced since 1985.[34]

Strengths and Weaknesses

Employee stock purchase plans offer a number of unique benefits to both employee and employer. Employees are given the opportunity to share in the fortunes of the company through a share purchase that includes an employer contribution and has no administrative fees. The main advantage to employers comes from the benefits of ownership. An employee who becomes a shareholder, so the theory goes, will no longer "act like a hired hand." Share ownership allows employees to identify with the company and its future.

This was by far the major strength of stock purchase plans, as reported by our respondents. Other noted strengths are variants on this overall theme, such as providing an entrepreneurial spirit, helping employees identify more closely with the firm's financial performance, and tying the interests of the employee to those of the shareholder.

A number of weaknesses were also mentioned. The major one concerned share prices. Although the employer contribution is intended in part to cushion against the stock price downside risk, our survey participants feel that falling share prices have a negative effect on employee morale. Also cited was the weak motivational aspect of this type of incentive. Within a broad-based plan, it was mentioned, individual employees at lower levels in the organization realistically have little opportunity to affect the short- or long-term performance of the company.

Implementing Long-Term Incentives

The results of one study by consultants McKinsey and Company, Inc. indicate that the simple expedient of giving managers stock options may be the simplest and wisest route to providing long-term incentives for top executives. In the McKinsey

stock purchase plans

study about one-half of the companies surveyed had stock options only and about one-half had performance-based plans in which managers were given cash bonuses for long-term performance.

The results indicated that in most cases the return to shareholders of companies with long-term cash performance incentives did not differ significantly from those companies which had only stock-based incentive plans (like stock options). This was so even though companies that paid cash bonuses had spent more to fund their incentive plans. Their most serious problem in awarding cash bonuses lay in identifying the proper performance measures. The survey concludes that successful long-term incentive plans should: (1) use measures of performance that correlate with shareholder wealth creation (that is, return on equity and growth), not earnings per share growth; (2) establish valid target levels and communicate them clearly to participants; and (3) provide for target adjustment under certain well-defined circumstances (in other words, the performance standards can be modified if market conditions warrant it.)[35]

INCENTIVES FOR SALESPEOPLE

Compensation plans for salespeople have typically relied heavily on incentives in the form of sales commissions, although the use of commissions varies by industry. This is illustrated in Table 13.1 which shows how companies in various industries have used salary, commission, or both to pay salespeople. In the tobacco industry, for instance, salespeople are usually paid entirely via commissions, while in the transportation equipment industry salespeople tend to be paid by salary. As can be seen, the most prevalent approach is to use a combination of salary and commissions to compensate salespeople.[36]

The widespread use of incentives for salespeople is due to three things: tradition, the unsupervised nature of most sales work, and the assumption that incentives are needed to motivate salespeople. And, unlike most other employees, salespeople do seem to clearly prefer being paid on an incentive basis: over 95% of the respondents in one study said they preferred to be paid on an incentive basis.[37] The pros and cons of salary, commission, and combination plans follow.

Salary Plan

salary plan

In the **salary plan** the salespeople are paid a fixed salary, although there may be occasional incentives in the form of bonuses, sales contest prizes, and the like.38 For example, a field sales engineer who is paid on a salary basis might have the following duties:

- Developing and executing sales and product training programs for the distributor's sales force
- Doing missionary work with selected manufacturers and major oil companies to encourage them to recommend his or her products to their dealers
- Participating in national and local trade shows
- Suggesting ideas for new products and promotional program[39]

Jobs like these are often found in industries that sell technical products; this is one reason why both the aerospace and transportation equipment industries have a relatively heavy emphasis on salary plans for their salespeople.

TABLE 13.1 How Salespeople Are Paid by Industry

Industry	Number of companies	Salary %	Commission %	Combination %
Aerospace	5	60%	—	40%
Appliance (household)	8	25	25%	50
Automobile parts and accessories	12	34	16	50
Automobile and truck	10	30	30	40
Beverages	6	50	—	50
Building materials	23	17	13	70
Casualty insurance	5	20	20	60
Chemicals	13	23	23	54
Cosmetics and toilet preparations	9	33	34	33
Drugs and medicines	12	25	25	50
Electrical equipment and supplies	19	26	10	64
Electronics	21	19	9	62
Fabricated metal products	26	26	19	55
Food products	14	43	14	43
General machinery	26	19	15	65
Glass and allied products	8	60	20	20
Housewares	12	25	25	50
Instruments and allied products	10	30	20	50
Iron and steel	10	20	—	80
Life insurance	5	20	20	60
Nonferrous metals	6	50	—	50
Office machinery and equipment	7	14	29	57
Paper and allied products	12	33	—	67
Petroleum and petroleum products	4	50	25	25
Printing	17	24	47	29
Publishing	14	10	30	60
Radio and television	7	—	—	100
Retailing	4	50	25	25
Rubber	8	25	—	75
Service industries	21	15	40	45
Textiles and apparel	6	33	33	34
Tobacco	4	—	100	—
Tools and hardware	11	18	36	46
Transportation equipment	5	100	—	—

Note: Method of payment (salary vs. commission) depends on industry.

SOURCE: Reprinted by permission of the *Harvard Business Review*. Exhibit from "How to Pay Your Salesforce" by John P. Steinbrink (July/August 1978). Copyright © 1978 by the President and Fellows of Harvard College; all rights reserved.

There are several advantages to paying salespeople on a straight salary basis. Salespeople know in advance what their income will be, and the employer also has fixed, predictable sales force expenses. It can develop a high degree of loyalty among the sales staff. Commissions tend to shift the sales person's emphasis to "making the sale" rather than prospecting and cultivating long-term customers.

The main disadvantage of the salary plan is that it does not depend on results.[40] In fact, salaries are often tied to seniority (rather than to performance), and this can be demotivating to potentially high performing salespeople, who see seniority—not performance—being rewarded.

Commission Plan

commission plan

Here salespeople are paid in direct proportion to their sales—for results, and only for results. The **commission plan** has several advantages. Salespeople have the greatest possible incentive, and there is a tendency to attract high-performing salespeople who see that effort will clearly lead to rewards. Sales costs are proportional to sales (rather than fixed), and the company's selling investment is reduced. The commission basis is also easy to understand and compute.

But the commission plan also has drawbacks. Salespeople focus on making a sale and on high-volume items; cultivating dedicated customers and working to push hard-to-sell items may be neglected. Wide variances in income between salespeople may occur; this can lead to a feeling that the plan is inequitable. More serious is the fact that salespeople are encouraged to neglect non-selling duties like servicing small accounts. In addition, pay is often excessive in boom times and very low in recessions.

Combination Plan

Most companies pay their salespeople a combination of salary and commissions, and there is a sizable salary component in most such plans. The most frequent percentage split reported in one study was 80% base salary and 20% incentives.[41]

Combination plans provide some of the advantages of both straight salary and straight commission plans, but also some of the disadvantages of each. Salespeople have a floor to their earnings so their families' security is ensured. Furthermore, the company can direct its salespeople's activities by detailing what services the salary component is being paid for, while the commission component provides a built-in incentive for superior performance. However, the salary component is not tied to performance, and the employer is therefore trading away some of the incentive value of what the person is paid. Combination plans also tend to become complicated, and misunderstandings can result.

INCENTIVES FOR OTHER PROFESSIONALS AND WHITE-COLLAR EMPLOYEES

Merit Pay as an Incentive

merit pay

Merit pay or a merit raise is any salary increase that is awarded to an employee based on his or her individual performance. It is different from a bonus in that it represents a continuing increment, whereas the bonus represents a one-time payment. Although the term merit pay can apply to the incentive raises given to any employees—exempt or nonexempt, office or factory, management or non-management—the term is more often used with respect to white-collar employees and particularly professional, office, and clerical employees. In one survey, for instance, more than 95% of the responding companies use a merit only pay plan. By contrast, in the wider business community only 59% report using a merit only pay system.[42]

Merit pay has both its advocates and detractors and is the subject of much debate.[43] Advocates of merit pay argue that only pay (or other rewards) that is tied directly to performance can motivate improved performance. They contend that the effect of awarding pay raises across the board (without regard to individual performance) may actually detract from performance by showing employees that they will be rewarded the same regardless of how they perform.

On the other hand, detractors of merit pay present some good reasons why merit pay plans can backfire. One is that the usefulness of the merit pay plan depends on the validity of the performance appraisal system, and if performance appraisals are viewed as unfair, so, too, will the merit pay that is based on them.[44] Similarly, supervisors often tend to minimize differences in employee performance when computing merit raises; they instead give most employees about the same raise, either because of a reluctance to alienate some employees or because of a desire to give everyone a raise that will at least help them stay even with the cost of living. A third problem is that almost every employee thinks he or she is an above-average performer; being paid a below-average merit increase can thus be demoralizing.[45] However, while problems like these can undermine a merit pay plan, there seems little doubt that merit pay can and does improve performance if the performance appraisals are carried out effectively.[46]

In general, many companies today are moving away from traditional pay practices based on seniority and toward pay practices based on employee performance. Among these new practices are the wide use of merit pay. Others include pegging pay to specific results and a pay-for-skill system, specifically, one that provides individual incentive for upgrading skills.[47] According to a recent survey by the Conference Board of Canada, merit pay continues to be the predominant factor in determining distribution of pay increases. Among responding companies, 59% planned to give merit-only increases in 1991, and 35% planned to use a general-plus-merit system for distributing increases.[48]

Incentives for Professional Employees

Professional employees are those whose work involves the application of learned knowledge to the solution of the employer's problems, including lawyers, doctors, economists, and engineers. Professionals almost always reach their positions through prolonged periods of formal study.[49]

Pay decisions regarding professional employees involve unique problems. One is that for most professionals money has historically been less important than it has been for other groups of employees. This is partly because professionals tend to be paid well anyway, and partly because they tend to be more driven by the desire to produce high-calibre work and receive recognition from colleagues in their profession. As a result (and as just a rule of thumb), professionals who go to work for employers do not do so with high-income expectations unless their plan is to move into management. What they do expect is reasonable pay progress and equitable treatment, and without these they will quickly becomes dissatisfied.

However, that is not to say that professionals do not like to receive financial incentives (and, in fact, the use of such plans is gaining popularity, especially among high-tech firms, as explained below). For example, studies in science-based industries like pharmaceutical and aerospace consistently show that firms with the most productive research and development groups have incentive pay plans for their professionals, usually in the form of bonuses. Here there is usually a conservative relationship between bonus and salary; in other words, a tendency to reward smaller portions of total pay in the form of a bonus.

Rewarding Key Contributors

Today, as never before, employers have to single out and reward key contributors—mostly selected managers and professionals—for their roles in making the firm successful. Among the factors fuelling this trend are the demand for innovation in firms doing business in a competitive world market, deregulation (which has firms in many industries battling for a foothold in a newly competitive environment), and a flood of venture capital that has created a multitude of small start-ups all battling for market position.

How do organizations typically reward their key contributors? According to a recent Hay Executive and Key Contributor Compensation Survey of high-technology firms, about 76% of the participants reported having some type of formal or informal key contributor plan.

In the high-tech survey, cash was the most common reward and was typically a one-time lump sum. Other rewards used included automobiles, trips, and research funding, as well as sabbaticals, public recognition, freedom-to-choose projects, and "general work-life improvements."[50]

Scanlon Plan

Many employers have installed incentive plans in which virtually all employees can participate; one of the most popularly used is the Scanlon plan, developed by Joseph Scanlon, a United Steel Worker's Union Official, in the United States in 1937.

Scanlon plan

The **Scanlon plan** has three basic features. The first is the philosophy of cooperation on which it is based. It assumes that managers and workers have to rid themselves of the "us" and "them" attitudes that normally inhibit employees from developing a sense of ownership in the company, substituting instead a climate in which everyone cooperates because he or she understands that economic rewards are contingent on honest cooperation. A pervasive philosophy of cooperation must therefore exist in the firm for the plan to succeed.[51]

The second feature of the plan is the involvement system.[52] This takes the form of two levels of committees—the departmental level and the executive level. Productivity-improving suggestions are presented by employees to the appropriate departmental-level committees, which then selectively transmit valuable suggestions to the executive-level committee. The latter then decides whether to implement the suggestion.

The third element of the plan is the sharing of benefits formula. Basically, the Scanlon plan assumes that employees should share directly in any extra profits resulting from their cost-cutting suggestions. (See our previous discussion on employee suggestion plans.)

The Scanlon plan has been very successful in terms of reducing costs and increasing a sense of sharing and cooperation among employees. In one recent study, labour costs were cut by 12%, and grievances were cut in half after implementation of such a plan.[53]

Yet a number of Scanlon plans have failed, and we know there are certain conditions required for their success. They are usually more effective where there is a relatively small number of participants, generally less than 1000. They are more successful where there are stable product lines and costs, since it is important that the labour costs/sales ratio remain fairly stable. Good supervision and healthy labour relations seem essential. And, of course, it is crucial that there be strong commitment to the plan on the part of management, particularly during the confusing phase-in period.[54]

DEVELOPING EFFECTIVE INCENTIVE PLANS

Incentive Plan Problems

There are a number of reasons why incentive plans fail, most of which can be explained in terms of what we know about human motivation. For motivation to take place, the worker must believe that effort on his or her part will lead to reward, and he or she must want that reward. In most cases where incentive plans fail, it is because one or both of these conditions are not met.[55] Unfair standards—standards that are too high or unattainable—are thus one cause for incentive plan failure. A second is the real or imagined fear that rates will be cut or standards raised if performance exceeds the standard for too long a time. Rate cuts have long been the nemesis of incentive plans, and the problem persists to this day, for instance among manufacturers who reduce a salesperson's territory as soon as his or her commissions become "excessive." Group restrictions and peer pressure can work both for and against the plan; if a group views the plan as fair, it can keep loafers in line and maintain high production. But the opposite is also true, and if for any reason the group views the plan as unfair it will—through education, ostracism, or punishment—see that the production levels of group members are held down. Other plans fail because employees do not understand them either because the plan is too complex or because it is not communicated to employees in an understandable way.

In summary, incentive plans can motivate employees. For example, two experts conclude that "there is considerable evidence that installation of such plans usually results in greater output per [working] hour, lower unit cost, and higher wages in comparison with outcomes associated with the straight payment system."[56]

But we also know that incentive plans can fail. So far we've discussed some of the causes of such failures. Now let us turn to some specific guidelines for developing effective incentive plans.[57]

Effort and rewards must be directly related. Our motivation model shows that for an incentive to motivate employees, they must see that effort will lead to their obtaining the reward. An effective incentive plan should therefore reward employees in direct proportion to their increased productivity. Employees must also perceive that they can actually do the tasks required. Thus, the standard has to be attainable, and employees must be provided with the necessary tools, equipment, and training.[58]

The reward must be valuable to the employees. For an incentive to motivate an employee, the reward must be attractive. Since people's needs differ, the attraction of various incentives also differs. Where other needs—for achievement, for recognition, etc.—are paramount, financial incentives may have little or no effect on performance.

Methods and procedures must be carefully studied. Effective incentive plans are generally based on a meticulous work methods study. This usually requires the services of an

COMPUTER APPLICATION IN FINANCIAL INCENTIVES

Appraisal Statistics

While individual supervisors are concerned with the mechanics of the appraisal process for merit pay purposes, HRM and upper management are interested in analyzing the overall results of the process. Some supervisors "grade" more stringently than others; some truly have mostly stars; and others are subject to the traditional rating errors. Comparing the results of various departments or divisions may flag certain areas for closer examination. Effective merit pay plans are always built on a foundation of fair and accurate appraisals.

It is helpful to accumulate data from various departments and/or supervisors, extracting a particular area(s) for review. More than one area at a time may be extracted by sorting the data first by department (in ascending alphabetical order) and then by supervisor's last name (again in ascending alphabetical order).

An examination of statistical averages and variances is then necessary. Too little variance indicates a central tendency—a supervisor who does not want to distinguish between employees, so all are rated average. Looking at the minimum and maximum scores actually awarded will tell whether or not there is a restricted range; in other words, another indication of little differentiation between employees. Of course, the range may be restricted on the high side (an "easy grader") or the low side. If there is very little difference in ratings, then superior performers are not getting reinforcement and poor performers are not being given clear expectations of what they must do to improve. Penley and Penley point out that small variance indicates "... undifferentiated feedback to the employees."[1]

It is also possible to develop an index based on (1) the ratings on any particular appraisal item and/or (2) the overall rating, by summing the rating for each person in the department. The value of this is to show either the tendency of the supervisor to rate high/low/neutral or to identify those departments with superior performers (and possibly good leadership) or potential problem areas.

An examination of the timeliness of appraisals may also be helpful. If the company's policy is to appraise the employee on or before the anniversary of hiring date, then that month and day are entered. In another column, the date on which the appraisal was actually done is entered. Subtracting the appraisal date from the hire date enables a quick view of the timeliness of appraisals. This is possible because packages such as Lotus 1-2-3 store Gregorian dates based on the number of days since December 31, 1899.[2]

By analyzing the results of the appraisal process, it is possible to see problem areas which demand further training. Or, perhaps the analysis, and subsequent questions, will lead a company to develop a whole new appraisal process with the input of all employees, not just supervisors. Viewing performance appraisals only on an individual basis lets management lose much of the value of the process.

---

[1] Larry E. Penley and Yolanda E. Penley, *Human Resources Simulation: Using Lotus 1-2-3* (Carrolton, Texas: South-Western Publishing Co., 1988), p. 121.

[2] Gregory T. LeBlond and Douglas Ford Cobb, *Using Lotus 1-2-3* (Indianapolis: Que Corporation), 1983, p. 169.

industrial engineer or other methods expert. Through careful observation and measurement they define fair performance standards.

The plan must be understandable and easily calculable by the employees. Employees should be able to easily calculate the rewards they will receive for various levels of effort (remember it is important for them to see the effort-reward link). Therefore, the plan should be easily understandable and easily calculable.

Effective standards must be set. Standards on which the incentive plan is built should be effective, which requires several things. The standards should be viewed as fair by the subordinates. They should be set high, but reasonable—there should be

On the Front Line

The question of whether to pay Carter Cleaning Centre employees an hourly wage or an incentive of some kind has always intrigued Jack Carter.

His basic policy has always been to pay employees an hourly wage, except that his managers do receive an end-of-year bonus depending, as Jack puts it, "on whether their stores do well or not that year."

He has, however, experimented in one store with incentive plans, with mixed results. Jack knows that a presser should press about 25 "tops" (jackets, dresses, blouses) per hour. Most of his pressers do not attain this ideal standard, though. In one, for instance, a presser named Walt was paid $6 per hour, and Jack noticed that regardless of the amount of work he had to do, Walt always ended up making about $180 at the end of the week. If it was a holiday week, for instance and there were a lot of clothes to press he might average 22 or 23 tops per hour (someone else did pants) and so he'd earn perhaps $190 to $200 and still finish up each day in time to leave by 3:00 p.m. so he could pick up his children at school. But when things were very slow in the store his productivity would drop to perhaps 12 to 15 pieces an hour, so that at the end of the week he'd still end up earning close to $180, and in fact not go home much earlier than he did when it was busy.

Jack spoke with Walt several times and while Walt always promised to try to do better, it gradually became apparent to Jack that Walt was simply going to earn his $180 per week no matter what. While Walt never told him so directly it dawned on Jack that Walt had a family to support and was not about to earn less than this "target" wage regardless of how busy or slow the store was. The problem was the longer Walt kept pressing each day the longer the steam boilers and compressors had to be kept on to power his machines

and the fuel charges alone ran close to $5 per hour. Jack clearly needed some way short of firing Walt to solve the problem, since the fuel bills were eating up his profits.

His solution was to tell Walt that instead of an hourly $6 wage he would henceforth pay him $.25 per item pressed. That way, said Jack to himself, if he presses 25 items per hour at $.25 each he will in effect get a small raise. He will also get more items pressed per hour and will therefore be able to shut the machines down earlier.

On the whole, the experiment worked well. Walt generally presses 25 to 35 pieces per hour now. He gets to leave earlier and with the small increase in pay he generally earns his target wage. Two problems have arisen though. The quality of Walt's work dipped a bit, and his manager has to spend a minute or two each hour counting the number of pieces Walt pressed that hour. Otherwise Jack is fairly pleased with the results of his incentive plan and he's wondering whether to extend it to other employees and other stores.

Jennifer's questions are as follows:

1. Should this plan in its present form be extended to pressers in the other stores?

2. Should other employees be put on a similar plan? Why? Why not?

3. Is there another incentive plan you think would work better for the pressers?

4. A store manager's basic job is to keep total wages to no more than 30% of sales and to maintain both the fuel bill and the supply bill at about 9% of sales. Managers can also directly affect sales by ensuring courteous customer service and by ensuring that the work is done properly. What suggestions would you make to Jennifer for an incentive plan for store managers?

about a 50-50 chance of success of reaching them. And the goals should be specific—this is much more effective than telling someone to "do your best."

The standards must be guaranteed. Around the turn of the century employers often raised production standards (or cut the piece rate) whenever employee's pay became "excessive." Today, employees remain suspicious that exceeding the standard will result in raising the standards, and to protect their own long-term interests they do not produce above standard, and the incentive plan fails. Therefore, it's important to view the standard as a contract with employees. Once the plan is operational, use great caution before decreasing the size of the incentive in any way.[59]

An hourly base rate must be guaranteed. It is usually advisable to guarantee employees' base rates particularly in the case of plant personnel.[60] They will therefore know that no matter what happens they can at least earn a minimum guaranteed base rate.

When to Use Incentive Plans

There are two bases on which companies can compensate employees: time and output. Straight salary or wages involve compensating employees based on increments of time (such as hourly, daily, or weekly). Incentive plans (calling for piecework or commissions) involve compensating employees based on their output.[61] Under what conditions should employers pay employees on a time basis? On an output (incentive) basis? Here are some guidelines (as summarized in Figure 13.2).

FIGURE 13.2
When to Pay on a Time Basis

Pay based on time is preferable:

1. *When units of output are difficult to distinguish and measure.* Employers should be able to clearly distinguish and identify each worker's output to pay them on an incentive basis. Where employers cannot do so then straight salaries or wages (or perhaps a group incentive plan) are more appropriate.

2. *When employees are unable to control quantity of output.* Where employees have little control over the quantity of output (such as on machine-paced assembly lines) pay based on time is more appropriate.

3. *When there is not a clear relationship between effort and output.* Similarly, if there is no clear, direct relationship between the worker's effort and his or her output—as when jobs are highly interrelated—pay based on time is more appropriate.

4. *When delays in the work are frequent and beyond employees' control.* It is clearly impractical to tie worker's pay to their output if production delays are beyond workers' control.

5. *When quality considerations are especially important.* Virtually all incentive plans tie pay to the quantity, rather than the quality of output. When quality is a primary consideration (as with engineering and other professions) pay based on time is more appropriate.

6. *When precise advance knowledge of unit labour costs is not required by competitive conditions.* Installing an incentive plan requires a substantial investment in industrial engineering, methods analysis, and computation of unit labour costs. If this type of precise cost control is not required by competitive conditions, it is probably not worthwhile to develop them just to install an incentive plan.

When Payment Should be Based on Output (Incentive Plans)

Similarly, pay based on output would be preferable when

1. Units of output can be measured.

2. There is a clear relationship between employee effort and quantity of output.

3. The job is standardized, the work flow is regular, and delays are few or consistent.

4. Quality is less important than quantity or, if quality is important, it is easily measured and controlled.

5. Competitive conditions require that unit labour costs be definitely known and fixed in advance of production.[62]

SUMMARY

1. The scientific use of financial incentives can be traced back to Frederick Taylor. While such incentives became somewhat less popular during the human relations era, most writers today agree that they can be quite effective.

2. Piecework is the oldest type of incentive plan. Here a worker is paid a piece rate for each unit produced. With a straight piecework plan, workers are paid on the basis of the number of units produced. With a guaranteed piecework plan each worker receives his or her base rate (such as the minimum wage) regardless of how many units he or she produces.

3. Other useful incentive plans for plant human resources include the standard hour plan and group incentive plans. The former rewards workers by a percent premium that equals the percent by which their performance is above standard. Group incentive plans are useful where the workers' jobs are highly interrelated.

4. Several incentive plans are discussed for white-collar personnel. Most sales human resources are paid on some type of salary plus commission (incentive) basis. The trouble with straight commission is that there is a tendency to focus on "big ticket" or "quick sell" items and to disregard long-term customer building. Management employees are often paid according to some bonus formula that ties the bonus to, for example, increased sales. Stock options are one of the most popular executive incentive plans.

5. The Scanlon Plan is an example of organization-wide incentive plans. The problem with such a plan is that the link between a person's efforts and rewards is sometimes unclear. On the other hand such plans may contribute to developing a sense of commitment among employees.

6. When incentive plans fail it is usually because (1) the worker does not believe that effort on his or her part will lead to obtaining the reward, or (2) the reward is not important to the person. Specific incentive plan problems therefore include: unfair standards, fear of a rate cut, group restrictions, lack of understanding, and lack of required tools, or training.

7. We suggest using incentive plans when units of output are easily measured, employees can control output, the effort/reward relationship is clear, work delays are under employee's control, quality is not paramount, and the organization must know precise labour costs anyway (to stay competitive).

KEY TERMS

fair day's work	attendance incentive plan	stock purchase plan
scientific management	employee suggestion plan	salary plan
piecework	short-term incentive bonuses	commission plan
straight piecework	cash bonus plan	merit pay
guaranteed piecework	profit sharing plan	Scanlon plan
standard hour plan	long-term incentive plan	
group incentive plan	stock option	

DISCUSSION QUESTIONS

1. Compare and contrast six types of incentive plans.
2. Explain five reasons why incentive plans fail.
3. How could the expectancy model of motivation we presented in Chapter 11 be applied to the question of incentives?
4. Describe the nature of some important management incentives.
5. When and why should a salesperson be paid a salary? A commission? Salary and commission combined?

EXPERIENTIAL EXERCISE

Purpose The purpose of this exercise is to provide practice in reviewing:

1. The conditions under which time versus performance-based incentives are appropriate.
2. The advantages of company-wide versus individual incentives.
3. The standards (sales, productivity, etc.) to which incentives can be tied.

Required Understanding Familiarity with our discussion of financial incentives and with the following case incident:

A Case of Incentives: The Ezell Musical Instrument Company (EMI) is located in Fredericton, New Brunswick. It is a medium-sized operation that has grown out of a family-owned company. Like many companies, it has to face tough competition at home and abroad. M. G. Ezell III is now the president of the firm.

Several years ago, when Ezell first took over, he thought about how he might build morale in the company. He felt that the company had good workers and that he would like to reward them for past services to encourage them to be more productive. EMI was not unionized. He hesitated to raise base wages because it might make the firm uncompetitive if foreign competition increased.

EMI was having an exceptionally good year, both for sales and profits. As a result, Ezell thought that the best way to reward the employees was to give them a Christmas-New Year's bonus. As he said to Abe Stick, his personnel manager, "Nothing like the old buck to make a man work harder." His bonus system was as follows:

Wages or Salary	Bonus
<$15 500	$500
$15 501-17 500	$600
$17 501-19 500	$700
$19 501-21 000	$800
>$21 000	8% of salary or wage

The bonuses were well received. Many people thanked the president, and Stick heard lots of good comments from the supervisors in January about how much harder the employees were working.

The next year, more foreign competitors entered the market. Materials were harder to get and more expensive. Sales were down 5%, and profits were down 15%. Ezell did not feel he could afford the same bonuses as last year. As a result, the bonuses were decreased as follows:

Wages or Salary	Bonus
<$15 500	$250
$15 501-17 500	$300
$17 501-19 500	$350
$19 501-21 000	$400
>$21 000	4% of salary or wage

This time, Stick heard little from the supervisors about increased productivity. He asked Harry Bell, one of the supervisors, what the reaction was to the bonuses.

BELL: To tell you the truth, Abe, I have morale problems. My people worked hard this year. It wasn't their fault sales or profits were down. Many expected last year's bonus or better. So they spent most of the old figure for Christmas gifts. When they got that letter from M. G. telling them they were getting only half of last year's on December 27, there was gloom and doom and some mumblings. Some of my people seem to be working less hard than at any time I can remember.

STICK: But that's not fair, Harry. They never received any bonuses before. Now they should be glad they received anything.

BELL: That's not the way they see it!

Stick decided not to discuss the matter with Ezell. Stick figured the problem would blow over. But the next year was even worse. Sales held but were not up to the prior years' levels. Profits were almost nonexistent. The board of directors decided to omit the dividend.

At this point Ezell came to Stick and said, "Abe, I don't see how we can pay any bonus this year. Do you think we can get by without causing a big drop in morale?"

How to Set Up the Exercise Divide the class into groups of four or five students. Everyone should briefly review "A Case of Incentives."

Instructions for the Exercise After discussing the case each group should develop answers to the following questions:

1. What does this case illustrate about the motivational impact of bonuses and incentives?
2. What could Mr. Ezell have done to prevent this problem in the first place?
3. Why should Mr. Bell expect that the employees would react negatively to the reduction in bonuses when they are not guaranteed as part of an employee's compensation?
4. Have rewards been accurately tied to performance by the Ezell compensation policy? If not, how might this failure be the cause of their problems?
5. What alternative formula or policy for discussing extra income to employees would you suggest?
6. What would you do now if you were Ezell? Stick?

If time permits, the class should discuss their recommendations.

CASE INCIDENT: Incentive or Exploitation?

Concourse Engineering employs over 200 employees in its metal stamping operations. Concourse makes various automotive parts used in the production of various North American cars. Twenty percent of its work force are salaried. These individuals include the general manager, administrative staff, plant foremen, plant forewomen, and quality control inspectors. Eighty percent of its work force are hourly paid shift workers. Pay at Concourse is comparable to other nonunion companies in the industry but slightly lower than unionized companies. Employment is considered secure, and the company has never laid off any workers in its many years of operations.

Late last year the company decided to implement a wage incentive plan for its hourly paid employees. Under the plan workers would be paid 80% of their base wage rate and the balance would be based on performance. This would be calculated on factors such as units produced beyond the minimum standard, error rate, and sales. According to management's projections employees could make up to 30% more in earnings. This plan would be phased in over six months. During the phase-in period workers were guaranteed that their pay would not fall below their existing wage rate.

Most employees were opposed to the plan. Some argued that "the employer was making a deliberate attempt to exploit the workers—trying to increase production while reducing wages." Others argued, saying, "We are already making a sacrifice working for Concourse, since workers are paid more in unionized companies and they have better benefits and job protection." "Maybe we should consider joining a union," said one employee. Others said, "this plan could cause us increased stress, burnout, and financial hardship."

Questions

1. Explain the reasons for the workers reacting negatively to the incentive plan.
2. How could management have avoided the negative reception with which the incentive plan was met?
3. Management is committed to the plan; what should it do?

NOTES

1. Richard Kopelman, "Linking Pay to Performance Is a Proven Management Tool," in *The Personnel Administrator*, Vol. 28 (October 1983), pp. 60-61.

2. Edward E. Lawler, III, *Pay and Organization Development* (Menlo Park, CA: Addison-Wesley Publishing Company, 1983), p. 81.

3. Richard I. Henderson, *Compensation Management* (Reston: Prentice Hall Company, 1985), p. 484.

4. For an excellent discussion of obstacles to incentive compensees, see Philip M. Podsakoff, Charles N. Greene, and James M. McFillen, "Obstacles to the Effective Use of Reward Systems," in S. L. Dolan and R. S. Schuler, eds., *Canadian Readings in Personnel and Human Resource Management* (St. Paul, Mn: West Publishing Co. 1987), pp. 245-259.

5. *Paying for Performance: The Growing Use of Incentives and Bonus Plans*, by Patricia L. Booth, Report 22-87, (Ottawa: The Conference Board of Canada, 1987), p. 1. See also Edward E. Lawler III, "New Approaches to Total Compensation" in Richard M. Steers and Lyman W. Porter, eds., *Motivation and Work Behaviour*, 4th ed. (New York: McGraw-Hill Book Company, 1987), pp. 254-267.

6. Booth, p. 4. See also *Lawler, Pay and Organizational Development*, p. 81 and Edward E. Lawler III, "The Design of Effective Reward Systems" in R.M. Steers in L.W. Porter, eds., *Motivation and Work Behavior*, 5th ed. (New York: McGraw-Hill Inc., 1991), pp. 507-531.

7. John R. Schermerhorn, Jr., James G. Hunt, and Richard N. Osborn, *Managing Organizational Behaviour*, 4th ed., (New York: John Wiley & Sons Inc., 1991), p. 178. See also, for example, Robert Opshal and Marvin Dunnette, "The Role of Financial Compensation in Industrial Motivation," *Psychological Bulletin*, Vol. 66 (1966), pp. 94-118. For a good example of how to implement a performance-based pay plan, see Stuart Freedman, "Performance-Based Pay: A Convenience Store Case Study," *Personnel Journal*, Vol. 64(July 1985), pp. 30-34; Rosabeth Moss Kanter, "The Attack on Pay," *Harvard Business Review*, Vol. 66(March-April 1987), pp. 60-67; Michael Smith, Edward O. Dowd, and George Christ, "Pay for Performance—One Company's Experience," *Compensation and Benefits Review*, (May-June 1987), pp. 19-27; and Robert L. Heneman and others, "The Relationship Between Pay for Performance Perceptions and Pay Satisfaction," *Personnel Psychology*, Vol. 41, no. 4 (Winter 1988), pp. 745-760; see also Richard I. Henderson, *Compensation Management* (Englewood Cliffs, N.J.: Prentice Hall Inc., 1989), pp. 363-367.

8. This is based on *Strategic Rewards Management: The Variable Approach to Pay* by Patricia L. Booth, Report 52-90, (Ottawa: The Conference Board of Canada, 1990), p. 7-12.

9. According to the results of the 1990 survey conducted by the Conference Board of Canada this wide-range distribution of responses was not unexpected, as some orga-

nizations use variable compensation as a management tool more strongly than others. Moreover, some companies employ large numbers of part-time employees who are often not eligible for these plans. In addition, slightly different interpretations of the question were apparent, with a few companies not including profit sharing and stock purchase plan eligibility when responding to this question.

10. Robert Rice, "Survey of Work Measurement and Wage Incentives in the USA," *Management Services* (January 1978), p. 10.

11. Robert Sibson, *Compensation* (New York: AMACOM, 1982), pp. 166-167.

12. Richard Henderson, *Compensation Management* (Englewood Cliffs, N.J.: Prentice-Hall Inc., 1989), pp. 360-363.

13. David Belcher, *Compensation Administration* (Englewood Cliffs, N.J.: Prentice-Hall, 1973), p. 314.

14. Measured day work is a third type of individual incentive plan for production workers. See, for example, Mitchell Fein, "Let's Return to MDW for Incentives," *Industrial Engineering* (January 1979), pp. 34-37.

15. Henderson, *Compensation Management*, pp. 367-368. See also David Swinehart, "A Guide to More Productive Team Incentive Programs," *Personnel Journal*, Vol. 65, no. 7 (July 1986).

16. John P. Alston, "Awarding Bonuses the Japanese Way," *Business Horizons*, Vol. 25 (September-October, 1982), pp. 6-8.

17. See, for example, Peter Daly, "Selecting and Assigning a Group Incentive Plan," *Management Review* (December 1975), pp. 33-45. For an explanation of how to develop a successful group incentive program, see K. Dow Scott and Timothy Cotter, "The Team That Works Together Earns Together," *Personnel Journal*, Vol. 63 (March 1984), pp. 59-67.

18. Manuel London and Greg Oldham, "A Comparison of Group and Individual Incentive Plans," *Academy of Management Journal*, Vol. 20, no. 1 (1977), pp. 34-41. Note that the study was carried out under controlled conditions in a laboratory setting. See also Thomas Rollins, "Productivity-Based Group Incentive Plans: Powerful, But Use with Caution," Compensation and Benefits Review, Vol. 21, no. 3 (May-June 1989), pp. 39-50; discusses several popular group incentive plans, including gainsharing, and lists dos and don'ts for using them.

19. Dale Schlotzhauer and Joseph Rosse, "A Five-Year of a Positive Incentive Absence Control Program," *Personnel Psychology*, Vol. 38, no. 3 (Autumn 1985), pp. 575-585.

20. George Schneller IV and Richard Kopelman, "Using Incentives to Increase Absenteeism: A Plan That Backfired," *Compensation Review* (second quarter 1983), pp. 40-45.

21. W. Carr "Communicating with ESP: Current Matters/New Ideas" *Human Resources Management in Canada* (Toronto: Prentice-Hall Canada Inc., 1985), p. 5,342.

22. *Strategic Rewards Management: The Variable Approach to Pay*, Booth, p. 11.

23. Ibid.

24. *Paying for Performance*, Booth, p. 25.

25. *Strategic Rewards Management*, Booth, p. 9.

26. *Paying for Performance*, Booth, p. 28.

27. *Strategic Rewards Management*, Booth, p. 9.

28. *Paying for Performance*, Booth, pp. 21-23.

29. Bruce Ellig, *Executive Compensation—A Total Pay Perspective* (New York: McGraw-Hill, 1982), p. 187.

30. F. Dean Hildedrand, Jr., "Individual Performance Incentives," *Compensation Review*, Vol. 10 (third quarter 1978), p. 32.

31. Edward Redling, "The 1981 Tax Act: Boon to Managerial Compensation," *Personnel*, Vol. 57 (March-April 1982), pp. 26-35.

32. *Paying for Performance*, Booth, pp. 7-10.

33. Ibid, pp. 17-19.

34. *Strategic Rewards Management*, Booth, p. 9.

35. Jude Rich and John Larson, "Why Some Long-Term Incentives Fail," *Compensation Review*, Vol. 16 (First Quarter 1984), pp. 26-37. See also Eric Marquardt, "Stock Option Grants: Is Timing Everything?" *Compensation and Benefits Review*, Vol. 20, no. 5 (September-October 1988), pp. 18-22

   Jone L. Pearce, "Why Merit Pay Doesn't Work: Implications from Organization Theory" in R.M. Steers and L.W. Porter, eds., *Motivation and Work Behavior*, 5th ed. (New York: McGraw-Hill Inc., 1991) pp. 498-506

36. This section is based primarily on John Steinbrink, "How to Pay Your Sales Force," *Harvard Business Review*, Vol. 57 (July-August 1978), pp. 111-122.

37. Belcher, *Compensation Administration*, pp. 505-507.

38. Straight salary by itself is not, of course, an incentive compensation plan as we use the term in this chapter.

39. Steinbrink, "How to Pay,", p. 112.

40. T.H. Patten, "Trends in Pay Practices for Salesmen" *Personnel*, Vol. 43 (January-February 1968), pp. 54-63.

41. Steinbrink, p. 112.

42. *Pay for Performance*, Booth, p. vii.

43. See, for example, Herber Meyer, "The Pay for Performance Dilemma," *Organizational Dynamics* (Winter 1975), pp. 39-50; Thomas Patten, Jr., "Pay for Performance or Placation?" *Personnel Administrator*, Vol. 24 (September 1977), pp. 26-29; William Kearney, "Pay for Performance? Not Always," *MSU Business Topics* (Spring 1979), pp. 5-16. See also Hoyt Doyel and Janet Johnson, "Pay-Increase Guidelines with Merit," *Personnel Journal*, Vol. 64 (June 1985), pp. 46-50.

44. Nathan Winstanley, "Are Merit Increases Really Effective?" *Personnel Administrator*, Vol. 27 (April 1982), pp. 37-41. See also William Seithel and Jeff Emans, "Calculating Merit Increases: A Structured Approach," *Personnel*, Vol. 60, no. 5 (June 1985), pp. 56-68.

45. James T. Brinks, "Is There Merit in Merit Increases?" *Personnel Administrator*, Vol. 25 (May 1980), p. 60.

46. *Merit Pay: Fitting the Pieces Together* (Chicago: Commerce Clearing House, 1982).

47. Rosabeth Moss Kanter, "From Status to Contribution: Some Organizational Implications of Changing Basis for Pay," *Personnel*, Vol. 64, no. 1 (January 1987), pp. 12-37. For a lively discussion on why merit pay systems fail see W. Clay Hamner, "How to Ruin Motivation with Pay," in Richard M. Steers and Lyman W. Porter, eds., *Motivation and Work Behaviour*, 4th ed. (New York: McGraw Hill Book Company 1987), pp. 242-253.

48. *Compensation Planning Outlook 1991* by Judith Lendvay-Zwicki, Report SR25 (Ottawa: The Conference Board of Canada, 1990), p. 4.

49. This section is based primarily on Robert Sibson, *Compensation* (New York: AMA-COM, 1981), pp. 189-207.

50. Michael Sprat and Bernadette Steele, "Rewarding Key Contributors," *Compensation and Benefits Review*, Vol. 17 (July-August 1985), pp. 24-37.

51. J. Kenneth White, "The Scanlon Plan: Causes and Correlates of Success," *Academy of Management Journal*, Vol. 22 (June 1979), pp. 292-312.

52. Moore and Ross, *The Scanlon Way*, pp. 1-2.

53. George Sherman, "The Scanlon Plan: Its Capabilities for Productive Improvement," *Personnel Administrator* (July 1976).

54. White, "The Scanlon Plan," pp. 292-312.

55. See Ronald Goettinger, "Why Isn't Your Incentive Compensation Working?" *Personnel Journal*, Vol. 60 (November 1981), pp. 840-841.

56. Robert Opsahl and Marvin Dunnette, "The Role of Financial Compensation in Industrial Motivation," *Psychological Bulletin*, Vol. 66 (1966), pp. 94-118, in Larry Cummings and William Scott, *Readings in Organizational Behavior and Human Performance* (Homewood, Ill.: Irwin/Dorsey, 1969). See also Behling and Schriesheim, *Organizational Behavior*. Both sets of authors point out, though, that the installation of an incentive plan is not (and cannot be) an isolated event. Improved work methods, and clearer policies, always accompany incentive plans, and it is often hard to determine whether it is the incentive plan or these other improvements that led to the improved performance.

57. Based on R. D. Pritchard, C. W. VonBergan, Jr., and P. J. DeLeo, "An Evaluation of Incentive Motivation Techniques in Air Force Technical Training," Air Force Human Resources Laboratory Technical Report (1974); Robert Pritchard, Philip DeLeo, and Clarence W. VonBergan, Jr., "A Field Experiment Test of Expectancy-Valence Incentive Motivation Techniques," *Organizational Behavior and Human Performance*, Vol. 15 (1976), pp. 355-406; J. K. Louden and Jay Wayne Deagan, *Wage Incentives* (New York: Wiley, 1959), pp. 25-28; Opsahl and Dunnette, *The Role of Financial Compensation in Industrial Motivation*, pp. 350-368. See also Thomas Rollins, "Pay for Performance: The Pros and Cons," *Personnel Journal*, Vol. 66, no. 6 (June 1987), pp. 104-111.

58. Opsahl and Dunnette, *The Role of Financial Compensation in Industrial Motivation*.

59. Gary Yukl and Gary Latham, "Consequences of Reinforcement Schedules and Incentives Magnitudes for Employee Performance: Problems Encountered in an Industrial Setting," *Journal of Applied Psychology*, Vol. 60 (June 1975).

60. Louden and Deagan, *Wage Incentives*, p. 26.

61. Based on Belcher, *Compensation Administration*, pp. 309-311. See also Edward Lawler III, "Reward Systems," in J. R. Hackman and J. L. Suttle, *Improving Life at Work* (Santa Monica, Calif.: Goodyear, 1977), pp. 191-219. See also Kent E. Romanoff, "The Ten Commandments of Performance Management," *Personnel*, Vol. 66, no. 1 (January 1989), pp. 24-28.

62. Belcher, *Compensation Administration*, pp. 309-310.

SUGGESTED READINGS

Paying for Performance: The Growing Use of Incentives and Bonus Plans by Patricia L. Booth, Report 22-87. Ottawa: The Conference Board of Canada, 1987.

Strategic Rewards Management: The Variable Approach to Pay by Patricia L. Booth, Report 52-90. Ottawa: The Conference Board of Canada, 1990.

Bowers, M.H. and R.D. Roderick. "Two-Tier Pay Systems: The Good, the Bad, and the Debatable." *Personnel Administrator*, June 1987. pp. 101-112.

Curington, W.P., N. Gupta, and G.D. Jenkins, Jr. "Labor Issues and Skill-Based Compensation Systems." *Labor Law Journal* 37(8), 1986. pp. 581-586.

Lawler, Edward E., III. Pay and Organization Development, Reading, Mass.: Addision-Wesley, 1981.

Lawler, Edward E. III. *Strategic Pay: Aligning Organizational Strategies and Pay Systems*. San Francisco: Jossey-Bass Publishers, 1990.

Miller, C.S. and M.H. Schuster. "Gainsharing Plans: A Comparative Analysis," *Organizational Dynamics*, Summer 1987. pp. 44-67.

Thompson, Michael A. "Incentive Pay: Linking Compensation to Performance" in *Human Resources Management in Canada*. Toronto: Prentice-Hall Canada Inc., 1988. pp. 40,543-40,549.

Thompson, Michael A., and J. Mary Lee. "Implementing Incentives: Should You Do It? How Should You Do It?" in *Human Resources Management in Canada*. Toronto: Prentice-Hall Canada Inc., 1989. pp. 40,571-40,581.

Thompson, Michael A. and J. Mary Lee. "What's Wrong with Pay for Performance?" in *Human Resources Management in Canada*. Toronto: Prentice-Hall Canada Inc., 1990. pp. 40,597-40,607.

CHAPTER
FOURTEEN Employee Benefits and Services

After studying this chapter, you should be able to

1. Explain the purposes and importance of employee benefits and services.

2. Understand the differences between direct and indirect compensation.

3. Explain the differences between mandatory, universal, and employer-provided benefits.

4. Explain the difference between Canada Pension Plan and Quebec Pension Plan.

5. Understand the Pension Benefits Standard Act.

6. Understand private pension plans.

7. Discuss the reasons for employee assistance programs.

8. Discuss internal and external coordination of benefits.

9. Explain flexible benefits.

OVERVIEW

The main purpose of this chapter is to describe the different types of benefits that are provided to employees. We discuss the government role in the field of employee benefits mandatory benefits, (such as the Canada Pension Plan), universal benefits (such as provincial health insurance plans), employer-provided benefits (such as private pensions), and employee services (such as employee assistance programs). We discuss the differences between direct and indirect compensation and explain how benefits are used to meet individual, organizational, and societal objectives. We explain the growing importance of two employee services, employee assistance programs and cafeteria (flexible) benefits. We also discuss issues involved in the administration and coordination of employee benefits and services.

INTRODUCTION: EMPLOYEE BENEFITS AND SERVICES

Employee benefits and services are very important to the well-being and security of employees. Benefits and services provide financial protection against such risks as accidents, unemployment, illness, and retirement. They are also important to organizations in that they assist them in competing for, recruiting, and retaining qualified and desirable employees. In addition, organizations are well aware that prompt and proper medical care of illnesses yields a healthier and more productive work force. Employers, by providing many benefits and services to employees, strive to enhance their self-image as organizations that care and are concerned about the general well-being of their employees. Finally, organizations provide benefits in order to meet employees' changing needs and preferences for a particular form of benefits and services.

Benefits differ from wages in many important respects. For instance, payments made by the employer for benefits normally are paid to an outside party (e.g., insurance carriers, auto leasing firms, etc.), while wages, which are paid directly into the employee's hands, permit more personal discretion in spending. Payments from benefit plans also usually have deferred characteristics: the actual benefit can only be realized in the event of some future occurrence (often with the negative personal implications such as disability). Also, for most companies, benefit programs are a smaller proportion of compensation than are wages.[1]

Many benefits are mandated by the government, while others are provided voluntarily by employers. A large component of most organizations' benefits are due to collective bargaining agreements. Benefits represent a substantial portion of employers' compensation costs whether they are voluntarily provided or legally required. Figure 14.1 illustrates the results of annual surveys, from 1954 to 1986, conducted by the management consultants Peat Marwick Stevenson & Kellogg. As shown the total employee benefits, as a percentage of total payroll, has grown from 15.1% in 1954 to 36.3% in 1986. This represents a substantial growth in benefits costs for Canadian companies over the past 20 years. Figure 14.2 illustrates the breakdown of the benefits cost in relation to total compensation cost. This provides a better understanding of the total cost of different components.

Purposes and Importance of Employee Benefits and Services

The purposes and importance of employee benefits and services are to

- Attract and retain the desired number of qualified employees by maintaining a competitive position in the employment market[2]
- Motivate efficient on-the-job performance
- Maintain or improve employees' morale
- Encourage increased productivity by rewarding above average performance
- Maintain or improve employees' job satisfaction
- Ensure that the benefit program is and appears to be internally equitable
- Reduce employees' turnover
- Meet collective bargaining demands in the most cost-effective way
- Enhance the organization's image among employees
- Continually endeavour to maximize the levels of benefit coverage with the benefit dollars available
- Meet required legal and social obligations

FIGURE 14.1

Benefits and Other Nonwage and Salary Cost Comparisons for Canadian Companies from 1954 to 1986

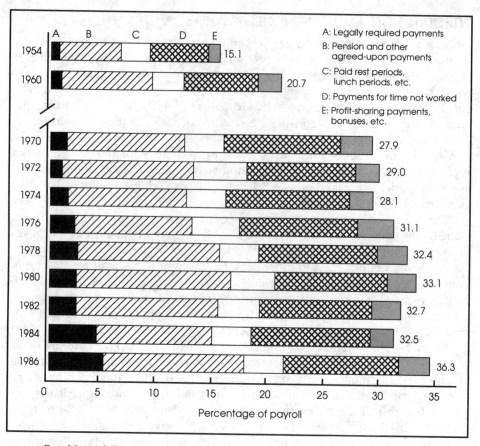

A: Legally required payments
B: Pension and other agreed-upon payments
C: Paid rest periods, lunch periods, etc.
D: Payments for time not worked
E: Profit-sharing payments, bonuses, etc.

SOURCE: Peat Marwick Stevenson & Kellogg, "Employee Benefits in Canada." *Annual Surveys from 1954–1986.* Used with permission.

THE ROLE OF GOVERNMENTS

Canadian governments influence employee benefits through a wide network of legislations, laws, and regulations. These laws and legislations cover such areas as health care, unemployment, retirement, and workers' safety. Canadian government programs have evolved since World War I, beginning with Workers Compensation in Ontario, to cover the emerging problems caused through job related injuries and illnesses in a new industrial economy. The greatest expansion of benefit programs came during and after World War II. During that time wages were frozen by the Order-in-Council 7440, passed in 1940. Because there was intense competition among organizations for scarce labour, management and labour used increased benefits as a means of getting around the wage freeze. It was during this time that the federal government passed the Old Age Pension Act and a bill providing widow's allowances.[3]

Today, the federal and various provincial governments appear to be actively transferring the costs of various social welfare programs to the private sector. For example, the federal government has transferred the cost of funding the unemployment insurance programs to the private sector and to premiums paid by em-

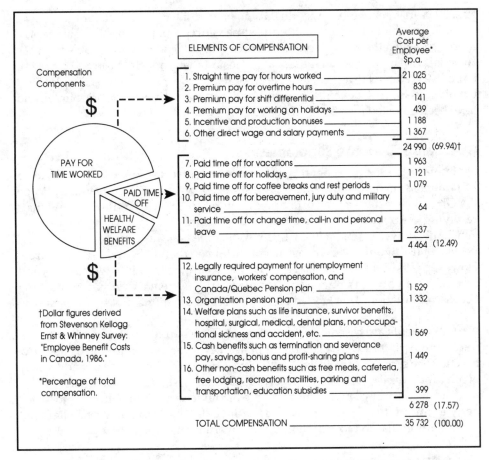

FIGURE 14.2
The Total
Compensation
Concept and Average
Costs

ELEMENTS OF COMPENSATION	Average Cost per Employee* $p.a.
Compensation Components	
1. Straight time pay for hours worked	21 025
2. Premium pay for overtime hours	830
3. Premium pay for shift differential	141
4. Premium pay for working on holidays	439
5. Incentive and production bonuses	1 188
6. Other direct wage and salary payments	1 367
	24 990 (69.94)†
7. Paid time off for vacations	1 963
8. Paid time off for holidays	1 121
9. Paid time off for coffee breaks and rest periods	1 079
10. Paid time off for bereavement, jury duty and military service	64
11. Paid time off for change time, call-in and personal leave	237
	4 464 (12.49)
12. Legally required payment for unemployment insurance, workers' compensation, and Canada/Quebec Pension plan	1 529
13. Organization pension plan	1 332
14. Welfare plans such as life insurance, survivor benefits, hospital, surgical, medical, dental plans, non-occupational sickness and accident, etc.	1 569
15. Cash benefits such as termination and severance pay, savings, bonus and profit-sharing plans	1 449
16. Other non-cash benefits such as free meals, cafeteria, free lodging, recreation facilities, parking and transportation, education subsidies	399
	6 278 (17.57)
TOTAL COMPENSATION	35 732 (100.00)

PAY FOR TIME WORKED

PAID TIME OFF

HEALTH/ WELFARE BENEFITS

†Dollar figures derived from Stevenson Kellogg Ernst & Whinney Survey: "Employee Benefit Costs in Canada, 1986."

*Percentage of total compensation.

SOURCE: David L. McPherson and John T. Wallace, "Employee Benefits Plans," *Human Resources Management in Canada* (Scarborough, Ont.: Prentice-Hall Canada Inc., 1986). Used with permission.

ployees. This became effective January 1, 1991.[4] The government of Ontario has transferred the cost of funding Ontario Hospital Insurance Plan to the private sector through a payroll tax.[5]

UNIVERSAL BENEFITS

Universal benefits are benefits that are provided by governments without the requirement for direct contributions from either employees or employers. Two benefits fall under this category: old age security, and guaranteed income supplement. A third benefit, a health insurance plan, is universal in most provinces, but in four provinces premiums are paid by individuals, employers, or both.

universal benefits

Old Age Security

The **Old Age Security Act** of Canada came into effect on January 1, 1952 and for the first time provided full universal pensions as a right, without a means test.[6] Old Age Security pension is provided to all Canadians who have resided in Canada for at

Old Age Security Act

least 40 years after age 18. Individuals who have resided in Canada for less than 40 years (beyond age 18) receive a reduced pension proportionate to their years of residence. When the Act was passed it provided $40.00 per month payable from age 70. However, in 1965 when the Canada Pension Plan came into force, the age criterion was reduced to age 65, and the amount of the pension increased. Since 1972 the old age security benefits have been indexed to the consumer price index and have been adjusted on a quarterly basis.

Guaranteed Income Supplement[7]

On January 1, 1967 the federal government amended the OAS Act to provide a **"guaranteed income supplement" (GIS)** of $30 per month to Canadians. When the GIS was enacted, it was primarily intended to ensure that those individuals receiving OAS would receive a minimum income, particularly while Canada Pension Plan was reaching its maturity. When the GIS was introduced, it was expected that it would be reduced in importance when CPP and QPP matured. However, GIS was expanded substantially and became fully interwoven into, and a permanent part of the Canadian social security system as a result of indexing because of inflation. This has led to an increase in the number of pensioners who qualify for GIS.

GIS benefits are based on an *income test*.[8] The amount paid to a recipient is reduced by $1.00 for every $2.00 that a pensioner receives besides his or her OAS benefits. The spouse of an old age security pensioner, who is between 60 and 65, may qualify for a *spouse's allowance*, subject to residence test and an income test.

The majority of provinces also provide guaranteed minimum incomes to the elderly to top up the benefits provided by the federal government. The eligibility criteria are similar to those of the federal government.

Provincial Insurance Health Plans[9]

All Canadians are covered for basic hospital and medical care through a system of interlocking provincial health insurance plans. These plans must meet minimum standards of service and administration in order to qualify for substantial federal government funding under the Canada Health Act (1984).

According to the provisions of the Canada Health Act, in order for a provincial health program to be eligible for the full federal contribution, it must meet the following criteria and conditions:

1. *Public Administration.* The program must be administered on a nonprofit basis by a public body that is appointed by and accountable to the provincial government.

2. *Comprehensiveness:* The program must cover all necessary hospital and medical services, and surgical-dental services rendered in hospitals.

3. *Universality:* 100% of the province's residents must be entitled to insured health services.

4. *Portability:* Coverage must be portable from one province or territory to another. The waiting period for new residents must not exceed three months.

   Insured health services must be made available to Canadians temporarily out of their own province.

5. *Accessibility:* Insured services must be provided on uniform terms and conditions for all residents. Reasonable access to insured services must not be precluded or impeded, either directly or indirectly, by charges or other mechanisms.

Besides these criteria, the Act states that extra-billing and user charges, other than user charges allowed by the regulations, must not be allowed.

All medically required services provided by physicians, surgeons, or other qualified professionals are covered by these provincial plans. Also covered are all necessary costs of hospitalization at standard ward accommodation rate levels. This includes all hospitalization services. However, "luxury" services such as semi-private or private rooms and private duty nursing are not covered.

MANDATORY BENEFITS

Mandatory benefits are those benefits that employers must provide to their workers by law. These benefits are considered essential to provide workers with a basic level of financial protection in the event of unemployment, illness, accidents, or retirement.

mandatory benefits

Canada Pension Plan and Quebec Pension Plan (CPP and QPP)

The **Canada Pension Plan** and the **Quebec Pension Plan** were enacted into law in April 1965 and came into effect January 1, 1966. These plans are comprehensive, contributory, and mandatory for all employees and self-employed individuals in Canada. All Canadians have universal portability of their benefits. This means that employees may change employers, change residences, and move anywhere in Canada and their Canada or Quebec Pension will move with them. Since 1974 all have been indexed to the consumer price index and have been adjusted annually (January 1, each year) to reflect changes in the cost of living.[10]

Canada Pension Plan
Quebec Pension Plan

These plans are intended to provide different types of pension incomes to Canadians. The different types of pension incomes include: retirement pensions, disability pensions, and pensions and benefits to children of disabled workers. Pension benefits are also paid to surviving spouses of contributors and orphans' benefits are paid for the dependent children of deceased contributors.

As contributory plans, CPP and QPP are funded by contributions paid by employers and employees. There is no government contribution to the plans. On January 1, 1987, major changes in contribution rates and new benefit programs were introduced to the Canada Pension Plan. These changes created greater flexibility for contributors. As a result of the changes, contributors may collect full pension at age 65 or collect reduced CPP pension between age sixty and seventy. A unique new feature is the option of splitting CPP pensions following separation of legal or common-law spouses. This means that pension credits earned by one or both spouses during the years of their relationship may be divided equally between them on the dissolution of the marriage or relationship. Spouses in a continuing relationship can apply to share their CPP pension benefits. Figure 14.3 illustrates the total retirement income among private pension plan recipients 65 years and older. As can be seen, mandatory benefits (CPP/QPP and OAS) constitute a substantial portion of Canadians' retirement incomes. Private pension plan benefits constitute another substantial share of retirement income for Canadians as can also be seen.

The payment of retirement pensions is not automatic, and neither are any other pension benefits automatic. Application must be made to a local office of Health and Welfare Canada. The retirement pension benefit is approximately 25% of the contributor's earnings in the previous three years. This is paid monthly for the contributor's (pensioner's) lifetime.

Workers' Compensation

workers' compensation

All ten provinces and the territories have a **workers' compensation** act to protect workers in the event of job-related accidents and industrial illnesses or diseases. The objectives of workers' compensation acts are to help protect employees from financial loss of income, provide financial benefits and medical care for disabilities, and help rehabilitate injured employees from accidents or illnesses suffered on the job.

The workers' compensation act of each jurisdiction places responsibility for the *adjudication of claims* in the hands of workers' compensation boards. The administration of the act is based on the concept of collective liability. This means that compensation is paid to injured workers collectively. The workers' compensation act covers virtually all industries. Industries are classified into groups based on their special industrial hazards. These groups of employers collectively pay the cost of compensation for all injured employees who are employed by the industries in their particular groups.

Employers are required to pay annual premiums to the workers' compensation board. These premiums are determined on a pro rata basis according to the employer's annual compensation data. However, an employer may be assessed an annual premium higher than those paid by other industries within its group. This may occur whenever there are higher than average accidents and claims from that employer's firm. Premiums paid by employers are tax deductible. However, payments to injured workers or their spouses are not subject to federal or provincial income taxes.

The workers' compensation legislation of each jurisdiction provides a variety of benefits to injured workers. These benefits include medical care for hospital, dental, and other medical expenses related to accidents causing personal injury; financial compensation in fatal cases, including lump-sum death payments to a surviving spouse, burial expenses, and pensions to a spouse and dependent children; and financial compensation in non-fatal cases, including wage-loss payments for temporary total disability and temporary partial disability. In cases of permanent disability, benefits may be paid in the form of a lump-sum payment or as a permanent disability pension. Rehabilitation services are also provided, including both medical and re-employment assistance in overcoming disabilities. The benefits that workers compensation provides are subject to a maximum ceiling. Table 14.1 illustrates the maximum wage ceiling in each province.

Unemployment Insurance

unemployment insurance

In 1940 the federal government, through an amendment to the British North America Act (BNA) 1867, presently known as the Canada Act 1982, enacted **unemployment insurance** legislation that gave it the sole jurisdiction in matters relating to unemployed workers in Canada. Following the amendment to the BNA Act the federal government implemented a variety of programs. The programs were designed to relieve or lessen the impact of workers' financial burdens during their transition from one job to the next.

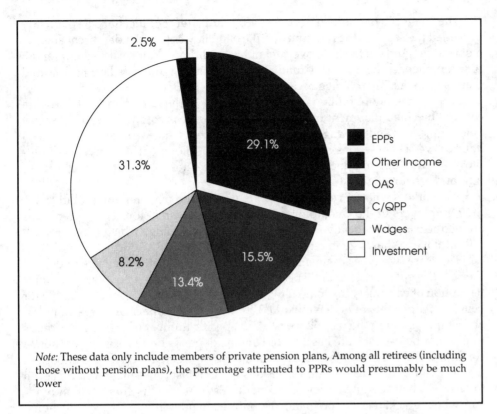

FIGURE 14.3
Distribution of Total Retirement Income among Private Pension Plan Recipients 65 Years and Older

EPPs
Other Income
OAS
C/QPP
Wages
Investment

2.5%
29.1%
31.3%
15.5%
13.4%
8.2%

Note: These data only include members of private pension plans, Among all retirees (including those without pension plans), the percentage attributed to PPRs would presumably be much lower

SOURCE: Statistics Canada, *Pension Plans in Canada* (Ottawa: Minister of Supply and Services Canada, 1986). Reproduced with the permission of the Minister of Supply and Services Canada, 1991.

TABLE 14.1 Maximal Earnings Covered Under Provincial Workers' Compensation Acts

PROVINCE	EARNINGS	ENACTED
Alberta	$40 000	1982
British Columbia	41 300	1988
Manitoba	33 000	1988
New Brunswick	32 900	1988
Newfoundland	45 500	1983
Nova Scotia	28 000	1986
Ontario	35 000	1988
Prince Edward Island	22 000	1988
Quebec	36 500	1988
Saskatchewan	48 000	1985
Northwest Territories	38 800	1987
Yukon Territories	36 000	1988

SOURCE: *Canadian Labour Law Report*, CCH Canadian Ltd., 1988.

The Unemployment Insurance Act, 1971 and later modifications have greatly expanded the scope of the program and the eligibility criteria. Under recent amendments to the Act, the federal government has withdrawn financial support for UI. As a consequence the full cost of funding the program is now shared by workers and their employers. This change became effective on January 1, 1991.

Approximately 12 million individuals or 95% of the Canadian work force are covered by Unemployment Insurance (UI). Coverage is compulsory for all salary paid employees and all wage (hourly) paid workers who work for at least fifteen hours a week. These jobs are called insurable employment. However, self-employed individuals and individuals over age 65 are not required to pay UI premiums and are not eligible for benefits.

All workers who are covered by UI are required to pay premiums jointly with their employers to the Unemployment Insurance Commission. These premiums are deducted automatically from each employee's earnings which together with the employers' shares go into the unemployment insurance fund.

There are two types of unemployment insurance benefits available under UI. These are regular benefits and special benefits. Individuals who have had an interruption of earnings (due to no fault of their own) for seven days are eligible for benefits. Applicants must have worked for a specific number of weeks in insurable employment in the past 52 weeks. The specific number of weeks individuals must work before they are eligible for benefits depends on the existing economic conditions and the unemployment rate in the region where they live. It is important to note that individuals who quit their jobs without just cause must wait for seven to 12 weeks before being eligible for benefits. Special benefits are paid to individuals who are sick, injured, pregnant, or confined in quarantine. A special one-time benefit is paid to those individuals who have reached age 65 who are no longer eligible for UI coverage.

The benefits payable to individuals depend on their weekly insurable employment earnings. However, the maximum weekly benefit payable is $384.00. In 1990 there were over three million UI recipients and the total benefits paid to claimants exceeded $13 billion. Table 14.2 illustrates a summary of government benefit levels and contribution rates.

EMPLOYER PROVIDED BENEFITS
Private Pension Plans

employer pension plan

There are three basic types of **employer pension plans**.[11] In the *group pension plans*, the organization (and possibly the employee) makes a set contribution to a pension fund. A second type of pension plan is actually a *deferred profit-sharing plan*. Here a certain percentage of profits is credited to each employee's account. These benefits are then distributed to the employee (or his or her dependents) upon his or her retirement or death. Finally, under *saving plans*, employees set aside a fixed percentage of their weekly wages for their retirement; the company usually matches from 50 to 100% of the employees' contribution.

Various types of employee savings and deferred compensation plans are, in fact, becoming increasingly popular. An employee savings plan may (but need not) have as its main aim an assured retirement income. In some cases savings plans are actually for shorter-range goals like paying college tuition for the employees' children. But whether used for a pension or some other goal, all savings plans encourage systematic savings by employees, with two added incentives:

TABLE 14.2 Summary of Government Benefit Levels and Contribution Rates, 1990

THE CANADA/QUEBEC PENSION PLAN*

	CPP	QPP
Year's Maximum Pensionable Earnings (YMPE)	$28 900	$28 900
Year's Basic Exemption (YBE)	2 800	2 800
Contribution Rate (employer and employee)	2.2% of employment earnings in excess of the YBE up to the YMPE	
Maximum Annual Employee/Employer Contribution	574.20	574.20
Maximum Monthly Retirement Pension (at 65)	577.08	577.08
Maximum Monthly Surviving Spouse's Pension		
—under age 55	324.37	493.12
—age 55 to 64	324.37	570.42
—age 65 and over	346.25	346.25
Maximum Lump-Sum Death Benefit	2 890.00	2 890.00
Maximum Monthly Disability Pension		
—contributor's benefit	709.52	709.52
—children's benefit (each)	107.96	29.00

OLD AGE SECURITY PROGRAM

Maximum Monthly Benefit (per person)	January 1, 1990†
Old Age Security (OAS)	348.07
Spouse's Allowance (SpA)	603.30
Guaranteed Income Supplement (GIS)	
—single	404.13
—couples	263.23

UNEMPLOYMENT INSURANCE PROGRAM

Benefit Level	60% of insurable earnings
Maximum Weekly Insurable Earnings	$640.00
Maximum Weekly Benefit	384.00
Premium Rates (% of weekly insurable earnings):	
Employee	2.25%
Employer (without premium reduction)	3.15
Employer (with partial premium reduction)	2.85
Employer (with full premium reduction)	2.79
Maximum Weekly Premiums:	
Employee	14.40
Employer	20.16

† Currently payments are indexed quarterly to reflect changes in the cost of living.
* Currently payments are indexed to reflect changes in the cost of living.

SOURCE: David L. McPherson and John T. Wallace, "Employee Benefit Plans," *Human Resources Management in Canada* (Scarborough, Ont.: Prentice-Hall Canada Inc., 1990). Used with permission.

(1) the employer usually matches employees' contributions; and (2) some form of income tax deferral occurs. Contributions to the plan are made by employees from after-tax earnings and these are partially or fully matched by the employer, who typically contributes 50 cents for each $1.00 contributed by the employee.[12] From the point of view of the employer, contributions are immediately tax deductible and in some cases company stock rather than cash can be used as the employer's contribution, thus giving employees stock ownership in the company. From the point of view of the employee, the employer's matching contributions are not taxed as income when made and investment income (such as interest on invested funds) are tax deferred, so that taxes on this income need not be paid until the employee receives his or her cash payment. If the payment occurs after retirement the tax savings to the employee can be substantial, since in most cases the person is then in a much lower tax bracket.

The entire area of pension planning is an extremely complicated one, partly because of the many federal laws governing pensions. For example, companies want to ensure that their pension contributions are tax deductible and it is therefore necessary to adhere to the pertinent income tax codes. In unionized companies, the union often must be allowed to participate in the administration of the pension plan. Table 14.3 illustrates membership of Canadians in private pension plans. As can be seen there are two primary groups: defined contribution plans and defined benefit plans.

TABLE 14.3 **Membership in Different Private Pension Plans**

Type of Pension Plan	Pension Plans		Membership	
	Number	Percent	Number	Percent
Defined contribution plans				
General defined contribution	8 613	48.6%	252 498	5.5%
Profit sharing	417	2.4	16 125	0.4
Subtotal: Defined contribution	9 030	51.0	268 623	5.9
Defined benefit plans				
Final earnings	3 472	19.6	2 720 709	59.6
Career average earnings	3 562	20.1	592 030	13.0
Flat benefit	1 352	7.6	930 509	20.4
Subtotal: Defined benefit	8 386	47.3	4 243 248	93.0
Combination and other plans	295	1.7	52 752	1.2
Grand total	17 711	100.0%	4 564 623	100.0%

SOURCE: Statistics Canada, *Pension Plans in Canada* (Ottawa: Minister of Supply and Services Canada, 1986), text table M. Reproduced with the permission of the Minister of Supply and Services Canada 1991.

Defined Contribution Plans

A defined contribution plan specifies the amount to be contributed each year to the plan by the employer (and the employee, if the plan is contributory). Defined contribution plans are also called money-purchase plans. Contributions to the plan are usually expressed as a percentage of each member's earnings. Funds contributed are invested on behalf of the member. The pension that will be received is whatever amount the contributions and accumulated investment and interest provide. Therefore the amount that will be received upon retirement will depend on the amount contributed and how well the funds were invested. There are many advantages to this plan. It is easy to administer; there is no need for actuarial valuations; the employer's costs are always known and predictable as a function of plan membership and members' earnings; and they are easily communicated to employees. There are certain disadvantages as well. Benefits may be difficult to forecast because of the fluidity of interest and investment returns; and the amount that older members can receive will be less because of insufficient time remaining for interest to compound.

Defined Benefit Plans

A defined benefit plan defines specifically the amount of retirement benefit that each member will receive based on service, earnings, or other factors. There are three types of defined benefit plans:

- *Final average benefit.* This is specified as a pension equal to 2% of the member's average annual earnings in the final five years of employment, multiplied by the number of years of service.
- *Flat benefit.* This is specified as a pension of $10 per month (for example) at retirement for each year of service.
- *Career average benefit:* This is specified as a pension equal to 2% of the member's average annual employment earnings, multiplied by the number of years of service.

While an employer usually has to develop a pension plan to meet its own unique needs, there are several key policy issues that must be considered,[13] including membership and retirement requirements, the benefit formula, and funding.

Vesting is another critical issue in pension planning. It refers to the money that the employer and employee have placed in the latter's pension fund that cannot be forfeited for any reason. Naturally, the employees' contributions always represent their own money and cannot be forfeited. But suppose a person worked for a company for 30 years, and then the company went out of business one year before the person was to retire at age 65. Unless the employee's rights to the company's pension contributions were vested—due to a union agreement or company policy, for instance—the employee might well find himself or herself with only his or her portion of the pension contributions.

Pension Benefits Standard Act

The Pension Benefits Standard Act of the government of Canada regulates all private pension plans in industries and applies to all employees in any province or territory who works for companies that fall under federal jurisdiction. These firms include crown corporations, banks, radio and communication companies, railways, and insurance firms. Most provinces (Alberta, Manitoba, Nova Scotia, Newfoundland, Ontario, Quebec, and Saskatchewan) have enacted their own pension benefits acts. The contents of these provincial government acts are similar to those of the federal Act. Pension plans in the remaining provinces are required to conform to certain criteria of the federal legislation in order to qualify for income tax deduction.

According to the provisions of the Pension Benefits Standard Act, pension funds must be held in trust for members and must have an administrator who is responsible for the proper operation of the plan. However, the plan cannot be held under the complete custody and control of either employers or the employees. This includes the employees' union. The appropriate procedure to follow in administering private pension plans is to administer it through a trust company in Canada, a corporate pension society, a registered life insurance company in Canada, or by some arrangement administered by the government of Canada or by a province.

Supplementary Health Care Plans

supplementary health care benefits

Most employers provide to employees some form of **supplementary health care benefits** coverage to help meet the costs of some health care that are not covered by government plans. Some supplementary health care benefits include hospital plans and major medical plans.

Hospital Plans

Some employers provide to employees semi-private or private room coverage. This type of coverage usually costs above the ward rate. Provincial health insurance plans only cover ward rates.

Major Medical

Some employers provide to employees major medical benefits coverage for health care cost such as: prescription drugs, prosthetics, chiropractic services, speech therapy, and ambulance services.

It is often the case that major medical health care coverage is subject to an annual deductible (usually $10-$25) and co-insurance deductible per claim. Co-insurance ranges from 50% employer and 50% employee to 80% employer and 20% employee. (For example, whenever an employee submits a claim for prescription drug, the employee would receive 80% of the claims cost.)

Dental Insurance

Dental insurance is one of the fastest growing and one of the most popular benefits offered by companies. In a recent survey over 86% of employers who responded said that they offered dental insurance benefits to their employees.[14] This suggests that dental insurance is incorporated into most employee benefits programs. Dental insurance is usually provided in three major areas. These are: *basic services*, diagnostic services such as examinations, consultations, and X-ray, preventive treatments, and prosthetic repair; *major services*, major reconstruction and replacements such as complete dentures, creation of fixed bridges, crowns, and oral surgery; and *orthodontic* services, required dental treatment to correct malocclusion of the teeth. Dental insurance is available from most insurance companies and other health care providers in Canada and is usually custom designed to allow employers to select the mix of services that meet their needs. Some provinces have "denticare" coverage which is usually limited to children and individuals over 65 years of age.[15]

Holidays

All jurisdictions in Canada have specified a minimum number of paid holidays that employees must be provided with each year. This ranges from nine, required by the federal government, to five, required by the province of Newfoundland. These government-mandated holidays are called statutory holidays. Employers are required to pay employees regular pay for statutory holidays and two and one-half times regular pay for statutory holiday days worked. The federal statutory holidays include: New Year's Day, Good Friday, Victoria Day, Canada Day (Dominion Day), Labour Day, Christmas Day, Thanksgiving, and Boxing Day. Many collective agreements require that employees be provided with additional paid holidays.

Vacation

Every jurisdiction in Canada requires that employers provide their employees with minimum vacation after a specified period of time. The amount of vacation entitlement is usually based on the employee's length of service with the employer. Most organizations have policies governing when vacation may be taken by employees. Some organizations close down their operations during designated periods each year and employees are required to take their vacations during that time. Other organizations allow employees to take their vacation anytime during the year. In 1990 CAW negotiated a unique clause with Ford, GM, and Chrysler whereby they will pay each worker a $500 vacation bonus each year to help with vacation expenses.[16] For a discussion of employee vacation entitlement in each jurisdiction see Chapter 16.

Minimum Wages

All jurisdictions in Canada have **minimum wage** legislation that applies to most categories of workers, except for farm workers and domestic workers. Table 14.4 illustrates the minimum wage rate in all jurisdictions. As can be seen minimum wage rates varies among each jurisdiction. These rates are for individuals 18 years and older. Minimum wage rate for individuals who are less than 18 years old are lower. Minimum wage rates are imposed by means of minimum wage orders that are periodically issued as per the legislation.[17] Minimum wages are paid primarily in the service sector. Table 14.5 illustrates the average hourly wage rate paid in different Canadian industries. As can be seen the average wage rate in all industries exceeds the minimum wage rate.

minimum wage

TABLE 14.4 Minimum Hourly Wage Rates (1991 Status)

Federal (all employees 17 years of age and over)	$4.00
Alberta (all employees 18 years of age and over)	$4.50
British Columbia (all employees 18 years of age and over)	$5.00
Manitoba (all employees 18 years of age and over)	$5.00
New Brunswick (no special rates with respect to age)	$4.75
Newfoundland (all employees 16 years of age and over)	$4.75
Northwest Territories (all employees 17 years of age and over)	$7.00
Nova Scotia (all employees 18 years of age and over)	$4.75
Ontario (all employees 18 years of age and over)	$6.00
Prince Edward Island (all employees 18 years of age and over)	$4.75
Quebec (all employees 18 years of age and over)	$5.30
Saskatchewan (all employees 18 years of age and over)	$5.00
Yukon Territory (all employees 17 years of age and over)	$6.24

SOURCE: *Human Resources Management in Canada* (Scarborough, Ont.: Prentice-Hall Canada Inc., September 1991). Used with permission

TABLE 14.5 Average Hourly Wage, by Industry, 1980-1988

MANUFACTURING	1980	1981	1988
Food and Beverages	$7.65	$8.62	$12.08
Rubber Products	8.22	9.37	12.94
Leather Products	5.35	5.97	8.09
Textile Products	6.44	7.07	10.26
Clothing	5.31	5.68	7.37
Wood Products	8.86	9.63	12.58
Furniture, Fixtures	6.37	6.99	9.06
Paper and Products	9.77	11.25	16.16
Printing, Publishing	8.98	9.97	13.95
Primary Metals	9.56	10.93	16.11
Metal Fabricating	8.52	9.58	12.65
Machinery	8.83	9.92	12.87
Transportation Equipment	9.33	10.39	14.84
Electrical Products	7.35	8.17	11.97
Non-metallic Mineral Products	8.92	10.05	13.35
Petroleum and Coal Products	11.12	12.53	16.60
Chemicals and Chemical Products	8.50	9.54	13.66
All Manufacturing	8.19	9.97	12.75
Other Industries:			
Mining and Milling	10.80	13.30	17.23
Construction:			
Building	12.47	14.07	14.84
Engineering	11.41	13.04	16.12
Urban Transport	9.44	10.44	15.32
Highway, Bridge Maintenance	7.79	8.69	13.18
Laundries, Cleaners, and Pressers	4.76	5.24	7.30
Restaurants, Caterers, and Taverns	4.50	4.89	8.38

SOURCE: Statistics Canada, Labour Division, June 1988. Reproduced with the permission of the Minister of Supply and Services Canada, 1991.

Maternity Leave

maternity leave

The Canada Labour Code and the employment standards laws in all other jurisdictions, except the Territories, provide rights to pregnant employees. Table 14.6 illustrates the type of entitlements and protection provided to pregnant employees in each jurisdiction. As can be seen pregnant employees under federal jurisdiction with six months continuous service are entitled to 17 weeks **maternity leave** and 24 weeks of child-care leave. An employee, on her written request, is entitled to be notified while on leave of every employment promotion or training opportunity for which she is qualified that become available during her leave. Pension, health, and disability benefits must continue to accumulate as long as the employee continues to make any required contributions.

In Saskatchewan, Alberta, and B.C. maternity leave rights are similar. However, in B.C. employees are not required to have a minimum length of service before they are entitled to maternity leave. In Manitoba there is no provision in the legis-

TABLE 14.6 Maternity Leave Status

Jurisdiction	Law	Minimum Length of Time on the Job	Pregnancy Leave Entitlement	Additional Parental Leave Entitlement	Employee Entitled to Reinstatement to Former Position	Employer Prohibited Terminating, or Laying off Employees Who Have Begun Maternity Leave	Employers May Require Employee to Commence Maternity Leave if Pregnancy Interferes with Job Performance
Federal	Canada Labour Code	6 Months	17 Weeks	24 Weeks	X	X	X
Alberta	Employment Standards Code	12 Months	18 Weeks		X	X	X
British Columbia	Employment Standards Act	No minimum	18 Weeks		X	X	X
Manitoba	Employment Standards Act	12 Months	17 Weeks		X	X	
New Brunswick	Employment Standards Act	12 Months	17 Weeks		X	X	X
Newfoundland	The Labour Standards Act	12 Months	17 Weeks		X	X	X
Nova Scotia	Human Rights Act	12 Months	17 Weeks		X	X	X
Ontario	Employment Standards Legislation	13 Weeks	17 Weeks	18 Weeks	X	X	
PEI	Labour Act	12 Months	17 Weeks		X	X	X
Quebec	Regulations Respecting Labour Standards	20 Weeks	18 Weeks		X		X
Saskatchewan	Employment Standards Act	12 Months	18 Weeks		X	X	X

HUMAN RESOURCE MANAGEMENT IN ACTION

Judge Awards $5 500 to Woman Fired During Maternity Leave

HALIFAX—A pharmacist who was dismissed during her maternity leave in 1988 has been awarded more than $5500 by a Nova Scotia Supreme Court. Judge William J. Grant awarded Debra Anne Moffatt $2646 for lost wages, $434 for lost benefits, as well as $2500 in punitive damages for the "unnecessarily insensitive, humiliating, and wrong manner" in which she had been dismissed by Canso Pharmacy (1983) Ltd. Moffatt had begun working for Canso in late 1985, spending half her time working at a pharmacy in Guysborough, N. S. and the other half at one in Canso, N. S. In June 1987, Moffatt learned she was pregnant and advised her employers. She later gave notice that she wanted to begin her maternity leave on February 2, but actually commenced her leave on January 25 and gave birth on February 8. In March, Canso hired another pharmacist to replace Moffatt at the Canso pharmacy, saying her services were no longer required there. But she was told she could still work at the Guysborough pharmacy, and perhaps at another pharmacy that operated drug stores in two other towns. Moffatt refused the other positions because they would require her to travel on a highway that was known for bad winter driving conditions. She received a termination notice on April 26 but continued on her maternity leave until May 23. She found a new job one month after that, and then sued the Canso and Guysborough pharmacies for wrongful dismissal. Judge Grant said Moffatt was entitled to damages because the terms of her employment had been changed "without her consent or consultation." As well, the new terms entailed her to drive on a dangerous road, to work in a different pharmacy for a person she didn't know, and to be prepared for overnight stays. The judge said the cumulative effect of these changes, as well as the fact that Moffatt had never received any complaints about her work, amounted to constructive dismissal and as such wrongful dismissal.

SOURCE: *Human Resources Management in Canada*, Report Bulletin no. 90 (Scarborough, Ont.: Prentice-Hall Canada Inc., August 1990) pp. 5-6. Used with permission.

Pregnancy Top Reason for Illegal Firing, Report Shows

QUEBEC—Pregnancy is the leading reason Quebec women were fired illegally from 1985 to 1990, Canadian Press reports. Statistics from the province's labour standards commission show that 42% of complaints about illegal dismissals were made when women were fired after getting pregnant. An additional 8% were fired when they had to meet family obligations. Most women fired illegally worked at sales jobs, hotels, restaurants, or in the textile industry.

SOURCE: *Human Resources Management in Canada*, Report Bulletin no. 95 (Scarborough, Ont.: Prentice-Hall Canada Inc., January 1991), p. 3. Used with permission.

Severance Notice Can't Overlap Maternity Leave

KAMLOOPS, B.C.—A company that laid off a female employee so that her severance notice would coincide with her maternity leave has come out the loser in a Supreme Court decision. Referring to the Employment Standards Act—which says vacation time cannot overlap with termination notice—Justice Robert Robinson said the same rules should apply to maternity leave. The employee, Maria Aimola, had been a costing clerk at Cooper Market Ltd. in Kamloops for 10 years, when the company merged with a competitor and laid off several workers. Aimola was told her job would be eliminated on October 31, 1987 and that she would be laid off January 31, 1988. Aimola went on maternity leave at the end of October 1987. Cooper Market paid her benefits until the end of January but refused to pay her salary, even though it would have constituted her severance notice, because the company claimed she was not available for work. The judge awarded Aimola six months' salary in lieu of notice.

SOURCE: *Human Resources Management in Canada*, Report Bulletin no. 80 (Scarborough, Ont.: Prentice-Hall Canada Inc., October 1989), p. 6. Used with permission.

lation allowing employers to require employees to commence maternity leave if the employee cannot reasonably perform her duties because of pregnancy.

In New Brunswick, P.E.I., New Foundland, and Nova Scotia maternity leave rights are similar. Ontario has the lowest minimum *specified* length of service on job before employees are entitled to maternity leave rights. Recent changes to the Employment Standards Act remove the rights of employers to require pregnant employees to go on pregnancy leave when they cannot reasonably perform their duties on account of pregnancy. The Quebec maternity leave provision of the Regulation Respecting Labour Standards is silent regarding the dismissal of an employee due to pregnancy. However, a recent court decision held that absenteeism caused by pregnancy is not just cause for dismissal.

In all jurisdictions aggrieved employees may seek redress under the human rights acts, and also under the Charter of Rights and Freedom. Although discrimination on account of pregnancy is prohibited in all jurisdictions there is an exception to this rule in jurisdictions such as Ontario and Quebec, if an employer can establish a bona fide occupational requirement defence. However, the employer must establish that it cannot accommodate the employee without undue hardship.[18]

The labour laws and employment standards laws of most jurisdictions require employers to give male employees whose wives are expecting a child paternity leave without pay. This usually for a period of up to eighteen weeks. Some jurisdictions also require employers to provide women who adopt children with parental leave.

Short-Term Disability (STD)

Many Canadian companies provide some form of income replacement benefits for their employees. This is intended to provide them with full or partial wage and salary payments in the event that they are unable to work due to illness or injuries. There are various types of **short-term disability** plans. Some plans are funded entirely by employees while others are funded entirely by employers. It is usually the case that STD plans are administered by the employer or by an insurance company. The duration of STD plans ranges from four to six months. Short-term disability plans are growing in usage in Canada. According to one survey conducted by the Pay Research Bureau all of the participating 171 companies offered some form of paid sick leave plan.[19]

short-term disability

Long-Term Disability (LTD)

Long-term disability plans provide partial income continuance to employees who are disabled for a prolonged period and have exhausted their short-term disability benefits. Long-term disability plans usually come into effect after a six month waiting period. They are usually integrated with government benefits provided through Canada Pension, Workers' Compensation, and Unemployment Insurance.

long-term disability

Supplementary Unemployment Benefits

Some employers provide "guaranteed annual income." This is often called **supplementary unemployment benefits**. These benefits are often found in industries such as auto making. They are provided whenever there is a shutdown to reduce inventories or to change machinery. Supplementary unemployment benefits are

supplementary unemployment benefits

paid by the company and supplement unemployment insurance benefits, thus enabling the workers to better maintain their standards of living. Supplementary benefits are becoming more prevalent in collective bargaining agreements and provide supplemental unemployment benefits (over and above unemployment insurance) for three contingencies: layoffs, reduced work weeks, and relocation.

Under the terms of the recent agreement between Canadian Auto Workers (CAW) and Ford Canada, the company pays into a fund to provide all laid-off workers who have more than one year's seniority with income protection of almost 95% of take-home pay (70%-72% of straight-time pay) plus benefits. The duration of the benefits depends on the state of the SUB Fund and on the worker's seniority. A worker with less than five years seniority can draw up to one year of SUB. Workers with five to nine years seniority can draw SUB for one full year independent of the state of the fund. Workers with 10 or more years seniority can draw SUB for two full years independent of the state of the fund.[20] Both GM and Chrysler contracts have similar provisions.

Life Insurance Plans

Most employers provide group life insurance plans for their employees. Group plans contain several important advantages for employers and employees. As a group, employees can obtain lower rates than if they bought such insurance as individuals. And group plans usually contain a provision for including all employees—including new ones—regardless of health or physical condition.

In most cases the employer pays 100% of the base premium, which usually provides life insurance equal to about two years' salary. Additional life insurance coverage is then paid for by the employee. In some cases the cost of even the base premium is split 50/50 or 80/20 between the employer and employee, respectively. In general, there are three key human resource policy areas to be addressed: the benefits-paid schedule (benefits are usually tied to the annual earnings of the employee); supplemental benefits (continued life insurance coverage after retirement, double indemnity, and so on); and financing (the amount and percent that the employee contributes).[21]

Employee Services

While an employer's insurance and retirement benefits usually account for the major portion of its benefits costs, most employers also provide a range of *employee services* including stock purchase plans, credit unions, food services, educational opportunities and subsidies, social and recreational activities, counselling, legal services, moving and/or transfer allowance, and child care. Child care is one of the most important services that employers can provide, therefore it is the focus of our discussion.

Child Care

child care

Child care is emerging as an important benefit in the 1990s. This has come about because of the large numbers of women (see Chapter 1) and single parents who are in the work force. This has created a substantial demand for good, safe child-care centres conveniently located near the parents' place of employment. In a survey conducted by Ontario Hydro, 72% of female employees viewed day care as a social right and over two-thirds said that they were in favour of day care becoming a bargaining issue. But, in the same survey, a higher percentage of men were not in favour of day care becoming a bargaining issue.[22] Ontario Hydro subsequently established a 62-space day-care facility in its building on University avenue in Toronto.

The results of a 1989 Financial Post survey showed that out of 1280 polled, 45% strongly agreed that companies with more than 100 employees should contribute financially to day care for their employees.[23] Kirsteen MacLeod of Financial Post argued that corporations that provide space for day-care centres for workers help to ease family stresses that affect employee performance.[24]

Accordingly to a study conducted by the Conference Board of Canada, on-site child-care centres help to alleviate personal problems, reduce absenteeism, reduce turnover, increase staff loyalty, reduce stress, and help to reduce distractions among the parents since they know where their children are and that they are being well cared for.[25] However, of the 2600 chief executive officers who responded to a survey by Arthur Anderson & Company, 52% feel child care is the worker's responsibility, while 9% favour company supported on- or off-site daycare.[26]

The provision of day-care facilities benefit both the parent(s) and the organization. For the parent(s) day-care programs help to meet their needs for facilities to provide care and nurturing to their young child while they work. For the organization the provision of benefits reduces absenteeism and turnover, increases morale and improves the organization's ability to attract qualified employees.[27] Various Canadian organizations have reported positive results due to their involvement in day-care programs. For example, Riverdale Hospital in Toronto reported that the number of qualified applicants increased by 40% within six months after the day-care centre was opened. A British Columbia company reported that its on-site day-care program reduced the average absenteeism for all employees from 12 to 5 days per year.[28]

Various organizations are providing on-site day-care facilities to their employees and tenants. In Toronto for example,[29] Orlando Corp has a day-care centre with space for 80 children in its 1200-acre Hearthland business park. Orlando paid for the construction and pays half the rent. Heartland tenants are given priorities for available space. Cumrost Development Corp has a 50-space day-care centre in the Royal Bank building in North York. Campeau Corp incorporated day-care space into its Water Park Place and Scotia Plaza properties. Hammerson Canada Inc., at its Bow River Square Complex in Calgary, has a 6600 square foot day-care facility with an outdoor playground, library, two nurseries, and four classrooms. This centre has space for 80 infants, toddlers, and pre-schoolers. The centre is available only to the 350 employees of Bow River Square's tenants. The Apple Tree Cambridge Community Child-care Centre that was opened in November 1990 was planned and partially funded by Allen-Bradley which contributed 20% of the $80 000 cost, with the provincial government paying the rest.

Table 14.7 illustrates the other different types of private-sector child-care facilities in the workplace across Canada. As can be seen employer-assisted child-care programs are of several kinds and sometimes have a combination of features. In Canada on-site facilities are more commonly found in the public sector rather than in the private sector. For instance, over 100 municipalities, hospitals, and other public sector organizations in Canada have established on-site day-care facilities whereas only a small number of private sector organizations have child-care facilities.[30]

Martha Friendly of the University of Toronto Child Care Resource and Research Centre estimates that no more than 50 companies in Canada make some kind of contribution to day-care facilities.

TABLE 14.7 Some Workplace Child Care Arrangements in the Private Sector

Name of Centre	Employer Contribution	Weekly Parent Fees (per child)	Number of Spaces	Number of Staff
Garderie Pomme de Reinette Montreal, Quebec Banque Nationale du Canada	Phone, maintenance, rent, computer services, postage	$65 for infants, $55 for toddlers and preschoolers	40	6 staff, 1 supervisor, 1 cook
Garderie sur une Patte Drummondville, Quebec Celanese Canada	Space, food, maintenance, and accounting	$50	60	9 staff, 1 supervisor, 1 cook, 7 full-time, and 2 part-time instructors
Down's Child Centre Winnipeg, Manitoba Horsemen's Association	Rent and utilities, loans as needed	$39	26	
Garderie L'Enfanfreluche Montreal, Quebec Lavalin Inc.	Accounting, payroll, subsidy 1 hot meal and 2 snacks	$50 and $37 for 2 children	60	8 staff full-time, 1 supervisor, 1 secretary, part-time 2 cooks, 2 p/t staff, 4 on call
Mutual Life Assurance Co. of Canada Day Care Centre Waterloo, Ontario Mutual Life of Canada Limited	All capital costs, some administrative services, (renovations and equipment to be paid back out of any profits)	$65 (to increase January 1985)	40	5 staff with E.C.E., 1 supervisor
7/11 Daycare Centre Burnaby, B.C. Southland Canada	Rent, utilities, repairs and maintenance, administrative support, and food	$46 toddlers $35 preschoolers	25	
Garderie de la Place Ville Marie Montreal, Quebec Trizec	Space, services	$85	30	1 director 1 staff
Nanisivik Daycare Centre Nanisivik, NWT Strathcona, Mineral Services	Employer covers all costs	No charge to users		

SOURCE: Susan Deller, "The Daycare Dilemma," *Benefits Canada* (April 1986), pp. 15-20. Reproduced with permission of Benefits Canada magazine.

Employee Assistance Program (EAP)

Employee assistance programs (EAPs) are specially designed programs that use technical, administrative, and professional human services, on either a contractual or employment basis, so that employees who have problems on or off the job have a recourse to professional assistance. Some of the problems that EAPs are designed to address include:

- Alcohol abuse—whether by employee, spouse, or other family member
- Drug abuse—whether by employee, spouse, or other family member
- Marital problems
- Illness—whether suffered by employee, spouse, or other family member
- Financial problems
- Legal problems
- Anxiety-related stresses—precipitated or aggravated either on or off the job[31]

Alcoholism is one of the most serious problems faced by employees in Canada. It has been estimated that 3.5%-7% or 350 000-700 000 members of the Canadian work force experience severe alcohol-related problems. These problems contribute to increased absenteeism, lower productivity, reduced employee morale, and increased accident rates. These problems also may contribute to increased medical costs, increased disability costs, and increased workers' compensation claims. It has been estimated to cost Canadian industries approximately $21 million per day.[32] Severe alcohol abusers are said to be characterized by personality changes, altered perception, faulty judgment, and unreliable memory. They are also characterized by blackouts, repression, and a sense of euphoria, all of which tend to distort recall, which then restricts the alcoholic's "personal insight into the reality and severity of the illness."[33] According to the Gallup International Research Institute Canadians are among the "world leaders" in alcohol consumption. The Institute noted that 77% of the adult Canadian population consume alcohol. Of this percentage, 17% consume a moderate amount of alcohol and 26% consume a great quantity.[34]

In order to deal with this growing problem, various types of employee assistance programs have been developed to help the employee deal with his or her problems. Some of the approaches developed include[35]

- In-house programs with the company providing its own staff of professionals;
- Public service agency programs (e.g., the Addiction Research Foundation, Canadian Mental Health Association, Family Service Association);
- Consortium programs in which several companies join to provide the necessary professional assistance;
- The Employee Recovery Program developed by the Canadian Labour Congress. This program trains union members as facilitators in linking the troubled employee with the appropriate resource; and
- Programs developed through the services of management consultants.

The implementation of EAPs can result in a variety of savings for employers. These savings occur through[36] reduced absenteeism, a decline in disciplines and grievances, fewer accidents, fewer visits to the medical health unit, reductions in benefit costs, and improved job performance.

employee assistance program (EAP)

Various Canadian companies that have implemented EAPs have reported substantial cost savings. According to the Canadian Mental Health Association's Project HELP unit, one of its clients, Warner-Lambert Canada Limited, estimates that the company has cut costs by between \$180 000 and \$200 000 per year as a result of their EAP. About 80% of the savings is due to a reduction in absenteeism, the other 20% being divided between group insurance savings and reduced loss of time as a result of accidents.[37] Another Canadian company, Eldorado Resources Limited, reported that it has been able to reduce its absenteeism rate by nearly 17% as a result of the implementation of EAP.[38]

The implementation of EAPs by organizations provide employees with the opportunity to get assistance so that they may deal effectively with their problems, and enable to the organization to maintain a more productive work force.

Other Employee Services[39]

Many companies provide service benefits in the form of basic services that most employees need at one time or another: these include credit unions, legal services, counselling, and social and recreational opportunities. Credit unions are usually separate businesses that are established with the assistance of the employer. Employees can typically become members of a credit union by purchasing a share of the credit union's stock for a nominal amount. Members can then deposit savings that accrue interest at a rate determined by the credit union's board of directors. And, perhaps more importantly to most employees, loan eligibility and the rate of interest paid on the loan are generally much more favourable than those found in financial institutions like chartered banks and trust companies. Employers are also providing an increasing range of counselling services to employees. These include financial counselling (for example, in terms of how to overcome existing indebtedness problems), family counselling (covering marital problems and so on), career counselling (in terms of analyzing one's aptitudes and deciding on a career), "out-placement" counselling (for helping terminated or disenchanted employees find new jobs), and pre-retirement counselling (aimed at preparing retiring employees for what many find is the "trauma" of retiring). Some employers also make available to employees a full range of legal counselling through legal insurance plans.

The Canadian Auto Workers' Union, which was instrumental in the introduction of dental benefits to Canada, has successfully negotiated with General Motors, Ford, and International Harvester to provide the first employer-paid legal aid for its members in Canada.[40] Many organizations provide recreational facilities for their employees. For instance Manulife Financial pays the capital costs for the facilities and the operating cost is paid by employees who use the facilities. Dofasco in Hamilton provides a 100-acre park including tennis courts, a baseball diamond, two hockey rinks, and an all-weather track for employees; Brock University provides among other things an Olympic-size, all weather swimming pool.

Finally, some employers also provide a wide range of social and recreational opportunities for their employees including company-sponsored athletic events, dancing clubs, annual summer picnics, craft activities, and parties.

ADMINISTRATION AND COORDINATION OF EMPLOYEE BENEFITS AND SERVICES[41]

The administration and coordination of employee benefits and services are two critical concerns in organizations. The provision of government regulated and em-

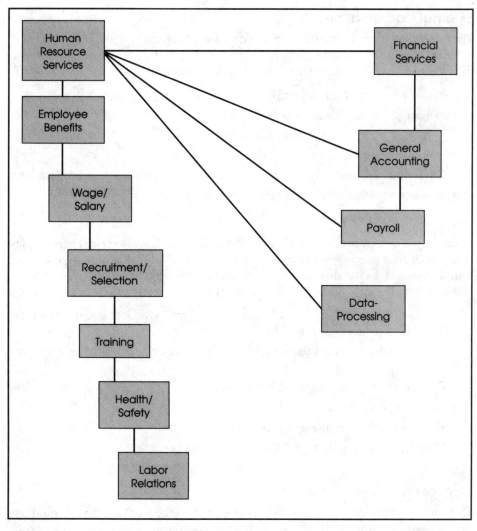

SOURCE: David L. McPherson and John T. Wallace, "Employee Benefits Plans," *Human Resources Management in Canada* (Scarborough, Ont.: Prentice-Hall Canada Inc., 1986). Used with permission.

ployer provided benefits is costly. As a consequence, employers must ensure that careful attention is paid to the design, implementation, administration, and coordination of employee benefits and services. Benefits may be coordinated in two ways: internally or externally.

Internal Coordination

Internal coordination of employee benefits is achieved through a network of certain administrative functions. Illustrated in Figure 14.4 are the basic relationships between these different functions. As the figure indicates the different functions required to coordinate employee benefits and services effectively include human resource services, accounting, payroll, employee benefits section, and labour relations.

External Coordination

The benefits section must often coordinate internal activities with those of several external organizations that are benefit carriers and that provide services related to benefits. Some of these external organizations include

- Insurance companies that are benefit carriers
- Insurance companies for rates and coverage
- Actuaries and outside accountants for verification and auditing purposes
- Unions for problems affecting contract provisions
- Government agencies for assistance in complying with laws and regulations
- Trustees for trustee benefit plans
- Other companies participating in industry-wide plans

Many organizations require the services of *benefit specialists*, also called benefit consultants. Benefit specialists provide organizations with skilled expertise, often not found in-house, in the design, implementation, and administration of employee benefits. Benefits specialists provide a variety of services. These include

- Conducting market surveys of benefit programs in the local, regional, or national labour markets or within an industry
- Assessing the general adequacy, efficiency, and effectiveness of existing programs
- Designing and implementing benefit plans
- Providing consulting services during labour negotiations
- Developing communication programs
- Liaising with benefit carriers on coverage and costs

Control and Development

The control of the day-to-day activities of employee benefits is an important aspect of benefits administration. Establishing standards and implementation of control mechanisms are often difficult tasks. However, they are very important to control cost, for the efficient and effective operation of benefit plans and to ensure that the cost data are valid and reliable.

The importance of implementing control mechanisms that are appropriate and effective has not been lessened by the increasing use of computerized systems. The ease and speed of computer reports should not lull organizations into eliminating manual checks. Great care must be taken to ensure that specific computer data and analyses systems accurately reflect the status of benefit plans. Whatever administrative control systems are implemented, computerized reports need to be periodically verified.

Costing

The cost of employee benefits and services is a significant part of organizations' payroll expenditures. These costs have been increasing more rapidly than salaries. It is therefore important that organizations develop rules to monitor ongoing benefits expenditures as well as the implementation of cost-control mechanisms for cost containment. Some of the cost containment techniques that organizations may use include:

- Increasing the co-insurance or deductible for employees
- Reducing current benefit levels
- Reducing the total cost of financing and administering existing benefits
- Creating "fitness" or "wellness" programs for employees

Communicating Employee Benefits

Many benefits and services employers provide to employees are often not communicated properly to employees. Often times the benefits that employers provide are discussed with employees during the orientation process, a time when the newcomers are under stress and are being pressured with other more important matters. As well, some organizations provide employees with a booklet containing the benefits and services available to them. The information in this booklet is often difficult to read, does not make for interesting reading, and is therefore ignored by employees. Many employees are unaware of some of the benefits that their employers provide. Many also tend to underestimate the costs of those benefits of which they are aware, and often take benefits for granted.

Effective communication about employees' benefits and services is not only desirable, it is mandatory in certain circumstances. Under existing labour legislation in Canada, unions have the right, in most cases, to receive financial data on the status of benefits that are covered by the collective agreement. Under the provisions of the federal Pension Benefits Standards Act as well as under the pension acts of various provinces, employers operating a pension plan covered by these acts must provide specific information to employees on the status of their pensions, usually on an annual basis.

A variety of communication media are available for conveying essential information about the different types of benefits to employees. Table 14.8 provides a comparison of these various media. As indicated, some of these media include:

- employee booklets
- letters and leaflets
- posters
- personalized payroll/benefit statements

A good communication policy manual should include a variety of these media for different purposes.

Cafeteria Benefits

The **cafeteria benefits plan**, also called flexible benefits, enables employees to pick and choose from available options and, literally, to develop their own benefit plans. Right now these cafeteria plans are offered mostly to salaried employees, but there is no doubt that their use will spread to non-salaried workers as well.

The basic idea of such plans is to allow the employee to put together his or her own benefit plan, subject to two constraints. First, the organization has to carefully set total cost limits. (This limits what it will spend for each total benefit package.) Second, each benefit plan must include certain mandatory items. These include,

cafeteria benefits plan

TABLE 14.8 Comparison of Communication Vehicles

TYPE	KEY FEATURES	ADVANTAGES	DISADVANTAGES
EMPLOYEE BOOKLETS	Readable (understandable to average employee) Index of benefits by contingency Summary of benefits as well as full details Compact as possible	Best vehicle for providing full details of plan features Serves as a reference source which employees can continually consult	Problems of employees unwilling to read such detail or not comprehending what is written
LETTERS, NEWSPAPERS LEAFLETS	Should be short and visibly attention-getting Should look personalized and convey important information.	Brief and inexpensive Can be produced on short notice	Easy to disregard. Not enough detail may be given to explain thoroughly
POSTERS	Should be colorful and eye-catching. Should be located in high-traffic areas. Should be changed frequently.	Highly visible. Easily read and understood.	May not contain sufficient detail to make worthwhile. May not be changed often enough to keep interest.
CALENDARS	Should be colorful and eye-catching. Should be a usable calendar.	Highly visible. Easily read and understood.	May not contain sufficient detail to make worthwhile. May not be used.
AUDIO-VISUAL PRESENTATIONS	Format should be both visibly and audibly attention-keeping. Groups should be fairly small.	Probably the best vehicle for conveying detailed information which an individual can instantly perceive and understand.	Relatively expensive to make and present. Need experienced personnel.
MEETINGS AND COUNSELLING	Groups should be fairly small for maximum interpersonal communications and feedback. Two-way communication should be emphasized.	Specific problem areas can be clarified. Communication is very personalized. Misunderstanding can be cleared up quickly.	Time-consuming. May require additional staff.
PERSONALIZED PAYROLL/BENEFIT STATEMENTS	Should be concise but understandable. What the company and employee pays should be differentiated.	Financial impact of benefits is clearly perceived. Relationship to direct wages is emphasized.	Extra work for payroll department.

SOURCE: David L. McPherson and John T. Wallace, "Employee Benefit Plans," *Human Resources Management in Canada* (Scarborough, Ont.: Prentice-Hall Canada Inc., 1986). Used with permission.

for example, Canada Pension, workers' compensation, and unemployment insurance. The amount of cafeteria dollars provided by employers is usually tied to each employee's base wage. Therefore as each employee's salary increases the cafeteria dollar is adjusted accordingly.

Subject to these two constraints, employees can pick and choose from the available options. Thus, a young married employee might opt for the company's life and dental insurance plans, while an older employee opts for an approved pension plan. Cafeteria benefits provide suitable benefits for different types of workers. The variation that may be allowed is limited only by the organization's administrative capacity. Cafeteria benefits provide a degree of cost control over benefit programs by eliminating the expense of across-the-board improvements that may not benefit the entire work force or by removing the duplication of benefits for two-income families.

Cafeteria benefits represent a dynamic approach to employee benefit planning primarily because they are intended to meet differences in the needs of individual employees, the changing needs of employees throughout their career, and the requirements of a rapidly changing business environment.[42] Lawler believes that cafeteria benefit programs can contribute to organizational effectiveness and that they have the potential to decrease absenteeism and turnover and allow the organization to attract a more competent work force. Since individuals receive the benefits they want rather than the benefits someone else thinks they want, working for the organization become more attractive.[43] The results of employee surveys conducted by Reichhold at its operations in North Bay and Thunder Bay, and by Cominco in B.C. appear to confirm many of Lawler's points. Many employees commented that the introduction of the cafeteria benefit program was a positive indication that the company treats its employees as responsible, mature adults.

Lawler argues that the traditional benefit programs do not take into account differences in employees' need, tastes, and preferences. The value of benefits varies widely from employee to employee. Such things as age, marital status, and number of children influence which benefit a person prefers. For example, young unmarried individuals prefer more time off the job whereas young married individuals prefer less time off. Likewise, older employees prefer greater retirement benefits. Lawler also believes that a cafeteria style benefit program makes the compensation system more competitive without increasing the cost of the benefits. Matching employee benefits to individual needs increases their perceived value.[44]

Various Canadian companies have implemented cafeteria benefits programs. These include Pepsi-Cola Canada Ltd., 3M Ltd., Reichhold Ltd., IMC in Saskatchewan, and Cominco Ltd. of Vancouver.[45] Cafeteria benefit programs provide employees with the flexibility of making changes to the mix of benefits they receive as their circumstances changes. Figure 14.5 illustrates the changes initiated by employees to the mix of their benefits. As can be seen employees at this Canadian company made a wide array of changes to the composition of their benefits.

The list of possible options can be quite long and would probably include many of the benefits discussed in this chapter: vacations, insurance benefits, pension plans, educational services, and so on.

Building this type of individual choice into a benefit plan can obviously be advantageous, but there are also disadvantages. The main problem is that the implementation of a cafeteria plan can involve substantial implementation and administrative costs. Each employee's benefits have to be carefully priced out. For instance, Xerox Canada decided against implementing a cafeteria style benefit pro-

FIGURE 14.5
Changes to Flexible
Benefits at Reichhold
Ltd.

- 98 percent of participants made at least one change to their benefits when the flexible dollar plan was introduced in 1986.
- 62 percent opted for a different life insurance plan: 40 percent increased their core coverage of two times earnings; 22 percent reduced the coverage.
- 54 percent changed their dental coverage with most shifting to a more comprehensive plan.
- 23 percent reduced their major medical coverage; virtually all of these were able to integrate with plans provided by their spouse's employer.
- 75 percent opted for one of the 12 accidental death options; the other 25 percent dropped the coverage.
- 88 percent elected to retain the higher of two long-term disability options.
- 11 percent were able to waive provincial medical premiums because they were covered by their spouse's plan.
- 11 percent elected to sell some vacation days.

SOURCE: Susan Deller, "Flexing Your Benefits," *Benefits Canada* (March 1986), pp. 31–35. Reproduced with permission of Benefits Canada magazine.

gram after a feasibility study revealed that the start-up cost would exceed $200 000. Two Canadian companies incurred substantial start-up costs when they implemented cafeteria benefits program. Pepsi's plan cost $80 000 to implement for its 600 salaried staff and Cominco's plan cost approximately $190 000 for its 1800 salaried staff. The cost and availability of many benefits, such as insurance plans, are based on the number of people who are covered by them. It may therefore be difficult to price a benefit plan and to determine its availability in advance so that employees may make an informed decision about participating in it. This problem is not likely to be a serious one for larger companies since a minimum number can usually be determined in advance. Small firms can try to solve this problem by negotiating a special arrangement with insurance companies.[46]

The other problem is the cost of administering the plan. The mix of employee benefits must be updated periodically, so even a medium-sized company would undoubtedly have to use a computer to administer such a plan.[47] Although most employees favour flexible benefits, many do not like to spend the time involved in choosing among available benefit options. Various consulting firms therefore have developed computerized games such as one called "FlexSelect," a user-friendly interactive program for personal computers that helps employees make choices under a flexible benefits program.[48] There are also mainframe and microcomputers to help organizations in administering cafeteria style benefits.

Employees' Preferences for Various Benefits

Two researchers carried out a study that provides some useful insights into employees' preferences for various benefits.[49] They mailed questionnaires covering seven possible benefit options to 400 employees of a midwest public utility company. Properly completed questionnaires were received from 149 employees (about 38% of those surveyed). The seven benefit options were as follows:

1. A five-day work week with shorter working days of 7 hours and 35 minutes.

2. A four-day work week consisting of 9 hours and 30 minutes each day.

3. Ten Fridays off each year with full pay. This includes 10 three-day week-ends per year, in addition to any three-day weekends previously scheduled.

4. Early retirement through accumulating ten days per year until retirement age. The retirement age is 65, minus the number of accumulated days. Full pay continues until age 65 is reached.

5. Additional vacation of two weeks per year with full pay. The additional vacation is added to the present vacation.

6. A pension increase of $75 per month.

7. Family dental insurance. The company pays the entire cost of family dental insurance.

Finally, employees were also asked to show their relative preference for a pay increase of 5%, in addition to any general wage increase negotiated.

Results

Overall results are presented in Figure 14.6. Note that two extra weeks of vacation was clearly the most preferred benefit while the pay increase was second in preference. Overall, the shorter work day was by far the least preferred benefit option.

But this is not the full story: as can be seen in Table 14.9 the employee's age, marital status, and sex influenced his or her choice of benefits. For example, younger employees were significantly more in favour of the family dental plan than were older employees. Younger employees also showed a greater preference for the four-day work week. As might be expected, preference for the pension option increased significantly with employee age. Married workers showed more preference for the family dental plan than did single workers. The preference for the family dental plan increased sharply as the number of dependents increased.

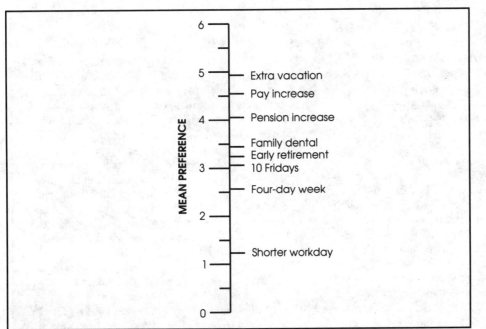

FIGURE 14.6
Preference for Various Benefits

SOURCE: Reprinted from the November 1975 issue of *Personnel Administrator*, copyright 1975, The American Society for Personnel Administration.

TABLE 14.9 How Different Employees Ranked Eight Benefits

Ranking of Employee Preference by Age, Marital Status, Sex, and Number of Dependents

Option	Age in Years			Marital Status		Sex		Dependents		
	18-35	36-4	50-65	Single	Married	Males	Females	0	1-3	4 or more
Extra Vacation	1	2	2	1	1	1	1	2	1	1
Pay Increase	2	1	3	2	2	2	3	1	3	3
Pension Increase	6	3	1	3	3	3	2	3	2	4
Dental Plan	3	4	7	7	4	4	7	8	5	7
Early Retirement	7	5	4	4	5	5	5	4	4	6
10 Fridays	5	6	5	5	6	6	4	5	6	7
Four-Day Week	4	7	6	6	7	7	6	6	7	5
Shorter Workday	8	8	8	8	8	8	8	7	8	8

1 is low, 8 is high

SOURCE: Reprinted from the November 1975 issue of *Personnel Administrator*, copyright 1975, The American Society for Personnel Administration.

COMPUTER APPLICATIONS IN BENEFITS

Benefits Spreadsheet

In the 1990s, companies will continue to be concerned about controlling benefits costs. One prerequisite to this is to be fully aware of how much the benefits offered are actually costing the company, on an ongoing basis. A benefits spreadsheet will provide this information.

The spreadsheet should list each employee (by name or number); the job code pay rate (annual, monthly, or hourly, since subsequent spreadsheet formulas will then calculate the appropriate rate for the benefit being considered); each department; and each benefit, all in separate columns. In order to accurately track current liabilities for benefits accrued but not used, separate columns for liability and use of these benefits should be listed.

For example, suppose the organization wants a report on a accrued vacations. In the liability column, accumulation minus use, times current hourly rate of pay can be calculated. It is this column that will highlight how costly it is to allow employees to accumulate vacation or sick leave from year to year. If an employee accrues at a $10 an hour rate now but does not use the vacation time until retirement, the cost of those hours could easily double or triple, as his or her pay rises.

In the use column, the number of vacation hours used should first be recorded. Then, in a separate column, the cost of the use (hours times hourly rate) should be calculated to compare months, quarters, and/or annual vacation cost to the company. In some instances, it may also be appropriate to add to this calculation the cost of paying someone else to fill in while the employee is gone. (This may be due to the hiring of a temporary employee or having to pay another regular employee time-and-a-half for extra hours.)

In order to prepare reports tied to specific benefits without affecting the overall spreadsheet, the column-width of those columns that should not appear as zero may be adjusted. The columns will still be in the spreadsheet but will not appear in the printed report. The benefits spreadsheet may be used to calculate possible profit sharing formulas, stock options, and to perform other useful human resource activities.

Once a firm has established a spreadsheet, it may also print individual employee reports from the overall spreadsheet. Periodic reports to employees help to keep the value of the benefit package meaningful. This report could show how much vacation and sick leave have accrued, how much was used in a given period, who the beneficiary of the life insurance plan is, as well as what options the employee has not selected. It also could show what the employee is paying for the benefits as well as the company's contribution. With these reports, the company could keep the employee informed, and also give the employee accurate and complete information.

HUMAN RESOURCE MANAGEMENT

On the Front Line

Carter Cleaning Centres have traditionally provided only legally required benefits for their employees. These include Ontario Health Insurance, Canada Pension Plan, and Workers' Compensation. The principals of the firm—Jack, Jennifer, and their families—have individual, family-supplied health and life insurance.

At the present time, Jennifer can see several things wrong with the company's policies regarding benefits and services. First, she wants to do a study to determine whether similar companies' experiences with providing health and life insurance benefits suggest they enable these firms to reduce employee turnover and perhaps pay lower wages. Jennifer is also concerned with the fact that at the present time the company has no formal policy regarding vacations, paid days off, or sick leave. Informally, at least, it is understood that employees get one week's vacation after one year's work. Sometimes employees who have been on the job only four months are paid fully for one week vacation while at other times employees who have been with the firm for six months or more have been paid for only half a week. Jennifer knows that this policy must be made more consistent.

She also wonders whether it would be advisable to establish some type of day-care centre for the employees' children. She knows that many of the employees' children either have no place to go during the day (they are preschoolers) or have no place to go after school, and she wonders if a benefit such as day care would be in the best interests of the company.

1. Draw up a policy statement regarding vacations, sick leave, and paid days off for Carter Cleaning Centres.

2. What are the advantages and disadvantages to Carter Cleaning Centres of providing its employees with additional health, hospitalization, and life insurance programs?

3. How should Jennifer go about determining whether a day-care centre would be advisable for the company?

Implications

The expectancy model of motivation holds that employees will be motivated to obtain rewards only if they view the rewards as attractive. From this study it is apparent that factors like the worker's age, marital status, and sex affect which rewards (in terms of benefits) he or she views as most desirable. One implication is that it seems advisable for organizations to attempt to determine employee's preferences concerning various benefit plans, and to individualize their benefit plans. Ironically (in most organizations), benefit plans are designed to apply equally to all employees, irrespective of differences in individual preferences.[50]

SUMMARY

1. Benefits provide to employees protection against such risks as illnesses and unemployment. Benefits help employers compete for and recruit qualified job candidates. They also help employers retain, satisfy, and motivate their work force. Employee benefits are available to all employees based on their membership in the organization.

2. Many federal and provincial laws influence the type and level of employees benefits provided by employers. By law, many benefits are universal, such as provincial health insurance plans. By law many benefits are mandatory, such as Canada Pension Plan, Workers' Compensation, and Unemployment Insurance. Some laws regulate voluntary benefits to ensure fairness, proper administration, and nondiscriminatory practices.

3. Surveys suggest two conclusions regarding employee's preferences for benefits. First, overall, time off (such as two extra weeks vacation) seems to be the most preferred benefit. Second, the employee's age, marital status, and sex clearly influence his or her choice of benefits. (For example, younger employees were significantly more in favour of the family dental plan than were older employees.) This suggests the need for individualizing the organization's benefit plans.

4. The cafeteria approach allows the employee to put together his or her own benefit plan, subject to total cost limits and the inclusion of certain nonoptional items. Several firms have installed cafeteria plans; they require considerable planning and computer assistance.

KEY TERMS

universal benefits

Old Age Security Act

guaranteed income supplement (GIS)

mandatory benefits

Canada Pension Plan

Quebec Pension Plan

workers' compensation

unemployment insurance

employer pension plan

supplementary health care plans

minimum wage

income replacement benefits

maternity leave

short-term disability

long-term disability

supplementary unemployment benefits

child care

employee assistance program (EAP)

cafeteria benefits plan

DISCUSSION QUESTIONS

1. What is indirect compensation?
2. Explain the purposes and importance of employee benefits and services.
3. What is an employee assistance program?
4. Explain the difference between universal and mandatory benefits.
5. Explain the importance of the coordination and administration of benefits.
6. What are cafeteria benefit programs?

CASE INCIDENT: Drinking for Fun

Lunch time at Crystal Distributing meant going to the Open Arms Steak and Tavern for their juicy burgers and generous servings of french fries. For many years both management and staff met at this tavern for lunch. Besides lunch they usually had a few jugs of beer, some schnapps, and some martinis. Conversations often ranged from general office politics, such as who was next in line to become supervisor, to discussions on major social and political issues of the day.

The group was often unable to conclude its discussions so it was common for some members to meet at the tavern after work to continue to talk. More than once the discussions went on for many hours. The tavern provided live and imaginative entertainment at nights for the benefits of its customers. Nicholas Lovejoy, Cassandra Loren (daughter of the firm's president), and David Darling were usually the last to leave each night. Often they stayed behind to continue enjoying the entertainment and to consume more bubbles. This practice went on for over five years.

About nine months ago Nicholas started coming to work late. On some occasions when he arrived at work he appeared obviously ineberated, and on a few occasions left work early because he was feeling ill. He missed completing various assignments. On those occasions David stepped in and completed them for him. This was done without the knowledge of the supervisor. Cassandra's late night activities at the tavern also were having an adverse effect on her work. On various occasions she missed important deadlines, misfiled important documents, was unable to concentrate on her duties, became forgetful, and missed a few staff meetings.

A little over a month ago someone anonymously sent a brown envelope to Wanda Springs, manager of human resources, informing her of the above noted problems.

Questions

1. How should Wanda handle this situation?
2. What type of policy would you recommend for Crystal Distributing?
3. What obligations, if any, does Crystal have for the social and emotional welfare of its employees?

NOTES

1. David L. McPherson and John T. Wallace, "Employee Benefit Plans," *Human Resources Management in Canada* (Toronto: Prentice-Hall Canada Inc., 1988), p. 45,014.

2. McPherson and Wallace, p. 45,015.

3. McPherson and Wallace, p. 45,031; see also Kalburgi M. Srinivas, ed., *Human Resource Management: Contemporary Perspectives in Canada* (Toronto: McGraw-Hill Ryerson, 1984) pp. 403-404.

4. *Human Resources Management in Canada*, Report Bulletin No. 76 (Toronto: Prentice-Hall Canada Inc., June 1989), p. 3.

5. *Human Resources Management in Canada*, Report Bulletin No. 77 (Toronto: Prentice-Hall Canada Inc., July 1989), p. 1.

6. The material in this section is drawn from Laurence E. Coward, *Mercer Handbook of Canadian Pension and Welfare Plans* (Toronto: CCH Canadian Limited 1991), p. 106.

7. Coward, pp. 108-109.

8. An income test may be defined as the total income of a family, excluding assets, that is used by the government to determine eligibility for benefits. The calculation of the total individual or family income usually excludes OAS benefits.

9. Coward, pp. 241-245.

10. Some portions of the materials in this section are drawn from: Laurence E. Coward, pp. 113-125; and McPherson and Wallace, pp. 45,034-45,038.

11. See Richard Henderson, *Compensation Management*, 5th ed. (Englewood Cliffs, N.J.: Prentice-Hall, 1989), pp. 383-384; Famularo, Handbook, pp. 37.1-37.9.

12. Edward Katz, "The Unsung Benefits of Employee Savings Plans," *Personnel Journal* (January 1979), pp. 30 and 31.

13. Robert E. Sibson, *Wages and Salaries: A Handbook for Line Managers* (New York: American Management Association, 1967), p. 234.

14. Employee Benefit Cost in Canada, 1986. Toronto: Thorne Stevenson & Kellog, p. 13.

15. McPherson and Wallace, pp. 45,064-45,065.

16. CAW/Ford, *Report: Highlights of the Agreement between the CAW-Canada and Ford Canada* (September 1990), p. 8.

17. *Canadian Labour Law Reports* (Toronto: CCH Canadian Limited, 1988) p. 771.

18. Parts of this material are drawn from "Pregnancy Rights: Where Does The Law Stand?" *The Employment Law Report*, Vol. 12, no. 1 (January 1991) pp. 1-4.

19. Pay Research Bureau, *Benefits and Working Conditions*, Vol. 1 (Ottawa: Public Service Staff Relations Board, January 1, 1980), p. 76.

20. CAW/Ford, p. 4.

21. Robert E. Sibson, *Wages and Salaries: A Handbook for Line Managers* (New York: American Management Association, 1967), pp. 235.

22. Bureau of Municipal Research, *Work-Related Day Care—Helping to Close the Gap* (Toronto: BMR, 1981).

23. Kirsteen MacLeod, "Firms take adult approach to day-care dilemma," *The Financial Post* (April 15, 1991) p. 36.

24. MacLeod, p. 36.

25. MacLeod, p. 36.

26. *Human Resources Management in Canada*, Report Bulletin no. 85 (Toronto: Prentice-Hall Canada Inc., March 1990), p. 3.

27. George Milkovich and Luis Gomez, "Day Care and Selected Employee Work Behaviours," *Academy of Management Journal* (March 1976), pp. 111-115. See also Kathleen Mahoney, "Day Care and Equality in Canada," *Manitoba Law Journal*, Vol. 14, no. 3 (1985), pp. 305-334.

28. See Bureau of Municipal Research, *Work-Related Day Care*, p. 30; Jay Paul, "How to Boost Productivity—Put a Nanny on Your Payroll," *Canadian Business* (March 1986), pp. 122-123. See also "Day Care Becoming Management Issue," *Financial Post*, October 18, 1986.

29. MacLeod, p. 36.

30. See Judith Martin, "High Quality Child Care: A Precondition to Equality of Employment," *Canadian Women Studies*, Vol. 6, no. 4 (1985) pp. 91-93. See also Link Byfield, "Feminism's $11 Billion Baby," *Alberta Report* (April 7, 1986), pp. 10-15.

31. Don Wheeler, "Quality of Working Life and Employee Motivation," *Human Resources Management in Canada* (Toronto: Prentice-Hall Canada Inc., 1987), p. 65,031.

32. Ministry of National Health and Welfare and the Ministry of Supply and Services, Canada, *Special Report on Alcohol Statistics*, (Ottawa: Ministry of Supply and Services, 1981), p. 22.

33. Dolores A. Rumpel, "Motivating Alcoholic Workers to Seek Help," in *Management Review*, Vol. 78 (July 1989), p. 38.

34. *La Presse*, (August 2, 1985), p. A4.

35. Wheeler, p. 65,032.

36. Wheeler, p. 65,034.

37. "Project HELP," Canadian Mental Health Association, Metropolitan Toronto Branch, (Toronto, 1983); see also Wheeler, p. 65,034.

38. B. Conway, "Employee Assistance at Eldorado," *Human Resources Management in Canada* (Toronto: Prentice-Hall Canada Inc., 1983), pp. 5085-5091.

39. Parts of this section are drawn from Richard I. Henderson, *Compensation Management*, 5th ed. (Englewood Cliffs, N.J.: Prentice-Hall Inc., 1989), pp. 437-449.

40. Virginia Galt, "Workers Are Winners on Prepaid Legal Aid," *The Globe and Mail*, (July 15, 1985), p. B3; "Prepaid Legal Services—The Newest Benefit," *Contract Clauses*, 9, no. 5 (December 1985), pp. 1-2.

41. The material in this section is drawn heavily from McPherson and Wallace, pp. 45,018-45,031.

42. Coward, p. 184.

43. Edward E. Lawler, *Pay and Organization Development* (Reading, Mass.: Addison-Wesley Publishing Company, 1983), pp. 72-74.

44. Lawler, pp. 72-73.

45. Frank Livsey and Robert J. McKay, "Flexible Compensation Schemes Catching on Slowly," *Financial Post* (February 8, 1986), p. 44; Susan Deller, "Cominco's Flex-Com: A Canadian Prototype," *Benefits Canada* (April 1984), pp. 22-26.

46. Lawler, pp. 74-75.

47. Henderson, p. 312, "Flexible Benefits Are Spreading Fast," *Dun's Business Month* (September 1981), pp. 82-84.

48. For information about this program, contact Towers, Perrin, Forster, and Crosby, 245 Park Avenue, New York, N.Y. 10167. Hewitt Associates similarly has a program called FlexSystem (Hewitt Associates, New York, N.Y.).

49. J. Brad Chapman and Robert Ottemann, *Employee Preference for Various Compensation and Fringe Benefit Options* (Berea, Ohio: ASPA Foundation, 1975).

50. Chapman and Ottemann; see also William White and James Becker, "Increasing the Motivational Impact of Employee Benefits," *Personnel* (January-February 1980), pp. 32-37.

SUGGESTED READINGS

Canadian Mental Health Association. Program Literature on Project HELP, an Employee Assistance Program. Canadian Mental Health Association, Metropolitan Toronto Branch.

Coward, Laurence E. *Mercer Handbook of Canadian Pension and Welfare Plans*, 10th ed. Toronto: CCH Canadian Limited, 1991.

DeSouza, Jackie. "Employee Assistance Programs: An Overview" in *Human Resources Management in Canada*. Toronto: Prentice-Hall Canada Inc., 1989. pp. 65,523-65,537.

Health and Welfare Canada. *Straight Facts about Drugs and Drug Abuse*. Ottawa: Ministry of National Health and Welfare, 1983.

McPherson, David L. and John T. Wallace. "Employee Benefit Plans" in *Human Resources Management in Canada*. Toronto: Prentice-Hall Canada Inc., 1988. pp. 45,018-45,031.

Patton, Garry. "How Will the GST Affect Employee Benefits." *The Employment Law Report*, Vol. 11 no. 4, April 1990. pp 25-27.

CHAPTER FIFTEEN
QUALITY OF WORK LIFE AND NONFINANCIAL MOTIVATION TECHNIQUES

After studying this chapter, you should be able to

1. Define quality of work life.
2. Explain how to set up a management by objectives program.
3. Discuss team-centred quality of work life programs.
4. Explain how to implement a quality circle program.
5. Discuss the pros and cons of flextime.

OVERVIEW

The main purpose of this chapter is to explain how to use several quality-of-work-life and nonfinancial "motivation" techniques and programs to improve the company culture, quality of work life, and performance of an enterprise. After explaining what is meant by "quality-of-work life" programs, we focus in on four important programs—management by objectives, team-centred QWL, quality circle programs, and alternate work arrangements. Each contributes to the quality of work life in the enterprise by providing employees with more opportunities for flexibility, creativity, and responsibility than they might have otherwise. And, in so doing, each program contributes to intrinsic motivators (recall Chapter 11) like the needs for achievement and to self-actualize, and thereby, hopefully, to improved performance at work.

INTRODUCTION

Many changes are occurring in the environment of human resource management. Information technology (PCs, etc.) increasingly demands a more sophisticated, better-trained work force. The majority of jobs that are being created in the Canadian economy today are in the service sector (like consultants, salespeople, food service workers, and nurses, jobs that do not readily lend themselves to highly restrictive work rules or supervisory practices. At the same time the supply of available labour is growing more slowly than in the past, and the average age of that work force is rising—two more factors that are putting a premium on using new methods for getting the best out of the work force. Finally, there are changes in work itself (and in how modern businesses are managed) that reflect the increasing globalization and need for responsiveness that corporate success today requires. As Dr. van Beinum of Ontario Quality of Worklife Centre observes, the challenge lies in matching people with technology.[1]

These changes are naturally influencing the human resource management methods employers use, and no where is this more apparent than in their worker reward and involvement systems. In particular, employers are increasingly utilizing nonfinancial motivation techniques like quality improvement programs and flexible work arrangements. Programs like these, as we will see in this chapter, aim at eliciting the best that workers can offer, by treating them responsibly, by giving them more discretion over their jobs, and in general by providing them with the opportunity to use their problem-solving skills to accomplish difficult jobs and thereby satisfy their needs to achieve and to self-actualize. Some of the most important of these nonfinancial human resource motivation/involvement methods are discussed in this chapter.

Quality of Work Life

Quality of work life (QWL) may be defined as the degree to which employees are able to satisfy their important personal needs by working in the firm. In this view programs like management by objectives, team QWL programs, quality circles, and alternative work arrangements all contribute to the quality of work life by contributing to

quality of work life (QWL)

1. Fair, equitable, and supportive treatment of employees
2. An opportunity for all employees to use their skills to the utmost and to self-actualize—to become all that they are capable of becoming
3. Open, trusting communications between all employees
4. An opportunity for all employees to take an active role in making important decisions that involve their own jobs
5. Adequate and fair compensation
6. A safe and healthy environment

While the phrase *quality of work life* is quite new, its conceptual foundations were actually laid some years ago, with the work of behavioural scientists such as Chris Argyris. At the time, Argyris was mostly concerned with the emotional health of workers. Basically, he argued that as people mature into adults they develop needs for independence, broader interest, and superordinate positions—an overall need, in other words, to control their own destinies. And, said Argyris, the typical company, with its rigid rules (such as having the boss determine the exact hours that employees must work), actually stifles employees' needs to control their lives and grow. Employees must be given more freedom, said Argyris, and his position helped set the stage for today's QWL movement.

Purposes and Importance of Quality of Work Life and Nonfinancial Motivation Techniques

The purposes and importance of quality of work life and nonfinancial motivation techniques are to

- Promote better cooperation between workers and management to increase productivity and improve the conditions of working life
- Heighten the level of participation and involvement by workers in matters affecting their work environment
- Provide workers with more meaningful work to increase their job satisfaction, motivation, and commitment to the organization
- Allow workers greater involvement and control in their jobs and an active input into the decision-making process in the organization
- Help reduce employee job dissatisfaction, stress, absenteeism, turnover, and recruitment costs

Quality of work life programs are widely used in the public and private sectors in Canada. There are over 300 Canadian companies that used one or more techniques of QWL programs. These include General Motors of Canada Ltd., the Toronto-Dominion Bank, Ford Motor Company of Canada, Northern Telecom Ltd., and McCains Food Ltd.[2] As a concept, quality of work life was formally introduced in Canada by the federal government in 1978 when it established a QWL Unit in the Employment Relationships Branch of Labour Canada. Since its formation the Unit has undertaken a wide diversity of activities designed to educate the public about the benefits of QWL programs. Some of the activities include the creation of a network of qualified experts to advise interested parties about the uses and benefits of QWL and the publication and distribution of literature about the effects of QWL on employees and organizations. It has also undertaken various research and training programs in QWL.[3]

Various provincial governments have also established QWL Centres. The location of these Centres varies from one province to the next. For example, in Ontario the Centre is located in the Ministry of Labour, whereas in Quebec QWL Centres are established at McGill University and the University of Montreal. In British Columbia the QWL Centre is operated by the British Columbia Research Council.[4]

The Role of the Human Resource Department

The human resource department has an important role to play in the design and implementation of programs that aim to improve employee's involvement and the overall quality of work life. The HR department can help to secure the commitment and support of top management. It can then act as the crucial coordinative link in securing the support and involvement of unions, line managers, and supervisors in joint planning and development of the program.

The human resource department's involvement is essential to ensure that any program of this nature is in harmony with the overall organizational policies and aims regarding human resources. The human resource department is usually staffed with a specialist who can critically diagnose the potential benefits of a plant-wide productivity and quality of working conditions incentive program such as flex-time and recommend the approaches that should be taken to ensure its effectiveness. Union and nonunion employees often perceive certain types of QWL participation as management manipulation in which workers are expected to contribute something for nothing. The HR department's role here is vital in communicating to the parties the benefits to be derived from such programs. However, many organizations have delegated responsibility for QWL to a senior executive to ensure that QWL objectives are achieved throughout the organization.[5] But these executives are usually supported by a small staff and therefore must rely on the HR department to conduct training and obtain feedback from employee attitude surveys.[6]

QWL at General Motors[7]

General Motors began experimenting with QWL programs in 1970 and remains a leader in this field. Its extensive work with QWL derives partly from former President F. James McDonald, a QWL advocate, partly from the fact that GM has the resources to study these programs, and partly from the notoriously unattractive jobs auto assembly workers hold.

At General Motors, QWL programs are characterized by the following:

- Union and management participation in the process
- Participation on the part of employees is voluntary
- Employees are assured of job security
- Periodic plant and team meetings are held to discuss such matters as schedules, quality, safety, and customer orders
- The use of quality circles through which employees meet to discuss problems affecting the plant performance and their work environment
- Training programs in team problem solving

A description of one of the QWL programs at the GM plant helps to illustrate the thrust of QWL at General Motors. The program here is centred around a production line in which foam rubber car seats are formed in aluminum molds. Bending over a hot conveyor line, the workers must use short, shovel-like tools to scrape off excess rubber buns that have extruded through holes in the molds. Then they remove the cushions and toss them onto another conveyor for shipping.

In an attempt to raise the quality of work life of the crew, GM implemented a process called sociotechnical system, or STS for short. Basically, STS is a method for giving the workers who actually do the job an opportunity to affect how the engineers design their jobs. The objective is to help ensure that the human considerations of the job carry equal or greater weight than the technical. In this particular program, the president of the local union and two assistants, along with several plant superintendents, serve on a redesigning committee that makes the final decision on workers' proposals. Selected hourly and salaried workers serve on task forces, the purpose of which is to encourage and identify suggestions from workers regarding how their jobs could be improved. These suggestions are then passed to the redesigning committee for a final decision.

Figure 15.1 illustrates a comparison of the different uses of QWL by two companies.[8]

FIGURE 15.1 Comparisons of QWL Approaches

THE SOCIALIZATION AND RECRUITMENT SYSTEM

ALCAN, GRANDE BAIE	GENERAL FOODS, TOPEKA	TRADITIONAL
Team meetings held monthly	Team meetings held frequently	Team meetings non-existent
Team supervisor hires replacements	Team hires replacements via team committee	Management hires replacements
Team members perform a variety of functions	All team members have the opportunity to rotate jobs	Job rotation restricted
	Dismissals controlled by team committee	Dismissals controlled by management
	Team members learn a variety of jobs and skills	Job, skill enrichment limited to task

THE CONTROL AND REWARD SYSTEM

ALCAN, GRANDE BAIE	GENERAL FOODS, TOPEKA	TRADITIONAL
Discipline and control provided by first-level management with peer pressure	Discipline and control of team members provided internally by the team	Discipline and control of work force provided by management
Team problem solving negates the need for a formal grievance procedure	Team problem solving negates the need for a formal grievance procedure	Formal grievance procedure as set by company policy or union-management contract
		Structured benefits plan based on a role
	Higher than average pay rate	Average or less than average pay rate
No probation period for new employees	No propation period for new employees	Probation period for new employees
	Attendance incentive	No attendance incentive
On full year net salary plus long-term disability plan		Limited sick leave with benefits benefits
Workers evaluated by supervisor	Workers evaluated by peers/team members	Workers evaluated by supervisor or special department

THE VALUE SYSTEM

ALCAN, GRANDE BAIE	GENERAL FOODS, TOPEKA	TRADITIONAL
Management expresses trust and confidence in ability of workers	Management is concerned about attitudes, interests, and goals of individuals	Management is concerned primarily with profit

FIGURE 15.1 (continued)

THE VALUE SYSTEM

ALCAN, GRANDE BAIE	GENERAL FOODS, TOPEKA	TRADITIONAL
Status symbols minimized (e.g., parking and common rooms are common areas)	Status symbols minimized (e.g., parking and lunch rooms are common areas)	Status symbols entranched (e.g., preferred parking, executive-only lunch rooms)
High worker morale, commitment, self-esteem, etc.	High worker morale, commitment, self-esteem, etc.	Morale, loyalty average or worse

SPECIFIC INDICATORS

ALCAN, GRANDE BAIE	GENERAL FOODS, TOPEKA	TRADITIONAL
Absenteeism significantly lower than in traditional management plant	Absenteeism low (2%)	Absenteeism relatively high, 7 to 15%
High safety and housekeeping standards	Safety and housekeeping standards (a team responsibility) above industry norms	Safety and housekeeping standards (via specialized departments) average
Management–employee relations are cooperative; win–win	Employee relations, labour negotiations cooperative; win-win	Labour negotiations adversarial; win–lose
Lower than average employee turnover	Lower than everage employee turnover	Average-to-high employee turnover
	Demeaning, repetitive, dirty work either shared or eliminated	Demeaning, repetitive work specified by job, not as part of shared function

PRODUCTIVITY, OUTPUT, AND PERFORMANCE

ALCAN, GRANDE BAIE	GENERAL FOODS, TOPEKA	TRADITIONAL
Productivity superior to other plants, given innovative technology	Outperforms similar plants on any standard	Productivity average or worse
No work stoppages	Strikes nonexistent	Strikes common
Individuals are multiskilled	Teams are function-oriented	Individuals are task-oriented
	Workers highly motivated	Workers poorly motivated
	Quality control unsurpassed in industry	Quality control average and variable
	Overhead costs relatively low	Overhead costs relatively high

SOURCE: M. Chadwick and F. Clark, *Design of a New Plant at CSP Foods*, Statistics Canada, cat. #1188-83E, pp. 8–11. Reproduced with the permission of the Minister of Supply and Services Canada, 1991.

MANAGEMENT BY OBJECTIVES PROGRAMS

Management by objectives (MBO) is in some respects the forebear of QWL techniques; the idea that employees should have a say in making job-related decisions has long been popular, and MBO was for many years the most widely used technique for putting this idea into practice. Stripped to its essentials, MBO, as discussed in Chapter 9, involves setting specific measurable goals with each employee and then periodically discussing his or her progress toward these goals. MBO programs consist of six main steps.

1. *Set the organization's goals.* An organization-wide plan for next year and set goals is established.

2. *Set departmental goals.* Department heads and their supervisors jointly set goals for their departments.

3. *Discuss departmental goals.* Department heads discuss the department's goals with all subordinates in the department (often at a department-wide meeting) and ask them to develop their own individual goals, asking, in other words, how each employee can contribute to the department's attaining its goals.

4. *Define expected results (set individual goals).* Department heads and their subordinates set short-term performance targets.

5. *Performance reviews: measure the results.* Department heads compare expectations for each employee with actual performance.

6. *Provide feedback.* Department heads hold periodic performance review meetings with subordinates to discuss and evaluate each subordinate's progress in achieving expected results.

The Three Foundations of MBO

MBO developed out of the practical experiences of managers, but it is also based on three sound psychological foundations: (1) goal setting, (2) feedback, and (3) participation.

For example, MBO involves mutual goal setting, and employees who have clear goals usually perform better than those who do not.[9] Clear, obtainable goals help channel energies in specific directions and let employees know the basis on which they will be rewarded. Employees who receive frequent feedback concerning their performance are usually more highly motivated than those who do not. Feedback that is specific, relevant, and timely helps satisfy the need most people have for knowing where they stand.

Allowing subordinates to participate genuinely in setting their own goals can also increase their commitment to these goals and thereby their performance. It can also make them feel more involved and can thus appeal to their higher level needs. While participation is not effective under all conditions—such as with more authoritarian employees who prefer more direction, for instance—in most situations it can lead to increased performance.

Some Benefits to Expect from MBO

Many MBO programs are quite successful. The following are some of the benefits.

MBO improves commitment and motivation. The process of participating in setting one's own goals leads to increased acceptance and commitment to those goals and thus to increased motivation and performance. Employees under MBO are usually shooting for targets that are clear and obtainable, which also leads to improved motivation.[10]

MBO directs work activity toward the organization's goals. MBO also results in a means/ends chain: managers at successively lower levels in the organization establish targets that are integrated with those at the next higher level. As a result, each person's work is directed toward contributing to the organization's goals since a chain of goals and subgoals develops to link lower and higher level work groups. In other words, MBO helps ensure that everyone's activity is ultimately aimed toward the organization's goals.

MBO forces and aids in planning and control. MBO forces top management to establish an overall plan and set of goals for the entire organization. It also requires other managers to set their own targets and plan how they will reach them. Furthermore, the goals or targets that emerge from the MBO process provide clear standards for control—standards (such as "increase sales by 30% this year") against which each employee's performance can be monitored, appraised, and controlled.

MBO identifies potential problems early. Frequent performance review sessions are an integral part of MBO. This increased interaction between managers and subordinates should help identify problems early, before they get too big.

MBO aids in the development of human resources. MBO serves a development function in that it helps identify performance deficiencies and enables managers and subordinates to set individualized self-improvement goals.

How to Set Effective Objectives

There are five things to keep in mind here. First, objectives must always be based on output, not process. "Selling cars" is a process. "Sell ten cars in June" is an output-based objective.

Second, objectives can be set in four main areas: quantity, quality, timeliness, and dollars. For each, choose a yardstick and then set an objective. For example:

Area	Yardstick	Objective
Quantity	Number of products produced	Produce 14 units per month
Quality	Number of rejects	No more than 10 rejects per day
Timeliness	Percent of sales reports in on time	Submit 90% of sales reports on time
Dollars	Percent of deviation from budget	Did not exceed budgeted expenses by more than 5% during year

Third, it should be clear from this example that objectives must always be measurable and specific. If something cannot be measured, it is not an objective. Research also shows that asking people to do their "best" rarely yields the results that can be achieved from specific, mutually agreed upon, goals.[11]

Fourth, always set stretch objectives. This means setting the new objective just high enough so it is challenging but not impossible. Raising quotas about 15 to 20% yearly is often about right.

Fifth, make sure the objective is attainable. Setting impossible goals will backfire: the person, knowing the task is hopeless, gives up and performance drops. Sometimes the best approach is to break the new objective into subgoals. For instance, suppose you want the person to handle 50 more calls per month. Break this into subgoals: have the person handle two extra calls the first day, three more than that two days later, and gradually build up to the 50-call increase. (Behaviour management experts call this "shaping" behaviour.)

To what extent should subordinates participate in setting the objectives? As much as is possible. If the supervisor knows enough about the job and the person's ability, he or she can just assign a challenging objective. This is usually easiest when dealing with clerical and blue-collar jobs. (Contrary to popular opinion, it works as well or better than "participative management" as long as one knows enough about the job to set attainable, challenging objectives.) With more complex jobs, it is usually best to have some give and take between the supervisor and the subordinate.

Problems to Avoid

There are three problems in using MBO. Setting unclear, unmeasurable objectives is the main problem. Setting an objective such as "will do a better job of training" is useless. "Will have four subordinate promoted during the year," on the other hand, is a clear, measurable objective.

Second, MBO is time consuming. Taking the time to set objectives, to measure progress, and to provide feedback take several hours per employee per year over and above the time already spent on each person's appraisal. Many managers believe the extra time is worth it, but this is an individual decision.

Third, setting objectives with the subordinate sometimes turns into a tug of war, with the manager pushing for higher quotas and the subordinate pushing for lower ones. This is why knowing the job and the person's ability is so important. To motivate performance the objectives must be fair and attainable.

In summary, here are some Dos and Don'ts of MBO:

- Do define the person's job responsibilities and duties.
- Do learn as much as possible about what reasonably challenging objectives would be for the job.
- Do set specific measurable output objectives.
- Do make the subordinate stretch to attain the objective.
- Do make sure the objective is viewed as fair and attainable.
- Don't let MBO be too time consuming.
- Don't get into a tug of war in setting the subordinate's goals.

QUALITY CIRCLE PROGRAMS

quality circle

A **quality circle** is a formal, institutionalized mechanism for productive and participative problem-solving interaction among employees.[12] QCs can be used to solve problems in productivity, safety, cost, and quality. QCs involves a significant amount of worker participation in decision making on matters previously regarded as solely the responsibility of supervisors.[13]

A quality circle is a group of five to ten specially trained employees who meet for an hour once a week for the purpose of spotting and solving problems in their work area. The circle is usually composed of a normal work group—a group of people who work together to produce a specific component or service.

Steps in Establishing a Quality Circle[14]

The four steps in establishing and leading a quality circle include planning, training, initiation, and operating.

Planning the Circle

The planning phase usually takes about one month and typically begins with a top-level executive making the decision to implement the quality circle (QC) technique. This usually leads to identifying and selecting a consultant who will assist top management in implementing the quality circles in the firm, although in some cases an in-house facilitator will be identified and set out for special circle methods training. The facilitator then returns to the firm and handles the tasks the consultant would otherwise have been responsible for.

One of the most important steps in this first phase involves selecting the quality circle steering committee. The steering committee becomes the group that directs quality circle activities in the organization. The committee is usually multidisciplinary in that it draws on employees from functions such as production, human resources, quality control, training, marketing, engineering, finance, and the union. Committees usually contain up to 15 members, and the chief executive is often a member. (The success of the quality circle concept often hinges on how committed to the technique the workers feel top management is; therefore, the steering committee almost always has at least one or two top managers as members.)

The steering committee has several responsibilities. Perhaps most importantly, it should establish circle objectives in terms of the kinds of bottom-line improvements they would like to see. Yardsticks include reduced errors and enhanced quality, more effective teamwork, increased job involvement, increased motivation, and an increased attitude of problem prevention. At the same time, the steering committee determines actions that are considered outside the charter of the circles—for instance, benefits and salaries, employment practices, and policies on discharging employees, personalities, and grievances.

The steering committee also chooses the in-house facilitator, the person who will be responsible for daily coordination of the firm's quality circle activities. In most cases the facilitator devotes full time to the quality circle tasks and is responsible for such specific quality circle duties as coordinating the activities of the circles; training leaders for each circle; attending circle meetings and providing expert advice and back up coordination; and maintaining records to reflect circle achievements.

During this first phase, the steering committee, working with the facilitator, selects leaders for the pilot program. (Two or three work areas are usually chosen as pilot areas for the QC program.) Although the steering committee is responsible for choosing these leaders, in practice the supervisor/leaders are usually selected by the managers of the departments where the pilot programs will operate; they are then confirmed by the steering committee.

Initial Training

In the second phase, the facilitator and pilot project leaders meet (usually with the consultant) and are trained in basic QC philosophy, implementation, and operation. This training course typically takes four days and includes various activities. On the first day, the consultant meets with the trainees to discuss the nature and objectives of quality circles. On the remaining days, trainees use case studies to learn quality circle leadership techniques.

Initiating the Circles

The third phase involves initiating the pilot program's circles. This usually begins with department managers conducting quality circle familiarization meetings with employees, the facilitator, circle leaders, and (ideally) an executive participating as speakers. Employees are told they will be contacted later for their decisions regarding whether or not they want to join a circle. Then, circle leaders contact each employee to determine circle membership, and the circles are constituted. The facilitator distributes member manuals for circle leaders at this point; the manuals contain an overview of the QC idea, as well as an explanation of data collection and problem-solving techniques. The basic techniques are usually learned by each circle in about eight weeks.

The Circle in Operation

Next, each circle can turn to its real job: problem solving and analysis. In practice, this involves five steps: problem identification, problem selection, problem analysis, solution recommendations, and solution review by management.

Problem Identification

The problems identified by circle members are usually mundane and are not particularly interesting to anyone outside the circle's work area. These problems might include how to keep the area cleaner, how to improve the work group's product quality, or how to speed up the packing of the work group's crates. Problems such as these may seem uninteresting to those outside the work group, but to the group they represent small impediments that, taken as a whole, reduce the group's performance. And, they are exactly the sort of problems for which the work group members are, in a very real sense, the resident experts at solving.

Notice that circle members generally do not spend their time identifying big interdepartmental organizational problems—not only would that be beyond their scope, but it would also be demoralizing to circle members to feel that management was "stuffing a problem down their throats."

Problem Analysis

In this next step, circle members collect and collate data relating to the problem and analyze them using data collection, analysis, and problem-solving techniques for which they are especially trained.

It is important to stress that it is the group members, rather than outside experts or the group leader/supervisor, who solve the problem. A big benefit—perhaps the biggest benefit—derived from quality circles is the sense of satisfaction that members get from being involved in the actual problem analysis process.

If they are prohibited from analyzing the problem by an inept leader, they will not only miss this sense of satisfaction but may actually resent (rather than be committed to) implementing the solution. Quality circles are as much a people-building opportunity as a quality-improving one, and to derive all the benefits from a circle the members themselves must be involved in the problem selection, analysis, and implementation. Workers generally derive a great sense of satisfaction and commitment from this sort of challenge, and solving the problem without the worker's involvement is really missing the point of the quality circle idea.

Solution Recommendations

The group's solution is then presented to management orally by group members, with the aid of charts and graphs they prepare themselves. The presentation is usually oral rather than written and more often than not is prepared by employees on their own time at break, lunch, and after work. Most group members derive a great sense of excitement and challenge out of being able to prepare this presentation and sell their ideas.

Solution Review and Decision by Management

Quality circles operate through the normal management chain of command. The presentation is made to the individual to whom the supervisor (normally the circle leader) reports, not to the steering committee or to somebody on the executive level. Top managers may be present as observers, but the rule is to adhere to the chain of command for any approvals required.

According to one source, 85% to 100% of circle suggestions are approved by the manager, often in the presentation meeting itself. Occasionally the manager will need some verification of studies done and may even ask a staff person to assist in the verification. In those unusual instances in which a manager must decline a recommendation, he or she is trained to explain why it was turned down, so as not to dampen the enthusiasm of the circle members.

Problems That Quality Circles Encounter

Quality circle expert Donald Dewar says that circles typically encounter certain problems. But he also says that if these problems can be anticipated, recognized, and dealt with by a firm's managers, then the effectiveness of their quality circle program will be enhanced. Some important recurring problems follow.

"This Is Just 'Another' Program"

One problem is that employees are often sceptical of the quality circle program, assuming either that it is just another participation program (such as suggestion program) or a device for tricking the workers into producing more.

The solution here is to confront this issue head on, before the subject is brought up. The worst thing to do is not mention it at all and let the workers' resentment and scepticism grow. If there is one factor that separates successful from unsuccessful quality circle programs, it is a management that stresses that the program is a people-building program first and a cost-reduction program second.

"Management Pays No Attention to Our Ideas"

Sometimes employees complain that management pays no attention to their ideas, either because management does, in fact, ignore the quality circle's suggestions or because previous participation programs (such as a suggestion program) resulted in little or no feedback from management.

Part of the solution here is to emphasize that circle members are not being asked to generate a list of problems to be turned over to management. Instead, they are being asked to identify problems and their causes and then to solve these problems, largely on their own. Another point to make is that the employees will not be asked to write down their suggestions; instead, they will be able to communicate them face-to-face in stand-up management presentations.

Selecting Problems Outside the Circle's Area of Expertise

Dewar says that "perhaps the number one pitfall to successful quality circle operation is the selection of problems outside the member's areas of expertise." Sometimes, for instance, a new circle completes its training and proceeds to pick a problem in someone else's area—as when a production group tries to solve a shipping problem or when a circle tries to grapple with a more complex interdepartmental problem.

The leader of a circle can avoid this problem by keeping the circle's members on track. Thus, when the circle is about to begin generating a list of problems to consider, they should be cautioned to focus on problems within their own areas—where they are the experts.

Problems That Are Too Difficult to Handle

Problems from outside a circle's area of expertise should always be considered too complex. Sometimes, though, problems even from their own area turn out to be too complex, given the backgrounds and training of circle members.

The firm's facilitator can be useful here. He or she can encourage the circle to call in an expert for temporary guidance; thus, the circle might draw on the firm's quality control manager or personnel manager.

"We Can't Start Circles Now—Meetings Will Hurt the Schedule"

Coming from managers and supervisors, this is exactly the sort of statement that will undermine the circle program, in that it seems to reflect management's less than wholehearted support for the program. From the supervisor's point of view, of course, their concerns seem well founded, since the prospect of eight to ten people sitting around for an hour talking every week can easily be translated into an extra several hundred dollars in costs and missed schedules.

Solving (or avoiding) this problem involves, first, showing managers and supervisors data regarding the past success of quality circles. Many circle programs have, in fact, been responsible for some huge successes, and even when the successes have been more minor, management has generally concluded that the benefits have far exceeded the costs. The facilitator can also point out that organizations generally never relax their schedules to accommodate circle meetings. Finally, he or she can invite reluctant supervisors or managers to attend a circle meeting or to speak with one or more circle leaders concerning how they feel about the program.

Fear of Interference from the Union

According to Dewar, unions are rarely an obstacle. When they have expressed concern, he says, it is usually because they think quality circles might take up such issues as wage levels, human resources matters, or grievances. These are normally the prerogatives of the union and are not, as we pointed out earlier, within the purview of the quality circle.

COMPUTER APPLICATIONS IN INCENTIVES

Attitude Surveys

According to a Louis Harris survey reported by *Industry Week*,[1] in 1989 fewer employees were satisfied with their jobs than in 1988. The reasons given were based on a dissonance between expectations and experience in ethical management behaviour, concern for employees, and communication. Mergers and acquisitions have only exacerbated the feelings of mistrust of management. Companies that value their workers apparently get input from them on company policies, perceptions of management, work or company restructuring, benefit packages (current and proposed changes), or reasons for turnover.

The use of employee attitude surveys has grown since 1944 when the National Industrial Conference Board "had difficulty finding fifty companies that had conducted opinion surveys."[2] Today most companies are aware of the need for employee anonymity, the impact of both the design of the questions and also their sequence, and the importance of effective communication, including the purpose of the survey before it is taken and feedback to the employees after it is completed. Computerization of surveys can provide anonymity, if there is no audit trail to the user, especially for short answers that are entered rather than written or typed on a distinguishable machine.

Survey software packages are available that generate questions on a number of standard topics and can be customized by modifying existing questions or by adding questions. If the survey is computerized, then reports can be generated with ease to provide snapshots of a given period of time, trend analyses, and breakdowns according to various demographics. Responses may be classified according to the respondents' age, sex, job category, department, division, function, or geographical location.

The survey may be conducted by placing microcomputers in several locations convenient for employee use. Employees are advised where the computers will be, for how long, and when the data will be collected (e.g., daily at 5 P.M. for a week). The screen should not be viewable by supervisors or passersby. While there may be some risk that employees will take the survey more than once, there are comparable risks with other methods. (For example, who completes the survey mailed to the employee's home?)

In addition to the survey topics listed above, managers may be interested in knowing how they are perceived by their peers and subordinates. Packages that may be customized are available which allow the manager to complete a self-assessment tool used to compare self-perception to the opinions of others. This comparison may assist in the development of a more effective manager. The same protection for anonymous participation is required, as is the necessity for communicating the purpose of the assessment, and feedback to participants.

Employees who are leaving the company are often asked their opinions during a formal or informal exit interview. Concerned about future references, employees often state innocuous reasons for leaving; reasons known to be acceptable to the company. However, if the existing employees could respond to computer questions (such as, If you could change some aspect of supervision, what would it be? If you could change some aspect of our benefits, what would it be?) and be assured that answers would not be looked at until several people had responded, more helpful information might be learned.

---

[1]Stanley J. Modio, "Whatever It Is, It's Not Working," *Industry Week*, Vol. 238, no. 14 (July 17, 1989), p. 27.
[2]Martin Wright, "Helping Employees Speak Out About Their Jobs and the Workplace," *Personnel*, Vol. 63 (September 1986), p. 56.

Therefore, the union president, says Dewar, should be invited to take a seat on the steering committee. Also, union stewards should be invited to be members of circles and the circles themselves should be presented as helping to create a more competitive organization that will provide greater job security for all.

Dewar suggests informing union officials of circle activities prior to initiation of those activities in an organization. This gets them involved at the start, avoids putting them in the position of not being able to answer members' questions about the circles, and also gives management an opportunity to assure them that the circle program is not a speed-up technique.

Various companies in Canada have implemented QCs and have reported much cost savings as a result. For instance, Vickers Inc., a manufacturer of hydraulic and pneumatic products and systems which employs approximately 7000 employees, reported that it is saving $250 000 because of the use of QCs programs.[15] Maritime Beverages which employs about 400 workers reported that grievances have dropped by 75% since the implementation of QCs.[16]

ALTERNATIVE WORK ARRANGEMENTS

Employers are increasingly instituting new flexible work arrangements that involve, for instance, giving workers more freedom to choose the hours that they work. These include flextime, a reduced work week, and job sharing.

Flextime

flextime

Flextime is a plan whereby employees' flexible workdays are built around a central core of midday hours, such as 11 to 2. It is called flextime because workers determine their own starting and stopping hours. For example, they may opt to work from 7 to 3 or 11 to 7.

Flextime in Practice

In practice, most employers who use flextime allow employees only limited freedom regarding the hours they work. This is summarized in Table 15.1 which shows the earliest starting time, latest starting time, and core periods that are most popular. As shown, employers still try to hold fairly close to the traditional 9 to 5 day. For example, in 67% of the companies employees cannot start work before 7 A.M., and in almost all firms employees must not clock in before 6 A.M. Similarly, in about half of the firms, employees cannot start work later than 9 A.M., and employees in about 40% of the firms must be in by 10 A.M. Therefore, the effect of flextime for most employees is to give them about 1 hour leeway in terms of starting before 9 or leaving after 5. Similarly, about 15% of the employers made 9 A.M.-3 P.M. their core period, while another 28% made their core period 9 A.M.-4 P.M.

The Pros and Cons of Flextime

Some flextime programs have been quite successful.[17] Because less time is lost due to tardiness, the ratio of worker-hours worked to worker-hours paid (a measure of productivity) increases. It has also been shown to reduce absenteeism and to cut down on "sick" leave being used for personal matters. The hours actually worked seem to be more productive, and there is less slowing down toward the end of the workday. Workers tend to leave early when work is slack and work later when it

TABLE 15.1 Typical Flextime Schedules

FLEXTIME STARTING TIMES

Earliest Starting Time	Percent of Respondents	Latest Starting Time	Percent of Respondents
Before 6 A.M.	10%	8–9 A.M.	55%
6–7 A.M.	21%	9–10 A.M.	31%
7–8 A.M.	67%	10–11 A.M.	9%
8–9 A.M.	2%	11–12 Noon	0%
After 9 A.M.	0%	After 12 Noon	5%

FLEXTIME CORE HOURS		WORK WEEK SCHEDULING	
Time	Percent of Respondents	Scheduling Plan	Percent of Respondents
8 A.M.–3 P.M.	5%	5 days, 40 hours	64%
8 A.M.–4 P.M.	19%	5 days, 37 1/2 hours	18%
8 A.M.–5 P.M.	10%	5 days, 35 hours	8%
9 A.M.–3 P.M.	15%	5 days, 38 3/4 hours	3%
9 A.M.–4 P.M.	28%	5 days, 36 1/4 hours	2%
9 A.M.–5 P.M.	6%	4 days, 40 hours	1%
10 A.M.–2 P.M.	4%	All others	4%
10 A.M.–3 P.M.	3%		
10 A.M.–4 P.M.	5%		
11 A.M.–3 P.M.	3%		
Noon–6 P.M.	1%		

Note: Types of industries represented are business and human services (including government agencies, medical institutions, educational institutions, nonprofit organizations, employment agencies, consulting firms, and publishing firms), 39%; banking/financial insurance, 28%; manufacturing/processing, 21%; retail/wholesale sales and distribution, 7%. Number of employees in represented companies: very small companies (1-100), 24%; small companies (101-1000), 27%; medium-sized companies (1000-10 000), 24%; large companies (over 10 000), 10%.

SOURCE: *1986 AMS Flexible Work Survey* (Willow Grove, Pa: Administrative Management Society, 1986), pp. 3, 4, 9.

is heavy. The use of flextime also seems to related to an increased receptiveness on the part of employees to changes in other procedures.

Flextime is also advantageous from the worker's point of view. It may reduce the tedium associated with the timing of their work and democratize their work. It also tends to reduce the distinction between managers and workers and requires more delegation of authority by supervisors.

There are also disadvantages. Flextime is complicated to administer and may be impossible to implement where large groups of workers must work interdependently.[18] It also requires the use of time clocks or other time records, and this can be disadvantageous from the point of view of workers.

Surveys covering some 445 employees (including drug companies, banks, electronics firms, and government agencies) indicate that the percentage of employees reporting productivity increases as a result of flextime programs range from a low of 5% or 10% in some firms to about 95% in one airline. On the whole, about 45% of employees involved in flextime programs report that the program has resulted in improved productivity.[19] The failure rate of flextime is also remarkably low, reportedly 8%, according to one study.[20]

Conditions for Success

There are several things that can be done to make flextime programs more successful.[21] Management resistance—particularly at the supervisory level and particularly before the program is actually tried—has torpedoed several programs before they became operational, so supervisory indoctrination programs are important prerequisites to success. Second, flextime is usually more successful with clerical, professional, and managerial jobs, and less so with factory jobs (the nature of which tends to demand interdependence among workers). Third, experience indicates that the greater the flexibility of a flextime program, the greater the benefits the program can produce (although the disadvantages, of course, multiply as well). Fourth, how the program is installed is important: a flextime project director to oversee all aspects of the program should be appointed, and frequent meetings should take place between supervisors and employees to allay their fears and clear up misunderstanding. A pilot study, say, in one department, is advisable.[22]

Also, flextime may be especially valuable for the employer when the group must share limited resources. For example, computer programmers often spend as much as two-thirds of their time waiting to make computer runs. In situations like these flextime may be especially beneficial. As one researcher concludes, "because flextime expands the amount of time that the computer is available to the programmer, this allows its usage to be spread over more hours, and the time in queues to make runs and get output back is reduced."[23]

Three- and Four-day Work Weeks

four-day work week

A number of employers have also switched to a **four-day work week**. Here employees work four 10-hour days instead of the more usual five 8-hour days.[24]

Advantages

Compressed work week plans have been fairly successful since they have several advantages (see Table 15.2). Productivity seems to increase since there are fewer start-ups and shutdowns. Workers are more willing to work some evenings and Saturdays as part of these plans.

TABLE 15.2 Advantages and Disadvantages of Flextime (in rank order)

RANK ORDER	ADVANTAGES
1	Improves employee attitude and morale
2	Accommodates working parents
3	Results in fewer traffic problems—workers can avoid congested streets and highways
4	Increases production
5	Decreases tardiness
6	Accommodates those who wish to arrive at work before interruptions begin
7	Facilitates employee scheduling of medical, dental, and other types of appointments
8	Decreases absenteeism
9	Accommodates the leisure-time activities of employees
10	Decreases turnover

	DISADVANTAGES
1	Lack of supervision during all hours of work
2	Finding key people unavailable at certain times
3	Causes understaffing at times
4	Accommodating employees whose output is the input for other employees is a problem
5	Inability to schedule meetings at convenient times
6	Employee abuse of flextime program
7	Keeping track of hours worked or accumulated is a problem
8	Planning work schedules is difficult
9	Inability to coordinate projects

SOURCE: *1986 AMS Flexible Work Survey* (Willow Grove, Pa.: Administrative Management Society, 1986), p. 4.

However, there has not been a lot of experience with short-ended work weeks, and it is possible that the improvements are short-lived. In one study, for instance, four-day weeks resulted in greater employee satisfaction and productivity and less absenteeism when evaluated after 13 months, but these improvements were not found after 25 months.[25] A recent review of a 3-day, 38-hour work weeks concluded that compressed work-week schedules have significant positive and long-lasting effects on the organization if handled properly. Regardless of individual differences, those employees who have experienced the 3/38 schedule reacted favourably to it, particularly if they had participated in the decision to implement the new program and if their jobs have been enriched by the schedule change. Fatigue did not appear to be a problem in this survey.[26]

Disadvantages

There are also some disadvantages, some of them potentially quite severe (see Table 15.2). Tardiness, for example, may become a problem. Of more concern is the fact that fatigue was cited by a number of firms as a principal drawback of the four-day work week (note that fatigue was a main reason for adopting 8-hour days in the first place).

Other New Flexible Work Arrangements

job sharing

work sharing

flexiplace

Employers are also taking other steps to accommodate the needs of their employees. **Job sharing** is a concept that allows two or more people to share a single full-time job; for example, two people may share a 40-hour-per-week job, with one working mornings and the other working afternoons. About 10% of the firms questioned in one survey indicated that they allow for job sharing.[27] **Work sharing** refers to a temporary reduction in work hours by a group of employees during economic hard times as a way of preventing layoffs; thus 400 employees may all agree to work (and get paid for) only 35 hours per week in order to avoid having the firm lay off 30 workers. **Flexiplace**, in which employees are allowed or encouraged to work at home or in a satellite office closer to home, is another example of a flexible work arrangement that is becoming more popular today.

Telecommuting is another option. Here employees work at home, usually with video displays, and use telephone lines to transmit letters, data and completed work back to the home office. The Human Resource Management in Action feature outlines a telecommuting program at the Bank of Montreal.

Still other employers, especially in Europe, are switching to a plan they call *flexyears*. Under this plan, employees can choose (at six-month intervals) the number of hours they want to work each month over the next year. A full-timer, for instance, might be able to work up to 172 hours a month. In a typical flexyear arrangement, an employee who wants to average 110 hours a month might work 150 hours in January (when the children are at school and when the company needs extra help to cope with the January sales). In February, she may work only 70 hours because she wants to, say, go skiing. In March, she may then work the full 173 hours to build up her credit, which will enable her to accompany her husband on a business trip abroad in the following month.[28]

HUMAN RESOURCE MANAGEMENT IN ACTION

Tele-commuting: The Bank of Montreal Experience—A Success Story

In February 1991, the Bank of Montreal, one of the largest banks in Canada, undertook a pilot project titled the "Alternative to Bank Premises—Pilot Project" or "Floating Office." The pilot project aimed to decide whether an alternate work environment is viable and desirable and could result in value-added to the bank. The objectives were to eliminate traditional bank premises in favour of a

"work where the work is" environment; facilitate and improve customer service; and improve employee quality of work life and morale. Other major benefits expected to accrue comprised two elements: a reduction in occupancy costs and cost avoidance for the surplus furniture.

Before undertaking this initiative, the Bank discovered that there was almost a total absence of information from which to work. The Bank had to resort to instinct, advice, and generic experience to build a vision of what a "Floating Office" would look like in reality. The Bank sought inputs from various internal departments including Legal, Corporate Risk and Insurance, Corporate Benefits, Taxation, Real Estate, and Employee Relations. The University of Western Ontario also provided some consulting.

During the analysis of the requirements for a "Floating Office" concerns were expressed over what this type of environment would do to people, to the team. The nature of the concerns included:

- the effect on the manager/subordinate relationship including the manager's ability to judge the subordinate's performance
- the absence of structure on people who depend on it
- the replacement of the social interaction with colleagues and peers including the value of the informal network on education and information exchange
- the ability to maintain a strong sense of teamwork and commitment with a decentralized group

After much discussion and assessment several conclusions emerged, specifically:

- that effective and professional management would be unaffected by the introduction of a "Floating Office"
- that much of the concern raised centred on trust and that either you have it or you don't have it despite the environment
- most people respond to increased freedom and autonomy in a positive way
- management and staff alike would have to be proactive and stay tuned in and anticipate problems as they evolved
- some attention would be required to bring the people together regularly to provide the true team focus

Participants came from the Bank's Business Systems Groups. Members included: Oone Senior Manager, five Business Systems Specialists, five Project Managers and fifteen Business Systems Analysts. Each participant received a personal computer, a second telephone line installed in their home, various computer software such as electronic mail, and numeric pagers. Pagers were chosen because of cellular phones' limitations. All individuals were required to wear their pagers during core hours. The Bank maintained a core site staffed by an Administrative Assistant. This person acted as a facilitator when direct access was not possible between individuals.

Several months after the pilot had been running, an Employee Relations Survey was initiated. Ninety-three percent responded favourably to the "Floating Office" and indicated that they would not want to go back to traditional banking. A side-effect of the move into a "Floating Office" has proven to be the ability of the group, on an individual basis, to get into flex-time management or "time shifting." Time shifting is the option to complete assigned tasks any time during the day or night so long as the work gets done and the person remains available during the "Core Hours." The actual design and detail of each day is a matter of personal choice.

Measuring the success of the pilot project included financial results compared to plan; the successful delivery of projects according to department commitments to the various customer groups; and employee satisfaction.

Over the course of the five months since the pilot project began every commitment was met on time. Each of the four lines of business has continued to run as effectively as before. Employee team spirit, morale and cooperation have increased. Many individuals have reacted to the increased empowerment and trust with improvements in performance and attitude. The increase in personal freedom through time-shifting has afforded personnel the opportunity to juggle home and work priorities more effectively. The project was also featured on the CBC at 6 television program initially telecast on October 16, 1991.

The Bank will realize a savings of $592.5M over five years from the implementation of the "Floating Office" in the Business Systems Division. It is currently expanding this system to other areas of the Bank.

SOURCE: Post-Implementation Review, Alternative To Bank Premises Pilot Project, July 1991. Reproduced by permission of D.B. Chamberlain, Senior Manager, Bank of Montreal, Business Systems, Financial Institution & Government Services, 55 Bloor Street West, 10th Fl., Toronto, Ontario M4W 3N5.

On the Front Line

As a recent graduate and a person who keeps up with the business press, Jennifer is not unfamiliar with the benefits of nonfinancial motivation such as quality circle programs.

Jack has actually installed a quality of work life program of sorts at Carter, and it has been in place for about five years. He holds employee meetings periodically but particularly when there is a serious problem in a store—such as very poor quality work or too many breakdowns—in which case he schedules a meeting with all the employees in that store and meets with them as soon as the store closes. Hourly employees get extra pay for these meetings, and they actually have been fairly useful in helping Jack to identify several problems. Jennifer is now curious as to whether these employee meetings should be formalized and perhaps a formal quality circle program initiated.

1. Would you recommend a quality circle program to Jennifer? Why? Why not?

2. Given what you know about the supervision of these stores, would you recommend a management by objectives program for store managers? Why or why not?

3. Are new work arrangements such as flextime or four-day work weeks practical at Carter? Why?

SUMMARY

1. *Quality of work life* refers to the degree to which employees are able to satisfy their important personal needs by working in the organization. It reflects such things as fair, equitable treatment; an opportunity for each worker to use his or her skills to the utmost; and an opportunity for all employees to take an active role in making important job-related decisions.

2. *Management by objectives*, a forebear of QWL programs, involves six steps: setting the organization's goals, setting the department's goals, discussing the department's goals, defining the expected results (setting individual goals), reviewing performances, and providing feedback. Goal setting, feedback, and participation are the three foundations of MBO.

3. A *quality circle* is a group of five to ten specially trained employees who meet for an hour once a week for the purpose of spotting and solving problems in their work area. QCs can be used to solve problems in productivity, safety, cost, and quality.

4. Steps in establishing a quality circle program include planning, training, initiating, and operating. Problems to be aware of include: attitudes such as, "This is just another program;" "Management pays no attention to our ideas;" selecting problems outside the circle's expertise; problems that are too difficult to handle; scheduling problems; and fear of interference from the union.

5. *Flextime* is a plan whereby employees' flexible workdays are built around a core of midday hours, such as 11 to 2. It seems to improve employee attitudes and morale, increase production, and decrease tardiness; however, unavailability of key people at certain times and, generally, scheduling activities like meetings can be problems. Flextime and other flexible work arrangements,

such as four-day work weeks, job sharing, work sharing, and flexiplace, are aimed in part at tapping employees' needs to be treated as responsible human beings, and to that extent they boost the quality of work life.

KEY TERMS

quality of work life (QWL)

management by objectives (MBO)

quality circle

flextime

four-day work week

job sharing

work sharing

flexiplace

DISCUSSION QUESTIONS

1. Define what is meant by a quality circle.
2. Explain the steps involved in operating a circle (including problem identification and problem selection).
3. Explain how you would set up a management by objectives program.
4. Describe several team-centred quality of work life programs.
5. Explain the pros and cons of flextime and the four-day work week.

CASE INCIDENT: Why Can't Goldstar Get It Right?

Everyone at Goldstar Products was excited when the Quality Circles program was implemented. For many years workers had expressed interest in participating in such a program since many employees heard from friends and relatives how well it worked in other companies. They felt that such participation would give them the opportunity to make some meaningful changes in working conditions at Goldstar.

For over five years Goldstar had an Employee Suggestion Plan (ESP). The plan offered employees a variety of rewards, including cash, additional vacation days, and special letters of commendation. Two years ago Goldstar had to discontinue that program because of lack of employee support and involvement. When the Quality Circles program was established management felt that it would be more successful than ESP because it would provide employees with direct input into their working conditions.

The program began six months ago with groups of 20 employees in each of the seven departments. But after five months none of the groups provided any recommendations that were considered useful. Four groups did not provide any recommendations. Group meetings were often noisy: some members engaged in shouting matches, disputing who was in charge, and others tried to dominate the proceedings. After observing the conduct of the groups, management decided to suspend the Quality Circles program. It hired a consultant to analyze the problems and to provide recommendations on how to improve the program.

Questions

1. What are the reasons the Quality Circles program failed at Goldstar?
2. Recommend a course of action the employer should follow to get the program working properly.

NOTES

1. Hans van Beinum, "New Technology and Organizational Choice," *QWL FOCUS*, Publication of the Ontario Quality of Worklife Centre of the Ontario Ministry of Labour.

2. Brent King "Quality Circles have Achieved Acceptance" in *Financial Post*, January 18, 1986, p. 15.

3. J. Mears and L. Brunet, "Overview: QWL Activities in Canada" in N.Q. Herrick, ed., *Improving Government: Experiments with QWL Systems* (New York: Praeger, 1983), pp. 5-11.

4. Harvey F. Koledny "Canadian Experience in Innovative Approaches to High Commitment Work Systems," in Shimon L. Dolan and Randall S. Schuler, eds., *Canadian Readings in Personnel and Human Resource Management* (St. Paul: West Publishing Co., 1987), pp. 313-321.

5. William B. Werther Jr. and William A. Ruch, "Chief Productivity Officer" Working Paper, Bureau of Business Research, College of Business Administration, Arizona State University, 1982.

6. William B. Werther Jr. and William A. Ruch, "Productivity Strategies at TRW," *National Productivity Review* (Spring 1983), p. 16.

7. Except as noted this section is based on "The New Industrial Relations," *Business Week*, (May 11, 1981).

8. M. Chadwick and F. Clark, "Design of a New CSP Foods," *Quality of Working Life Case Study Series*, Labour Canada, Catalogue No. L44-1188/83 1984.

9. Gary Latham and J. James Baldes, "The Practical Significance of Locke's Theory of Goal Setting," *Journal of Applied Psychology*, Vol. 60, no. 1 (February 1975).

10. Steven Carroll and Henry Tosi, *Management by Objectives* (New York: Macmillan, 1973), pp. 130-138.

11. Ibid. See also Joseph Leonard, "Why MBO Fails So Often," *Training and Development Journal*, Vol. 40, no. 6 (June 1986), pp. 38-42.

12. R. Lozano and Philip C. Thompson, "QC Implementation in the Space Shuttle External Tank Program at the Michoud Marietta Corporation," ASQC 34th Annual Technical Conference Transactions, 1980 as quoted in Olga Crocker, in *Quality Circles*, (Toronto: Methuen Publications, 1984), p. 6.

13. Crocker, p. 8.

14. This section based on Donald Dewar, *The Quality Circle Guide to Participation Management* (Englewood Cliffs, N. J.: Prentice-Hall, 1980). See also James Thacker and Mitchell Fields, "Union Involvement in Quality-of-Work Life Efforts: A Longitudinal Investigation," *Personnel Psychology*, Vol. 40, no. 1 (Spring 1987), pp. 97-112. They conclude that unions' fears of QC's may be misplaced and that after quality-of-work life involvement, "a majority of the rank and file members who perceived QWL as successful gave equal credit for the success to both union and management. The rank and file members who perceived QWL as unsuccessful tended to blame management for the lack of success." See also Anat Rafaeli, "Quality Circles and Employee Attitudes," *Personnel Psychology*, Vol. 38 (Fall 1985), pp. 603-615; Mitchell Lee Marks, Edward Hackett, Philip Mirvis, and James Grady, Jr., "Employee Participation in a Quality Circle Program: Impact on Quality of Work Life, Productivity, and Absenteeism," *Journal of Applied Psychology*, Vol. 71, no. 1 (February 1986), pp. 61-69, and "Quality Circles: A New Generation," *BNA Bulletin to Management*, Vol. 38, no. 2 (January 1987), pp. 10-15.

15. Brent King, "Quality Circles have Achieved Acceptance," *Financial Post*, January 18, 1986, p. 15.

16. Ibid.

17. Donald Peterson, "Flextime in the United States: The Lessons of Experience," *Personnel*, Vol. 57 (January-February 1980), pp. 21-37; 1987 *AMS Flexible Work Survey* (Willow Grove, Pa: Administrative Management Society, 1987), p. 22.

18. Stanley Nollen, "Does Flexitime Improve Productivity?" *Harvard Business Review*, Vol. 56 (September-October 1977), pp. 12-22.

19. Ibid.

20. Stanley Nollen and Virginia Martin, *Alternative Work Schedules Part One: Flexitime* (New York: AMACOM 1978), p. 44.

21. Peterson, "Flextime in the U.S.," pp. 29-31.

22. Another problem is that some employers let workers "bank" extra hours by working, say, 45 hours one week so they need work only 35 hours the next week. The problem is that in the 45-hour week the employees should, strictly speaking, be paid an overtime rate for the extra 5 hours worked. Some employers handle this problem by letting hours worked vary from day to day but requiring each week to be a 40-hour week. Others are experimenting with letting workers accumulate hours and be paid overtime if necessary. See J. C. Swart, "Flexitime's Debit and Credit Option," *Personnel Journal*, Vol. 58 (January-February 1979), pp. 10-12.

23. David Ralston, David Gustafson, and William Anthony, "Employees May Love Flextime, but What Does It Do to the Organization's Productivity?" *Journal of Applied Psychology*, Vol. 70, no. 2 (1985), pp. 272-279.

24. Janis Hedges, "New Patterns for Working Time," *Monthly Labour Review*, February 1973, pp. 3-8.

25. John Ivancevich and Herbert Lyon, "The Shortened Work Week: A Field Experiment," *Journal of Applied Psychology*, Vol. 62, no. 1 (1977), pp. 34-37.

26. Janina Latack and Lawrence Foster, "Implementation of Compressed Work Schedules: Participation and Job Redesign as Critical Factors for Employee Acceptance," *Personnel Psychology*, Vol. 38, no. 1 (Spring 1985), pp. 75-92. Interestingly, one way to determine how employees will react to a 4/40 or flextime work schedule apparently is to ask them ahead of time. One study suggests that these will be the reactions that actually emerge three to six months after commencement of the program. See Randall B. Dunham, Jon L. Pierce, and Maria B. Castaneda, "Alternative Work Schedules: Two Field Quasi-Experiments," *Personnel Psychology*, Vol. 40, no. 2 (Summer 1987), pp. 215-242.

27. Ideas and Trends, *Commerce Clearing House*, February 26, 1982, p. 61.

28. "After Flexible Hours, Now It's Flexiyear," *International Management*, March 1982, pp. 31-32.

SUGGESTED READINGS

Crocker, Olga. *Quality Circles*. Toronto: Methuen Publications, 1984.

Fitch, Gavin. "Beyond QWL: Enhancing the Quality of Non-working Life through Flexible Working Arrangements" in *Human Resources Management in Canada*. Toronto: Prentice-Hall Canada Inc., 1988, pp. 65,509-65,521.

Hackman, R.J. and G.R. Oldham. *Work Redesign*. Toronto: Addison-Wesley, 1980.

Nadler, D.A. and E.E. Lawler III. "Quality of Work Life: Perspectives and Directions," *Organizational Dynamics*, Winter 1983, pp. 20-30.

Ouchi, William G. *Theory Z*. New York: Avon Books, 1981.

O.W.L. Focus. *The Emergence of Q.W.L. Domains*. Toronto: The News Journal of the Ontario Quality of Working Life Centre, 1986.

Portis, B.P. and D. Fullerton. "Effective Use of Quality Circles," *Business Quarterly*. Fall 1985.

Taylor, Harold L. *Personal Organization—The Key to Managing Your Time and Your Life*. Toronto: Time Management Consultants, Inc., 1983.

Wheeler, Don. "Quality of Working Life and Employee Motivation" in *Human Resources Management in Canada*, Toronto: Prentice-Hall Canada Inc., 1987, pp. 65,011-65,044

PART FIVE

EMPLOYEE RIGHTS, SAFETY, AND REPRESENTATION

CHAPTER SIXTEEN
EMPLOYEE RIGHTS AND MANAGEMENT RIGHTS

After studying this chapter, you should be able to

1. Explain the purposes and importance of employee rights and management rights.
2. Understand Canadian common law provisions regarding the employer-employee relationship.
3. Explain the meaning of just cause.
4. Discuss the concept of constructive dismissal.
5. Understand sexual harassment and organizational strategies for dealing with the subject.
6. Explain progressive discipline.

OVERVIEW

The main purposes of this chapter are to describe those contractual rights, implied rights, and legal rights of employees as well as those legal and contractual rights of management. We discuss the role of Canadian common law in regulating the employment relationship. We describe the concept of just cause, a method under which employees may legally be terminated by employers. We outline various remedies available to employees when they have been terminated without just cause.

We discuss the unique concept of constructive dismissal—a concept that refers to unilateral changes in the terms and conditions of the employment contract that are considered unacceptable to the employee. We discuss the remedies available to the employee.

We discuss sexual harassment in the workplace, various case laws on the matter, and various strategies that organizations should pursue in combatting this problem.

INTRODUCTION: WHAT ARE EMPLOYEE AND MANAGEMENT RIGHTS?

An organization hires an employee to perform assigned tasks to enable the organization to meet established objectives. The organization expects the employee to perform his or her job competently, reliably, carefully, and safely. It also is the organization's expectation that the employee will follow established policies, procedures, and rules. An employee expects to receive equitable compensation, to be treated with respect and dignity, to be provided with a safe and healthy work environment, and not to be subject to any unfair management practices. In most cases, both the employer and the employee are able to fulfil their respective obligations in a mutually satisfactory manner. However, on various occasions the organization fails to pursue the policies, procedures, practices, and other courses of action that meet the employee's expectations; or the consequences of management leadership style, philosophy, and values as well as the general organizational climate and culture infringe on the employee's contractual rights, implied rights, legal rights, or human rights. An employee, on various occasions, may also fail to fulfil his or her obligations by not conforming to the policies, procedures, and rules of organizations. Examples include insubordination, alcohol and drug abuse, theft of property, poor performance, and poor productivity.

Regardless of the origin of management and/or employee problems, whenever they occur they can be disruptive, costly, time-consuming, and counterproductive.

Employee rights include those rights protected by federal laws and policies, such as the Human Rights Act, Canada Labour Code, Charter of Rights and Freedoms, employment equity programs, and health and safety programs. They also include those rights protected by provincial and territorial governments laws and policies such as human rights acts, employment standard programs, and pay equity programs. Further, employee rights include formal contractual rights contracted with the employers (including collective bargaining agreements) and implied rights provided under Canadian Common Law and Quebec Civil Code.

Management rights include the rights to plan, organize, lead, coordinate, and control those processes and activities needed to accomplish the organization's designated objectives. Further, management rights include the rights to exercise its prerogatives to develop and administer policies and procedures to attract, recruit, and maintain an effective work force. Additionally, management rights include the rights to retain desirable employees, discipline employees who violate organizational rules, and to dismiss undesirable employees.

Purposes and Importance of Employee Rights and Management Rights

The purposes and importance of employee rights and management rights are to

- Ensure that employees are treated fairly, with respect, with dignity and equality, regardless of race, sex, national origin, colour, age, and religion
- Ensure that the organization's policies, procedures, rules, and practices do not treat employees unjustly or discriminate against any employee
- Ensure that employees' formal contractual rights and implied contractual rights are honoured by the employer

- Ensure procedural fairness in the administration of the employer's disciplinary rules, processes, procedures, and practices
- Ensure that the employer's disciplinary rules are reasonable, just, consistently and equally applied; that employees are aware of the rules, aware of any alleged infractions, and given the opportunity to be heard
- Ensure that the employer does not penalize employees for engaging in legal union activities, or attempt to directly or indirectly influence or undermine labour unions, but bargains in good faith and fairly with the employees' union
- Ensure that the physical well-being of employees is protected through the promotion of sound preventive health and safety programs and practices, as well as ensuring that prompt action is taken to correct any problems that arise
- Ensure that employees recognize, respect, and fulfil their moral and legal obligations to their employers
- Ensure that employers are able to organize and operate their organizations in the best interest of all parties
- Ensure that employees' statutorily protected rights are not violated
- Ensure that employees are not terminated arbitrarily
- Ensure that employees do not violate their contractual, legal, or implied responsibilities to their employers
- Ensure that management's rights to plan, organize, and control work processes for the accomplishment of organization's objectives are respected
- Ensure that management's expectations regarding employee performance, appropriate conduct, and behaviour are honoured by employees

CANADIAN COMMON LAW PROTECTION

Canadian common law

Quebec Civil Code

Under **Canadian common law** the employer-employee relationship is governed by an employment contract.[1] The Canadian common law applies to all provinces except Quebec, where the employment relationship is regulated by the **Quebec Civil Code**.[2] Nonetheless, in both cases much has not been regulated and has been left instead to the interpretation of the courts.

A contract is a formal agreement made between the parties involved. It is usually the case that an employment contract specifies the terms and conditions of employment and includes an expiration date. When an expiration date is specified, the duration of the contract automatically ends at that date. While the contract is in force an employee cannot be prematurely dismissed without just cause. If an employee is dismissed before the expiration of the contract, he or she may commence an action for breach of contract and wrongful dismissal.[3]

In Canada, the majority of the employees are hired under an *implied contract*. An implied contract means that the agreement between the employer and the employee is for an indefinite period of time and may be terminated only when given reasonable notice by either party to the implied contract. A contract of employment is implied once an offer is made and the company sets out the employee's duties and responsibilities, offering a salary in return, and the terms and conditions are accepted by the individual.[4] However, employers cannot hire and fire employees at will. They can legally terminate employees without reasonable notice only when just cause exists. If just cause does not exist, then the termination is considered wrongful dismissal.

Certain categories of employees do not fall under the wrongful dismissal doctrine, although they are clearly employees. These employees include workers covered by a collective agreement, regardless of employment status. Such workers are bound by the collective agreement terms as to termination and are therefore not entitled to common law action for wrongful dismissal. Nevertheless, for employees covered by collective agreements, the issue of just cause for dismissal is often similar to common law.

Some employees whose employment is created by statute, or who are provided with a statutory right to arbitration or other statutory dismissal remedy, may not be entitled to pursue a common-law wrongful dismissal action. Such employees in most provinces include Crown and municipal employees, teachers, police officers, fire fighters, and ministers.[5]

Just Cause[6]

Just cause is defined as any conduct by an employee inconsistent with the fulfillment of the express or implied condition of service. It is any action by the employee that could seriously affect the operation, reputation, or management of an organization. Just cause includes specific acts of disobedience, incompetence, dishonesty, insubordination, personality conflict, intoxication, persistent absence from work, or lateness. (The specific circumstances under which these actions by an employee constitute just cause will be discussed later). However, what constitutes just cause in a particular situation depends not only on the category and possible consequences of the misconduct, but also on both the nature of the employment and the status of the employee. Thus the existence of misconduct sufficient to justify cause cannot be looked at in isolation. Whether or not misconduct constitutes cause has to be analyzed in the circumstances of each case. Misconduct must be more serious in order to justify the termination of a more senior, longer-service employee who has made positive contributions to an organization.[7]

just cause

The term just cause is intended to provide fairness to the employee. Even though management has the right to develop, establish, and enforce its policies and disciplinary procedures, these rules must be fair and reasonable; well-known to the employees; and applied equally, consistently, and fairly.[8]

Conduct of the employee amounting to just cause for dismissal constitutes a breach of the employee's fundamental obligations to the employer, and this is what gives the employer the right to put an end to the contract. If just cause exists, there is no right to "some" notice before dismissal, even in the case of long-service employees.[9] Conduct inconsistent with fulfillment of the employer's express or implied conditions of service will justify dismissal.[10]

The general rule has been stated as follows:

> If an employee has been guilty of serious misconduct, habitual neglect of duty, incompetence, or conduct incompatible with his [or her] duties, or prejudicial to the employer's orders in a matter substance, the law recognises the employer's right summarily to dismiss the delinquent employee.[11]

Further, just cause means that an employer can terminate an employee for a valid job-related reason that could seriously have an adverse effect on the operation, reputation, financial resources, or management of the organization.[12] Cause must be determined objectively, that is, it must be established that there are reasonable grounds for the termination.[13]

Just Cause for Dismissal[14]

Under Canadian common law an employee may be dismissed for just cause if the employer has objective proof of incompetence (poor performance), fraud, wilful disobedience, insubordination, dishonesty, fraudulent misrepresentation of qualifications, excessive absenteeism, forgery, personality conflict, or intoxication.

Since dismissal for just cause is an exception to the employee's usual rights, summary dismissal can be utilized only for very serious misconduct or serious breaches of a fundamental nature.[15] The determination of whether misconduct is serious enough to justify dismissal must be assessed individually and objectively in each case.[16]

According to one judge:

> the causes which are sufficient to justify dismissal must vary with the nature of the employment and the circumstances of each case. Dismissal is an extreme measure, and not to be resorted to for trifling causes. The fault must be something which a reasonable [person] could not be expected to overlook ...[17]

The implication of the above is that an employer is not entitled to seize upon a minor instance of misconduct in order to avoid his or her duty to give reasonable notice. It is usually the cause that a single incident is not sufficient to establish cause,[18] particularly if the conduct is provoked or aggravated by the employer,[19] or if the employee was not wholly responsible for the problem.[20]

It is only in exceptional circumstances that a single act of misconduct can justify summary dismissal. Examples would include acts that are extremely prejudicial to the employer,[21] or acts, the consequences of which are likely to persist over time. Cases of dishonesty or revelation of immoral character that cause a complete failure of trust in the employee qualify as exceptional circumstances. One judge has said that a single incident of misconduct or disobedience must be wilful, deliberate, and show gross incompetence to justify dismissal without a prior warning.

The cumulative effect of a number of minor instances or misconduct can also justify dismissal in some cases. However, to constitute just cause, the series of events must cause either serious deterioration in the business relationship of the parties or cause the employee to be unable to properly perform his or her duties and conduct the employer's business.

In cases where a gradual deterioration of performance or the accumulation of a number of minor failings is relied upon as cause for dismissal, the employer should ensure that the employee is warned and is given time to improve his or her performance before the dismissal.

Under Canadian common law, an employer is entitled to dismiss an employee upon discovery of conduct constituting just cause, even if such conduct occurred previously, without the employer's knowledge. Misconduct that occurs after dismissal, including constructive dismissal, is not just cause and cannot be relied upon, since it is only conduct occurring during the course of employment that can be taken in account.

The onus of proving the existence of just cause is on the employer.

Disobedience

It is usually the case that a single act of disobedience will not be serious enough to justify dismissal without a warning.[22] In order to justify dismissal on the basis of a single act of disobedience, the act must be wilful, or deliberate.[23] The act must also be so serious as to show that the worker is repudiating one of the essential conditions of the contract,[24] or must be incompatible with the faithful discharge of his or her duties.[25]

A reasonable excuse for disobedience, even a personal reason, may eliminate the right to dismiss for cause.[26] For instance, the failure of a manager to accept a phone call from the president while the manager was embroiled in a crisis would not be sufficiently serious enough to justify dismissal.[27] Nor would a manager's visit to his or her office during suspension pending investigation of allegations of misconduct.[28] But the following acts were held to be serious acts of disobedience that justified dismissal: a refusal to attend an important meeting,[29] a refusal to work assigned shift work where the assignment was within the terms of the contract,[30] a refusal to rehire an employee dismissed contrary to instructions,[31] the refusal or failure to follow important safety procedures,[32] and the failure to follow instructions with regard to overdraft approvals.[33]

Failure to comply with rules or refusal to perform the job in the exact way specified may be just cause if the employer's business is prejudiced by the refusal;[34] if constant supervision would be required to ensure compliance;[35] or if the refusal is conduct incompatible with the faithful discharge of the employee's duties.[36]

A complete refusal to cooperate,[37] a refusal to perform specific job duties,[38] and a refusal to comply with the reasonable company rules about medical leave,[39] or loan authorization[40] have all been held to constitute just cause.

Likewise, neglect of duties or refusal to perform the job can amount to just cause for dismissal.[41] This includes the situation where a worker, anticipating his dismissal, abandons his or her position. But it is important to note that where there is some justification for the neglect or refusal, a warning may be required.[42]

Incompetence

Substandard performance by an employee is just cause for dismissal. But employers are not entitled to dismiss employees for mere dissatisfaction with their work; there must be actual incompetence[43] or inability to carry out duties[44] or substandard work that persists after a warning to improve performance. The employee's standards must fall below an objective standard of performance[45] and a mere failure to meet goals set by the employer does not necessarily establish incompetence[46] especially where the goals, or consequences of not meeting them, have not been communicated to the employee. In cases where an employer changes performance standards, it may be necessary to prove that an employee has agreed to these revised standards before there will be just cause for dismissal for failing to meet them.[47] The employer may also have to prove that it has applied its standards equally to all employees before the dismissal of one employee will be just.[48] The employer's performance standard must be reasonable, fair and non-discriminatory. Figure 16.1 illustrates other conditions which must exist to justify the dismissal of an employee for incompetence.

FIGURE 16.1
Just Cause for Dismissal Due to Incompetence

In order for incompetence to constitute just cause for dismissal, the following conditions must exist:

1. The employee's job duties and the standards of performance established by the organization must be clearly communicated.

2. The employee who is performing poorly must be made aware that there is a discrepancy between his or her performance and the standards for the job. Recent positive feedback or evaluations will seriously weaken the evidence of incompetence.

3. Incompetence will not be acceptable as a grounds for dismissal if other employees with similar job duties are also performing below standard but are not recognized by the organization as poor performers.

4. The employee must be provided with adequate training or, if already trained, must be informed of what to do to improve the unsatisfactory job performance.

5. The employee must be given a reasonable amount of time to improve performance after he or she has been warned. Similarly, if new to the job, the employee must be given a reasonable opportunity to learn the job.

6. If the performance continues to be below standard, the employee must be informed that his or her job is in jeopardy.

7. In order to establish incompetence, the employee's poor performance must not have been partly due to actions of the company (such as failing to provide the necessary support) or, in some cases, factors beyond the employee's control.

8. If employees are routinely dismissed for failing to attain a specific standard of performance, this must be made clear to the employee at the time of hire.

9. The organization cannot use incompetence as a justification for dismissal where the employee's performance is improving or where there is a reasonable belief that the poor performance is temporary.

SOURCE: Abridged and adapted from Howard A. Levitt, *The Law of Dismissal in Canada* (Aurora: Canada Law Book 1985), pp. 105–112. Reproduced with the permission of Canada Law Book Inc., 240 Edward Street, Aurora, Ont. L4G 3S9.

Dishonesty

An employee may be dismissed for just cause because of his or her dishonesty. Just cause for dismissal due to dishonesty falls into two categories: those where the employee's dishonest conduct is seriously prejudicial to the employer's interests or reputation, and those where the misconduct, although less serious, reveals such a untrustworthy character that the employer is not obliged to continue the employee in a position of responsibility or trust. For just cause to exist in either situation, the employer must have proof that the employee has committed the dishonest act. A mere suspicion of dishonesty or mere poor judgment is not sufficient to justify dismissal.[49]

Seriously Dishonest Conduct

Seriously dishonest conduct that would justify dismissal includes theft from the employer,[50] falsifying expense accounts or personal credits,[51] taking unauthorized breaks in breach of rules after warnings not to do so, breaching store security rules or cash handling procedures, misapplication of the employer's funds due to the employee's contractual dispute with the employer,[52] claiming unauthorized overtime payment,[53] making unjustified demands for payment of large commissions,[54] taking unauthorized raises advances, or bonuses,[55] taking "kickbacks" or secret commissions,[56] and purposely misrepresenting products to clients of the employer.[57]

Untrustworthy Character

Revelations of *untrustworthy character* that would be just cause for dismissal of an employee include: exchanging personal goods with office goods and refusing to comply with the company's accounting procedures,[58] misappropriating the employer's property,[59] padding or cheating on an expense account or improperly charging personal expenses to the employer,[60] taking an unauthorized loan from company funds,[61] unauthorized approval of overdrafts,[62] obtaining an employee loan improperly,[63] misappropriating promotional travel tickets for personal use,[64] forgery of a signature on a company report by a manager,[65] resume fraud,[66] cheating on a qualifying exam where the position required the highest moral character,[67] and improper financial dealings with customers or suppliers.[68]

Insubordination

Insubordination justifies dismissal where the remarks made or language used by the employee are incompatible with the continuance of the employment relationship.

This is so even in cases of a single or isolated incident in the following instances: when the conduct is so serious as to destroy harmonious relations between the parties,[69] when it indicates conduct incompatible with the employee's duties and prejudicial to the employer's business,[70] or when it seriously undermines management's authority.[71] An employee's mere poor judgment, insensitivity, or resentment is not sufficient to constitute just cause.[72]

However, if an employee's insubordination has been provoked or aggravated by the employer or caused by conduct amounting to constructive dismissal, there will be no just cause for dismissal.[73]

There can be no insubordination where the employee is unaware that the individual to whom he or she speaks is a person of authority.[74] But if a manager, in front of many lower ranked employees, challenged management's plans and took the side of the subordinates, then his or her conduct would be considered prejudicial to the employer and would be just cause for dismissal.[75] An employee who harangued his or her manager for half an hour in front of other employees by swearing, insulting the manager and the company, and by using aggressive and abusive language may be dismissed for just cause.[76]

Personality Conflict

An employee may be dismissed for cause in the following instances: when a *personality conflict* or attitudinal problem escalates to the level of total inability to get along with superiors, co-workers, or subordinates,[77] or when such an attitudinal problem puts the employee into constant conflict in the workplace,[78] substantially interferes with production,[79] or causes large staff losses,[80] or when cooperation is a fundamental part of the job.[81] Similarly, creating difficulties not only with staff but with clients may justify dismissal where the employee refuses to improve his or her attitude.[82] Inability to get along with co-workers or superiors will not be grounds for dismissal where the fault for poor relationships lies at least partly with the other workers or when the employer has demonstrated a lack of guidance and support.[83]

Intoxication

Intoxication may be considered just cause for dismissal. However, if a company encourages its salespeople to socialize with clients then it could not complain if a salesperson occasionally returned from a business lunch somewhat intoxicated, where there was no excessive use of alcohol.[84] Similarly, an isolated instance of drunkenness and misconduct at the company Christmas party is not considered prejudicial or inconsistent with the employee's continued faithful discharge of his duties.[85] However, an employee who became drunk and abusive at a company dinner was dismissed for cause, since he had been warned in the past about similar behaviour.[86] It is important that the organization ensures that it has sufficient and objective evidence to justify the dismissal. The following case illustrates how costly it can be to dismiss an employee with insufficient evidence.

Algoma Steel Corp. must pay a manager over $200 000 in damages because it failed to give him the union-level job to which he was entitled upon termination. The case derives from a 1986 incident where an employee of Algoma ran over a stop sign with a van on company property. His supervisor concluded he had been drinking and terminated him immediately. The employee at the time held the position of foreman, a managerial-level job at Algoma. Mr. Justice B. Thomas Granger found insufficient evidence to justify the employee's firing and ruled he had been unjustly dismissed. More importantly, the judge said that Algoma had erred in handling the termination: the terms of the collective agreement stated that an employee promoted out of the bargaining unit (as he was) who then loses his managerial job is entitled to return to the bargaining unit with full seniority. He noted that because Algoma is a major employer in a single-industry town, it owes its employees longer notice periods. Granger said the nine months' notice that Algoma gave him was unfair because it did not take into account his age (48 at the time), lack of alternate employment opportunities in the region, and his "potential mobility." He granted the man the 24-month notice period because Algoma was an "employer who sought a lifetime commitment from its employees," and awarded him $304 000 in lost income and benefits. (See Johnston v. Algoma Steel Corp. Ltd., Supreme Court of Ontario, 1009/86.)[87]

Absence from Work and Lateness

Absence from work without the employer's permission may amount to just cause, depending on the circumstances. A one-day absence may not be sufficient,[88] nor may occasional absences,[89] but frequent, unauthorized absences may justify dismissal,[90] as may an absence that remains unexplained, in breach of company rules.[91] Further, a brief unjustified absence at a critical time may constitute just cause,[92] as may providing false reasons for an unauthorized absence.[93] (An employee who obtained authorization through false reasons was held by the court to have been dismissed for just cause.[94]) Similarly, an employee who failed to report for work, or seek a leave of absence, or communicate her intentions after the expiry of her sick leave was justly dismissed; as was an employee who failed to respond to requests for information and failed to return to work as soon as he had recovered from an illness.[95]

Moral Character and Off-the-Job Conduct

An employee may be dismissed for cause for his or her private conduct, if that conduct is wholly incompatible with the proper discharge of the employee's duties or if it would tend to prejudice the employer. Importantly, however, the existence of just cause depends on the seriousness of the conduct in relation to the exact nature of the employee's job and on the *objective* view of the conduct, in relation to the community's moral standards, rather than the employer's subjective view.[96] For instance, an important public position, such as a city manager, may require conduct, both public and to a reasonable degree private, that will hold the public's trust and confidence.[97] Any moral misconduct beyond a triviality would justify dismissal.

A manager who had an affair with a subordinate and allowed their personal relationship to affect the working atmosphere was dismissed for cause.[98] An employee convicted of gross indecency for conduct occurring away from work was not justly dismissed, since there was no evidence the matter would adversely affect the employer even if known to his co-workers and customers.[99] However, the fact that an employee used the employer's premises for immoral purposes with members of the opposite sex might support dismissal.[100] A supervisor convicted of sexual assault on a minor was properly dismissed—the confidence and respect of his

1. Refusal by an employee to accept a transfer or demotion.
2. Adverse economic conditions.
3. Corporate, divisional, or other company reorganization.
4. Redundancy.
5. Refusal to do unsafe work.
6. Sale of a business.
7. Resignation by the employee.
8. Garnishment.

subordinates had been destroyed, and this would have had serious production and safety implications in a dangerous workplace.[101]

Figure 16.2 illustrates some conditions that do not constitute just cause for dismissal. These factors do not constitute just cause for termination because they are not related to an employee's conduct while just cause is generally based on misconduct.[102]

CONSTRUCTIVE DISMISSAL

constructive dismissal

The concept of **constructive dismissal** refers to unilateral changes in the terms and conditions of the employment contract that are unacceptable to the employee. Whenever the employer commits a major breach of a major term of the employment relationship then the employee may take the position that a dismissal has taken place. Under common law this is so although the employer has not actually given the employee formal notice of termination.[103] Its important to note that the breach by the employer must be major, and not just a minor or incidental breach.[104] A minor change in the employment relationship by the employer is not viewed as constructive dismissal. Consequently, this does not give an employee a right to resign and sue as if there had been discharge.[105]

Whenever there is a breach of a term of the employment arrangement by the employer that gives rise to a constructive dismissal, it is the responsibility of the employee to inform the employer that the change is not acceptable. An attempt must be made by the employee to either get the employer to reconsider the change or the employee must attempt to negotiate an appropriate alternative. The employee should not resign before there has been an attempt to negotiate with his or her employer.[106] If the employee is unable to negotiate a mutually satisfactory alternative, then he or she must then resign and sue for wrongful dismissal. Should the employee elect not to resign, but choose to continue to work under the new working conditions then the changes or new condition will be deemed to have been accepted by the employee and will become part of the employment agreement.[107] Any major change in the employment relationship may give rise to constructive dismissal, however, the most common changes in employment status that are generally considered constructive dismissal are

- Unjustifiable demotion
- Unilateral reduction in salary or benefits
- Forced resignation

- Forced early retirement
- Forced transfer
- Unilateral changes in job duties and responsibilities

One employee was informed by a letter from her employer that she was being re-assigned to special project work due to a corporate reorganization. The employer further suggested in the letter that "If this proposed working arrangement does not work out to our mutual satisfaction, I think it will be necessary for you to seek satisfaction in employment elsewhere." The letter also stated that her first assignment was to train her subordinate to assume her former responsibilities. She sued for constructive dismissal. The court agreed. The court found that "while the new proposal involved no less money for her, it represented a vastly different situation from that which prevailed before ... she was stripped of her title and supervisory functions ... was moved from a salaried position for an indefinite term to what was in effect a probationary period with no guarantee of continued employment."[108]

In another case, the court ruled that the employer's unilateral change in job responsibilities altered the employee's employment contract so fundamentally as to constitute constructive dismissal.[109]

DAMAGES

Under Canadian Common Law the courts cannot order the reinstatement of an employee who was wrongfully dismissed by his or her employer. Nor can the court order a change of the breach in the employment relationship that gave rise to a constructive dismissal. Instead the courts determine the amount of salary and benefits that the employee would have been entitled to if the employer had given sufficient notice. In one case the judge stated that "the law is that an employees' claim for damages is not limited to the wages or salary he would have received had he been given proper notice. The dismissal, if wrongful, is a breach of contract, and all damages flowing therefrom are recoverable."[110]

Damages for Mental Distress

A recent development under common law is the awarding of **damages for mental distress** resulting from factors such as the suddenness of the dismissal and the loss of reputation. However, the mental distress must result from the way the termination was handled—the inadequacy of the notice that was provided to the dismissed employee—and not from the fact of the termination.[111] If the employer provides sufficient notice then the employee may not sue for mental distress.[112] Evidence of mental distress must exist.[113] There must also be evidence that the termination was conducted in a callous and arbitrary manner.[114] In one case the judge established the following four-fold test for the determination of mental distress:

damages for mental distress

1. The mental distress must have been caused by a breach of the contract, i.e., failure to give reasonable notice.
2. The breach must have been of a wanton or reckless character.
3. The breach must have been of such a character that mental distress would have been in the reasonable contemplation of the parties when the contract was made, i.e., it was not too remote.
4. The mental distress must arise independently of pecuniary loss.[115]

Aspects of employers' behaviour that have influenced courts in awarding mental distress damages have included unsubstantiated allegations of dishonesty or incompetence,[116] continuing unfounded allegations of just cause, despite a lack of any evidence, right up until trial,[117] malice or bad faith,[118] unfair treatment (particularly in failing to give reasons for the termination or to give the employee a chance to refute the allegations against him),[119] insufficient investigation of serious misconduct charges that are later shown to be untrue,[120] terminating the employee by telephone while he was sick in bed,[121] refusing to deal with an employee's unreasonable workload that was ruining her health,[122] assurances of job security,[123] enticement away from a previous, secure job,[124] misrepresentation of the job,[125] and abrupt, insensitive termination.[126]

The effects on the employee that have been held to constitute mental distress include depression, withdrawal, anxiety,[127] loss of confidence or self-esteem,[128] effects on family life,[129] sleeplessness and/or eating disorders,[130] headaches,[131] and excessive consumption of alcohol.[132]

Mental distress may be aggravated where the employee is a member of a small community[133] or small ethnic community.[134] Although it would seem to breach the law against damages for loss of reputation, loss of standing in the community has been mentioned as a rationale for awarding general damages.[135]

In one case an employee was terminated from his position from a bank. He was accused of various acts of theft and fraud. The manager at the branch engaged the services of one of his personal friends, a security officer, to build a case against him. However, none of allegations against him were substantiated at the trial. The court ruled that the employer had acted in a "brutal and cold," "shocking, [and] miserable" fashion. In addition the court also found that the employer acted spitefully and maliciously toward the employee and on several occasions went so far as to fabricate information to support unfounded allegations of criminal activity. The employee was awarded $10 000 for punitive damages and another $10 000 for damages for mental distress.[136]

The Terminated Employee's Duty to Mitigate

An employee who has been terminated and is suing for damages has, under common law, a *duty to mitigate* his or her losses or lower the employer's damages by making every effort to find alternately comparable employment elsewhere. In one case the judge stated that "It was the duty of the plaintiff to attempt to secure other employment and to make all reasonable efforts to secure such a position as one could reasonably expect him to take under all the circumstances." However, an employee is not obliged to accept an inferior position elsewhere, which, if it had been assigned by the employee's former employer, could have been refused by the employee on grounds that it would have constituted constructive dismissal.[137]

Nevertheless it is the responsibility of the employer to prove the employee's failure to mitigate.[138] It is also the employer's responsibility to prove that the terminated employee could have found another comparable job if he or she had searched for one.[139] However, if the court finds that an employee did not attempt to mitigate and that an alternately comparable job was available and could have been located earlier, then the court will reduce the damages by deducting the amount that the employee could have earned if he or she had been working.[140] In one case an employee was dismissed without cause and was provided with 12 months' severance pay plus relocation counselling. The court noted that the most important factors in determing proper notice were age, length of service, responsibility, and availability of suitable work. The court ruled that the 12 months' notice provided was appropriate and that he should have mitigated by making more full use of the relocation centre and by sending out more applications.[141]

WRONGFUL RESIGNATION

Under Canadian common law, as well as under government statutes, when an employee resigns he or she is required to provide the employer with reasonable notice. If the employee does not provide reasonable notice, then the employer can sue for **wrongful resignation**. The employer can sue for damages but cannot sue to obtain a court order to force the employee to return to work. The courts have generally awarded damages when the employer can demonstrate that it actually incurred damages because of the employee's failure to give sufficient notice. The primary reason for providing adequate notice is to enable the employer to hire a replacement for the employee.[142]

wrongful resignation

HUMAN RESOURCE MANAGEMENT IN ACTION

Winnipeg Firm Gets Damages for "Wrongful Resignation"

WINNIPEG—A Manitoba Court of Queen's Bench has ordered a former manager for Westfair Foods Ltd. to pay the company $1057 for her "wrongful resignation" about two years ago. Nadene Henderson had sued Westfair for wrongful dismissal, but Judge Jeffrey J. Oliphant instead ruled in favour of the company's counterclaim that Henderson had wrongfully terminated her employment contract in June 1988. In his decision, Oliphant said Henderson had breached a section of the Employment Standards Act that requires workers and employers alike to give a minimum of one pay period's notice of termination.

Henderson began working for one of Westfair's Winnipeg stores in 1981. Following several promotions over the next few years, she was promoted to the position of assistant divisional manager in January 1988, which paid her a salary of $27 500 plus bonuses, bringing her annual earnings to about $44 000. In April 1988, Westfair announced its plans to move its head office to Calgary as of September 1 of that year. Henderson had known since the spring of 1987 the company's intention to move. In a written notice, Henderson indicated that she wished to continue working for Westfair but did not intend to move to Calgary. The company's divisional manager, Rose Darkazanli, and her husband, the vice-president of corporate development, designed a plan which would allow Henderson to remain employed in Winnipeg as an assistant divisional manager. On May 10, 1988, the plans were announced to Henderson and other staff who would be affected by the changes. Henderson was ambivalent about the plan and said she would have to talk to her husband before accepting the proposal. On May 11, Henderson advised Darkazanli that she would not accept the new job. That meant she would no longer be employed with Westfair as of September 1, the day the head office move took effect. Relations between Henderson and Darkazanli soured during the rest of the month, and Henderson did not return to work after June 1. She eventually sued for damages, alleging constructive dismissal. However, Judge Oliphant said the employment contract was terminated when Henderson refused to accept the position created for her in Winnipeg, and that this refusal was tantamount to a resignation.

SOURCE: *Human Resources Management in Canada*, Report Bulletin no. 91 (Scarborough, Ont.: Prentice-Hall Canada Inc., September 1990), pp. 5-6.

The courts have generally awarded damages for advertising costs to recruit a new employee, placement agency fees, and the cost incurred for overtime paid to other employees. Any wage cost saved by not having to pay that particular employee's salary are usually deducted from the damages.[143] The employer is obliged to mitigate the employee's damages by hiring a replacement as soon as possible.

SEXUAL HARASSMENT

sexual harassment

One of the most important, controversial, and complex issues surrounding human resource management is the problem of **sexual harassment**. As a result of changing social values and the implementation of government public policies (e.g., Human Rights Act) actions and activities that were once tolerated, ignored, considered horseplay, or innocent flirtation are now prohibited.

Sexual harassment is a form of workplace harassment. In recent years various human rights commissions across Canada have reported a large number of sexual harassment complaints. During this time various boards of inquiry have ruled on the issue and strongly condemned the existence of sexual harassment in the workplace. In the precedent-setting case a human rights board of inquiry stated that "there is no reason why the law, which reaches into the workplace so far as to protect the work environment from physical or chemical pollution or extremes of temperature, ought not to protect employees from negative psychological and mental effects where adverse gender-directed conduct emanating from a management hierarchy may reasonably be construed to be a condition of employment."[144]

Sexual harassment includes[145]

- demand for sexual favours in return for hiring, promotions, transfers, and tenure
- sexual gestures
- patting, pinching, or brushing against the body
- derogatory sexual statements
- unwelcome sexual advances
- request for sexual favours
- lewd sexual comments
- leering, ogling
- teasing with photographs of nude or scantily clad individuals
- placing obscene cartoons at a place of work
- grabbing in intimate areas of the body
- sexual innuendos
- unwelcome remarks about the individual's body, attire, age, and race
- verbal abuse or threats
- unwelcome invitations or requests
- condescending actions that undermine the person's self-respect
- physical assault

In one case the tribunal found that a manager had sexually harassed employees consistently and deliberately over a period of months and that the effect of this conduct had been to poison the work environment. The tribunal ruled that an employer's failure to

- recognize that sexual harassment is prohibited conduct;
- deal with complaints of sexual harassment as a serious matter;
- advise its employees that sexual harassment that affects the employment relationship is improper; and
- make both supervisors and employees aware of the significance and consequences of sexual harassment.

will lead to it being held liable for discrimination.[146]

In other words the tribunal ruling means that organizations are responsible for the consequences of sexual harassment unless they establish corporate personnel harassment policies, communicate the policies to all employees, and enforce the policies, equally, fairly, and consistently.

Employers' liability for the consequences of sexual harassment has been confirmed by various court decisions and human rights decisions.[147]

It is important that the individual states that the sexual advances are unwelcome. The following case illustrates:

A man was terminated for sexually harassing a subordinate. Both of them were found by the court to be "touchers," commonly putting their hands on fellow employees when they spoke with them. They attended a convention together in Montreal. They had meals together and the complainant accepted the gentleman's invitation to go sightseeing. When she became cold he put his hand around her. She did not complain. They had dinner together and he again put his arm around her shoulders. She did not complain. When he walked her back to her hotel room, he kissed her. At that point, she protested and he immediately left. The next day they sat together and again, he touched her from time to time and she did not protest.

The court found that the complainant was either not angry or had skillfully suppressed her emotions to conceal them from the plaintiff. The court noted, citing a human rights decision that "an invitation to dinner is not an invitation to complaint." In order for sexual harassment to be a cause for dismissal, the sexually oriented practice must be unwanted, and known to be unwanted by the person who is accused of harassing. In this case, there was no suggestion of any demand for sexual favours, express or implied. Since the complainant never indicated that she found the plaintiff or his actions offensive, he had no reason to believe that they were unwanted. The court found that if he had known that his actions were not wanted, he would have immediately stopped, as he did on the one occasion when it was made clear.[148]

An amendment to the Canada Labour Code in 1985 has made it mandatory for all companies that operate under federal jurisdiction, such as banks and insurance companies, to develop and implement sexual harassment policies.

Since the late 1980s companies, unions, and government agencies have been mounting programs to teach workers their rights and encourage them to fight the problem of sexual harassment in the workplace. An informal national survey by the

Globe and Mail shows that complaints of sexual harassment to human rights commissions have remained steady or declined slightly in years.[149] Table 16.1 illustrates the results of the survey.

TABLE 16.1 Sexual Harassment Complaints to Human Rights Commissions

	1988		1987	
	Number of complaints	As a % of total human rights complaints	Number of complaints	As a % of total human rights complaints
BRITISH COLUMBIA	61	16	60	21
ALBERTA	60	21	42	18
SASKATCHEWAN	15	7	37	15
MANITOBA	not available		not available	
ONTARIO	106	6	146	8
QUEBEC	67	10	69	10
PRINCE EDWARD ISLAND	1	3	1	3
NOVA SCOTIA	10	6	15	8
NEW BRUNSWICK	6	5	7	6
NEWFOUNDLAND	9	11	24	28

SOURCE: Jane Coutts, "Workplace Programs Easing the Fight Against Sexual Harassment," *The Globe and Mail* (August 12, 1989), p. A8. Reprinted by permission of The Globe and Mail.

Recently the United Steelworkers of America introduced a policy on sexual harassment, including clauses bargained into collective agreements. Other unions including the Canadian Union of Public Employees and the Canadian Auto Workers Union have adopted similar policies.

According to Alan Ardison of the B. C. Human Rights Commission, sexual harassment destroys productivity and has other negative economic impacts on organizations that tolerate it in the workplace.[150]

As a Crown corporation, Petro-Canada was required to institute a policy on sexual harassment in the wake of the Robichaud decision. Sheila O'Brian, director of public affairs for Petro-Canada, said that having the policy benefits both the company and workers.

> I think employees are more productive when the environment is free of that kind of difficulty, and I think in the past, in companies without policies, it was just easier for people to leave, and you lose that skill and experience and you have a much tenser population. The policy saves money on staff turnover, complaints and just the general climate on the job.[151]

Ms O'Brien, formerly a commissioner on the Federal Human Rights Commission, believes it is preferable for a sexual harassment complaint to be handled internally because employees will feel very comfortable if they can face it straight on

FIGURE 16.3
Employer Strategies:
Sexual Harassment

Policy Development

- Establish clear and precise written policies defining sexual harassment and prohibiting sexual harassment in the workplace.
- Develop specific code of conduct to govern the behaviour of all employees.
- Establish an internal administrative system to handle sexual harassment complaints.
- Appoint a sexual harassment coordinator to administer the policy. Effective policy administration will encourage settlements of sexual harassment complaints and discourages employees from going outside the organization to the Human Rights Commission or the courts to complain and seek justice.
- Establish a specific set of penalties and sanctions, within a framework of progressive discipline, to be levied against sexual harassers.

Policy Communication

- Communicate to all employees exactly what the organization's sexual harassment policies are.
- Ensure that all employees are aware of their rights to be free from all forms of sexual harassment, and ensure that they are aware of the remedies available to those employees who have been victims of sexual harassment.
- Communicate the organization's strong disapproval of managers, supervisors or anyone in authority requesting sexual favours from their subordinates or engaging in any practices that constitute sexual harassment.
- Communicate to all employees that those whose rights have been violated should complain without any fear of retaliation.
- Communicate prohibitions and expectations to all employees through a variety of media (sources), e.g. the employee handbook, newsletters, notice boards, seminars, and staff meetings.

Policy Enforcement

- Ensure that all complaints are investigated.
- Ensure that all complaints are handled promptly, consistently, impartially, fairly, and confidentially.
- Ensure that all employees found guilty of harassment are disciplined equally.
- Provide counselling services to assist victims of sexual harassment.

and know it will be dealt with—and not to the determent of the complainant. Figure 16.3 illustrates strategies employers should follow in dealing with sexual harassment.

Recent court decisions have held that sexual harassment is just cause for dismissal. An employee who sexually harassed his secretary, causing her to file a complaint with the Human Rights Commission, was justly dismissed,[152] as was a manager who left the employer open to a human rights complaint by sexually harassing a coworker, even though no human rights complaint was filed.[153]

Further, a man who had an affair with a subordinate and showed her favouritism in the office, thus creating a poor working atmosphere, also was justly dismissed.[154] The use of an employer's premises for immoral purposes also could support a dismissal.[155]

To ensure that the rights of employees are protected, organizations must develop policies on sexual harassment. Figure 16.3 illustrates the type of strategies that employers should follow in developing sexual harassment policies. As can be seen, to be effective, a policy must consist of three major criteria: 1) policy development, 2) policy communication; and 3) policy enforcement.

EMPLOYEE DISCIPLINE

The purposes of discipline are to correct an employee's undesirable behaviour or unacceptable level of performance and to encourage compliance with the organization's policies, procedures, rules, standards and practices. It seeks to shape attitudes and mould norms of acceptable behaviour and responsible employee conduct. A sound and effective progressive disciplinary policy will communicate to employees the organization's expectations, and the sanctions that will be applied to offenders. As such it will provide an adequate warning system, ensure that enforcement is consistent among all employees, match penalties with offenses, and ensure due process. Before disciplinary action is taken against an employee, management should review the problem and the penalty to be imposed. Figure 16.4 presents a list of offenses that should lead to disciplinary actions.

There are three major types of discipline. These are preventive, corrective, and progressive discipline.

Preventive Discipline

preventive discipline

Preventive discipline is the development, maintenance, and communication of standards of behaviour and conduct expected of employees. Employees like to know where they stand and the criteria against which infractions are assessed. For instance an organization by developing absenteeism and lateness policies and communicating these policies to employees helps to prevent employee absenteeism and lateness, since employees will endeavour to ensure compliance to avoid the

FIGURE 16.4
**Offenses that Should
Lead to Disciplinary
Actions**

1. Wilful damage to, tampering with, defacing or unauthorized discarding of company property.
2. Dishonesty, deception, or fraud
3. Excessive absence
4. Theft, misappropriation of company property, or stealing trade secrets
5. Leaving worksite without permission
6. Insubordination
7. Failure to obey safety rules, procedures, and practices
8. Sexual harassment
9. Failure to meet and maintain required job performance quality and quantity standards
10. Fighting, or engaging in horseplay
11. Unauthorized absence
12. Albohol or drug abuse, or possession of liquor or illegal drugs.
13. Indecent and/or immoral behaviour or conduct on company premises
14. Use of abusive, vulgar, threatening or intimidating language at the workplace
15. Repeated tardiness
16. Possession of unauthorized weapons, or carrying concealed weapons or firearms on company premises
17. Sleeping on the job
18. Reporting to work in an intoxicated state
19. Unauthorized work stoppage, slow down or walkout
20. Unauthorized disclosure of company to competition or any one else
21. Smoking in a restricted area
22. Refusal to comply with a reasonable job-related request by the employer
23. Disrupting other workers' job performance
24. Falsification of, or alteration to company documents or records
25. Gambling on the job
26. Clock-punching another's time card

penalties that usually accompany these policies. Often times companies reward employees for not being sick and some circulate employees' attendance and safety records to inspire the avoidance of safety infractions and to promote better attendance records.

Corrective Discipline

Corrective discipline is designed to discourage infractions of organizational rules, procedures, and regulations and stimulate compliance with established policies and procedures. The main objectives of corrective discipline are to correct unacceptable behaviour and to improve employee conduct; to maintain consistent and effective group behaviour and conduct; and to discourage others from engaging in similar types of behaviour.

corrective discipline

One of the most effective corrective disciplinary techniques is the *hot stove rule*. Figure 16.5 illustrates its components.

The hot stove rule is based on the idea that like a hot stove, effective disciplinary actions should 1) include a warning (the heat from a hot-stove sends out a warning to discourage individuals from touching it); 2) include immediate feedback to ensure that the violator sees the connection between the rule violation and the discipline (a hot stove provides immediate feedback to anyone who touches it); 3) be consistently applied to ensure fairness, so as not to discriminate and to ensure that

FIGURE 16.5
The Hot Stove Rule

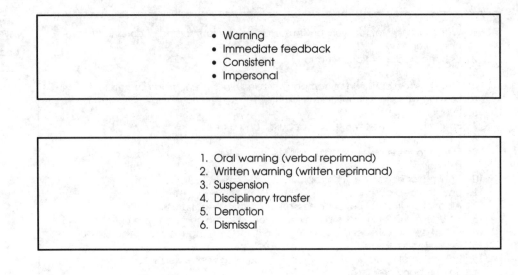

- Warning
- Immediate feedback
- Consistent
- Impersonal

FIGURE 16.6
Progressive Disciplinary Procedures

1. Oral warning (verbal reprimand)
2. Written warning (written reprimand)
3. Suspension
4. Disciplinary transfer
5. Demotion
6. Dismissal

everyone is treated equally (a hot stove consistently burns everyone who touches it); and 4) should be administered impersonally. That is, the focus of the discipline must be on the infraction and not on the sex or personality of the offender (a hot stove does not play favourites).

Progressive Disciplinary Procedures

progressive discipline

The concept of **progressive discipline** means that management responds to the first offence by an employee with minimal action but applies stronger or more serious penalties to repeated offenses. The sequence of action involved in progressive discipline are illustrated in Figure 16.6.

Oral Warning

This is the first step in the process and is the mildest form of reprimand. The employee should be informed of the infraction that has been committed and the problem that this rule violation has caused. The employee should be given an opportunity to state what happened and to help develop a solution to the problem. The manager or supervisor should ensure that the employee is aware of what type of follow-up action will be taken if the problem is repeated. Although oral warning is an informal process, it may be useful for the supervisor to document the problem and outcome, have the employee sign it, and maintain a copy in his or her file for future reference.

Written Warning

This is the second step in the process, and is the first *formal* stage in the progressive disciplinary procedure. This step is a serious one as the written warning becomes part of the employee's official file in the human resource department. As with the oral warning the employee is informed of the rule violation(s) and the potential consequences of repeated violations. Many organizations allow employees to purge their files of written warnings after a period of time has elapsed. This usually occurs if the employee demonstrates that the past deviant behaviour has been corrected and as long as there are no other infractions.

Suspension

This is the third step in the process and may be as short as a few hours to several days or as long as several weeks. The length of the suspension usually depends on the seriousness of the employee's infraction and the prevailing circumstances. Suspensions of one month or more are rare.

Disciplinary Transfer

This is the fourth step in the process. It is primarily useful when it is demonstrated that the primary cause of the persistent or recurring problem/infraction is a personality conflict. A transfer may help to diffuse the situation.

Demotion

This is the (optional) fifth step in the process, and may be used as an alternate to dismissal. This step may be used by management that feels itself legally or ethically bound to retain an employee who may be a very long-serving one. It may also be used in the case of an employee who may have the capability of performing the job but is in need of some "shock treatment." It also tells the employee that management is not prepared to put up with or let her or him "get away" with flagrant abuses or gross disregard of the organization's rules, policies, and procedures. It may be noted that demotion is not commonly used as a disciplinary procedure because it has serious consequences for the punished employee as well as other workers. The demotion of an employee is a constant punishment to the demoted employee and can be demoralizing to other workers.

Dismissal

This is the final step in the disciplinary process and is regarded as the ultimate disciplinary punishment which is used as a last resort when all else fails. Because it is such a dramatic, drastic, and at times painful recourse, it should be used only for the most serious infractions.

A recent development is the integration of employee discipline with counselling. Such counselling usually falls under employee assistance programs (EAP). These programs were discussed in Chapter 15. Where there is a collective agreement in force, the disciplinary action is usually spelled out in that collective agreement. We discuss this in Chapter 19.

STATUTORY NOTICE OF TERMINATION

The federal, provincial, and territorial governments have all established **statutory notices of termination**, labour codes that include specific provisions for notice periods or for payment of financial compensation in lieu of notice to employees upon termination. The federal statute is called the Canada Labour Code and applies to all companies that operate under federal jurisdiction, such as banks, insurance companies, communication companies, and crown corporations. As Table 16.2 indicates, the required notice period depends on the individual's length of service and varies from one jurisdiction to another. The notice periods set out in the exhibit

statutory notice of termination

TABLE 16.2 Termination of Employment Notice by Employer and Employee

JURISDICTION	LENGTH OF SERVICE OR EMPLOYMENT	NOTICE TO BE GIVEN BY	
		EMPLOYER	EMPLOYEE
Federal	3 months	2 weeks	n/a
Ontario	3 months but less than 1 year 1 year but less than 3 years 3 years but less than 4 years 4 years but less than 5 years 5 years but less than 6 years 6 years but less than 7 years 7 years but less than 8 years 8 years or more	1 week 2 weeks 3 weeks 4 weeks 5 weeks 6 weeks 7 weeks 8 weeks	1 week if less than 2 years 2 weeks if employed 2 years or more
Quebec	3 months but less than 1 year 1 year but less than 5 years 5 years but less than 10 years 10 years or more	1 week 2 weeks 4 weeks 8 weeks	Quebec Civil Code stipulates 1 week if hired by week 2 weeks if hired by month 1 month if hired by year
British Columbia	6 months consecutive 3 years 4 years or more	2 weeks 3 weeks 1 additional week for each subsequent year up to a maximum of 8 weeks	n/a
Manitoba	2 weeks	1 pay period where wages are paid less often than once a month reasonable notice otherwise	Same as for Employer
Alberta	3 months or less 3 months but less than 2 years 2 years or more	none 1 week 14 days	n/a
Saskatchewan	3 months but less than 1 year 1 year but less than 3 years 3 years but less than 5 years 5 years but less than 10 years 10 years or more	1 week 2 weeks 4 weeks 6 weeks 8 weeks	n/a
Nova Scotia	3 months or longer 2 years but less than 5 years 5 or more years but less than 10 years 10 years or more	1 week 2 weeks 4 weeks 8 weeks	1 week if less than 2 years 2 weeks if 2 years or more
P.E.I.	3 months or longer	1 week	1 week
Newfoundland	1 month but less than 2 years 2 years or more	1 week 2 weeks	1 week 2 weeks
New Brunswick	6 months 5 years	2 weeks 4 weeks	
Northwest Territories	No legislation, but reasonable notice should be given		
Yukon	6 months or more	1 week	Same as for employer

SOURCE: Kathy Bullock, "Termination of Employment," *Human Resources Management in Canada* (Scarborough, Ont.: Prentice-Hall Canada Inc., 1989), pp. 75,017-75,018. Used with permission.

are minimum entitlements. Various court decisions have affirmed that many factors should be taken into account to determine appropriate notice, such as age, length of service, and position.

Reasonable Notice

The rationale for giving **reasonable notice** is to provide the terminated employee with a reasonable amount of time to find a similar position elsewhere at a similar salary without suffering financial or emotional loss.[156]

reasonable notice

The objective of giving reasonable notice is to put the employee in the same position he or she would have been in if the employer had not breached the contract by dismissing the employee.[157] In order to properly compensate the employee, the notice period must be an estimate of the time it will take the employee to obtain a similar job with similar pay in the same geographical area.[158] It is not the goal of the notice period to guarantee the finding of new employment; thus the actual time necessary to find a new job is not always the same as the length of reasonable notice.[159] Under common law there are no established specific notice periods that constitute reasonable notice beyond the statutory minimums established by various federal, provincial, and territorial governments. Various rulings by judges over the years on a multitude of individual cases indicate that the following criteria are taken into account:

- age
- length of service
- experience and training

- level of responsibility
- degree of specialization
- method of recruitment[160]

Repercussions for Employers

It is very important that an employer view termination not only from the basis of its legal rights, but also from the standpoint of potential repercussions. The following should be recognized:

1. *Potential liability.* This includes not only the severance settlement but the cost of counsel as well as the share of the litigating employee's counsel that the employer is required to pay.

2. *The amount that the employee is likely to settle for at different stages of the proceeding.* Each case should be analyzed within the context of the psychology of the employee in question. (i.e., the one in need of a quick settlement and the one who can afford to sustain a lengthy proceeding.)

3. *The incentive given by severance settlements to other employees to litigate.* Just as excessively low settlements will discourage litigation, so excessively high settlements will encourage it.

4. *The effect that a suit may have on the morale of the remaining employees.* If existing employees believe that the employer has handled itself badly, they will lose trust in the company and seek employment elsewhere when the market improves.

5. *The effect that losing at trial will have on both the morale and readiness to litigate of remaining employees.* Litigating and losing can result both in losing the respect of staff and in further motivating them toward litigating if they are terminated.

6. *The effect that winning at trial will have on both the morale and readiness to litigate of other employees.* When the employer succeeds, the remaining employees will be both less likely to sue if they are terminated and will have more confidence in the employer's judgement of what constitutes a "termination with cause."

7. *The effect that litigation with a particular employee will have on customers and suppliers.* An employee's rapport with customers and suppliers can be vitally important. Often during litigation, an employee in a position to do so, will use the tactic of soliciting letters of reference from those customers and suppliers with whom a relationship has developed. Having customers approached by a hostile employee complaining to them about the manner in which he or she was treated could be far more costly then any reasonable severance settlement.

8. *The effect that litigation with a particular employee will have on the company's competitive position.* There are some employees who should be paid amounts significantly more, upon termination, than a court might award. For example, senior executives could cause significant damage if they started complaining to the remaining employees, customers, suppliers, bankers, and the general industry about the state of the company and the reasons for the termination. Further, the risk that such an individual might provide confidential information or the use of his or her knowledge and skills to a competitors should be considered as part of the settlement.

9. *The effect that litigation with a particular employee will have on the company's reputation in the community.* As a result of the scrutiny government and the public lend to responsible employers, and the media attention a large-scale and improperly planned termination can create, termination should be carefully thought out so as to appear to the public as fair, humane, and reasonable.

10. *The cost of litigation—in legal fees, severance settlements, and management time.* All of these factors should be considered at every stage of the litigation.[161]

Dismissed Employee's Strategies

1. *Review the options.* Although it may appear to be more economical to proceed with a lawsuit instead of accepting the company's initial offers, the drawbacks of a lawsuit must be taken into account.

   a) A lawsuit could take up to two years before the court renders a decision. (However, most unjust dismissal actions are settled within six months, out of court.)

   b) Just as there are skeletons in many companies' closets, such is also the case with many employees.

   c) The legal expenses of litigation make it reasonable to accept a slight reduction in the severance settlement.

   d) There is generally a greater need for severance monies immediately after termination.

   e) The results are uncertain.

2. *See a legal specialist.* Many companies are prepared to negotiate more seriously when an employee is represented by counsel.

3. *Establish a case by documents.* All memorandum sent by the employer critical of job performance should be responded to in a respectful manner so as not to create cause in itself.

4. *Obtain a job description.* The employer will have to prove upon dismissal that the discharge resulted from failure to perform only those duties contained in this job description, or from incompetence in performing them.

5. *Solicit a reference.* This is a very good time to obtain evidence. Generally, the employer is feeling embarrassed, even remorseful about having to terminate the employee.

6. *Ask for reasons.* The terminated employee should ask the employer to provide reasons for the termination.

7. *Record the termination interview.* After the lawsuit is commenced, it is customary for employers to allege a number of causes for discharge about which the employee had never been warned.

8. *Build a file.* An employee terminated for "cause" can generally assume that the employer will have been documenting a case against him or her. The employee should be doing the same.

9. *Mitigate damages.* Trial judges resent employees who utilize the fact of being dismissed as an opportunity to take a vacation. The following suggestions should be considered:

a) send out five letters per day

b) reapply to all prior employers

c) register with a Canada Employment Centre and a few placement agencies

d) send letters to all former employer's competitors

e) keep track of all expenses of searching for a job.

10. *Substantiate mental distress.* The courts generally require medical evidence, and they are generally more impressed with the certificate of a psychiatrist than that of a general practitioner.

11. *Be cautious in starting a business.* Employees have a duty to mitigate their damages by trying to find comparable alternate employment. If the employee puts full efforts into starting a business and not enough in finding an alternative comparable job, the court will reduce the amount of notice to which the employee would otherwise have been entitled.

12. *Avoid impropriety.* An employee should always be careful to maintain an appearance of integrity during the litigation.[162]

PLANT CLOSURES

The federal and most provincial governments have established various public policies to cushion the impact of mass terminations due to, among other factors, plant closures. Each jurisdiction has established minimum notice requirements that must be provided to employees affected by large-scale terminations. The larger the number of workers to be terminated, the longer the required notice period must be. Companies are also required to provide advance notice to the employees' union, the Minister of Labour, and Canada Employment and Immigration.

The federal government and some provinces have established special programs to intervene when there is information about impending plant closures. The purpose of the intervention is to try to minimize the individual, social, and economic disruption that may be created by the mass termination. In the federal jurisdiction, and in Ontario and Quebec, the statutes require the formation of special committees comprising employees, employee representatives (e.g., union), management, and a ministry of labour representative. The purpose of the committee is to try and find a way to avoid the mass termination. If this approach is unsuccessful, the committee works to formulate measures to find new jobs for the displaced workers and to help them deal with their new situation.

The jurisdiction of Ontario has established a special section within the Ministry of Labour called the Employment Adjustment Branch. The purposes of the branch are to

• Identify plants that are likely to close;

• Determine what steps, if any, may be taken to prevent impending plant closure(s);

• Facilitate the meeting of employees, unions, and employers to resolve any contentious issues, and ensure that workers' rights are protected.

The federal, Ontario, and B.C. government statutes require that special severance pay be provided to compensate for the loss of job. This special severance is in addition to the compensation that must be paid for the advance notice period.

On the Front Line

Several weeks after she began working with her father it was necessary for Jennifer to fire one of the store managers. The problem was that there were several thousand dollars in sales receipts unaccounted for and she was personally sure that it was the store manager who had taken the cash. Of course there was no "smoking gun," in that no one actually caught the manager pocketing the cash. There was no doubt, however, that based on a physical inventory that Jennifer and her father made, the orders had gone out and the money for them was unaccounted for, and in this particular case there was virtually no one else who could have taken the cash.

Both Jack and Jennifer were distressed when the manager refused to resign; in fact, he threatened to sue for wrongful discharge if he were fired. His basic position was that he had done nothing wrong and that to be summarily dismissed like this would besmirch his character and make it impossible for him to get an-

other job. He also pointed out that Jack had promised him (when he was hired away from a competitor) that if he got sales up 40% (which he did) and expenses in line with those budgeted for that new level of sales, his performance would be rated outstanding and he would get a 10% raise. In fact, he did increase sales and reduce expenses, so he was now contending not only that he should not be fired, but that he should be kept on with a raise. He offered to take a polygraph exam. But given the ambiguity surrounding such results, Jack felt it was best to simply terminate the man. Jennifer's questions include:

1. Was summarily terminating this man in this way without further investigation a sound move? Should it have been done differently?

2. Does it appear that the manager has a basis upon which to file a wrongful-discharge suit?

3. How should the matter be handled now?

SUMMARY

1. Employee rights are protected by federal laws and policies, such as the Human Rights Act, Canada Labour Code, Charter of Rights and Freedoms, employment equity programs, and health and safety programs.

2. Management rights include the rights to plan, organize, and control those activities necessary to meet the organization's objectives, including recruiting and maintaining an effective work force.

3. Under Canadian common law the employer/employee relationship is governed by an employment contract. Most employees are hired under an *implied* contract.

4. Under Canadian common law an employee may be dismissed for just cause if the employer has objective proof of certain types of infractions that we discussed at length. Summary dismissal can be used only for serious breaches of a fundamental nature.

5. Management must develop sound policies, procedures, and practices that protect employee rights, and must be willing to correct any unfair decisions and remedy any real or perceived injustices.

6. Management must ensure that its policies and procedures avoid discrimination and unfair and unjust practices. It must develop strong policies against all

form of discrimination and ensure that there are appropriate mechanisms in place to monitor and enforce these policies.

7. Management should ensure that due process is established and that all disciplinary actions including terminations are thoroughly reviewed and that any and all legal requirements are followed to be fair to the employee as well as to avoid future litigation. Further, management must establish sound policies to facilitate the attainment of its objectives.

8. Management policies that should be implemented include policies on sexual harassment, health and safety, employee discipline, and termination.

KEY TERMS

employee rights

management rights

Canadian common law

Quebec Civil Code

just cause

constructive dismissal

damages for mental distress

wrongful resignation

sexual harassment

preventive discipline

corrective discipline

progressive discipline

statutory notice of termination

reasonable notice

DISCUSSION QUESTIONS

1. How do Canadian common law and the Quebec Civil Code affect an organization's employment practices?

2. Identify and discuss some just causes for dismissal.

3. What is meant by the concept of constructive dismissal?

4. What is sexual harassment and what are its implications for organizations?

5. Outline the basic steps for an employer to follow when developing and administering employee discipline.

6. Identify and discuss how an employer can properly manage the termination process.

CASE INCIDENT: The Supervisor's Private Phone Calls

A large British Columbia forestry company hired a logger. Thirteen years later he was promoted to the position of supervisor. That put him in charge of a crew of 25 men engaged in log clearing operations. The supervisor was responsible for his crew's safety and productivity and was classified as a confidential employee. As such, he was permitted to charge long distance calls to the company's telephone account, provided that the calls were related to his employment duties.

The supervisor's promotion required him to move to another geographical location. Both he and his wife were very attached to their respective families and wanted to keep in touch with them. As a result, their personal telephone bills began to mount. The supervisor then decided to bill these calls to the company. He made frequent personal long distance calls from his office and his wife did so from their house. In spite of the supervisor's warnings not to do so, his wife charged her calls to the company's phone number.

The supervisor had been in his position for about three years when he was called to a staff meeting. His manager was concerned because the division's phone budget of $70,000 had been exceeded by $20,000. The manager, believing that the problem was due to unnecessary long distance calls, instructed the supervisory personnel to be more frugal in making those calls.

After the staff meeting the supervisor and his wife stopped charging their personal calls to the company. However, about a month after the meeting, the company decided to audit previous long distance telephone bills. The audit revealed that many calls originating from the supervisor's office and home had been made to families and friends, but were billed to the company. These charges amounted to over $750.

When asked for an explanation, the supervisor readily admitted that he had billed the company for personal calls made by himself and his wife. He said that they had stopped making those calls after the staff meeting and this was confirmed by the records. The supervisor also offered to reimburse the company. The manager suspended the supervisor and told him to return the next afternoon. When the supervisor returned the manager told him that he was dismissed for theft. The supervisor subsequently sued the company for wrongful dismissal.

In court the supervisor, referring to his 17 years of "good and loyal" service to the company, said that discharge was too harsh a punishment. He contended that the company should have regarded his misbehaviour "as simply poor judgment ... deserving only of progressive discipline by way of reprimand and suspension without pay for a set period." Dismissal would only be warranted if there would be "future repetition of the same sort of transgression."

Questions

1. Do you think charging personal long distance calls to a company is a serious offence that justifies dismissal? Explain.

2. Since the supervisor offered to reimburse the company and since he had long served the company, do you agree that the company could have been more lenient with him? Why or why not?

3. What are some of the steps management can take to avoid a similar situation?

SOURCE: *The Employment Law Report*, Vol. 12, no. 8 (August 1991), p. 76. Reproduced by permission of Concord Publishing Ltd, 14 Prince Arthur Avenue, Toronto, Ontario M5R 1A9.

CASE INCIDENT: The Baker, the Baker's Wife, and the Manager

A baker, trained in Italy, began working for a British Columbia grocery store. Three years later the store's owners transferred him to their bakery. Fourteen years later the bakery hired a new manager.

The new manager asked the employees to advise him as soon as possible when they wished to take their vacations. The manager wanted to make sure that there would be no production problems arising from an overlapping of holidays of key employees.

There was only one employee senior to the Italian-trained baker. The senior employee immediately reserved the first two weeks in July. Another employee reserved the last week in July and the first week in August.

Before vacation time arrived, the bakery received an exceptionally large order requiring the doubling of production. Unfortunately, the senior employee then decided to retire and the manager was unable to hire a replacement.

In June, the Italian-trained baker's wife decided to visit their daughter in Toronto. Without telling her husband, she bought airline tickets departing for Toronto on July 15th and returning on August 9th. Toward the end of June the baker became aware of his wife's plans and immediately notified the manager.

The manager told the baker that he could not take his planned vacation because there were large orders on hand and the bakery was short-staffed. The manager pointed out that he had tried to hire additional staff but was unable to do so. Moreover, the manager told the baker that another employee had reserved the last week in July and the first week in August for her vacation.

There was an unfortunate conflict between the two men who had been friends for many years. At one point the baker said that he would forego his vacation if the bakery paid the cancellation fee for his airline tickets. The manager refused to do so. Finally, the manager told the baker that if he went on vacation there would be no job for him when he returned.

In spite of the manager's warning the baker left for his vacation on July 15th. When he returned he found that he no longer had a job at the bakery despite his 18 years of service. He sued for wrongful dismissal.

At the trial the bakery argued that it had not dismissed the baker. It said that it had given the baker the choice of going on vacation or retaining his job. According to the bakery, the baker's decision to go on vacation amounted to a resignation.

The bakery also argued that even if the baker's conduct had not qualified as a resignation, his insubordination was just cause for dismissal.

The baker testified that shortly before he went on vacation his brother died. He added that he had been working long hours because of the bakery's increased production schedule. The baker claimed that "due to his long service with the company and the stress due to overwork and the death of his brother, he should be excused for the incident." He said he was entitled to "a reasonable amount of severance pay in lieu of notice."

In his testimony the baker pointed out that the bakery had survived his three-week absence. According to the baker, this indicated that the bakery was unreasonable when it refused to grant him permission to take his vacation.

Questions

1. Was the baker wrongfully dismissed? Explain.
2. Did the baker's conduct constitute insubordination, and if so was it just cause for dismissal? Explain.
3. How should this situation have been handled? Why?

SOURCE: *The Employment Law Report*, Volume 12, Number 8 (August 1991), pp. 72-73. Reproduced by permission of Concord Publishing Ltd, 14 Prince Arthur Avenue, Toronto, Ontario M5R 1A9.

NOTES

1. I. Christie, *Employment Law in Canada* (Toronto: Butterworths, 1980) as quoted in Giles Trudeau, "Employee Rights versus Management Rights: Some Reflections Regarding Dismissal" in Canadian Readings in Personnel and Human Resource Management, Dolan and Schuler, eds., (St. Paul, Min.: West Publishing Company, 1987), p. 368.

2. Trudeau, p. 370.

3. Edward A. Aust, *The Employment Contract* (Cowansville: les Editions Yvon Blais Inc., 1988) as quoted in Ellen E. Mole, *Wrongful Dismissal Practice Manual* (Toronto: Butterworths Canada Ltd., 1989), p. 31.

4. Kathy Bullock, "Termination of Employment" in *Human Resources Management in Canada* (Toronto, Ont.: Prentice-Hall Canada Inc., 1989), pp. 75,105.

5. Mole, p. 43.

6. Parts of the information in this section are drawn from Mole and from Levitt, *The Law of Dismissal in Canada* (Aurora, Ont: Canada Law Book Inc., 1985). Used with permission.

7. Levitt, p. 66.

8. Trudeau, p. 373.

9. See *Degelman* v. *Anderson Industries Ltd.* (1987), 61 Sask. R. 85 (Q.B.).

10. See *Denham* v. *Patrick* (1910), O.L.R. 347 (C.I.).

11. See *Port Arthur Shipbuilding Co.* v. *Arthurs et al.,* (1969), S.C.R. 485.

12. Levitt, p. 65.

13. Levitt, p. 66.

14. Parts of the material in this section are drawn from Ellen E. Mole, *Wrongful Dismissal Practice Manual*, Vol. 1 & Vol. 2 (Toronto: Butterworths Canada Ltd., 1967), pp. 403-547. Used with permission.

15. *MacDonald v. Richardson Greenshields of Canada Ltd.* (1985), 69 B.C.L.R. 58 (S.C.).

16. *Hardie* v. *Trans-Canada Resources Ltd.* (1976), 71 D.L.R. (3d) Alta. C.A.; see also *Durand* v. *Quaker Oats Co. of Canada Ltd.* (1990), 45 B.C.L.R. (2d) 354 (C.A.), revg C.C.E.L. 223.

17. *Stein* v. *B.C. Housing Management Commission* (1984), unreported, Hutchinson J. (B.C.S.C.) WDPM 844-02303 (18 pp.)

18. See the following cases: *Buchanan* v. *Continental Bank of Canada* (1984), 58 N.B.R. (2d) 333 (Q.B.); *MacNeil* v. *Ronscott Inc. c.o.b. as Shoreline Motor Hotel* (1988), 88 C.L.L.C. 14,015 (Ont. S.C.); *Brown* v. *Block Bros. Realty Ltd.* (1988) unreported, Gibbs J. (B.C.S.C.) WDPM 745-040-3 (5 pp.); *Durand* v. *Quaker Oats Co. Canada Ltd.* Supra. note 16.

19. *Blainey* v. *F. R. Kickey Ltd.* (1985), unreported, Conant Dist. Ct. J. (Ont. Dist. Ct.) WDPM 535-021-3 (9 pp.). See also D.E.L.D. Issue 3, Sept. 9, 1986, pp. 23-24.

20. *Van Aggelen* v. *I.C.G. Liquid Gas Ltd.* (1988), unreported, Provenzano L.J.S.C. (B.C.S.C.) WDPM 828-020-3 (11 pp).

21. *Stilwell* v. *Audio Pictures Ltd.,* (1955), O.W.N. 793 (C.A.).

22. Mole, pp. 404-405.

23. See the following cases: *Bell* v. *Izak Walton Killan Hospital for Children* (1986), 14 C.C.E.L. 276 N.S.S.C.; *Murphy* v. *Sealand Helicopters Ltd.* (1988), 72 Nfld & P.E.I. R. 9 (Nfld. S.C.); *Elliott* v. *Parksville* (City) (1990), 66 D.L.R. (4th) 107 B.C.C.A., affirming 89 CLLC 14,038 (S.C.).

24. See the following cases: *Parks* v. *H. H. Marshall Ltd.* (1984), 62 N.S.R. (2d) 142 (S.C.); *Pierce* v. *Canada Trust Realtor* (1986), unreported, Gray J. Ont. H.C. WDPM 601-013-3 (25 pp.); *Pombert* v. *Brunswick Mining and Smelting Corp. Ltd.* (1987), 84 N.B.R. (2d) 296 (C.A.) affd 1987, 79 N.B.R. (2d) 79. For examples, see: *Bell* v. *Society for Promotion of Education and Activities for Children in the Home* (1984), 6 C.C.E.L. 156 affd 47 Sask. R. 290 (C.A.); *Kozak* v. *Aliments Krispy Kernels Inc.* (1988), 22 C.C.E.L. 1 (Ont. Dist. Ct.); *English* v. *NBI Can. Inc.* (1989), C.C.E.L. 21 (Alta, Q.B.).

25. *Macdonald* v. *Canada Games Park Commission* (1986), 58 Nfld. & P.E.I. R 29 (Nfld. Dist. Ct). See also D.E.L.D., Issues, Sept 1986 p. 4.

26. *Barkley* v. *Weyerhaeuser Canada Ltd.* (1987); unreported, Houghton L.J.S.C. (B.C.S.C.) WDPM 726-001-3 (29 pp.) *Briant* v. *Gerber (Canada) Inc.* (1989) T.L.W. 925-027 (Ont. S.C.) See also *MacNeil* v. *Ronscott Inc. c.o.b. as Shoreline Motor Hotel* (1988), 99 C.L.L.C.; *Stephens* v. *Morris Rod Weeder Co. Ltd.* (1989), 27 C.C.E.L. 92 (Sask. Q.B.).

27. *Vlooswyck* v. *Elevator Builders Construction Ltd. et al.* (1978), 11 A.R. 388 (S.C.).

28. *Pierce* v. *Canada Trust Realty* (1986), unreported, Gray J. (Ont. H.C.) WDPM 601-013-3 (25 pp.).

29. *Bechard* v. *Chrysler Canada Ltd.* (1979), 108 D.L.R. (3d) 576 (Alta. Q.B.).

30. *Ironmonger* v. *Moli Energy Ltd.* (1990), T.L.W. 1012-025 (B.C. Co. Ct).

31. *Warner* v. *Richmond Lions Long-Term Care Society et al.* (1986), unreported, Macdonnell J. (B.C.S.C.) WDPM 607-019-3 (14 pp.).

32. *Delaney* v. *MacKenzie & Feimann Ltd.* (1986), unreported, Taggart, J.A. (B.C.C.A.) WDPM 546-01B-3 (12 pp.); see also *Wilson* v. *Champion Forest products (Alta.) Ltd.* (1988), 90 A.R. 338 (Q.B.).

33. *Granoff* v. *National Trust Co. Ltd.* (1986) unreported, Houghton J. (B.C.S.C.) WDPM 607-021-3 (6 pp.).

34. *Geoff Coleman Yacht Sales Ltd.* v. *C. & C. Yachts Ltd.* (1983), 45 B.C.L.R. 66 (S.C.); *Cooke* v. *Canada Trust Co. et al.* (1983), unreported, Conant Co. Ct. J. (Ont. Co. Ct.) WDPM 221-024-3 (11 pp.); *Ennis* v. *C.I.B.C.* (1986), 13 C.C.E.L. 25 (B.C.S.C.); *Cox* v. *C.N.R.* (1988), 84 N.S.R. (2d) 271 (N.S.S.C.); *Taylor* v. *Sears Canada Inc.* (1990), 95 N.S.R. (2d) 170 (S.C.).

35. *Funnell* v. *Peat, Marwick, Mitchell & Co.* (1979), 11 B.C.L.R. 47 (S.C.).

36. *Miller* v. *K-Mart Canada Ltd.* (1987), unreported, Aylward J. (Nfld. S.C.); *Durand* v. *Quaker Oats Co. of Canada Ltd.* (1990), 45 B.C.L.R. (2d) 354 (C.A.) revg 20 C.C.E.L. 223.

37. *Russell* v. *Smith Industries North America Ltd.* (1979), 10 B.C.L.R. 248 (S.C.).

38. *Lewis* v. *Associated Laboratories Ltd.* See also *Ellchuk* v. *Int'l. Stage Lines Inc.* (1989), 28 C.C.E.L. 309 (B.C. Co. Ct.).

39. *Kearley* v. *Iron Ore Co. of Canada* (1980), 30 Nfld & P.E.I. R. 293 (Nfld. S.C.).

40. *Berger* v. *Royal Bank of Canada* (1986), 45 Man. R. (2d) 167 (Q.B.); *Stock* v. *Bank of N. S.* (1988), 22 C.C.E.L. 217 (B.C.S.C.).

41. See *Poole* v. *Chick Adam Ltd. et al.* (1985), unreported, Van Camp J. (Ont. H.C.) WDPM 511-028-3 (24 pp.); *Wilmot* v. *Keenlyside et al.* (1988), unreported, Callaghan J. (B.C.S.C.) WDPM 828-006-3 (10 pp.).

42. See *Smallman* v. *Copperfield's Hotels Ltd.* (1984), unreported, Honey Co. Ct. J. (Ont. Co. Ct.) WDPM 322-030-3 (19 pp.); *Webster* v. *Gold Medal Data Systems Ltd.* (1985), 39 Sask. R. 114 (Q.B.); *Gibson* v. *Snackery Foods Ltd.* (1987), unreported, Oppal J. (B.C.S.C.) WDPM 729-012-3 (9 pp.).

43. See the following cases: *Vorvis* v. *Insurance Corp. of B. C.* (1984), 53 B.C.L.R. 63 varg 134 D.L.R. (3d) 727 (A.) affd. (1989), 58 D.L.R. (4th) 193 (S.C.C.); *Morby* v. *Toyer Plymouth Chrysler Ltd.* (1986), 14 C.C.E.L. 221 (N.B.Q.B.); *Penney* v. *Labrador Inuit Dev't Corp.* (1987), 65 Nfld. & P.E.I. R 153 (Nfld. S.C.).

44. *Fogarty* v. *Palmeter's Country Home Ltd.* (1977), 27 N.S.R. (2d) 306 (S.C.).

45. *Cormier* v. *Hostess Food Products Ltd.* (1984), 52 N.B.R. (2d) 288 (Q.B.); see also *Cheetham* v. *Barton* (1990), T.L.W. 947-001 (Ont. Dist. Ct.).

46. *Goldberg et al.* v. *Western Approaches Ltd.* (1985), 7 C.C.E.L. 127 (B.C.S.C.); *Shulman* v. *Xerox Canada Inc.* (1986), 75 N.S.R. (2d) 7 (S.C.); *Ellchuk* v. *Int'l. Stage Lines Inc.* (1989), 28 C.C.E.L. 309 (B.C. Co. Ct.). See also *English* v. *NBI Can. Inc.* (1989), 24 C.C.E.L. 21 (Alta. Q.B.).

47. *McHugh* v. *City Motors (Nfld.) Ltd.* (1988), Nfld & P.E.I. R. 68 (Nfld. S.C.) vard on other grounds (1989), 74 Nfld. & P.E.I. R. 263.

48. *Priestman* v. *Swift Sure Courier Services Ltd.* (1989), unreported, Boyd L.J.S.C. (B.C.S.C.) WDPM 844-025-3 (10 pp.).

49. See the following cases: *Thorvaldson* v. *Famous Players Ltd.* (1983), 22 Man. R. (2d) 79, affg 17 Man. (2d) 391 (A.A.); *Langlois* v. *Farr Inc.* (1988), 26 C.C.E.L. 249 (Que. C.A.); see also *Delorme* v. *Banque Royale Du Canada* (1987), 19 C.C.E.L. 298 (Que. S.C.).

50. *Meszaros* v. *Simpsons-Sears Ltd.* (1979), 19 A.R. 239 (Q.B.); *Neigum* v. *Wilkie Co-operative Assoc. Ltd.* (1987), 55 Sask. R. 210 (Sask. Q.B.); *Bellefleur* v. *Enflo Canada Ltd.* (1988), 22 C.C.E.L. 181 (N.B.Q.B.).

51. *Laverty* v. *Cooper Plating Inc.* (1987), 17 C.C.E.L. 44 (Ont. Dist. Ct.). See also *Boisvenue* v. *St. Stephen (Town)* (1988), 22 C.C.E.L. 116 (N.B.Q.B.).

52. *Clarke Estate et al.* v. *Dale and Co. Ltd.* (1985), 51 Nfld. & P.E.I. R. 244 (Nfld. S.C.); *Iacono et al.* v. *Mitchell* (1985), unreported, Rutherford J. (Ont. H.C.) WDPM 534-017-3 (9 pp.).

53. *Taylor* v. *Sears Canada Inc.* (1990), 95 N.S.R. (2d) 170 (S.C.).

54. *Stevenson* v. *Osler Wills Bickle Ltd.* (1985), unreported, Keith J. (Ont. H.C.) WDPM 504-027-3 (34 pp.).

55. *Warner* v. *Richmond Lions Long-Term Care Society et al.* (1986), unreported, Macdonnell J. (B.C.S.C.) WDPM 607-019-3 (14 pp.); *Tallon* v. *Rural Mun. of Greenfield No. 529* (1990), T.L.W. 944-004 (Sask. Q.B.).

56. *Melanson* v. *Rexdale Lions Club* (1986), unreported, McRae J. (Ont. H.C.) WDPM 605-011-3 (12 pp.).

57. *Kiff* v. *Allstate Insce. Co. of Canada et al.* (1986), unreported, R.E. Holland J. (Ont. H.C.) WDPM 616-009-3 (16 pp.).

58. *Spence* v. *Wyeth Ltd.* (1983), unreported, Gray J. (Ont. H.C.) WDPM 208-205-3 (23 pp.). See also *LeFurgey* v. *Royal Bank of Canada* (1984), 56 N.B.R. (2d) 286 (Q.B.); *Eskelson* v. *Demaine and District Cooperative Ass'n Ltd.* (1984), 37 Sask. R. 12 (Q.B.).

59. *Mackin* v. *Kings Regional Rehabilitation Centre*, (1990), 95 N.S.R. (2d) 238 (S.C.).

60. *Taggart* v. *Tilden Rent-A-Car System Ltd.* (1978), 13 A.R. 334 (S.C.); *Ferguson* v. *Canadian Vehicle Leasing Ltd.* (1983), unreported, Reid J. (Ont. H.C.) WDPM 222-023-3 (12 pp.); *Ball* v. *MacMillan Bloedel Ltd.* (1989), 29 C.C.E.L. 99 (B.C.S.C.).

61. *Aston* v. *Gander Aviation Ltd.* (1981), 32 Nfld. & P.E.I. R. 148 (Nfld. S.C.); *Bruce Marshall Service Centre Ltd.* v. *Marshall* (1983), unreported, Vanini Co. Ct. J. (Ont. Co. Ct.) WDPM 221-021-3 (21 pp.).

62. *Granoff* v. *National Trust Co. Ltd.* (1986), unreported, Houghton, J. (B.C.S.C.) WDPM 607-021-3 (6 pp.); See also *Berger* v. *Royal Bank of Canada* (1986), 45 Man. R. (2d) 167 (Q.B.).

63. See *Lefurgey* v. *Royal Bank of Canada* (1984), 56 N.B.R. (2d) 286 (Q.B.); *Ennis* v. *CIBC* (1986), 13 C.C.E.L. 25 (B.C.S.C.).

64. *Durand* v. *Quaker Oats Co. of Canada Ltd.* (1990), 45 B.C.L.R. (2d) 354 (C.A.), revg (1988), 20 C.C.E.L. 223 (B.C.S.C.); *Anderson* v. *Pioneer Sports-World Inc.* (1990), T.L.W. 1020-019 (Ont. Dist Ct.). See also D.E.L.D. Issue 8 (May 8 1990) p. 62.

65. *Jewitt* v. *Prism Resources Ltd.* (1980), 110 D.L.R. (3d) 713, affd. 127 D.L.R. (3d) 190 (B.C.C.A.).

66. *Cornell* v. *Rogers Cablesystems Inc.* (1987), 87 C.L.L.C. 14,054 (Ont. Dist. Ct.); *Schafer* v. *Pan Matric Informatics Ltd.* (1987), unreported, Power J. (Alta. Q.B.) WDPM 715-032-3 (21 pp.).

67. *Takoff* v. *Toronto Stock Exchange* (1986), 11 C.C.E.L. 272 (Ont. H.C.).

68. *Warner* v. *Richmond Lions Long-Term Care Society et al.* (1986), unreported, Macdonnell J. (B.C.S.C.) WDPM 607-019-3 (14 pp.).

69. *Codner* v. *Joint Construction Ltd.* (1989), 74 Nfld. & P.E.I. R. 219 (Nfld. S.C.); *Clare* v. *Moore Corp. Ltd.* (1989), 29 C.C.E.L. 41 (Ont. Dist. Ct.).

70. *Laird* v. *Sask. Roughriders Football Club* (1982), 18 Sask. R. 333 (Q.B.); *Holden* v. *Metro Transit Operating Co.* (1983), 1 C.C.E.L. 159 (B.C.S.C.).

71. *Belliveau* v. *Dylex Ltd.* (1987), 79 N.B.R. (2d) 141 (Q.B.).

72. *Leblanc* v. *United Maritime Fisherman Co-op* (1984), 60 N.B.R. (2d) 341 (Q.B.); *Schwanke* v. *Para-Med Health Services Inc.* (1985), 9 C.C.E.L. 314.40 Alta. L.R. (2d) 10 (Q.B.).

73. *Spong* v. *Westpres Publications Ltd.* (1982), 2 C.C.E.L. 228 (B.C.S.C.); *Blainey* v. *R. F. Hickey Ltd.* (1985), unreported, Conant Dist. Ct. J. (Ont. Dist. Ct.) WDPM 535-021-3 (9 pp.); *Paitich* v. *Clarke Institute of Psychiatry* (1988), 19 C.C.E.L. 105 (Ont. H.C.).

74. *Tremblett* v. *Bernard W. Barlle Ltd.* (1977), 19 Nfld. & P.E.I. R. 397 (Nfld. S.C.).

75. *Mullen* v. *Neon Products Ltd.* (1981), 33 A.R. 51.(Q.B.).

76. *Clare* v. *Moore Corp. Ltd.* Supra, n. 69.

77. See *Fonceca* v. *McDonnell Douglas Canada Ltd.* (1983), C.C.E.L. 51 (Ont. H.C.).

78. *Ma* v. *Columbia Trust Company Ltd.* (1985), 9 C.C.E.L. 300 (B.C.S.C.).

79. *Boryski* v. *Chef-Redi Meats Inc.* (1983), 22 Sask. R. 257 (Q.B.); see also *Mellquist* v. *Lake of the River (Rural Municipality)* (1987), 62 Sask. R. 165 (Q.B.).

80. *Forgarty* v. *Palmeter's Country Home Ltd.* (1977), 27 N.S.R. (2d) 306 (S.C.).

81. *Richie* v. *Intercontinental Packers Ltd.* (1982), 14 Sask. R. 206, 16 Business Law Report (B.L.R.).

82. *Funnel* v. *Peat Marwick, Mitchell & Co.* (1979), 97 D.L.R. (3d) 459, 11 B.C.L.R. 47 (S.C.); *Trotter* v. *Chesley* (Town) (1990), T.L.W. 944-035 (Ont. Dist. Ct.).

83. *Waite* v. *LaRonge Child Care Co-operative* (1985), 40 Sask. R. 260 (Q.B.); *Munro* v. *M.S.A. Cablesystem Ltd.* (1990), T.L.W. 1004-002 (B.C.S.C.).

84. *Hardie* v. *Trans-Canada Resources Ltd.* (1976), 71 D.L.R. (3d) 668 (Alta. C.A.).

85. *Buchanan* v. *Continental Bank of Canada* (1984), 58 N.B.R. (2d) 333 (Q.B.).

86. *Snider* v. *N. B. Telephone Co. Ltd.* (1986), 69 N.B.R. (2d) 8 (Q.B.), affd (1987) 78 N.B.R. (2d) (C.A.).

87. *Human Resources Management in Canada*, Report Bulletin no. 78 (Toronto: Prentice-Hall Canada Inc., 1989), p. 4.

88. *Reece* v. *Kanata Hotels Ltd. et al.,* (1984) unreported, Fleury Co. Ct. J. (Ont. Co. Ct.) WDPM 410-029-3 (20 pp.).

89. *McIntyre* v. *Hockin* (1889), 16 O.A.R. 498 (C.A.). See also *Webster* v. *Gold Medal Data Systems Ltd.* (1985), 39 Sask. R. 114 (Q.B.); *Sloane* v. *Toronto Stock Exchange* (1988), 24 C.C.E.L. 52 (Ont. S.C.).

90. *MacDonald* v. *Azar,* (1948), 1 D.L.R.. 854 (N.S.S.C.).

91. *Kearley* v. *Iron Ore Co. of Canada* (1980), 30 Nfld. & P.E.I. R. 293 (Nfld. S.C.).

92. *Nossal* v. *Better Business Bureau of Metropolitan Toronto Inc.* (1985), 51 O.R. (2d) 279 (C.A.).

93. *Port Arthur Shipbuilding Co.* v. *Arthurs et al.,* (1967), S.C.R. 85, revg (1969). See also *Cox* v. *C.N.R.* (1988), 84 N.S.R. (2d) 271 (S.C.).

94. *Cox* v. *C. N. R.* (1988), 84 N.S.R. (2d) 271 (S.C.).

95. *Prest* v. *Ottawa Roman Catholic Separate School Board* (1980), 29 O.R. (2d) 678, affd 128 D.L.R. (3d) 384 (C.A.); *Athabasca Realty Co. Ltd.* v. *Merenick et al.* (1982), 36 A.R. 507 (Q.B.).

96. *Reilly* v. *Steelcase Canada Ltd.* (1979), 26 O.R. (2d) 725, 103 D.L.R. (3d) 704 (H.C.J.).

97. *Boisvenue* v. *St. Stephen (Town)* (1988), 22 C.C.E.L. 116 (N.B.Q.B.).

98. *O'Malley* v. *Pacific Customs Brokers (Airport) Ltd. et al.* (1984), 10 C.C.E.L. 98 (B.C.S.C.).

99. *Goodwin* v. *Canada Trustco Mortgage Co.* (1986), unreported, Smith Dist. Ct. J. (Ont. Dist. Ct.) WDPM 541-015-3 (5 pp.).

100. *Manolson* v. *Cybermedix Ltd. et al.* (1985), 5 C.P.C. (2d) 291 (Ont. S.C.).

101. *Brenton* v. *Potash Co. of America* (1985), 63 N.B.R. (2d) 62 (Q.B.).

102. Levitt, p. 121.

103. *Varrelmann* v. *Phoenix Brewery Co.* (1984), 3 B.C.R. 135 (Div. Ct.).

104. *Longman* v. *Federal Business Development Bank* (1982), 131 D.L.R. (3d) 533, 36 B.C.L.R. 115 (S.C.).

105. Levitt, p. 43; see also *Scott* v. *City of Windsor* (1984), 4 C.C.E.L. 145 (Ont. S.C.).

106. *Page* v. *Jim Patterson Industries Ltd.* (1982), 5 W.W.R. at 101, Sask. R. 125 at 130. See also Levitt, pp. 43-45.

107. Levitt, p. 44.

108. *Reid* v. *Crock Inc.* (1985), 33 A.C.W.S. (2d) 375 (Ont. Dist. Ct.) West D.C.J. (14 pp.). See also D.E.L.D. Issue 2 (July 15, 1986) pp. 11-12.

109. *Robinson* v. *Tirgley* (1988), 20 C.C.E.L. 263 (N.B.Q.B.).

110. See *Stevens* v. *LeBlanc's Welding and Fabricating Ltd. et al.* (1982), 40 N.B.R. (2d) 389 (Q.B.).

111. *Brown* v. *Waterloo Regional Board of Commissioners of Police* (1983), 37 O.R. (2d) 277, 136 D.L.R. (3d) 49, 17 B.L.R. 299 (H.C.J.).

112. *Pilon* v. *Peugeot Canada Ltd.* (1980), 29 O.R. (2d) 711, 114 D.L.R. (3d) 378, 12 B.L.R. 277 (H.C.J.).

113. *Hilts* v. *Euroclean Canada Inc.* (1982), 16 A.C.W.S. (2d) 244 (Ont. Co. Ct.).

114. *Grant* v. *MacMillan Bloedel* (1983), 83 C.L.L.C. 14,002 (Ont. H.C.J.).

115. *Rahemtulla* v. *Vanfed Credit Union* (1984), 4 C.C.E.L. 113 (Ont. H.C.).

116. *Cody* v. *Coffee Mill Canada Ltd.* (1986), 76 N.B.R. (2d) 211 (Q.B.); *Thomas* v. *Chaleur Auto Sales Ltd.* (1988), 87 N.B.R. (2d) 312 (Q.B.).

117. *Jivrag* v. *City of Calgary et al.* (1986), 45 Alta. L.R. (2d) 343 (Q.B.) revd in part (1987), 18 C.C.E.L. xx(n) (C.A.).

118. *Jivrag* v. *City of Calgary et al.,* supra, no. 117.

119. *Kowton* v. *Edmonton* (1985), 38 Alta. L.R. (2d) 397 (Q.B.); *Stewart* v. *Standard Broadcasting Corp.* (1989), 29 C.C.E.L. 290 (Que. S.C.).

120. *Delorme* v. *Banque Royale du Canada* (1987), 19 C.C.E.L. 298 (Que. S.C.).

121. *Thom* v. *Goodhost Foods Ltd.* (1987), 17 C.C.E.L. 89 (Ont. H.C.).

122. *Horvat* v. *NCR Canada Ltd.* (1989), unreported (Ont. Dist. Ct.).

123. *Young* v. *Huntsville District Memorial Hospital et al.* (1984), 5 C.C.E.L. 113 (Ont. H.C.).

124. *Steer* v. *Aerovox Inc. et al.* (1984), C.C.E.L. 130 (N.S.T.D.) (tort liability); *Colasurdo* v. *CTG Inc. et al.* (1988), 18 C.C.E.L. 264 (Ont. H.C.).

125. *Carle* v. *Comite Paritaire Due Vetement Pour Dames* (1987), 22 C.C.E.L. (Que. S.C.).

126. *Thom* v. *Goodhost Foods Ltd.* (1987), 17 C.C.E.L. 89 (Ont. H.C.).

127. These factors are mentioned in virtually every mental distress damages award.

128. *Young* v. *Huntsville District Memorial Hospital et al.* (1984), 5 C.C.E.L. 113 (Ont. H.C.); *McOnie* v. *River Pub Ltd. et al* (1987), 79 N.S.R. (2d) 379 (S.C.).

129. *Desseroit et al* v. *Delta Hotels Ltd.* (1985), unreported, Lazier Dist. Ct. J. (Ont. H.C.) WDPM 422-018-3 (139 pp.); *Heffernan* v. *Barry Cullen Chevrolet Oldsmobile Ltd.* (1986), unreported, Steele J. (Ont. H.C.) WDPM 634-020-3 (15 pp.).

130. *Lindsay* v. *Superior Acceptance Corp.* (1986), unreported, Lazier Dist. Ct. J. (Ont. Dist. Ct.) WDPM 630-030-5 (5 pp.); *Moran* v. *Atlantic Co-operative Publishers* (1988), 23 C.C.E.L. 205 (N.S.S.C.).

131. *Rahemjtulla* v. *Vanfed Credit Union* (1984), 4 C.C.E.L. 113 (Ont. H.C.).

132. *Mackow* v. *A. Berger Precision Ltd.* (1985), unreported, Bernstein Dist. Ct. J. (Ont. Dist. Ct.) WDPM 424-027-3 (11 pp.).

133. *Johnson* v. *Canadian Association for the Mentally Retarded, Arboreg Branch* (1985), 37 Man. R. (2d) 12 (Q.B.).

134. *Jivrag* v. *City of Calgary et al*, supra, no. 117.

135. *McHugh* v. *City Motors (Nfld.) Ltd.* (1988), 22 C.C.E.L. 187 (Nfld. S.C.) revd (1989), 58 D.L.R. (4th) 453 (C.A.). See also D.E.L.D., Issue 3 (October 3, 1989), p. 21.

136. *Ribeiro* v. *Canadian Imperial Bank of Commerce* (1989), 67 O.R. (2d) 385 (H.C.). See also D.E.L.D. Issue 2 (July 15, 1986), p. 15.

137. *Gardner* v. *Rockwell International of Canada* (1975), 9 O.R. (2d) 105, 59 D.L.R. (3d) 513 (H.C.J.).

138. *Mayhew* v. *Canron Inc.* (1982), 50 N.S.R. (2d) 278 and 349 (S.C.T.D.).

139. *Red Deer College* v. *Michael et. al.* (1976), S.C.R. 324 affg 44 D.L.R. (3d) 447 (1974) 2 W.W.R. 416 *Doyle* v. *Auld* (1990), 33 C.C.E.L. 95 (P.E.I. T.D.).

140. *Clark* v. *Babcock and Wilcox Canada Ltd.* (1982), 9 A.C.W.S. (2d) 184 Ont. (H.C.J.).

141. *Wright* v. *Westar Mining Ltd.,* (1987), T.L.W. 725-037 (B.C.S.C.).

142. Levitt, p. 267.

143. *Red Deer* v. *Michaels* (1976), 2 S.C.R. 324 affg 44 D.L.R. (3d) 447, (1974) 2 W.W.R. 416.

144. *Cherie Bell & Ann Korcczak* v. *Ernest Ladas & The Flaming Steak Tavern* (1980), as quoted in Harish C. Jain, "Human Rights Issues in Employment" in *Human Resources Management in Canada* (Toronto, Ont.: Prentice-Hall Canada Inc., 1989), p. 50,035.

145. This definition includes the definition provided by the Canadian Human Rights Act, the Ontario Human Rights Act, and other human rights acts.

146. See *Kotyk* & Allary v. *Canadian Employment and Immigration Commission*, as quoted in Jain, p. 50,035.

147. For example, in *Rocichaud* v. *Treasury Board* (1987), as quoted in Jain, p. 50,036. The Supreme Court of Canada ruled that the Department of National Defence was liable for the act of a supervisor who was found guilty of sexual harassment by a CHRC tribunal.

148. *Shiels* v. *Saskatchewan Government Insurance* (1988), 20 C.C.E.L. 55 (Sask. Q.B.). See also D.E.L.D., Issue 2 (August 9, 1988), p. 10.

149. Jane Coutts, "Workplace Programs Easing the Fight Against Sexual Harassment," *The Globe and Mail* (August 12, 1989), p. A8.

150. Coutts, p. A8.

151. Coutts, p. A8.

152. *Himmelman* v. *King's-Edgehill School* (1985), 7 C.C.E.L. 16 (N.S.S.C.); see also *Ma* v. *Columbia Trust Co. Ltd.* (1985), 9 C.C.E.L. 300 (B.C.S.C.); *Murphy* v. *Truck Bodies (1982) Ltd. et al.* (1986), 58 Nfld. & P.E.I. R. 271 (Nfld. S.C.); *Neigum* v. *Wilkie Cooperative Association Ltd.* (1987), 55 Sask. R. 20 (Sask. Q.B.).

153. *Tellier* v. *Bank of Montreal* (1987), 17 C.C.E.L. 1 (Ont. Dist. Ct.). See also *Boisvenue* v. *St. Stephen (Town)* (1988), 22 C.C.E.L. 116 N.B. (Q.B.).

154. *O'Malley* v. *Pacific Customs Brokers (Airport) Ltd. et al.* (1984), 10 C.C.E.L. 98 (B.C.S.C.).

155. *Dismissal and Employment Law Digest* (Aurora, Ont.: Canada Law Book, Inc., April 18, 1989), p. 48.

156. Bullock, p. 75, 016.

157. *Ansari et al.* v. *B. C. Hydro and Power Authority* (1986), 2 B.C.L.R. (2d) 33 (S.C.).

158. Mole, p. 906.

159. *Lesiuk* v. *British Columbia Forest Products Ltd.* (1984), 56 B.C.L.R. 216 revd on other grounds 8 B.C.L.R. (2d) 297 (C.A.).

160. *MacDonald* v. *United Tire & Rubber Co. Ltd.* (1984), 25 A.C.Q.S. (2d) 218 (Ont. H.C.); *Anderson* v. *Pirelli Cables Inc.* (1984), 26 A.C.W.S. (2d) 202 (Ont. H.C.).

161. Adapted and abridged from Levitt, pp. 306-309. Used with permission.

162. Adapted and abridged from Levitt, pp. 287-294. Used with permission.

SUGGESTED READINGS

Bullock, Kathy. "Termination of Employment" in *Human Resources Management in Canada*. Toronto: Prentice-Hall Canada Inc., 1989, pp. 75,011-75,065.

CCH Canadian Limited. *Canadian Master Labour Guide*. Toronto: CCH, 1990.

Christie, I. *Employment Law in Canada*. Toronto: Butterworths, 1990.

Grant, James D. and Terry H. Wagar. "Dismissal for Incompetence: An Analysis of the Factors used by Canadian Courts in Determining Just Cause for Termination." Administrative Sciences Association of Canada (Personnel and Human Resources Division), Proceedings of the Annual Conference, June 1991, pp. 1-10.

Levitt, Howard A. *The Law of Dismissal in Canada, 2nd ed*. Aurora, Ont.: Canada Law Book Inc., 1992.

McShane, Steven. and D. McPhillips. "Predicting Reasonable Notice in Canadian Wrongful Dismissal Cases." *Industrial and Labor Relations Review*, 41, 1987, pp. 108-117.

Mole, Ellen E. *Wrongful Dismissal Practice Manual*, Vols. 1 & 2. Toronto: Butterworths, 1990.

Powell, Michael Lane and William Roger Angus. "Constructive Dismissal: Dead or Alive?" in *Human Resources Management in Canada*. Toronto: Prentice-Hall Canada Inc., 1990, pp. 75,523-75,531

Rhodes, Susan R. and Richard M. Steers. *Managing Employee Absenteeism*. Reading, Mass.: Addison-Wesley Publishing Company, 1990.

Sherman, V. Clayton. "Eight Steps to Positive Discipline of Problem Employees" in *Human Resources Management in Canada*. Toronto: Prentice-Hall Canada Inc., 1989, pp. 70,549-70,569.

CHAPTER SEVENTEEN
EMPLOYEE HEALTH AND SAFETY

After studying this chapter, you should be able to

1. Explain the purposes and importance of employee health and safety management.
2. Explain different federal and provincial safety acts in Canada.
3. Discuss government administrative structures for health and safety.
4. Discuss the purposes of joint health and safety committees.
5. Explain accident reporting and investigation requirements.
6. Discuss employees' rights to safe and healthy work environments.
7. Explain what causes unsafe acts.
8. Understand the problem of stress.
9. Explain the problem of burnout.

OVERVIEW

This chapter presents the essential characteristics of health and safety legislation in Canada. Today, every manager needs a working knowledge of occupational health and safety standards, so we discuss them at length. Specifically, we review Canadian jurisdictional framework for health and safety, how health and safety legislation operates, and government administrative structures for health and safety. We also emphasize the importance of supervision in maintaining and promoting safety. We discuss several specific techniques for preventing accidents.

We discuss the problem of stress and provide some techniques for coping with it. We also discuss other health-related issues such as AIDS, drugs, and VDTs.

INTRODUCTION: HEALTH AND SAFETY MANAGEMENT

Health and safety management is an important function of human resource management. Organizations' health and safety policies are influenced by a variety of sources including governments, unions, the public, and the economic cost. Governments influence organizations' health and safety policies by establishing legislations that require organizations to protect workers from unsafe working conditions, workplace hazards and risks, and to protect the community from pollution, the effects of toxic substances, and other forms of health hazards. Unions have traditionally been strong advocates for the maintenance and improvement of safe working conditions. Many unions have included health and safety issues among their bargaining priorities. Increased public awareness and concern about the dangers of environmental pollution and exposure to toxic substances have also resulted in increased pressures on organizations to develop and promote more effective and substantive health and safety policies.

The development, promotion, and maintenance of employee safety and health policies protect organizations' most important and valuable assets—human resources. Sound safety and health policies assist the organization to control healthcare costs associated with illnesses, accidents, or other disabilities. These economic costs can be substantial and include:

- The cost of wages paid to workers who are attracted to the accident site and therefore not working
- Equipment or work in process that is interrupted, spoiled, or damaged.
- Interruptions in the work of the injured person as well as the work of those who come to the scene, leading to slowdowns at later production stations.
- The repair of damaged equipment or work in process.
- Cleanup costs.
- Payments to the injured employee in excess of workers' compensation.
- Dispensary services provided by the plant nurse, company infirmary, and so on.
- The diminished productivity of the injured person after his or her return to the job but before full work output can be sustained.
- Cost of supervisory time (incurred because accidents must be investigated, and reports must be made and processed).
- Extra overtime costs occasioned by the initial interruption of work.
- Costs associated with the recruitment, selection or transfer, and training of a replacement for the recuperating worker.
- Costs associated with the higher scrap, spoilage, or generally lower efficiency of the replacement.
- Legal costs for advice with respect to any potential claim.
- Costs of rental equipment placed temporarily in service while unsafe equipment is repaired or replaced.[1]

Purposes and Importance of Health and Safety Management

The purposes and importance of health and safety management are to

- Ensure the physical safety and well-being of employees at their place of work

- Ensure the provision and maintenance of safe and healthy working conditions in the workplace
- Ensure that the workplace is free from hazards
- Deal effectively with workers' health and safety concerns and complaints
- Design, develop, establish, and promote health and safety policies, programs, and procedures at the workplace

HEALTH AND SAFETY LEGISLATION IN CANADA

Government legislation in the area of workplace health and safety has, historically, had two major aims. First, it has been directed toward ensuring that the injured worker receives compensation and that the employer accepts liability for the injury. Second, it has sought to prevent accidents resulting in injury or illness by laying down minimum standards for safety in the workplace and providing a means of enforcing such standards. Workers' compensation legislation was introduced in the various Canadian provinces in the second decade of this century. Accident prevention legislation began earlier, in the second half of the 19th century with the introduction of health and safety legislation. Both types of legislation remain today in Canada, although their scope and direction have undergone major changes, particularly in the last decade.

It is important that those concerned with human resource management in Canadian industries have an understanding of the various types of health and safety legislation and their implications for human resource management strategies and programs.

The legislative framework in Canada and the effects of provincial or federal legislation on a particular workplace must also be understood, as should the trends and directions of health and safety legislation generally in Canada, so that they may be taken into account when company policies are designed. The way in which jurisdiction for health and safety is divided between the provincial and federal governments should also be understood, since it is possible for a large company to come under both provincial and federal jurisdiction.

Figure 17.1 illustrates the major health and safety laws of the federal and provincial governments and their various administrative bodies.

Jurisdictional Framework

Canada differs from the United States in the extent of federal jurisdiction for workplace health and safety. In Canada, there is no national equivalent to the U.S. Federal Occupational Safety and Health Act. By contrast, in Canada there are 13 different jurisdictions that regulate health and safety. The Constitution of Canada (Canada Act 1982) determines the parameters of federal and provincial jurisdiction over workplace health and safety. Under that act, the federal government's power to legislate is limited to federal government employees and to industries coming under federal jurisdiction. Federally-regulated industries include interprovincial railways, communications, pipelines, canals, ferries, shipping, air transport, banks, grain elevators, uranium mines, certain crown corporations, and atomic energy. Generally, the federal government's power to regulate is related to areas of national, international, or interprovincial nature. Each province, on the other hand, has wide regulatory powers over matters within its boundaries relating to the working environment and the employer/employee relationship in the workplace.

FIGURE 17.1
Health and Safety:
Major Acts and
Agencies

FEDERAL	**MAIN AGENCY**
Canada Labour Code, Part IV, amended 1984 (Applies to federal civil servants and to those workers in industries covered by federal jurisdiction, such as transportation, banking, broadcasting, and people working on grain elevators, pipelines, and nuclear power)	Labour Canada and Health and Welfare Canada
BRITISH COLUMBIA	
Workers' Compensation Act, 1979, amended 1980	Workers's Compensation Board
Industrial Health and Safety Retulations, amended 1979, Factory Act, 1979	
Occupation Environment Regulations, Mines Act, 1980 (for health and safety provisions)	
ALBERTA	
Occupational Health and Safety Act, 1976, amended 1983.	Community and Occupational Health Ministry
SASKATCHEWAN	
Occupational Health and Safety Act, 1977; Occupational Health and Safety Regulations, amended 1981	Department of Labour, Occupational Health and Safety Division
MANITOBA	
Workplace Safety and Health Act, 1976, amended 1983.	Department of Environment and Workplace Safety and Health
ONTARIO	
Occupational Health and Safety Act, 1978	Ministry of Labour, Occupational Health and Safety Division
QUEBEC	
An act Respecting Occupational Health and Safety, 1979; Environment Quality Act, 1977; Quality of the Work Environment, 1981; Worker's Compensation Act, 1964	Health and Safety Commission of the Department for Social Development (which consists of fifteen members—seven from labour, seven employers, and a full-time chairman appointed by the government)
NEW BRUNSWICK	
Occupational Health and Safety Act, 1983	Occupational Health and Safety Commission (which consists of seven members—three from labour, three employers, and an independent full-time chairperson appointed by government—and is responsible to the Ministry of Labour and Manpower)

NOVA SCOTIA

Industrial Safety Act, 1967, amended 1981; Health Act, 1967

Ministry of Labour, Occupational Safety (Industrial Safety) Division

Occupational Health Regulations, amended 1977

PRINCE EDWARD ISLAND

Workers' Compensation Act, 1974, amended 1980

Workers' Compensation Board

Industrial Safety Regulations, 1974

NEWFOUNDLAND

Occupational Health and Safety Act, 1978, amended 1980: The Workers' Compensation Act, 1970, amended 1980

Department of Labour and Manpower, Occupational Health and Safety Division

SOURCE: Dilly Robertson, "Occupational Health and Safety," *Human Resources Management in Canada* (Scarborough, Ont.: Prentice-Hall Canada Inc., 1987), pp. 60,028–60,030. Used with permission.

Thus, each province has its own health and safety legislation with its own unique features, although there are common themes and trends. In the Northwest Territories and the Yukon, territorial jurisdiction is exercised through a commissioner and a territorial government that has power to issue ordinances over a wide range of local matters, including health and safety. Some such ordinances—for example, Mining Safety and Workers' Compensation—deal specifically with occupational health and safety.

How Does Health and Safety Legislation in Canada Operate?

The major ways in which governments in Canada use legislation to exercise a degree of control over health and safety in the workplace are common to all jurisdictions. They are as follows:

- *By setting out general duty clauses in the legislation.* The effect of a general duty clause is to place an overall responsibility upon the party concerned. It can be a catch-all clause to be applied to a hazardous situation for which no specific regulation exists.

- *By issuing regulations under authority of the act.* Most of the provincial acts can be described as "enabling legislation" in the sense that they provide the government with authority to issue specific regulations on a wide range of health- and safety-related matters.

  Usually, regulations can be issued at any time to become effective. However, in some provinces, all or certain regulations must be the subject of public hearings or comment before they can be proclaimed.

- *By setting out statutory rights.* In provincial legislation in Canada, statutory rights are set out for employees that relate to the right to refuse to work, the right to involvement in joint committees, and the right to receive certain information.

- *Through enforcement procedures.* Enforcement procedures relate to the power of government-appointed inspectors to enter workplaces and issue orders where the act is not being complied with and, ultimately, to institute prosecutions for violations of the act. Generally, inspectors are given wide powers to issue orders, including shutting down a machine or an entire production process or facility.

- *By referencing standards and codes.* These may be referenced in legislation so that compliance, or proof of the intent of compliance, becomes mandatory; this is often the case with CSA Standards on personal protective equipment such as safety shoes.

GOVERNMENT ADMINISTRATIVE STRUCTURES FOR HEALTH AND SAFETY

Major changes have taken place in most of the provinces in recent years in the administrative structures applying to health and safety legislation. Two trends can be noted: consolidation of standard-setting and enforcement functions under one government body, and the establishment of tripartite, consultative, or policy-setting forums.

Essentially there are three functions concerned with government occupational health and safety administration: legal standard-setting and enforcement; workers' compensation; and accident-prevention education, information, and advice. These functions are not all integrated under one government agency in all of the provinces. The Government of Alberta, for instance, has recently moved in a somewhat different direction from other provinces in its administration of occupational health and safety. It has in fact combined community health (public health) with occupational health and safety to form a combined Community and Occupational Health Ministry. In other provinces (Quebec and New Brunswick), all these functions come under the general policy direction of a commission.

- In Newfoundland, Nova Scotia, Ontario and Saskatchewan, the major administering body for occupational health and safety legislation is the provincial ministry of labour

- In British Columbia and Prince Edward Island, the major administering body is the provincial workers' compensation board.

- Quebec and New Brunswick have established commissions that include labour and management representation, and these commissions effectively provide policy direction for the setting, administration, and enforcement of health and safety law, as well as compensation and accident prevention.

- Manitoba, Saskatchewan, Alberta, Ontario, and Prince Edward Island have advisory councils established through legislation which provide for representations from management and labour. The councils also provide their respective provincial ministers of labour with advice on health and safety matters.

- In most of the provinces, accident prevention information, advice, and education are provided through either the ministry of labour, the workers' compensation board, or the commission.

- In Ontario, the position is somewhat different in that accident prevention associations were established early in the century and their funding was ensured through statutory provisions in the workers' compensation act.

Although funding is provided through the WCBs, these associations are directed by volunteer directors from member companies. The largest two of these associations are the Construction Safety Association of Ontario and the Industrial Accident Prevention Association.

The Quebec Act allows for industrial sector-based associations to be set up through joint agreement between employers' associations and unions. Once established, the object of each sector-based association is to provide training and assistance to the workplaces in the sector. They are funded through the Commission.

An understanding of the governmental administrative structure for developing regulations, enforcing the law, providing education, and handling workers' compensation is important for those concerned with safety management so that reporting requirements to various government departments can be complied with and contacts and sources of information on health and safety matters can be identified.

Joint Health and Safety Committees

The federal government and all the provinces except Nova Scotia and Prince Edward Island have legal provisions requiring the establishment of **joint health and safety committees** for specified types of workplaces. The overall intent of governments is to place emphasis on the necessary role of workers in health and safety programs and to encourage employers to resolve health and safety problems through their own internal responsibility systems.

joint health and safety committees

The support of governments for the role of joint committees in occupational health and safety can be seen in two ways:

1. In the statutory provisions with regard to committees and their rights and responsibilities, and

2. In the way in which joint committees are drawn into the government inspection and enforcement process.

The legal role of joint committees varies between the provinces. In general, Quebec's and Saskatchewan's legislations give joint committees more legislative authority than do the other provinces. In any event, wherever joint committees are required by law, the human resource manager should ensure that they are encouraged and enabled to play an effective role in the company's health and safety program. Table 17.1 illustrates a list of types of information that should be provided to workers—when, how, and to whom.

Where Joint Committees Are Required

Basically two approaches are used. In some cases, joint committees must be established in every workplace covered by the relevant act where more than a specified number of people are employed, e.g., 29 or more in Ontario, and 10 or more in Newfoundland. In others, they are required in classes of industry so designated or by order of the minister in individual cases.

Accident Reporting and Investigation Requirements

In all of the Canadian jurisdictions, there are requirements for employers to report accidents causing injury or occupational diseases to the workers' compensation boards. These requirements are for the purposes of administering compensation and rehabilitation programs.

TABLE 17.1 Employees' or Representatives' Access to Information: Information to be Provided by Employer

TYPE OF INFORMATION PROVIDED	WHEN & HOW	TO WHOM
Names and work locations of Joint Health and Safety Committee members	permanently posted in the workplace	Workers
Copy of the Act and any explanatory material published by the Ministry	permanently posted in the workplace, in English and majority language.	Workers
Copy of written health and safety policy	prominently posted in the workplace	Workers
Results of health and safety reports and copies of written reports	to be made available to:	JHSC or Rep.
	to be advised of results and provided copies, upon request	Workers
If prescribed to keep exposure records of workers, who have access to those records	to be made available	To each worker his or her exposure record
Where required to do air sampling under regulation, air sampling results	post in workplace	Workers
Measures and procedures, where required to have these by regulation	when applicable, in writing	Affected Workers
Director's order made under S.20	post in workplace, and on receipt from Director, copies to:	Workers, JHSC or Rep.
A Ministry inspector's order or report	post in workplace, with copies to:	Workers, JHSC or Rep.
Employer's notice of compliance with inspector's order	post in workplace	Workers
Notices required to be sent to Ministry in cases of injury, death or accident	at the same time as provided to the Ministry, copies to:	JHSC members or Rep., and Trade Union
Necessary information required by JHSC member or representative for carrying out workplace inspection	as required for inspection	designated worker JHSC member, or Rep.
Health and safety experience and work practices of similar industries, of which the employer is aware	as requested	JHSC members or Rep.
Annual summary of workplace injury experience received by employer from WCB in response to request from any person in the work place	post in workplace	Workers

Where a designated substance regulation applies, assessment results	copies to:	each JHSC member
Control program for designated substance, where applicable	copies to: acquaint with its provisions: and make available in English and majority language:	each JHSC member affected Workers Workers
Inventory of hazardous materials and hazardous physical agents	copies to be made available to:	Workers, JHSC, or Rep.
Floor plan showing names and locations of all hazardous materials	to be accessible to:	Workers
Notice of location of floor plan	post in workplace	Workers
Unexpired material safety data sheets (MSDSs)	to be made available to:	Workers, JHSC, or Rep.
Hazardous Materials Assessment	to be made available to:	—as above—
Information on things that emit hazardous physical agents	to be made available to:	—as above—
Warning signs in locations of above	post in locations	Workers

SOURCE: *A Guide to the Provisions of Ontario's Occupational Health and Safety Act, 9th ed.* (Toronto: Industrial Accident Prevention Association, 1990), pp. 28-29. Used with permission.

Regardless of the particular legal provisions that apply in a jurisdiction, the following are, in practical terms, important components of any effective health and safety plant program:

- All accidents that have caused an injury or have the potential to cause serious injury should be investigated by a trained, competent person or team.

- The purpose of such investigations should be to identify all the circumstances (conditions, acts, procedures) that contributed to the accident and to determine the steps that can be taken to prevent a recurrence.

- Records of all accidents and serious incidents should be kept; such records enable regular analysis to be made of the types of accidents occurring, their frequency, causes, etc.

Immediate Notification/Written Reports

Most jurisdictions, as a minimum, require immediate notification to the responsible ministry of any accident that causes a death or a critical injury or in the event of an explosion whether or not injuries were caused. Such notification must be done by telephone or telegram. In some jurisdictions (e.g., Alberta and New Brunswick) such immediate notification also applies to accidents that have the potential to cause serious injury. Quebec requires immediate notification in the case of a death, where one worker is disabled for 10 consecutive days, where several workers are disabled for one day or more, or where property damage in excess of $50 000 has been caused by the accident.

Most jurisdictions also require, in addition to immediate telephone or telegram notification, that a written report be submitted within a specified time. The details required include such matters as the circumstances leading to the accident, probable causes, preventive steps to be taken to avoid such accidents in future, and names and addresses of witnesses. Ontario and Manitoba, for example, specify the type of information to be included in such written reports.

There is usually also a requirement to notify the appropriate ministry when an employer is informed that an employee has contracted an occupational disease or illness.

Note that "critical injury" is defined in a regulation under Ontario's Act; "serious injury" is defined in a regulation under Alberta's Act. These definitions are important since they determine the type of accidents for which the special reporting requirements apply under the respective Acts.

Duty to Investigate Accidents

Some jurisdictions place a specific duty on the employer to investigate accidents. Companies coming under federal jurisdiction are under a duty to have a suitably qualified person investigate any accident and to take remedial action. There is a similar requirement in Newfoundland and British Columbia. In B.C., the duty to investigate applies to any accidents that caused death, a critical injury, or an injury requiring medical attention, or accidents that might have caused serious injuries. The information to be contained in such investigation reports is prescribed and copies must be given to the workers' compensation board and to the health and safety committee. In Alberta, employers must undertake an investigation for accidents that caused serious injury or an injury requiring medical attention, or accidents that might have caused serious injuries. Section 6 of British Columbia's Industrial Health and Safety Regulations, that serves as a useful guide to any thorough accident investigation report, lays a duty on the employer to ensure that an accident investigation report is prepared containing:

- the place, date, and time of the accident;
- the names and job titles of persons injured in the accident;
- the names of witnesses;
- a brief account of the accident, including a statement of the events that preceded the accident;
- identification of any unsafe conditions, acts, or procedures that contributed in any manner to the accident;
- corrective action recommended to prevent similar accidents; and
- the names of persons who investigated the accident.[2]

EMPLOYEES' RIGHTS TO SAFE AND HEALTHY WORK ENVIRONMENTS

A distinctive feature of the reforms that have taken place in most Canadian health and safety legislations is the provision of protection for a worker's right to refuse unsafe work. Prior to such reforms, workers had a right under common law to refuse work that would put them in imminent danger. It should be noted that most existing legislation laid a duty on workers not to do unsafe work. However, pursuing such rights in common law was usually expensive, difficult, and time consuming, and was therefore never a practical right for most workers.[3]

When the right was first introduced into legislation in various provinces, many employers expressed concern that the right would be abused—particularly by trade unions—and that this legal right would prove to be potentially disruptive to industry. However, with few exceptions, these fears have so far proved to be generally unfounded. An employee's right to refuse work considered unsafe is not based on that worker's ability to demonstrate that a work hazard exists. In most instances all that is required of the worker is to demonstrate that there is "reason to believe" that the work is unsafe and hazardous. It is important to note that in most Canadian jurisdictions this right is not extended to certain type of jobs. For example, in Ontario workers in hospitals, police officers, fire fighters, workers in correctional institutions, etc. are specifically excluded.[4]

Most of the health and safety acts established by the federal, provincial, and territorial governments provide ample detail of a worker's right to refuse work and the procedure that should be followed in the event that a worker exercises that right.

Most of the acts state that a worker may not be disciplined for exercising his or her right to perform a duty as laid down by relevant health and safety acts. This does not mean that the employer cannot discipline an employee who refuses to work. If the employer were to discipline a worker, the worker could complain that the discipline was in effect a penalty. When this happens the onus is on the employer to prove that the worker was not exercising his or her right under the act but was acting frivolously and unreasonably.[5]

Many of the acts are silent as to whether an employer may reassign another worker to work refused on grounds of safety, if the employer believes that no hazard exists. One act (in Ontario) states that another worker may be reassigned to do the work (pending investigation and resolution) provided that the worker is informed of the original employee's refusal and the reason for it. Figure 17.2 illustrates the sequences of steps that must be followed in Ontario when a worker has reason to believe work is likely to endanger him- or herself or another person.

WHAT CAUSES ACCIDENTS?

Unsafe Conditions

As the word itself suggests, chance occurances are sometimes causes of "accidents." In reality, unsafe conditions are one main cause of accidents. They include such things as:

- improperly guarded equipment
- defective equipment
- hazardous arrangement or procedure in, on, or around, machines or equipment
- unsafe storage—congestion, overloading
- improper illumination—glare, insufficient light
- improper ventilation—insufficient air change, impure air source[6]

While accidents can happen anywhere, there are some "high danger" zones. About one-third of industrial accidents occur around forklift trucks, wheelbarrows, and other handling and lifting areas, for example. The most serious accidents usually occur near metal and woodworking machines and saws, or around transmission machinery like gears, pulleys, and flywheels. Falls—on stairs, ladders, walkways, and scaffolds—are the third most common cause of industrial accidents. Hand tools (like chisels and screwdrivers), and electrical equipment (extension cords, electric drop lights, etc.) are other big accident causers.[7]

On a day-to-day basis many supervisors find that a brief checklist of "unsafe conditions" can be very useful for spotting problems. One such checklist is presented in Figure 17.3.

Personal Traits and "Unsafe Acts"

There is little doubt that unsafe acts (not unsafe conditions) are the major cause of accidents, and that people cause these unsafe acts.

Most safety experts and managers long ago discovered that it is impossible to eliminate accidents simply by reducing unsafe conditions. This is because people cause accidents, and to date no one has found a sure-fire way to make employees work safely. The result is a number of unsafe acts like:

- failing to secure equipment
- failing to use safe attire or personal protective equipment
- throwing materials
- operating or working at unsafe speeds, either too fast or too slow
- making safety devices inoperative by removing, adjusting, disconnecting them
- using unsafe equipment, or using equipment unsafely

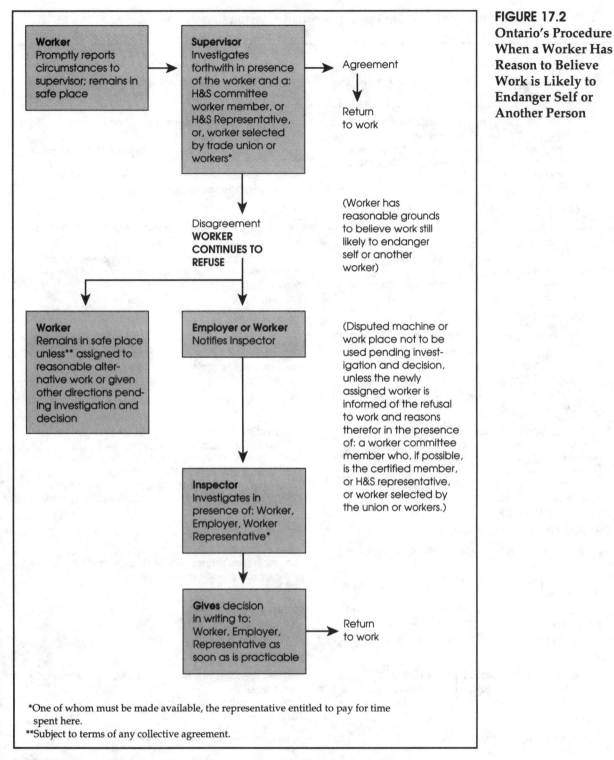

FIGURE 17.2
Ontario's Procedure When a Worker Has Reason to Believe Work is Likely to Endanger Self or Another Person

Worker	Supervisor
Promptly reports circumstances to supervisor; remains in safe place	Investigates forthwith in presence of the worker and a: H&S committee worker member, or H&S Representative, or, worker selected by trade union or workers*

Agreement → Return to work

Disagreement
WORKER CONTINUES TO REFUSE

(Worker has reasonable grounds to believe work still likely to endanger self or another worker)

Worker
Remains in safe place unless** assigned to reasonable alternative work or given other directions pending investigation and decision

Employer or Worker
Notifies Inspector

(Disputed machine or work place not to be used pending investigation and decision, unless the newly assigned worker is informed of the refusal to work and reasons therefor in the presence of: a worker committee member who, if possible, is the certified member, or H&S representative, or worker selected by the union or workers.)

Inspector
Investigates in presence of: Worker, Employer, Worker Representative*

Gives decision in writing to: Worker, Employer, Representative as soon as is practicable

Return to work

*One of whom must be made available, the representative entitled to pay for time spent here.
**Subject to terms of any collective agreement.

SOURCE: *A Guide to the Provisions of Ontario Occupational Health and Safety Act, 9th ed.* (Toronto: Industrial Prevention Association, 1990), p.21. Used with permission.

FIGURE 17.3 Checklist of Mechanical or Physical Accident-Causing Conditions

I. General Housekeeping

Adequate and wide aisles—no materials protruding into aisles

Parts and tools stored safely after use—not left in hazardous positions that could cause them to fall

Even and solid flooring—no defective floors or ramps that could cause falling or tripping accidents

Waste cans and sand pails—safely located and properly used

Material piled in safe manner—not too high or too close to sprinkler heads

Floors—clean and dry

Firefighting equipment—unobstructed

Work benches orderly

Stockcarts and skids safely located, not left in aisles or passageways

Aisles kept clear and properly marked—no air lines or electric cords across aisles

II. Material Handling Equipment and Conveyances

On all conveyances, electric or hand, check to see that the following items are all in sound working conditions:

Brakes—properly adjusted

Not too much play in steering wheel

Warning device—in place and working

Wheels—securely in place; properly inflated

Fuel and oil—enough and right kind

No loose parts

Cables, hoods or chains—not worn or otherwise defective

Suspended chains or hoods—conspicuous

Safely loaded

Properly stored

III. Ladders, Scaffold, Benches, Stairways, etc.

The following items of major interest to be checked:

Safety feet on straight ladders

Guard rails or hand rails

Treads, not slippery

Not splintered, cracked or rickety

Properly stored

Extension ladder ropes in good condition

Toe boards

IV. Power Tools (stationary)

Point of operation guarded

Guards in proper adjustment

Gears, belts, shafting, counterweights guarded

Foot pedals guarded

Brushes provided for cleaning machines

Adequate lighting

Properly grounded

Tool or material rests properly adjusted

Adequate work space around machines

Control switch easily accessible

Safety glasses worn

Gloves worn by persons handling rough or sharp materials

No gloves or loose clothing worn by persons operating machines

V. Hand Tools and Miscellaneous

In good condition—not cracked, worn, or otherwise defective

Properly stored

Correct for job

Goggles, respirators, and other personal protective equipment worn where necessary

VI. Welding

Arc shielded

Fire hazards controlled

Operator using suitable protective equipment

Adequate ventilation

Cylinder secured

Valves closed when not in use

VII. Spray Painting

Explosion-proof electrical equipment

Proper storage of paints and thinners in approved metal cabinets

Fire extinguishers adequate and suitable; readily accessible

Minimum storage in work area

VIII. Spray Painting

Properly serviced and tagged

Readily accessible

Adequate and suitable for operations involved

SOURCE: Courtesy of the American Insurance Association. From "A Safety Committee Man's Guide," 1-64

- using unsafe procedures in loading, placing, mixing, combining
- taking unsafe positions under suspended loads
- lifting improperly
- directing, teasing, abusing, startling, quarrelling, and horseplaying[8]

Unsafe acts like these can short-circuit even the best attempts to minimize unsafe conditions.

METHODS OF REDUCING UNSAFE ACTS

Basic Approaches to Preventing Accidents[9]

In practice, accident prevention boils down to two basic activities: reducing unsafe conditions and reducing unsafe acts. Reducing unsafe conditions is primarily in the domain of safety engineers: their task is to remove or reduce physical hazards. (However, supervisors and managers also play a role in reducing unsafe conditions, particularly with regard to identifying and eliminating unsafe conditions like unguarded machinery and slippery floors.) Reducing unsafe acts, on the other hand, is an activity in which supervisors and managers play a major role. Methods for reducing unsafe acts include selection and placement, persuasion, training, and behaviour modification.

Reducing Unsafe Acts Through Selection and Placement

One way to reduce accidents is to screen out "accident-prone" individuals before they are hired. Psychologists have in fact had some success in screening out persons who might be accident-prone for some specific job. The basic technique involves identifying the personal factor (such as visual skill) that might be related to accidents on the job, then determining whether scores (on this characteristic) are indeed related to accidents on the job. Biographical (application blank) data, tests, and interview questions are some of the tools that can be used.

THE PROBLEM OF JOB STRESS

Stress is the general term applied to feelings of anxiety, tension, pressure, and **stress** other types of physical and psychological discomfort that individuals experience.[10] When stress begins to build it can have adverse consequences on an individual's emotions, thought processes, and physical condition. When stress becomes excessive, the affected employee may develop various symptoms of stress that can harm his or her health, job productivity, and even threaten the ability to cope with either the work environment or his or her private life. Figure 17.4 illustrates some common symptoms of stress. As can be seen some of the symptoms of stress include tension, anxiety, alcohol abuse, sleep disorders, and job dissatisfaction.

Probably one of the most frequent manifestations of stress is alcohol abuse. (See Chapter 14 for a comprehensive discussion of this problem.) Table 17.2 illustrates some observable patterns that indicate alcohol-related problems. As can be seen, alcohol-related problems range from tardiness (in the earliest stages of alcohol abuse) to prolonged unpredictable absences in its later stages.[11]

TABLE 17.2 Observable Behaviour Patterns Indicating Alcohol-Related Problems

STAGE	ABSENTEEISM	GENERAL BEHAVIOR	JOB PERFORMANCE
I Early	Tardiness Quits early Absence from work situations ("I drink to relieve tension")	Complaints from fellow employees for not doing his or her share Overreaction Complaints of not "feeling well" Makes untrue statements	Misses deadlines Commits errors (frequently) Lower job efficiency Criticism from the boss
II Middle	Frequent days off for vague or implausible reasons ("I feel guilty about sneaking drinks"; "I have tremors")	Marked changes Undependable statements Avoids fellow employees Borrows money from fellow employees Exaggerates work accomplishments Frequent hospitalization Minor injuries on the job (repeatedly)	General deterioration Cannot concentrate Occasional lapse of memory Warning from boss
III Late Middle	Frequent days off; several days at a time Does not return from lunch ("I don't feel like eating"; "I don't want to talk about it"; "I like to drink alone")	Aggressive and belligerent behavior Domestic problems interfere with work Financial difficulties (garnishments, and so on) More frequent hospitalization Resignation: does not want to discuss problems Problems with the laws in the community	Far below expectation Punitive disciplinary action
IV Approaching	Prolonged unpredictable ab-	Drinking on the job (probably)	Uneven

TABLE 17.2
(continued)

Terminal Stage	sences ("My job interferes with my drinking")	Completely undependable Repeated hospitalization Serious financial problems Serious family problems: divorce	Generally incompetent Faces termination or hospitalization

Note: Based on content analysis of files of recovered alcoholics in five organizations. From *Managing and Employing the Handicapped: The Untapped Potential,* by Gopal C. Pati and John Adkins, Jr., with Glenn Morrison (Lake Forest, Ill.: Brace-Park, Human Resource Press, 1981).

SOURCE: Gopal C. Pati and John I. Adkins, Jr., "The Employer's Role in Alcoholism Assistance," *Personnel Journal,* Vol. 62, no. 7 (July 1983), p. 570.

The Canadian Institute of Stress estimated in 1991 that job stress costs Canadian business over $15.4 billion annually. This cost is reflected in lowered productivity, disability payments, and replacement payments.[12]

Stress can lead to physical disorders that result from changes in an individual's internal body system when it attempts to adjust and cope with the stress.[13] The duration and intensity of stress may be either temporary or long-term, mild or severe. The severity of the impact of stress depends on how powerful its symptoms and causes are and on the individual's ability to both cope with and recover from it. Stress can affect shop floor employees as much as executives.

Causes of Stress

Conditions or factors that cause stress are known as stressors. There are two major types of stressors, these are job-related (environmental) factors and individual factors.

Job Factors

A variety of job factors can lead to stress. Figure 17.5 illustrates the various causes of job stress. As can be seen, work-related stress arises from a variety of sources. It

---

Tension and anxiety	Heart disease
Anger and aggression	Irritability and boredom
Increased smoking or consumption of alcohol	Sleep disorders
Changes in appetite and digestive problems	Reduced productivity
Job dissatisfaction and increased absenteeism	Increased blood pressure
Increased incidents of sexual problems	Chronic worry and inability to relax
Lack of concentration	Increased accidents
	Substance abuse
	Forgetfulness
	High cholesterol levels
	Reduced commitment to the organization

FIGURE 17.4
Typical Symptoms of Stress

Using Computers to Monitor Safety

Companies that must comply with federal and provincial health and safety laws are obligated to file federal and provincial reports, to monitor employee exposure to various hazards, and note trends, and to provide employees with information on hazards in their workplaces. Computers can assist in all three areas.

if, for example, a given decibel level indicates increased friction. Trends of various hazards can also be plotted for work redesign to make the workplace safer.

Reporting

Most federal and provincial forms can be formatted and formulated on a company's computer so that only the raw data needs to be entered. The computer will perform the instructed calculations and print out the results in an acceptable format. If a piece of information has been input in error, only that figure needs to be changed. Recalculations are automatic. With some forms, the typing of results takes several hours. This task is completed in minutes with a computer.

The federal government is encouraging increased use of computers. Integration Management Information Systems (IMIS) was established to find ways in which computers can facilitate agency work. Rather than completing forms by hand that then must be keyed by data entry clerks, computers can facilitate the entering of data directly.

Monitoring

Computers can track personal exposure level (PEL) for noise, particulate, vapours, or other contaminates for a given location, giving timely warnings of trigger points. A dosimeter sensor can be plugged directly into a personal computer to translate readings on an hourly basis. Not only does this protect, say, the hearing of workers, but it can also spot equipment that needs servicing

Communicating

The effectiveness of training in any area depends in part on the Hawthorne Effect: the degree to which the student feels that the training is important and accurate. In communicating the hazards of a workplace, employees might not listen because they feel that they will not be exposed to those particular hazards, or that they are already careful, or that their work situation does not support those safeguards. If the supervisors push for results to the point of ignoring torn gloves, holes in respirators, inadequate ventilation, or workers who are not wearing safety glasses, then employees will ignore the training. Also, employees may not understand key parts of the training.

Interactive computers can help with some of these problems. If an employee is assigned to work with a hazardous substance that was discussed with her or him a few weeks before, the knowledge may have become hazy. Access to personal computer can allow the employee to refresh her or his memory on how to handle the substance and what to avoid doing. If there are words within the explanation that are not clear, an interactive program will allow the employee to question that word (and any words in the subsequent definition) until she or he is ready to return to the original explanation. How recently an employee has reviewed the information correlates with the degree of retention, and computer-assisted instruction provides training anytime the employee needs help.

may result from role ambiguities, work overload, time pressures, or interpersonal conflicts with coworkers, subordinates, supervisors or clients. For instance role ambiguity[14] exists when there is a lot of uncertainty surrounding job expectations, job definition, and the scope of the individual's responsibilities. Individuals who do not know how their jobs will be evaluated can be experience a great deal of stress.

Work overload and time[15] pressures are causes of stress when individuals are asked to produce much more than they are capable of, or much more than is reasonable. Time pressures can result in high anxiety and high stress when individuals are asked to meet unrealistic deadlines.

Health and Safety Aspects of Alcohol and Drug Use

There is a high correlation between heavy use of alcohol or drugs and health and safety problems in the workplace, according to Bruce Cunningham, a consultant for the Addiction Research Foundation of Ontario.

Speaking at a conference on Drug Testing in the Workplace, organized by the Canadian Centre for Occupational Health and Safety, Mr. Cunningham noted that there is evidence of such a relationship from working with people who are undergoing treatment for a dependency problem. "People in treatment centres, whether they're referred from the workplace or seek help on their own, frequently report poor work performance, behaviour that proved a cost to the organization, and a higher frequency of accidents than would normally be expected."

There is evidence of such a relationship too in looking at persons referred to employee assistance programs. Their performance, he said, improves tremendously in the year after treatment.

More striking evidence of a relationship between alcohol and drug use and workplace accidents comes from surveys conducted by the Addiction Research Foundation which correlated what people said about the amount of alcohol or drugs they used and the extent to which their work activity was curtailed by injuries (on or off the job) during the past year. As shown in the accompanying tables, "once we get beyond the people who don't drink at all, we have an almost linear relationship. As reported frequency of usage went up, people having to curtail their work activity also went up." (Mr. Cunningham noted that among the non-drinkers, for whom the injury rate was higher than for those consuming less than 2 drinks a day, there may have been some people who used to drink heavily).

"We're convinced," said Cunningham, "that there is some risk to health and safety in the workplace from the consumption of alcohol and other drugs." They may not cause many accidents by themselves, but they are probably a factor in some.

There are various ways of intervening, he said. Education of the work force about the health and safety risks associated with the use of alcohol and drugs can be a powerful weapon. "In a study of 100 people who were arrested for marijuana use, the ones who said they intended to stop cited health concerns based on information they had received as the reason for stopping." Many other interventions also have been found to be effective, including training supervisors to recognize some of the patterns that indicate a person is moving in the direction of becoming a safety risk, employee assistance programs, union counselling programs, and alerting security staff. "In some situations, urine tests may be relevant for certain jobs."

RELATIONSHIP BETWEEN ALCOHOL USE AND LOST TIME INJURIES IN 1987

Alcohol use	Employees surveyed	Number with lost time injuries	% of total
Average daily alcohol consumption			
0 drinks	404	12	3.0
>2 drinks	739	13	1.8
2-3 drinks	52	3	5.8
3-4 drinks	31	2	6.5
>4 drinks	35	4	11.4

RELATIONSHIP BETWEEN DRUG USE AND LOST TIME INJURIES IN 1987

Drug use	Employees surveyed	Number with lost time injuries	% of total
Never used drugs	1 163	29	2.4
Rarely used drugs	116	6	5.2
Occasionally/Often used drugs	84	6	7.1

SOURCE: Addiction Research Foundation, *The Worklife Report*, Vol. 6, No. 2, 1988, p. 4.

FIGURE 17.5
Some Causes of Job Stress

Role ambiguity	Frustrations
Task demands	Interpersonal conflicts
Career concerns	Time pressures
Work overload	Organizational climate
Management style	Work schedule
Job secutiry	Design of the individual's job
Pressures created by other employees	

Individual Factors

A variety of personal factors can lead to stress. A major personal factor that can produce stress is both magnitude and frequencies of changes in an individual's life. For example, a major change such as the death of a spouse or a divorce can have a very strong impact on an individual's health. Two researchers[16] have developed a 100 point scale which shows what degree of stress different factors generate. Table 17.3 illustrates the scale of stressful life events. An individual may use this scale by reading each of the events and checking those that have happened to them during the past 12 months. The points are then totalled.

The researchers found that if a person experiences changes that add up to more than 200 scale points in a given year, he or she has a 50-50 chance of incurring a serious health problem in the upcoming year. If a person experiences changes which add up to more than 300 scale points in a given year, then he or she has a 75% chance of developing serious health problems in the following year.

Stress and the Individual Personality

No two people will react to the same job in the very same way, since personal factors also influence the person's stress. For example, "Type A" personalities—people who are "workaholics" and who feel driven to always be on time and meet deadlines—normally place themselves under greater stress than do others. Similarly, a person's impatience, self-esteem, health and exercise, tolerance for ambiguity, and work and sleep patterns can similarly affect how he or she reacts to stress.

Yet job stress is not always bad. DuBrin makes the point that some stress can actually have positive consequences for the person and the organization. Some people, for example, only work well under at least modest stress, and find they are more productive as a deadline approaches. Others find that stress may result in a search that leads to a better job or to a career that makes more sense given the person's aptitudes. A modest level of stress may even lead to more creativity if a competitive situation results in new ideas being generated.[17] As a rule, however, employers do not worry about the sorts of modest stress that lead to such positive consequences. Instead, and for obvious reasons, they focus on dysfunctional stress and its negative consequences.

Dr. Selye has defined stress as the non-specific response of the body to any demand placed upon it. In other words, it is the way in which the body produces the appropriate energy to adapt to the demand being faced. An example would be the body's production of adrenalin in response to a frightening situation. Stress, of itself, cannot be good or bad—it is simply part of the reality of living and the

TABLE 17.3 Relative Weights of Life Changes

Life Event	Scale Value
Death of spouse	100
Divorce	73
Marital separation	65
Jail term	63
Death of a close family member	63
Major personal injury or illness	53
Marriage	50
Fired from work	47
Marital reconciliation	45
Retirement	45
Major change in health of family member	44
Pregnancy	40
Sex difficulties	39
Gain of a new family member	39
Business readjustment	39
Change in financial state	38
Death of a close friend	37
Change to a different line of work	36
Change in number of arguments with spouse	35
Mortgage or loan for major purchase (home, etc.)	31
Foreclosure of mortgage or loan	30
Change in responsibilities at work	29
Son or daughter leaving home	29
Trouble with in-laws	29
Outstanding personal achievement	28
Spouse begins or stops work	26
Begin or end school	26
Change in living conditions	25
Revision of personal habits	24
Trouble with boss	23
Change in work hours or conditions	20
Change in residence	20
Change in schools	20
Change in recreation	19
Change in church activities	19
Change in social activities	18
Mortgage or loan for lesser purchase (car, etc.)	17
Change in sleeping habits	16
Change in number of family get-togethers	15
Change in eating habits	15
Vacation	13
Christmas	12
Minor violations of the law	11

SOURCE: T.H. Holmes and L.O. Rahe, "Scaling of Life Change: Composition of Direct and Indirect Methods," *Journal of Psychosomatic Research*, 15 (1971). Used with permission.

process of adapting to different demands and situations; however, each individual's reaction to stressors differs. It has been demonstrated that over a period of time, stress can result in physical harm, such as high blood pressure, heart attacks, or peptic ulcers. While a certain amount of stress is both necessary and inevitable in daily life, chronic overexposure to stressful situations will result in health impairment and affect job performance.[18]

BURNOUT—A COMPANION PROBLEM OF STRESS

burnout

Burnout is the feeling that individuals experience of total depletion of all physical and mental resources. Dr. Herbert Freudenberger, an expert on the overachiever, defined burnout as the total depletion of all physical and mental resources caused by excessive striving to reach some unrealistic work-related goal. Burnout, he contends, is often the end result of too much job stress, especially when that stress is combined with the fact that an individual becomes preoccupied with attaining unattainable work-related goals. In his book, *Burnout: How to Beat the High Cost of Success*, Freudenberger lists some of these other signs of possible impending burnout.[19] These are listed in Figure 17.6.

Who Suffers from Burnout?

Burnout, Freudenberger says, is mostly limited to dynamic goal-oriented individuals or idealists who are overdedicated to whatever they undertake. The potential burnout victim thrives on intensity, often setting his or her life to lurch from crisis to crisis, deadline to deadline. Burnout victims usually don't lead well-balanced lives, in that virtually all their energies are focused on achieving their work-related goals. The burnout victim is usually a workaholic for whom the constant stress of seeking unattainable goals to the exclusion of other activities can lead to physical and perhaps mental collapse. Figure 17.7 provides a burnout checklist.

Stress Management

The management of stress, as far as the individual is concerned, concentrates on helping the individual to cope with stress and avoid overexposure to stress-causing situations.[20]

There are a number of things that can be done to alleviate stress, ranging from common-sense remedies such as getting more sleep and eating better (so as to build up resistance to stress) to more exotic remedies such as biofeedback and meditation. Finding a more suitable job, getting counselling, and planning and organizing each day's activities are other sensible responses.[21] In this book "Stress and the Manager," Dr. Karl Albercht suggests the following to reduce stress on the job.[22]

- Build rewarding, pleasant, cooperative relationships with as many colleagues and employees as possible
- Do not bite off more than can be chewed
- Build an especially effective and supportive relationship with supervisors
- Understand the boss's problems and help the boss to understand the subordinate's
- Negotiate realistic deadlines on important projects with the boss. Be prepared to propose deadlines, instead of having them imposed

FIGURE 17.6
The Burnout Checklist

	Mostly True	Mostly False
1. I feel tired more frequently than I used to.	_____	_____
2. I snap at people too often.	_____	_____
3. Trying to help other people often seems hopeless.	_____	_____
4. I seem to be working harder but accomplishing less.	_____	_____
5. I get down on myself too often.	_____	_____
6. My job is beginning to depress me.	_____	_____
7. I often feel I'm headed nowhere.	_____	_____
8. I've reached (or am fast reaching) a dead end in my job.	_____	_____
9. I've lost a lot of my zip lately.	_____	_____
10. It's hard for me to laugh at a joke about myself.	_____	_____
11. I'm not really physically ill, but I have a lot of aches and pains.	_____	_____
12. Lately I've kind of withdrawn from friends and family.	_____	_____
13. My enthusiasm for life in on the wane.	_____	_____
14. I'm running out of things to say to people.	_____	_____
15. My temper is much shorter than it used to be.	_____	_____
16. My job makes me feel sad.	_____	_____

Interpretation: The more of these questions you can honestly answer mostly true, the more likely it is that you are experiencing burnout. If you answered twelve or more of these statements mostly true, it is likely you are experiencing burnout or another form of mental depression. If so, discuss these feelings with a physical or mental health professional.

SOURCE: A.J. Dubrin, *Contemporary Applied Management* (Plano, Texas: Business Publications, 1982), p. 243. Reprinted with permission. The checklist is based in part on the questionnaire printed on the dust jacket of *Burn Out* by Freudenberger.

FIGURE 17.7
Symptoms of Burnout

Inability to relax.

Tendency to identify too closely with activities.

The positions that the individual worked so hard to attain often seem meaningless once reached.

Increased work activities but decreased enjoyment.

Increasing need for a particular crutch such as smoking, liquor, or tranquilizers.

Constant irritability—family and friends often comment that the individual does not look well.

The individual is described as a workaholic constantly striving to obtain work-related goals to the exclusion of almost all outside interest.

Quebec Crown Attorneys Suffer High Burnout Rate

MONTREAL—A new study shows that more than 50% of Quebec's 250 Crown attorneys are suffering from stress-related burnout, and that one in five needs treatment for psychiatric problems and alcoholism. Jean-Pierre Major, president of the Quebec Association of Crown Attorneys, which commissioned the study, says that the 90 Crown attorneys working in Montreal, for example, handle more than 25 000 criminal prosecutions a year, and are often called upon to make up to 40 court appearances a day. A report issued last year by the Quebec justice ministry found that the work of Crown attorneys begins to suffer after 15 daily court appearances. The current situation has led to lawyers not having a chance to read files or meet clients before arriving in court. Major says the provincial government should hire more Crown attorneys, provide treatment for those suffering from work-related problems, build more courts, and conceive a better system to rehabilitate prisoners so they do not return to a life of crime. The study also found that 99% of Crown attorneys are dissatisfied with their employer—the justice ministry—and that 81% believe the legal system is suffering because they are overworked. The association has hired one of the study's researchers, Dr. Shimon Dolan, to refer attorneys in the advanced stages of burnout to psychiatrists, cardiologists, alcohol and drug-treatment centres, and fitness programs.

SOURCE: *Human Resources Management in Canada*. Report Bulletin no. 80 (Scarborough, Ont.: Prentice Hall Canada Inc., October 1989), p. 2. Used with permission.

Truck Driver First to Get Compensation for Stress

TORONTO—A long-haul truck driver has become what's believed to be the first Canadian worker to get workers' compensation because of chronic stress on the job. The driver, who isn't named in the judgement, was laid off in June 1985 because of dizziness, headaches, and fainting. He lost his original case with the Workers' Compensation Board in 1986, but won in late April before the board's appeals tribunal. The driver had 32 years of trucking experience, beginning when he was 16 years old. His job-related stress included having to supervise a driver who routinely used narcotics while driving and another trucker who wouldn't drive at night at more than 65 kilometres an hour. The driver routinely made runs from North Bay and Sudbury to Vancouver, covering nearly 190 000 kilometres between July 1984 and June 1985. On one trip, he nearly ran over the body of a dead driver, and on another, he had to drag two children out of a smashed truck past the body of their dead grandmother. The board noted that although the driver felt no immediate effects from his exposure to the accident, every time he drove by that particular spot on the highway he visualized the grandmother's dead body. The case may mean that other workers suffering chronic job stress are eligible for compensation as well. It has not been decided how much the driver will receive.

SOURCE: *Human Resources Management in Canada*. Report Bulletin no. 88. (Scarborough, Ont.: Prentice-Hall Canada Inc., 1990). Used with permission.

- Study the future. Learn as much as possible about likely coming events and get as much lead time as possible to prepare for them
- Find time every day for detachments and relaxation
- Take a walk now and then to keep the body refreshed and alert
- Make a noise survey of the office area and find ways to reduce unnecessary racket
- Get away from the office from time to time for a change of scene and change of mind

- Reduce the amount of trivia to which attention is given. Delegate routine paperwork to others whenever possible
- Limit interruptions. Try to schedule certain periods of "uninterruptibility" each day and conserve other periods for own purposes
- Know how to delegate effectively
- Do not put off dealing with distasteful problems such as counselling a problem employee
- Make a constructive "worry list." Write down the problems that are of concern and beside each write down what should be done about it, so that problems do not simply hover.

Implications for Human Resource Management

The subject of stress is important, not only because of the effects on the working organization (productivity, absenteeism, accident rates, etc.) but also because, to some extent at least, it is associated with the growing concern for the quality of working life. Some implications for the human resource managers are:

- Medical programs to identify individuals whose health may be being affected by stress
- The establishment of employee fitness programs
- Employee counselling programs
- Individual stress-management programs that help individuals learn to cope with stress
- Work design and organization—knowledge of stressors in work situations may be taken into account in the redesign of work or the introduction of a new organizational structure

The organization and its human resource specialists and supervisors also play a big role in identifying and remedying job stress. For the supervisor, this typically involves monitoring each subordinate's performance in order to identify the symptoms of stress and then informing the person of the organizational remedies that may be available, such as job transfers or counselling. The human resource specialist's role includes using attitude surveys to identify organizational sources of stress (such as high-pressure jobs), refining selection and placement procedures to ensure the most effective people-job match, and making available career planning aimed at ensuring that the employee moves toward a job that makes sense in terms of his or her aptitudes and aspirations.

DRUG TESTING

A controversy concerning drug testing and employment has surfaced recently in the media.[23] Fears have been raised that employers could use **drug testing** as a means of screening out applicants or ridding themselves of employees they consider undesirable. The potential for human rights abuses is great. In response to the debate surrounding drug testing, both the Ontario Human Rights Commission (OHRC) and the Canadian Human Rights commission (CHRC) issued policies in recent years on employment-related drug testing.

    The OHRC policy, announced on October 23, 1987, prohibits testing for drug and alcohol use during the application and interview stages. This policy is part of

drug testing

the OHRC's broader policy on employment-related medical examinations. In other words, the OHRC considers a drug test to be a medical test, which is prohibited at the pre-employment stage. Employment-related medicals are considered "reasonable and bona fide" by the OHRC in the following cases only:

- after a written offer of employment
- where the specific physical abilities required to perform the essential duties of a position have been identified;
- where they are limited to determining the person's ability to perform the essential duties of the position; and
- where reasonable accommodation for those failing to pass the test is included as part of the process.

While an employer cannot test at the pre-employment stage, it can make a written job offer conditional on the applicant successfully completing a job-related medical examination. This examination may include testing for alcohol or drugs only if such testing is necessary to ensure that the prospective employee is able to perform the essential duties of the job; and only if the employer makes reasonable accommodation for those individuals who do not pass the medical examination.

The federal (CHRC) policy states that the use of "positive" results from drug testing to disqualify an applicant from employment consideration may be discriminatory on prohibited grounds. These include disability (drug dependency), age (younger individuals, 18 to 29 years of age, being the majority of drug users), and race (visible minorities with higher levels of melanin pigment in their skin). The policy further states that employers must establish that drug testing is relevant in determining whether the individual has the capacity to perform the job safely, efficiently, and reliably. The CHRC goes on to state that where drug testing is carried out, it must be done in a valid, reliable, and accurate manner. In addition, the employer may be required to avoid any discriminatory effect, that is, to reasonably accommodate individuals who fail a drug test.[24]

AIDS

AIDS

AIDS (acquired immune deficiency syndrome) is caused by a virus called human immune-deficiency virus (HIV) that attacks and disrupts the body's immune system, its defence against disease.[25]

The World Health Organization (WHO) estimates that by 1993 between 500 000-3 000 000 people will be affected with AIDS.[26] In Canada it is estimated that 50 000 individuals are infected with the AIDS virus.[27]

In May, 1988, the Canadian Human Rights commission (CHRC) released an eight-page policy paper. The CHRC recognized three occupational situations that could justify treating an employee with HIV differently than other employees:

- where the individual carries out invasive procedures (i.e., the puncturing or incision of the skin or the insertion of an instrument or foreign material in the body, as in surgery or other medical procedures);
- where he or she is required to travel to countries where AIDS carriers are barred; or
- where a sudden deterioration of brain or central nervous system functions would compromise public safety.

The Ontario Human Rights Commission has declined to establish a separate policy on AIDS. In the OHRC's view, AIDS should be treated as similar to other handicaps.

In a recent cases, an Ontario board of inquiry found that Ron Lentz, a nurse with AIDS, was terminated because of his disability. The Toronto Western Hospital was ordered to reinstate him six months later. A similar finding was made in a grievance arbitration involving Pacific Western Airlines and the Canadian Airline Flight Attendants Association in 1987. The griever, a flight attendant, was suspended with pay when the employer suspected that he had contracted AIDS. A federal arbitration board held that the suspension from work with pay was a breach of the collective agreement. The arbitrator found, based on medical evidence, that AIDS is not transmitted though casual contact. Hence there was no risk to passengers or fellow employees. The employee had the right to continue to work as long as he was physically able to do the job.[28]

The Government of Ontario recently announced that doctors are no longer required to automatically report to public health authorities the names of patients infected with HIV virus or who are infected with AIDS. However, it states that the government will continue to collect other vital statistics such as age, sex, and risk factor. They also announced that the government spend about $800 000 on anonymous testing of HIV.[29]

VIDEO DISPLAY TERMINALS

The introduction of **video display terminals** into thousands of workplaces—in factories as well as in offices—in recent years has resulted in concerns being raised about the possible health hazards posed to operators, particularly operators who

video display terminals

HUMAN RESOURCE MANAGEMENT IN ACTION

Job Pools, Not Computers, to Blame for Boring Work

MONTREAL—Blaming the growing use of computers and other office technologies for making jobs boring and repetitive is a mistake. Many companies, faced with rising turnover rates because they seem to offer "dead-end" jobs, are beginning to re-evaluate the organization of their offices especially clerical functions and "pools" of specialists. British financial institutions, among the first companies to fragment jobs into typing or filing pools, are reconsidering their approach to office organization in an effort to become more competitive. In a recent address to the second international scientific conference on Work with Display Units, British industrial sociologist Juliet Webster told her audience that traditional approaches to clerical work—fragmenting tasks into filing or typing pools—are inefficient and create

boring, dead-end jobs. Webster says that many managers blame office automation for recruitment and retention problems that are more the result of political decisions about how to organize office work. She encourages companies that currently fragment jobs into repetitive, specialized tasks to change them into jobs that broaden people's talents and challenge them. Webster points out that typing pools were once thought to be the most efficient way to complete that particular task, although in reality many people were making mistakes because they did not understand the context of the work.

SOURCE: *Human Resource Management in Canada*, Report Bulletin no. 80 (Scarborough, Ont.: Prentice-Hall Canada Inc., 1989), p. 3. Used with permission.

On the Front Line

Employee health and safety is a very important matter in the laundry and cleaning business. Each facility is a small production plant in which machines, powered by high-pressure steam and compressed air, work at high temperatures washing, cleaning, and pressing garments often under very hot, slippery conditions. Chemical vapours are continually produced, and caustic chemicals are used in the cleaning process. High temperature stills are almost continually "cooking down" cleaning solvents in order to remove impurities so that the solvents can be reused. If a mistake is made in this process—like injecting too much steam into the still—a "boilover" occurs, in which boiling chemical solvent erupts out of the still and over the floor and anyone who happens to be standing in its way.

As a result of these hazards and the fact that chemically hazardous waste is continually produced in these stores, several government agencies have instituted strict guidelines regarding the management of these plants. For example, posters have to be placed in each store notifying employees of their right to be told what hazardous chemicals they are dealing with and what the proper method for handling each chemical is. Special waste-management firms must be used to pick up and properly dispose of the hazardous waste.

A chronic problem the Carters (and most other laundry owners) have is the unwillingness on the part of the cleaning-spotting workers to wear safety goggles. Not all the chemicals they use require safety goggles, but some—like the hydroflurous acid used to remove rust stains from garments—are very dangerous. The latter is kept in special plastic containers, since it dissolves glass. The problem is that wearing safety goggles can be troublesome. They are somewhat uncomfortable. They also become smudged easily and thus cut down on visibility. As a result, Jack has always found it almost impossible to get these employees to wear their goggles. Jennifer has several questions:

1. How should her firm go about identifying hazardous conditions that should be rectified?

2. Would it be advisable for her firm to set up a procedure for screening out accident-prone individuals?

3. How would you suggest she get all employees to behave more safely at work? Also, how would you advise her to get those who should be wearing goggles to wear the goggles?

work with VDTs on a more or less continual basis throughout the working week. Much, but not all, of the concern has focused around the possibility of operator exposure to radiation that might be emitted by VDTs, especially in the case of pregnant operators.

So far, research undertaken in Canada, the United States, and in Europe has failed to find any evidence of ionizing radiation (e.g., X rays) being emitted from VDTs at detectable levels. There is some evidence that non-ionizing (e.g., radio frequency) radiation may be emitted in low doses. Current evidence therefore suggests that there is little or no hazard posed by radiation, assuming that the equipment is kept in good condition.

VDTs pose other potential hazards to the health of operators, however. These hazards can generally be considered in three categories:

1. *Eye strain and fatigue* resulting from inappropriate or badly placed lighting, glare on the screen, improper placement of the screen in relation to the opera-

tor's eye level, insufficient rest for the eyes, poor colour contrast of symbols on the screen, and so on. Labour Canada suggests that there be at least a 15-minute break during the morning and afternoon for operators. In addition, units should be placed so that the operator can look beyond the screen at frequent intervals.

2. *Muscular stress.* Strain of the muscles in the back and neck may arise as a result of poorly designed seating or improper placement of the unit in relation to the operator, especially with regard to the height of the keyboard.

3. *General fatigue and psychological stress.* General fatigue may result from eye strain or muscular stress. Psychological stress may result from general fatigue, unpleasant working conditions (including background noise, and isolation from other workers which some VDT work demands), and from work which is paced entirely by the VDT and not by the operator.[30]

SUMMARY

1. In this chapter we discussed the important role of health and safety in organizations. We examined various federal and provincial occupational health and safety legislations created to ensure that employees' workplaces are free from unsafe working conditions, risks, hazards, and unsafe work behaviours. These legislations also are designed to ensure that employers develop and implement and maintain health and safety programs. One feature of most health and safety acts is the requirement that organizations establish joint safety committees.

2. Supervisors play a key role in safety since there will always be accidents unless workers want to act safely and do so. A commitment to safety on the part of top management, and a filtering down of this commitment through the management ranks, is an important aspect of any safety program.

3. There are three basic causes of accidents: chance occurrences, unsafe conditions, and unsafe acts on the part of employees. Unsafe conditions (like defective equipment) are one big cause of accidents.

4. Unsafe acts on the part of employers are a second basic cause of accidents. Such acts are to some extent the result of certain behavioral tendencies on the part of employees, and these tendencies are possibly the result of certain personal characteristics.

5. There are several approaches that can be used to prevent accidents. One is to reduce unsafe conditions (although this is somewhat more in the domain of safety engineers). The other approach is to reduce unsafe acts, for example through selection and placement, training and behaviour modification, persuasion and propaganda, and top management commitment.

6. Stress and burnout are other potential health problems at work. Reducing job stress involves such things as getting away from work for a while each day, delegating, and developing a "worry list."

7. Alcoholism, drug addiction, video display terminal-related health problems, and AIDs are other employee health problems discussed in this chapter.

KEY TERMS

joint health and safety committees

stress

burnout

drug testing

AIDS

video display terminals

DISCUSSION QUESTIONS

1. Explain how to provide a safer environment for your employees to work in.
2. Discuss how to minimize the occurrence of unsafe acts at the workplace.
3. Explain what employees can do when unsafe conditions exist in the workplace.
4. Explain what causes unsafe acts.
5. Describe at least five techniques for reducing accidents.
6. Analyze the legal and safety issues concerning AIDS.
7. Explain the symptoms and causes of stress.
8. What is the relationship of burnout to stress?

CASE INCIDENT: Asbestos and the Workers' Compensation Board

A worker's widow claimed for burial and dependency benefits, arguing that her husband's death from lung cancer resulted from workplace exposure to asbestos. After a detailed investigation of the workplace, a WCB Appeals Adjustor denied the widow's claim. The widow appealed to the Workers' Compensation Appeals Tribunal (WCAT).

At the outset of the hearing the WCAT Panel said that lung cancer in asbestos workers is clearly an industrial disease compensable under the Workers' Compensation Act (the "Act"). The Panel then referred to the WCB's policy in dealing with lung cancer claims.

WCB's policy is that "lung cancer claims be favourably considered" when there is

(a) "a clear and adequate history" of at least ten years' occupational exposure to asbestos and
(b) a minimum interval of ten years between the first exposure to asbestos and the appearance of lung cancer.

Where these criteria have not been established, claims will be judged on an individual bases, and the worker will be given the "benefit of the doubt."

At the hearing the parties agreed that there was an interval of over 20 years between the husband's first exposure to asbestos and the appearance of lung cancer. The Panel, therefore, said, "What remains to be demonstrated ... is whether there is a clear and adequate history of at least ten years occupational exposure to asbestos."

The husband, who was 59 years of age when he died from lung cancer, had been employed as a rigger for almost 25 years. His function was to dismantle, erect, and move heavy equipment and structures. In determining the extent of his workplace exposure to asbestos, the Panel relied on the testimony of riggers with similar work experience.

The widow tried to show that the typical rigger had ongoing, regular contact with substances containing asbestos. The employer then tried to show that the worker's level of exposure was minimal and well within safe limits. According to the employer, "there was simply very little asbestos in the air when a given rigger was working on a given job." In support of its argument the employer presented several analyses which indicated that the total concentration of airborne fibre was low.

After hearing both sides the Panel decided that "exposure to some level of asbestos occurred on an occasional but regular basis." The Panel thought that if the rigger had been exposed to dangerous levels of asbestos, that exposure would have emanated from two sources. One source was a particular location in the plant. The other source was a particular piece of equipment found generally though the plant.

The particular location in question was the mould ship, an extremely dusty area. The evidence suggested that a rigger might be in that area not more than two or three times a year. But this limited exposure could be dangerous because of the presence of an extremely high concentration of airborne fibre. The evidence indicated that the riggers generally worked without protective masks.

The second potentially dangerous source of asbestos exposure involved the riggers' relatively constant contact with asbestos gaskets. Riggers encountered these gaskets in much of the repair and maintenance work. The evidence indicated that riggers seldom wore protective masks when removing gaskets.

The WCB denial of the widow's claim was largely based on a report prepared by one of its medical consultants. That doctor had concluded that the husband's exposure to asbestos had been minimal and that his lung cancer occurred solely as a result of his smoking. The doctor had also concluded that the husband's exposure to asbestos "was such that he fell below the threshold point at which asbestos and cigarette smoking can be said to have a `multiplicative or synergistic effect.' "

Questions

1. Why would you agree or disagree with the decision of the WCB Appeals Adjustor?

2. What do you believe was the outcome of the appeal to the Workers' Compensation Appeals Tribunal? Why?

3. What can an organization do to protect workers from exposure to asbestos?

SOURCE: *The Employment Law Report*, Volume 11, Number 5, May 1990, pp. 39-40. Reproduced by permission of Concord Publishing Ltd, 14 Prince Arthur Avenue, Toronto, Ontario M5R 1A9.

EXPERIENTIAL EXERCISE

Purpose: The purpose of this exercise is to provide practice in identifying unsafe conditions.

Required Understanding: Familiarity with material covered in this chapter, particularly that on unsafe conditions and that in Figure 17.3.

How to Set Up the Exercise/Instructions: Divide the class into groups of four or five students.

Assume that you are a safety committee retained by the school to identify and report on any possible unsafe conditions in and around the school building.

Each group will spend about 45 minutes in and around the building you are now in for the purpose of identifying and listing possible unsafe conditions. (*Hint*: Make use of Figure 17.3.)

Return to the class in about 45 minutes, and a spokesperson from each group should list on the board the unsafe conditions they think they have identified. How many were there? Do these also violate government standards? How would you go about checking?

NOTES

1. Don Petersen, *Safety Supervision* (New York: Amacom, 1976), pp. 50-53.
2. A portion of the material in the preceding sections draws heavily on Dilys Robertson, "Occupational Health and Safety" in *Human Resources Management in Canada* (Toronto: Prentice-Hall Canada Inc., 1990), pp. 60,001-60,120.
3. Robertson, p. 60,040.
4. Robertson, pp. 60,053-60,060.
5. Robertson, p. 60,061.
6. "A Safety Committee Man's Guide," Aetna Life and Casualty Insurance Company, Catalog 872684.
7. Ibid, pp. 17-21. See also "Safety Program: High Priority," Bureau of National Affairs, *Bulletin to Management* (May 4, 1989), p. 144, for safety programs with regard to office design and work station safety.
8. List of unsafe acts from "A Safety Committee Man's Guide," Aetna Life and Casualty Insurance Company.
9. Lester Bittel, *What Every Supervisor Should Know* (New York: McGraw-Hill, 1974) p. 249.
10. Keith Davis and John W. Newstrom, *Human Behaviour at Work*, 8th ed. (New York: McGraw Hill Book Company, 1989), pp. 482-483.
11. Gopal Pati and John Adkins Jr., "The Employer's Role in Alcoholism Assistance" *Personnel Journal*, Vol. 62, no. 7 (July 1983), pp. 568-572. See, also, Commerce Clearing House, "How Should Employers Respond to Indications an Employee May have an Alcohol or Drug Problem?" *Ideas and Trends* (April 6, 1989), pp. 53-57.
12. Canadian Institute of Stress, Toronto, 1991.
13. Davis and Newstrom, pp. 482-483.
14. Davis and Newstrom, pp. 482-483.
15. Gene Deszca, Ronald Barke, and Victor N. MacDonald, "Organizational Correlates of Role Stress of Administrators In the Public Sector" ASAC (Organizational Behaviour Division) Meeting Proceedings (Vol. 3, Part 5, 1982), pp. 100-109; V.V. Baba, M.J. Baba and M.H. Harris, "Strain and Absence: A Study of White-Collar Workers in Quebec," *Working Paper #83-010* (Montreal: Concordia University, Faculty of Commerce, 1983).
16. K. Albercht, *Stress and the Manager* (Englewood Cliffs, N.J.: Prentice-Hall Inc., 1979), p. 35. See also J.A. Lischeron, *Occupational Health: Psychological Management—Contemporary Perspectives in Canada* (Toronto: McGraw-Hill Ryerson Ltd., 1984), p. 437.
17. Thomas H. Holmes and Richard H. Rahe, "The Social Readjustment Rating Scale," *Journal of Psychosomatic Research* (August 1967).
18. Andrew DuBrim, *Human Relations: A Job-Oriented Approach* (Reston): Reston Publishing, 1978), pp. 66-67.

19. Herbert Freudenberger, *Burn-Out* (Toronto: Bantam Books, 1980). See also Susan Jackson, Richard Schwab, and Randall Schuler, "Toward an Understanding of the Burnout Phenomenon," *Journal of Applied Psychology*, Vol. 711, no. 4 (November 1986), pp. 630-640, and James R. Redeker and Jonathan Segal, "Profits Low? Your Employees May Be High!" *Personnel*, Vol. 66, no. 6 (June 1989), pp. 72-76.

20. Robertson, p. 60,037.

21. John Newman and Terry Beehr, "Personal and Organizational Strategies for Handling Job Stress: A Review of Research and Opinion," *Personnel Psychology* (Spring 1979), pp. 1-43. See also, Bureau of National Affairs "Work Place Stress: How to Curb Claims," *Bulletin to Management*, April 14, 1988, p. 120.

22. Karl Albercht, *Stress and the Manager* (Englewood Cliffs, N.J.: Spectrum, 1979).

23. Harish C. Jain, "Human Rights: Issues in Employment," *Human Resource Management in Canada* (Toronto: Prentice-Hall Canada Inc., 1989), pp. 50,025-50,026.

24. Canadian Human Rights Commission, *Drug Testing*, Policy 88-1, Ottawa (January 1988).

25. Jain, p. 50,026.

26. *"AIDS" The Bulletin*, (William M. Mercer Meidinger Hansen Inc., June 1988), no. 156.

27. Ibid.

28. Jain, p. 50,026.

29. Paula Todd "AIDS Patients Granted Privacy," *Toronto Star* (April 16, 1991), pp. 1, 22.

30. Robertson, pp. 60,086-60,087.

SUGGESTED READINGS

Atherley, Gordon. "The Conflict Between Medical Monitoring and Human Rights" in *Human Resources Management in Canada*. Toronto: Prentice-Hall Canada Inc., 1986, pp. 60,501-60,510.

Nash, Michael. *Canadian Occupational Health and Safety Law Handbook*. Toronto: CCH Canadian Limited, 1983.

Robertson, Dilys. "Identifying Joint Health and Safety Committee Training Needs" in *Human Resources Management in Canada*. Toronto: Prentice-Hall Canada Inc., 1990, pp 60,567-60,575.

———— *Ontario Health and Safety Guide: A Dictionary of Legal Compliance*. Toronto: Richard DeBoo Limited, 1984.

Wong, Roland. "Aids in the Workplace" in *Human Resources Management in Canada*. Toronto: Prentice-Hall Canada Inc., 1987, pp. 60,511-60,518.

CHAPTER EIGHTEEN LABOUR RELATIONS

After studying this chapter, you should be able to

1. Explain the purposes and importance of labour relations.
2. Discuss the history of the labour movement.
3. Explain contemporary trends in labour relations.
4. Explain the reasons for the growth of labour unions.
5. Present examples of what to expect during the union certification drive.
6. Discuss union goals and philosophy.
7. Explain the organizing and certification process.

OVERVIEW

The main purpose of this chapter is to provide basic information about the labour movement. After briefly discussing the history of the Canadian labour movement we describe some basics of labour legislation, including the subject of union growth, union goals and philosophy, and union membership in the blue collar and white collar industries. We explain the role that labour relations boards play in the process and we also discuss the organizing process and the certification process.

INTRODUCTION: THE LABOUR MOVEMENT

The term *labour relations* refers to the ongoing interactions between labour unions and the management in organizations. *Labour unions* refer to the organization of individuals who have joined together for the purposes of presenting a united front or collective voice in dealing with management in order to secure and further the social and economic interests and well-being of their membership. Labour unions reduce managerial discretion and flexibility in implementing and administering human resource policies, procedures, practices, management, and wage determination.

Purposes and Importance of Unionization

The purposes and importance of unionization are to

- Influence managerial policies, decisions and practices, as well as employment conditions
- Assist workers to achieve higher wages and influence the wage setting process
- Assist workers to obtain job security, improve working conditions, and achieve human needs fulfillment—job satisfaction and the social need for affiliation
- Assist workers to achieve greater control over their jobs
- Influence the rules and procedures covering discipline, transfers, promotions, grievances, and layoffs

The following brief survey of the history of the labour movement will provide some insight into the development and growth of unions in Canada.

A BRIEF HISTORY OF THE LABOUR MOVEMENT IN CANADA

The Canadian labour movement had its beginnings in the late 18th and early 19th centuries.[1] Unions, or groupings of employees formed to better their working conditions, were found as early as 1794. While the first union on record was an organization of boot and shoe workers in Montreal in 1827, printers are usually regarded as being the first occupational group to establish permanent unions in Canada. Since few unions kept lasting records, it is difficult to trace in detail the early developments in the growth of the Canadian labour movement. The little evidence that exists suggests that early unions were generally found in urban areas in Ontario, Quebec, and Nova Scotia.

Attempts by unions to join together for mutual support often ran afoul of common law, as conspiracy in restraint of trade. The criminal conspiracy doctrine was based on the idea that the existence of trade unions was against the common good. As a result, during that era, involvement in union activities was a criminal offence.[2] Combinations for the purpose of setting wages, taking strike action, and performing other organizational activities were generally deemed unlawful. However, prosecutions were not numerous, since those employers who were opposed to unionism were generally successful in keeping their employees nonunionized without recourse to court action.

At the time of Confederation there were some early craft unions in existence in Canada. These craft unions were affiliated with international unions, either from Great Britain or the United States. Although a few unions existed at federation, there were severe legal restrictions on union organization that made it difficult to organize and establish unions. In 1872, there was a strike of the Toronto printers that ended with violence and arrests. The unrest resulted in the public demand for labour law reforms in Canada. The Canadian Trade Union Act was enacted in 1872, legalizing the trade union movement. Another act that passed in the same year was the Criminal Law Amendment Act which legalized peaceful strikes and picketing.

During the late 1870s some provinces also implemented mediation and arbitration to prevent work stoppages. However, since these required the mutual agreement of labour and management to be operational, they were rarely used because mutual agreement was often difficult to achieve.

The Dominion Conciliation Act of 1900

Dominion Conciliation Act

In 1900, Parliament passed the **Dominion Conciliation Act** which gave the minister of labour the power to appoint a conciliation board at the minister's initiative or at the request of either management or the union. The aim of the Act was to regulate industrial disputes.[3] However, the Act did not make the conciliation process compulsory. It was based upon the voluntary submission of a dispute.[4] The Act required that the conciliation board be tripartite in nature, consisting of one union representative, one representative from management, and a neutral chairperson. The Board had a fact-finding role and it was required to make and to publish specific recommendations on ways to settle disputes between unions and management. Parliament felt that the publication of these recommendations would mobilize public opinion against the malingering side.

The Industrial Disputes Investigation Act (IDI) 1907[5]

Industrial Disputes Investigation Act

In 1907 Parliament passed a landmark legislation called the **Industrial Disputes Investigation (IDI) Act**. The IDI Act was introduced by the Minister of Labour, MacKenzie King, who later became prime minister. This Act made conciliation compulsory. It delayed the right to strike or to lockout, thereby freezing the conditions of employment in order to allow a conciliation board to investigate the dispute and make a recommendation to the minister of labour. Delaying work stoppage prevented strikes at important and strategic times and provided warning of future economic action against the employer. The objectives of the Act were "to bring about a settlement of the dispute" as quickly as possible, and to bring outstanding disputes to a tripartite conciliation board. The board was given the power to investigate disputes, compel testimony to find out the cause of the dispute, and to recommend a settlement. This principle was adopted by most provinces and is, today, present in the labour legislations of most jurisdictions in Canada. It is a distinctive feature of Canadian labour that distinguishes it from American and British law.

One case that has had a profound impact on the effectiveness of the IDI Act was the *Toronto Electric Commission* v. *Snider* case in 1923.[6] The case arose out of the refusal of the Toronto Electric Commission to recognize the authority of a conciliation board appointed under the Act to deal with the dispute between the commission and its workers. The commission argued before the court that the federal government did not have jurisdiction to apply the Act to municipal employees or to enact laws affecting civil rights. The highest appellate[7] at that time ruled that the IDI Act was indeed unconstitutional. From that moment, the future of Canadian labour law rested primarily in the domain of the provinces.

Today, approximately 90% of labour relations are governed by provincial statutes. The remaining 10%, mainly federal departments, crown corporations and agencies, transportation, communications, and banking, fall under the federal government. Following the *Snider* case the IDI Act was amended in 1925 "to cover only those labour disputes upon or in connection with any work undertaking business which is within the legislative authority of the Parliament of Canada."[8] This in principle is embodied in the Canada Labour Code, and has been upheld as constitutional.[9] The 1925 amendment also provided that the provinces could pass legislation to make the Act applicable within the provinces. By 1932, all the provinces except P.E.I. had passed legislation to that effect.

The U.S. Wagner Act

In 1935 the **Wagner Act** (National Labour Relations Act) was passed in the United States. This was a powerful, innovative labour relations act. The Wagner Act dealt with recognition issues requiring management to recognize a certified union as the exclusive bargaining agent for that group of workers. It also listed unfair labour practices and cited those activities management could not engage in during a union organizing drive, such as interfering with, restraining, or coercing employees. Many provisions of the Wagner Act were adopted and incorporated into Canadian labour legislations. These include freedom of association and collective bargaining.

Wagner Act

In 1944, PC1003 was passed in Canada. This was a federal statute, under the national emergency clause, that paralleled the Wagner Act in the States. It set up the War Labour Relations Board and ultimately served as the prototype statute for the provinces.

The Public Service Staff Relations Act of 1967

In 1967 Parliament passed the **Public Service Staff Relations Act** that gave federal public servants the right to join a union. The Act provided public servants with the choice to determine whether to opt for compulsory arbitration or the right to strike. The Act also provided for the designation of certain services as essential services. The groups of public servants responsible for these essential services were only allowed the option of compulsory arbitration.

Public Service Staff Relations Act

Public servants in Saskatchewan and Quebec had previously won the right to unionization in 1944 and 1964 respectively. Following the passage of Public Service Staff Relations Act, all other jurisdictions, except Ontario and Alberta, passed similar legislations.

LABOUR RELATIONS AND CONTEMPORARY LAW

General Purposes

Canadian labour laws have two general purposes. The first is to provide a common set of rules for fair negotiation. The laws do not change the nature of union-management interaction but rather regulate the way in which this interaction is conducted, so that both parties can have an equal chance to negotiate an agreement that is mutually satisfactory.

The second objective of the labour laws is to ensure the protection of the public interest. Labour legislations aim to prevent the impact of labour disputes from inconveniencing the public. As a result these laws serve to ensure that a delicate balance is established between the rights of the public and the rights of the parties in the negotiations.

The cornerstone of Canadian labour legislation is the **Canada Labour Code** which became effective in 1971. The Canada Labour Code is the successor of the Industrial Disputes Investigation Act of 1907. It too provides for a conciliation procedure that parties are required to follow before they are in a legal position to strike or to lockout. It is usually the case that this procedure comes into effect after the expiration of the old agreement or after notice to negotiate the first agreement. This procedure may, however, be implemented at any time once bargaining has commenced even though the old agreement is still in effect.

Jurisdiction

As with human rights statutes, primary jurisdiction regarding labour laws resides with the provinces. The exceptions to this rule are as follows: times of national emergency (for example, wars), and all air, rail, shipping, and trucking operations that are interprovincial or international. These enterprises fall under federal jurisdiction.

This procedure of many separate jurisdictions within one country has several advantages over other legislative models (for example the U.S.). It allows for some diversity of legislation so that one jurisdiction can see how a certain new law works in other provinces before enacting it in its own province. This may be likened to a field experimentation procedure and can definitely lead to an improvement in the overall system. However, the procedure is not without its disadvantages. For one thing, it can become very confusing for a multiprovincial union and/or company to know which set of rules it belongs under, and it can become expensive to sort out this confusion. It can also become time consuming, especially when one considers that while the laws are different in each jurisdiction, the purposes are the same, yet much time must be spent ascertaining whether a particular procedure will be legal in one jurisdiction but not in another.

There exist common characteristics among the legislation in all the jurisdictions in Canada that have labour laws. These common characteristics may be summarized as follows:

- All jurisdictions have procedures for the certification of a union to represent the employees in a particular bargaining unit. It is important to note that a bargaining unit may consist of all employees in a specific occupation, in one or more plants, or in a branch or a department of a company.

- All jurisdictions require that a collective agreement must be in force for a minimum of one year.

- All jurisdictions (except British Columbia and Saskatchewan) create procedures that must be followed by all parties before a resort to strike or lockout may be put into effect.

- All jurisdictions (except Saskatchewan) outlaw strikes or lockouts during the life of an agreement.

- All jurisdictions provide for the arbitration of disputes over matters arising from an interpretation of the collective agreement.

- All jurisdictions prohibit certain specified "unfair practices" on the part of labour and management.

- All jurisdictions provide for a labour relations board or the equivalent to administer and enforce the provisions of the legislation. These boards are also responsible for deciding who is eligible to participate in collective bargaining and which bargaining unit is sanctioned to represent certain group of employees.

Labour Relations Boards

All jurisdictions in Canada have established **labour relations boards** (LRBs) to administer their labour relations acts. In all jurisdictions, labour relations boards are tripartite. That is, they are composed of union representatives, management representatives, and a neutral chair or a vice-chair. (This person is usually a representative of the government). Labour relations boards have some degree of autonomy from the minister of labour, and much flexibility in their operating procedures. LRBs are typically empowered to investigate violations of labour laws.

labour relations boards

The scope of their authority includes the power to decide whether an organization is an appropriate unit for collective bargaining purposes. They have the power to accept or modify the unit described in the union's application. The boards may make changes in order to ensure that the unit accurately represents the characteristics of the employing organization. The boards also have the power to decide whether an individual is an employee for the purposes of the law, whether a collective agreement is in force, and whether the parties are bound by it. Board rulings, by being tabled in the appropriate court, become in effect court orders.

Conciliation and Mediation

All jurisdictions in Canada provide for **conciliation** and **mediation** services. A conciliator or a mediator may be appointed by the federal or provincial minister of labour or at the request of management, the union, or both. However, the legislation in each jurisdiction varies in scope. (For example, in all jurisdictions, except British Columbia and Saskatchewan, strike action is not allowed until a conciliation effort has been undertaken and failed. In Quebec a strike is permitted 90 days after a union has requested the appointment of a conciliation officer).

conciliation
mediation

Conciliation may be defined as the intervention of a third party whose primary purpose is to bring the parties together and keep them talking in order to enable them to reach an agreement. The conciliator's role is a passive one. He or she is not permitted to make any direct input into the negotiation process.

Mediation may be defined as the intervention of a third party whose primary purpose is to help the parties to fashion an agreement that is mutually satisfactory to both parties. The mediator's role is an active one. He or she is allowed to make direct input into the negotiation process. It is often the case that the mediator meets with each side separately and attempts to assist them to bridge the existing gap between the parties.

Arbitration

All jurisdictions in Canada, except Saskatchewan, require that all collective agreements include a provision for final settlement by **arbitration** of all unresolved issues, without work stoppage. This means that the parties must commit themselves to arbitration and cannot engage in strikes or lockouts.

arbitration

Employers' Rights

An employer has the right to manage its affairs and maintain an efficient business enterprise and an employee has an obligation to perform work in return for remuneration.[10] As a result, section 71 of Ontario Labour Relations Act and its counterparts in other jurisdictions[11] state that nothing in the statute authorizes anyone to persuade to become or refrain from becoming a member of a trade union at the workplace during working hours. This provision represents an attempt to balance an employee's statutory rights to engage in union activity with an employer's proprietary and commercial rights.

The following is a list of some of the actions an employer may engage in under the law. All of these are based on an employee's right under the law not to join, as well as to join, a union.

1. Employers have a right to express their opinions, views, and sentiments regarding unions in general and the organizing union in particular.

2. Employers may state their position on whether employees should or should not vote for the union, or on any other matters involved in the organizing campaign.

3. Employers may prohibit distribution of union literature on their own property on company time. But they must allow solicitation on free time, subject to reasonable regulations respecting safety and proper conduct.

4. Employers may prohibit distribution of union literature on their premises, provided that they customarily prohibit distribution of all forms of literature.

5. Employers may increase wages, make promotions, and take other human resource actions if they would do so anyway in the normal course of business. In most jurisdictions, however, once an application for certification is received by the board, wages, fringes, and working conditions are frozen until the application is disposed of.

6. Employers may assemble employees during working hours and state opinions respecting the election, if one is to be held, as long as they avoid threats and promises. Employers have no obligation to give the union the same opportunity. In some jurisdictions, there is a "quiet period" specified before an election (e.g., in Ontario it is 72 hours), during which campaigning by either side may not take place. If this prohibition is violated, then the election may be set aside.

Legal Constraints on Management

During an organizing drive, Canadian labour laws place constraints on management actions. As a result management is not free to engage in whatever practices it chooses to oppose the formation of the labour union. The following are examples **unfair labour practices** of **unfair labour practices**:

- Interference with the rights of employees to select the union of their choice for collective bargaining purposes, or discrimination against employees for union *activity*. This generally means that employers cannot dismiss, discipline, or threaten employees for exercising their rights under the legislation. They cannot make promises that will influence an employee's choice of a union—for example, promising better benefits should the employee select one union rather than another or vote for no union. These provisions, however, do not prevent employers from making their case in support of one union or another, or for no union. What the employer can say under these circumstances, the manner in which it is said, and the forum use are matters that are susceptible to review by the relevant labour relations board.

- Participation in the formation, selection, or support—financial or otherwise—of unions representing that employer's employees.
- Unilaterally changing the terms of collective agreements or changing or threatening to change the wages and working conditions during certification proceedings or during collective bargaining, if the purpose is to undermine the union. They are compelled, as are unions, to bargain in good faith—that is, to demonstrate serious bargaining.
- Taking any action that the labour board believes deceived the employees on vital issues to a degree that they are unable to vote freely.

Labour boards will look at all employer actions in the context of the employer's total response to the organizing campaign. Where that campaign involves elements of strong anti-union propaganda, for example, what might ordinarily appear to be innocent language or actions could be viewed by the board as less than benign.[12]

Legal Constraints on Unions

Canadian labour laws also place major prohibitions on the conduct of labour unions during the organizing process. Some **unfair union labour practices** are

unfair union labour practices

- Interference with or participation in the formation or administration of an employers' organization.
- Interference with the bargaining rights of a certified union.
- Discrimination against union members or employees in the bargaining unit.
- Intimidation or coercion of employees to become or remain members of the union.
- Forcing employers to discriminate against, dismiss, or discipline union members.
- Failure to provide fair representation for all employees in the bargaining unit, whether in collective bargaining or in grievance procedure cases.

Other unfair practices include striking or locking out, or threatening to strike or lockout, before the time period specified in the legislation has elapsed.

LABOUR UNION GROWTH AND MEMBERSHIP

The history of the growth of the labour movement in Canada has shown a dramatic expansion between the years 1911 and 1983. In 1911, the first year official statistics were collected, there were 133 000 workers who belonged to trade unions in Canada. This figure grew to 3 563 000 or 40% of the work force by 1983. Since 1983 union membership has been declining at a steady rate.

Figure 18.1 shows the latest available statistics on union membership in Canada. Note that in 1989 union membership stood at 3 944 000 or 36.2% of the work force. This represents a decline of 3.8% since 1983. Various factors are responsible for the continuing decline of membership in unions. Some of these factors include the increase in service sector jobs, increase in white collar jobs, and decline of employment opportunities in heavy industries that are traditionally heavily unionized. Another factor includes much more effective nonunion strategies being utilized by nonunionized organizations.

Figure 18.2 shows union membership of the 15 largest unions in Canada. As can be seen the Canadian Union of Public Employees (CUPE) was the largest union in Canada in 1989, with 356 000 members. Figure 18.3 illustrates the level of membership in various unions in Canada. As shown there were 2 280 520 members in 1989.

The large number of workers that belong to unions particularly in the white collar industry reflects the workers' concern that their job security can be threatened by the introduction of new technology, or lesser demand for the services of certain classes of workers. Both can, and have, affected both blue and white collar workers. For many years blue collar unions have negotiated contracts that include provisions for layoffs, severance pay, and company assistance in locating new sources of employment. Teachers' unions, which are white collar unions have also successfully negotiated contracts that provide for some degree of job security in light of declining enrolment. These activities on behalf of workers are intended to provide workers with protection and to make the problem of redundancy and job insecurity less frightening to them.[13]

FIGURE 18.1
Union Membership in Canada

Year	Union membership (thousands)	Union membership as percentage of civilian labour force	Union membership as percentage of non-agricultural paid workers
1972	2 388	27.8	34.6
1973	2 591	29.2	36.1
1974	2 732	29.4	35.8
1975	2 884	29.8	36.9
1976	3 042	30.6	37.3
1977	3 149	31.0	38.2
1978	3 278	31.3	39.0
1979	n.a.	n.a.	n.a.
1980	3 397	20.5	37.6
1981	3 487	30.6	37.4
1982	3 617	31.4	39.0
1983	3 563	30.6	40.0
1984	3 651	30.6	39.6
1985	3 666	30.2	39.0
1986	3 730	29.7	37.7
1987	3 782	29.8	37.6
1988	3 841	29.6	36.6
1989	3 944	29.7	36.2

SOURCE: Labour Canada, *Directory of Labour Organizations in Canada*, 1989. Reproduced with the permission of the Minister of Supply and Services Canada, 1991.

FIGURE 18.2
Unions with 50 000 or
More Members, 1989

		Membership (thousands)
1.	Canadian Union of Public Employees (CLC)	356.0
2.	National Union of Provincial Government Employees (CLC)	297.2
3.	Public Service alliance of Canada (CLC)	171.9
4.	United Food and Commercial Workers International Union (AFL-CIO/CLC)	170.0
5.	National Automobile, Aerospace and Agricultural Implement Workers Union of Canada (CLC)	160.4
6.	United Steelworkers of America (AFL-CIO/CLC)	160.0
7.	International Brotherhood of Teamsters, Chauffeurs, Warehousemen and Helpers of America (AFL-CIO)	100.0
8.	Social Affairs Federation Inc. (CNTU)	94.6
9.	School Boards Teachers' Federation (CEQ)	75.0
10.	Service Employees International Union (AFL-CIO/CLC)	75.0
11.	Canadian Paperworkers Union (CLC)	69.0
12.	International brotherhood of Electrical Workers (AFL-CIO/CFL)	64.4
13.	United Brotherhood of Carpenters and Joiners of America (AFL-CIO)	62.0
14.	International Association of Machinists and Aerospace Workers (AFL-CIO/CLC)	58.4
15.	IWA-Canada (CLC)	50.0

SOURCE: Labour Canada, *Directory of Labour Organizations in Canada*, 1989. Reproduced with the permission of the Minister of Supply and Services Canada, 1991.

FIGURE 18.3
Union Membership by
Congress Affiliation,
1989

Congress Affiliation	Membership	
	Number	Percent
CLC	2 280 520	57.8
AFL-CIO/CLC	819 811	20.8
CLC only	1 460 709	37.0
CNTU	210 810	5.3
CFL	213 901	5.4
AFL-CIO/CFL	204 521	5.2
CFL only	9 380	0.2
AFL-CIO only	230 360	5.8
CEQ	102 314	2.6
CSD	60 836	1.5
CCU	32 420	0.8
CNFIU	3 780	0.1
Unaffiliated International Unions	15 386	0.4
Unaffiliated National Unions	675 508	17.1
Independent Local Organizations	118 492	3.0
TOTAL	**3 944 327**	**100.0**

SOURCE: Labour Canada, *Directory of Labour Organizations in Canada*, 1989. Reproduced with the permission of the Minister of Supply and Services Canada, 1991.

Why Do Workers Organize?

A tremendous amount of time and money has been spent trying to analyze "why workers organize," and many theories have been proposed, yet there's no simple answer to the question, partly because each worker probably joins for his or her own unique reasons. It does seem clear however that workers do not unionize just to get more pay or better working conditions. While these are important factors, the urge to unionize seems to boil down to the belief on the part of workers that it is only through unity that they can get their fair share of the "pie" and also protect themselves from the arbitrary whims of management. In practice, this usually means that low morale is a main determinant of unionization.

Research Findings

Several recent studies confirm the fact that low morale is a major reason why workers turn to unions. In one study, the researchers conducted an attitude survey to determine how satisfied employees were with various aspects of their jobs, including supervision, kind of work, and pay. By coincidence, attempts were made several months later to unionize employees in various units of this company. The results of this study showed that employees who were more dissatisfied were more prone to subsequently engage in unionization activity and to unionize. For example, in all cases employees in the units where no unionization activity took place were more satisfied than those in the units with unionization activity. An interesting aspect of this study was that (in retrospect) the company found that it had enough information from the attitude survey to have predicted the degree of future union activity in its organization.[14]

Generally, it is often dissatisfaction with basic bread and butter issues that leads to pro-union voting, rather than noneconomic issues such as opportunities for achievement on the job (although noneconomic issues are often important as well). One researcher found that employee dissatisfaction with basic issues such as job security and wages was most strongly correlated with a vote for the union, while the employees' satisfaction with such things as supervisor and type of work were less so.[15] The author of this study contends, by the way, that dissatisfaction alone will not automatically lead to unionization. First, she says dissatisfied employees must believe they are without the ability to influence a change in the condition causing the dissatisfaction. Then, she adds, a large enough group of employees would have to believe it could improve things through collective action.

The bottom line (to repeat) is that the urge to unionize often boils down to the belief on the workers' part that it is only through unity that they can get their fair share of the pie and also protect themselves from the arbitrary whims of management. Here is how one writer describes the reasons behind the early unionization of automobile workers:

> In the years to come, economic issues would make the headlines when union and management met in negotiations. But in the early years the rate of pay was not the major complaint of the autoworker.... Specifically, the principal grievances of the autoworkers were the speed-up of production and the lack of any kind of job security. As production tapered off, the order in which workers were laid off was determined largely by the whim of foremen and other supervisors. The system encouraged workers to curry favor by doing personal chores for supervisory employees—by bringing them gifts or outright bribes. The same applied to recalls as production was resumed. The worker had no way of knowing when he would be laid off, and had no assurance when, or whether,

he would be recalled.... Generally, what the workers revolted against was the lack of human dignity and individuality, and a working relationship that was massively impersonal, cold, and nonhuman. They wanted to be treated like human beings—not like faceless clockcard numbers.

Union Goals and Philosophy

The primary goals and philosophy of a union are to promote, protect, maintain, and enhance the economic and social interests of its membership.[16] Other goals include an attempt to fulfil various human needs of its membership. These include job security, improved job satisfaction, a greater sense of fair treatment, the betterment of the members' standard of living, and improved working conditions at the workplace. The pursuit of these aims is also intended to preserve the union's own welfare.

Job Security

Job security is one of the principal goals of unions. Unions strive to ensure job security for their members in order to provide a cushion against the impact of fluctuations in economic conditions, arbitrary termination, layoffs, and other forms of unjust treatment by employers. Unions provide job security by participating in the rules governing the work environment, resisting productivity-improvement techniques such as robotics, resisting the use of part-time workers, and contracting jobs to outside companies.

Improved Economic Conditions

Improved economic conditions constitute one of the primary aims of unions. They pursue this aim by negotiating for higher wages, increased benefits, and cost of living adjustments (COLA) to protect the erosion of their members' paycheques during inflationary times.

Better Working Conditions

Better working conditions are another important aim of unions. Over the years unions have successfully negotiated a variety of improvements in working conditions for their members. These include shorter work weeks, safer working conditions, longer breaks, and reduced compulsory overtime.

Fairness and Equality

Fairness and equality are important aims of unions. They often achieve these aims by successfully negotiating a seniority clause into the contract. This clause often means that major human resource decisions, such as promotions, transfers, wage increases, and layoffs are based on seniority. Unions often argue that without this provision management would likely engage in the practice of favouritism and thereby treat employees unfairly.

STRUCTURE AND FUNCTION OF LABOUR UNIONS IN CANADA

Labour unions in Canada are organized on three levels: local, national and international, and central labour congresses. Figure 18.4 illustrates the structure of the Canadian Labour Congress and its affiliation with segments of the Canadian labour movement and international unions.

FIGURE 18.4
The Structure of the
CLC-Affiliated
Segment of the
Canadian Labour
Movement

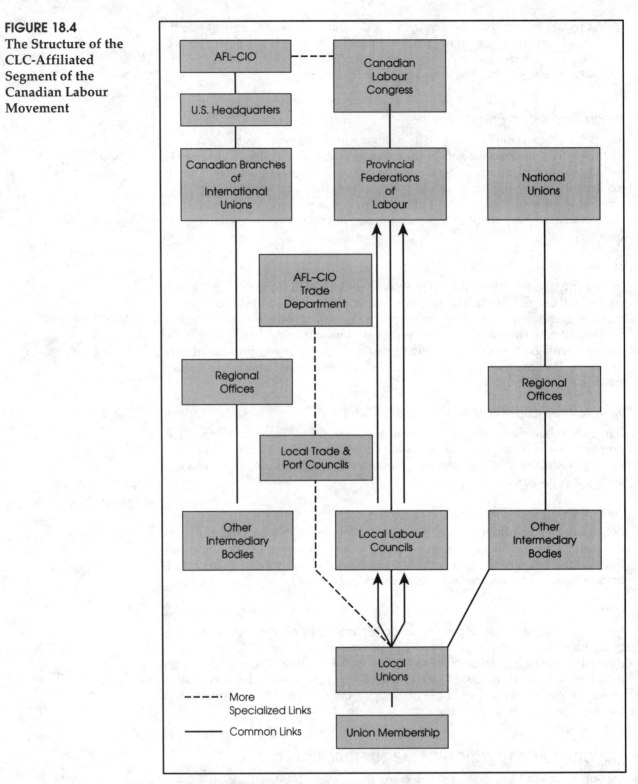

SOURCE: John Crispo, *International Unionism* (Toronto: McGraw-Hill Co. of Canada Ltd. 1967), p. 167.
Used with permission of the author.

Local Unions

The **local union** is the primary unit of labour union organization. There are three types of local labour organizations in Canada. The first is the independent local union. This type of local union is not affiliated with any other national or international labour organization. The second type is the local union that is affiliated with a national or international union. The third type is the local union that is directly chartered by a central labour congress. A typical local union consists of a president, secretary/treasurer, business agent, grievance committee, bargaining committee, and shop steward(s). Union leaders are elected by their members, usually for a specific period. The local union is usually responsible for negotiating collective agreement with employers. It is also responsible for handling grievances.

National and International Unions

Most local unions in Canada are part of a **national union**. These local unions must comply with the provisions of the constitution of the parent union. National unions provide a wide range of services to local unions. They provide assistance during negotiation, grievance handling, strike activities, and the arbitration process.

When we speak of **international unions** in Canada, we generally mean those that operate unions in Canada and the United States of America. The services they provide, broadly speaking, are similar to those provided by national unions. The headquarters of all international unions are located in the parent country, however, most select a senior Canadian executive, usually at the vice-presidential level. Most members of international unions belong to the AFL-CIO which is similar to the CLC. Most Canadian members of international unions belong to both the CLC and the AFL-CIO.

Canadian Labour Congress

The **Canadian Labour Congress (CLC)** is an organization affiliated with various unions, directly chartered locals, and provincial federations of labour and local councils for the purpose of broadly coordinating their activities at the national level, including the relations between unions and government and establishing relations with organized workers internationally.[17] It is composed of 77 national and international unions. The CLC is responsible for looking after the interest of its members at the provincial and national levels. Figure 18.5 illustrates the CLC organizational chart. The affiliates in the provinces function in a similar manner to the CLC except that they do not charter local unions. Funds are obtained through a per capita tax on all affiliates.[18]

THE UNION ORGANIZING PROCESS

In order for a union to become the bargaining unit for a group of employees it must be certified by a labour relations board. To secure certification it must show evidence that it has obtained the minimum level of membership support required by the labour board. The initiative for the first contact between the employees and the union may come from the employees, from a union already representing other of the firm's employees, or from a union representing workers elsewhere. Often when one or more nonunionized companies operate in a highly unionized region, the union takes the lead in trying to unionize the nonunionized companies. For

FIGURE 18.5
Canadian Labour
Congress Organization

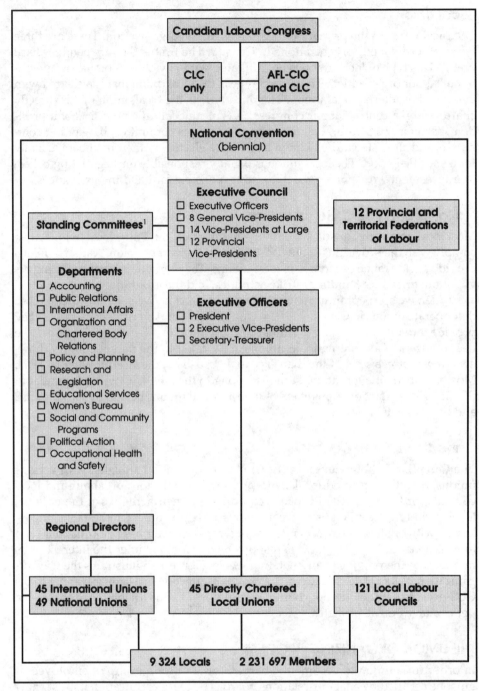

SOURCE: Adapted from Kumar, Pradeep, *The Current Industrial Relations Scene in Canada, 1988*. (Kingston: Queen's University, Industrial Relations Centre), p. 547.

instance, the National Automobile, Aerospace, and Agricultural Implement Workers Union of Canada (CAW-Canada) has made repeated attempts to organize the workers at the Michelin Tire plants in Nova Scotia but so far has been unsuccessful. Probably the main factor frustrating its efforts has been the provincial legislation passed as part of the deal that brought the company to the province. The bill makes organizing at these plants more difficult. Another example is the same Union's attempt to organize the employees of Magna International, a large auto-parts manufacturer. Despite a significant effort, as of this writing the organizing attempt has resulted in the certification of only 47 of Magna's 14 000 employees. The Union's lack of success has been attributed to the company's organization—most of its plants have only about 100 employees—and its generous profit-sharing plan, in which ten percent of pre-tax profits goes to employees.[19]

Getting the organizing drive started, particularly where it has not been initiated by employees, can often be challenging. Finding an initial contact within the plant can be a major problem. Bob White of the CAW tell of his early work at organizing plants, when he and a colleague stationed themselves outside the plant gate, identified individuals who "looked promising," followed them home to find out where they lived, and then returned later that evening to their homes to make a "cold call" to investigate their interest in representation by the union.[20]

Certification of Bargaining Units[21]

While all jurisdictions differ slightly in their **union certification** procedure, the norm is for unions to present their membership information for a bargaining unit, which they have defined, to the appropriate labour relations board in order to be certified. The labour relations board then determines whether the actual bargaining unit is based upon some community of interests among the workers, and awards recognition if the union membership in that unit is higher than some minimum percentage.

union certification

There are three basic ways in which a union can obtain recognition as a bargaining unit for a group of workers: 1) voluntary recognition, 2) the regular certification process, and 3) a prehearing vote.

Voluntary Recognition

An employer in all Canadian jurisdictions, except Quebec, may voluntarily recognize and accept a union and commence collective bargaining with that union.

Regular Certification

The regular certification process involves the union submitting the required minimum membership evidence to the labour relations board. It is important to note that in Canada, documenting trade union membership[22] serves as a labour board's primary means for determining employee support for collective bargaining. In all jurisdictions except B.C. and Nova Scotia, labour boards need not resort to a representation vote if the applicant union can demonstrate by documentary evidence that it has sufficient membership in the proposed bargaining unit. Unions are required to satisfy the board that they have secured a prescribed minimum of membership support. The usual way in which membership is provided is by presenting the board with signed membership cards and the evidence that initiation dues or fees have been paid,[23] but in each Canadian jurisdiction the labour relations board

FIGURE 18.6 A Comparison of Provisions Dealing with Certification

Jurisdiction	% support needed to apply for certification	% support where boards are mandated to certify without a vote	% support needed to apply for a prehearing vote	% support necessary to certify a union when a vote is taken	
				50% of those in the bargaining unit	50% of those voting
Federal	35	50 or more	35		X
Newfoundland	50		40	X	
Prince Edward Island	50		N/S		X
Nova Scotia	40	50 or more	N/S		X
New Brunswick	40–60	50 or more	40	X	
Quebec	35	50 or more	35	X	
Ontario	45–55	55 or more	35		X
Manitoba	45-55	55 or more	45	X	
Saskatchewan	25		N/S		X
Alberta	40	must conduct a vote	N/S		X
British Columbia	45	must conduct a vote	45		X

N/S—Not specified.

SOURCE: A.J. Craig, *The System of Industrial Relations in Canada*, 3rd ed. (Scarborough, Ont.: Prentice-Hall Canada Inc., 1991), p. 125. Used with permission.

COMPUTER APPLICATIONS IN LABOUR RELATIONS

Computers Assist both Labour and Management

Both sides of labour-management relations may benefit from the use of computers. Management may track grievances to see where and on what subjects training is needed. Labour may find that computers provide new ways to assist members.

Management is able to track trends in grievances within any given time period for the whole company, a division or department, or a particular supervisor or group of supervisors. For example, the researcher might hypothesize that supervisors with less than one year of experience in their positions might generate more grievances than experienced supervisors. If this proves

to be true, then either new supervisors should be trained before starting in the position or they should be offered frequent training sessions during their first year. However, research might prove that in some departments this hypothesis is not true. Thus, if there are a number of grievances from a large department, an investigation might reveal the need for (1) managerial training, probably defined by the subject of the grievances, (2) better communication on a topic (such as the importance of following safety rules), or (3) the development of a process that allows more input from employees before instituting new policies. Grievance topics may be coded for easy computer tracking. Grievances may incorporate more than one code.

Labour, too, can benefit from computerization. With the demographic changes in the workplace, labour is searching for new ways to meet the needs of its members and potential members. One area of concern which has continued for many years is a concern for job security due to mergers and acquisitions that have cost many employees their jobs. Another is the trend toward service industries and away from manufacturing that has led to a need for knowledgeable workers who are more highly educated. A third is the many low-paying jobs that have been generated by the service industry. When closed shops were legal, the union hall was the place to find a job. This function has now generally been replaced by temporary employment agencies.

However, unions could still fulfil this function for the benefit of their members. Not only are there many craft and skill workers who need the kind of expertise offered by unions to adequately find placement, there are many technical and knowledge-based workers who need to keep up to date on skills, equipment, and procedures through both information sharing and hands-on training. Computer-based networks nationwide would help to adjust the unemployment caused by having skills in one location and jobs in another. As Hallett suggests, unions could become "the single best source of information, training, standards, and individuals (with) specific skills and talents." With the support of international unions, locals could be linked effectively and relatively inexpensively (using telephone lines) to provide this source of information, thus assuring their members a degree of job security.

SOURCE: Geoffrey J. Hallet, "Unions in Our Future?" *Personnel Administration*, Vol. 31 no. 4 (April 1986), pp. 40-94.

may order a representation vote regardless of the extent of documentary evidence (although it is not general practice to require one as a pre-condition for certification.)

If the board is satisfied that the applicant union has met the statutory requirements regarding membership evidence, the board may certify the unit without a vote. Figure 18.6 illustrates the certification requirements in different jurisdictions.

Prehearing Votes

A prehearing vote may be conducted where there is evidence of irregularities, such as evidence that the employer is engaging in unfair labour practices. In such a case a "quickie" or prehearing vote may be ordered to measure the support of workers for unionizing before the employer infringes further on workers' rights to engage in union activities.

In those jurisdictions where a prehearing vote is allowed, the board conducts the vote and seals the ballots pending the outcome of its investigation. The vote also generally includes those workers whose eligibility for inclusion has been challenged by one side or another. Consequently the ballots are not counted until the board has ruled on which employees should be included or excluded in from the bargaining unit. If the board determines that the bargaining unit is appropriate and that the majority of members in the bargaining unit supports the union, it will certify the union.

When an application is submitted to a board, the board must first determine the scope of the bargaining unit. A vote is then held and if the majority votes against the union, it is decertified.

Labour relations boards take the following factors into account when deciding on the appropriateness of a proposed bargaining unit:[24]

On the Front Line

Last week something happened at one of the Carter stores that upset Jack and Jennifer. As is often the case, one of the workers involved with cleaning and spotting had to be fired because of poor-quality work. The nature of the business is such that employees are continually quitting, being fired, and being rehired somewhere else, and in fact it is not unusual for a worker in the industry to have worked in all or most of the stores in a geographic area during the period of five or so years. Because job switching is so much a part of the industry, Jack and Jennifer were therefore taken aback when Bob, the man who was fired, reacted almost violently. He threw a bottle of chemicals to the floor, began shouting that Jack was "incompetent, unfair, and unfit to be an employer" and proceeded to warn that he was forthwith driving to the local headquarters of the textile workers union to get them to begin organizing the Carter's firm. Subsequently, several of Carter's store managers reported that employees were talking among themselves much more animatedly during lunch than they usually do and that a man who one manager believes is a local union representative has been meeting with the employees after work as well. Jennifer has several questions:

1. Is it possible that her firm is in the first stages of an organizing campaign? How could she find out for sure?

2. What steps should she take now to determine if such organizing activity is going on?

3. If this firm is being organized, what steps should she take next?

- the community of interest among employees
- viability of the unit
- custom and practice
- desires of employees
- geographic, skill, or craft distinctions
- lines of advancement and demotions
- history of collective bargaining (has the unit been agreed to in a previous organizing campaign?)
- organizational structure of the employer
- common duties, wages, wage payment methods, working conditions, and
- desirability of separating white-collar from blue-collar employees

Interest Dispute

interest dispute
rights dispute

Following the certification of a bargaining unit, both the employer and the union are legally required to bargain in good faith over the terms and conditions of a collective bargaining agreement. All jurisdictions require that the term of a collective agreement must be for a minimum of one year. Thus the first agreement may last for one year or more. Prior to the expiration of an agreement either party may serve notice that it intends to bargain for a revised collective agreement. This process is known as contract negotiation or an **"interest" dispute**. This is intended to distinguish it from contract interpretation or a **"rights" dispute**. In rights disputes the clauses of the collective agreement provide guidelines to the arbitrator in the determination of his or her decision about the dispute. But in interest disputes there are no existing guidelines to assist the negotiators in reaching a decision.

Decertification

All labour relations acts provide procedures for workers to apply for the decertification of their unions. Generally, members may apply for decertification if a majority of members are dissatisfied with the performance of the unions. Dissatisfaction may arise because members feel that the union is ineffective, weak, indifferent, or inefficient. Applications must be submitted to the appropriate labour relations board.

SUMMARY

1. Union membership has been alternately growing and shrinking since as early as the 1870s.

2. A uniquely Canadian approach to labour relations was created in 1907 with the passing of the Industrial Disputes Investigation Act, which required compulsory conciliation before either side could resort to economic force.

3. The passage of the Wagner Act in the U.S. served as a landmark piece of legislation in North American Labour relations and was the base for all subsequent Canadian labour relations laws.

4. The unique characteristics of Canadian labour laws include certification procedures, grievance procedures, union security, labour relations boards, interest arbitration boards, and court reviews.

5. The purposes of the Canadian labour laws are to provide a set of common rules for a fair fight, to ensure the protection of the public interest, and to encourage or least allow union growth where there is some sentiment for it.

6. The primary goals of unions are to promote, protect, maintain, and enhance the economic and social interests of their memberships, as well as to ensure job security, better working conditions, and fairness and equality.

7. Labour unions in Canada are organized on three levels: local, national and international, and central labour congresses.

8. In order for a union to become the bargaining unit for a group of employees, it must be certified by a labour relations board. The three basic ways in which recognition is obtained are: 1) voluntary recognition, 2) the regular certification process, and 3) a prehearing vote.

KEY TERMS

Dominion Conciliation Act

Industrial Disputes Investigation Act

The Wagner Act

Public Service Staff Relations Act

Canada Labour Code

labour relations boards

conciliation (CLC)

mediation

artitration

unfair labour practices

local union

unfair union labour practices

national union

international union

Canadian Labour Congress

union certification

interest dispute

rights dispute

DISCUSSION QUESTIONS

1. Explain the history of the Canadian labour movement.
2. Discuss the structure and function of the CLC.
3. Explain the goals and philosophy of unions.
4. What is the difference between conciliation and mediation?
5. Explain the union drive and election process.
6. What is the purpose of the Canada Labour Code?

CASE INCIDENT: A Matter of Economics or Unfair Labour Practice?

Edper Furniture Manufacturing has been in existence since 1960. It manufactures furniture for upscale department stores. The company employs 30 individuals in its design and production department. All factory workers are hourly paid.

The company is not unionized. However, it monitors wage settlements at its major unionized competitors, and always matches their wages, but its benefits package is lower. Many workers at the firm feel that they are slightly ahead of workers in the unionized companies anyway, since they do not pay union dues. Edper's practice has contributed to a good working relationship between its workers and management.

One bright sunny day, two employees, Barbara Dallas and Alex Springate, started talking about life at the company over lunch. Both agreed that although the firm generally matched base pay of unionized companies, the benefits it provided were not very good. According to Alex, "we do not have any pension plans, disability plan, dental plan, or job security. The firm can let us go tomorrow and we would not have anything to show for 20 years of service." Barbara agreed, saying, "The same things have crossed my mind recently, and I bet other workers must be thinking the same thing. This year when the company announced our wage increase I thought they would have done something about the benefits but nothing was done." "Obviously if they were going to change the benefits they would have done so by now," Alex replied. After a moment, Barbara said, "If we approach management about our concerns they might think that we are trouble-makers and fire us." Lunch ended at this point and they agreed to talk to some of their close friends to get their input.

The next time Barbara and Alex met they exchanged notes. They were surprised to find out that most workers shared their concerns and felt that they should consider unionizing. Contacts were established with the CAW and the sign-up process began in the summer of 1991. During that period the company suffered severe financial losses because of the recession. It lost 50% of its market share. Its financial advisors informed the firm that 30% was probably lost permanently due to cross-borders shoppers. The company decided to lay off half of its work force. Alex and Barbara were among those laid off. Workers claimed that the layoff was an intimidating tactic by management and filed an unfair labour practice claim against the company.

Questions

1. Was the action by the employer unfair labour practice?
2. What do you believe was the outcome of their complaint?

NOTES

1. Parts of the section are based on George Saunders, *Union-Management Relations: An Overview in Human Resources Management in Canada* (Toronto: Prentice-Hall Canada Inc., 1983), pp. 55,011-55,075; and John Anderson and Morley Gunderson, *Union-Management Relations in Canada* (Don Mills, Ont.: Addison-Wesley Publishers, 1982); and Alton Craig, *The System of Industrial Relations in Canada* (Toronto: Prentice-Hall Canada Inc., 1991).

2. George W. Adams, *Canadian Labour Law* (Aurora, Ont: Canada Law Book Inc., 1985), pp. 3-6; see also Alton W. Craig, *The System of Industrial Relations in Canada*, 3rd ed. (Toronto: Prentice-Hall Canada Inc., 1991), pp. 36-37.

3. Adams, p. 6.

4. Ibid.

5. Parts of this section are drawn from Adams, pp. 8-10; and Craig, pp. 112-115.

6. *Toronto Electric Power Commission v. Snider* (1923) OLR at p. 455 (S.C.), rev'd OLR. loc. cit. p. 454 (1924) 2 ALR. 761 (S.C. App. Div.).

7. The highest appellate court of that time was the Judicial Committee of the British Privy Council. The case was heard initially before the Supreme Court of Ontario which upheld its constitutionality. But the then highest appellate court, the Privy Council in England, ruled that it was unconstitutional because the nature of an employment relationship was a matter of civil rights, a power assigned exclusively to the provinces under section 92 of the BNA Act.

8. An act to amend the Industrial Disputes Act 1907.

9. See reference re Industrial Relations and Disputes Investigated Act, etc. 1955, as quoted in Adams, p. 10.

10. For an excellent discussion of employer property rights and employer freedom of speech, see George W. Adams, *Canadian Labour Law: A Comprehensive Text* (Aurora, Ont: Canada Law Book, 1985), pp. 519-543.

11. See also B. C. Labour Code s.4; Alberta Labour Relations Act s 136(b); Canada Labour Code s.185 (d), and N.B. Industrial Relations Act s.4 (1)

12. Parts of this section were drawn from David A. Peach and Paul Bergman, *The Practice of Labour Relations*, 3rd ed. (Toronto: McGraw Hill Ryerson Limited, 1991), pp. 50-51.

13. Craig, pp. 52-53.

14. W. Clay Hamner and Frank Schmidt "Work Attitude as Predictors of Unionization Activity," *Journal of Applied Psychology*, Vol. 63, no. 4 (1978), pp. 415-521. See Amos Okafo, "White Collar Unionization: Why and What to Do," *Personnel*, Vol. 62, no. 8 (Aug. 1985), pp. 17-20.

15. Jeanne Brett, "Why Employees Want Unions," *Organizational Dynamics* (Spring 1980); John Fossum, *Labour Relations* (Dallas, Tex.: Business Publications, 1982) p. 4.

16. P. Kumar "Union Growth in Canada: Retrospect and Prospect" in W. C. Riddell, ed., *Canadian Labour Relations* (Toronto: University of Toronto Press, 1986), p. 103; see also Craig, pp. 72-74.

17. Bureau of Labour Information, Labour Canada, *Directory of Labour Organization in Canada 1988* (Ottawa: Supply and Services Canada, 1988), p. 232.

18. Ibid.

19. *Canadian Human Resources Reporter*, June 27, 1988.

20. Bob White, *Hard Bargains* (Toronto: McClelland and Stewart, 1987), p. 21.

21. Craig, pp. 122-126.

22. For a comprehensive discussion of membership evidence see Adams, pp. 355-368.

23. See for instance Canada Labour Relations Board Regulations and Ontario Labour Relations Act.

24. A. W. R. Carrothers, E. E. Palmer, and W. B. Rayner, *Collective Bargaining Law in Canada*, 2nd ed. (Toronto: Butterworths 1986, p. 376); Peach and Bergman, pp. 38-39.

SUGGESTED READINGS

Adams, George W. *Canadian Labour Law*. Aurora, Ont.: Canada Law Book Inc., 1985.

Aderson, John, Morley Gunderson, and Allen Ponak. *Union-Management Relations in Canada*, 2nd ed. Toronto: Addison-Wesley Publishers, 1989.

Coates, Mary Lou. "Industrial Relations in 1990: Trends and Emerging Issues" in *Human Resources Management in Canada*. Toronto: Prentice-Hall Canada Inc., 1990, pp. 55,589-55,599.

Craig, Alton J. *The System of Industrial Relations in Canada*, 3rd ed. Toronto: Prentice-Hall Canada Inc., 1991.

Kumar, Predeep, Mary Lou Coates, and David Arrowsmith. *The Current Industrial Relations Scene in Canada*. Kingston, Ont.: Industrial Relations Centre, Queen's University, 1988.

Labour Canada, *Directory of Labour Organizations in Canada*. Ottawa: Supply and Services Canada, 1989.

Peach, David A. and Paul Bergman. *The Practice of Labour Relations*, 3rd ed. Toronto: McGraw-Hill Ryerson, 1991.

Whitehead, J. David and Carman Cullen, "The New Employee in Industrial Relations" in *Human Resources Management in Canada*. Toronto: Prentice-Hall Canada Inc., 1989, pp. 55,551-55,559.

CHAPTER NINETEEN
COLLECTIVE BARGAINING

After studying this chapter, you should be able to

1. Explain the purposes and importance of collective bargaining.
2. Understand the significance of a collective agreement and be familiar with many of its typical provisions.
3. Describe the major bargaining strategies.
4. Understand contract administration and the grievance-arbitration process.
5. Discuss the impact that pay equity has on the collective bargaining approach.

OVERVIEW

This chapter describes the purposes and importance of collective bargaining. We explain approaches to working out the collective agreement and cover the provisions found in most collective bargaining agreements. Major bargaining strategies such as integrative bargaining and distributive bargaining are highlighted, and we also present a comprehensive discussion of the grievance-arbitration process. Finally we also discuss the implications of pay equity for collective bargaining.

INTRODUCTION: WHAT IS COLLECTIVE BARGAINING?

collective bargaining

Collective bargaining is the process through which representatives of management and the union meet to negotiate a labour agreement. The term includes the organization process as well as the negotiation process and the administration of the contracts or collective agreements that are the result of those negotiations.[1] These collective agreements specify the economic rewards, working conditions, rights, and responsibilities of each union member. The collective bargaining process allows individual workers an opportunity to participate in the decision-making process which governs the employment relationship between management and labour.

The nature and type of the actual bargaining process depends, to a significant extent, on the nature of the atmosphere that characterizes the relationship between management and labour. It also depends on the respective strengths of management and the union and the degree of cooperation that exists between them.

Purposes and Importance of Collective Bargaining

The purposes and importance of collective bargaining are to

- Negotiate, in *good faith*, a collective agreement that describes the scope of management rights and responsibilities and union rights and responsibilities
- Achieve an agreement that is acceptable to management, labour union representatives, and the union membership
- Develop a framework for labour relations in the organization, including the provision of an orderly mechanism to clarify the interpretation and application of the contract and to resolve conflicts which may arise

Figure 19.1 illustrates the environmental factors that affect collective bargaining from a systems perspective. Using a simplified explanation of open systems theory (see Chapter 1 for a discussion of open systems theory) it is possible to define the labour relations system as comprising "a complex of private and public activities, operating in a specified environment, which is concerned with the allocation of rewards to employees for their services and the conditions under which these services are rendered."[2] The framework shown here was developed by John Dunlop.[3] It consists of four basic components: i) internal inputs expressed as the goals, values, and power of the participants in the system that are influenced by various subsystems such as economic, political, legal, and social factors; ii) the complex of private and public processes for converting the inputs into outputs; iii) the outputs comprising the material, social, and psychological rewards workers receive in exchange for services; and iv) a feedback loop through which the outputs flow not only directly into the labour relations systems itself but also into the environmental subsystem.

As can be seen there are three major groups in the model. These are labour, government and private agencies, and management. Each of the groups has different goals. For instance, the goals of labour include the acquisition of power, survival, growth, and securing improved working conditions, better wages, and job security for workers. The goals of management include increasing market share, growth, profit, and the preservation of managerial prerogatives to direct the work force as it sees fit. The goals of government include protection of individual rights, fairness, and equality in the workplace and stability and growth in the economy. The compatibility or incompatibility of these goals, particularly those of labour and management, help to shape the negotiating climate of the collective bargaining process.[4]

FIGURE 19.1 Environmental Factors Affecting Collective Bargaining

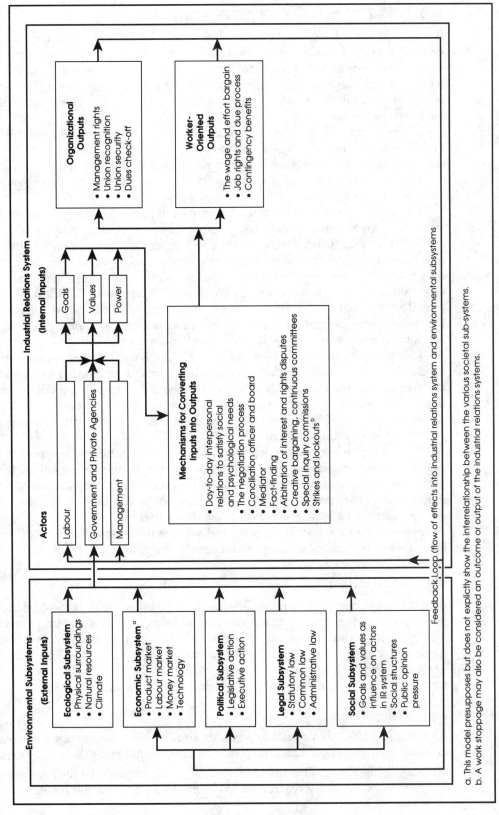

a. This model presupposes but does not explicitly show the interrelationship between the various societal sub-systems.
b. A work stoppage may also be considered an outcome or output of the industrial relations systems.

SOURCE: A.W. Craig, *The System of Industrial Relations in Canada*, 3rd ed. (Scarborough, Ont.: Prentice-Hall Canada Inc., 1990), p.3. Used with permission.

WORKING OUT THE LABOUR AGREEMENT[5]

collective agreement

All Canadian jurisdictions have established three essential requirements for a valid **collective agreement**: it must be made between an employers' organization and a trade union or council of trade unions, it must contain provisions regarding the terms and conditions or employment, and it must be in writing.[6] Although there are slight variations in the statutory language between jurisdictions, the essence of all the provisions is the same.

The collective agreement is the cornerstone of our labour relations system. It sets out the terms and conditions of dispute to be resolved by binding arbitration, it confirms bargaining rights, and its existence is used as the basis to determine the legality or illegality of various activities which are engaged in by an employer, a trade union or employees.[7]

All collective agreements must be written documents. Mere verbal understandings between management and labour are not collective agreements and will not be enforced as such.[8] But parties to collective bargaining do not normally execute a formal document until some time after the bargaining process has been completed. Instead, the agreement of the parties is usually reduced to a memorandum of agreement subject to ratification by the respective principals. (Ratification is the formal approval of a collective agreement by union members who are affected by that collective agreement.) A memorandum of agreement can serve as a collective bargaining agreement once the conditions set out in it are satisfied.[9]

Following the successful negotiation of a collective agreement between management and the union negotiating team, the contract is submitted to the union membership for ratification. A collective agreement may be binding without ratification.[10] However, ratification may be made necessary by the parties, in which case the memorandum of agreement does not become a collective bargaining agreement until ratification has occurred.

The collective bargaining process includes many activities surrounding the negotiation and implementation of the terms of collective agreements. If the terms of collective agreements meet the needs and expectations of the workers and are spelled out clearly, and the parties share a common understanding of them, then these terms may be implemented with few difficulties.[11]

Negotiating a contract is complex and at times time-consuming and difficult. Nevertheless both parties are legally required to bargain in good faith.

What Is "Good Faith"?

good faith

Bargaining in **good faith** is necessary for effective union-management relations. It means that both parties communicate and negotiate. It means that proposals are matched with counterproposals and that both parties make every reasonable effort to arrive at an agreement.[12] It does not mean that either party is compelled to agree to a proposal. Nor does it require that either party make any specific concessions (although as a practical matter, some may be necessary).

When Is Bargaining Not "in Good Faith"?

As interpreted by labour relations boards and the courts, a violation of the requirement for good faith bargaining may include the following:

1. *Surface bargaining*. This involves merely going through the motions of bargaining, without any real intention of completing a formal agreement.

2. *Concession.* Although not required to make a concession, the courts' and boards' definitions of good faith suggest that a willingness to compromise is an essential ingredient in good faith bargaining.

3. *Proposals and demands.* Labour relations boards consider the advancement of proposals as a factor in determining overall good faith.

4. *Dilatory tactics.* The parties must meet and confer at reasonable times and intervals. Obviously, refusal to meet at all with the union does not satisfy the positive duty imposed on the employer.

5. *Imposing conditions.* Attempts to impose conditions that are so onerous or unreasonable as to indicate bad faith will be scrutinized by labour boards.

6. *Unilateral changes in conditions.* This is viewed as a strong indication that the employer is not bargaining with the required intent of reaching an agreement.

7. *Bypassing the representative.* An employer violates its duty to bargain when it refuses to negotiate with the union representative. The duty of management to bargain in good faith involves, at a minimum, recognition that this *statutory representative* is the one with whom the employer must deal in conducting bargaining negotiations.

8. *Commission of unfair labour practices during negotiations.* Such action may reflect upon the good faith of the guilty party.

9. *Providing information.* Information must be supplied to the union, upon request, to enable it to understand and intelligently discuss the issues raised in bargaining.

10. *Bargaining items.* Refusal to bargain on a "mandatory" item (one *must* bargain over these) or insistence on a "permissive" item (one may bargain over these) is usually viewed as bad faith bargaining.[13]

Typical Provisions in Collective Agreements

The following are some of the typical provisions found in collective agreements:

1. Arbitration clause
2. Union recognition clause
3. Union security clause
4. No strike or lockout provision
5. Management rights
6. Grievance procedures
7. Disciplinary procedures
8. Compensation rates and benefits
9. Hours of work and overtime
10. Health and safety provisions
11. Employee security/seniority provisions
12. Contract expiration date

Of the 12 items listed above, five deserve closer scrutiny.

Arbitration Clause

arbitration clause

All Canadian jurisdictions, with the exception of Quebec and Saskatchewan, require that all collective agreements contain an **arbitration clause** providing for the final and binding settlement or arbitration of all disputes arising during the term of a collective agreement over the application and interpretation, or administration of that agreement. Arbitration will be further discussed later in this chapter.

Recognition Clause

union recognition clause

The **union recognition clause** is perhaps one of the most basic clauses. This provision is integral to the regime of collective bargaining as it is practised in Canada, and accordingly, it is required as a mandatory provision of each collective agreement by various statutes governing labour relations. It determines the scope of the bargaining unit and the work that falls within the unit. Additionally, it is this clause that fetters management's ability to negotiate individual agreements with its employees without the consent of the union. It prevents management from unilaterally imposing more punitive disciplinary terms, altering wage rates, or instituting bonus plans. Ontario and New Brunswick require a clause in the collective agreement recognizing the union as the exclusive bargaining agent for the employees in the bargaining unit specified in the labour board's certification order. In all jurisdictions, the certification order forms the basis for the negotiation of the collective agreement, and a recognition clause is generally included in collective agreements where it is not required by law so as to provide a clear indication in the contract of the group to whom the contract applies.

Union Security Clause

union security clause

All Canadian jurisdictions permit the inclusion of **union security clauses** in collective agreements that provide for the protection of the status of the union. The right to enforce such clauses as conditions of employment was firmly established by the Supreme Court[14] in 1959. The normal method of enforcement would be the use of the grievance and arbitration procedure provided by the collective agreement.[15]

There are various forms of union security clauses. These include i) closed shop, ii) modified union shop, iii) Rand formula or agency shop, iv) open shop, and v) checkoff.[16]

- Closed shop is the most restrictive form of union security—only members of the union may be hired by the employer.
- Modified union shop is a slight variation on closed shop clauses. All present and future employees must become and remain union members. However, the employer may hire individuals who are not union members at the time they are hired.
- The Rand Formula or agency shop is a union security arrangement that does not require union membership but does require all members of a bargaining unit to pay dues to the union.
- Open shop is a situation where there are no requirements for union membership or payment of dues.

checkoff

The process by which union dues are collected by the employer via payroll deduction and remitted to the union is known as **checkoff**. Checkoff provisions may be used with any of the other union security provisions. All Canadian jurisdictions provide that the employer must checkoff union dues when authorized to do so by the employee. All collective agreements in Canada have a checkoff clause. In five Canadian jurisdictions—British Columbia, Manitoba, Ontario, Quebec, and the Federal—the employer must deduct union dues from all employees in the bargaining unit and remit them to the union, if the union requests. Therefore, in these jurisdictions, the minimum union security provision in collective agreements is the Rand formula.

No Strike or Lockout Provision

All Canadian jurisdictions, except Saskatchewan, prohibit strikes and lockouts during the term of a collective agreement. Collective agreements in New Brunswick, Ontario, and Prince Edward Island must contain a **no strike or lockout provision**. In other jurisdictions, the required arbitration clause must have a "no cessation of work" provision.[17]

no strike or lockout provision

Management Rights Clause

The **management rights clause** clause describes the areas where management may exercise its prerogatives without discussion with or concurrence from the union, or the rights that are reserved to management that are not subject to collective bargaining, systematizing, centralizing, or sophistication of the employer's personnel policies, procedures, and rules. With unionization, for instance, the employer might take steps to 1) advise all plant managers that union-related questions should be referred to the headquarters's labour-relations specialist; 2) formulate a compensation plan and particularly a system of wage classes; and 3) develop an improved, more objective procedure for appraising employee performance, so that union challenges might be more easily defended against.

management rights clause

MAJOR BARGAINING STRATEGIES

There are two major bargaining strategies: distributive bargaining and integrative bargaining.[18]

Distributive Bargaining

Distributive bargaining is one of the most common forms of bargaining. It is called *distributive* because it involves the distribution of things that are available in limited quantities. This type of bargaining usually occurs when management and labour are unable to resolve outstanding issues, such as wages, working conditions, and rules of administration of the contract, in a proposed collective agreement. Distributive bargaining is sometimes referred to as "win-lose" bargaining, because the gains of one party are normally achieved at the expense of the other party.

distributive bargaining

The essential characteristics of distributive bargaining are illustrated in Figure 19.2. As indicated, distributive bargaining is characterized by three distinct components: the initial point, the target point, and the resistance point. On one hand, the labour union's initial demand point is usually higher than what the union expects to receive from management. The union target point is next, and represents what the union considers a realistic assessment of what is achievable from management. The union's final phase is the resistance point. This represents its minimally acceptable level. On the other hand, these points are essentially reversed for management. Its initial point is its lowest level that is used to commence negotiation.

FIGURE 19.2
Distributive
Bargaining

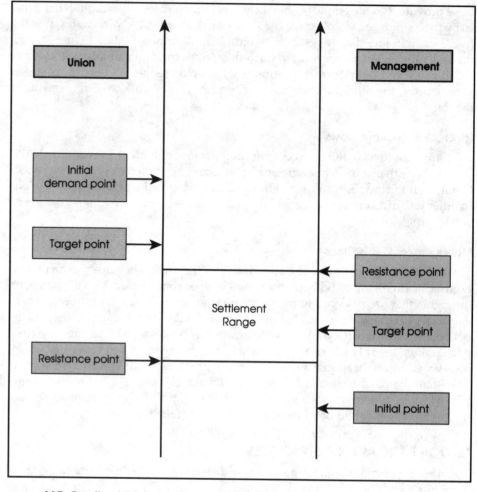

SOURCE: M.R. Carrell and F.E. Kuzmits, *Personnel: Human Resource Management*, 2nd ed., 1986, p. 466. Reproduced by permission of Macmillan Publishing Company.

Next is its target point, the area where management would like to reach an agreement with the union. Management's final phase is its resistance point that represents its ceiling or upper limit. The actual settlement range generally lies between the target point of management and the target point of the union. However, when both sides are unable to bridge the gap and reach a settlement, then a negative settlement range exists and a bargaining impasse results.[19]

Integrative Bargaining

integrative bargaining   The objective of **integrative bargaining** is to establish a creative negotiating relationship that benefits both labour and management. The integrative strategies require that both management and the union drop their combative attitudes and adopt a genuine interest in the joint exploration of creative solutions to common problems. Labatts Breweries have used a unique negotiating approach called "single team bargaining" that involves special seating arrangements, a focus on prob-

COMPUTER APPLICATION IN COLLECTIVE BARGAINING

Estimating Offers and Costs with Computers

Management students, whether they ultimately work for management or labour, are usually introduced to gaming—computer simulations that answer "what-if ..." questions. Sometimes the simulations are complex strategies; sometimes they are as basic as looking at cash-flow projections. These same concepts may be applied to labour-management negotiations. When labour suggests a 5% wage increase the first year, followed by 3% each of the next two years, management counters with 3, 3, 5, understanding that their proposal will cost less over the course of the three years. However, costing out other benefits may not be as easily understood. Therefore, programs which rapidly calculate the dollar cost of benefits (both direct and indirect costs) offer the opportunity for more knowledgeable bargaining.

To quickly calculate the costs of offers or counter offers, a simple table based on the percent of (1) each step in salary range, or (2) each employee's annual pay, or (3) a particular benefit can be altered. For example, if each wage step is 4% higher than the one below, and the first step of each grade equals the middle step of the previous grade, simply changing the first grade's first step in the table of the wage plan will update it. Then, by linking this table to the rate each employee is paid (keyed to that table), the new total cost is available. If an employee is paid at the rate of step 4, grade 3, a cell address next to that employee's name tells the company what is budgeted for that employee. If that employee has worked an average of 100 hours overtime each of the last three years, a formula would be placed next to the employee's name which includes the cell address plus the hourly rate (if the wage plan is not in hourly figures) times 100 (to represent the 100 hours).

If one side suggests that the benefits package should be raised by 7% to include so many dollars for child care, the negotiator should have available the number of employees who have expressed an interest in this benefit and how many children are involved as well as a range of possible costs of child care in the area. By combining this information with the current percentage of payroll assigned to benefit costs, it will be clear whether or not the 7% is a realistic figure of probable costs. The negotiator might be willing to give 5% and, with data of probable use and cost figured in, be able to negotiate a wording of the benefit that will better control costs, keeping them within the intended range.

For success at the bargaining table, the negotiators must be prepared not only in terms of what their organization (management or labour) would like, or must get, or can give up, but also in terms of what the other side is likely to suggest. Decision trees suggest guestimates in ranges of low, mid, and high probabilities of subjective variables.

The Art of Negotiating, a labour-management negotiations program developed by a father-son team of attorneys with a programmer,

> creates an interactive session between user and computer in which the user is prompted with questions at every step. The program then reincorporates the user's answers with further questions that develop a framework for the upcoming negotiation.[1]

This scientific approach to bargaining is based on the father's win-win, expanded thinking philosophy. The program forces each negotiator to think about the needs, limitations, and possible strategies of the other side. The novice will benefit by learning how to approach the bargaining table with facts, reasonable estimates, and a strategy: the veteran will find that possibilities are developed more quickly.

Computers, then, help to prepare the negotiator for the bargaining sessions, and could possibly shorten the time spent bargaining. If bargaining is done off-site, portable or laptop computers with 30 or 40 megabyte memories provide support.

---

[1] M. Steven Potash, "A Scientific Approach to Bargaining," *ABA Journal* (January 1986), p. 58.

lem-solving, off-the-record discussions, and wide participation.[20] The objective is to create "win-win" situations where both labour and management can "win" and to avoid win-lose situations.[21]

Quality of Work Life programs are one form of integrative bargaining in which management and labour participate in jointly-sponsored projects designed to improve productivity and the quality of the workers' working conditions. There are two other types of integrative bargaining: productivity bargaining and concessionary bargaining.

Productivity Bargaining

productivity bargaining

One of the primary purposes of **productivity bargaining** is to improve the effectiveness of the organization by eliminating work rules and inefficient work methods that inhibit productivity. Getting labour's agreement to eliminate old, ineffective work habits is not always easy. Unions may often fear that this form of bargaining will eventually lead to the loss of union jobs and a weakening of the union's power base and strength. However, notwithstanding the reluctance of many unions, many changes have been made to improve productivity, indicating a shift from distributive to productivity bargaining. A union's acceptance of new, improved work rules and practices may be due to a belief that jobs will become more secure as the employer's operation become more efficient and effective as productivity improves.

Concessionary Bargaining

concessionary bargaining

Concessionary bargaining is a special type of bargaining strategy utilized by employers when they are experiencing severe economic problems that have come about as a result of general economic recession or financial difficulties. During concessionary bargaining, employers usually seek agreement from their union to freeze economic rewards such as wages and benefits. In some instances management may seek reductions, sometimes called "give backs," in wages, benefits, and cost of living adjustments. It is usually the case that in exchange for these concessions, management would guarantee job security.

CONTRACT ADMINISTRATION

After a collective agreement has been negotiated, labour and management are required to abide by the terms and conditions of the provisions of the agreement. The results of the collective bargaining process that is implemented to ensure that they do so is known as **contract administration**. Notwithstanding the amount of time, effort, care, and attention put into the writing of the actual contract, it is almost inevitable that problems will arise regarding the application, and interpretation of the agreement.

contract administration

Disagreements between management and labour about the application and interpretation of the contract do not necessarily indicate bad faith on the part of either party. Instead, genuine differences of opinion about the intent of certain clauses may exist. In addition, differences of opinion may exist because of misunderstandings, unclear contract language, and changing circumstances. When disagreements or problems arise in the interpretation and application of the collective agreement, they are usually handled and settled through the grievance procedure.

The Grievance-Arbitration Process

The **grievance-arbitration process** is found universally in all labour-management agreements and is supported by public policy in all jurisdictions in Canada. It can generally be said that grievance-arbitration procedures have been effective in solving day-to-day problems under a labour agreement, in identifying areas where contract language and supervision require improvement, and in minimizing work stoppages and sabotage.

grievance-arbitration process

Purposes of the Grievance-Arbitration Process

The primary purpose of the grievance-arbitration process is to seek an application of the contract with a degree of justice for both parties that makes a resort to a strike or a lockout unnecessary. There are, indeed, some related, secondary purposes as well. One such purpose is to interpret the language of the agreement. Since life in an organization is dynamic, problems frequently arise during the period of the contract that were not anticipated by the parties involved and consequently were not provided for in the contract. In addition, problems of disagreement in the interpretation of clauses in the contract are also a source of contention that at times triggers the grievance-arbitration process.

When a grievance is filed, the parties must reach an agreement on applying the contract to the particular problem or they must submit the matter to an outsider for a decision. Another purpose of the grievance procedure is to provide a communicative device from the rank-and-file workers to higher management.

Generally, the grievance procedure tends to "take the pulse" of the organization, notifying management of potential trouble spots and areas of discontent. It also indicates places where managerial attention is needed. Further, it sometimes serves a political purpose within the union in that stewards or other union officers will push employees' grievances to demonstrate the usefulness of the union hierarchy.

Yet another purpose of the grievance-arbitration procedure is to call to the attention of the union, management, or both, those areas of the contract requiring clarification or modification in subsequent negotiations. It is usually the case that contracted clauses under which grievances constantly seem to arise are in need of careful examination and correction.

The grievance-arbitration process involves systematic union-management deliberation of a complaint at successively higher organizational levels. The problem may be settled at any of these levels, and if not, the complaint may be submitted to an impartial outside party whose decision is final and binding. The complaint is usually made by an employee. Though management sometimes uses grievance procedures to process a complaint about the union, such use is rare. All contracts contain grievance procedures, and most contain provisions for arbitration as a final step.[22]

Grievance arbitration is an adjudicative process through which disputes arising out of the application and operation of a collective agreement are finally resolved. As such, it performs the same functions for the parties to a collective bargaining agreement as the courts do in resolving issues and disputes arising from the operation of contracts in society generally. In essence, it is a quasi-judicial system created for each collective bargaining relationship.

Grievance arbitration is one of two quite distinct processes, both of which are commonly characterized as labour arbitration. The other, **interest arbitration**, from

interest arbitration

which grievance arbitration must be distinguished, is a form of dispute resolution in which the *arbitrator* makes the terms, conditions, and rules that govern the employer-union-employee relationship. So characterized, interest arbitration functions as a surrogate for collective bargaining, and the awards of arbitrators in these circumstances take the form of and serve the same purpose as collective agreements. Normally, they do not contain reasons for decision nor do they make findings of "right" or "wrong."[23]

In the vast majority of grievances alleging that an employee has been disciplined improperly, a board of arbitration must make two independent decisions. First, it must determine whether the employee actually engaged in some form of misconduct. Then, if it answers that question in the affirmative, it must decide whether such misconduct warrants the particular discipline imposed, including a consideration of whether the nature of discipline imposed violated the collective agreement.

Most collective agreements recognize an employer's right to discipline its employees in ways other than by terminating the employment relationship. However, virtually all agreements restrict the employer's common-law rights to use its disciplinary powers by requiring it to show "just or reasonable cause" for whatever sanction is imposed. The most immediate effect of such a provision is to deny the employer the right to terminate the employment relationship simply by giving reasonable notice. Of course, by contract or by collective agreement, the parties may expressly provide for the termination of persons employed for stipulated periods on the provision of reasonable notice.[24]

As noted, most collective agreements restrict an employer's right to discipline its employees by expressly requiring it to prove that it had just or reasonable cause for the discipline it imposed. Arbitrators are agreed that to satisfy this standard in instances of dismissal, an employer must affirmatively establish that as a result of some misconduct or disability the grievor has demonstrated his or her incompatibility or has seriously prejudiced or injured the reputation or some other legitimate interest of the employer.[25] Figure 19.3 illustrates the typical grievance procedure formed in collective agreement.

As can be seen, the typical first step of the grievance procedure in a labour contract occurs when an aggrieved employee or a union steward on behalf of the employee brings a complaint to the employee's immediate supervisor. Most labour contracts require that the grievance be presented in writing at the first step. The sequence of steps may vary in some contracts.

Usually, if the problem is not resolved to the satisfaction of the employee at the first step, he or she may then take the problem to the next higher managerial level designated in the contract, and so on through all the steps provided for in the contract. In Ontario, the most common practice is for labour contracts to provide for three steps, exclusive of arbitration.

In the grievance-arbitration process, the managerial people concerned will ordinarily seek the advice of the industrial-relations experts of the company's human resource department at some point in the process. This is usually done at step 2. This particular department is usually involved in the managerial decision at the final steps within the organization. Many contracts specify participation of the general manager, the chief executive officer, or the president of the company at the final step in the grievance process.

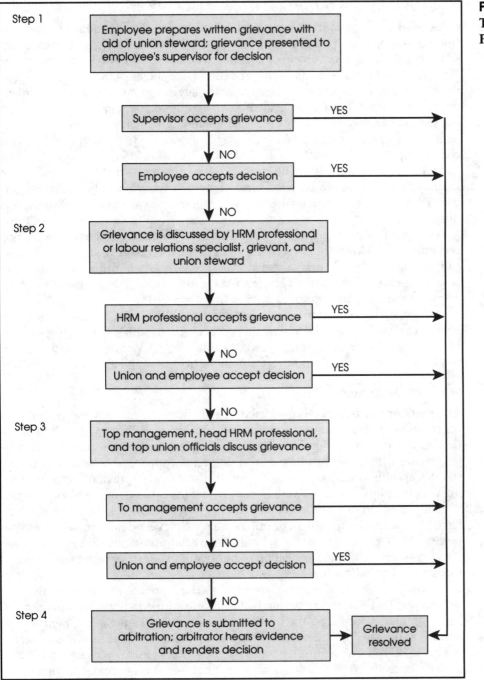

FIGURE 19.3
Typical Grievance
Process

Step 1

Employee prepares written grievance with aid of union steward; grievance presented to employee's supervisor for decision

Supervisor accepts grievance — YES

NO

Employee accepts decision — YES

NO

Step 2

Grievance is discussed by HRM professional or labour relations specialist, grievant, and union steward

HRM professional accepts grievance — YES

NO

Union and employee accept decision — YES

NO

Step 3

Top management, head HRM professional, and top union officials discuss grievance

To management accepts grievance

NO

Union and employee accept decision — YES

NO

Step 4

Grievance is submitted to arbitration; arbitrator hears evidence and renders decision

Grievance resolved

Difficulties Commonly Encountered

Some grievances stem from perceived injustices or injured feelings rather than from contract violations on the part of management. When such grievances arise the union has the difficult problem of deciding whether to process the complaint and face the possibility of rebuffs during the successive stages of the grievance procedure or whether to attempt pacification of the aggrieved employee. Management, on the other hand, must also decide how to handle such grievances.

One author suggests that a partial solution through a "clinical approach," in contrast to "legalistic" one, is a better device for morale and face-saving.[26] With the clinical approach, the steward or stewards attempt to assess the emotional and social aspects of the complaint and deal with the problem at that level. Simply permitting the employee to blow off steam may provide a partial solution. In any event, careful listening and analysis may permit the steward or supervisor to identify the real problem.

Another difficulty in the use of the grievance procedure is the possibility of it becoming a vehicle for the respective parties to test their relative strengths. As a result, the union may file grievances at every opportunity in order to wring every possible concession from management. On the other hand, management may fight every grievance in an attempt to contain the union.

Under such circumstances, the grievance procedure can hardly adjust problems at the lowest possible organizational level. On the other hand, the use of the grievance machinery, including arbitration, under such circumstances does serve to clarify the limits of the contract for both parties.

Role of the Arbitrator[27]

An arbitrator's jurisdiction is derived primarily from the collective agreement and the submission to arbitration and, in most provinces in Canada, it is founded in the legislative requirement that collective agreements contain an arbitration clause to provide a final and binding dispute settlement process. In addition, public statutes and the common law may provide a secondary source of decision-making power or authority. As well, in certain instances, there may be other factors affecting an arbitrator's jurisdiction in a dispute. For example, the grievance may have been withdrawn, settled, or otherwise conclusively determined before arbitration. Furthermore, just as the submission to arbitration initiates the arbitrator's jurisdiction in each case, completion of the award exhausts or terminates the specific grant of jurisdiction.

The collective agreement is recognized as the fundamental source of the subject-matters that may come within the arbitrator's jurisdiction. Accordingly, unless it grants a specific power to the arbitrator to "make the agreement for the parties" as opposed to "interpret and apply" it, arbitrators have held that they cannot do so. That is, an arbitrator whose jurisdiction is to be a "rights" arbitrator under a collective agreement cannot assume jurisdiction to make an "interests" determination. Often this limitation is recognized and given effect by arbitrators in their dismissal of a grievance on the basis that the agreement is silent or that the subject-matter of the dispute does not come within the terms of the agreement, or is premature. For example, it is now firmly settled that a provision in the agreement which provides for the arbitration of unjust dismissals will not, standing alone, permit an arbitrator to review the compulsory retirement of any employee, nor an early retirement agreement made between an employer and an employee.

In the grievance-arbitration process the arbitrator's role is generally considered quasi-judicial, that is, analogous to or approaching the role of a judge. He or she is expected to listen to evidence, weigh it impartially and objectively, and make a decision based on the labour contract. There are some significant differences between the arbitrator's role and that of a judge, however.

First, arbitration hearings tend to be much more informal than courtroom proceedings. The parties may or may not have legal counsel present at the hearings, and the proceedings are not bound by the rules of evidence as in the court of law. However, the proceedings are expected to be conducted with dignity and fairness. They are most likely to include the cross-examination of the parties or witnesses and the submission of documents as evidence.[28]

Secondly, the role of the arbitrator differs from that of the judge in that the arbitrator is not bound by precedents to the extent that the judge is usually held.[29] Although the arbitrator may study decisions of other arbitrators in order to sharpen understanding of the issues, and even though both parties may cite arbitrational decisions in support of their positions, an arbitrator is not bound by the decisions of other arbitrators. On the other hand, following precedents established in arbitration awards earlier in the relationship between the parties gives consistency to the particular relationship and may minimize unnecessary grievances.

A union may be subjected to considerable pressures from an aggrieved worker to push a grievance to further steps or to arbitration. Likewise, a union official may wish to press a certain case as a test of strength or to "get back" at management.

Similarly, a human resource manager may be pressured by other members of management to settle or not to settle the grievance. The urgency to "settle" is very much dependent on the current labour relations climate in the organization.

The grievance-arbitration process is interrelated with the process of contract negotiation. What the parties intended when they negotiated the contract may become an important element in an arbitration decision, and the arbitrator's decision may prompt one or both parties to seek a revision in the contract. Similarly, ambiguous or vague contractual clauses may precipitate grievances to test the meaning of the contract language. In addition, if a high degree of controversy and hostility characterize negotiations, a similar spirit may carry over into the administration of the contract and vice versa.

THE IMPLICATIONS OF PAY EQUITY FOR COLLECTIVE BARGAINING

Although the **pay equity** timetable may be such that it cannot wait for the expiration of some collective agreement, where possible it should be integrated into collective bargaining.

pay equity

Ontario's new Pay Equity Act is one of the most significant interventions by government into the process of setting wages in Canada since the advent of modern labour relations legislation in the 1940s.[30]

In essence, the Act forces employers to reassess the way they compensate employees on the basis of a new factor, known as "value." More specifically, the act requires that companies pay women working in traditionally female jobs the same wages that men working in equivalent, traditionally male jobs receive, provided that the work performed by both is found to be roughly the same under a job-evaluation plan.

Although other Canadian jurisdictions have laws requiring equal pay for work of equal value, the Ontario act is the most comprehensive of its kind for two reasons.

First, it applies to both the public and private sectors. (Manitoba has a pay equity law similar in form and intent to the new Ontario act, but it only applies to the public sector.) Second, Ontario's act is "proactive," meaning that the onus is on employers to take remedial steps to establish pay equity by evaluating jobs, implementing wage increases where necessary, and keeping their employees fully abreast of all related developments. Manitoba, Nova Scotia, and Ontario are the only jurisdictions in Canada to take a legislated approach to pay equity, although Prince Edward Island recently introduced similar legislation. The federal and Quebec jurisdictions both have equal pay legislation, but their schemes differ in that while an employer is expected to maintain pay equity practices, the process is complaint-driven, or "reactive."

While pay equity will have major implications for employers generally, there are numerous provisions in the Ontario act that will specifically affect union-management relations.

The most important implication of the Pay Equity Act for union-management relations is the requirement, in section 14(2), that an employer negotiate in good faith and endeavour to agree on a pay equity plan with the bargaining agent representing its employees. While employers who operate in a union-free environment will be able to exercise full control over the development of their pay equity plans, those who must deal with a trade union will have to share this control, to seek consensus or compromise and possibly to face adjudication of their plan if no agreement can be reached.

Although employers and trade unions will have to agree on what job evaluation plan will be used, employers should do their homework prior to the negotiations and decide beforehand on the job-evaluation plan which best meets their requirements.

Trade union groups have already indicated that they would like to conduct pay equity negotiations in sessions totally separate from regular contract negotiations. It is likely that they want to ensure that the gains from pay equity adjustments will not cut into what they would otherwise be able to negotiate for members during regular contract talks.

An interesting aspect of an employer's duty to negotiate pay equity with a trade union is the approval process. Once a trade union and an employer have agreed to a pay equity plan and the plan is posted in the workplace, the act specifies that the Pay Equity Commission is deemed to have given its approval to the plan. The act also specifies that the terms of a pay equity plan that have been agreed upon will automatically be incorporated into the relevant collective agreement and that they will take precedent over any other provisions in the agreement which might conflict with the establishment of pay equity. In a unionized environment, therefore, no individual employee has the right to appeal the content of the plan to the Commission.

Conflicting Jurisdictions

The duty to negotiate under the Pay Equity Act raises another concern for employers that have unionized employees. This requirement is similar to the duty articulated in the Ontario Labour Relations Act and other collective bargaining statutes. What then would be the appropriate forum for adjudication of a pay equity dispute should a bad-faith bargaining charge be laid?

On the Front Line

Being in the laundry and cleaning business, the Carters have always felt strongly about not allowing employees to smoke, eat, or drink in their stores. Jennifer was therefore surprised to walk into a store and find two employees eating lunch at the front counter. There was a large pizza in its box, and the two employees were sipping colas and eating slices of pizza and submarine sandwiches off paper plates. Not only did it look messy, but there were also grease and soda spills on the counter and the store smelled of onion and pepperoni, even with the four-foot-wide exhaust fan pulling air out through the roof. In addition to being a turnoff to customers, the mess on the counter increased the possibility that a customer's order might actually become soiled in the store.

While this was a serious matter, neither Jennifer nor her father felt that what the counter people were doing was grounds for immediate dismissal, partly because the store manager had apparently condoned their actions. The problem was they didn't know what to do. It seemed to them that the matter called for more than just a warning, but less than dismissal. Jennifer had these questions:

1. Should a disciplinary system be established at Carter's Cleaning Centres?

2. If so, what should it cover, and how would you suggest they deal with the errant counter people?

Under the Pay Equity Act, if the parties were not able to agree on one or more issues, the matter would ultimately be settled by the Pay Equity Commission. However, under regular collective bargaining, the parties could ultimately resort to a strike or a lockout to settle their differences. This raises a further question: if a pay equity issue leads to a bargaining impasse, would employees be barred from striking, or the employers from locking them out, while they each have rights, respectively, to do so under normal collective bargaining law? Unfortunately, it is too early to answer these thorny questions.

Ontario's new Pay Equity Act introduces a number of new and formidable obstacles between employers and trade unions. As in normal collective bargaining, however, the two sides will have the opportunity to overcome their differences through negotiation. Because the act is unequivocal in intent and quite detailed in setting out a timetable for achieving pay equity, companies might feel that they are behind the eight ball. However, management should not be put off, but should approach the adoption of pay equity with the same resolve to maintain operational control that it would take into any set of negotiations. Considering the potential costs and the kinds of organizational changes that the act will force companies to undertake, managers must make a special effort to ensure that the pay equity program they choose fits in with and complements their overall business objectives.

SUMMARY

1. Collective bargaining is the process of organizing employees to negotiate together with their employer. Collective bargaining enables worker to participate in the decision-making process that formulates the policies, procedures, and rules that govern the employment relationship.

The bargaining involves negotiation of a contract, administration of the contract, enforcement of the contract, and a mechanism for interpreting disputes which may arise during the term of the contract.

2. Bargaining in good faith is necessary for effective union-management relations. Both parties must make every reasonable effort, through communication and negotiation, to arrive at a collective agreement.

3. The collective agreement, the cornerstone of our labour-relations system, sets out the terms and conditions of dispute to be resolved by binding arbitration, confirms bargaining rights, and is used to determine the legality of various activities. Typical provisions include an arbitration clause, a recognition clause, a union security clause, a no strike or lockout provision, and a management rights clause.

4. There are two major bargaining strategies: distributive bargaining, that involves the distribution of things that are available in limited quantities (i.e., "win-lose" bargaining), and integrative bargaining, that seeks to establish a creative negotiating relationship that benefits both labour and management (i.e., "win-win" bargaining).

5. Contract administration seeks to ensure that labour and management abide by the provisions of the collective agreement. The grievance-arbitration process involves systematic union-management deliberation of a complaint at successively higher organizational levels.

6. In the grievance-arbitration process, the arbitrator's role is considered quasi-judicial: he or she listens to evidence, weighs it impartially, and makes a decision based on the labour contract.

7. Ontario's Pay Equity Act forces employers to compensate employees on the basis of value, requiring companies to pay women working in traditionally female jobs the same as men working in equivalent traditionally male jobs.

KEY TERMS

collective bargaining
collective agreement
good faith
arbitration clause
union recognition clause
union security clause

checkoff
no strike or lockout provision
management rights clause
distributive bargaining
integrative bargaining
productivity bargaining

concessionary bargaining
contract administration
grievance-arbitration process
interest arbitration
pay equity

DISCUSSION QUESTIONS

1. What is collective bargaining?
2. Explain the significance of the collective agreement.
3. What is a grievance?
4. Explain the role of the arbitrator.
5. What is the objective of Ontario's Pay Equity Act, and explain how the duty to negotiate under the Act concerns employers that have unionized employees.

CASE INCIDENT: Whose Side Are You On?

Mary O'Neill became union steward two years ago after Ted Stevens was promoted into a managerial position. It was common practice at Bramalee Products International to promote former union stewards to supervisory positions.

Stuart Smith has worked for Bramalee Products International for over 10 years. Early one Tuesday morning Stuart and his supervisor were engaged in an argument over the appropriate way to complete an assigned task. The argument was lengthy and at times heated. The supervisor felt that Stuart was challenging his position and authority, and was disrespectful to him. Stuart claimed that there was an honest disagreement between the two individuals, which is part of the dynamics of working life. Stuart also noted he was merely engaging in a competitive exchange of ideas with the supervisor, trying to arrive at the best solution to enhance production. Stuart was suspended for insubordination. He filed a grievance against the suspension. The grievance remained unresolved after step 3 in the grievance process (see Figure 19.3). At this point Mary told Stuart that she would like to talk to him about "where we go from here."

MARY: "As you know, I fully support your grievance and believe you were wronged by your supervisor. But I do not believe you can win this case at arbitration. I say this based on two years' experience handling grievances. I know how the process works. I have read various arbitration rulings. It grieves me to tell you that cases similar to yours are usually won by management. I believe that the arbitrator's rulings on those decisions were unfair. But the reality is that management has won them consistently. On the bright side I think we have made our point to management. I sensed that they got the message that they cannot overreact to situations like these, or they will stifle creativity and innovation. I feel certain they will ensure that this does not happen again. Arbitration can be costly both financially and emotionally. Because of these factors and because the odds are stacked against us, my recommendation is that we do not pursue this matter any further."

STUART: "I am not very pleased with what you have told me. You are supposed to be representing my interests, but you seem to be speaking for management. In fact, I should tell you that I am not pleased with the way you have handled this grievance. You allowed management to walk all over us during the meetings. You appear to maintain a too friendly and cozy relationship with management. You did not represent my interests as forcefully as you could. You are doing a better job trying to sell me on the merits for not going to the next step than you did defending me during the various stages of the grievance process. It appears that you are using this position to gain a promotion into the managerial ranks. There has been talk around the office that you will not hesitate to undermine the members who you are supposed to represent in order to advance your career. You seem to be playing a very dangerous and hypocritical game."

Questions

1. Do you believe that Mary's maintenance of good and harmonious relations with management clouded her judgment? Elaborate.

2. In your opinion, should the fact that management consistently wins cases similar to Stuart's discourage the union from taking such grievances to arbitration? Explain.

3. What impact, if any, does management's practice of promoting union stewards into managerial positions have on the grievance-arbitration process?

NOTES

1. David A. Peach and Paul Bergman, *The Practice of Labour Relations*, 3rd ed. (Toronto: McGraw-Hill Ryerson, 1991), p. 2.

2. A. W. J. Craig, *The System of Industrial Relations in Canada*, 3rd ed. (Toronto: Prentice-Hall Canada Inc., 1990), p. 2.

3. J. R. Dunlop, *Industrial Relations Systems* (New York: Holt, 1958); for details on the initial Canadian applications of this model see H. Jain (ed.), *Canadian Labour and Industrial Relations: Private and Public Sectors* (Toronto: McGraw-Hill Ryerson Ltd., 1975), pp. 2-12. For a more recent and comprehensive application of this model see A.W.J. Craig, *The System of Industrial Relations in Canada*, 3rd ed. (Toronto: Prentice-Hall Canada Inc., 1990), pp. 1-16.

4. Craig, pp. 1-16.

5. Parts of this section are drawn from George W. Adams, *Canadian Labour Law* (Aurora, Ont: Canada Law Book Inc., 1985), pp. 670-673.

6. *Canada Labour Code RSC (1970); Labour Relations Act (1980)*. See also Adams, pp. 670-673.

7. *OLRB* May 22, (Ontario: Graphic Centre, 1967).

8. Donald William Movers Ltd. (1975) Canadian LRBR.

9. Canteen of Canada Ltd., 1984, 15 LAC.

10. *OLRB*, (Canada: Sperry Vickers Division, Sperry Inc. 1983).

11. Craig, pp. 149-150.

12. Dale Yoder, *Personnel Management* (Englewood Cliffs, N.J.: Prentice-Hall, 1972), p. 486.

13. Quoted in Reed Richardson, *Collective Bargaining by Objectives* (Englewood Cliffs, N.J.: Prentice-Hall, 1977), p. 150; adapted from Charles Morris, ed., *The Developing Labor Law* (Washington, D.C.: Bureau of National Affairs, 1971), pp. 271-310.

14. Adams, p. 694.

15. Ibid.

16. Peach and Bergman pp. 122-124.

17. Donald J. M. Brown and David M. Beatty, *Canadian Labour Arbitration*, 3rd ed. 1991. p. 9-1. Used by permission of Canada Law Book Inc., 240 Edward St., Aurora, Ontario. L4G 3S9.

18. For a comprehensive discussion of distributive bargaining and integrative bargaining see Richard E. Walton and Robert B. McKenzie, *A Behaviourial Theory of Labour Negotiations*, (New York: McGraw-Hill, 1965), pp. 4-6.

19. See Howard Raiff, *The Art and Science of Negotiation* (Cambridge, Mass.: Belknap Harvard University Press, 1982), pp. 44-65.

20. "One Way to Avoid Strikes: Defuse the Confrontation Method," *The Financial Post*, November 8, 1975, p. 11.

21. Roger Fisher and William Ury, *Getting to Yes* (New York: Penguin Books), 1983.

22. Wendell French, *Human Resources Management*, 2nd ed. (Boston: Houghton Mifflin Company), 1990, p. 601.

23. Brown and Beatty, p. 1-1; See also A. Brown, "Interest Arbitration," *Task Force on Industrial Relations*, Study No. 18, (Ottawa: Information Canada 1970), pp. 5-8.

24. Brown and Beatty pp. 7-1-7-2.

25. Ibid p. 7-22.

26. See Benjamin M. Selkam, *Labour Relations and Human Relations* (New York: McGraw-Hill, 1947).

27. Brown and Beatty, pp. 2-1-2-6.

28. French, p. 605.

29. See Jay E. Grenig, "Stare Decisis, Re Judicata and Collecteral Estoppel and Labour Arbitration," *Labour Law Journal* 38 (April 1987), pp. 195-205.

30. This section draws on Arthur Potts, "The Implications of Pay Equity for Collective Bargaining" in *Human Resources Management in Canada* (Toronto: Prentice-Hall Canada Inc. 1987), pp. 55,519-55,524.

SUGGESTED READINGS

Arthurs, H.D., D.D. Carter, and H.J. Glasbeek, *Labour Law and Industrial Relations in Canada*, 2nd ed. Toronto: Butterworths, 1984.

Brown, Donald J.M. and David M. Beatty, *Canadian Labour Arbitration*, 3rd ed. Aurora, Ont.: Canada Law Book, 1991.

Herman, E.E. *Determination of the Appropriate Bargaining Unit by Labour Relations Boards in Canada*. Ottawa: Canada Department of Labour, 1966.

Palmer, E.E. *Collective Agreement Arbitration in Canada*, 2nd ed. Toronto: Butterworths, 1983.

CHAPTER
TWENTY

STRATEGIC ISSUES IN HUMAN RESOURCE MANAGEMENT

After studying this chapter, you should be able to

1. Discuss the trends influencing the nature of work and the work force in the 1990s.
2. Explain the impact these trends will have on the human resource management (HRM) function.
3. Conduct an HRM audit.
4. Identify the international issues in human resource management and describe how HR managers may meet these challenges.

OVERVIEW

The purpose of this chapter is to discuss strategic issues in human resource management and in particular human resource management's evolving role in creating and implementing strategic planning. We explain how various trends such as demographic trends will influence human resource management. At the end of this chapter we tie together what we have said in this book to this point. This serves to help develop a unifying philosophy of human resource management.

TRENDS INFLUENCING HUMAN RESOURCE MANAGEMENT (HRM)

We are speeding through a period of transition for HRM that reflects changing social values, new work force expectations and composition, new legislation and government regulations, changing economic conditions, and the onslaught of competition.[1] These trends and pressures will dramatically influence the nature of work and the Canadian work force in the years ahead and will shape the evolving role of human resource management. We have to understand these trends to understand their impact on HRM.

Demographic Trends

There are, first, dramatic demographic shifts taking place in Canada. As we discussed in Chapter 1, the baby boomers who crowded into the labour market in the 1970s and 1980s are advancing toward middle age. If Canada's fertility rate remains low then the average age of the population will increase substantially. This demographic trend will result in a smaller pool of younger, qualified individuals from which the organization may recruit. This shrinking pool will increase competition for the limited supply. HRM specialists must ensure that the organization adopt or strengthen its policies to train and upgrade the skills of older workers to meet the challenge of rapidly changing technology. They must also ensure that more emphasis is placed on benefits (pensions, medical) than on direct compensation. Consequently the human resource policies that attracted and motivated employees of the 1980s will no longer be appropriate for an aging population.

Trends in the Nature of Work

The nature of the work that employees will have to do is changing too. Perhaps the biggest change involves the shift from manufacturing to services. Today, for example, nearly two-thirds of the work force is employed in producing and delivering services; in fact, the blue collar industrial work force has declined. While about one million new jobs are projected for the 1986-2000 period, the goods-producing industries are projected to have almost no growth in employment during these years. Service-producing industries, therefore, will account for nearly all of the projected growth in new jobs.

Along with this shift from manufacturing to services, some occupational groups are projected to expand faster than average over the next ten years. Technicians, service workers, professional workers, sales workers, and executive and management employees will all experience faster than average employment growth between now and the year 2000. New jobs will increasingly require a higher level of education. If the labour available does not have the requisite skills and education, the HR specialists will have to develop programs for skills training and make selections on the basis of training potential. Programs to encourage continuing education will thus take on added importance over the next few years.

Technological Trends

At the same time technological advances will continue to shift employment from some occupations to others while contributing to gradual increases in productivity. For example, telecommunication already makes it relatively easy for many workers to work at home. Computer-aided design/manufacturing systems plus robotics will also increase rapidly. By 1990, for instance, General Motors had about 14 000 robots building automobiles (compared to about 1000 in 1984). Manufacturing advances will obviously eliminate many blue collar jobs, replacing them with fewer but more highly skilled jobs. Similar changes are taking place in office automation, where personal computers, word processing, and management information systems continue to change the face of office work.

The skills required to operate these new technologies will obviously have major effects on all levels of organizational functioning. Labour-intensive blue collar and clerical functions will decrease while technical, managerial, and professional functions will increase. Here again the nature of work will change and with it the nature of the work force with which HRM must cope.

Political/Legal Trends

Human resource managers will also have to continue to cope with changing political and legal trends. The unwillingness of Newfoundland and Manitoba to ratify the Meech Lake Agreement has brought about new political uncertainties. Although the resolution of these uncertainties will be orderly, changes of any kind (particularly political changes) can be stress-inducing on workers and their families. These could have adverse impacts on employee health and productivity. HRM specialists must ensure that the organization takes the necessary steps to deal with such factors if and when they arise. One of the most important trends is the adoption and implementation of employment equity and pay equity programs.

Competitive and Managerial Trends

Increasing international and domestic pressures will also continue to shape organizations. Competition is already international and this trend can only intensify. Competition today is not just intense, it is intense across national borders, and there is no doubt that every company will have to seek performance improvements in the years ahead.

At the same time, several factors are boosting the intensity of domestic competition as well. The international nature of competition is itself one factor, injecting new competitors into the Canadian scene. The wave of mergers (prompted, in part, by deregulation, junk bonds, and increasingly aggressive managers) will continue to create the need for more cost-effective performance on the part of companies.

One result is that downsizing today has become a continuing corporate activity. Witness the downsizing at CBC, Air Canada, and Esso. Fewer than half the employers that downsized in 1988-89 cited a "business downturn"—actual or forecast—as the reason. About 57% of the human resource managers in one survey listed "improved staff utilization," mergers and acquisitions, and other reasons (such as budget cuts) for their staff cuts. Only about 43% of the 1084 employers responding were forced to make reductions due to economic slowdowns.[2] Of the 424 companies that downsized, 30% planned to do so again in the next 12 months. And companies are not just getting leaner: increased competition and shorter product life cycles are creating an even greater need for more flexible, adaptable companies that are more decentralized and participative. They increasingly rely on cooperative project teams to come up with new products to ensure meeting the customers' needs. HRM must assume an innovative role in helping companies make the required changes.

THE EVOLVING ROLE OF HUMAN RESOURCE MANAGEMENT[3]

Conference Board of Canada Survey Results

In a survey conducted by the Conference Board of Canada of senior HR executives, the majority of survey respondents (54%) indicated that HRM has undergone considerable change during the last five years. Thirty-two percent stated that the function has experienced some change and only about 8% indicated that the function has stayed the same.

Human resource executives noted a significant change in top management's perception of the HR function. According to some respondents, the HR role was at one time normally designated to a secondary function. Today, HRM is springing to centre stage, actively courted by many CEOs and required by the top hierarchy to make a business contribution to the organization. About 78% of survey respondents stated that the HR function wields a greater influence within the organization than it did five years ago.

Senior management recognizes HRM as a significant force in driving organizational effectiveness. As Urban Joseph, Executive Vice-President, Human Resources Division, The Toronto-Dominion Bank, stated, "Organizations that select better employees, train and develop them more effectively, organize them better, evaluate them, and compensate their performance on an equitable and effective basis have a better chance of implementing their strategic objectives."

The importance attached by the top hierarchy to HRM varies among organizations. According to Robert Dods, Principal, William M. Mercer Limited, top management's perception of the strategic importance of the HR function within the organization is directly related to

- The role played by the vice-president of HR in the development and formulation of the corporate strategic planning process.

- The ability of the vice-president of HR to develop and communicate a set of meaningful corporate-wide HR strategies.

- The significance that HR strategies have on various business plans and facilitating the implementation of the corporate strategic plan.

- The extent to which the HR function can be an ongoing contributor to the organization at the same time becoming more proactive, adaptive, and lean.

- The extent to which the HR executive provides leadership role in managing cultural change and productivity improvement initiatives.

The influence of HR executives within organizations will, according to Mr. Dods, be directly proportional to the degree to which they are successful in achieving these goals.

Many respondents indicated "encouraging signs of higher corporate profile" as they started serving on corporate strategies, tactical, planning, and finance committees. One respondent noted that in his organization, the president and the vice-presidents of planning and systems, operations, finance, and human resources form the management structure. This group meets regularly and decides on the strategic direction of the firm. The HR executive is, in this instance, a major contributor to management philosophy and corporate direction.

Another example of the prominence of HRM is found in the growing number of senior HR executives reporting to CEOs. Many HR executives indicated that changes in their reporting relationship during the last five years elevated them to a direct reporting relationship to the CEO. About 76% of survey respondents indicated that they reported directly to CEOs. The rest reported to other executives such as corporate vice-presidents.

Harold Giles, Corporate Vice-President, Human Resources, General Electric Canada Inc., argued that the absence of a direct reporting relationship to the CEO perpetuates the purely administrative role of the function and negates the strategic role that the HR function must be called upon to play.

Don Champion, Vice-President, Administration, British Columbia Telephone Company, stated that HRM has been traditionally "the conscience of the organization" and is regarded as a vehicle of hope for employees. He saw a relationship between the high profile of the senior HR executive within an organization and the morale and commitment of employees. "If the profile of the senior HR executive is kept up within an organization, employees perceive the importance the organization attaches to the `human' side of the business and consequently morale goes up," he added. He stressed that an organizational design that insulated the senior HR executive from the CEO "would be a very bad signal" to employees and could be an impediment to "getting the work done."

Strategic Partnership with Line Management

Some respondents indicated that the influence and power of the HR function will stem from a strategic alliance with line management. "Establishing a close link with line managers is key to our relevance to management in our divisional operations. Human resource professionals and line managers must become business partners," stated one respondent.

The shift away from a bureaucratic approach to a consultative role is also dictated by the imperative of bottom-line orientation of the HR function. For instance, Mr. Ellsworth, Vice-President, Northern Telecom Canada, mentioned that with respect to compensation, HR managers used to develop merit pay guidelines, pay-off matrices, and a "host of delivery systems" for line managers to adopt. The present thrust in many firms is to move away from the system-wide compensation approach toward holding the line manger accountable for his or her compensation cost.

Human Resource Management at the Strategic Level

The HR function is also evolving from a "record-keeping and fire-fighting function" to a more proactive, professional service directly involved in strategic planning.

In a few large firms, administrative activities are being transferred out of the function to other departments such as finance and information systems. For instance, General Electric Canada is divorcing the HR function from the record-keeping role of the past by creating an administrative centre that looks after payroll and the administration of benefits under the company's department of finance. In a few organizations, HR executives contend that by the year 2000, many of the purely administrative functions such as payroll and benefits may be contracted out.

Ken Benson, Vice-President, Personnel and Administration, Canadian Pacific Limited, sees the HR function moving away from a creative, administrative function to becoming an integral part of the company's strategic, tactical, and operational process.

Involvement by HRM in strategic planning activities is reported to have increased in the past five years and respondents indicated that it will increase further in the future. About 84% of survey respondents stated that they participate in strategic planning.

Partners with Profit

The traditional view of the HR department as an expensive staff centre with no connection to bottom-line profitability is no longer valid. Ed Taylor, Vice-President, Human Resources, Westinghouse Canada Inc., argued that in the new business environment, the HR function can no longer continue being a staff support department with no interest in the financial impact of its actions on the organization.

Ensuring Organizational Effectiveness

Organizational effectiveness is largely contingent upon the optimal contribution of each employee. Consequently, HRM is focusing increasingly on creating an environment aimed at generating the maximum output from the most efficient utilization of employees.

Mr. Ellsworth of Northern Telecom stated that in the present competitive context, it is imperative for HRM to create a work environment that will motivate employees to "apply a discretionary effort" at work, by willingly adding much greater value to the business on their own accord.

Ensuring organizational effectiveness is one of the fundamental objectives of HRM at The Toronto-Dominion Bank. Urban Joseph argued that the bank's HR department is adding to corporate value through the systematic use of the following five "technologies": acquisition of human assets, organization design, performance appraisal, compensation practices, and employee relations.

Measurement of HRM's Contribution

Human resource executives argued that one of the key functions of senior management in the future would be to measure results in a more exact fashion. This concern over a cost-benefit relationship is a major step in making sure that HRM remains a vital and respected part of the organization. Mr. Giles of General Electric Canada predicted that HRM will fail if its contribution cannot be measured. Robert Algar, Vice-President, Personnel and Industrial Relations, Trimac Transportation System, agrees: "The role of HRM will fail to be significant unless its performance can be measured. Management resources demand measurement."

Trends like these will demand a change in the traditional role of the human resource management department, one that shifts it more from "staff" to "line," and from being a reactor to top management's plans to a partner in developing and implementing strategy.

Specific Changes

In the "Survey of Issues in HRM," by the Conference Board of Canada, HR executives were presented with a list of 17 issues to consider. They were asked to identify in order of importance the five major issues confronting HRM in the next five years. As Figure 20.1 shows, the issues identified by survey respondents are

- linking HR planning to the strategic business plan
- leadership within the organization

FIGURE 20.1

Major Issues Confronting Human Resource Management in the Next Five Years (94 respondents)

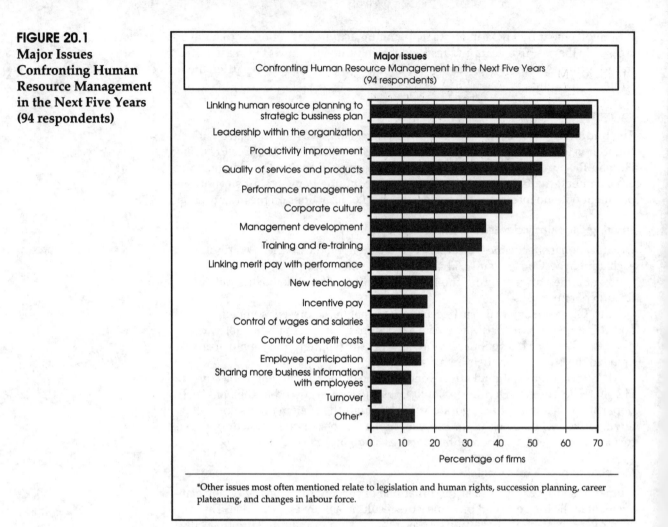

Major issues
Confronting Human Resource Management in the Next Five Years
(94 respondents)

Percentage of firms

*Other issues most often mentioned relate to legislation and human rights, succession planning, career plateauing, and changes in labour force.

SOURCE: *Human Resource Management: Charting a New Course*, by Prem Benimadhu, Report 41-89 (The Conference Board of Canada, 1989).

- productivity improvement
- quality of services and products
- performance management

Most of these issues, as well as those such as changing the "corporate culture," which was selected by 43% of respondents, are broad organizational issues related to the overall structure.

Linking Human Resource Planning to the Strategic Business Plan

Sixty-seven percent of respondents indicated that linking HR planning to the strategic business plan will be a significant HR issue in the next five years. The integration of HR planning into the corporate plan is imperative for business success. Respondents indicated that many well-conceived business plans went awry because HR implications of a strategic thrust were not considered.

Leadership within the Organization

The issue of leadership within the organization was selected by 64% of the respondents. Many respondents indicated that the survival of the firm in the next decades will require a significant change in the way organizations have operated in the past. They view their role as agents of change, playing a leadership role and providing a strong impetus to transforming the organization to meet the challenges in the business environment.

Productivity Improvements

Fifty-nine percent of the respondents indicated that productivity improvement will be of crucial importance to HRM in the next five years. Productivity improvement is imperative because, although Canada's productivity level remains high and the country is still capable of sustaining a high standard of living, it is not maintaining as high a growth on productivity as some other western countries. James Marchant, Vice-President, Human Resources, Canron Inc., stated that competitive pressures are forcing HR executives to institute productivity enhancement programs.

Quality of Services and Products

Human resource executives also feel that they have an important role to play in enhancing the quality of services and products. Fifty-two percent of respondents indicated that quality will be a fundamental issue facing their organizations. The emphasis on quality is all the more important because Canadian business today has continental and international opportunities and quality will be a major component in its winning combination. HR executives also argued that quality begins in-house—with the people. Without a quality work force and without a work force committed to quality, organizations cannot produce quality products and services.

Performance Management

Human resource executives identified another crucial issue during the interviews: performance management is receiving considerable attention, often in relation to a firm's emphasis on productivity improvement. Overall, 46% of respondents felt that performance management will be a major issue in the next five years.

Other Issues

The identification of the following issues further underscores HRM's strategic orientation rather than the operational direction that involves more routine concerns. The selection of these issues clearly shows that HR executives view their role more as participants at the strategic business level than merely as support staff, and that there are some other specific ways in which the human resources function will change.[4]

Employee Benefits

Changing demographics and the changing work force will demand changes in employee benefits. For instance, elder care—direct or indirect care provided to aging relatives—will become more popular as employees and their relatives get older. Furthermore, the tendency toward earlier retirement seems to have bottomed out. The expectation for the next decade is for a very gradual increase in the retirement age. Canada has already adopted a gradual increase in the normal retirement age for Canada Pension Plan purposes.

Consistent with the gradually rising retirement age, employers will have to cope with elder care, motivating plateaued workers, upgrading employees' skills, and instituting more flexible work hours.

Designing New Organizations

Peter Drucker contends that automation will require changes in job design, in the flow of work, and in organizational relationships.[5] Automation on the factory floor requires, for instance, that first-line supervisors change into genuine managers. The traditional functions of first-line supervision are being eroded by automation and either transferred to the work force or built into the process. And, of course, implementing "people" changes like these is traditionally the responsibility of the human resource management function.

Adjusting to Knowledge Workers

Even in the smokestack industries the manual labour component of the work force now accounts for no more than 25%. In most other industries, it is down to one-sixth or less. Productivity of white-collar workers and especially of the rapidly growing groups of knowledge workers is thus the big productivity challenge in developed countries. (The term "knowledge workers" encompasses such professionals as systems analysts, professors, accountants, management consultants, and marketing specialists.) The critical factors in knowledge work productivity are things like attitudes, work flow, job relationships, and the designs of jobs and teams. Above all, knowledge work productivity depends on placing the right person on the job. And, again, says Drucker, these are all jobs for the human resources managers.

Restructuring Career Ladders and Compensation

The shift to knowledge work and knowledge workers also creates a need to rethink and to restructure career ladders, compensation, and recognition.[6] The traditional career ladder in most businesses has only managerial rungs. But for most knowledge workers, a promotion to a management job is a wrong reward, says Drucker. The good ones often prefer to keep on doing professional or technical work. The shift to knowledge work will also force us to rethink the traditional organizational structure. The existing structure—derived from the nineteenth-century military—sees the managers as the boss, with everybody else as the subordinate. In the knowledge-based organization, knowledge workers are the "bosses," and the "manager" is in a supporting role as their planner and coordinator. But this means that jobs—their responsibilities, relationships, and rewards—have to be thought through and redesigned, again, probably, by the human resource management group.

Recruitment

As discussed, the number of new workers available to the labour force is expected to grow much more slowly over the next 10 years than it has in the past. This will make recruitment more difficult. As one expert puts it: "In a scarce labour market, the human resources department needs to differentiate itself and the company from the competition so that they can attract the desirable, highly qualified job seekers who are in demand."[7] Recruiting top-notch candidates during the next ten years will therefore be a very challenging task. And, probably, without an effective human resource management group, the employer will not have the workers it needs to conduct its business effectively. In its quest for good employees, an employer's human resource management group will have to work more closely with a select group of universities, perhaps providing them with information about jobs and career planning to help build a mutually supportive relationship.

Training

The training function will take on added importance in the next 10 years as increasingly complex knowledge jobs must be filled in part by a work force that is often ill prepared educationally to meet the new challenges.[8] Increasingly, human resource management will be called upon to implement a growing range of training programs, from basic skills and literacy training up through computer skills training and training in interpersonal communications and leadership. Thus in this area, too, the role of human resource management will have to expand in the next few years.

The Changing Role of Human Resource Management

The role of human resource management will change in three other major ways as well. There will be an expansion of its consultative role, a new emphasis on its line function, and its role in developing and implementing corporate strategy will be expanded.

First, human resource managements' traditional role as consultant to the company should increase in the years ahead; in fact, top HRM jobs are increasingly demanding a proven track record in providing top-notch consulting services on previous jobs. As firms must cope with shorter product life cycles, increased competition, and a more sophisticated work force, HRM's expert advice in areas like redesigning organizations, monitoring attitudes, instituting quality improvement teams, and molding company culture will be in high demand.

Paradoxically, while human resource management's consultative/staff role will expand, its line role will expand as well. Drucker points out, in fact, that there are already quite a few precedents for human resource departments carrying out a line function. He notes that it has always been so in the largest Japanese firms and in the military. And the Vatican's "personnel department," which picks and appoints the bishops of the Catholic church, is strictly a "line department." To make the jump to a more line-oriented role, the way these departments are staffed will probably change, too. For example, the vice-president for human resource management may increasingly have a top-level operating background and come up though the ranks before assuming the human resource manager's role.

But perhaps the most striking change in human resource management will be its evolving role in developing and implementing corporate strategy. Traditionally corporate strategy—the company's plan for how it will balance its internal strengths and weaknesses with external opportunities and threats in order to maintain a competitive advantage—was a job primarily for the company's operating (line) managers. Thus Company X's president might decide to enter new markets, drop product lines, or embark on a five-year cost-cutting plan. He or she would then more or less leave the human resource implications of that plan (hiring or firing new workers, hiring outplacement firms for those fired, and so on) to be carried out by the human resource department. But today things are different. Strategies increasingly involve merging employees from different firms, and companies face the demographic and work force changes described above. It is now increasingly necessary to involve personnel in the earliest stages of developing the firm's strategic plan. Human resource management will move from "reactor" to "developer and implementer" of strategy.

INTERNATIONAL ISSUES IN HUMAN RESOURCE MANAGEMENT

It is not necessary to look very far to see how important international business has become to companies here and abroad. In Canada, exports are expected to increase as a result of the free trade agreement between Canada and the United States and other external activities.

This rapid growth of exports reflects the fact that many more Canadian-based companies are focusing their marketing efforts not only here, but abroad. Huge "global" companies like Seagrams, and Olympia and York have long had extensive overseas operations. However, with the European market unification of 1992, the opening up to Eastern Europe, and the rapid development of demand in other areas of the world, more and more companies are going to find that their success (and perhaps their survival) depends on their ability to market and manage overseas. And, of course, to foreign companies Canada is "overseas" and thousands of foreign firms already have thriving operations on (and beyond) our shores.

As a result of this internationalization, companies must increasingly be managed globally, even though such globalization confronts managers with some herculean challenges. Market, product, and production plans must often now be coordinated on a worldwide basis for instance, and organization structures capable of balancing centralized home-office control with adequate local autonomy must be created.

Some of the most pressing challenges facing employers concern the impact of globalization on a company's human resource management system. These challenges range from (1) general issues like how to select, train, and compensate managers who must be sent to foreign posts, to (2) dealing with country-specific differences that demand corresponding country-specific fine tuning of a firm's human resource management policies. These two sets of challenges are addressed next.

The trend toward international business and global competition is likely to continue into the next century.[9] As one researcher observed, the Canadian economy provides an even more dramatic example of the growing importance of international business activity than the United States:

> There are over 500 Canadian-based companies with foreign subsidiaries, a figure which has climbed 43% since 1974. Nearly one-quarter of all goods consumed by Canadians are imported from other countries, and the same percentage of Canada's gross national product is exported abroad. More than half of Canada's manufacturing capacity is owned by foreigners.[10]

One of the implications of the internationalization of business and global competition is the increasing need for organizations to properly manage their human resources and to be knowledgeable about the unique issues and dimensions of international HRM. In addition, with the increasing trend toward the globalization of business, more Canadian corporations will seek business opportunities in foreign countries and will require managers to work with persons from diverse cultures and backgrounds. This will entail an ever-increasing need for managerial talent who share an international outlook and the ability and willingness to do business in foreign countries whether in foreign subsidiaries or in joint venture agreements. This of course has important implications for the future curriculum of management educations.[11]

As we have already touched on at several points in this book, there are at least three major general HRM issues a global company has to address: selecting managers for overseas assignments, orienting and training these people, and then compensating them.

Selection and Training for Multinational Management

Organizations selecting multinational managers must be as careful to define the job demands and human requirements as they would for any domestic job. Many companies make the mistake of evaluating only the technical (such as manufacturing knowledge) demands of the overseas job, while ignoring the cultural demands and need for adaptability that characterize such overseas jobs. Thus, as one vice-president for international human resources puts it: "There is too much emphasis on executives' technical abilities and too little on their cultural skills and family situation ... when international executive relocations fail, they generally fail either because expatriates cannot fathom the customs of the new country or because their families cannot deal with the emotional stress that a company's relocation entails."[12] In the same vein, one expert on Japanese multinational enterprises argues that Japanese multinationals have had better success rates with the employees they send overseas than do U.S. firms; she argues that this is largely a product of superior selection and training.[13]

One researcher argues that an important implication of the internationalization of business is an increased need for international managers. Given the increasing trend toward the internationalization of business and global competition, one would hope and expect that schools of management and business are keeping pace by adjusting their curriculum. She further argues that "somewhere in the business curriculum there be made room for a consideration of the underlying philosophy of international business."[14]

Another researcher believes that courses in international business will become even more important in the management curriculum and that existing courses should be made more rigorous, with more multidisciplinary and analytical content. Besides economics, functional fields and organization and management strategy, international business education may very well include competency in foreign languages, knowledge of other cultures through the study of history, literature, sociology, and religion in addition to periods of living, learning, and working in foreign countries. Other dimensions that can be included in international business are studies of comparative governments and policies, comparative commercial law, comparative sociology, international labour relations, transfer of technologies, and international accounting standards and practices. At any rate, much original thought is required to make international business courses more pertinent for the future.[15]

According to one researcher, while the international business curricula at the undergraduate level in Canadian universities is an area of neglect, at the graduate level it is adequate. He found a greater number of international business courses in the curricula at the graduate level much higher on average than at the undergraduate level. However, despite the importance and range of international personnel and human resource issues, there are no international business courses on IHRM at either the undergraduate or graduate level at any Canadian university.[16] It is important, according to another researcher, for managers to understand diverse and changing foreign cultures and national aspirations and to adopt their decision making to them.[17]

A realistic preview is an important technique that could be used. Both the potential transferee and his or her family need to have all the information that can be provided to them on the problems to expect in the new job (such as mandatory private schooling for the children) as well as any information obtainable on the cultural benefits, problems, and idiosyncrasies of the country in question. In any case, the golden rule here is to "spell it out ahead of time," as Ciba-Geigy, a major conglomerate consisting of 80 groups of companies, does for its international transferees.[18]

The question arises as to whether there are paper-and-pencil tests that can be used to more effectively select employees for overseas assignments and here the answer seems to be "yes." Generally speaking, of course, the development and use of any such test should ideally be company-specific and validated as a tool for placing candidates overseas. However, companies have developed and validated general-purpose tests that focus on the aptitudes and personality characteristics of successful candidates overseas. One such assessment tool is called the Overseas Assignment Inventory. Based on 12 years of research involving more than 7000 cases the test's publisher indicates that it is useful in identifying characteristics and attitudes such candidates should have.[19]

International Issues in Compensation Management

Generally speaking, the whole area of international compensation management[20] presents some tricky problems. On the one hand, there is a certain logic in maintaining company-wide pay scales and policies so that, for instance, divisional marketing directors throughout the world are all paid within the same narrow range. This reduces the risk of perceived inequities and dramatically simplifies the job of keeping track of disparate country-by-country wage rates.

And yet not adapting pay scales to local markets can present an HR manager with more problems than it solves. The fact is that it can be enormously more expensive to live in some countries (like Japan) than others (like Greece), and if these cost-of-living differences are not considered it may be almost impossible to get managers to take "high cost" assignments.

Yet even here the answer is usually not just to pay, say, marketing directors more in one country than in another. For example, this could cause resistance when telling a marketing director in Japan who's earning $2000 per week to move to the division in Spain, where her pay for the same job (cost of living notwithstanding) will drop by half. One way to handle this problem is to pay a similar base salary company-wide and then add on various allowances according to individual market conditions.[21]

The problem here is that determining what equitable wage rates should be in many countries is no simple matter. As we explained in Chapter 12, there is a wealth of "packaged" compensation survey data already available in Canada, but such data is not easy to come by overseas. As one expert on the matter has said, "Unfortunately, local sources of compensation information in foreign counties are hard to find, and often only compound the problem rather than helping to bridge the gap."[22] As a result, he says that "one of the greatest difficulties in managing total compensation on a multinational level is establishing a consistent compensation measure between countries that builds credibility both at home and abroad."

Some multinational companies deal with this problem by conducting their own annual compensation surveys. For example, Kraft conducts an annual study of total compensation in Belgium, Germany, Italy, Spain, and the United Kingdom. Kraft tries to maintain a fairly constant sample group of study participants (companies) in its survey. It then focuses on the total compensation paid to each of ten senior management positions held by local nationals in these firms. The survey covers all forms of compensation including cash, short- and long-term incentives, retirement plans, medical benefits, and prerequisites.[23] The company then uses this data to establish a competitive value for each element of pay. This information in turn becomes the input used for annual salary increases and proposed changes in the benefit package.

One international compensation trend of growing importance concerns the awarding of long-term incentive pay to overseas managers. While it may not seem particularly logical, many U.S. multinationals only permit the top managers at corporate headquarters to participate in long-term incentive programs like stock option plans.[24] Equally problematic is the fact that many of the multinationals that do offer overseas managers long-term incentives (32 out of 40 doing so in one survey) only use overall corporate performance criteria when awarding incentive pay. Since the performance of the company's stock on a Canadian stock market may have little relevance to, say, a French manager in its subsidiary in France, the incentive value of such a reward is highly suspect. This is particularly so in that, as one expert writes, "Regardless of size, a foreign subsidiary's influence on its parent company's stock price (Canadian dollars) is more likely to result from exchange rate movements than from management action."[25]

The answer, more multinationals are finding, is to formulate new long-term incentives specifically for overseas executives. More and more Canadian multinationals are thus devising performance-based long-term incentive plans that are tied more closely to performance at the subsidiary level. These can help build a sense of ownership among key local managers while providing the financial incentives needed to attract and keep the people needed overseas.

Impact of Inter-Country Differences on Human Resource Management

There are two basic sets of issues in international HRM management. One, as explained above, is the more general set of issues regarding how to select, train, and compensate managers, given the unique demands that dealing with new and different cultures places on international transferees. The second set of thorny international HRM issues derives from the fact that there are wide-ranging differences in legal systems, labour availability, and so on among countries. As a result, multinationals must, to some extent, fine tune their HRM policies to the unique needs of each country in which they do business.

To a large extent companies operating only within the borders of Canada enjoy the luxury of dealing with a relatively limited set of economic, cultural, and legal variables. Notwithstanding the range from liberal to conservative, for instance, Canada's is basically a capitalist competitive society. And, while a multitude of cultural and ethnic backgrounds are represented in Canada's work force, various shared values (such as an appreciation for democracy) help to blur the otherwise sharp cultural differences. And while the different provinces (as explained in Chapter 2) certainly have their own laws affecting HRM, a basic legal framework as laid down by federal law helps to produce a fairly predictable set of legal guidelines regarding matters such as employment discrimination, labour relations, and safety and health.

A company operating multiple units abroad is generally not blessed with such relative homogeneity. For example, minimum legally mandated holidays may range from none in the United Kingdom to five weeks per year in Luxembourg. And, while there are no formal requirements for employee participation in Italy, employee representatives on boards of directors are required in companies with more than 30 employees in Denmark. The point is that the management of the human resource function in multinational companies is complicated enormously by the need to adapt human resource management policies and procedures to the unique differences among the countries in which each subsidiary is based. We turn now to a closer examination of the sorts of inter-country differences that demand such adapting.[26]

Cultural Factors

There are wide-ranging cultural and ethnic differences from country to country which demand corresponding differences in human resource practices among a company's foreign subsidiaries. We might generalize, for instance, that given the cultural background of the Far East and the importance there of the patriarchal system, the typical Japanese worker's view of his or her relationship to his or her employer has an important impact on how that person works. Human resource incentive plans in Japan therefore tend to focus on the work group while in the West the more usual prescription is to focus on individual worker incentives.[27]

In addition to mediating for differences in HR practices these sorts of cultural differences also suggest that HR staff in a foreign subsidiary is best comprised of citizens of the subsidiary's host country. A high degree of sensitivity and empathy for cultural and attitudinal demands of co-workers is always important when selecting employees to staff overseas operations, as we explained above. However, such sensitivity is especially important when the job is HRM and the work involves all those "human" jobs like job interviewing, testing, orienting, training, counselling, and (if need be) terminating. As one expert puts it, "An HR staff that shares the employee's cultural background is more likely to be sensitive to the employee's needs and expectations in the work place—and is thus more likely to manage the company successfully."[28]

Economic Factors

Differences in economic systems among countries also influence the role played by HRM. In free enterprise systems, for instance, the need for efficiency tends to favour HR policies that value high productivity, efficient workers, and staff cutting where market forces dictate it. Moving along the scale toward more socialist systems, on the other hand, HR practices tend to shift more toward preventing unemployment, even at the expense of sacrificing competitive advantage.

Labour Cost Factors

Differences in labour costs may also produce corresponding differences in HR practices. High labour costs can require a focus on efficiency, for instance, and on all those HR practices aimed at improving employee performance. On the other hand, the lower labour costs associated with some less developed countries may make it cost effective to spend less on employee productivity-boosting activities.

Industrial Relations Factors

Industrial relations (and particularly the relationship between the worker, the union, and the employer) varies dramatically from country to country and has an enormous impact on human resource management practices. In the Federal Republic of Germany, for instance, "co-determination" is the rule. Here employees have the legal right to have a voice in setting company policies. In this and several other countries workers elect their own representatives to the supervisory board of the employer, and there is also a vice-president for labour at the top management level.[29] On the other hand, in many other countries the state interferes very little in the relations between employers and unions. In Canada, for instance, HR policies on most matters such as wages are set not by the state but by the employer or by the employer in negotiations with its labour unions. In Germany, on the other hand, the various laws on co-determination including the Works Constitution Act, (1972), the Co-Determination Act (1976), and the ECSC Co-Determination Act (1951) largely determine what HR policies will be in many German firms.

Europe 1992[30]

As of 1992 the twelve separate countries of the European community are unified into a common market for goods, services, capital, and even labour. Generally speaking, tariffs for goods moving across borders from one EC country to another disappeared, and employees (with some exceptions) found it easier to move relatively freely between jobs in various EC countries.

Figure 20.2 summarizes current employment practices and policies among EC countries. The figure underscores two things. First (in line with our discussion of inter-country differences, above), there are some wide-ranging differences in HR practices amongst EC countries. Thus as shown in Figure 20.2 many countries have minimum wages while others do not, and maximum hours permitted in the work day and work week vary from no maximum in the United Kingdom to a maximum of 48 hours per week in Greece and Italy. Similar differences are apparent in matters like minimum annual holidays, minimum notice to be given by employer, termination formalities, and employee participation.

Second, the impact of "1992" will be to gradually reduce these sorts of differences among member countries. However, these changes will be gradual. Social legislation and examinations by the European Commission are at the present time slowly harmonizing some of these differences. However, even if all of these differences summarized in the figure are eventually eliminated, cultural differences will no doubt require that HR practices will still differ from country to country. Even into the far distant future, in other words, managing human resources multinationally will present some tricky problems for HR managers.

FIGURE 20.2 Current Employment Practices and Policies Among EC Countries

Country	Employment Formalities	Minimum Pay	Max. Hours (Including overtime)	Minimum Annual Holiday	Minimum Notice to be Given by Employer	Termination Formalities	Employee Participation
Belgium	Certain terms must be in writing	Yes	8 per day; 40 per week	4 weeks.	Workers: 14–28 days. Others: 3 months for up to 5 years' service = 3 max. for every 5 years service. Higher paid employees notice period agreed on when notice given or decided by Court.	Can terminate without notice for gross misconduct (but this does not include all instances of incompetence). Redundancy payments.	Work councils.
Denmark	Contracts usually oral.	No, but conform to one of 2 compulsory wage systems.	Depends on collective agreement.	2.5 days per month.	Workers: depends on collective agreement. Others: 1–6 months.	Can terminate without notice for gross misconduct; unfair dismissal and redundancy payments.	Employee representatives on board of directors where there are more than 30 employees.
France	Contracts in writing. Collective agreements may be generally binding.	Yes	10 per day; 39 per week.	2.5 days per month (includes 5 Saturdays).	1 month after 6 months' service; 2 months after 2 years's service.	Unfair dismissal. Redundancy payments. Authorization of redundancies required.	Employee and union representatives. Works councils.
Germany	Fixed-term agreements restricted; collective agreements may be generally binding	No, but if a collective agreement, this must make provision.	8 per day, 48 per week.	18 days.	Workers: 2 weeks to 3 months. Others: 6 weeks to 6 months from end of calendar-year quarter.	Unfair dismissal. Prior consultation on redundancies or dismissals with works council and in some cases the labor authorities	Works councils.
Greece	'No substantial formalities.	Yes	48 per week.	4 weeks (after 1 year's employment).	Workers: none. Others: 1 month to 2 years	Severance payments of 5–52 days' pay for workers or 1–24 months' pay for other employee. If notice given, only .5 payable	Employee committees.

Country							
Ireland	Employees may require employers to supply written statements of terms of employment	No	No generally applicable statutory maximum	3 weeks	1–8 weeks.	Unfair dismissal. Redundancy payments.	No formal requirements.
Italy	Contracts in writing. National collective agreements.	Collective agreement.	48 per week. 8 per day.	Collective agreement.	Collective agreement.	Severance payments. Can dismiss only for redundancy or good cause.	No formal requirements.
Luxembourg	Written contracts must be provided. Agreements may be binding on a sector	Yes	40 per week. 8 per day.	25 working days (5 days' holiday equals one week).	4 weeks to 6 months, depending on category of worker and length of service.	Severance payments. 1–12 months. Prior notification of redundancy and redundancy payments.	Employees's representatives. Joint works councils. Employee directors.
The Netherlands	No substantial formalities.	Yes	48 per week. 8.5 per day. 5.5 days per week.	4 weeks.	Interval of payment (usually 2 weeks or 1 month) or a period of up to 13 weeks (26 weeks for older employees) based on length of service, whichever is longer.	Authorization of labor office usually required to dismiss with notice. May need to go to the Court; either procedure can take several months.	Works council in undertakings with 35 or more employees.
Portugal	Fixed-term contracts must be in writing.	Yes	Office workers: 42 hours per week. Others: 48 per week; 8 per day.	Not less than 21 days nor more than 30 days.	Redundancy notice period fixed when conditions of redundancy established.	Can dismiss only for "just cause" or redundancy. Prior notification of redundancies.	Workers' Commissions and registered trade unions.
Spain	No substantial formalities.	Yes	40 per week. 9 per day	2.5 days per month.	1 month after 1 year's service, 3 months after 2 years.	Only for specified causes. Dismissal for other causes; compensation to 45 days pay per year of service.	No formal requirements.
United Kingdom	Written statement of terms of employment.	No	No	No	1–13 weeks.	Unfair dismissal. Redundancy payments. Prior notification of redundancies.	No formal requirements.

SOURCE: SEDEL, RAE, "Europe 1992: HR Implications of the European Unification." *Personnel*, October 1989, p.22 (reprinted with permission of the publisher from *Personnel Today*, April, 1989).

AUDITING THE HRM FUNCTION

While the firm's human resource management policies and focus should be consistent with the company's strategic plan, the bottom line should always be: "To what extent is HRM effectively carrying out its function?" In other words designing a set of policies and an HRM philosophy that is consistent with where the company wants to go is only part of the job. Effectively carrying out those functions is another.

Several suggestions have been made for how to assess how HRM in a firm is actually doing. One approach is to use accounting and statistical techniques to calculate the cost of human resources, for instance the dollar investment in human assets that good training provides. In this way the bottom-line contribution of HRM can be concretely assessed.[31] For an employer with the wherewithal to conduct such a program, it may well be worth considering. A second, less rigorous, but still effective approach follows.

The HR Review

At a minimum, a less mathematically exacting but still highly valuable "HR review" should be conducted, one aimed at tapping top managers' opinions regarding how effective HRM has been. While an "HR review" is comprehensive, its value lies in its simplicity. Such a review should contain two parts: what should be and what is.[32]

The question "what should be?" refers to the broad aims of the HRM department and involves two things. It should start, first, with a very broad philosophy or vision statement. This might envision HRM as being "recognized as an excellent resource rather than a bureaucratic entity, a business-oriented function, and the conscience of the company," and so forth. This vision might also enumerate the characteristics of the HRM staff, for instance, as "experts in their areas of responsibility, demonstrating a commitment to excellence, and being creative, analytical problem solvers." The vision statement should thus set the tone for HRM.

Second, this broad vision gets more focus with an HRM mission statement. This describes what the mission of the department should be, for instance "to contribute to the achievement of the company's business objectives by assisting the organization in making effective and efficient use of employee resources and, at the same time, assisting employees at all levels in creating for themselves satisfying and rewarding work lives."[33]

Second, the focus of the HR review then shifts to an evaluation of "what is?" This part of the evaluation consists of six steps and involves input from the corporate HRM staff, division heads, divisional HRM heads, and those other experts (like the benefits administrator) that report directly to the head of corporate HRM. The issues to be addressed are as follows:

1. *What are the HRM functions?* The participants listed above (division heads and so forth) provide their opinions about what they think HRM's functions should be. The list can be extensive, ranging from pay equity enforcement and managing health benefits, to employee relations management, recruitment and selection, training, and even community relations management. The important point is to crystallize what HRM and its main "clients" believe are HRM's functions.

2. *How important are these functions?* The participants then rate each of these functions on a 10-point scale of importance, ranging from low (1-3) to medium (4-7) to high (8-10). This provides an estimate of how important each of the 15 or 20 identified HRM functions are in the views of by HRM executives and their clients (like division managers).

3. *How well is each of the functions performed?* Next, the same participants evaluate how well each of these HRM functions are actually being performed. For example, the evaluators may find that four functions—say, employee benefits, compensation, employee relations, and recruiting—receive "high" ratings from more than half of the raters. Other functions may get "medium" or "low" ratings.

4. *What needs improvement?* The next step is to determine which of the functions rated "most important" rate as high, or medium, or low in terms of "how well is each of the functions performed?" Functions (like "labour relations") that are assessed as highly important but evaluated as low in terms of performance will require the quickest attention. To formalize the comparison of importance and performance ratings, have the participants compare the median importance and performance ratings for each of the 15 to 20 functions identified in step 1. Then, each of the participants should be asked what can be done to increase the importance or improve performance of each of the 15 to 20 functions. In terms of importance, it could turn out that some functions are and should be much less important than others and that some functions (like community relations) are best administered though other departments like public relations. In any event, this step in the HR review will help to reveal if such changes are needed.

   More important, the discussions at this stage will help identify the HRM functions in which the department has to improve its performance. The discussions arising at this point should help to pinpoint specific problems that contributed to the "low performance" ratings and help provide recommendations for improving HRM's performance on low-rated functions (say, selection or training).

5. *How effectively does the corporate HR function use resources?* This next step of checks is to determine if the HRM budget is being allocated and spent in a way that is consistent with the functions HRM should be stressing. First, an estimate of where the HRM dollars are being spent should be made—for instance, on recruiting, employment equity compliance, compensation management, and so on. Also ongoing work and new programs (such as a quality improvement program that may be installed two years hence) must be distinguished. Questions to ask are: "Is expense allocation consistent with the perceived importance and performance of each of the HRM functions?" and "Should any dollars be diverted to low performing functions to improve their effectiveness?"

6. *How can HR become optimally effective?* This final step is aimed at allowing one last, broader view of the areas that need improvement and how they should be improved. For example, at this step it may be apparent that a large, divisionally organized company needs to strengthen divisional and on-site HRM staffs so that responsibilities for certain HRM functions can be moved closer to the user.

Expert Systems In HRM

An Expert System is a program that attempts to simulate how human experts solve problems. This is done by entering knowledge from one or more "expert" sources into what is known as a "knowledge base." This knowledge base includes the rules for solving a specific type of problem. When a user queries the expert system, the rules are evaluated, and the user is presented with an "expert" answer.[1] The value to HRM is that, within an hour, the person knowledgeable in a given area (such as) can put together a program that recognizes complex rules of logic. The software is user friendly, and some packages have very good graphics.

Users of electronic spreadsheets (like Lotus 1-2-3 and VP Planner Plus) are already building knowledge systems to handle complex problems. Current uses include producing sales reports quickly when products, data, or rules change frequently. One-time reports using relatively small data bases can be combined with macros to use the time of the manager or professional more efficiently. This type of system is called a performance aid. The user sets the rules (if this is the situation, do that, otherwise do this), which can be combined (AND) or contrasted (OR) with other rules.

In HRM, knowledge systems are useful in several areas. For example, as cafeteria benefit plans proliferate, the interaction of decisions made by employees may violate a rule that requires that at least 60% of the employees must choose term life insurance in order for that benefit to be offered at a group rate. The computerized HRM aid could alert management to that fact, as well as allow employees to ask "what-if" questions to see the impact of various decisions on outcomes such as income tax rate, total retirement income, early retirement, or net pay after deferring income.

Knowledge systems are also valuable in reviewing the impact of changes in career ladders, in the weighting of elements in job analysis, and in the effect of recruitment on such outcomes as total wage and benefits costs, employment equity categories, and promotional opportunities as well as estimated aging of the work force of that particular company. Risk mangers can more accurately assess the cost of various combinations of benefit packages and differing experience ratings of health plans. Supervisors can more clearly differentiate the impact of merit pay with systems that establish percentage increases based on performance ratings. The company can also judge the bottom line impact of various percentage raises for various levels of demonstrated accomplishment based on performance appraisal. While small knowledge systems are useful in contract negotiations, large expert systems will give more accurate estimates of strategic decisions without bias or emotion and without overlooking significant details.

With the demographic shifts in Canada and the increasing rate of change in the external environment, HR managers must be able to offer ways for companies to remain competitive domestically and internationally. Knowledge-based expert systems will become a part of the arsenal.

---

[1] Mary Lynn Manns, unpublished manuscript, February 19, 1990.

TOWARD A PHILOSOPHY FOR HUMAN RESOURCE MANAGEMENT
The Need for a Philosophy

In Chapter 1 we said that people's actions are always based in part on the assumptions they make and that this was especially true in regard to human resource management. The basic assumptions that are made about people—"Can they be trusted?" "Do they dislike work?" "Can they be creative?" "Why do they act as they do?"—together comprise a philosophy of human resource management. And the people hired, the training provided, and leadership style all reflect (for better or worse) this basic philosophy.

Throughout this book we have emphasized the "nuts and bolts" of human resource management by focusing mainly on the concepts and techniques all managers need to carry out their human resource management related tasks. It is therefore easy to lose sight of the fact that these techniques, while important, cannot be administered effectively without some unifying philosophy. For, to repeat, it is this philosophy or vision that helps guide the organization in deciding what people to hire, what training to provide, and how to motivate employees.

A Broader View of the Role of Human Resource Management: The Quality of Work Life

We also saw that managers are increasingly measuring their actions in terms of quality of work life, which means the degree to which employees are able to satisfy their important personal needs by working in the organization. In practice, this means providing employees with fair, equitable treatment; an opportunity to use their skills to the utmost and to self-actualize; open, trusting communications; an opportunity to take an active role in making important job-related decisions; adequate and fair compensation; and a safe and healthy environment.

We explained several techniques, including management by objectives and quality circles, that are aimed at improving the employee's quality of work life. Quality of work life goes beyond mere techniques, in that the quality of work life that prevails in an organization will reflect not just techniques but basic attitudes and assumptions about people.

Related to this, virtually every human resource management-related action taken affects the quality of work life in some way. Thus selection should emphasize placing the right person the right job, where that person can have the most satisfying, rewarding (and motivating) experience. Similarly, an equitable grievance procedure will help protect employee rights and dignity and therefore contribute to the quality of work life. Every human resource management action taken, in other words, affects the employee's quality of work life, and the employer's action will in turn reflect basic assumptions about people. It is when human resource management actions should be geared not just to satisfying the organization's staffing needs but also to satisfying the employee's need to grow and self-actualize that a personnel management system can be properly referred to as a human resource management system.

SUMMARY

1. Demographic, social, economic, and technological trends are forcing changes on organizations and human resource management. These trends include, for instance, a dramatic slowdown in the growth of the labour force, an increasing emphasis on knowledge-based work, and an increasingly internationalized competition.

2. In the face of trends like these, the role of human resource management is evolving. Specific ways in which the human resource management function will change include changes in employee benefits, new organization structures, restructuring career ladders, dealing with an aging work force, experimenting with new recruitment methods, and doing more training of workers to help them cope with the new knowledge-based jobs.

3. Perhaps the most striking change in human resource management will be its evolving role in developing and implementing corporate strategy. A company's strategic plan outlines the course of action the firm plans to pursue in becoming the sort of enterprise that it wants to be given its external opportunities and threats and its internal strengths and weaknesses. To this end, human resource management helps top management to formulate and execute the company's strategic plan by helping to supply intelligence regarding the company's external opportunities and threats, by supplying intelligence about the company's internal strengths and weaknesses, and by helping execute the plan, for instance, by eliminating a weakness that could be an impediment to the plan.

4. The impact of globalization on HRM comprises challenges ranging from how to select, train, and compensate managers in foreign posts, to dealing with inter-country differences, including cultural, economic, labour cost, and industrial relations factors.

DISCUSSION QUESTIONS

1. Why is HRM seen as a partner in developing and implementing strategy?
2. Discuss the evolving role of human resource management.
3. Discuss the five major issues confronting HRM in the next five years.
4. What are some of the issues regarding selection for multinational management?

NOTES

1. *Human Resource Management: Charting a New Course*, by Prem Benimadhu, Report 41-89 (Ottawa: Conference Board of Canada, 1989), p. 1.

2. American Management Association Survey, *Personnel (New York: AMA, October 1989)*.

3. *Human Resource Management: Charting a New Course* by Prem Benimadhu, pp. 1-19.

4. This is based on Edward E. Lawler III, "Human Resources Management: Meeting the New Challenges," *Personnel* (January 1988), p. 27; Michael Driver, Robert Coffey, and David Bowen, "Where is HRM Management Going?" *Personnel* (January 1988), pp. 28-31; Erick G. Flamholtz and others, "Personnel Management: The Tone of Tomorrow," *Personnel* (July 1987), pp. 43-48; and Laura Herren, "The New Game of HR: Playing to Win," *Personnel* (June 1989), pp. 19-22.

5. Peter Drucker, *The Wall Street Journal*, January 20, 1988.

6. Ibid.

7. Herren, "The New Game of HR," p. 20.

8. Ibid., p. 22.

9. Alan M. Saks and Daniel A. Ondrack, "International Human Resource Management: Trends and Implications for Management Education," Administrative Sciences Association of Canada (Personnel and Human Resources Division), *Proceedings of Annual Meeting*, Vol 9, part 9 (1988), p. 1.

10. N. J. Alder, "Women in International Management: Where are They?" *California Management Review*, 26 (4), (1984), p. 78.

11. Saks and Ondrak, pp. 1-2.

12. Paul Blocklyn, "Developing the International Executive," *Personnel* (March 1989), p. 44.

13. Rosalie L. Tung, "Human Resource Planning in Japanese Multinationals: A Model for U.S. Firms?" *Journal of International Business Studies*, Vol. 15, no. 2 (Fall 1984), pp. 139-149.

14. J. G. Maisonrouge, "The Education of a Modern International Manager," *Journal of International Business Studies*, 14 (1) (1983), p. 144.

15. W. A. Dymsza, "The Education and Development of Managers for Future Decades," *Journal of International Business Studies*, 13 (3) (1982), p. 15.

16. C. L. Hung "International Business Curricula in Canadian MBA Programs," Administrative Sciences Association of Canada (International Business Division) Proceeding of Annual Meeting 1989.

17. Dymsza, p. 12.

18. Blocklyn, p. 45.

19. Madelyn Callahan "Preparing the New Global Manager," p. 30.

20. For an excellent discussion of international issues in Compensation Management, see Steven L. McShane, Kim Miller, and Tom Prescott, "Compensating Expatriate Employees: A Review and Exploration of Canadian Practices," Administrative Sciences Association of Canada (Personnel and Human Resources Division) *Proceedings of Annual Meeting*, Vol. 9 (1988), pp. 11-19.

21. James Stoner and R. Edward Freman, *Management*, 4th ed. (Englewood Cliffs, N.J.: Prentice Hall, 1989), p. 783.

22. Hewitt Associates, "On Compensation," (May 1989), p. 1 (Hewitt Associates, 86-87 East Via De Ventura, Scottsdale, Arizona 85258).

23. Hewitt Associates, "On Compensation," p. 2.

24. This is based on Eduard Gaugler, "HR Management: An International Comparison," *Personnel* (August 1988), pp. 24-30.

25. Brooks, "Long-Term Incentives: International Executives Need Them, Too," p. 41.

26. These are based on Gaugler, p. 26.

27. For a discussion of this see Gaugler, p. 26.

28. Gaugler, p. 27. See also Simcha Ronen and Oded Shenkar, "Using Employee Attitudes to Establish MNC Regional Divisions," *Personnel* (August 1988), pp. 32-39.

29. This is discussed in Gaugler, p. 28.

30. This is based on Rae Sedel, "Europe 1992: HR Implications of the European Unification," *Personnel* (October 1989), pp. 19-24.

31. For a discussion along these lines, see Joel Lapointe and Joe Ann Verdin, "How to Calculate the Cost of Human Resources," *Personnel Journal* (January 1988), pp. 34-45.

32. This is based on Bruce R. Ellig, "Improving Effectiveness Through an HR Review," *Personnel* (June 1989), pp. 56-64.

33. Ellig, p. 57.

SUGGESTED READINGS

Human Resource Management: Charting a New Course by Prem P. Benimadhu, Report 41-89. Ottawa: The Conference Board of Canada, 1989.

Globalization: Canadian Companies Compete by Catharine G. Johnson, Ottawa: The Conference Board of Canada, 1990.

McShane, Steven L., and Tom Prescott. "Compensating Expatriate Employees: A Review and Exploration of Canadian Practices" Administrative Sciences Association of Canada (Personnel and Human Resources Division) *Proceedings of Annual Conference*, 1988. pp. 11-19.

Mendenhall, Mark and Gary Oddou. *International Human Resource Management: Readings and Cases*. Boston: PWS-Kent Publishing Company, 1991.

Saks, Alan M. and Daniel A. Ondrack. "International Human Resource Management: Trends and Implications for Management Education." Administrative Sciences Association of Canada (Personnel and Human Resources Division) *Proceedings of the Annual Conference*, 1988. pp. 1-10.

Major Employment and Labour Laws in Canada

APPENDIX A

FEDERAL LAWS:

Canada Labour Code
Canadian Charter of Rights and Freedoms
Canadian Bill of Rights
Canadian Human Rights Act
Department of Labour Act
Employment Equity Act
Fair Wages and Hours of Labour Act (Applied to Contractors)
Holidays Act
National Training Act
Public Service Employment Act
Public Service Staff Relations Act
Trade Unions Act

PROVINCIAL LAWS:

ALBERTA:

Apprenticeship, Training and Certification Act
Construction Industry Collective Bargaining Act
Department of Career Development and Employment Act
       (Formerly Manpower Development Act)
Department of Labour Act
Employment Standards Act
Individual Rights Protection Act
Industrial Wages Security Act
Labour Relations Act
Occupational Health and Safety Act
Workers' Compensation Act

BRITISH COLUMBIA:

Employment Standards Act
Factory Act (Industrial Health and Safety Regulations)
Human Rights Act
Industrial Relations Act
Labour Regulation Act
Mines Act (Occupational Environment Relations)
Ministry of Labour Act
Wage (Public Construction) Act
Workers' Compensation Act

MANITOBA:

Apprenticeship and Trades Qualification Act
Employment Standards Act
Construction Industry Wages Act
Department of Labour Act
Human Rights Act
Labour Relations Act
Pay Equity Act (Public Sector)
Payment of Wages Act
Vacations with Pay Act
The Workplace Safety and Health Act

NEW BRUNSWICK:

Employment Standards Act
Fair Wages and Hours of Labour Act
Human Rights Act
Industrial Relations Act
Industrial Training and Certification Act
Occupational Health and Safety Act

NEWFOUNDLAND:

Apprenticeship Act
Department of Labour Act, 1984
Industrial Standards Act
Labour Relations Act, 1977
Labour Standards Act
Newfoundland Human Rights Code
Occupational Health and Safety Act
Workers' Compensation Act

NOVA SCOTIA:

Apprenticeship and Tradesmen's Qualification Act
Department of Labour and Manpower Act
Human Rights Act
Industrial Safety Act
Labour Standards Code
Minimum Wage Act Regulations and Orders
Trade Union Act
Workers' Compensation Act

ONTARIO:

Apprenticeship and Tradesmen's Qualification Act
Employment Standards Act
Government Contracts Hours and Wages Act
Hospital Labour Disputes Arbitration Act
Industrial Standards Act
Labour Relations Act

Ministry of Labour Act
Pay Equity Act, 1987
Occupational Health and Safety Act
Ontario Human Rights Code, 1981
Workers' Compensation Act

QUEBEC:

Abolition of Compulsory Retirement Act
Charter of Human Rights and Freedoms
Construction Safety Code
Labour Code
Labour Relations, Vocational Training and Manpower Management in the
Construction Industry Act
Labour Standards Act
Manpower Vocational Training and Qualification Act
National Holiday Act
Occupational Health and Safety Act
Professional Syndicates Act

SASKATCHEWAN:

Apprenticeship and Trade Certification Act
Construction Industry Labour Relations Act
Department of Labour Act
Labour-Management Dispute (Temporary Provisions) Act
Labour Standards Act
Occupational Health and Safety Act
Saskatchewan Human Rights Code
Trade Union Act

NORTHWEST TERRITORIES:

Apprentices and Tradesmen's Act
Fair Practices Act
Labour Standards Act
Occupational Training Agreements Act
Workers' Compensation Act

YUKON:

Apprentice Training Act
Employment Standards Act
Human Rights Act
Occupational Training Act

APPENDIX B

Interrelationships Between Human Resource Management Functions

FIGURE A (Chapter 3) **The Relationship of Human Resource Planning to Other HRM Functions**

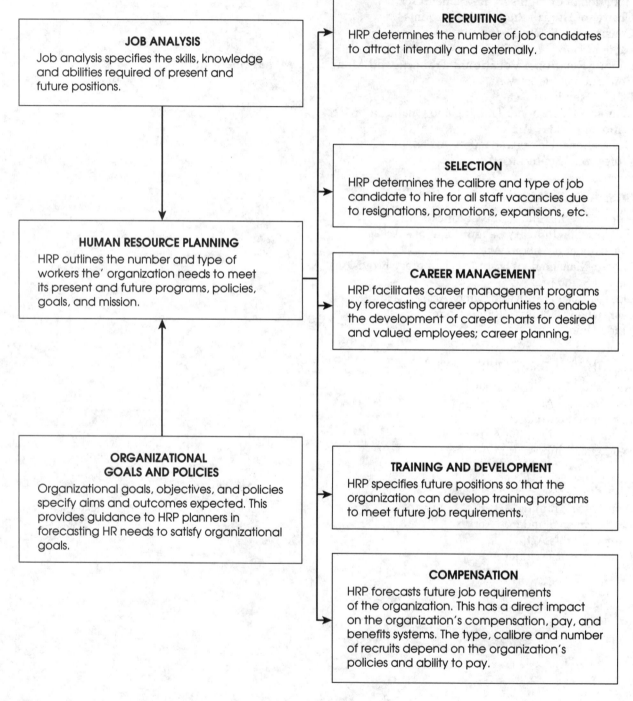

JOB ANALYSIS
Job analysis specifies the skills, knowledge and abilities required of present and future positions.

HUMAN RESOURCE PLANNING
HRP outlines the number and type of workers the' organization needs to meet its present and future programs, policies, goals, and mission.

ORGANIZATIONAL GOALS AND POLICIES
Organizational goals, objectives, and policies specify aims and outcomes expected. This provides guidance to HRP planners in forecasting HR needs to satisfy organizational goals.

RECRUITING
HRP determines the number of job candidates to attract internally and externally.

SELECTION
HRP determines the calibre and type of job candidate to hire for all staff vacancies due to resignations, promotions, expansions, etc.

CAREER MANAGEMENT
HRP facilitates career management programs by forecasting career opportunities to enable the development of career charts for desired and valued employees; career planning.

TRAINING AND DEVELOPMENT
HRP specifies future positions so that the organization can develop training programs to meet future job requirements.

COMPENSATION
HRP forecasts future job requirements of the organization. This has a direct impact on the organization's compensation, pay, and benefits systems. The type, calibre and number of recruits depend on the organization's policies and ability to pay.

FIGURE B **(Chapter 5) The Relationship of Recruitment to Other HRM Functions**

JOB ANALYSIS

Job analysis determines the appropriate skills, knowledge, and abilities required for the job to be performed. To determine the pay it provides employees on the basis of job content and job performance, the organization must be able to accurately identify the required tasks, knowledge, and skills and the conditions under which they must be performed.

RECRUITMENT OF HUMAN RESOURCES

Recruitment involves searching for and obtaining qualified job candidates at the right time and place so that the organization may select those applicants that meet its requirements.

SELECTION

Selection criteria affect recruitment sources, methods, and efforts.

The calibre and quantity of job applicants available may affect the degree of the organization's selectivity.

HUMAN RESOURCE PLANNING

HRP is a prerequisite to recruitment planning. Through the process of HRP, the numbers and types of employees needed by the various levels, and as well as the time period within which needs must be met, can be determined. HRP influences the strategies for attracting applicants, applying valid selection methods, and smoothing the "joining up" process of new hires.

COMPENSATION MANAGEMENT

The level of compensation which the organization offers can assist or impair the recruitment process.

The supply and demand of job applicants may affect compensation rates.

LEGAL ENVIRONMENT

An organization's recruiting efforts are affected by legal constraints, including those provided by the Human Rights Act. The human rights acts of every province, territory, and the federal government prohibit various types of discrimination in recruitment. Organizations must ensure that they comply with all of the provisions of these acts that relate to recruiting.

PERFORMANCE APPRAISAL

The quality of job candidates being recruited will affect the organization's performance standards.

Performance appraisal provides important feedback for evaluating the effective-ness of the recruiting process.

TRAINING AND DEVELOPMENT

The skills, knowledge, and other qualifications of job applicants affect training needs. The availability of training programs may affect recruiting efforts.

FIGURE C (Chapter 6) The Relationship of Selection to Other HRM Functions

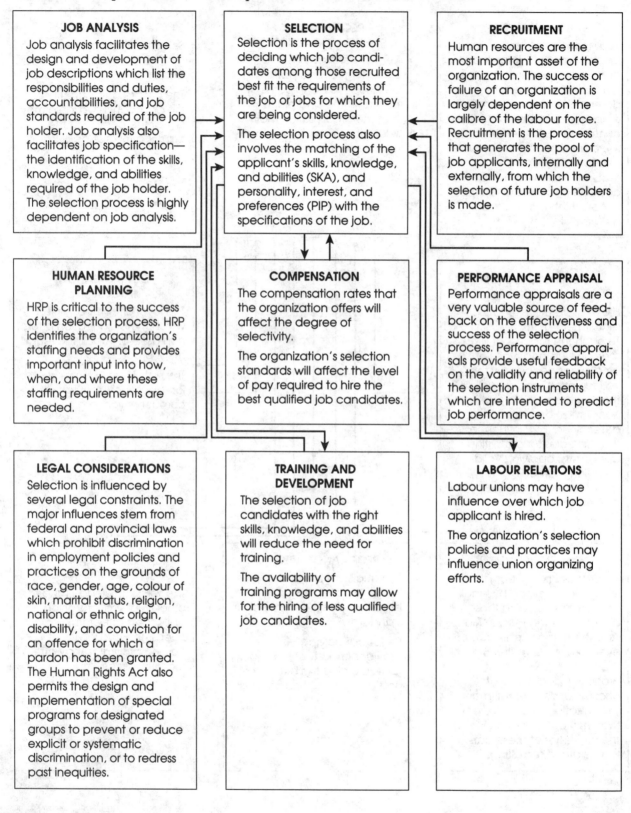

JOB ANALYSIS

Job analysis facilitates the design and development of job descriptions which list the responsibilities and duties, accountabilities, and job standards required of the job holder. Job analysis also facilitates job specification—the identification of the skills, knowledge, and abilities required of the job holder. The selection process is highly dependent on job analysis.

SELECTION

Selection is the process of deciding which job candidates among those recruited best fit the requirements of the job or jobs for which they are being considered.

The selection process also involves the matching of the applicant's skills, knowledge, and abilities (SKA), and personality, interest, and preferences (PIP) with the specifications of the job.

RECRUITMENT

Human resources are the most important asset of the organization. The success or failure of an organization is largely dependent on the calibre of the labour force. Recruitment is the process that generates the pool of job applicants, internally and externally, from which the selection of future job holders is made.

HUMAN RESOURCE PLANNING

HRP is critical to the success of the selection process. HRP identifies the organization's staffing needs and provides important input into how, when, and where these staffing requirements are needed.

COMPENSATION

The compensation rates that the organization offers will affect the degree of selectivity.

The organization's selection standards will affect the level of pay required to hire the best qualified job candidates.

PERFORMANCE APPRAISAL

Performance appraisals are a very valuable source of feedback on the effectiveness and success of the selection process. Performance appraisals provide useful feedback on the validity and reliability of the selection instruments which are intended to predict job performance.

LEGAL CONSIDERATIONS

Selection is influenced by several legal constraints. The major influences stem from federal and provincial laws which prohibit discrimination in employment policies and practices on the grounds of race, gender, age, colour of skin, marital status, religion, national or ethnic origin, disability, and conviction for an offence for which a pardon has been granted. The Human Rights Act also permits the design and implementation of special programs for designated groups to prevent or reduce explicit or systematic discrimination, or to redress past inequities.

TRAINING AND DEVELOPMENT

The selection of job candidates with the right skills, knowledge, and abilities will reduce the need for training.

The availability of training programs may allow for the hiring of less qualified job candidates.

LABOUR RELATIONS

Labour unions may have influence over which job applicant is hired.

The organization's selection policies and practices may influence union organizing efforts.

FIGURE D (Chapter 7) The Relationship of Employee Training to other HRM Functions

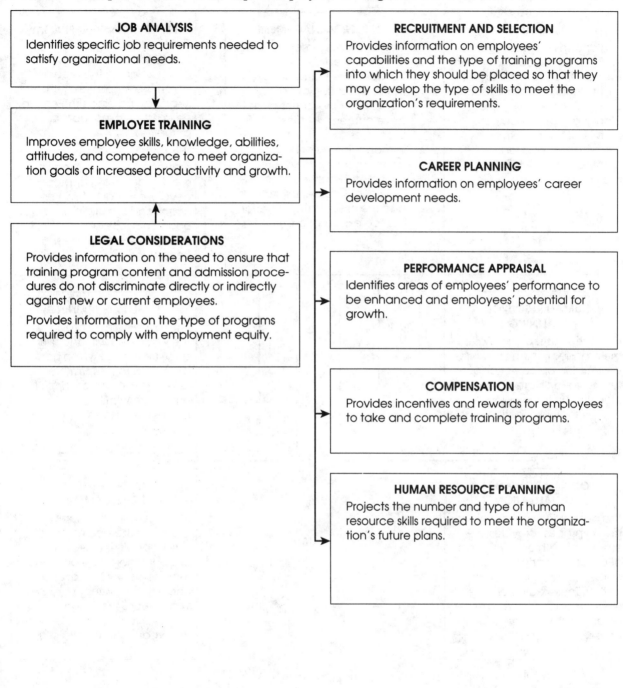

JOB ANALYSIS

Identifies specific job requirements needed to satisfy organizational needs.

EMPLOYEE TRAINING

Improves employee skills, knowledge, abilities, attitudes, and competence to meet organization goals of increased productivity and growth.

LEGAL CONSIDERATIONS

Provides information on the need to ensure that training program content and admission procedures do not discriminate directly or indirectly against new or current employees.

Provides information on the type of programs required to comply with employment equity.

RECRUITMENT AND SELECTION

Provides information on employees' capabilities and the type of training programs into which they should be placed so that they may develop the type of skills to meet the organization's requirements.

CAREER PLANNING

Provides information on employees' career development needs.

PERFORMANCE APPRAISAL

Identifies areas of employees' performance to be enhanced and employees' potential for growth.

COMPENSATION

Provides incentives and rewards for employees to take and complete training programs.

HUMAN RESOURCE PLANNING

Projects the number and type of human resource skills required to meet the organization's future plans.

FIGURE E (Chapter 10) The Relationship of Career Management to Other HRM Functions

JOB ANALYSIS

Job analysis provides vital information for job description and job specification requirements so that employees may undertake their own career planning with an accurate picture of the performance expectations and requirements of jobs in which they are interested.

CAREER MANAGEMENT

Career management includes the mutual establishment between the individual and the organization of career goals, planning, paths and development. All these processes assist the individual in managing his or her career and in ensuring that there is a fit or match between the individual's career aspirations and the organization's performance expectation.

PERFORMANCE APPRAISAL

The feedback which is provided to the employee communicates the areas in which the employee needs to improve and assists the employee in establishing realistic career goals.

The feedback provided to management assists management in designing appropriate developmental training programs and realistic career goals and provides the employee with accurate career counselling.

HUMAN RESOURCE PLANNING

HRP forecasts job vacancies in the organization. This provides information on career opportunities to facilitate career planning by the employee and by the organization.

EMPLOYEE TRAINING

Employee training provides the employee with the skills and knowledge which he or she needs to perform the job effectively. It also provides the employee with learning experiences necessary for goal achievement.

ORIENTATION AND SOCIALIZATION

The orientation and socialization process provides the employee with an awareness of career opportunities and career equity in the organization. These data help the newcomer to decide whether he or she could have a fulfilling career in the organization.

MANAGEMENT DEVELOPMENT

Management development facilitates the attainment of career goals. It takes into account short-term and long-term career planning, and charting the paths of progression upward within the structure to fill vacancies within the organization.

FIGURE F (Chapter 12) The Relationship of Compensation Management to Other HRM Functions

JOB ANALYSIS

Job analysis is the foundation of two essential compensation functions. It provides key information on the essential characteristics of the basic task requirements of each job. This is used to conduct job evaluations to determine the relative worth of each job so as to establish internal equity.

Job analysis data are essential for conducting salary surveys. Accurate job analysis facilitates the determination of the similarity of jobs for making salary compensations with other companies to ensure external equity.

COMPENSATION MANAGEMENT

Compensation is the rewards employees receive in exchange for the contribution of time, effort, and certain abilities.

Compensation serves to attract qualified job candidates, motivate and satisfy employees, and ensure equity.

Compensation represents a substantial part of an organization's operating cost. An organization's success depends on how much productivity is gained from employees in exchange for compensation and on its control of labour costs.

LABOUR RELATIONS

Labour unions influence the determination, cost, and administration of compensation. In unionized firms, management has less flexibility in compensation management since such firms must negotiate all aspects of pay.

Labour unions also influence the wages in non-unionized firms where those firms often feel obliged to pay wages similar to those paid by unionized firms because of their fears that their employees may join a union.

HUMAN RESOURCE PLANNING

HRP influences, and may be influenced by, the organization's compensation. HRP's forecast of an organization's HR needs and supply affects the firm's overall compensation program. Thus, if there is a shortage in the labour market of the type of HR skills required, then the organization may have to offer a higher starting salary to attract qualified job candidates.

EMPLOYEE BENEFITS

Employee benefits are influenced by direct compensation. It is often the case that employee benefits increase in proportion to the level of employee pay rates. Particular benefits are often available only to individuals in certain income brackets.

RECRUITMENT/SELECTION

Recruitment and selection efforts are influenced by compensation policies. An organization may use compensation for such objectives as: attracting, retaining, and motivating employees. The type of policy followed will influence the quality of job candidates that the organization will be able to attract.

LEGAL CONSIDERATIONS

The organization's compensation management must ensure compliance with various government laws and regulations such as employment standard acts, human rights acts, pay equity laws, and income tax laws.

PERFORMANCE APPRAISAL

Performance appraisal is very important in linking reward to performance.
Performance appraisal is the technique used to enhance employee performance.

Performance appraisal is also useful in measuring an employee's potential for promotion.

FIGURE G (Chapter 13) The Relationship of Incentive Compensation to Other HRM Functions

JOB ANALYSIS

Job analysis defines the essential characteristics of each job. It is against these job characteristics that employees' performances are measured and compensated.

It is therefore essential that the tasks to be performed are accurately defined and are job related.

INCENTIVE COMPENSATION

Incentive compensation is intended to link the compensation of employees more closely to their contributions.

The success of the type of incentive compensation used is contingent upon the organizational climate, employees' acceptance of the plan, and its suitability to the organization's needs rather than on the techniques of the plan.

PERFORMANCE APPRAISAL

Performance appraisal serves as a very important procedure in the incentive compensation process. When employees' compensation is linked to performance, it is essential that their performance be accurately measured on the basis of objective criteria.

The performance appraisal used must be objective, reliable, fair, consistently applied, effective, and free from biases.

LEGAL CONSIDERATIONS

Incentive compensation is influenced by various legal considerations. These include the human rights acts, Canada Labour Code, employment standard acts, and pay equity acts.

LABOUR RELATIONS

Labour unions exert much influence over the implementation and administration of incentive compensation. Labour has traditionally opposed incentive systems for a variety of reasons including concern that such systems will rob workers of their fair share of measured productivity, that standards are set unfairly, and that such systems are designed to deny workers well-deserved pay increases.

Labour unions often cooperate with management when they are convinced that incentive systems are fair, when employees are able to control the performance on which the ncentive is based, and when the performance appraisal system is free of biases and equity exists.

FIGURE H (Chapter 14) The Relationship of Employee Benefits and Services to Other HRM Functions

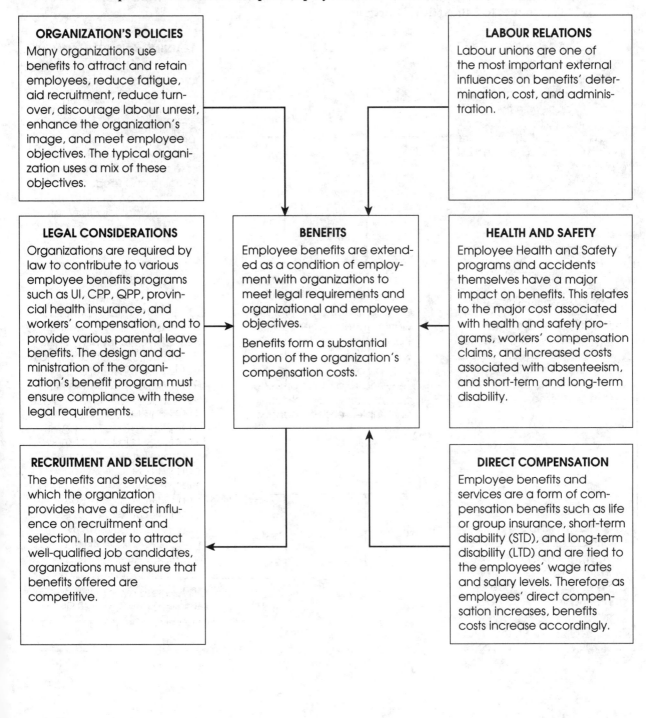

ORGANIZATION'S POLICIES
Many organizations use benefits to attract and retain employees, reduce fatigue, aid recruitment, reduce turnover, discourage labour unrest, enhance the organization's image, and meet employee objectives. The typical organization uses a mix of these objectives.

LABOUR RELATIONS
Labour unions are one of the most important external influences on benefits' determination, cost, and administration.

LEGAL CONSIDERATIONS
Organizations are required by law to contribute to various employee benefits programs such as UI, CPP, QPP, provincial health insurance, and workers' compensation, and to provide various parental leave benefits. The design and administration of the organization's benefit program must ensure compliance with these legal requirements.

BENEFITS
Employee benefits are extended as a condition of employment with organizations to meet legal requirements and organizational and employee objectives.

Benefits form a substantial portion of the organization's compensation costs.

HEALTH AND SAFETY
Employee Health and Safety programs and accidents themselves have a major impact on benefits. This relates to the major cost associated with health and safety programs, workers' compensation claims, and increased costs associated with absenteeism, and short-term and long-term disability.

RECRUITMENT AND SELECTION
The benefits and services which the organization provides have a direct influence on recruitment and selection. In order to attract well-qualified job candidates, organizations must ensure that benefits offered are competitive.

DIRECT COMPENSATION
Employee benefits and services are a form of compensation benefits such as life or group insurance, short-term disability (STD), and long-term disability (LTD) and are tied to the employees' wage rates and salary levels. Therefore as employees' direct compensation increases, benefits costs increase accordingly.

FIGURE I (Chapter 15) The Relationship of Quality of Work Life (QWL) and Nonfinancial Motivation Techniques to Other HRM Functions

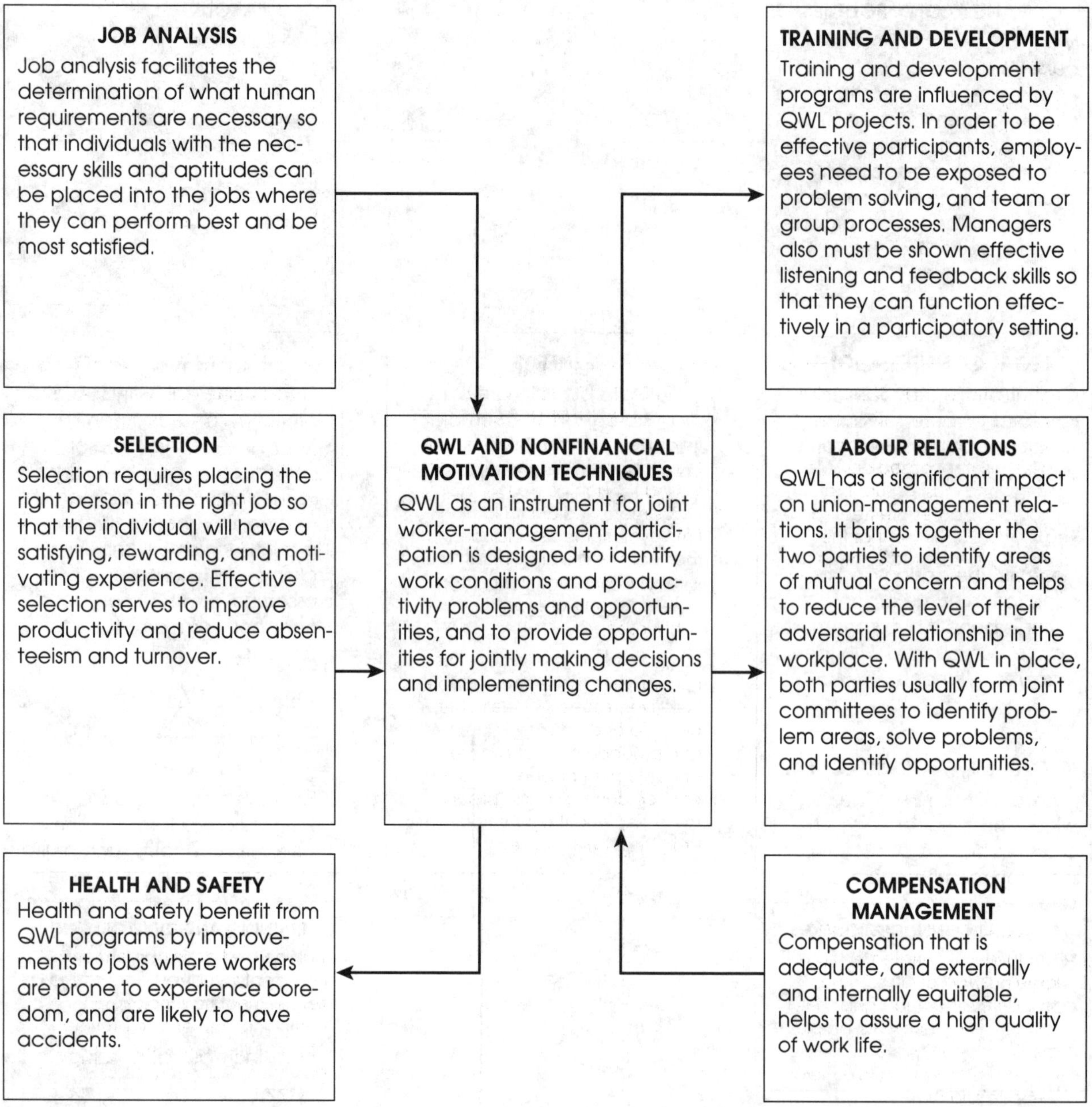

JOB ANALYSIS

Job analysis facilitates the determination of what human requirements are necessary so that individuals with the necessary skills and aptitudes can be placed into the jobs where they can perform best and be most satisfied.

TRAINING AND DEVELOPMENT

Training and development programs are influenced by QWL projects. In order to be effective participants, employees need to be exposed to problem solving, and team or group processes. Managers also must be shown effective listening and feedback skills so that they can function effectively in a participatory setting.

SELECTION

Selection requires placing the right person in the right job so that the individual will have a satisfying, rewarding, and motivating experience. Effective selection serves to improve productivity and reduce absenteeism and turnover.

QWL AND NONFINANCIAL MOTIVATION TECHNIQUES

QWL as an instrument for joint worker-management participation is designed to identify work conditions and productivity problems and opportunities, and to provide opportunities for jointly making decisions and implementing changes.

LABOUR RELATIONS

QWL has a significant impact on union-management relations. It brings together the two parties to identify areas of mutual concern and helps to reduce the level of their adversarial relationship in the workplace. With QWL in place, both parties usually form joint committees to identify problem areas, solve problems, and identify opportunities.

HEALTH AND SAFETY

Health and safety benefit from QWL programs by improvements to jobs where workers are prone to experience boredom, and are likely to have accidents.

COMPENSATION MANAGEMENT

Compensation that is adequate, and externally and internally equitable, helps to assure a high quality of work life.

FIGURE J (Chapter 16) The Relationship of Employee Rights and Management Rights to Other HRM

JOB ANALYSIS

Job analysis provides the essential data for the preparation of job descriptions and job specifications. Job descriptions describe job performance standards and expectations against which employees' performances are evaluated.

UNION-MANAGEMENT RELATIONS

Collective bargaining agreements are instrumental in creating a variety of employee rights. These include job security; the use of seniority in promotions, layoffs, and recall; dispute resolution mechanisms; and dismissal with just cause.

Nonunionized companies must ensure that they treat employees with respect, dignity, and fairness to avoid stimulating unionizing activities.

RECRUITMENT AND SELECTION

The recruitment and selection processes must be free of biases, must be based on valid criteria, and must ensure that all job candidates are treated equally and fairly, so that the rights of job candidates are not violated.

EMPLOYEE RIGHTS AND MANAGEMENT RIGHTS

Employee rights include the right to be treated fairly, justly and equally, and the right to be free from harassment and discrimination. Employee rights also include the right not to be arbitrarily dismissed without cause, and the right to have contractual, legal, or implied rights respected.

Management rights include the right to have management's prerogatives respected; the right to develop and administer policies and procedures to attract, recruit, and select employees; the right to enforce corrective disciplinary measures; and the right to dismiss employees with cause.

PERFORMANCE APPRAISAL

Performance appraisal standards must be accurate and evaluations must be done properly. Since performance appraisal results may be the basis for termination, they may thus become the basis of court challenges for unjustifiable dismissal.

LEGAL CONSIDERATIONS

Employees are protected by a large network of laws. These include contractual rights (collective agreements, employment contracts) statutory laws (human rights laws, employment standards, the Canada Labour Code) and implied rights (common laws). Employers must ensure due process is followed in matters such as discipline and dismissal. Employees must ensure that they conform to the employers' performance expectations, standards of conduct, and standards of behaviour.

TRAINING AND DEVELOPMENT

Training and development are important in fulfilling legal obligations in meeting employment equity requirements to provide opportunities for women, visible minorities, Native people, and the physically disabled.

Training programs must be fair and just and must not violate any human rights of employees. When violations occur, organizations are held accountable.
(See Chapter 2)

FIGURE K   (Chapter 17) The Relationship of Health and Safety to Other HRM Functions

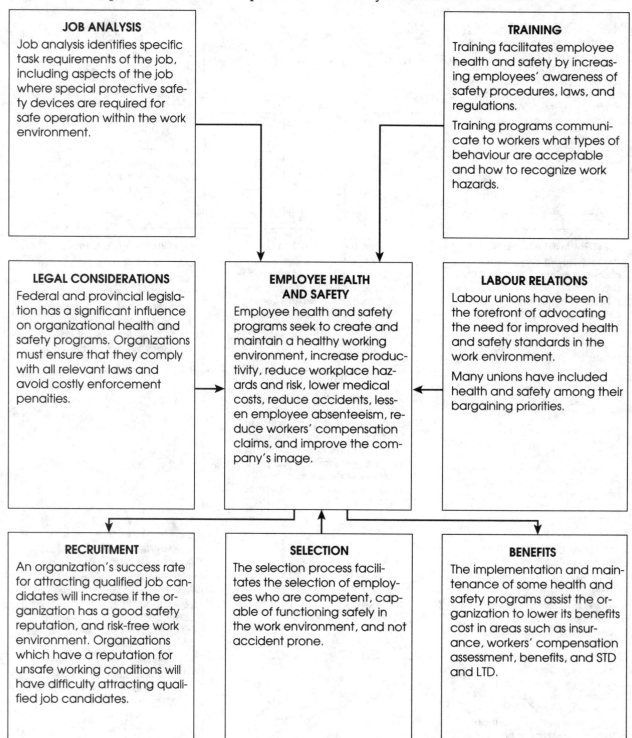

JOB ANALYSIS
Job analysis identifies specific task requirements of the job, including aspects of the job where special protective safety devices are required for safe operation within the work environment.

TRAINING
Training facilitates employee health and safety by increasing employees' awareness of safety procedures, laws, and regulations.

Training programs communicate to workers what types of behaviour are acceptable and how to recognize work hazards.

LEGAL CONSIDERATIONS
Federal and provincial legislation has a significant influence on organizational health and safety programs. Organizations must ensure that they comply with all relevant laws and avoid costly enforcement penalties.

EMPLOYEE HEALTH AND SAFETY
Employee health and safety programs seek to create and maintain a healthy working environment, increase productivity, reduce workplace hazards and risk, lower medical costs, reduce accidents, lessen employee absenteeism, reduce workers' compensation claims, and improve the company's image.

LABOUR RELATIONS
Labour unions have been in the forefront of advocating the need for improved health and safety standards in the work environment.

Many unions have included health and safety among their bargaining priorities.

RECRUITMENT
An organization's success rate for attracting qualified job candidates will increase if the organization has a good safety reputation, and risk-free work environment. Organizations which have a reputation for unsafe working conditions will have difficulty attracting qualified job candidates.

SELECTION
The selection process facilitates the selection of employees who are competent, capable of functioning safely in the work environment, and not accident prone.

BENEFITS
The implementation and maintenance of some health and safety programs assist the organization to lower its benefits cost in areas such as insurance, workers' compensation assessment, benefits, and STD and LTD.

FIGURE L (Chapter 18) **The Relationship of Labour Relations to Other HRM Functions**

RECRUITMENT AND SELECTION

In unionized organizations, labour unions exert significant influence over the staffing process, particularly internal recruiting and selection. Unions usually insist on seniority as the major criterion for promotion whereas management prefers to base promotion on merit. In practice, preference usually goes to the individual with the most seniority when all applicants are of equal ability and experience.

In some industries such as construction, unions have direct control over who is hired. Only union members may be hired by employers under what is known as a closed shop agreement.

HEALTH AND SAFETY

Labour unions influence an organization's health and safety policies and programs. Safe and healthy working conditions are often the subject of negotiation between union and management. Union representatives usually have membership on joint union-management safety committees.

LEGAL CONSIDERATIONS

Labour unions in unionized firms impose on these firms a variety of legal obligations and the need to ensure that policies and procedures comply with labour laws.

The union organizing process imposes constraints on management; management is legally obliged to recognize and bargain with a legally established bargaining unit. Management is required to comply with all relevant provisions of the Labour Relations Act. The presence of unions restricts management flexibility. Management must use the dispute resolution mechanism of grievance arbitration to settle disputes.

LABOUR RELATIONS

Labour relations refers to the interaction between labour and management in the determination, administration, and interpretation of those policies and practices that govern employer-employee relations. Where unions exist, management and labour jointly determine wages, working conditions, and dispute resolution mechanisms.

TRAINING AND DEVELOPMENT

Labour unions are often instrumental in putting training programs in place. During the collective bargaining process, unions often agree to automation on condition that the organization implement retraining programs for their members.

COMPENSATION AND BENEFITS

Labour unions are instrumental in the determination and administration of all aspects of compensation and benefits. When disputes arise over the interpretation of clauses regarding compensation and benefits, unions are heavily involved in resolving such disputes through the grievance arbitration process.

GLOSSARY

Accommodation The second step in the socialization process in which the newcomer, upon entering (joining) the organization, attempts to become a functioning member of it.

Action learning A training technique by which management trainees to work full time analyzing and solving problems in departments other than their own.

AIDS The disruption of the body's immune system caused by a virus called human immune-deficiency virus (HIV).

Alternation ranking method A method for evaluating employees that ranks them from best to worst on some trait.

Anticipatory socialization The first step in the socialization process in which individuals develop certain attitudes, values, and expectations about what it will be like working and succeeding in their chosen organizations.

Appraisal interview A process of communicating to employees the outcomes of their performance assessment for the past appraisal period.

Aptitude test The measurement of an individual's aptitude or potential to perform an array of tasks, provided the individual is given proper training.

Aptitudes and special talents Intelligence, numerical aptitude, mechanical comprehension, and manual dexterity play an important role in career decisions and have long been used by career counsellors to help guide their clients.

Arbitration Definitive third party intervention in which the arbitrator usually has the power to determine and dictate the settlement terms.

Arbitration clause All collective agreements must contain a clause providing for the final and binding arbitration on all disputes arising during the term of a collective agreement over the application, interpretation, or administration of that agreement.

Attendance incentive plan A plan for reducing employee absence, for instance, by allowing unused sick leave to be converted to additional pay or vacation at the end of the year.

Baby boomers Individuals who were born after World War II and before 1965 who now determine the dominant characteristics of the Canadian labour force.

Behaviour description interview An interviewing technique involving identifying important behavioural dimensions of a job and then assessing the job applicants against those dimensions.

Behaviour modelling A training technique that involves (1) showing the trainee the right (or "model") way of doing something, (2) letting the person practise the right way to do it, and then (3) providing feedback regarding his or her performance.

Behaviour modification/operant conditioning Changing or modifying behaviour through the use of rewards or punishment.

Behavioural observation scales (BOS) BOS are based on carefully developed job analysis.

Behaviourally anchored rating scale (BARS) A scale that combines the benefits of narrated critical incidents and quantified ratings by anchoring a quantified scale with specific narrative examples of good or poor performance.

Benchmark jobs Jobs used to anchor the employer's pay scale and around which other jobs are then slotted based on their relative worth to the firm.

Blind ads A *want ad* that omits the identity and street address of the hiring employer.

Burnout The feeling that individual experiences of total depletion of all physical and mental resources caused by excessive striving to meet some unrealistic, work-related goal.

Cafeteria benefits plan Also called flexible benefits, this plan enables employees to pick and choose from available options and, literally, to develop their own benefit plans.

Canada Employment Centres The purpose of these government-operated centres is to assist employers find suitable job candidates in the labour market to meet their labour force needs, and to assist job seekers to find suitable employment at no cost to either the employer or the job seeker.

Canada Labour Code The successor of the *Industrial Disputes Investigation Act* of 1907. It provides for a conciliation procedure that the parties are required to follow before they are in a legal position to strike or to lock out.

Canada Pension Plan A comprehensive, contributory plan mandatory for all employees and self-employed individuals in Canada, providing retirement pensions, disability pensions, and pensions and benefits to children of disabled workers.

Canadian Classification and Dictionary of Occupations An excellent source of standardized occupational information and describes and classifies jobs by specific occupation.

Canadian Human Rights Act The Act states that: "every individual should have an equal opportunity with other individuals to make himself or herself the life that he or she is able wishes to have, consistent with his or her duties and obligations as a member of society without being hindered in or prevented from doing so by discriminating practices base on race, national or ethnic origin, colour, religion, age, sex, marital status, or conviction for an offence for which a pardon has been granted or by discriminatory employment practices based on physical handicap."

Canadian common law Under Canadian common law, the employer-employee relationship is governed by an employment contract. The Canadian Common Law applies to all provinces except Quebec.

Canadian Human Rights Commission This Commission administers the *Canadian Human Rights Act*, and is comprised of the Chief Commissioner, a Deputy Commissioner, and anywhere from three to six part-time members, all appointed by the Governor-in-Council.

Canadian Labour Congress (CLC) An organization affiliated with various unions, directly chartered locals, and provincial federations of labour and local councils, for the purpose of broadly coordinating their activities at the national level, including the relations between unions and government and establishing relations with organized workers internationally.

Career All the jobs an individual has occupied over the span of his or her life.

Career anchor A concern or value an individual will not give up if a choice has to be made.

Career cycle The different stages through which a person's career evolves.

Cash bonus plan The provision of cash bonuses, in addition to regular compensation, based on the achievement of established performance goals.

Central tendency effect The tendency of appraisers to rate employees as average or around the middle point for all performance qualities of the rating scale.

Charter of Rights and Freedoms The Charter provides the following fundamental rights to every Canadians: freedom of conscience and religion; freedom of though, belief, opinion, and expression, including freedom of the press and other media communication; freedom of peaceful assembly; and freedom of association.

Checkoff The process by which union dues are collected by the employer via payroll deductions and remitted to the union.

Child care The provision of company-sponsored or on- or off-site day-care facilities.

Classes Dividing jobs into classes based on a set of rules for each class, such as amount of physical effort required.

Classification (or grading) method The method by which jobs are categorized into groups.

Collective agreement A written agreement entered into between an employers' organization and a trade union or council of trade unions, containing provisions regarding the terms and conditions of employment.

Collective bargaining The process through which representatives of management and the union meet to negotiate a labour agreement.

Commission plan A pay system in which salespeople are paid in direct proportion to their sales — for results, and only for results.

Compensable factor Fundamental, compensable elements of a job, such as skill, effort, responsibility, and working conditions.

Compensation All financial rewards received by employees as a result of their employment relationship with an organization.

Computer-assisted instruction The use of computers to facilitate the training process. Systems like Control Data's PLATO have several advantages. They provide self-paced, individualized instruction that is one-on-one and easy to use, and trainees get immediate feedback to their input.

Computerized forecasting A software package developed by an HRM specialist, in conjunction with line managers, compiling the necessary information (i.e., productivity, sales projections), in order to forecast HR requirements using a computer.

Concessionary bargaining A strategy used by employers experiencing severe economic problems caused by a general economic recession or financial difficulties.

Conciliation The intervention of a third party whose primary purpose is to bring two parties together and keep them talking in order to enable them to reach an agreement.

Construct validity A psychological concept, attribute, or quality that explains just what a particular test is measuring.

Constructive dismissal Under common law, whenever an employer commits a major breach of a major term of the employment relationship, the employee may take the position that a dismissal has taken place even though he or she has not received formal termination notice.

Content validity A test that is "content valid" is one which contains a fair sample of the tasks and skills actually needed for the job in question.

Contract administration The process implemented to ensure that labour and management abide by the terms and conditions of the provisions of the collective agreement.

Controlled experimentation In a control experiment used to evaluate training efforts, both a training group and a control (no training) group are used to determine to what extent any change in performance in the training group resulted from the training itself rather than from some organizational damage like a raise in pay.

Corrective discipline A disciplinary technique designed to discourage infractions of organizational rules, procedures and regulations, and to stimulate compliance with established policies and procedures.

Criterion validity A type of validity based on showing that scores on the test ("predictors") are related to job performance ("criterion").

Critical incident method Keeping a record of uncommonly good or undesirable examples of an employee's work-related behaviour and reviewing it with the employee at predetermined times.

Damages for mental distress A recent development under common law is the awarding of damages for mental distress resulting from factors such as the suddenness of the dismissal and the loss of reputation.

Decline stage A deceleration period in the career cycle during which may people are faced with the prospect of having to accept reduced levels of power and responsibility and have to learn to accept and develop new roles as mentors and confidantes for those who are younger.

Delphi technique A judgmental forecasting method used to arrive at a group decision.

Demographics The composition of individuals in the work force according to such characteristics as age, sex, marital status, and education level.

Distributive bargaining A form of bargaining involving the distribution of things that are available in limited quantity.

Dominion Conciliation Act This Act which came into effect in 1900, gave the Minister of Labour the power to appoint a conciliation board at the Minister's initiative or at the request of either management or the union to regulate industrial disputes.

Drug testing Medical examinations to determine whether an individual is using drugs or alcohol.

Employee assistance program Specially designed programs that use technical, administrative, and professional human services, on either a contractual or employment basis, so that employees who have problems on or off the job have a recourse to professional assistance.

Employee referrals Job applicants referred by present employees who are generally their friends or relatives.

Employee rights The rights protected by federal laws and policies, such as the *Canadian Human Rights Act*, *Canada Labour Code*, *Charter of Rights and Freedoms*, *Employment Equity Programs*, and health and safety programs.

Employee suggestion plan Employees are encouraged to submit suggestions on ways to improve some aspect of an organization's operations.

Employee training The process of teaching new or current employees new skills designed to improve their skills, knowledge, abilities, and attitudes in order to meet the organization's requirements for maintaining and increasing productivity and the individual's needs for further growth.

Employer pension plan There are three basic types of employer pension plans: group pension plans in which the organization (and possibly the employee) makes a set contribution to a pension fund; a deferred profit-sharing plan in which a certain percent of profits is credited to each employee's account; and savings plans, in which employees set aside a fixed percentage of their weekly wages for their retirement, and the company usually matches from 50 to 100% of the employees' contribution.

Employment agency The term "employment agency" includes a broad category of recruitment organizations and activities, such as Canada Employment Centres, temporary help agencies, and executive recruiting firms.

Employment equity Employment equity aims to remove those workplace barriers that prevent women, visible minorities and native people from achieving their full potential.

Equity theory of motivation The argument that people are strongly motivated to maintain a balance between what they perceive as their inputs, or contributions, and their rewards.

Essay method A performance appraisal method in which the appraiser describes, in essay form, the employee's performance within a number of broad categories.

Establishment stage The core of most people's work lives, spanning roughly from ages 24 to 44.

Executive recruiters These firms assist employers in finding middle and senior managers and professional people.

Expectancy theory of motivation The argument that a person's motivation to exert effort is based on his or her expectations of success.

Exploration stage The period of a person's career, roughly from ages 15 to 24, during which a person seriously explores various occupational alternatives, attempting to match these alternatives with what he or she has learned about them.

Factor comparison method This method is actually a refinement of the *ranking method*, in that the user ranks each job several times — one for each compensable factor chosen.

Fair day's work Frederick Taylor's observation that haphazard setting of piecework requirements and wages by supervisors was not sufficient, a careful, formal, scientific process of inspection and observation was needed to define acceptable production quotas for each job.

Fiedler's Leader match training A program that identifies types of leaders and teaches them how to fit their leadership style to their situation.

Flexiplace A flexible work arrangement in which employees are allowed or encouraged to work at home or in a satellite office closer to home.

Flextime A plan whereby employees can build their workday around a core of midday hours but can determine their own starting and stopping hours.

Forced distribution method A comparative evaluation rating technique similar to "grading on a curve."

Four-day work week A 40-hour work week comprising four ten-hour days instead of the more usual five eight-hour days.

Functional control The control exerted by human resource management specialists as coordinators of human resource activities.

Functional job analysis A method used for classifying jobs by taking into account the extent to which instructions, reasoning and judgments, and verbal facility are necessary for performing job tasks.

Federal Contract Compliance Program Companies that employ 100 or more employees and wish to bid on federal contracts of $200 000 or more to provide goods and services to the federal government are required to implement employment equity programs and to certify in writing their commitment to implement employment equity as a condition of the bid.

Good faith The legal requirement that both parties negotiating a contract bargain honestly, fairly, and sincerely.

Grades A job classification system synonymous with classes. Grade descriptions are written based on compensable factors listed in classification systems, and often contain dissimilar jobs, such as secretaries and mechanics.

Graphic rating scale A scale that lists a number of traits and a range of performance for each. The employee is then rated by identifying the score that best describes his or her level of performance for each trait.

Grid training A formal approach to team building designed by Blake and Mouton.

Grievance-arbitration process Systematic union-management deliberation of a complaint at successively higher organizational levels.

Group incentive plan This plan involves setting work standards for each member of the group and maintaining a count of each member's output. Members are then paid based on one of three formulas: (1) all members receive the pay earned by the highest producer; (2) all members receive the pay earned by the lowest producer; or (3) all members receive payment equal to the average pay earned by the group.

Group norms The acceptable standard of conduct that influences workers' behaviour and is enforced by a variety of social pressures.

Growth stage The stage of an individual's career that lasts roughly from birth to age 14. It is a period during which the person develops a self-concept by identifying with and interacting with other people such as family, friends, and teachers.

Guaranteed income supplement When GIS was enacted, it were primarily intended to ensure that those individuals receiving *OAS* would receive a minimum income, particularly while Canada Pension Plan was reaching its maturity.

Guarantee piecework A pay system in which the employee is paid by the hour (the minimum wage) whether or not he/she produces the number of pieces required. As an incentive he or she is also paid at the piece rate for each piece produced over the required number.

Halo effect The tendency of appraisers to allow one rating they assign to one aspect of an employee's performance to excessively influence the evaluation and the rating assigned to other aspects of the employee's performance during an evaluation

Hersey-Blanchard Situational leadership theory A widely practical leadership model based on the contingency theory that successful leadership is achieved by selecting the right leadership style to match the maturity of the followers.

Human relations movement The primary aim of the human relations movement was an examination of jobs from the perspective of the workers.

Human resource information system A computerized data base process used to store detailed information on employees, HRM policies and procedures, government laws and regulations, and health and safety records.

Human resource management The management of people in organizations, including those activities in which organizations engage to meet individual's goals, society's objectives, and the organization's productivity and effectiveness.

Human resource objectives Provide a sense of direction to employees, communicate to them the organization's expectations, reduce uncertainty, establish standards against which to measure performance or productivity, and establish the priorities by which they can operate.

Human Resource Planning The process of forecasting an organization's human resource needs (demands).

Human resources accounting A process designed to measure the present cost and value of human resources as well as their future worth to the organization.

Hygiene factors Incentives that satisfy lower-level needs according to Herzberg's *motivator-hygiene theory of motivation.*

Incentive compensation A type of financial reward that ties and strengthens the link between individual workers' pay and performance. Also known as performance-based pay or variable compensation.

Industrial Disputes Investigation Act This Act made conciliation compulsory, by delaying the right to strike or to lockout thereby freezing the conditions of employment in order to allow a conciliation board to investigate the dispute and make a recommendation to the minister of labour.

In-house development centres A company-based method for exposing prospective managers to realistic exercises to develop improved management skills.

Integrative bargaining A bargaining style that seeks to establish a creative negotiating relationship that benefits both labour and management.

Intelligence tests A test of general intellectual abilities such as verbal comprehension, inductive reasoning, memory, numerical abilities, speed of perception, spatial visualization, and word fluency.

Interest arbitration A form of dispute resolution in which the arbitrator makes the terms, conditions, and rules which govern the employer-union-employee relationship.

Interest dispute Prior to the expiration of an agreement either party may serve notice that it intends to bargain for a revised collective agreement. This process is known as contract negotiation or "interest" dispute.

Interest test These test measure the relative strength of an applicant's interest in certain occupations or compares candidates' interests with those of other people performing the same kind of work.

International union Unions that operate both in Canada and the U.S. They provide services similar to those provided by *national unions.*

Job analysis A systematic procedure for identifying the duties and skill requirements of a job and the kind of person who should be hired for it.

Job description A written description of the activities, responsibilities, and working conditions of a job — one product of a job analysis.

Job enrichment Herzberg's method for building "motivators" into the job by making work interesting and challenging. By carefully structuring the work situation, employees can be given a chance to experience a sense of achievement, as in assembling a product from start to finish.

Job instruction training (JIT) Listing each of a job's basic tasks, along with a "key point" for each, in order to provide step-by-step training.

Job posting Written notification to all current employees of job vacancies within the company.

Job rotation A management training technique that involves moving a trainee from department to department to broaden his or her experiences, and identify strong and weak points.

Job sharing A concept that allows two or more people to share a single full-time job.

Job specification A list of the personal qualities, traits, skills, and background required a certain job — another product of a job analysis.

Joint health and safety committees The federal government and all the provinces except Nova Scotia and Prince Edward Island have legal provisions requiring the establishment of joint health and safety committees for specified types of workplaces. The intent is to emphasize the necessary role of workers in health and safety programs and to encourage employers to resolve health and safety problems through their own internal responsibility systems.

Just cause The law recognizes the employer's right summarily to dismiss an employee guilty of conduct inconsistent with the fulfillment of the express or implied conditions of service.

Labour market The geographic and demographic area from which an organization recruits employees and throughout which individuals seek employment.

Labour relations boards All jurisdictions in Canada have established labour relations boards (LBR) to administer the labour relations acts.

Labour unions The organization of individuals for the purposes of presenting a united front or collective voice in dealing with management in order to secure and further the social and economic interests and wellbeing of their membership.

Layoff A situation in which three conditions are present: (1) there is no work available for the employee who is being sent home, (2) management expects the no-work situation to be temporary and probably short-term, and (3) management intends to recall the employee when work is again available.

Learning principles Guidelines that should be familiar to all trainers, including making new material meaningful by providing a bird's-eye view and familiar examples, organizing the material, splitting it into meaningful chunks, using familiar terms, and employing visual aids.

Leniency effect The tendency for appraisers to give employees high evaluations on all aspects of performance regardless of their actual performance.

Line authority A type of authority possessed by managers of operating departments that authorizes these managers to make decisions about production and their subordinates.

Local union The primary unit of labour union organization. It may be independent, affiliated with a national or international labour organization, or directly chartered by a central labour congress.

Long-term disability This plan provides partial income continuance to employees who are disabled for a prolonged period and have exhausted their short-term disability benefits.

Long-term incentive plans Incentives intended to motivate and reward management for the corporation's long-term growth and prosperity and to inject a long-term perspective into the executive's decisions.

Maintenance stage During this latter period in the career cycle the person has typically created for himself or herself a place in the world of work and most efforts are now directed to securing that place.

Management by objectives (MBO) A goal-setting process that entails the setting of specific goals for selected task for a specified period of time.

Management development Training for managers, aimed at providing managers with the leadership skills they need to do their jobs.

Management rights The rights to plan, organize, lead, coordinate, and control those processes and activities needed to accomplish the organization's designated objectives.

Managerial grid Numerical ratings for managers in a grid or matrix configuration based on their leadership style.

Managerial judgment Despite the type of HR forecasting used, it is rare that any historical trend, ratio, or relationship will continue unchanged into the future; judgment is thus needed to modify the forecast based on factors which could change in the future.

Mandatory benefits Benefits that employers must provide to their workers by law. These benefits are considered essential to provide workers with a basic level of financial protection in the event of unemployment, illness, accidents, or retirement.

Markov analysis A method for forecasting an organization's future supply of human resources by specific categories such as position and sex. It is based on the development and use of transitional probability matrices.

Maternity leave The Canada Labour Code and the employment standards laws in all other jurisdictions, except the Territories, provide for leaves of absence to pregnant employees.

Mediation The intervention of a third party whose primary purpose is to help the parties to fashion an agreement that is mutually satisfactory to both parties.

Merit pay Any salary increase awarded to an employee for his or her individual performance.

Mid-career crisis substage It is often during this stage that the person is, for the first time, faced with the difficult decisions of what he or she really wants, what really can be accomplished, and how much must be sacrificed to achieve his or her goals.

Minimum wage All jurisdictions in Canada have minimum wage legislation that applies to most categories of workers, except for farm workers and domestic workers.

Mixed interview This interview format is a combination of structured and unstructured interviews.

Motivation People are motivated to accomplish those tasks which they feel will lead to rewards.

Motivator factors Incentives which satisfy higher-level needs.

Motivator-hygiene theory of motivation Herzberg's theory that higher-level needs, such as the need for recognition, are insatiable, unlike physiological needs, or *hygienes*.

Multiple regression analysis A forecasting method used to handle complex, or multiple, dependent and independent variables. See *Regression analysis*.

National union Most local unions in Canada are part of a national union, which provides assistance during negotiation, grievance handling, strike activities, and the arbitration process.

Need achievement theory The theory that focuses on one of Maslow's "esteem" needs — the need to achieve — and aims at predicting the behaviour of those who rank high or low in the need to achieve.

Needs hierarchy Maslow's view human needs form a hierarchy or ladder and that each need becomes active or aroused only when the lower needs are reasonably satisfied.

"9,9" managers Highest ranking on the grid program. A manager with this rating is highly concerned with people *and* production.

No strike or lockout provision All Canadian jurisdictions, except Saskatchewan, prohibit strikes and lockouts during the term of a collective agreement.

Nominal group technique An expert estimation technique of forecasting in which a group of individuals sit at a table and separately write their ideas on sheets of paper which are then presented, discussed, and ranked.

Occupational orientation The theory developed by John Holland that says there are six basic personal orientations that determine the sorts of careers to which people are drawn.

Occupational skills The skills needed to be successful in a particular occupation. The skills break down into three groups, depending on whether they emphasize data, people, or things.

Old Age Security Act An act that came into effect on January 1, 1952, providing full universal pensions as a right, without a means test. Old Age Security pension is provided to all Canadians who have resided in Canada for at least 40 years after age 18.

On-the-job training (OJT) Training a person learn a job by actually performing it.

Operational planning The determination of an organization's short-term needs, and the human resources and human resources programs and policies that are required to achieve the organization's objectives.

Organization chart A chart showing the titles of managers' positions and connecting them by lines indicating accountability and responsibility.

Organizational choice A process that involves a series of decisions an individual makes about joining an organization.

Organizational climate The prevailing atmosphere that exists in organizations and the impact it has on employees.

Organizational culture The core values, beliefs, behaviour patterns, understandings, assumptions, norms, perceptions, emotions, and feelings that are widely shared by the members in the organizations.

Organizational objectives Broad statements of the organization's mission and purpose for existence, values and philosophy.

Orientation The process of introducing new employees to their colleagues, supervisors, and work groups, as well as to their department, to the organization, to the organization's policies, and to the tasks to be performed.

Outplacement counselling A systematic process by which a terminated person is trained and counselled in the techniques of self-appraisal and securing a new job that is appropriate to his or her needs and talents.

Paired comparison method Ranking employees by making a chart of all possible pairs of the employees for each trait and indicating which is the better employee of the pair.

Panel interview An interview in which a group of interviewers question the applicant.

Participant diary/logs A method of collecting job analysis information in which an employee records each activity engaged in (along with the time) in a log

Pay equity The focus of pay equity is to eliminate the historical gap between the incomes of men and women and to ensure that the salary ranges correspond to the value of work performed.

Pay grades A pay grade is comprised of jobs of approximately equal difficulty or importance as determined by job evaluation.

Performance analysis Careful study of performance to identify a deficiency and correct it with new equipment, a new employee, a training program, or some other adjustment.

Performance appraisal The formal, systematic process of evaluating qualitatively and quantitatively employee job performance and potential for the future.

Personality tests An instrument used to measure basic aspects of an applicant's personality, such as introversion, stability, motivation, neurotic tendency, self-sufficiency, self-confidence, and sociability.

Physical ability tests One of the rationale for their use is to ensure that the applicants who are hired are physically capable of doing the job.

Piecework The oldest type of incentive plan, as well as the most commonly used. Earnings are tied directly to what the worker produces by paying the person a "piece rate" for each unit he or she produces.

Point method The job evaluation method involves identifying several compensable factors, each having several degrees, as well as the degree to which each of these factors is present in the job.

Position analysis questionnaire (PAQ) A questionnaire used to collect quantifiable data concerning the duties and responsibilities of various jobs.

Preference test An instrument designed to assess a person's activity preferences.

Preventive discipline The development, maintenance, and communication of standards of behaviour and conduct expected of employees.

Problem-solving interview The focus of problem-solving interviews is on simulation exercises or hypothetical situations which the job candidate is expected to analyze and solve.

Process chart A process chart provides more detailed understanding of the flow of work than can be obtained from the organization chart alone.

Productivity bargaining The attempt to improve the effectiveness of the organization by eliminating work rules and inefficient work methods that inhibit productivity.

Profit sharing plan Under this type of plan, the dollar payout to an individual employee is directly linked to corporate financial results and is normally paid in cash on a current rather than deferred basis.

Programmed learning A systematic method for teaching job skills, involving presenting questions, or facts, allowing the person to respond and providing immediate feedback on the accuracy of his or her answers.

Progressive discipline A disciplinary technique in which management responds to the first offence by an employee with minimal action and stronger or more serious penalties are applied to repeated offenses.

Public Service Staff Relations Act This Act provided public servants with the choice to determine whether to opt for compulsory arbitration or the right to strike. It also designated certain services as essential.

Quality circle A formal, institutionalized mechanism for productive and participative problem-solving interaction among employees.

Quality of work life (QWL) The degree to which employees are able to satisfy their important personal needs by working in the organization.

Quebec Civil Code In Quebec the employment relationship is regulated by the Quebec Civil Code. However, much has been left to the interpretation of the courts.

Quebec Pension Plan A comprehensive, contributory and mandatory for all employees and self-employed individuals in Quebec, providing retirement pensions, disability pensions, and pensions and benefits to children of disabled workers.

Ranking method The simplest job evaluation method involves ranking each job relative to all other jobs, usually based on some overall factor like "job difficulty."

Rate ranges Most employers do not just pay one rate for all jobs in a particular pay grade; instead, they develop rate ranges for each grade so that there might, for instance, be 10 levels or "steps" and 10 corresponding pay rates within each pay grade.

Ratio analysis An approach to forecasting human resource needs by determining the ratio between (1) some causal factor (like sales volume) and (2) number of employees required (for instance, number of salespeople).

Reality shock A period that may occur at the initial career entry when the new employee's high job expectations confront the reality of a boring, unchallenging job.

Reasonable notice The rationale for giving reasonable notice is to provide the terminated employee with a reasonable amount of time to find similar position elsewhere at similar salary without suffering financial loss or emotional loss.

Recency effect The tendency of appraisers to evaluate an employee's total performance based on the employee's last or most recent performance.

Recruitment The process of searching for and locating potential job candidates of high quality and in adequate numbers so that the organization may select the most appropriate individuals to staff its job requirements.

Regression analysis A method used for projecting future HR demands based on a past relationship between the organization's employment level (dependent variable) and some measurable factor of output (independent variable) such as revenues, sales, or production.

Reliability Refers to the degree of dependability, consistency, or stability of measurement of a measure (either predictors, criterion, or other variables).

Replacement planning The process of identifying when a position will become vacant and identifying the individuals with the potential to replace the incumbent.

Rights dispute A difference in interpretation of the clauses of a contract between two parties.

Role management The third stage of the socialization process in which newcomers must come to grips with, cope, and resolve any problems discovered during the *accommodation stage*.

Role playing A training technique in which trainees act out the parts of people in a realistic management situation.

Salary plan A plan in which salespeople are paid a fixed salary, although there may be occasional incentives in the form of bonuses, sales contest prizes, and the like.

Salary surveys Compensation or salary surveys play a central role in the pricing of jobs, and virtually every employer (regardless of size) therefore conducts such surveys for pricing one or more of its jobs.

Scanlon plan An incentive plan developed in 1937 by Joseph Scanlon and designed to encourage cooperative, involvement, and sharing of benefits.

Scientific management The process of "scientifically" analyzing manufacturing processes, reducing production costs, and compensating employees.

Selection Selection is the process of collecting and evaluating information about an individual in order to extend an offer of employment.

Serialized interview According to this format, the applicant is interviewed sequentially by several interviewers and then rated by each on a standard form.

Sexual Harassment Unsolicited or unwelcome sex- or gender-based conduct that has adverse employment consequences for the complainant.

Short-term disability This income replacement benefit is intended to provide the employees with full or partial wage and salary payments in the event that they are unable to work due to illness or injuries.

Short-term incentive bonuses Annual bonus plans aimed at motivating the short-term performance of managers and executives.

Similarity effect The tendency of appraisers to evaluate an employee's performance based on the characteristics they perceive the employee sharing with themselves.

Skill inventories A resource used for internal recruiting since they provide important quantitative and qualitative data of the human resources in the organization.

Socialization The process through which employees learn what is expected of them in terms of appropriate norms, behaviour, and acceptable performance.

Stabilization substage The stage during which firm occupational goals are set and the person does more explicit career planning to determine the sequence of promotions, job changes, and/or any educational activities that seem necessary for accomplishing these goals.

Staff authority A type of authority possessed by service managers that allows them to assist and advise, but not direct, line managers.

Standard hour plan The standard hour plan is very similar to the piece-rate plan, with one major difference: the worker is rewarded by a percent premium that equals the percent by which his or her performance is above standard.

Statutory notice of termination The federal, provincial and territorial governments have all established statutory notices of termination, labour codes that include specific provisions for notice periods or for payment of financial compensation in lieu of notice to employees upon termination.

Stochastic analysis A technique used to analyze employee career movement or mobility patterns of flow from one job to another within an organization.

Stock purchase plan Allowing employees to buy company shares on a voluntary basis, usually with their own funds.

Stock option The right to purchase a stated number of shares of company stock at a stated price during a stated period of time.

Straight piecework A pay system based simply on the number of pieces the employee produces; there is no guaranteed minimum wage.

Strategic planning The process of setting organizational objectives and deciding on comprehensive programs of action that will achieve these objectives.

Stress The general term applied to feelings of anxiety, tension, pressure, and other physical and psychological discomfort that individuals experience in response to job-related and individual stressors.

Stress interview An approach in which the applicant is asked a series of rapid-fire, sometimes harsh, and rude questions. This technique helps identify hypersensitive applicants and those with high or low stress tolerance.

Strictness effect The tendency of appraisers to evaluate employee's performance standards too harshly.

Structured interview Using this format the interviewer relies on a series of predetermined job-related questions. This method imposes constraints on both the interviewer and the interviewee.

Succession planning The process of making long-range management developmental plans to fill future management human resources needs.

Supervisory bias The tendency of appraisers to evaluate their subordinates based on individual differences among ratees in terms of characteristics like age, race, and sex. The bias affects the ratings an employee gets, often quite apart from the employee's actual performance.

Supplementary unemployment benefit This benefit is provided whenever there is a shutdown to reduce inventories or change machinery.

Supplementary health care plans Many employers provide to employees some form of coverage to help meet the costs of some health care not covered by government plans.

Systemic Discrimination Any company policy, practice, or action which is not openly or even intentionally discriminatory, but which has an indirectly discriminatory impact or effect on some individuals.

Frederick Taylor The use of financial incentives - financial rewards paid to workers whose production exceeds some predetermined standard - was popularized by Frederick Taylor.

Transactional analysis A method for facilitative on-the-job communication in which people analyze their own and other people's particular ego states. There are three such ego states: parent, adult, and child.

Trend analysis An initial, exploratory exercise in forecasting by studying the firm's employment trends over the last five years or so.

Trial substage The stage lasting from about ages 25 to 30. During this period the person determines whether or not the chosen field is suitable; if it is not, several changes may be attempted.

Unemployment insurance A program was designed to relieve and lessen the impact of workers' financial burdens during their transition from one job to the next.

Unfair labour practices During an organizing drive, Canadian labour laws place constraints on management actions. As a result management is not free to engage in whatever practices it chooses to oppose the formation of the labour union.

Unfair union labour practices Canadian labour laws also place major prohibitions on the conduct of labour unions during the organizing process.

Union certification The process in which unions present their membership information for a bargaining unit, which they have defined, to the appropriate labour relations board. The labour relations board then determines whether the actual bargaining unit is based upon some community of interest among the workers, and awards recognition if the union membership in that unit is higher than some minimum percentage.

Union recognition clause This provision determines the scope of the bargaining unit and the work that falls within it. It is required as a mandatory provision of each collective agreement by the various statutes governing labour relations.

Union security clause All Canadian jurisdictions permit the inclusion of union security clauses in collective agreements that provide for the protection of the status of the union.

Universal benefits Benefits provided by the government without the requirement for direct contributions from either employees or employers.

Unstructured interview The unstructured format is a conversational-style interview. The interviewer pursues points of interest as they come up in response to questions.

Valence Vroom's term for the value of a goal to a person.

Validity A test's validity is the accuracy with which the test measures what it is supposed to measure.

Vestibule or simulated training Training employees on special off-the-job equipment, as in airplane pilot training, whereby training costs and hazards can be reduced.

Video display terminals The introduction of video display terminals into the workplace in recent years has resulted in concerns being raised about the possible health hazards posed to operators, particularly operators who work with VDTs on a more or less continual basis throughout the working week.

Videotaped interview This interview is conducted in two stages. First, the traditional face-to-face interview is conducted and is videotaped. At the completion of the interview the job candidate is assessed by the interviewer. Second, the videotape is taken to the company for viewing by the hiring line managers and/or other interviewers.

Voluntary reduction in pay plan All employees agree to reduction in pay in order to keep everyone working.

Voluntary time off All employees agree to take time off which again has the effect of reducing the employer's payroll and avoiding the need for a layoff.

Vroom-Yetton leadership training A development program for management trainees that focuses on decision making with varying degrees of input from subordinates.

Wage curve The wage curve depicts graphically the pay rates currently being paid for jobs in each pay grade relative to the points or ranking assigned to each job or grade, as determined by the job evaluation.

Wagner Act An act passed in 1935 in the U.S. banning certain types of unfair labour practices and requiring management to recognize a certified union as the exclusive bargaining agent for that group of workers.

Walk-ins Individuals who voluntarily go to organizations to apply for jobs without having been invited by the organization and without referral.

Want ads Want ads describe the job, specifications and compensation, the hiring employer and the recruitment office to which to submit applications and/or resumes.

Weighted application blank A job application form in which items (such as age or geographical location) are weighted in accordance with their relationship to job performance.

Work sharing A temporary reduction in work hours by a group of employees during economic hard times as a way of preventing layoffs.

Workers' compensation The provision of employer-funded income and medical benefits to work-related accident victims or their dependents, regardless of fault.

Write-ins People who voluntarily submit unsolicited resumes to organizations.

Wrongful resignation Under Canadian common law as well as under government statutes, when an employee resigns, he or she is required to provide the employer with reasonable notice. If the employee does not provide reasonable notice, the employer can sue for wrongful resignation.

NAME INDEX

Blood, Milton, 106, 313
Bolles, Richard, 340
Boone, Mary, 249
Booth, Patricia L., 443, 444, 445
Borman, Walter C., 312, 313, 314
Bourqault, Luce, 106
Bray, Douglas, 341
Brett, Jeanne, 603
Brief, Arthur, 363
Brinks, James T., 445
Briscoe, Dennis R., 33
Brooks, Brian, 649
Brown, Donald J. M., 624, 625
Brunet, L., 506
Bullock, Kathy, 532, 541, 547
Burack, Elmer H., 106, 107
Burke, Ronald J., 73, 315

Charal, Elaine, 200, 214
Chemers, M. M., 279
Cherrington, David J., 340
Christie, I., 541
Cicero, J. P., 248
Clark, F., 506
Coffey, Robert, 648
Cohen, Robert M., 106
Conklin, David, 406
Constantin, S. W., 211
Conway, B., 483
Cornelius III, Edwin, 138, 171
Coutts, Jane, 547
Coward, Laurence E., 481, 483
Cox, Alan J., 171
Craig, A. W. J., 603, 624
Cranshaw, Steven, 213, 215
Crino, Michael, 171
Crocker, Olger, 506

C

Cabelly, Allan, 106
Caldwell, David, 172
Caldwell, Sharon, 211
Callahan, Madelyn, 649
Campbell, John T., 214, 363
Campbell, Richard, 341
Campion, James, 212
Carlson, R. E., 212
Carr, W., 444
Carroll, F. J., Jr., 405
Carroll, Stephen J., 314, 506
Carron, Theodore, 138
Carrother, A. W. R., 604
Carter, S. D., 73
Cascio, Wayne, 107, 138, 211, 312, 313
Catalano, R. E., 249
Cattaneo, R. J., 33, 195, 204, 205, 214, 215
Chadwick, M., 506
Chamberlain, D. B., 503
Champion, Don, 630
Chapman, J. Brad, 483
Charack, Larry, 106

D

Daft, Richards L., 33
Dale, Ernest, 138
Daly, Peter, 444
Daniel, Mark J., 100
Das, H., 107
Das, M., 107
Daum, Jeffery, 171
Davis, Keith, 580
Davis, Ryan, 314
Deagan, Jay W., 446
DeCenzo, David A., 247
Decker, P. J., 171
Decker, Robert L., 211
DeCotiis, Thomas, 313
Deitch, Clearance, 406
Delbecq, A. L., 106
DeLeo, P. J., 446
Denisi, Angelo, 138
Dessler, Gary, 363
Deszca, Gene, 580
Dewar, Donald, 506
Dewey, M., 215

Hall, Douglas T., 212, 247, 248, 341
Hall, Francine, 341
Hamner, W. Clay, 363, 603
Harris, Michael M., 211
Harvey, Edward B., 72, 73
Harvey, Robert, 138
Hathaway, Donald B., 107
Hawk, Roger, 106, 170
Hay, Edward, 404
Hedges, Janis, 507
Hellervik, Lowell, 212
Henderson, Richard, 138, 313, 405, 443, 444, 482, 483
Heneman, Herbert G., Jr., 106, 313
Herren, Laura, 648
Hersey, P., 267, 268, 280
Herzberg, Frederick, 138, 346, 348, 350, 351, 357
Hestwood, Thomas, 40
Hewitt Associates, 649
Hildedrand, F. Dean, Jr., 444
Hill, Jeff, 172
Hinrichs, John, 279
Hodge, B. J., 33
Hogan, Joyce, 214
Hogan, Robert, 214
Holland, John, 322, 323, 340
Hollandsworth, James, Jr., 212
Holmes, Thomas H., 580
Hough, Susan, 247
Howard, Ann, 214
Hulin, Charles, 313
Hung, C. L., 649
Hunt, James G., 443
Hunter, I. A., 72

I

Ilgen, D. W., 341
Ivancevich, John, 507

J

Jackson, Dave, 106, 107
Jain, Harish C., 72, 74, 107, 172, 205, 213, 215, 581
Jameson, Robert, 340
Janz, Tom, 187, 188, 212
Johnson, Robert, 315, 363
Jones, John W., 214
Joseph, Urban, 629, 630
Juriansz, Russel G., 406

K

Kanter, Rosabeth Moss, 445
Katz, Edward, 482
Kaufman, H. G., 341
Kazanas, H. C., 105
Keaveny, Timothy, 313
Kelly, John G., 72, 73, 74, 406
King, Brent, 506
Kirkpatrick, D. L., 249
Klatt, Lawrence A., 340
Koledny, Harvey F., 506
Kopelman, Richard, 443
Kraut, Allen, 279, 312
Kumar, P., 603

L

Ladinski, R. C., 212
Lamon, Wayne, 107
Landy, Frank, 211, 315
Lane, Irving M., 213
Larson, John, 445
Latack, Janina, 507
Latham, Gary, 248, 249, 279, 446, 506
Lawler III, Edward, 33, 106, 172, 393, 443, 475, 483, 648
Ledvinka, James, 106
Lee-Gosselin, H., 73
Lendvay-Zwickl, Judith, 404, 445
Lengnick-Hall, Cynthia, 105

Winstanley, Nathan, 445
Witzel, William, 315
Wolf, Michael N., 105
Wright, Patrick, 138

Y
Yao, Margaret, 406
Yates, Valerie, 314
Yetton, P., 265-67

Yoder, Dale, 405, 624
Yukl, Gary, 446

Z
Zaidi, Mahmood A., 33
Zedeck, Sheldon, 106
Zemke, Ron, 214
Zippo, Mary, 33
Zwacki, Robert, 405

SUBJECT INDEX

HIV, 48
 See also Health and safety
Holidays.
 See Employee benefits and services
Hot-stove rule of discipline, 530
Human relations movement, 5
Human resource:
 accounting, 103
 audit, 644
 information system,18, 81, 82
 planning, 26, 75
 recruitment, 26, 145
 See also Human resource
 management department
Human resource management:
 activities of, 1, 9, 10
 auditing the HRM function, 644
 challenges, 15
 defined, 1
 function of, 1, 7
 history of, 4
 impact of inter-country differences, 639
 international issues, 636, 638
 motivation and needs, 345-348
 the need for a philosophy, 646
 other issues, 633-635
 policies, 22
 purposes of, 3
 review, 644
 role of, 629-631, 635-636, 647
 selection and training for multinational management, 637
 specific changes, 631-633
 strategic issues, 31, 627
 systems view, 14
 trends, 627-628
Human resource management
 department:
 grievances. *See* Collective
 bargaining
 health and safety regulations.
 See Health and safety
Industrial relations department,
 8, 11

role in career management, 319
role in Quality of Work Life
 efforts, 486
role of, 8, 11
Human resource planning: 26, 75
 barriers to implementation,
 95-100
 defined, 76
 evaluation, 101
 external opportunities and
 threats, 78
 internal strengths and weaknesses, 78
 job analysis, 113
 operational planning, 79
 programs, 95
 purposes, 76
 strategic, 77
 successful execution, 79
Human resource planning
 process:
 needs forecasting, 80, 83
 program planning, 80
Human Rights Act, Canadian, 43
Human rights laws, 16

I

Imagined grievances. *See*
 Perceived injustices or injured
 feelings
Incentive compensation, 419
 defined, 419
 environments and practices, 421
 fund determination, 427
 individual awards, 428
 long-term, 428-430
 for managers and executives,
 426-427
 money and motivation, 419-421
 plans, 422-426
 problems, 435-438
 for professionals and white-
 collar employees, 432-434

rewarding key contributors, 434
role of human resources
  department, 421
for sales people, 430-432
uses, 419
when to use, 438
Incentives, financial, types of, 422
Indirect compensation. *See*
  Employee benefits and
  services,
Industrial Disputes Investigation
  Act, 584-585
Industrial relations department.
  See Human resource management department
Industrial unions. *See* Labour
  relations
Internal equity of pay, 368, 369
International hiring in compensation management, 638, 639
International unions. *See*
  Labour relations
Interviewers, error, 183
Interview major types, 185-190
Interviews:
  guidelines for, 190
  in job analysis, 116
  performance appraisal, 301-304
  in selection process, 181-183,
    185-189
  supervisory interviews, 177
  types, 185
Inventories:
  skill, 90, 150-151

J
Job:
  application forms. *See*
  Application forms
  classes, 390
  classification, 378
  description, 110, 399-403
  posting, 150

specification, 110
Job analysis:
  assessment, 63
  compensation, 113
  defined, 26, 110
  employee health and safety, 114
  format, 139-143
  labour relations, 114
  legal considerations, 112
  nature of, 110
  performance appraisal, 113
  purpose and importance of, 111
  recruitment, 113
  relation to other HRM func-
    tions, 112
  selection, 113
  steps in, 114, 115
  training and development, 113
Job design, 134, 349
  See also Quality of Work Life,
    484
Job enlargement, 134, 349
Job enrichment, 134, 349-352
  how to, 351
  implementing, 352
  pros and cons, 349
Job evaluation:
  factor comparison method, 379,
    408-417
  job grading, 378, 379
  job ranking, 377
  point system, 378
Job identification, 130
Job instruction training, 238-239
Job performance standards. *See*
  Performance appraisal,
  standards in
Job rotation, 134, 256, 349
Job sharing, 502
Job specifications, 134
Just Cause, 513
Just Cause for dismissal, 514
  absence from work or lateness,
    519
  dishonesty, 516

disobedience, 515
incompetence, 515
insubordination, 517-518
intoxification, 518-519
moral character and off-the-job
conduct, 519-520
seriously dishonest conduct, 516
untrustworthy character, 517

K
Knowledge tests, 196

L
Labour:
agreement. *See* Collective
bargaining
market, defined, 15
market, analysis, 15, 371
movement. *See* Unions
organizations as source of
recruits, 160
relations, 114, 582
unions, 16, 582
Labour relations:
and arbitration, 587
and contemporary law, 585-587
board, 587
certification of bargaining units,
597-599
conciliation, 587
decertification, 599
define, 583
the Dominion Conciliation Act
of 1990, 584
employer's rights, 588
the Industrial Disputes
Investigation Act (IDI)
1907, 584
Industrial unions, 582
International unions, 582
labour movement, 583

labour union growth and
membership, 589-592
legal constraints on management, 588-589
legal constraints on unions, 589
mediation, 587
the Public Service Staff Relations
Act of 1967, 585
structure and function of labour
unions in Canada, 593-595
union goals and philosophy, 593
union organizing process,
595-597
why workers organize, 592
Labour Relations Board (LRB),
587
Lay offs, 332-334
Leadership training, 235-236
Fiedler leader match, 263
Hersey-Blanchard's Situational
leadership, 267-268
transactional analysis, 269-270
Vroom-Yetton, 265-266
Learning principles, 235-236
Lectures, 239
Legal:
aspects, 37
environment, 25, 42
Legitimate grievances. *See*
Grievance-arbitration process
Leniency bias, 298
Life insurance. *See* Employee
benefits and services
Line authority, 7
Local unions, 595

M
Management, scientific, 4
Management by objectives
(MBO) in performance
appraisals, 294
Management development, 251,
252

appraisal. *See* Performance appraisal
  assessment, 271
  introduction to, 252
  needs, 254
  process, 254
  purposes and importance of, 252
  relationship of, 253
  techniques, 255-268
Management rights, 29, 510
  absence from work and lateness, 519
  Canadian common law protection, 512
  constructive dismissal, 520
  corrective discipline, 529
  damages, 521
  damages for mental stress, 521
  defined, 511
  dishonesty, 517
  dismissal, 510
  dismissed employee's strategies, 535
  disobedience, 515
  employee discipline, 528
  incompetence, 515
  insubordination, 517
  intoxification, 519
  just cause, 513
  moral character and off-the-job conduct, 519
  personality conflict, 518
  plant closures, 536
  preventive discipline, 528-529
  purposes and importance, 511-512
  reasonable notice, 533
  regarding collective agreements, 611
  repercussions for employers, 534
  sexual harassment, 524-528
  statutory notice of termination, 531
  terminated employee's duty to mitigate, 522

  wrongful resignation, 523
Managerial judgment, 86
Manpower planning. *See* Human resource planning
Manditory benefits:
  CPP and QPP, 453
  Minimum wages, 461
  Unemployment Insurance, 454
  Workers' Compensation, 454
Mandatory retirement, 66
Marital status, 46
Markov analysis, 94
Mediation. *See* Labour relations
Medical evaluation of applicants, 177, 198-199
Meech Lake, 628
Membership Card for Union, 597
Merit raise, 432-433
Methods of collecting job analysis information:
  authority, 132
  Canadian Classification and Dictionary of Occupations, 125
  diary/logs, 123
  functional job analysis, 125
  interview, 116
  interview guidelines, 117
  job identification, 130
  job summary, 130
  observations, 118
  position analysis questionnaire, 123
  procedures, 116
  pros and cons, 116
  quantitative job analysis techniques, 123
  relationships, 132
  responsibilities and duties, 132
  standards of performance, 132
  typical questions, 117
  who collects the job information, 116
  working conditions and physical environment, 133
  writing job descriptions, 130

Metropolitan Order Processing System (MOPS), 155-156
Minimum wages, 461
Minorities:
  labour market, 19
Mixed interviews, 186
Modern era, 6
Multiple Regression analysis, 90

N
National unions, 595
Negotiations. *See* Collective bargaining
Nominal Group Technique (NGT), 89

O
Observation:
  in job analysis, 118, 123
  in performance appraisal, 284, 295
Occupational descriptions. *See* Job, description
Old Age Security (OAS), 451-452
Ontario Pay Equity Act, 389, 390
Orientation, 219
  conducting the orientation, 223
  orientation techniques, 220
  purposes and importance of, 219
Organizational:
  climate, 23
  culture, 22
  defined, 166
  objectives, 83
  stage 1: attractiveness, 167
  stage 2: effort, 167
  stage 3: choice among job offers, 167-168
  stages in, 166
Organization charts, 109

P
Participation diary/logs, 123
Pay equity, 54, 387-390, 619-620
Pardoned offence, as prohibited ground of discrimination, 48
Part-time work, 20
Pay. *See* Compensation
Pension Benefits Standards Act, 459
Perceived injustices and injured feelings, 618
Performance appraisal, 28, 63, 113, 282
  behavioural observation scales (BOS), 295
  biases in, 296
  defined, 283
  development, 284, 285
  elements of, 284-287
  evaluation interview, 301-307
  feedback for human resource management, 283
  how to avoid problems, 299-301
  implementing, 296
  management by objectives (MBO), 294
  measures, 23
  methods, 287-293, 296
  problems, 296-299
  standards in, 284
  uses of, 283, 284
  who should do, 286
Personnel association of Ontario, 24
Physical handicap, 47-48
Piecework, 423
Placement Agencies. *See* Employment agencies
Planning:
  barriers, 95, 98-99
  human resource, 26, 75
  human resource programs, 95
  replacement, 91
  succession, 91
Point allocation method, 414